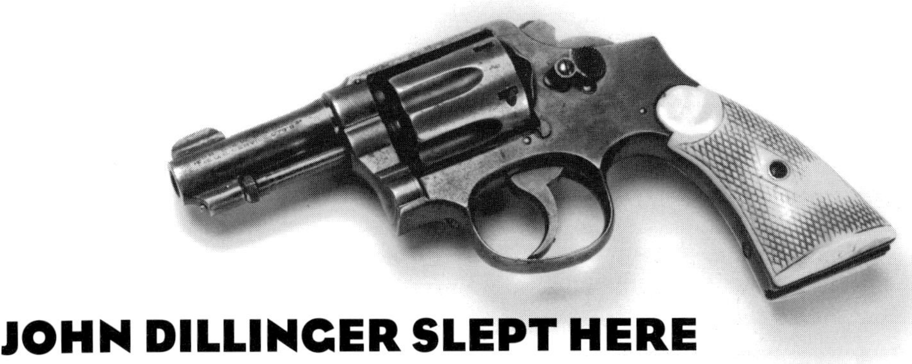

JOHN DILLINGER SLEPT HERE

A CROOKS' TOUR OF CRIME AND CORRUPTION IN ST. PAUL, 1920–1936

JOHN DILLINGER

Minnesota Historical Society Press *St. Paul*

PAUL MACCABEE

SLEPT HERE

A CROOKS' TOUR OF CRIME AND CORRUPTION IN ST. PAUL, 1920–1936

Cover: The revolver used by policeman Henry Cummings to wound John Dillinger in a March 1934 shootout (also, *title page*); the Lincoln Court Apartments, St. Paul; Dillinger FBI photograph and wanted poster.

Minnesota Historical Society Press
St. Paul 55102

Manufactured in the United States of America
10 9 8 7 6 5 4 3 2 1

International Standard Book Number 0–87351-315–0 (cloth)
0–87351-316–9 (paper)

∞The paper used in this publication meets the minimum requirements of the American National Standard for Information Sciences—Permanence for Printed Library Materials, ANSI Z39.48–1984.

Maccabee, Paul, 1955–
John Dillinger Slept Here— : a crooks' tour of crime and corruption in St. Paul, 1920–1936 / Paul Maccabee.
p. cm.
Includes bibliographical references and index.
ISBM 0–87351-315–0 (alk. paper). — ISBN 0–87351-316–9 (pbk. : alk. paper)
1. Crime—Minnesota—St. Paul—History—20th century.
2. Criminals—Minnesota—St. Paul—History—20th century.
3. Criminals—Homes and haunts—Minnesota—St. Paul. 4. St. Paul (Minn.)—Description and travel. I. Title
HV6795.S24M33 1995
364.1'09776'58109042—dc20 95–5236

CONTENTS

St. Paul's old Federal Courts Building, site of the 1935–36 trials of Dillinger and Barker-Karpis gang members; (inset) conspirators Elmer Farmer and Volney Davis leaving building after sentencing

John Dillinger in 1934, at his father's home with the wooden handgun used to escape jail in Crown Point, Indiana

PREFACE

“Of all the Midwest cities, the one that I knew best was St. Paul, and it was a crooks’ haven,” boasted Alvin “Creepy” Karpis, the kidnapper and bank robber whom J. Edgar Hoover anointed Public Enemy Number One. “Every criminal of any importance in the 1930’s made his home at one time or another in St. Paul. If you were looking for a guy you hadn’t seen for a few months, you usually thought of two places—prison or St. Paul. If he wasn’t locked up in one, he was probably hanging out in the other.”[1]

Visitors to Minneapolis and St. Paul today see few traces of the years when Karpis, John Dillinger, “Ma” Barker and her sons Fred and “Doc,” Lester “Babyface Nelson” Gillis, and George “Machine Gun Kelly” Barnes found refuge in this underworld haven. Instead, travel guides direct tourists to the homes of novelist F. Scott Fitzgerald and railroad magnate James J. Hill. No bronze plaque marks the St. Paul apartment building from which Dillinger machine-gunned his way out of an FBI trap in March 1934. Nor are there any signs identifying the West St. Paul home that served as a hideout for Ma Barker in April 1932. Until now, the locations of dozens of other 1930s gambling dens, Prohibition speakeasies, brothels, Murder Inc. assassination sites, and Dillinger gang safe houses have been known only to a few retired FBI agents and police detectives.

This gangland guide, based on nearly 100,000 pages of FBI files, retraces the steps of those underworld figures and explores the political and social environment that allowed the criminals to flourish in America’s Saintliest City. The crooks’ tour begins in 1928, with the slaying of Irish syndicate chieftain “Dapper Dan” Hogan, the supervisor of St. Paul police chief John O’Connor’s “layover agreement.” The agreement guaranteed safe harbor in St. Paul for the nation’s bank robbers, stickup artists, kidnappers, extortionists, and killers—with the understanding that they would not commit crimes within the city limits. The tour follows the fuse of civic corruption, lit by the flow of Prohibition bribes. It documents the burgeoning power of gangsters in the 1930s, as St. Paul was transformed into a market for criminal services: the laundering of stolen bank loot and the open sale of getaway vehicles, automatic weapons, and corrupt police officials.

The tour proceeds to the arrival of the Keating-Holden gang, a group as devoted to golf as to bank robbery; the intersecting careers of outlaws Frank “Jelly” Nash and Verne Miller as they collided with bloody consequences in the Kansas City Massacre; the crime waves of the Dillinger and Barker-Karpis gangs, climaxing with the kidnappings of two prominent

St. Paul citizens, William Hamm Jr. and Edward Bremer; and the 1935 and 1936 trials of the surviving gangsters in St. Paul federal court.

To J. Edgar Hoover's disgust, many law-abiding Minnesotans relished the wicked glamour of dancing and dining at the nightclubs—the Hollyhocks, the Boulevards of Paris—patronized by these public enemies. The Great Depression and less-than-great journalists contributed to the perception of sociopathic killers such as Babyface Nelson as outlaw legends. Widespread contempt for Prohibition laws had elevated local bootleggers, among them Benny Haskell of Minneapolis and Leon Gleckman of St. Paul, to the status of illicit entrepreneurs. Anger over banks foreclosing on loans led many people to view the bank robbers flooding St. Paul as machine gun-toting Robin Hoods.

"The papers say he was bad," Dillinger's sister Audrey Hancock told a reporter in 1934, echoing popular sentiment. "No doubt he was. I don't believe in killin' people, but about robbin' banks, well, I don't think Johnny was any worse than the bankers. The bankers robbed people, too, didn't they?"[2]

Adding to the public's confusion was the selective history of J. Edgar Hoover's public relations machine. His FBI ensured that accounts of the Twin Cities underworld remained a cobweb of Hoover-authorized fantasy hung over a skeleton of fact. Hoover, named in 1924 to reorganize and clean up a corrupt Bureau of Investigation in the Department of Justice, built his name and his bureau's image on the capture of flamboyant but relatively petty midwestern gangsters like John Dillinger. That reputation had important consequences: a trusting public believed Hoover when he denied the existence of a national crime syndicate—the Mafia.[3]

"History is always best written generations after the event," suggested journalist and historian Theodore H. White, "when clouded fact and memory have all fused into what can be accepted as truth, whether it be so or not." The absolute truth about the activities of the Barker-Karpis and Dillinger gangs is unknowable because the participants are dead. To construct the most accurate account of the gangster days possible, I began eleven years of research for this book with a review of thousands of pages of FBI files, obtained under the federal Freedom of Information Act (FOIA).

The FBI has been known variously as the Bureau of Investigation (1909), the U.S. Bureau of Investigation (1932), the Division of Investigation (1933), and, finally, the Federal Bureau of Investigation, which has been its name since July 1935. To avoid confusion, all of my references to the agency use the current name, Federal Bureau of Investigation (FBI), a title J. Edgar Hoover secured to reflect the additional powers granted by 1934 legislation in the wake of the Kansas City Massacre, Dillinger, and Lindbergh kidnapping cases.

I expected the files on Dillinger, Karpis, and others released by the FBI to be sanitized, much as Hoover had airbrushed his publicists' accounts of the bureau's pursuit of gangsters during the 1930s. In fact, the FBI's internal memoranda—which Hoover never imagined would be exposed to public view—are remarkably candid. What Hoover allowed to appear in public was often mythology, but what he and his agents wrote for their own consumption was freely peppered with their jealousies and triumphs, the capricious rages of the director, rivalries with local police and other federal agencies, the FBI's frustration with the local news media, and often astounding feats of behind-the-scenes detective work.

Complementing the FBI records that I used were Minnesota Bureau of Criminal Apprehension homicide files, St. Paul and Minneapolis police files, court records, prison inmate files, and federal Prohibition Department documents.

Most importantly, I interviewed more than 250 detectives, gangster family members, FBI agents, prosecutors, judges, gangster girlfriends, and criminal defense attorneys. The vast majority of these people speak here for the first time. Believing, as dramatist John Still wrote, that "the memories of men are too frail a thread to hang history from," I have tried to corroborate each interview with written records from the period. For example, the re-creation in chapter 5 of how the Barker-Karpis gang escaped from its West St. Paul hideout, tipped off by corrupt police, was built from interlocking sources. To the FBI's internal memoranda and newspaper accounts of Ma Barker's flight, I have added the evidence I found in state Bureau of Criminal Apprehension investigative reports and interviews with three surviving members of a family that lived side-by-side with the Barker-Karpis gang.

Preserved within the FBI's files, too, were more than a dozen confessions made by girlfriends and wives of Dillinger and Barker-Karpis gang members, including Paula Harmon, girlfriend of Fred Barker; Edna "the Kissing Bandit" Murray, lover of kidnapper Volney Davis; and Irene Dorsey Goetz, widow of hit man Fred "Shotgun George Ziegler" Goetz. These matter-of-fact accounts provide a unique antidote to Hollywood's portrayal of gangster life: the day-to-day fear of capture, lives marked by furtive abortions and venereal disease, and abandonment and beatings by their men.

I began this book as an investigative reporter in 1981, when a journalist in the newsroom of the *Twin Cities Reader* weekly newspaper mentioned that Isadore "Kid Cann" Blumenfeld—the Godfather of Minneapolis—had died of heart disease. Intrigued that sedate Minnesota had a history of organized crime, I filed the first of more than 200 FOIA requests for crime files possessed by the FBI, the Drug Enforcement Administration, the U.S.

Labor Department, the Immigration and Naturalization Service, and other agencies. A seven-year struggle with the Justice Department led to my testifying before the Senate Subcommittee on Technology and the Law in 1988 about the FBI's reluctance to open its files on mobsters.

My discovery of duplicate—yet uncensored—FBI documents in the National Archives in Washington, D.C., exposed precisely what the FBI was withholding. The National Archives files revealed that the Justice Department was deleting the names of corrupt police and political figures who had accepted bribes from the underworld and acted as "moles" for the gangsters. The FBI cited concern about "invasion of privacy" as justification for protecting the identity of these officials, many of whom had been dead for nearly half a century. Other censored FBI files dealt with law-enforcement strategies that could be embarrassing to the bureau, such as wiretapping, surveillance, and "mail covers" on the correspondence of people who knew the Dillinger and Barker-Karpis gangs.

Probing the history of crime in Minnesota is also complicated by the destruction of much of the written record of the gangster era. At the St. Paul Police Department, limited file space and the renovation of the central police station in the 1980s led to the destruction of thousands of pages of vintage police records. Into the garbage went every page of the files on John Dillinger, Ma Barker, Alvin Karpis, and other gangsters. Thick sheaves of fingerprint and identification records on hundreds of criminals were tossed into the trash; officers wandering by pulled out a few as souvenirs. Even the straw hat that Homer Van Meter of the Dillinger gang had been wearing when police officers shot him to death in 1934, saved for decades, disappeared. A purging of police files occurred in Minneapolis, too, where the entire intelligence file on syndicate boss Isadore Blumenfeld vanished; in Chicago, virtually every police department record from the Al Capone years, including evidence from the St. Valentine's Day Massacre, was thrown out; and in Kansas City, the police department's Kansas City Massacre investigation file has disappeared.[4]

Back in St. Paul, at the site of the old Ramsey County jail, a trash bin was filled with records stretching back to the days of Ma Barker. One witness remembers leaning into the open bin, jammed with city attorneys' records soaked by a light rain, and finding dripping pages of correspondence from the family of Homer Van Meter arguing that city officials should turn over his 1932 Ford coupe. Every page was destroyed.

At the Minnesota Bureau of Criminal Apprehension, when a comprehensive computer system arrived in the 1970s, hundreds of crime documents from the Dillinger era were fed into paper shredders. Index cards to old homicide records were destroyed.[5]

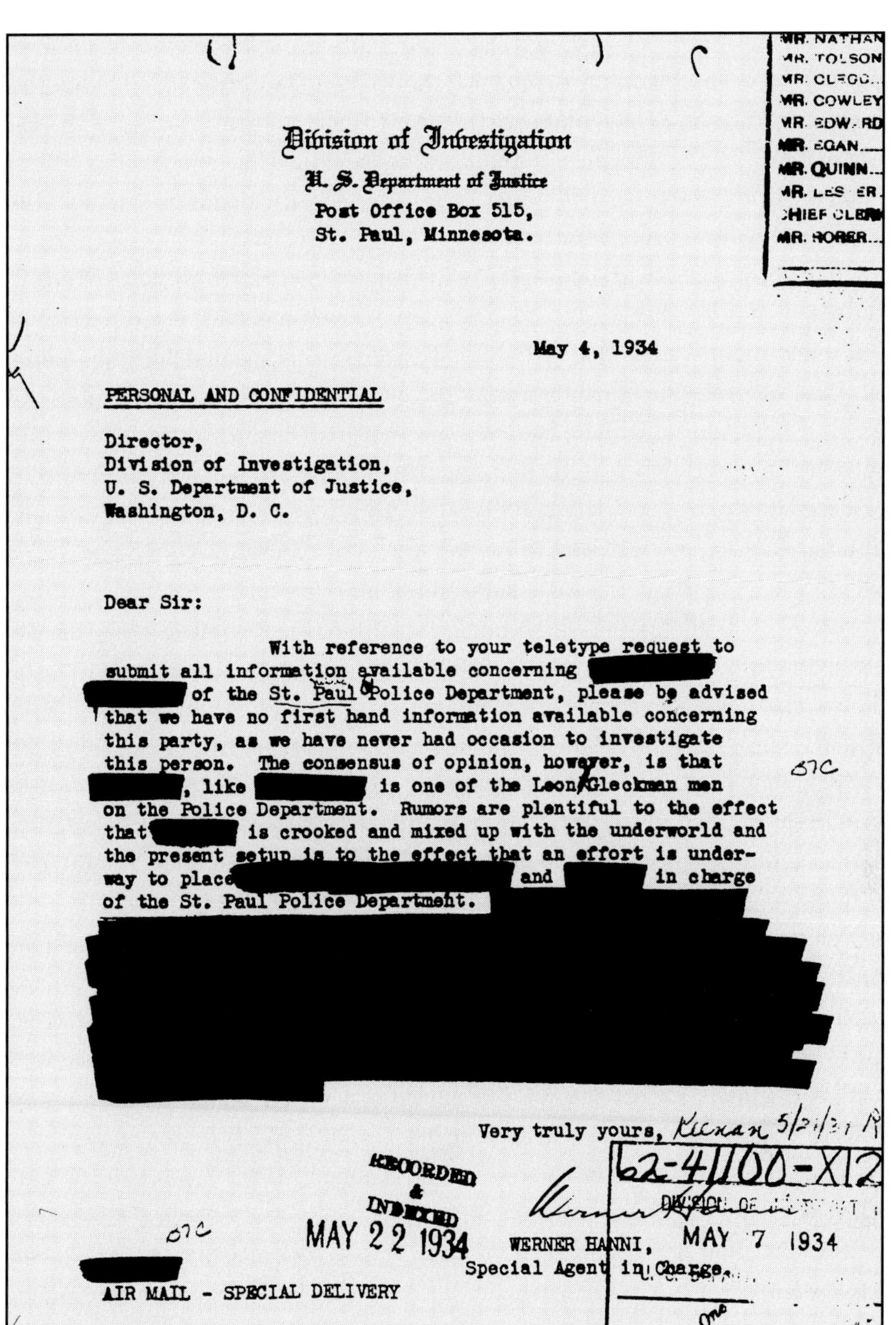
Division of Investigation
U. S. Department of Justice
Post Office Box 515,
St. Paul, Minnesota.

MR. NATHAN
MR. TOLSON
MR. CLEGG
MR. COWLEY
MR. EDWARDS
MR. EGAN
MR. QUINN
MR. LESTER
CHIEF CLERK
MR. HOMER

May 4, 1934

PERSONAL AND CONFIDENTIAL

Director,
Division of Investigation,
U. S. Department of Justice,
Washington, D. C.

Dear Sir:

With reference to your teletype request to submit all information available concerning [redacted] of the St. Paul Police Department, please be advised that we have no first hand information available concerning this party, as we have never had occasion to investigate this person. The consensus of opinion, however, is that [redacted], like [redacted] is one of the Leon Gleckman men on the Police Department. Rumors are plentiful to the effect that [redacted] is crooked and mixed up with the underworld and the present setup is to the effect that an effort is underway to place [redacted] and [redacted] in charge of the St. Paul Police Department.

[redacted]

Very truly yours, Keenan 5/21/34

RECORDED & INDEXED MAY 22 1934

62-41100-X12

DIVISION OF INVESTIGATION MAY 7 1934

WERNER HANNI,
Special Agent in Charge.

b7C

AIR MAIL - SPECIAL DELIVERY

A 1934 FBI memo about St. Paul bootlegger Leon Gleckman, with censored references to police corruption

According to the Federal Bureau of Prisons, the inmate files for most of the Dillinger and Barker-Karpis gang members imprisoned in Alcatraz and Leavenworth were thrown out in the early 1970s under a statutory thirty-year destruction rule. The handful of Leavenworth and Alcatraz files quoted in this book were saved accidentally, when they were set aside for study and federal officials simply forgot to destroy them.[6]

Why is the historical record of a city's racketeers worth saving? Because the story of Minneapolis and St. Paul, like that of any city, is a mingling of glory and infamy, of people with high integrity and others with low morals. St. Paul was built as much on a legacy of gamblers, scoundrels, and sinners as on a tradition of philanthropists, statesmen, and business barons. By probing the underworld—from homegrown criminals such as fixer Harry "Dutch" Sawyer to imported thieves like Dillinger—one gains a richer understanding of how citizens viewed their police force, their city government, and their vices of alcohol, gambling, and prostitution. St. Paul's experiment in accommodating the underworld also provides a lesson in the consequences of a government forging a partnership with criminals.

The story of the St. Paul underworld also offers a magnifying glass with which to view a defining moment in law enforcement. It was here, from 1933 to 1936, that J. Edgar Hoover demonstrated the viability of the national police force that he craved and that so many had opposed. The necessary elements rushed together in one city: a local police force so corrupt that it demanded a federal alternative; a series of high-profile interstate crimes that left clues in several parts of the country; a firestorm of media coverage, fed primarily by FBI publicity; and a series of clues that demanded a level of technology that few local police possessed. St. Paul served first as a haven, and then as a burial ground, for many members of the Barker-Karpis and Dillinger gangs, but it was also the birthplace of the modern FBI and the cult of Hoover as the nation's number-one G-man.

This book is organized so that it can be enjoyed in two ways: as a "crooks' tour" of the actual crime sites or as a history book to be read in the safety of your home. You will find the criminal events of *John Dillinger Slept Here* grouped around the underworld sites where they occurred, and as a result the chronology skips around a bit. To help you tell your Babyface Nelsons from your Machine Gun Kellys, miniature biographies of the most prominent St. Paul gangsters are offered in the Rogues and Reformers Gallery section. The Twin Cities Crime Chronology traces the major events of Minnesota gangsterdom.

One objective of this book is to explore the belief, espoused in most histories of the gangster era, that legitimate society remained aloof from the underworld during the 1930s—at least until the Barker-Karpis gang violated the O'Connor agreement by kidnapping businessmen Edward Bremer and William Hamm. But research in Justice Department and police files reveals that the overworld and underworld of Minnesota were far more intertwined than was previously acknowledged. The local banking, brewery, city government, and restaurant industries had found common ground with organized crime more than a decade before the Barker-Karpis and Dillinger gangs moved into St. Paul.

Evil can be enticing. The inherent drama of the lawbreakers' lives has made it easy for Hollywood to focus on their cruel dynamism and ignore their victims. Today, the nickname Babyface Nelson is as recognizable as the names of Harry Houdini and P. T. Barnum. Yet few people could identify Nelson's innocent victims, among them bystander Theodore Kidder and slain FBI agents W. Carter Baum, Herman Hollis, and Sam Cowley. Whenever possible, I have tried to give voice to the victims of the Dillinger and Barker-Karpis gangs. You will find here the fullest account yet published of the terror felt by the abducted Edward Bremer, blindfolded and bound to a point near paralysis, and the shock experienced by the children of Roy McCord, who was machine-gunned by the Barker-Karpis gang because his Northwest Airlines uniform made him look like a police officer.

"God cannot alter the past," quipped Samuel Butler, "but historians can." It is my hope that *John Dillinger Slept Here* will alter how we perceive the public enemies in the 1930s and the men who hunted them—that it will peel away the nostalgic glamour ascribed to the Dillinger and Barker-Karpis gangs; restore to public view the heroes of that tumultuous period (crusading *St. Paul Daily News* editor Howard Kahn, for example); place the triumphs and failures of J. Edgar Hoover and the FBI in perspective; and fully reveal the villainy of gangland collaborators like police chief Thomas Archibald Brown.

Now, pull on that black fedora, pick up your violin case, and prepare to take the crooks' tour.

Paul Maccabee
St. Paul, Minnesota
January 1995

ACKNOWLEDGMENTS

John Dillinger Slept Here benefits from the contributions of a network of gangland scholars that stretches from New York to Los Angeles. I owe much to crime historian William J. Helmer for his meticulous dissection of the weaponry and explosives mentioned in this book; also helpful were crime aficionados Rick Mattix, Tim Albright, Ross Opsahl, Jeff Maycroft, Kathi Harrell, Ellen Poulsen, Robert Bates, Dee Cordry of the OklahombreS, and Joe Pinkston of Indiana's John Dillinger Historical Wax Museum.

A tip of the cap to the three Minnesota police departments that opened their 1930s crime files: South St. Paul Police Capt. David Vujovich, who lent his records on the Barker-Karpis gang's payroll robbery; Minneapolis Police Department records officer Bev Johnson and Lt. Gary McGaughey; and St. Paul police librarian Edith Kroner, personnel staffer Mary Zupfer, and records officers Lt. Michael Moorehead and Sgt. Mark Johnston. St. Paul police historian Fred Kaphingst deserves a special epaulet for saving the 1928 file on Dan Hogan's murder from destruction.

Capt. Joseph O'Connor, former commander of the Philadelphia Police Department's Organized Crime Intelligence Unit, shared his files on Murder Inc. hit men George Young and Joseph Schaefer. David Finazzo of the Detroit Police Department provided access to the file on Verne Miller's murder, which contained a 1934 police interview with George "Machine Gun Kelly" Barnes that proved revelatory. Special thanks also go to Ramsey County Medical Examiner Michael McGee for his help in providing reports on the murders and suicides of gangsters.

The Minnesota Bureau of Criminal Apprehension (BCA) was singularly generous in offering unrestricted access to its 1930s murder files and crime identification records. Thanks go to Karen McDonald, BCA director of crime history and fingerprints; agent Mike Campion; and former superintendent Mark Shields.

The FBI's Freedom of Information Unit was most reluctant to release its files on the gangster era. I did, however, appreciate the help of FBI historian Susan Rosenfeld and Lawrence J. Heim, editor of the newsletter of the Society of Former Special Agents of the FBI, *The Grapevine,* in providing material on individual agents and cases.

Mike Robar, Freedom of Information officer with the Federal Bureau of Prisons, dedicated himself to locating critical files from Alcatraz and Leavenworth prisons that the bureau had thought were long destroyed.

More than 250 people offered their memories of the gangster era, often in multiple interviews lasting for hours. I am particularly indebted to Horace "Red" Dupont, employee of gangland fixer Tom Filben; former St. Paul police officers Charlie Reiter and Pat Lannon Sr.; the late Richard Pranke, FBI special agent; and Martin Rohling, Jack Peifer's doorman at the Hollyhocks Club. Members of the gangsters' families who were surprisingly open about their nefarious kin included Bruce Barnes, son of "Machine Gun Kelly" Barnes; Bruce Hamilton, nephew of Dillinger gang member John Hamilton; Albert Grooms, nephew of Alvin Karpis; Carole DeMoss, niece of Harry Sawyer; and Ann Michaud, niece of Dan Hogan.

Among the many librarians who contributed, I would like to give special thanks to the staffs of the Minneapolis *Star Tribune*'s library, the St. Paul Public Library, and the Minneapolis Public Library's Special History Collection for unearthing newspaper clippings and photographs. I am also grateful to the Nita Haley Stewart Memorial Library in Midland, Texas, for permission to quote from portions of J. Evetts Haley's five original interviews with bank robber Harvey Bailey.

Journalist Gareth Hiebert and researchers Jim "The House Detective" Sazevich of St. Paul and Sal Giacona of Detroit brought the outlines of madam Nina Clifford's world to life. Journalist Kara Morrison investigated Harry Sawyer's family in Lincoln, Nebraska; Alison Fitzgerald and *Chicago Tribune* reporter John J. O'Brien probed Alvin Karpis's family in Chicago.

The role of the Minnesota Historical Society (MHS) in the creation of this book has extended far beyond that of a publisher; its archives have been a haven and resource throughout this project. I am grateful for the enthusiasm and dedication of Jean A. Brookins and Ann Regan of the MHS Press, and I am astonished by the commitment of editors Marilyn Ziebarth, John Radzilowski, and Lynn Marasco and volunteer reader Pat Rolewicz. I also received assistance from the historical societies in Hennepin, Ramsey, Koochiching, and Dakota counties.

For his guidance through the jungle of publishing arcana, I appreciate the counsel of my literary oracle, Scott Edelstein, of Minneapolis. My parents, Rose and Ralph Fishman, continue to be my life's anchors.

Most of all, this book could never have been written without the unflagging energy and insight of my loving wife and partner in crime history, Paula. She spent hundreds of hours editing every sentence and reviewing every blurry photograph, providing her unerring advice on issues ranging from the legal, historical, and grammatical to the logical, philosophical, and aesthetic. Paula, this one's for you.

Paul Pioneer Press.

Sidelights on Edgar Markham column. See "Politics and editorial page.

ST. PAUL, MINN., WEDNESDAY, DECEMBER 5, 1928. C PRICE THREE CENTS

HOGAN DIES OF BOMB WOUN

'DAPPER DAN' HOGAN AND HIS BOMB-WRECKED CAR

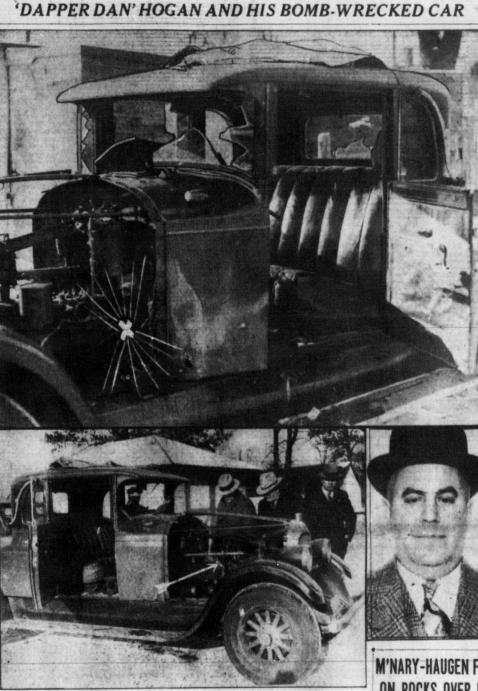

Scenes of the destruction wrought by the bomb which was planted in the automobile of "Dapper Dan" Hogan, restaurant man and underworld figure, were caught by a Pioneer Press photographer soon after the explosion. In the upper picture the approximate location of the death bomb is shown by the cross. The lines radiating from it show the double course of the explosion. Below the arrow points to the wire where the bomb was grounded on the engine. Inset, "Dapper Dan" Hogan, whose right leg was blown off above the knee by the explosion.

MUST
MATUM
RNANE

t Promised St.
hree Major
r in Day.

AID POLICE

ncy to Co-op-
rding Life
perty.

ust go."
imatum of Chief
urnane Tuesday
y of major crime
ich a restaurant
y hurt in a bomb
policeman was
nd a filling sta-
y a bandit who
the attendant.
Commissioner of
M. Clancy and
eller were shown
er, oon Dispatch
es of the three
emoval to Brain-
y, suspect in the
robbery. Mayor
be reached.

Enforced.

o be done about
ed.
gsters or undesir-
ey'll certainly be
f Murnane said.
t go. We intend
s and give St.
ble policing under

bomb explosion in
anny Hogan lost
nane said:
st time we have
of this kind and
will be taken to

City of St. Paul
nal way as other
ner Clancy said.
en unfortunate in
at times, we have
ld. We will con-
st possible service
nd property with
mmand."

d Murnane.

pledged co-opera-
urnane in ridding
rld characters.
we are with a
uipment, and no
oeller said. "we
e the chief all we
ur men, in stamp-
n St. Paul.
orce here in the
s has been used
ers, the care and
and in patroling
word, we have no
t. However, at
of the Minnesota
will be introduced
a department."

ET PART
0,000 ESTATE

(AP)—Two average
rls are about to
nobility and be-
to a $15,000,000
Isabelle and Mar-
d 8 years old, re-

U. S. DENIED CHANCE TO TRY BLACKMER

'Dapper Dan' Was 'King' to Scores Who Mourn as Death Seals Lips

M'NARY-HAUGEN FIRM ON ROCKS OVER BILL

Iowan Spurns Oregonian's Feeless Farm Measure as Ineffective.

By EDGAR MARKHAM.
(Pioneer Press Staff Correspondent.)

Washington, Dec. 4.—The farm relief firm of McNary-Haugen is on the verge of dissolution.

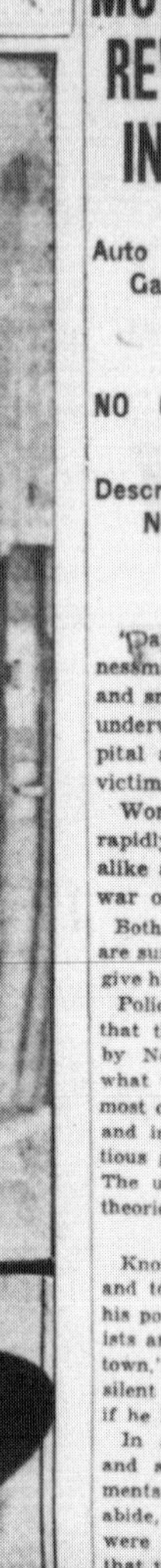

MUTTE
REVEN
IN UN

Auto Blast
Gang; Sl
Poli

NO CLUES

Description
Near Ga
Inv

"Dapper D
nessman, re
and smiling a
underworld,
pital at 8:55
victim of a g
Word of
rapidly and p
alike armed
war of repri
Both believ
are sure to fol
give him a cha
Police were
that the crim
by New Yor
what was ter
most cowardly
and incited b
tious gang of
The underwo
theories of its

Dies W

Known thr
and to some
his power to
ists and to "
town," Hoga
silent as to th
if he knew.
In soft dr
and small h
ments known
abide, mutter
were heard,
that they wo
lawless aid is
Mr. Hogan,
lived only a
hours after h
by at their h
street, shortl

GANGL

"Dapper
of attaching
tomobile s
world's new
the United
feuds, polic
night.
While ma
vogue and p
into their
method of
nihilate hi
starter of h
used in bu
cases.
Tuesday's
such case r
side large
exception o

his garage a
his car to tak
in-law downt

1

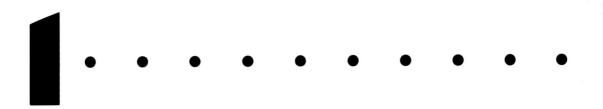

THE SEEDS OF CORRUPTION

The 1928 car-bomb murder of Dan Hogan stunned the underworld; John J. "the Big Fellow" O'Connor, architect of the O'Connor system.

1 **'I Didn't Know I Had an Enemy in the World!'**

Home of the Irish Godfather

1607 West Seventh Street, St. Paul

Just before 11:30 A.M. on December 4, 1928, St. Paul underworld czar Daniel "Dapper Dan" Hogan—heavy with a late-morning breakfast—walked toward his Paige coupe. The forty-eight-year-old Irishman had parked the car in the white stucco garage just behind his West Seventh Street home. Awaiting Hogan, hidden between the rear end of the engine block and the bottom of the footboard, was an explosive charge wired to the starter.[1]

Hogan had told a friend that he had seen someone hanging around the alley in back of his house several times and that he thought someone had it in for him. Hogan had installed a burglar alarm to warn of any attempts on his life, but the batteries that powered the garage alarm had expired. So, too, would Danny Hogan.[2]

"Some powerful explosive had been placed under the floor board near the starter," said the 1928 police report. "Wires had been attached to the bolt on the top of the block of the Motor . . . which made a complete electrical circuit to the explosive." Hogan climbed into the coupe, turned on the ignition, and stepped down on the starter pedal. Instantly, the bomb lodged beneath the floorboards detonated. The force of the blast rocketed the auto out of Hogan's garage and into the alley. Hogan's right leg was "practically blown off," said the police report. "The explosion blew the hood off of the car, went thru the top of the car, broke all the windows in the car, flattened the gears, blew the steering wheel completely off, tore part of the rear end of the engine off [and] broke all windows in the Garage."[3]

For a decade, Hogan had ruled the underworld from the tables of his Green Lantern saloon on Wabasha Street, just three blocks from the Minnesota Capitol. The "layover agreement," or O'Connor system of protection, named after Police Chief John O'Connor and supervised by Hogan, ensured that out-of-town gangsters visiting St. Paul would receive police protection if they followed three rules: check in with Hogan, donate a small bribe, and promise to commit crimes only outside the city limits.

Hogan's first arrest—for "room prowling" in Los Angeles—had earned the chunky laborer a stay in San Quentin prison in 1905, followed by time in Wisconsin, South Dakota, and Minnesota jails for robbing banks and stealing furs. Shortly after Hogan was first arrested in St. Paul, on November 29, 1909, he discovered his true calling—organizing major crimes from the sanctuary of St. Paul, selecting the criminal personnel for the job, and laundering stolen merchandise, particularly hard-to-fence government bonds.[4]

FBI files indicate that Hogan masterminded the 1924 robbery of $13,000 from the Finkelstein and Ruben collection wagon at the corner of Eighth and Cedar Streets in St. Paul. The wagon picked up the daily receipts from local movie houses, and Hogan shrewdly planned the robbery for a Monday morning so that he would profit from the Saturday and Sunday movie collections. In exchange for planning the robbery, Hogan and his partner received 10 percent of the loot.[5]

"Danny Hogan . . . today he'd probably be called a Godfather, sort of a father figure for hoods who were climbing the world of hoodlumism," said retired St. Paul newspaper reporter Fred Heaberlin.[6]

In the early 1920s, Hogan allied himself with his underworld counterpart in Minneapolis—a 6-foot, 2-inch Irishman named Edward G. "Big Ed" Morgan—to operate a gambling den under Minneapolis police protection. (Curiously, the FBI noted that "no liquor is allowed on these premises by Dan Hogan."[7]) Hogan and Morgan, a slot machine king and muckraking journalist for the *Twin City Reporter* scandal sheet, developed an amicable split of the Twin Cities underworld. Hogan commanded all of St. Paul, while Morgan, in a loose partnership with bootleggers Tommy Banks and Isadore "Kid Cann" Blumenfeld, handled Minneapolis crime out of the Dyckman Hotel and Brady's Bar on Hennepin Avenue.

"It is common knowledge in Minneapolis and St. Paul that Dan Hogan and Edward Morgan harbor criminals from other parts of the United States," stated a 1926 FBI memo.

> The police of Minneapolis and St. Paul are said not to interfere with these criminals, there being an understanding between Dan Hogan and the St. Paul Police and Edward Morgan and the Minneapolis Police that if the criminal gangs controlled by them refrain from committing crime in the Twin Cities, that they will not be disturbed. It is a well known fact in the community that a very little crime such as bank robberies, etc. is committed here, the criminals are safe as long as they live up to the pledge made by Dan Hogan and Edward Morgan to the local police.

Of special value to visiting hoods was St. Paul's tradition of refusing extradition requests made by cities outside the perimeter of the O'Connor system. "It is further rumored that the police have a tipoff system," explained the FBI file, "by which Dan Hogan or Morgan is informed when a member of the criminal gang controlled by them is wanted by either the U.S. authorities or another State, wherefor it is difficult to make such captures in the Twin cities."[8]

Gradually, the bribes of the O'Connor payoff system overflowed into the pockets of St. Paul police detectives, aldermen, grand jury members, judges, and even federal prosecutors. Hogan "is so entrenched politically and otherwise," lamented post office investigators that same year, "that law enforcement officers in St. Paul and Minneapolis fear him. In fact, give protection to members of his organization."[9]

The O'Connor system is more than a historical curiosity, an amusing interlude in a cartoon cops-and-robbers chase. It provides a cautionary tale about corruption, its corrosive effects on a midwestern city, and the rise of organized crime in America. Hogan's activities were only a small part of the scandal. Prohibition had offered lawbreakers a new industry and a sudden infusion of illicit money. Police had particular difficulty enforcing laws that a significant number of people refused to support. Citizens' tacit acceptance of corruption—and their inclination to romanticize criminals—helped the underworld flourish. Bootleggers began to attack and steal from each other; some moved on to robbing banks and kidnapping. Bystanders, police officers, and FBI agents were killed. J. Edgar Hoover and the FBI rose to prominence fighting these highly visible crooks—and ignored the more sophisticated and dangerous crime syndicates of Charles "Lucky" Luciano, Frank Costello, Meyer Lansky, and others.

By 1927, thanks to Dan Hogan's connections, St. Paul was known across the United States as the Wall Street for laundering hot bonds, stolen securities, and other ill-gotten financial paper. "Hogan is a nationally known character as a 'fence' for the disposal of stolen property and undoubtedly hundreds of thousands of dollars of stolen stamps and bonds and other valuable property have come into his hands," concluded a 1927 Justice Department memo. "He is doubtless one of the most resourceful and keenest criminals in the United States and has always been able to cover his tracks so as to avoid detection."[10]

Just how resourceful was demonstrated when the Hamilton County Bank in Cincinnati was robbed by Oklahoma bank robber Harvey Bailey on September 28, 1922. The Bailey gang jammed three laundry bags with more than $265,000 in securities, virtually cleaning out the bank's financial assets. Hogan's syndicate offered to return some of the stolen bonds in exchange for a cash ransom. When the U.S. Secret Service put Hogan under surveillance in the hope of locating the bonds, Hogan responded in kind, putting the Secret Service agents under the gang's surveillance.[11]

Then the FBI learned from an informant in Leavenworth prison that Hogan had personally handled $80,000 of the money stolen from the Denver Mint on December 18, 1922. That ninety-second robbery, which netted $200,000 in currency and left one bank guard dead, was labeled years later by the *Denver Post* "Denver's biggest robbery—a crime that set a new under-world high in an American era already spectacular with bootleg booze, bank robbery, gun molls and murder."[12]

Stolen bonds traceable to both the Denver Mint and the Hamilton County Bank robberies began to surface in St. Paul. Harvey Bailey, who relieved Upper Midwest banks of almost $1 million in cash and bonds—including $30,000 from the Olmsted County Bank and Trust in Rochester, Minnesota—provided an inside view of Hogan's operations. Decades later, Bailey explained in his autobiography, *Robbing Banks Was My Business,* how he met Hogan to explore a market for his loot and then decided to entrust Hogan with some $80,000 in stolen money. "Now listen, it may take me a month or it may take me six months to dispose of this, but I'll get with it," promised Hogan.[13]

Fixers like Hogan made St. Paul a favorite of expert criminals like Bailey, considered the dean of American bank robbers. "I would be lying if I said that I didn't find a market for that money, because I found the market. . . . I had wonderful connections during them years," wrote Bailey.

The usual underworld rate offered criminals thirty-five to forty cents on the dollar for stolen railroad or security bonds and eighty-five to ninety cents for Liberty Bonds. By August 1923, Hogan had successfully laundered most of the Denver Mint loot for Bailey. "We made him make it good and he did make it good. Oh yes, thieves is thieves, you know," said Bailey admiringly of Hogan. "But there's honesty among us."[14]

Although members of Hogan's gang were caught with portions of the Denver Mint money, none would implicate the boss. A triumphant Hogan gave Bailey a going-away gift—a tip-off that Bailey had been recognized at Jack Dempsey's Brainerd, Minnesota, prizefight—and Bailey left St. Paul to cool off in Chicago.

Nothing demonstrated Hogan's influence better than his response to being indicted in 1927 for a conspiracy to commit a 1924 robbery in which $35,000 was taken from the Chicago Great Western Railroad station in South St. Paul. The gangsters met Hogan at his saloon to plan the robbery, then held up the mail messenger and delivered a 10 percent cut to the Green Lantern. Hogan's robberies, unlike those of Bonnie Parker, Clyde Barrow, and other better-known bandits, nearly always reaped substantial profits and seldom resulted in gunplay.[15]

Hogan was imprisoned in the Ramsey County jail for the South St. Paul score, but his $100,000 bond—the largest ever demanded by a U.S. District Court judge in St. Paul—was covered by twenty-five bondsmen. The case against Hogan began to collapse when a key witness, Chicago robber Tommy O'Connor, escaped from a train. O'Connor went to the newspapers,

Family photo of Dan Hogan (left), relaxing at his Big Bass Lake cabin west of Bemidji with his wife, Leila, and father-in-law, Fremont Hardy

claiming that every word of his grand jury testimony implicating Hogan had been fabricated.[16]

"A few days prior to trial of Subjects at St. Paul, Minn., it was learned that the witnesses, all underworld characters, had changed their stories," an FBI agent wrote in a 1927 memo. "It is believed said witnesses were paid or intimidated after indictment and before trial, through the underworld connections and influence of Subject Hogan." Minneapolis police chief Frank Brunskill suddenly told postal inspectors that he could not help prosecute Hogan's gang, that he wouldn't "double-cross the boys." Postal inspectors were baffled: "Every prospective lead at Minneapolis was bungled in some mysterious way." By July 1927, all robbery charges against Hogan were dismissed.[17]

Those who did choose to speak against Hogan suffered a severely reduced life expectancy. Informant John Moran, reportedly a participant in the South St. Paul robbery who was to serve as a government witness against Hogan, died abruptly in the Atlanta penitentiary a week after Hogan visited him there. After being interviewed in 1927 about a mail robbery, two of the Hogan gang's girlfriends, Ann Grenville and Teddy Du Bois, were shot to death in Grenville's University Avenue apartment. A post office inspector told the FBI that Grenville's suite was a hangout for Hogan's gang. "She and her companion were killed by hirelings of Hogan," the inspector concluded, "because of their belief that she had knowledge of their criminal operations." When a cab driver was asked about his statement that the murdered women had visited Hogan's saloon—and that he saw Hogan on the day of the murder—the eyewitness abruptly changed his story. "I made a mistake," the cabbie protested to police. "I did not see Danny that night."[18]

The Justice Department estimated that in a ten-month span, Hogan's gang robbed seven post offices in Wisconsin and Minnesota, netting more than $250,000. "For years many crimes of violence, including Post Office burglaries, bank robberies and hold-ups within a radius of several hundred miles of St. Paul, upon investigation, have pointed to some complicity or responsibility on the part of the defendant Hogan," said an attorney general's memo.[19]

Now a gangster's car bomb had accomplished what the Justice Department's investigators could not. "One thing nearly saved Uncle Dan's life at the time," Hogan's niece, Ann Michaud, recalled of the explosion. "Danny was short with a big tummy, and to drive his coupe, he had to lean way back in order to reach the pedals. That's how he protected his head—they'd intended to blow his head off!"[20]

More than a hundred of Hogan's friends offered to donate blood for a transfusion; hospital phone lines were jammed by people calling to check on his condition. Going into surgery, Hogan looked up at his physician and quipped, "Doc, you'd *better* be good!" But Hogan slipped into a coma and, nine hours after the explosion, died. To the legions of gamblers, burglars, and con men in St. Paul, Hogan's death was a tragedy—a frightening upset in a universe of orderly corruption.[21]

"Hoarse voices, bearing the accent of the underworld, queried, 'I just heard Danny died. That ain't true, is it?,'" reported the *St. Paul Pioneer Press*. "Men who gathered at out of the way places, hardened men who have seen death before, who have seen their pals go by the hand of the gangster, spoke in hushed voices, punctuated now and then by threats of vengeance."[22]

Uppermost in their minds was this question: With Hogan gone, who could ensure that the corrupt legacy of Chief John O'Connor would continue, and that gangland peace would reign in the mob's capital city?

2 'A Haven for Criminals'

Old St. Paul Police Headquarters
110 West Third Street (now Kellogg Boulevard)
near Washington Street, St. Paul

Among tourists visiting Minnesota in the 1920s, St. Paul evoked images of a gracious metropolis built by railroad barons like James J. Hill, with Victorian mansions spread along Summit Avenue and around Irvine Park, near the rolling beauty of the Mississippi River. But the FBI saw the city as a refuge for gamblers, kidnappers, jewel thieves, and bank robbers who were protected by corrupt local police and politicians.

"This city was a haven for criminals," wrote an FBI agent in a 1934 briefing on crime conditions. "The citizenry knew it, the hoodlums knew it, and every police officer in the city knew. Hoodlums from the entire United States knew that they could come into St. Paul, make their presence known to the Chief of Police, and stay here with immunity, provided that they committed no crimes in the city. Everytime they moved they notified the police department. Other cities could try in vain to extradite or remove criminals from St. Paul."[23]

Bill Greer, a St. Paul crime reporter, explained how criminals and the police collaborated: "Usually you got off the train and there was a policeman at the depot who could recognize every face in crime. He'd say, 'If you're gonna stay here, you'd better go up and see so and so. . . .' We were going to have a clean town, even though they had some dirty birds living in it." Mobsters from Chicago would arrive at the depot with gold watches and chains in hand, ready to trade the jewelry for protection from the police.[24]

The architect of this system of crime containment was John J. "the Big Fellow" O'Connor, who supervised his underworld from police headquarters. Born in Louisville, Kentucky, to Irish immigrant parents in 1855, O'Connor moved to St. Paul in 1857 with his father, politician "Honest John" O'Connor. After a ten-year apprenticeship in the grocery business, the younger O'Connor joined the police, rising from the rank of detective in 1881 to serve as chief for nearly eighteen years (from 1900 to his resignation in 1912, and again from 1914 to his

Old St. Paul Police headquarters during Chief John J. O'Connor's administration; gold police badge presented to O'Connor, Christmas 1900

final resignation in 1920). A horse-racing fan who bet tens of thousands of dollars on a single race, O'Connor had a terrific memory, an obsessive dislike of barbershops and movie theaters, a taciturn personality, a massive physique, and an unhappy marriage. (His wife, Annie, divorced him in 1922 on charges of cruelty.)[25]

O'Connor devised his own system of dealing with the underworld. "If they behaved themselves, I let them alone," he admitted. "If they didn't, I got them. Under other administrations there were as many thieves here as when I was chief, and they pillaged and robbed; I chose the lesser of two evils." The police department's official 1904 souvenir book boasted that "thieves and criminals respect" Chief O'Connor. "When they are in the city they choose to retain him as their friend, and to do so avoid committing acts which will not only make him their enemy, but will be sure to result in their falling into the hands of the 'Big Boy,' as they familiarly call him." As a result of O'Connor's methods, the souvenir book proclaimed, "never in the history of St. Paul has human life and the property of citizens been so safe, and the virtue of women so assured."[26]

Cementing the chief's power was his relationship with his brother, Democratic party boss and former city alderman Richard T. "the Cardinal" O'Connor, who had much the same philosophy toward crime. "Gambling, which was rampant, was not subject to graft" under alderman O'Connor, according to the *St. Paul Daily News*. "Every game was run on the square and frequently visited by the best citizens and looked upon in the same spirit as it is today in our best clubs."[27]

The original go-between for Chief O'Connor, before Dan Hogan's reign in the late 1920s, was a crimson-haired character from New York named William H. "Reddy" Griffin. Born of Irish immigrant parents in 1848, Griffin—a "jeweler" by trade—lived with his daughter and his wife, Cora, in the Elmwood Apartments on prestigious Summit Avenue. Griffin held court during the early 1900s at the Hotel Savoy at 420 Minnesota Street, a gamblers' hangout in downtown St. Paul. (The Hotel Savoy site—near the corner of Seventh Place and Minnesota Street—is now occupied by the Bremer Tower and Metropolitan Building.)[28]

Griffin was responsible for collecting money from the brothels and gambling dens along St. Peter, Hill, and Washington Streets and bringing the crisp green tributes to O'Connor's police station. Through his friendship with O'Connor, Griffin would get visiting crooks inexpensive rooms along Wabasha Street and ensure that criminals checked in at police headquarters within twelve hours of their arrival.

"It was even rumored that pickpockets held practice sessions at the Savoy," wrote a St. Paul reporter. "They'd work on each other. The conmen gilded their bricks there. The yeggs mixed their 'soup'"—the safecrackers mixed their explosives.[29]

By 1912 Griffin had moved his St. Paul office to 14 West Sixth Street (adjacent to today's Garrick parking ramp). Griffin survived at least one underworld shootout, only to die of apoplexy in 1913 at the age of sixty-five in Shakopee, Minnesota, en route to the Mudcura Sanitarium.[30] Dan Hogan took his place as the mob's liaison with Chief O'Connor.

One newspaper noted that O'Connor "was criticized for his methods, the old school kind, by which he kept track of crooks. His enemies charged that he made St. Paul a refuge for crooks, allowing them to stay here and escape arrest as long as they did not commit crimes in this city." O'Connor responded to his critics by insisting that St. Paul was better off if his officers forced criminals to police themselves: "When a man knows that I know who and where he is, and that I can put my finger on him if I want him, he has every reason to behave himself."[31]

Yet the O'Connor system, while it reduced bank robberies and other major crimes during the 1920s, fostered an atmosphere that encouraged open gambling and prostitution. Former St. Paul police officer David Morgan recalled the days when his grandfather, the Reverend David Morgan, ran a downtown St. Paul mission during O'Connor's years as chief: "My grandfather was preaching against the wide open town of St. Paul, and especially preaching about those girls in the whorehouses." Chief O'Connor tried to strike a deal to get Reverend Morgan to ease off on his attacks on the St. Paul brothels, explaining that the men using them were from northern Minnesota, where there were no women. Morgan countered that he would stop preaching against sinful St. Paul if the women stopped walking the streets, kept to the brothels, and turned off their red lights.

A year later, Morgan noticed that the red lights were back on and the women were back on the sidewalks. He stormed up to O'Connor's office at police headquarters, charging him with failing to keep his side of the bargain. "I bet you a gold watch, Reverend, that the girls are *not* back on the street," scoffed the chief. To settle the issue, they stepped outside. The first woman they walked up to propositioned them both. "That Christmas, my grandfather received a large railroad watch," laughed Morgan's grandson. "Engraved on it was 'To Rev. David Morgan from Chief O'Connor, Christmas 1902.' My son, David, still has that watch today."[32]

Controversy dogged O'Connor. In 1910 the Minnesota Federation of Women's Clubs charged that the chief tolerated open dice games at cigar stands throughout St. Paul. (O'Connor replied that "women should attend to their own business in their homes.") An official with the Law Enforcement League sought to have O'Connor fired as police chief for failing to pursue liquor law violators. ("Tell your paper that if a _____ like that can put me out of office, I'll leave the city," O'Connor responded to the *St. Paul Dispatch*). Minneapolis mayor Wallace Nye charged in 1916 that police were unable to stem crime in his city because St. Paul under O'Connor had become a haven for crooks.[33]

New York columnist Westbrook Pegler first brought the O'Connor system to national attention, wryly noting that New York and Chicago would not be bothered by the reputation St. Paul had developed, since "those two cities have been called sinkholes of sin for many years and they have learned to take it, and even like it." Pegler told of the day when Detective Tommy Horn, O'Connor's watchdog on the St. Paul underworld, recognized a visiting pickpocket in Hogan's Green Lantern saloon. Horn asked the pickpocket if he had checked in with O'Connor. Not yet, said the pickpocket—he had just gotten off the train and stopped for a drink. Would Horn join him? The detective and the pickpocket had a drink together and then prepared to leave: "At the door, the visiting pickpocket turned and said mischievously, 'I am on my way, Tommy, and I seem to have your stickpin.' 'Yes,' said Detective Horn, 'I saw you. And you can keep it because it is a phony. And, anyway, I have got your watch.'"

Pegler noted that criminals who violated the O'Connor system would be locked in an office alone with Chief O'Connor. Minutes later, the hoodlums would limp out, savagely beaten. O'Connor, said Pegler, "took great pride in the fact that all this police work of his was done by hand." FBI director J. Edgar Hoover sent this Pegler column to the U.S. attorney general, noting soberly that although the article was meant to be humorous, it might furnish information on organized crime in St. Paul.[34]

Chief O'Connor did not mind if St. Paul's resident felons robbed banks in Minneapolis, kidnapped businessmen in Duluth, or burglarized safes in neighboring Iowa. His job was to keep the streets of St. Paul safe, regardless of the consequences for neighboring cities and states. Both FBI and Prohibition Bureau files suggest that until at least 1931, major criminals did restrict their felonious activity to areas outside St. Paul.

Lesser crimes were controlled by the system, too. After all, why should St. Paul gangsters tolerate a wave of purse snatchings downtown when the resulting uproar could jeopardize next week's $160,000 railroad robbery in South Dakota? "I often heard stories about some ambitious young man who would go out and snatch an old lady's purse on the street," reporter Bill Greer recalled. "Within a few hours . . . one or two rather determined gentlemen [would] walk up beside him and say, 'Son, we believe we'd better teach you some manners.' . . . It was a safer town to live in for most people when you had the criminals making sure that there was no crime."[35]

Police officer David Morgan witnessed an example of the mob's self-policing when he helped investigate a bank robbery in St. Paul's Midway area during the early 1930s. A policeman met with racketeer Leon Gleckman at the Hotel St. Paul and told him, "We're living up to the agreement, but you're not living up to your side." The bank robber was turned over to the police the next morning, ready to accept his punishment. "The gangsters," laughed Morgan, "didn't want the heat."[36]

O'Connor died in 1924 at the age of sixty-eight, from what newspapers termed "general ill health and the infirmities of age." Almost four thousand people attended his funeral at the St. Paul Cathedral, and local newspapers applauded his methods of crime prevention. "If it be said that Chief O'Connor's methods were those of a bygone day," wrote the *St. Paul Pioneer Press*, "the fact remains that they generally accomplished results." As long as the criminals "were on their good behavior, they were not molested. . . . And when they transgressed his unwritten rules, they could not escape him."[37]

Frank Sommers, a former Wisconsin city detective, succeeded O'Connor as chief and maintained O'Connor's system of crime containment. A scandal over Sommers's "vice investigations" forced him to resign. The chief had sent police to raid fifty-five gambling dens, brothels, and moonshine houses but reported that at thirty-five of the sites, no illegal activity could be found. Yet in parallel investigations, federal agents found ample evidence of lawbreaking at the same locations "raided" by Sommers's men. Justice Department files claimed that after Sommers's resignation he became a consultant to Dan Hogan's crime gang and provided Hogan's thieves with top-level protection through federal officials who could "fix" Prohibition cases.[38]

Chief O'Connor's legacy—the bribed police, compromised U.S. attorneys, corrupt judges, and network of fences for stolen property—laid the foundation that attracted the John Dillinger and Barker-Karpis gangs to St. Paul in the 1930s.

"St. Paul has been a sanctuary for the underworld long enough," complained one newspaper. "Do the police run this town, or do the gamblers, bootleggers, gunmen and other racketeers?"[39] Government records suggest that under Danny Hogan and John O'Connor, *both* did. Few members of that underworld flourished as profitably as Nina Clifford, the city's most acclaimed madam.

3 'A Very Respectable Brothel'

Nina Clifford's Brothel and Home
147 and 145 South Washington Street, St. Paul

The intertwining of St. Paul's underworld and overworld was most obvious between the sheets at Nina Clifford's brothel. "The story went that there were three important people in St. Paul," said reporter Fred Heaberlin, who was a teenager during Clifford's heyday. "They were James J. Hill, Archbishop John Ireland, and Nina Clifford."[40]

From the late 1880s through the 1920s, Nina's two-story brick mansion reigned as the most elegant house of sin in St. Paul. "In my younger days," recalled veteran St. Paul police officer Pat Lannon Sr., "Nina ran a very respectable brothel, just down below the police station. She was given some immunity. Nina didn't do anything to upset the apple cart—that is, she didn't do anything against the wishes of the police and the other powers that be. There was a lot overlooked." Clifford's house was well kept but not expensive, recalled Lannon. "Anyone was welcome at Nina's who had the bucks—their charges weren't exorbitant, not like some of these flash places."[41]

Clifford was born Hannah Crowe in Ontario in 1851 to British-Irish parents, Patrick and Ann Crowe. The Crowe family emigrated to the United States when Hannah was nine. She later married Conrad Steinbrecher, was widowed, and moved to St. Paul after her mother died in 1886. Hannah Steinbrecher, who lived on Cedar Street close by Third, a few doors down from the old Minnesota Club (located then at the southeast end of Fourth and Cedar), adopted the name Nina Clifford.[42]

In 1888 Clifford built her three-story brick-and-stone brothel at 147 Washington for a cost of $12,000. She lived next door, at 145 Washington. On her 1888 building permit, she described the purpose of the brothel building as "dwelling house"; a wag scribbled in the words "and seminary."[43]

The "vice districts" of St. Paul had moved away from the Fifth Street houses between Sibley and Cedar Streets toward the Hill and Washington Street district of Nina Clifford. The cheaper flophouses stretched along the 300 and 700 blocks of St. Peter and Wabasha. City plat maps openly refer to the Washington Street area as "female boarding houses," and prostitutes were identified in census records as "sports," "boarders," or "prostitutes."[44]

Clifford's brothel was built directly below the central police station and just across the street from the old county morgue at 164 Washington Street (where, legend has it, the prostitutes could get low-cost checks for venereal disease). Down the street was the infamous Bucket of Blood saloon and Mamie Porter's Chicken Shack, which offered butter-fried chicken to the men recovering from the Hill Street brothels.[45]

Nina Clifford's Washington Street brothel in 1937

By the year 1900, census records show, Clifford's brothel—with nine prostitutes ranging in age from eighteen to thirty-eight, a cook, a Norwegian housekeeper, three chambermaids, a male porter, and a Scottish musician—was thriving. The women came from England, Scotland, Arizona, New York, and Michigan.[46]

Former St. Paul police officer and cab driver David Morgan remembered that Clifford hired Blue and White taxis to drive the women who worked for her to Lake McCarron beach, first warning them not to sunburn their backs. Unlike the grim brothels along St. Peter Street, which were little more than second-story flophouses with mattresses, Nina Clifford's was an establishment, offering its customers such amenities as a waiting room furnished with lounges.[47]

Arthur Sundberg, who as a fifteen-year-old delivered dresses to the house from Atkinson's store, recounted to St. Paul newsman Gareth Hiebert just how elegant the brothel was:

> The public area downstairs . . . was all carpeted in the finest deep pile. Nina's office . . . was a beautiful large room with a wide, marble fireplace. . . . To the rear of the office was another large room . . . [with a] polished dance floor, lined with chairs and always someone playing piano. . . . All manner of drinks were available, provided by well-dressed help. . . . It was here that the visitors met the girls. . . .
>
> One day, when I was there delivering dresses, she called me to her

desk and opened a cigar box. In it were several hundred unset diamonds . . . no small ones. . . . She also had a dozen or more diamond rings with identification tags on each.

These were all stones that had been left as security for various obligations. Most of them were left by Westerners, cattlemen, miners and lumbermen, who had come to St. Paul on business and looking for big city pleasures which proved to be too much for their purses.

Sundberg claimed that Clifford would twist the stones out of the rings and throw the settings off the High Bridge into the Mississippi River so the stones could not be identified.[48]

"Nina Clifford has such a flourishing business at her rooming house . . . that it is necessary for her to maintain two phones," noted Police Chief Frank Sommers in a 1923 letter to the public safety commissioner. Although his officers were unable to enter the brothel, Sommers assured the commissioner that the madam "has a maid and a housekeeper there, but . . . there are no other girls living there."[49]

Such official protection helped guarantee the safety of Clifford's patrons, by legend the most prominent businessmen of her era. In turn, Clifford's women were exquisitely dressed when they rode down Summit Avenue on Sundays and visited the Metropolitan Theater for musical performances.[50]

Howard Guilford, editor of the *Twin City Reporter*, an anti-Semitic scandal sheet, was determined to puncture the women's respectability. In his florid 1920s exposé of Twin Cities brothels, *Holies of Holies of the White Slave Worshipper*, Guilford condemned the "pimps, procurers, white slavers, and bawdy house property owners" by name and identified each brothel. Guilford specifically attacked Clifford—"Nina Clifford is only an alias for a Jew name which is almost unpronounceable"—and described her brothel: "Expensive draperies and trappings are festooned from the walls, and imported rugs are on the floor."[51]

The legends of Nina Clifford are legion: how she adopted homeless women until they got back on their feet, how the sons of St. Paul's wealthy families came of age at Nina's.[52]

Clifford died of a stroke, three weeks short of her seventy-eighth birthday, during a visit to Detroit in July 1929. After a $490 funeral at St. Catherine's Church, she was buried beside her mother in Detroit's Mt. Elliott Cemetery.[53]

Her death was front-page news in St. Paul. The *Daily News* hailed her as "the queen of St. Paul's demi-monde," while the rival *Pioneer Press* referred to her as "a prominent figure in St. Paul's underworld," calling her brothel an "underworld resort."[54]

More than thirty-one relatives from Detroit, Omaha, and Seattle were listed in the probate petition for a piece of what newspapers referred to as Clifford's "large fortune," but all that was left of her estate for the Ramsey County probate court to verify were two fur coats worth a total of $150, $500 in household furniture, and the $8,800 real estate value of her brothel. It was rumored that Clifford gave her wealth to an adopted daughter that she put through an elegant eastern boarding school, while probate records suggest that Clifford invested her money back in Michigan: her Detroit estate included more than 133,000 shares of stock in a variety of gold and copper mines.[55]

Journalist Fred Heaberlin, who lamented that "everybody seems to have known Nina Clifford, except for me," told of a legendary prank on the day of the madam's death: "When word got around that Nina Clifford had died in Detroit, a bunch of movers and shakers who used to have fun together rented a room at the Lowry Hotel to . . . [play] practical jokes." The pranksters called St. Paul's most eminent politicians, attorneys, and businessmen (including Roy Dunlap, Heaberlin's managing editor) to inform them sadly that Clifford had passed away. But in her will, each victim was told, Clifford specified that he should be one of the pallbearers at her funeral. Those who caught on to the joke promptly joined the group at the Lowry Hotel for more phone calls to unwary pallbearers. "The fictional part of the story is that the night trains to Chicago were filled with prominent businesspeople who did not want to be pallbearers at Nina Clifford's funeral," Heaberlin said.[56]

Immediately after Clifford's death, claims one source familiar with St. Paul's underworld, Minneapolis gangster Isadore "Kid Cann" Blumenfeld installed his own girlfriend to operate the brothel. City directories indicate that one Lillian Lee, "saleswoman," ran it from 1931 through 1934.[57]

In the summer of 1933, Clifford's heirs, hoping to open a nightclub in her house, tried unsuccessfully to get a restaurant license for her 147 Washington property. Police Chief Thomas E. Dahill, the Guild of Catholic Women, and Mayor William Mahoney vigorously opposed reopening Nina's as a nightclub. In 1936 the house was put up for auction; the next year, St. Paul's most famous brothel was condemned and razed. The curious scavenged bricks from Clifford's house, and her doorknob and bell were salvaged by a Ramsey County engineer.[58]

Long after the destruction of Clifford's house, rumors persisted that the Minnesota Club, at 317 Washington Street, was connected by an underground tunnel extending from the club's basement to Clifford's back door, barely a block away. An underground passage extending from the Minnesota

Club to the site of what once was Clifford's brothel does exist. St. Paul utility maps document a six-foot-high water tunnel stretching from the basement of the Minnesota Club to within a hundred feet of what was once Clifford's back door. (One can still see the New Hill Street entrance to the tunnel just under Kellogg Boulevard, across from the Ramsey County medical examiner's office.)[59]

The Minnesota Club has continued to fan the flames of its connection with Nina Clifford. A portrait of a woman identified as Clifford hangs on the Washington Street wall of the club's main bar, the oval frame enclosing a demure, black-haired beauty in a silver-gray dress. The painting was donated to the club in 1980 through the efforts of *St. Paul Dispatch* columnist Gareth Hiebert.[60]

In the hallway outside the bar is a framed photograph of the first Minnesota Club, on Cedar Street, with a caption noting the apartment where Nina Clifford lived from 1887 to 1889. Attached to a red-brown brick allegedly salvaged from the ruins of Clifford's brothel is a plaque that reads: "This brick from Nina Clifford's house is presented to the Gentlemen of the Minnesota Club for their great interest in historic buildings."[61]

Legendary portrait of "Nina Clifford" hanging in St. Paul's Minnesota Club

4 'I Am Sure There Will Be Justice'

Dan Hogan's Final Resting Place
Calvary Cemetery, 753 Front Avenue, St. Paul

The bomb that killed Danny Hogan in 1928 failed to upset the corrupt traditions of the O'Connor system, the heritage of cooperation between police and the gangsters, gamblers, and madams of St. Paul.

More than three thousand mourners paid tribute before Hogan's casket at the O'Halloran and Murphy funeral home. Hogan's coffin and his grave were bedecked with five thousand dollars' worth of lilies, roses, and gold and white chrysanthemums sent by underworld friends in New York, Chicago, and the Twin Cities.[62]

"Hogan had one of the grandest funerals ever staged in St. Paul—the Chicago gangland-type funeral, with huge masses of flowers and a funeral mass at St. Mary's," reporter Fred Heaberlin recalled. "Somehow, one would rather be in Mr. Hogan's place than [in] that of his murderers," preached Father Nicholas J. Finn. Police detectives flooded the church as mobsters and businesspeople paid their last respects.[63]

"I am sure there will be justice," said Hogan's widow, Leila. "If Danny had lived, he would have gone on the one leg they left him and would have taken care of it himself."[64]

As if in tribute, the St. Paul underworld briefly went dark: slot machines were removed, brothels were demurely closed, gambling dens were emptied. George "Bugs" Moran, the Minnesota-born rival to Al Capone and a friend of Hogan, was seen pacing back and forth in front of Hogan's West Seventh Street residence, apparently to protect the Hogan family from further underworld attacks.[65]

Dan Hogan's grave is in Calvary Cemetery, on the north end of St. Paul. Two other architects of the O'Connor system—William Griffin and Chief John O'Connor—lie nearby. A cemetery staff member says that one of O'Connor's relatives visits to leave the chief a pint of Irish whiskey.[66]

A five-inch portion of the bell wire that connected the bomb to the starter of Hogan's car can be seen today—by special appointment—in the St. Paul Police Department's history exhibit at 110 East Eleventh Street. Although the police had this evidence, the investigation sputtered and Hogan's assassin or assassins were never caught.

"I don't believe the police *made* an attempt to find out who killed Dan Hogan," said retired officer Pat Lannon Sr., who joined the force the year that Dan Hogan was slain. "There were people who had a reason to do it, and the other people figured it was good riddance to eliminate a bad influence!"[67]

"I don't know who could have done it," protested Hogan on his deathbed. "I didn't know I had an enemy in the world." The underworld seethed with theories. "Mr. Hogan always told me everything with which he was connected in the Twin Cities," his widow told the *Minneapolis Tribune*. "He had no serious quarrels with anyone here. He had eastern connections though, which I didn't know much about."[68]

Many suggested that the bomb was long-distance vengeance from the East Coast syndicate. Perhaps the mob held Hogan responsible for the sawed-off pistol—traced to a St. Paul sporting goods store—that had been used to kill gambler Arnold "the Brain" Rothstein in New York one month earlier. If Rothstein's murder had been planned in St. Paul, New York gangsters could have concluded that Hogan must have known about it.[69]

"Uncle Danny knew who had killed him, but he'd never tell his family, because he was afraid the gangsters would come after *us*," said Hogan's niece, Ann Michaud. "Dan Hogan ruled the roost in St. Paul. When my uncle Danny was blown up, we learned that he'd told these small-time gangsters from Chicago that they could not rob a bank in St. Paul. He wanted to keep the worst element out of St. Paul, so it wouldn't attract attention!"

The most credible murder suspect would have to be Hogan's own underworld protégé, Harry "Dutch" Sawyer, a Nebraska butcher's son who had served as Hogan's assistant in fencing jewelry and other stolen goods at the Green Lantern saloon. Before his death, Hogan had told his wife that he had put $50,000 in a safe deposit box for her. Only two men had keys to the box—Dan Hogan and Harry Sawyer. When Hogan was killed, "Aunt Lee went to the bank and the money was all gone," recalled Michaud. "Harry Sawyer cleaned out his safe deposit box. I'm surprised that my uncle even gave Harry the key!"[70]

Daniel "Dapper Dan" Hogan

Sawyer felt that he had reason to be bitter about his mentor. Years later, Sawyer's wife, Gladys Rita Sawyer, told FBI agents that when Hogan was arrested for participating in the 1924 robbery of the South St. Paul Post Office, Sawyer raised the $100,000 bond. She said her husband personally furnished $25,000 of this bond. She continued that Hogan "jipped Harry out of this $25,000."[71]

Gladys Sawyer also claimed that Hogan had cheated her husband of his cut from the Hollywood Inn gambling casino in Mendota. "Some years ago Harry Sawyer, Danny Hogan, Fred Ulrich and Red Clare were jointly associated in the operation of a gambling place known as 'Hollywood Inn' near St. Paul," an FBI interviewer noted. Gladys Sawyer told the FBI that "Harry was jipped out of his share of a $36,000.00 cut through the operation of this place by Danny Hogan."[72]

Woody Keljik, a tour guide and historian for the old Federal Courts Building (now Landmark Center) who has studied St. Paul's gangster era, has no doubts about who killed Hogan. "When Dapper Danny Hogan was running the Green Lantern, it was a very profitable place," said Keljik. "The boys came here and instead of putting their money in the bank, they trusted Dan to leave it with him in the Green Lantern safe. Then a guy named Harry Sawyer, a small hood from Omaha, came to St. Paul under the O'Connor system, and Harry coveted the Green Lantern. Sawyer's the guy who fixed the car on Seventh Street with the bomb. Dapper Dan went to gangster heaven, and Harry Sawyer got the Green Lantern."[73]

Dan Hogan was a rarity in the 1920s underworld, a mob peacekeeper with as much clout at police headquarters as in the underworld. From the Green Lantern, Hogan could arbitrate disputes between competing gangs and cool violent tempers in a city jammed with alumni from the country's major prisons.

When Hogan died, Harry Sawyer inherited both the Green Lantern and control of the O'Connor system. In time, Sawyer's friends from across the

CITY OF ST. PAUL, MINN.

DEPARTMENT OF PUBLIC SAFETY—BUREAU OF HEALTH—DIVISION OF VITAL STATISTICS

CERTIFICATE OF DEATH

PLACE OF DEATH St. Paul Hospital — 2881

If death occurred in a hospital or institution, give the NAME instead of street and number.

1 FULL NAME Daniel Hogan

(2) Residence. No. 1607 W. 7th St. St. Ward 5 (Usual place of abode) (If non-resident, give City or Town or State)

Length of residence in city or town where death occurred 13 yrs. mos. ds How long in U. S., if of foreign birth? yrs. mos. ds.

PERSONAL AND STATISTICAL PARTICULARS

3 SEX: Male

4 COLOR OR RACE: White

5 Single, Married, Widowed or Divorced (Write the Word): Married

5a If Married, Widowed or Divorced HUSBAND of (or) WIFE of Jane Hardy

6 DATE OF BIRTH (month, day and year) Unknown 1880

7 AGE Years About 48 Months Days If Less than 1 day...hrs. or .....min.

8 OCCUPATION OF DECEASED

(a) Trade, Profession or particular kind of work Restaurant Prop

(b) General nature of industry, business or establishment in which employed (or employer)

(c) Name of employer

9 BIRTHPLACE (city or town) (State or country) California

PARENTS

10 NAME OF FATHER Daniel Hogan

11 BIRTHPLACE OF FATHER (city or town) (State or country) Unknown

12 MAIDEN NAME OF MOTHER Unknown

13 BIRTHPLACE OF MOTHER (city or town) (State or country) Ireland

14 Informant Mrs. Jane Hogan (wife) (Address) 1607 W. 7th St.

15 Filed 12-5-28 19 64461 Registrar.

Eug. F. Simon, M.D.

MEDICAL CERTIFICATE OF DEATH

16 DATE OF DEATH (month, day, and year) ~~December 4, 1928~~

17 I HEREBY CERTIFY, That I attended deceased from 19 to 19 that I last saw h alive on 19 and that death occurred, on the date stated above, at m. The CAUSE OF DEATH* was as follows:

Multiple injuries - shock right leg torn off 183

duration, years mos. ds.

CONTRIBUTORY (Secondary) caused by bomb in automobile

duration years mos. ds.

18 Where was disease contracted, if not a place of death?

Did an operation precede death? yes Date 12-4-28

Was there an autopsy? no

What test confirmed diagnosis?

(SIGNED) C.A. Ingerson, Coroner M. D.

19 (Address) M.J. Leonard, Dep.

*State the Disease Causing Death, or in deaths from Violent Causes, state (1) Means and Nature of Injury, and (2) whether Accidental, Suicidal or Homicidal. (See reverse side for additional space.)

19 PLACE OF BURIAL, CREMATION, OR REMOVAL: Calvary Cemetery — DATE OF BURIAL: 12-7-28 19

20 UNDERTAKER: O'Halloran & Murphy — ADDRESS: St. Paul

Certified to be a true and correct copy of the record on file with the Division of Public Health, City of St. Paul, Minnesota.

Alterations shown made under authority of Minnesota Statute 144.172, and Regulations of State Board of Health.

(Signed) [signature], this 18 day of June 1982.

Deputy Registrar, Vital Statistics

Dan Hogan's death certificate

Hogan's bombed Paige coupe with blown-out windows and cloth roof

country—public enemies like John Dillinger, Alvin Karpis, and Fred and Doc Barker—would be drawn to St. Paul, free to begin a five-year crime wave that might have appalled Hogan.

Sawyer had been a petty thief and bootlegger throughout the 1920s. Now, with the coming of Prohibition, Sawyer, like so many other hoodlums, was transformed from a small-time grifter into an underworld potentate.

2

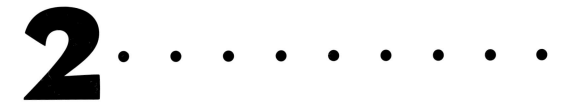

THE BOTTLING OF FORBIDDEN FRUIT

Moonshiners Florence Friermuth (at left) and Susie Friermuth Duffing after a 1921 liquor raid; Minnesota Congressman Andrew Volstead, author of the national Prohibition law

5 'Blind Pigs, Beer Flats, and Brothels'

Andrew Volstead's Prohibition Bureau
Old Federal Courts Building
75 West Fifth Street, St. Paul

"On Tuesday next the United States will go 'dry'—the first great nation to undertake this stupendous experiment in behalf of public morals," proclaimed the *St. Paul Pioneer Press* in 1919, in a burst of Prohibition-era optimism. "It has been the experience of those cities which have tried prohibition that crime—petty crime, that is—declines under a dry regime," the article went on. "The probabilities are, however, that little by little everybody will become accustomed to the new order. . . . The best thing for the United States to do is to forget as quickly as possible that it ever enjoyed the stimulation of alcohol."[1]

The naiveté now sounds quaint: in fact, the passage of Prohibition nourished the explosive growth of organized crime in every major city in the United States, turning the trickle of bribes to public officials into a torrent of political corruption. Small-time bootleggers like St. Paul's Jack Peifer, Harry Sawyer, and Leon Gleckman were elevated by Prohibition profits into power brokers who could fix a grand jury, buy off a judge, sheriff, or prosecuting attorney, secure a governor's pardon for a convict, and ensure the appointment of a lenient police chief.

The criminals who later hid out in St. Paul—robbers George "Machine Gun Kelly" Barnes, Alvin "Creepy" Karpis, Lester "Babyface Nelson" Gillis, Harvey Bailey, Frank "Jelly" Nash, Verne Miller, and John "Three Fingered Jack" Hamilton—were initiated into crime and civic corruption through the bootleg liquor trade. "Bootlegging was one of the few crimes in history condoned by the people, ignored by the law, and guaranteed to yield fabulous profit with a minimum of grief," concluded crime writer Dean Jennings. "It made millionaires out of illiterates, heroes out of homicidal Robin Hoods, and corrupt public figures out of honest men."[2]

The Volstead Act, passed by Congress in 1919 over the veto of President Woodrow Wilson, provided for enforcement of the Eighteenth Amendment —Prohibition. The act was named after its author, Republican congressman Andrew John Volstead of Granite Falls, Minnesota. Later appointed special counsel to the Prohibition Bureau at its St. Paul headquarters, Volstead drafted indictments against bootleggers from his office in the old Federal Courts Building.

"In 1925, Mr. Volstead was 65 years old," Prohibition Bureau clerk Helen Warren Pfleger recalled. "He was a dignified gentleman, quiet and unassuming, but most affable. . . . He had been a country lawyer before he became a congressman and was far from the 'hail-fellow, well-met' back-slapping type of politician. . . . I wonder how many of the thousands of persons who passed by Mr. Volstead on the streets of downtown St. Paul recognized him. I don't imagine many did, although his name was well-known all over the world."[3]

Ironically, Volstead's home state was uniquely positioned for maximum participation in the bootlegging industry that resulted from the legislation that bore his name. Because St. Paul was a major railroad center, it was easy for the city's bootleggers to export and import liquor disguised as "timber" or "kerosene." By sheer geographical good fortune, the hundreds of miles of wilderness in northern Minnesota and Canada provided an unpoliceable border for liquor smugglers. Prohibition agents said that every week they stopped about two thousand quarts of liquor from being smuggled across the Ontario-Minnesota line into northern Minnesota or from Manitoba into Bemidji.[4]

The German immigrants who came to the state in the 1800s had used its ample fresh water to found more than a hundred breweries; in 1887 Minnesota was the fifth largest beer-producing state in the country. During Prohibition, at least one major brewery—Schmidt—continued to produce limited quantities of illicit alcohol for sale in speakeasies, although it pretended to be making only soft drinks and nonalcoholic "near beer." In one five-month period in the 1920s, Northwest-area Prohibition agents confiscated 240,569 gallons of moonshine, seized more than fifty automobiles, destroyed 315 stills, and arrested 1,275 people. Minnesota's U.S. marshal made more than a thousand arrests for Prohibition offenses in 1920—a figure that did not include local arrests of bootlegging grocers, cab drivers, railroad cooks and Pullman porters, farmers, drugstore retailers, bartenders, and saloon keepers.[5]

"You could buy it if you knew a druggist. . . . They made their own gin and you could buy it in any drugstore," recalled St. Paul crime reporter Nate Bomberg. "And there were speakeasies and apartment houses where after hours you could buy a bottle and drink all night. . . . In fact, it was a joke. People didn't look down on Prohibition. . . . Forbidden fruit is the sweetest."[6]

Prohibition agents tried to uncover home breweries—hidden in outhouses and basements—by tracking deliveries of the oak chips used to color whiskey. "There will be moon," predicted St. Paul police chief Michael Gebhardt in 1922, "as long as the moon shines and people are just beginning to realize how many persons know how to make it." Gebhardt estimated that 75 percent of St. Paul citizens were distilling moonshine or making wine.[7]

The three dozen agents assigned to Minnesota were overwhelmed: in his *Plain Talk* magazine, crusading reporter Walter Liggett claimed that Minnesota harbored ten thousand bootleggers. The official Prohibition Survey of Minnesota winced over Liggett's charges that the state "is dripping wet; that speak-easies, blind pigs, beer flats, and brothels flourish in abundance . . . that gambling joints operate without fear of molestation; and that police and other local officers protect the bootlegger, the gambler, and the prostitute."[8]

The bootleggers of the 1920s were treated as outlaw folk heroes and tolerated by the wealthiest families. For Minnesota's society matrons and businessmen, the liquor baron of choice was Benny Haskell, who sold fine champagne, scotch, and gin out of the Radisson Hotel in Minneapolis. The Justice Department reported that Haskell catered "to a most exclusive clientele of prominent business and professional people in Minneapolis, St. Paul, and Winona, Minnesota."[9]

Opposing the moonshiners were Prohibition agents with a style reminiscent of the marshals who had patrolled the Wild West. St. Paul had Joseph "Two Gun" Alberts, who shot revolvers out of the hands of bootleggers, Malachi (Mel) Harney, who later helped put Al Capone in prison for tax evasion, and Maurice Silverman, who barely escaped death in 1930 after discovering a moonshine still near Robbinsdale, Minnesota. Attempting to arrest the bootleggers, Silverman jumped onto the running board of their getaway car and grabbed the steering wheel, oblivious to the shots the bootleggers fired at him.[10]

Machine guns were not the only hazard Prohibition agents faced during raids. "The life of a Prohibition agent is a demoralizing one due to the fact that he is necessarily and officially bound to consume considerable intoxicating liquor—good and bad, but mostly bad," noted Minneapolis Judge John McGee in a 1924 letter to the U.S. attorney general. "In time he becomes very much as does a criminal lawyer, about as bad morally as the people he operates among and deals with." The judge noted that one Prohibition agent testified to drinking 700 glasses of alcohol and 700 glasses of moonshine whiskey on the job; not surprisingly, dozens of Prohibition cases were dropped when cases fell apart in court.[11]

Meanwhile, the sheer size of distilling operations in Minnesota towns staggered Prohibition agents. In 1921, agents on power boats found moonshine distilleries built on islands in the Mississippi River, with hundreds of gallons of apricot and corn mash hidden under the greenery. They found distilleries hidden in the St. Paul city dump and on farms in Eagan, Mendota, Rosemount, White Bear Lake, New Brighton, Newport, Forest Lake, North St. Paul, and dozens of other communities.[12]

Prohibition inspired bootleggers to new heights of imagination. Gangsters smuggled liquor into Minnesota on railroad cars, disguising the alcohol as scrap iron shipments, hair tonic, castor oil, paint, varnish, "printer's supplies," and even "saddlery." Federal agents found illicit liquor hidden inside steam radiators. In April 1924, federal "dry agents" found a St. Paul bar owner hiding six pints of moonshine whiskey in bottles suspended from her girdle—three pints dangling against each leg.[13]

From stills in Minnesota's Stearns and Morrison Counties sprang a whiskey so popular it had a trade name—Minnesota 13—that came from its chief ingredient, Northern Dent No. 13 corn. Sold to retailers at up to $6.50 a gallon, Minnesota 13 was reportedly tastier than much of the whiskey available legally before Prohibition. "The best moonshine you could buy was made up around St. Cloud; they called it Minnesota 13," recalled Bob Burns, a former club musician. "They made it clean. Some of the moonshine made up in Minneapolis . . . it was so rotten that you'd take the cork out and just the smell of it would make you sick. But you'd hold your nose and gargle it down and throw up a couple of times and try to get some of it to stay down!"[14]

From Wisconsin came shipments of "miniature"—moonshine redistilled for a higher-proof kick. Best of all was 39B, alcohol legally delivered to cosmetics and pharmaceutical companies for hair tonic or perfume. The liquor syndicates diverted the "perfume" for redistillation, after which it become 139-proof "bang-up" liquor sold at up to fifteen dollars a gallon. Much of this imported liquor was spirited into Minneapolis and St. Paul in the railroad cars arriving daily in the Midway "Transfer District." Not surprisingly, some of the state's busiest redistillation factories and speakeasies sprouted along University Avenue in the Midway.[15]

The liquor syndicates discovered that the odoriferous process of creating moonshine from fermenting fruit in a still was inefficient. Instead, they could buy tax-free denatured alcohol from the federal government for "industrial" purposes and then redistill the poisonous mixture for sale to thirsty consumers.[16]

U.S. attorney Lafayette French admitted privately that Minnesota had "become flooded with various forms of specially denatured alcohol under the designation of body rub," thanks to a loophole in the Volstead Act that enabled drugstores in Minneapolis and St. Paul to legally import railroad cars full of Formula 39 "body rub." "Frankly," wrote French, "I believe it is futile to furnish this office with a prosecution broom and ask us to sweep back the sea of body rub which the government, through its permits, allows to come into the district."[17]

One of the more colorful bootleggers in the Midway area was boxer Sammy "the Fighting Tailor" Taran. In 1925 agents raided Taran's distillery at 817 North Wheeler Avenue (a brown-and-cream bungalow that still stands between Hubbard and Hewitt Avenues). The agents claimed that

Dumping illegal liquor at Pillsbury and Charles Streets, St. Paul, about 1925

Taran's distillery was part of a million-dollar alcohol ring that used the bungalow to redistill "body-rub alcohol" into "high-grade whiskey." But the liquid evidence against Taran disappeared: nearly every bottle of the alcohol seized from his home in 1925 was inexplicably destroyed by Prohibition agents. The jury was forced to acquit him of bootlegging charges, a verdict that inspired Judge Hugo Hanft to rail against the agents for failing to preserve the evidence against Taran. The incident reflected the most corrosive by-product of the bootlegging business—the tens of thousands of dollars in protection money required for local police, sheriffs, judges, prosecutors, and even Prohibition agents. The city of St. Paul, with its twenty-year tradition of corruption through the O'Connor system, provided rich soil for Prohibition bribery.[18]

As early as 1920, northwest Prohibition chief Paul D. Keller admitted that bootleggers had been "tipped off" to virtually every major raid he had undertaken in Minnesota during the previous fourteen days, inspiring an investigation of his entire Prohibition staff. In 1926 a liquor baron told Treasury agents that corruption was so complete in St. Paul that a local bootlegger was able to walk freely into the central police station and steal back his own confiscated liquor. Newspapers reported that when federal agents raided bars and distilleries, they found empty warehouses—and were jeered by moonshiners who had been notified that they were coming. It was only years later, when the FBI questioned Dillinger gang girlfriend Beth Green, that the government learned that in the late 1920s, Dan Hogan had installed a woman informant in the Prohibition Bureau in the Federal Courts Building.[19]

Then, on February 16, 1925, the murder of a St. Paul liquor hijacker named Burt Stevens split open the largest liquor conspiracy in the United States. The killing revealed the breadth of corruption extending from the St. Paul Police Department up to the most powerful federal prosecutors in Minnesota.

6 'A Lawless Business Grown to Gigantic Proportions'

The Murder of Burt Stevens
465 St. Peter Street, St. Paul

The *St. Paul Dispatch* described the 1925 slaying of liquor hijacker Burt Stevens and the revelations of corruption that followed as "the most scandalous episode that has ever disgraced these twin communities." The article noted that the scandal was "prohibition in its finest flower—larceny, banditry and murder superimposed upon bribery and violation of the liquor law."[20]

With 112 indictments for Prohibition violations, the Cleveland liquor case that followed the killing of Stevens became the largest liquor conspiracy case in the history of Prohibition. The collapse of the liquor syndicate began when Stevens was shot outside the Dreis Brothers' Drug Store on the southwest corner of the intersection of Seventh (then Ninth) Street and St. Peter, adjacent to what is today Mickey's Diner.

The reasons for the slaying went back to 1923, when St. Paul bootlegger Bennie Gleeman and Harry Gellman, a tailor from Minneapolis, formed the Gleeman-Gellman alcohol ring. Joining these underworld entrepreneurs were poolroom proprietor Morris Roisner, who acted as accountant and office manager; defense attorney Abe Ginsberg, the fixer and political connection; and an up-and-coming liquor mogul named Leon Gleckman, who would become the most powerful syndicate figure in St. Paul. Roisner dreamed up the front names (the Kevin Sweet Grass Developing Company was a poetic one) and rented the ring's headquarters in St. Paul's Builders Exchange Building. The ring began to ship scotch whisky and champagne, disguised as "lubricating oil," in trucks painted with the names of fictitious moving companies.[21]

The rival bootleggers of Minneapolis and St. Paul averted a liquor war by agreeing in 1924 to cooperate in importing liquor. The Minneapolis group, led by Isadore "Kid Cann" Blumenfeld and his friends Abe "Brownie" Brownstein and Edward "Barney" Berman, called themselves "the Minneapolis Combination." The St. Paul bootleggers, whose roster swelled to include Gleeman's brother Abe, now referred to their operation as "the Syndicate." The Syndicate received its liquor through Cleveland, where gangsters purchased denatured grain alcohol legally from the federal government. Organized along the lines of a corporation, the Cleveland liquor ring operated through underworld figures in St. Paul, Duluth, Minneapolis, and dozens of other U.S. cities. The Cleveland ring offered its affiliates protection through the bribery of local police officials and railroad men, warehouses to store the liquor in, and toughs to discourage liquor hijackers.

By the mid-1920s, the St. Paul Syndicate was importing two carloads of Cleveland alcohol a week, producing weekly revenues of between $100,000 and $200,000. With profits of $20,000 a week, the Syndicate decided, according to Bennie Gleeman, to set aside money to buy protection. Gleeman said that a bribery fund of 14 percent of Syndicate profits—nearly $3,000 a week—was turned over to Minnesota law-enforcement officers. One underworld rumor held that in the early 1920s, the Syndicate was paying the chief of the St. Paul police, Frank Sommers, one dollar for every gallon of illegal liquor sold.[22]

The Syndicate demonstrated its influence over local authorities in the winter of 1923–24, when the Prohibition Bureau seized 237 barrels of denatured alcohol from the Syndicate and stored the liquor at the Kedney warehouse in Minneapolis. Unperturbed, the Syndicate simply paid the warehouse clerk a $75-per-barrel bribe. In exchange, the Syndicate was allowed to steal back 170 barrels of its alcohol, replacing the incriminating evidence with tap water.[23]

A local bootlegger, under questioning by assistant U.S. attorney William Anderson, unexpectedly offered to expose the Syndicate members who had stolen back the Kedney liquor. Suddenly, all charges against the Syndicate were dropped, and Anderson ordered the evidence against the Syndicate destroyed. Ben Gleeman later told a grand jury that the Syndicate bribed Anderson to allow the gang to steal the liquor back. Justice Department informants reported that Anderson was taking thousands of dollars from the Syndicate, enabling the modestly paid official to outfit his $30,000 home with expensive oriental rugs and furniture. Anderson left the U.S. attorney's office in 1929 and became defense attorney for Syndicate bootlegger Leon Gleckman.[24]

The Syndicate's most troubling problem was not the police or even Prohibition agents, but the threat posed by hijackers determined to steal the Syndicate's liquor or extort hush money. Two Syndicate enforcers, Tommie

Webber and Morrie Miller, guarded liquor shipments as they were unloaded. In a prophetic aside, Morris Roisner said that they were "such bad men that they would not hesitate to shoot in broad daylight on as thickly a traveled street as Seventh and Wabasha in St. Paul." If Miller had killed one man, Roisner said, he had killed twenty.[25]

In February 1925 members of the Syndicate were at St. Paul's Milwaukee freight yards to load the latest shipment of alcohol. They were surprised by hijacker Burton Stevens, a twenty-two-year-old hoodlum from Chrechtenville, Iowa, and an accomplice. Stevens warned that Prohibition agents had spotted the liquor and would arrest them unless they paid Stevens a protection fee. The Syndicate guessed that Stevens's warning was a hoax, and Miller had to be restrained from killing Stevens on the spot.[26]

Days later, Bennie Gleeman, driving a truck carrying more than seventy-five cases of scotch whisky, found that he was being followed by Stevens. Gleeman confronted Stevens, saying, "You fellows put a scare into us, I thought you were Feds. I have some stuff in the garage, don't touch it."[27]

That afternoon, Stevens called the Syndicate from the Dreis Drug Store in downtown St. Paul. "I heard a couple of Jews are looking for me," he snarled. "Words don't mean anything on the telephone, come on over and see me." Bennie Gleeman and Morrie Miller drove through downtown, where Gleeman spotted Stevens in front of the drugstore. In a confrontation on the street, Stevens and Miller both brandished guns. Miller shouted, "You won't hijack my stuff anymore" and shot Stevens in the head and chest.[28]

The Syndicate assured Gleeman "that they were going to square everything with the Chief of Police in St. Paul and that all I had to do was to keep quiet and not involve anybody in the shooting." Bootlegger Leon Gleckman "had a drag with the St. Paul Police force, [and] would fix everything so that no one would get in trouble," the Syndicate's lawyer assured Gleeman.

The Syndicate shuttled the Gleeman brothers from hideout to hideout, terrified that the ring would be exposed if the police interviewed Bennie. Under pressure from the Syndicate, Abe Gleeman agreed to falsify testimony to protect his brother. As an extra incentive, the gang promised Abe that if he ever exposed the workings of the Syndicate, Morrie Miller would come back to Minnesota and kill him.[29]

Four days after the shooting, the Gleeman brothers turned themselves in. A first trial ended with a deadlocked jury, but in a second trial, in April 1925, with star prosecutor Pierce Butler Jr. at the helm, both Gleemans were found guilty of murder and sentenced to spend their lives in prison. Government prosecutors denied that Miller existed, calling him a "phantom gunman."[30]

The Gleeman brothers, Ben and Abe (at front), with escorts, after being sentenced to life in prison

In September the Gleemans demanded a third trial, filing fifty-six affidavits from eyewitnesses claiming they were innocent and identifying Morrie Miller as the murderer. Abandoned by the liquor ring, the Gleemans decided to split the Syndicate open. They confessed that the St. Paul group was merely a branch of a $140 million alcohol business run out of the Superior Industrial Alcohol Company in Cleveland.[31]

When agents raided Superior Alcohol, they seized 5,865 drums of denatured alcohol, stumbling over evidence that the conspiracy stretched both east and west: to Pittsburgh, Philadelphia, Baltimore, Atlantic City, Detroit, Chicago, St. Paul, Minneapolis, Duluth, and San Francisco. Nearly 900,000 gallons of liquor were distributed to bootleggers across the country each week. Most importantly, the Gleeman trial brought to light the millions of dollars in protection fees paid to corrupt police, railroad staff, and federal agents.[32]

Inspired largely by the Gleemans' confessions, Treasury agents immersed themselves in the Cleveland ring's trail of telegrams, bank transactions, and telephone calls. The government issued a 50,000-word indictment charging more than one hundred defendants with nearly a hundred illegal acts in twelve cities. Ben and Abe Gleeman, under life sentences at Minnesota's Stillwater State Prison, testified before a Cleveland grand jury that indicted more than sixty Minnesota residents tied to the liquor conspiracy. Of the 112 Cleveland liquor case defendants indicted in 1926, an astonishing 41 lived in St. Paul. The chief prosecutor, Cleveland district attorney A. E. Bernstein, called St. Paul "the most flagrant center of the nationwide alcohol ring."[33]

"Here is disclosed amongst us a lawless business grown to positively gigantic proportions," noted the *St. Paul Dispatch*. "According to the Gleemans, it ran in money to something like $200,000 a week, or approximately $10,000,000 a year. This is about as much money as is spent annually by the city of St. Paul." Unsympathetic to the Gleemans' claims that they had been framed, the *Dispatch* declared that if "they are not properly in the penitentiary for murder, by their own confessions they ought to be there for a variety of other crimes.... They are behind prison walls and that is surely where they belong."[34]

Throughout the Gleemans' trials, there were barely hidden overtones of anti-Semitism and nativism directed against bootleggers, many of whom were Jewish immigrants. U.S. attorney Lafayette French promised to deport foreign-born members of the alcohol syndicate. French said that "a large percentage of the leading figures in the illicit liquor business in the Northwest are not American citizens," reported the *St. Paul Pioneer Press*, "and the combined effort will be undertaken to drive those aliens convicted of major crimes from the country." One Prohibition Bureau survey of Minnesota analyzed obedience to prohibition laws by "foreign-born units of the population, as well as those of mixed and foreign parentage," noting that in Minnesota "a pronounced foreign strain characterizes the population." "I have no use for foreigners who come to this country and break laws with impunity," agreed federal judge John McGee in 1923, after sentencing soft drink parlor operator Sam Vannovich for Prohibition violations. "In my opinion they all should be sent back to the countries from which they came."[35]

Walter Liggett, in his *Plain Talk* magazine, summed up the attitudes of many Minnesotans toward Jewish bootleggers such as Bennie and Abe Gleeman with this doggerel: "Ten thousand Jews are making booze/ In endless repetition/ To fill the needs of a million Swedes/ Who wanted Prohibition."[36]

The O'Connor system of police protection held fast during the search for gunman Morrie Miller. A Los Angeles district attorney condemned the city of St. Paul for allowing Miller, then suspected of a California drug company robbery, to jump bond and escape prosecution for Stevens's murder.[37]

If "Miller is a phantom, local officialdom made him so," editorialized the

Pioneer Press. "The regular phantom factories are in St. Paul government. The police can make phantoms of criminals while you wait, the best in the business." Finally Miller was apprehended and brought to St. Paul in April 1929, but two Ramsey County grand juries failed to indict him for the Stevens murder. What St. Paul refused to do, the underworld handled on its own. After Miller became an assistant to East Coast bootlegger Irving "Waxey Gordon" Wexler, he was shot to death by New York mobsters in 1933.[38]

Although the O'Connor system could not protect the Syndicate from the Cleveland grand jury, the gang could employ the best defense lawyers in the Upper Midwest to fight the liquor charges. Assistant U.S. attorney M. E. Evans confessed privately that the conspiracy defendants from Minnesota were formidable opponents in court: each of the twenty-three defendants had one to five lawyers, who were remarkable for their "sheer cussedness."[39]

In 1927 thirteen of the defendants pleaded guilty. Morris Roisner and Sammy Harris were sentenced to prison time in Georgia, Harry Gellman was sentenced to fourteen months in an Atlanta prison, and others received workhouse sentences and jail terms.[40]

Although the trials destroyed the Gellman syndicate, two of the Cleveland defendants surfaced later. One was police officer Thomas A. Brown, arrested and temporarily suspended from the St. Paul Police Department when a federal judge ordered him to Cleveland on charges of participating in the liquor smuggling. All charges against Brown were dismissed; he rose to become chief of the St. Paul police from 1930 to 1932 and played a pivotal role in the John Dillinger and Barker-Karpis cases of the 1930s.[41]

In addition, the FBI discovered that Brown had an alter ego in the St. Paul underworld. According to a 1932 FBI report, "Brown, the former Chief of Police at St. Paul . . . [was] known to be intimately associated with Leon Gleckman and to have been controlled by Leon Gleckman while in the St. Paul Police Department." With the Gellman ring gone, Gleckman—bootlegger, power broker, underworld fixer—could step into the vacuum. The bootlegger's target was nothing short of the St. Paul mayor's office.[42]

7 'A Rendezvous for Gangsters'

The Hotel St. Paul Headquarters of Leon Gleckman
363 St. Peter Street, St. Paul

Every American city had its Prohibition beer baron. In Chicago, it was Alphonse "Scarface" Capone. In New York, it was Arthur "Dutch Schultz" Flegenheimer. And in St. Paul, it was Leon Gleckman.

Gleckman "played an active part in politics and in the affairs of this city generally and in that way became a strong factor in the city government," confided U.S. attorney Lewis L. Drill to the U.S. attorney general in 1933. He "was regarded by some as the Al Capone of St. Paul. That he had influence and acquired influential friends there is no doubt. Moreover, these friends and influences were not at all confined to characters of the underworld, so to speak. On the contrary they included bankers, lawyers, and in fact persons in practically all walks of life." Gleckman cultivated friends in very high places: prosecutors found records of phone conversations between Gleckman and the office of U.S. Senator Thomas Schall, prominent bankers, and Republican political leaders. Gleckman was even able to get Congressman Einar Hoidale to intercede with the U.S. attorney general in an attempt to postpone a criminal case against him in 1934.[43]

This unorthodox "politician" was born in 1894 in Minsk, Russia (today in Belarus), the third of eight children raised by Gershon and Nechama Gleckman. Gershon was described in his son's prison records as "a strict disciplinarian, a total abstainer and law-abiding man." Nechama (Nettie), originally from Austria and the daughter of a rabbi, was described in government files as "a religious, tolerant woman." The Gleckmans came to the United States from Minsk through London, Nova Scotia, and finally Port Huron, Michigan, during the winter of 1903. As a teenager, Gleckman married clerical worker Rose Goldstein, with whom he had three daughters. A salesman by inclination, a bootlegger by vocation, and a sports buff by avocation, Gleckman was described in prison records as "self-confident, glib, respectful."[44]

Psychological tests at Leavenworth prison highlighted Gleckman's intelligence. The prison analysis said Gleckman's problem-solving abilities and insight exceeded those of 92 percent of the inmates, "showing that this man is of a high degree of planfulness and efficiency." The prison file concluded by observing that Gleckman was "a rather aggressive, pleasant appearing cooperative hebrew. . . . His aggressiveness is characteristic of his general impressions derived from members of his race, but there is nothing offensive about them."[45]

Gleckman was first arrested in 1922, when Prohibition agents raided his Minnesota Blueing Company on University Avenue in Minneapolis. The government estimated that Gleckman's two-story factory, equipped with thirteen stills, was generating annual profits of a million dollars.[46]

Right away, Gleckman showed the inclination for bribery that was to elevate him to boss of the St. Paul underworld. After pleading guilty in U.S. District Court to liquor conspiracy, he was sentenced to eighteen months in Leavenworth; his attorney later claimed that Gleckman discussed a bribe with the prosecutor before the conviction and afterward paid the prosecutor to file a false confession of error in the Circuit Court of Appeals. But the appeals court did not buy the scheme and affirmed Gleckman's conviction.[47]

Gleckman was philosophical about the failure of the deal, telling his attorney that he would resign himself to serving his time in prison "if he could get his $30,000 back" from the bribery attempts. Imprisoned in Leavenworth in 1927, Gleckman was so well behaved that he was made a trusty and assigned to the greenhouse.[48]

When he was released, Gleckman turned the third floor of the Hotel St. Paul into his headquarters for summit meetings with gangsters and politicians, according to a Treasury Department probe. On January 18, 1930, Gleckman moved into suites 301–303, where, from an unlisted telephone, he made hundreds of phone calls to Chicago, New Orleans, Milwaukee, New York, Havana, and Montreal. His prominence in the underworld was such that in March 1932—at the height of the FBI's hunt for fugitive bank robbers Francis L. "Jimmy" Keating and Thomas Holden—the FBI rented room 309 to spy on Gleckman's visitors. The FBI also targeted the hotel in its search for prison escapee Frank Nash, noting that "the St. Paul Hotel . . . is believed to be a rendezvous for gangsters." On the other side of the law, Michael Malone, the Treasury Department agent who infiltrated Al Capone's syndicate in Chicago, maintained a room at the hotel.[49]

Interviewed by the FBI years later, Gleckman confirmed that he had "maintained offices" at the hotel "for the purpose of carrying on his political enterprises." According to FBI records, Gleckman's "political enterprises" chiefly involved payments of protection money to police, commissioners, city councilors, and other power brokers—which, in turn, gave Gleckman the power to assist others who wanted favors from these figures. An underworld informant told the FBI that Tom Brown, who was then chief of police, rented a room at the hotel to facilitate payoffs. Boxer Walter "Saph" McKenna of the Hollyhocks Club casino delivered weekly payments to Brown's room.[50]

Police officials Charles Tierney and Thomas Dahill told the FBI that from 1930 to 1932, when Brown was chief of police, all gambling in the city was controlled by Gleckman through his suite in the Hotel St. Paul. Gleckman confessed to FBI agents that he had used political connections to help his friend Tom Brown become police chief. Gleckman added that "with the return of legalized liquor [Gleckman] left the racket and, having a large amount of money, entered the political situation in St. Paul with the hope of some day becoming Mayor of St. Paul."[51]

Gleckman told the FBI that "he had excellent contacts in the political setup in St. Paul during that period [1930–32] and that he made more money

Hotel St. Paul in 1933, headquarters for bootlegging king Leon Gleckman (right)

through politically secured contracts than he ever made in the alcohol business." Gleckman boasted that he had purchased several city councilors as a way to "secure a foothold in politics."[52]

While Gleckman was engineering political deals upstairs, the hotel's circular driveway served as a bootleg distribution center. Austin Cravath, a Texaco filling station owner, was recruited by Minneapolis gangster Isadore "Kid Cann" Blumenfeld to manage his St. Paul alcohol operations hidden at the Dexheimer farm near Mendota and the Fransmeyer farm just off Highway 110 near Fort Snelling. Cravath's son Calvert, now a resident of Stillwater, Minnesota, recalled that "everybody either made it, sold it or drank it—no matter who they were, from preachers on down. There was no stigma to alcy [alcohol] at that time."

As a teenager, Calvert hid gasoline cans filled with alcohol under the hood of his father's Studebaker. The Cravaths would drive the car—customized with a souped-up engine capable of reaching speeds of a hundred miles per hour—into the curved driveway that still graces the Hotel St. Paul. "It was all arranged with the bellhop," Cravath recalled. The bellmen "knew exactly when you'd be there, they had $100 cash—$25 per gallon. The alcy cost us $3 to make, and sold wholesale for $8 per gallon." Cravath figured that his father's distilling operation made a profit of $2,000 a day—which, Cravath quipped, "gives you quite a cushion for the unexpected expenses."[53]

Protection payments were made at Fort Snelling, near where the liquor was made, Cravath said. Farmers and sheriffs operating near the distillery received a gallon of liquid bribery every week. As a result, the ring enjoyed advance notice of police raids. During these well-rehearsed operations, reporters were invited to watch the police plunge axes into a pair of sacrificial stills; the active stills were hidden behind blankets. When the reporters left, the ring picked up two new stills from a Minneapolis warehouse to guarantee that there would be no interruption in production.

By 1932, Austin Cravath's operations usually produced between 400 and 610 gallons of alcohol every twenty-four hours. The four-hundred-gallon stills had sixteen gas burners to cook the alcohol. ("You wore shorts and tennis shoes, with sweat rolling off you," recalled Cravath.) Guards equipped with submachine guns protected the Cravath operation against hijacking, but on occasion they would slip out to hijack someone else's load of liquor. "We were so big, that [once] one of our semi trucks left, the call [alarm signal] went off, and our hijackers hijacked our own stuff!" said Cravath. Cravath's liquor business operated freely through the fall of 1933. The bootlegging ring was then told the precise date on which its guaranteed police protection would expire. A convoy of trucks guarded by a crew of enforcers with sawed-off pump shotguns brought the surplus alcohol to a customer in Chicago by the name of Al Capone.[54]

8 'The Lousiest Crime in the World'

Leon Gleckman's Home
2168 Sargent Avenue, St. Paul

Leon Gleckman's considerable influence at City Hall and police headquarters could not protect him from an occupational hazard common to bootleggers of the 1930s—gangsters who kidnapped other gangsters. Gleckman was abducted on September 24, 1931, from his home, which he shared with his wife of eighteen years. He was held hostage for eight days in a cottage forty miles from Woodruff, Wisconsin. The initial ransom was thought to be as high as $200,000, but when the kidnappers contacted Gleckman's partner, Morris Roisner, the amount had dropped to $75,000. The final sum was precipitously reduced to $5,000, plus the $1,450 in cash that Gleckman had in his pockets. With the help of go-between John "Jack" Peifer of the Hollyhocks casino—newspapers hailed Peifer for performing an "errand of mercy" in negotiating with the kidnappers—Gleckman was released on October 2.[55]

The FBI discovered that there was far more to the Gleckman kidnapping than had made the newspapers; it involved suspicious intermingling of the underworld and the police. One of the four men who kidnapped Gleckman, Albert Tallerico, told his fellow inmates at Stillwater Prison that casino operator Peifer had engineered the kidnapping. Tallerico said that Gleckman's kidnappers "lived in mortal terror of Jack Peifer," claiming that St. Paul police chief Tom Brown and the county attorney had both warned the kidnappers that "if they knew what was good for them they would not mention the name of Jack Peifer" when the grand jury investigated the abduction.[56]

To be sure, there was no love lost between Leon Gleckman and Jack Peifer. An underworld informant detailed how Gleckman's syndicate had once hijacked Peifer's liquor; Peifer, accompanied by strongman William "Dutch" Canner, met with Gleckman and threatened to kill him if he ever interfered with Peifer's business again. "Some friends had recently told [Gleckman] that he would be surprised to know that some persons whom he regarded as friends had participated in the kidnapping," the FBI learned from Gleckman years later. Gleckman told the agents that he intended to investigate the rumors and "would take care of them in his own way."[57]

One of Gleckman's kidnappers, hotel proprietor Frank LaPre, was found on suburban St. Paul's Lake Vadnais Boulevard on October 3, 1931, dead of multiple gunshots in the face. Immediately after LaPre was killed, the other conspirators were apprehended and convicted of the kidnapping.[58]

Several stories were told to account for these events. Kidnapper Tallerico claimed that Jack Peifer and another member of the kidnap gang had driven out to see LaPre, who was allegedly holding out on returning $5,000 of Gleckman's ransom money. But according to a former St. Paul police officer, a list of the kidnappers was beaten out of LaPre just before he died; then Gleckman himself turned the list over to the police. Chief Tom Brown handed the list of suspects to a pair of officers, who promptly picked them up. "Fellas, you did a great job," Brown reportedly told the officers, relaxing in his office with Gleckman. The Gleckman ransom money, recovered from LaPre's hotel safe, was shifted into Brown's campaign fund to finance his unsuccessful run for Ramsey County sheriff.[59]

An FBI informant confirmed the latter story with a slightly different scenario: saloon keeper Frank Reilly told agents that "La Pre was killed by Brown and others and planted in an automobile to make it look like the kidnapping gang had killed LaPre, because he was thought to have double-crossed them." Taxi driver George Rafferty, Brown's brother-in-law, told the FBI that he too had heard rumors that the police killed LaPre and then planted his body in another car to make it look like he had been murdered by underworld companions.[60]

Improbably, the city's leading racketeer publicly hailed the police department, which Gleckman said "rescued me from possible death at the hands of kidnappers and within 26 hours had captured the gangsters and recovered the $5,000 ransom money." The bootlegger offered special praise for policeman Tom Brown, who had been under attack by mayoral candidate William Mahoney. "During the administration of Chief of Police Thomas A. Brown, there have been no gangland murders," said Gleckman to reporters, "and what few major crimes there have been have been promptly and effectively cleared up. . . . I feel it my duty to defend the department against any slurs that may be cast upon it by mud that is intended to be thrown at me."[61]

After the trauma of being kidnapped, the FBI reported, "Gleckman had a police guard near his house, ostensibly to guard against another kidnapping." For months after the kidnapping, Gleckman's protectors—not his bodyguards, but the St. Paul police—were on edge. One evening, a neighbor looking for his five-year-old daughter passed Gleckman's house a few times. Suddenly, the FBI said, the neighbor was "accosted, kicked around and generally abused by two city detectives who accused him of having designs on Gleckman's life." The man was able to convince the police that he was just looking for his errant daughter. Many underworld bosses across the United

States controlled members of their police departments, but how many gangsters could command police officers to stand guard outside their home?[62]

Despite the security, Gleckman's daughter Florence was kidnapped by gangsters in the summer of 1932 but was released without payment of the $50,000 ransom when the kidnappers ran into problems with their hideout. Gleckman told FBI agents that "kidnapping is the lousiest crime in the world." During the investigation of the William Hamm kidnapping in 1933, Gleckman told agents that he normally would not give them information, but because of his personal experiences with kidnappings he would help the FBI identify Hamm's kidnappers.[63]

After his daughter was kidnapped, Gleckman hired a sixteen-year-old girl to clean, cook, and walk the children home from school each day. Apart from the shock of finding a revolver under Gleckman's bedroom pillow ("I was scared to death, I'd never seen a gun before"), Gertrude Sletner remembered her four years as the Gleckman family's maid with pleasure.

Gleckman spent most of his time away from his Sargent Avenue residence on business. His evenings were spent at local movie theaters with wife, Rose. Gleckman would fall asleep the moment the movie began and wake up for the final credits. "Leon said it was the only way he could get any sleep," said Sletner.

The Gleckmans, for all their wealth, still had the simple tastes of immigrants from the eastern European shtetl; his favorite dishes were raw hamburger and barely cooked rump roast. The Gleckmans once asked Sletner to prepare some chopped liver for their dinner, and Sletner forgot the culinary assignment. Later, Rose Gleckman opened the refrigerator, stuck her finger in a bowl, and told Gertrude how terrific her chopped liver was. Puzzled by the comment, Sletner peeked inside the refrigerator. Mrs. Gleckman had been extolling the fine taste of a bowl of dog food.[64]

9 'See If He Wants to Be Mayor'

The Merchants Bank Building
Fourth and Robert Streets, St. Paul

Determined to break Leon Gleckman's hold on city government, in 1932 federal agents stepped up their surveillance by installing a telephone wiretap at his Republic Finance Company, an auto finance firm located in suite 713 of the Merchants Bank Building. To the Prohibition Bureau's dismay, the tap was located by telephone company representatives only four days after it had been installed at great inconvenience and expense ("four nights being necessary to complete same," noted the Prohibition Bureau director,

Liquor baron Leon Gleckman after his release by kidnappers, with wife, Rose, and daughters Lorraine and Helen Mae at their Sargent Avenue home in 1931

"the work being done at intervals when employees of the building were not present").[65]

Despite the government's electronic intrusion, Gleckman continued as unofficial czar of St. Paul. "Leon kept a jar on the desk where people would drop parking tickets," recalled Max Ehrlich, Gleckman's partner in Republic Finance. "At the end of the week, a big Irish cop would drop by, take a fistful of cigars and bring the tickets to City Hall—and that's the last you'd hear of them. . . . Leon Gleckman *was* the Mayor of St. Paul, at least indirectly!"

"I overheard this conversation with Leon," said Ehrlich. "'So and so doesn't want to be mayor.' And Leon said, 'Go call this fellow and see if *he* wants to be mayor!'" The candidate mattered little; Gleckman was already the chief executive officer of Minnesota's capital city.[66]

Gleckman's political power reached its zenith in early 1932, when Justice Department memoranda admitted that Gleckman "controlled the local government in the City of St. Paul." But then on May 3, 1932, William J. Mahoney was elected mayor after a campaign during which he claimed Gleckman had "one-man control" of the underworld. A Treasury Department agent reported that Mahoney had promised to "eliminate Mr. Gleckman from control in local affairs and rid the City of St. Paul from gangster influences." Gleckman responded by offering to donate $5,000 to charity if Mahoney "could prove his malicious charges." Mahoney called the offer a "gangster trick" and declined to take up Gleckman's challenge.[67]

When a Treasury Department investigation discovered evidence that Gleckman was laundering his income through Republic Finance Company, the business's records suddenly disappeared. Powerful forces pressed hard for a full investigation into Gleckman's power. The publisher of the *St. Paul Dispatch* wrote to the U.S. attorney general

> Gleckman is the real political boss in the city and . . . he controls the police and the Council and probably controls the liquor and gambling traffic. We have reached a point where I think something should be done and I am anxious to have something started in the very near future, because I feel that it is time for St. Paul to be rid of gangs and racketeers and gangsters who are now having so much influence in the political and social life of the city.[68]

Assistant U.S. attorney George A. Heisey seconded the publisher's outrage: "While in the past several years, Special Agents of the Prohibition Service have had the taxpayer [Gleckman] under close surveillance, [and] have had 'taps' on telephone wires at his home and at his office, they never have been able, since his release from the penitentiary in 1928, to connect him with the illegal liquor traffic."[69]

Michael Malone and J. N. Sullivan, the Internal Revenue agents who had helped bust Al Capone, were reassigned to work on Gleckman's tax case in 1932. Gleckman reported paying income taxes of $432, far short of the $69,443 the agents believed Gleckman really owed. Sullivan crisscrossed North America—from the St. Paul Boxing Club to Havana's Mill Creek Distillery—to obtain information on Gleckman's hidden assets. Identifying precisely how much Gleckman owned, and where, and with whom was an enormously complex task. "I am not sure how this case will work out," wrote one worried prosecutor. "We are apparently meeting terrific pressure on witnesses, for their memory is either bad or they are denying facts which our investigating leads us to believe existed."[70]

Gleckman's power was diminished by the repeal of the Eighteenth Amendment in 1933 (passed by Congress in February and ratified by 36 states on December 5), and then permanently limited by his 1934 conviction for tax evasion. The government proved that he had concealed $366,522 in income between 1929 and 1931. Gleckman had been clever enough to make the ledger sheets at the bank that documented his deposits disappear. Unfortunately, his envoys forgot to remove the deposit slips, which tipped off the government to the invisible transactions. He was convicted again in May 1937 in U.S. District Court of attempting to bribe a juror during his earlier tax evasion cases. But even as Gleckman's power waned, he could be found acting the role of "the Al Capone of St. Paul" at the Hotel St. Paul and the Boulevards of Paris nightclub.[71]

10–12 St. Paul's Roaring Nightlife

10. The Mystic Caverns
676 Joy Avenue, St. Paul
11. The Castle Royal
6 West Channel Street, St. Paul
12. The Boulevards of Paris and the Coliseum Ballroom
1100 West University Avenue, St. Paul

The flood of criminal talent drawn by the O'Connor system's leniency toward felons to St. Paul in the early 1930s—from the Ozarks, Los Angeles, Chicago, and New York—produced a roaring nightlife of jazz, fine liquor, and high-stakes gambling. By 1932 the 271,606 residents of St. Paul supported forty-four theaters and fourteen major hotels, along with innumerable speakeasies (or "blind pigs") and casinos.[72]

Among the most unusual of the gambling emporiums were the Mystic Caverns and the Castle Royal, two nightclubs built inside the cool sandstone mushroom caves along the Mississippi River bluffs. The Mystic Caverns, which featured fan dances by stripper Sally Rand, was a multichambered cave casino outfitted with roulette wheels and blackjack tables. Robert Brooks Hamilton, later of gangland's notorious Hollyhocks nightclub, and Chicago pickpocket Robert "Frisco Dutch" Steinhardt supervised gambling at the Mystic Caverns. "In the fall of 1933 Bob Hamilton put up a $500 bankroll to back a gambling game we operated in a cave in the side of a mountain near St. Paul," Steinhardt told FBI agents. "This cave was on the property of two brothers named Fester [actually Foster]," one of whom was director of the St. Paul Police Band.[73]

"The Mystic Caverns was the most beautiful place you ever saw," recalled Sarah Knutson, whose father helped maintain the nightclub, hauling out the white sand that sifted down from the cave walls. "The cavern had a monstrous chandelier, with lights flashing all different colors, [hung] two stories above the polished-wood dance floor. It was a thrill—people would walk from miles to get to the Mystic Caverns." The club boasted a full kitchen, a restaurant with white tablecloths, and a private penthouse for underworld business meetings. Knutson recalled surprises hidden throughout the club

—including men dressed as glow-in-the-dark skeletons and an Egyptian mummy in a casket; the mummy would change into an attractive woman, courtesy of the mirror-and-light illusion known to magicians as "Pepper's Ghost." In 1934 a Ramsey County grand jury investigation led to convictions for running an underground casino, closing the Mystic Caverns forever.[74]

In its heyday the Castle Royal (which most recently reopened as the Wabasha Street Caves) featured rich oriental carpets and glittering chandeliers, gambling in the back room, and performances by Cab Calloway, the Dorsey brothers, and Harry James. Although there is no proof that Dillinger and other gangsters frequented the Royal, current owners Donna and Steve Bremer have heard all of the gangland legends. "Ma Barker and her gang stopped into the club," claimed Donna Bremer. "In the 1930s, the underworld would come to these nightclubs on the weekend, and then the wealthy of Minneapolis and St. Paul would come just to see the gangsters."[75]

"The Castle Royal was built in a mushroom cave," recalled former St. Paul police officer Pat Lannon Sr. "They turned it into a nightclub, put in

Castle Royal nightclub, built into the Mississippi River bluffs; 1933 ad announcing club's grand opening

gambling—craps and poker and cards—in the back end." Lannon claimed that the Castle Royal's gambling operations figured in a scheme by Tom Brown (reassigned as a police detective) to destroy rival George Moeller's campaign for Ramsey County sheriff. Lannon took candidate Moeller on a guided tour of the Royal when the police held a party at the club. "But we skirted the gambling room and didn't take him there," laughed Lannon. "Next day, talk about a con, there's a newspaper article about gambling at the Castle Royal and the article said that [Moeller] was there. They put him on the spot and the grand jury was going to have an investigation to railroad Moeller!" Lannon went to Ramsey County Attorney Michael Kinkead and explained Brown's political maneuvering; formal charges were never brought against Moeller.[76]

When it opened in October 1933, the Castle Royal promoted itself in newspapers as "the World's Most Gorgeous Underground Nite Club." Its motto, "Fit for a King," referred to opening night entertainment by Juan King and his ten-piece Castle Royal Orchestra.[77]

The Mystic Caverns and the Castle Royal were dwarfed by the mammoth Boulevards of Paris nightclub at the southwest corner of Lexington Parkway and University Avenue and its adjacent dancehall, the Coliseum Ballroom. The Boulevards was "the fanciest place this side of New York," recalled Marguerite Junterman, daughter of its proprietor, John Lane. "If you hadn't made it to the Boulevards of Paris, you hadn't seen St. Paul!"[78]

The Coliseum, built as an ice rink in 1918, later got a vast dance floor—at 100-by-250 feet, the largest in the world at that time, its owner claimed. Three thousand revelers would sneak in bottles of ginger ale spiked with bootleg whiskey to enhance their enjoyment of such name acts as Fats Waller and Ben Pollack. The Coliseum catered to what Junterman called "the cheaper crowd," serving hot dogs rather than steaks.[79]

In contrast, the Boulevards of Paris offered elegant cigarette girls, twenty-five stage dancers performing a new show every Friday, and tuxedoed and gowned patrons. When it opened in 1929, the Boulevards promoted chef Karl Seidel's cuisine ("European dishes of Old World Origin and rare delicacy"), a ladies' waiting room decorated with black satin and mirrors, simulated Parisian sidewalks, and a full-scale reproduction of the American Bar in Paris.[80]

A basement casino, ringing with the sounds of poker, roulette, and craps, was supervised by gambling expert "Frisco Dutch" Steinhardt. "In about the year of 1930, Ben Harris and John Lane and Bob Hamilton were operating the Boulevards of Paris, a night club in St Paul," Steinhardt told the FBI. "I went into partnership with them, and we opened up a gambling casino at this place." Gambling executive Ben Harris, a former publicist for

The Coliseum Ballroom; impresario John Lane of the Boulevards of Paris

Minnesota governor Floyd B. Olson and a close friend of Minneapolis syndicate boss Isadore Blumenfeld, managed the Boulevards of Paris. The FBI reported that Gladys Sawyer, wife of St. Paul racketeer Harry Sawyer, had said that in 1930 and 1931, when Tom Brown was chief of the St. Paul police, "gambling in the city was permitted, but a payoff to the police was required . . . and all of the collecting for the county was handled by Benny Harris, who was operating the 'Boulevards of Paris.'"[81]

To skirt Prohibition violations, Lane's staff would serve customers setups (a glass, a bowl of ice, and ginger ale), and the customers brought their own illicit alcohol. "The customers were pretty savvy, they kept the booze hidden," said Junterman. "The police assigned to the Coliseum were all paid off, but nothing was flaunted." The police support helped discourage competition. Underworld informant Frank Reilly told the FBI that he had contemplated opening his own nightclub in St. Paul's Highland Park, but when the Boulevards opened— attracting mobsters from Toledo, Philadelphia, and Chicago—Reilly concluded it was useless to fight a club that "opened with the full consent of the police."[82]

Lane, a former telegram messenger, rose to become a Ramsey County commissioner (1926–30) with a deft skill at cultivating political connections. He brought an extravagant style to his life and to his nightclub: he once purchased a magnum of champagne and Rocquefort cheese for his granddaughter's first birthday, insisting that the girl should have only the best. When the spread of jukeboxes began to cut into venues for live music, Lane often let jazz musicians sleep in his basement while he sought work for them in the Twin Cities.[83]

Musical giants Fats Waller, Benny Goodman, and Louis Armstrong were among those who performed at the Boulevards. Many artists performed surprise shows at the Boulevards after Junterman sneaked backstage at the Orpheum Theatre, asked the entertainers if they wanted a free dinner after their show, and brought the hungry singers, actors, and comics to the Boulevards.

Lane had a genius for imaginative promotions, among them weight-reducing contests and a hundred-dollar bounty offered to anyone who could find a club with a larger dance floor. Junterman recalled another: "The parking lot between the Coliseum dance hall and the Boulevards would flood, so no one could park a car there. My dad capitalized on the flood—he put an advertisement in the newspaper that said, 'Come to Lexington and University and see the new Coliseum Lake!' He even put *rowboats* in the water. People took it seriously and would come to see our lake."

Perhaps most wondrous of all is the story of the installation of the Coliseum's famous dance floor. Lane hired his cousin, a carpenter, to install a dance floor on top of the Coliseum's roller-skating surface in the early 1920s. Thanks to a construction error (the floor supports were placed too far apart) and a damp climate, the floor swayed precariously. For anyone else, the unsteady floor would have spelled disaster, but Lane promptly advertised the world's only "floor that sways with motion." He boasted in posters and advertisements that "you'll never get tired of dancing at the Coliseum, because of our swaying floor—it sways with the dancers!"[84]

Part of the wicked fun of the Boulevards of Paris was the chance that you might bump into a gangster on the dance floor. During the 1932 hunt for Chicago bank robbers Jimmy Keating and Tommy Holden, the FBI learned that the Boulevards was a popular winter hangout for the duo, along with gangsters Frank Nash of Oklahoma and Capone hit man Fred "Shotgun George Ziegler" Goetz. The Boulevards may have played a more sinister role for the underworld: Dillinger gang member Tommy Gannon claimed that the Thompson submachine gun used by gangsters to assassinate Minneapolis journalist Walter Liggett in 1935 was secreted under the dance floor before being dumped in the Mississippi River.[85]

On September 18, 1929, unknown gangsters detonated a bomb inside the Boulevards of Paris. Built of concrete blocks, the building was barely damaged, even though the blast was heard more than two miles away.

Publicly, Lane insisted that the bombing was simply a reprisal for his having ejected some unruly thugs who had indulged in a birthday party brawl. "In attempting to operate a cafe for ladies and gentlemen of the community, it seems I have incurred the displeasure of gangsters," Lane told reporters. "The Boulevards of Paris management will not be intimidated by the racketeers who have adopted the Chicago method of terrorism." Privately, though, Lane told his family he believed that the bombing was the work of a vengeful gangster. (Some say John Dillinger; others claim it was New York beer baron Dutch Schultz.) Apparently Lane had thrown the drunken mobsters out of the Boulevards for playing catch with open ketchup bottles and making unwelcome passes at a waitress.[86]

In 1934 the Boulevards of Paris became the Vanity Fair dance hall; the dance palace degenerated into a ten-cent joint, shambling out of business by 1936. Lane died in 1952. Nine years later, the Boulevards of Paris building was razed. When the neighboring Coliseum was torn down in 1958, *St. Paul Dispatch* reporter Gareth Hiebert wrote: "There are many who still rub their eyes and can't believe that the Coliseum isn't there when they pass by."[87]

The demise of the Boulevards of Paris and the Coliseum coincided with the repeal of Prohibition and the rise of a different kind of criminal—the assassin-for-hire exemplified by Murder Incorporated. The trial of two Murder Inc. hit men in 1932 revealed that killers Joey Schaefer and George Young had visited the Boulevards of Paris to relax before planning their murders. The Murder Inc. enforcers were corporate killers sent across the United States to slaughter hundreds of men for calculated business purposes. One of their most sensational "contracts" occurred a few blocks from the Boulevards of Paris, at the corner of University and Snelling Avenues.[88]

13 A Slaying by Murder Inc.

The Green Dragon Cafe
469 North Snelling Avenue, St. Paul

"Bootlegging called for a more elaborate infrastructure than burglary," wrote crime historian William Weir:

A burglar can break into any place, anywhere. Bootlegging was a business that depended on steady customers. The customers had to know the bootlegger and know that they could depend on him. That tied the bootlegger to the area where his customers lived. Because there were a lot of other bootleggers, he had to defend his territory. That led to something new in American crime—the permanently employed, salaried gunman, the hoodlum.[89]

The practice of employing a stable of professional gunmen who killed for business reasons reached its height in the late 1920s and early 1930s, when labor racketeer Louis "Lepke" Buchalter, Benjamin "Bugsy" Siegel, and Mafia chieftain Meyer Lansky founded an assassination service, Murder Inc., in Brooklyn, New York.

Abe Wagner, a Murder Inc. victim, with his wife

On July 25, 1932, at the intersection of University and Snelling Avenues in St. Paul—in broad daylight, with a police car parked just a block away—a pair of Murder Inc. killers assassinated an underworld fugitive they had tracked across the country. Their target was bootlegger Abe Wagner, the twenty-six-year-old son of Jewish immigrants from eastern Europe. Wagner, who had briefly been a suspect in the murder of Charles Lindbergh's baby boy, narrowly survived a February 1932 attempt on his life by New York's Mazza gang, a syndicate that had already killed his brother Allie. Wagner fled to St. Paul, masquerading as a fruit peddler under the alias Abe Loeb. Five months later, Murder Inc. located Wagner and sent the "contract" for the bootlegger's murder to killers George Young and Joseph Schaefer.[90]

Police intelligence files described Young and Schaefer as "competent and dependable killers for Meyer Lansky, very closely aligned with the Italian element of the Mafia or La Cosa Nostra." George Young (whose real name was Albert Silverberg) was an immigrant from Odessa, Russia (today, Ukraine), with a rap sheet covering thirteen arrests for assault and battery, receiving stolen goods, robbery, and possession of burglar's tools. Joey Schaefer (real name Nathan Winger) was an Austrian-born bootlegger whose seven arrests included charges of carrying a concealed weapon, suspicion of murder, and assault and battery on a policeman.[91]

Both Young and Schaefer were former members of the Irving "Waxey Gordon" Wexler bootlegging mob. Both were being hunted themselves for the murder of Prohibition agent John Finiello, whom they may have killed in December 1930 during a raid on the Rising Sun Brewery in Elizabeth,

New Jersey. Murder Inc. sent Young and Schaefer to the safest city in America for crooks on the lam—St. Paul. During a 1931 visit, Schaefer had stayed in a third-floor apartment at 3310 South Fremont Avenue in Minneapolis—the same apartment building where, two years later, John Dillinger's gang would hide from the FBI. This time the two killers moved to the Hotel St. Paul, Young in room 1032 and Schaefer in 824.[92]

Apparently, the assassins had a series of assignments in Minnesota. The underworld's St. Paul territory had been challenged by Harry "Gorilla Kid" Davis, a small-time Philadelphia hoodlum whose nickname came from his reputation as the homeliest crook in Minnesota. To eliminate this rival who had "muscle[d] in on some of the rackets," according to Minnesota Bureau of Criminal Apprehension (BCA) reports, Murder Inc. arranged to have Davis "taken for a ride." The Gorilla Kid's body was found July 20, 1932, in a ditch near Big Marine Lake about twenty miles northeast of St. Paul. Nattily dressed in a golf suit with a white cap, Davis had two small-caliber bullet holes in the back of his head. The bureau desperately hunted for Abe Wagner for questioning, "but before [he] could be located the police were informed that Loeb [Wagner] had expressed his intention of going to the Police Department to clear himself of suspicion with regard to the [Davis] murder," said an FBI file.[93]

On the evening of July 25 Wagner's partner, Al Gordon, stepped into John Courtney's Drug Store at 1598 University Avenue to have a prescription filled. (Today, the Spruce Tree Center mall covers the entire murder scene.) In walked Wagner, with what the cashier called a "wild look." The two men stepped out of the drugstore and started to walk west along University Avenue; neither noticed Young and Schaefer stalking them.[94]

Seventeen-year-old Ellie Hallberg McLean was meeting her boyfriend at the corner of University and Snelling, a few yards from the pharmacy. A Chrysler coupe drove by the young couple, and McLean saw a passenger frantically waving at them to move away, but they ignored the mobster's warning. "A dark green Packard drove up alongside the coupe and two men got out—Joe Schaefer, with dark pants, blue shirt; and George Young, [who] had a panama suit with panama hat," recalled McLean. "We'd seen gangster movies, and we figured the two were going to rob some place.... The two men started walking toward Snelling on University.... Like fools, we started walking the same direction they were going. Hey, we were kids—we didn't know what we were going to see!"[95]

McLean saw the two killers run toward the Courtney Drug Store, where they fired .32- and .38-caliber revolvers at Al Gordon, fatally wounding him. The pair then began to chase Wagner east down University Avenue and south on Snelling Avenue toward the Snelling Hotel and the Green Dragon

The southwest corner of University and Snelling Avenues in about 1932, the murder site of bootlegger Abe Wagner (Loeb); the Green Dragon Cafe is at the far left, and John Courtney's Drug Store is at the right. A diagram from the magazine **Startling Detective Adventures** *shows how the murder happened.*

cafe at 469 Snelling (today the site of an Applebee's restaurant), firing as they ran and hitting Wagner, as well as nearby windows and walls. Young and Schaefer followed the bleeding Wagner into the Green Dragon, where they beat him over the head with their gun butts. With six bullets in his chest and stomach, Wagner died at Ancker Hospital without regaining consciousness. Young and Schaefer were immediately caught by a patrolman on Roy Street. Their companions in the Chrysler, parked outside 463 North Snelling to facilitate their getaway, were forced to flee without them.[96]

Dick Pranke, a St. Paul police employee and later an FBI agent, remembered the scene at police headquarters when Young and Schaefer were brought in for fingerprinting: "Half a dozen police officers had grabbed the killer—either Young or Schaefer, I can't remember—by his head and legs and arms and physically forced him to put his fingerprints down on the pad." The fingerprints identified Young and Schaefer as the men wanted for killing a Prohibition agent in New Jersey.[97]

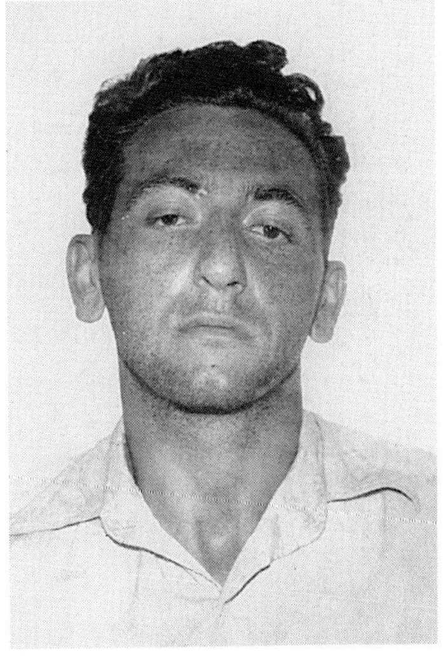

St. Paul police arrest photo of Joseph Schaefer, a Murder Inc. hit man

Gradually the FBI and the St. Paul police traced the killers' movements just before the Wagner and Gordon murders. Their getaway driver, William Weisman, was hiding at the St. Paul home of the Harry Smith family at 1892 Lincoln Avenue (a two-story ivy-covered red-brick and stucco house that still stands near the intersection of Lincoln Avenue and Howell Street). Trial testimony placed Young and Schaefer at 1892 Lincoln just an hour before they murdered Wagner. The FBI also found that they had stayed at the Thomas Edwards cottage at Third Street and Park Avenue in White Bear Lake during the summer of 1932. Their landlady remembered a crowd of men gambling and drinking, their guns scattered on the furniture, running up enormous telephone bills, often leaving the cottage at ten o'clock in the evening and returning at five the next morning.[98]

During a twenty-day trial, extraordinary efforts were made to get the killers acquitted. Two men were offered $100 each to fabricate false testimony for the defense. Horace "Red" Dupont, a former employee of underworld figure Tom Filben, said that the St. Paul police chief was offered a $25,000 bribe to free Young and Schaefer but turned the offer down. The state's four top criminal defense attorneys represented Young and Schaefer, while gangsters in New Jersey raised funds for the legal defense. Most surprisingly, St. Paul police drove to Holman Field on October 13 to welcome an aircraft carrying a strange mix of Young and Schaefer supporters: Congressman Ben Golder of Philadelphia and a then-unknown Meyer Lansky, later to become the most powerful non-Italian figure in organized crime.[99]

Despite their powerful connections, Young and Schaefer were convicted of murdering Wagner in Ramsey County District Court. On November 11, 1932, they were sentenced to life at hard labor in Minnesota's Stillwater Prison. But FBI files suggest that the mob's efforts to free Young and Schaefer had just begun. Burton Turkus, the assistant district attorney who prosecuted Murder Inc., claimed that a Brooklyn gangster named "Dandy Jack" was paid $35,000 to spring Young and Schaefer from Stillwater Prison with dynamite, an effort that was unsuccessful.[100]

While they were in Stillwater, the hit men confided in a gambler named Leonard Hankins, who had been imprisoned for murder related to the Barker-Karpis gang's 1932 robbery of the Third Northwestern National Bank in Minneapolis. Hankins told the FBI a remarkable tale of how the Murder Inc. duo benefited from bribes, favoritism, and underworld deals inside the Minnesota prison system. The bureau learned that when Bugsy Siegel realized that he could not free his two employees, he ensured that they were rewarded for their patience (and silence) in Stillwater.[101]

According to Hankins, the Murder Inc. duo "appear[ed] to run the prison." Young and Schaefer seldom ate what the other prisoners ate and at one time had a private room where they dined on steaks, Hankins said. Both had electric plates in their cell blocks so they could make coffee any time. Files from the Philadelphia Police Department confirm that "there was very little that they did without—with the exception of women. They had money, liquor, and food, as much as they wanted." A prison official confirmed in a 1956 letter to U.S. Senator Hubert Humphrey that Young and Schaefer enjoyed special privileges in Stillwater, including contraband whiskey, money, and fresh meat.[102]

The duo received a fifty-dollar weekly stipend from Murder Inc., which they passed on to prison officials for special privileges. Hankins revealed that in 1949 several Minneapolis nightclubs sent entertainers to put on shows for the Stillwater inmates: "Young, Schaefer and [convicted murderer] Rubin Shetsky were allowed to sit in a special section to watch the show," an FBI document said, "and he [Hankins] later heard through gossip that the women entertainers returned the following day and were taken to the basement of the prison, and thereafter Warden Utecht personally took Young, Schaefer and Shetsky to the basement, where he left them alone with some of the women entertainers."[103]

Most intriguingly, Hankins told the FBI that millionaire Charlie Ward, an ex-convict from Leavenworth who had transformed himself into the president of the printing firm of Brown and Bigelow, was secretly Young and Schaefer's guardian angel." Hankins claimed that Ward provided $100,000 to spring Young and Schaefer from prison. The hit men told Hankins that "a Hollywood, California gangster named Bugs Siegel is . . . the person who made the arrangements to get that money from Charles Ward." The FBI was able to confirm only that Ward "borrowed" $100,000 from Siegel and deposited it in St. Paul's Midway Bank.[104]

Siegel himself visited St. Paul in 1939 for a final attempt to spring Young and Schaefer from prison. His temporary headquarters would be the Lowry Hotel in downtown St. Paul.

14 'A Recognized Member of Murder Inc.'

Bugsy Siegel at the Lowry Hotel
339 North Wabasha Street, St. Paul

It was appropriate that mobster Bugsy Siegel stayed at the Lowry Hotel (now the Lowry Office Building), for it had developed a rich underworld history since its opening in 1927. Alvin "Creepy" Karpis often stayed at the Lowry during his 1932–33 crime sprees with Fred and Doc Barker. When Karpis was held in the Federal Courts Building (now Landmark Center), he gazed longingly out the windows of the FBI office toward the Lowry, three blocks away. Bootlegger Leon Gleckman, recovering from his 1931 gangland kidnapping, hid in a rooftop apartment at the hotel.[105]

But no Lowry Hotel resident was more infamous than Bugsy Siegel. Siegel and Meyer Lansky, youthful partners in the Bugs and Meyer mob of bootleggers, murderers, and extortionists, went on to found a coast-to-coast organized crime syndicate with Lucky Luciano, Frank Costello, and other Italian gangsters. By the time Siegel visited the Lowry Hotel, he was running West Coast criminal activities for the syndicate. An FBI Vice Conditions report confirmed that Siegel, "a recognized member of Murder, Inc.," paid a visit to Minnesota: "On December 4, 1939, [Siegel] was known to have visited St. Paul and stayed at the Lowry Hotel, at which time he attempted to make some sort of deal to have Joseph Schaefer and George Young released from Stillwater State Prison. These individuals were known killers of this Murder, Inc., who were sent to St. Paul to murder another member of the Syndicate."[106]

Young and Schaefer told fellow inmate Leonard Hankins that Siegel had tried and failed to get a $100,000 bribe into the prison to get them out. At that time, Hankins told the FBI, Siegel visited them at the prison about

The Lowry Hotel, Wabasha and Fourth Streets, where syndicate founder Ben "Bugsy" Siegel stayed in 1939

nine times in three months and three times during one week; Siegel's visits took place in private offices behind closed blinds. St. Paul police officer Joe Sherin claimed that the mob offered $100,000 to any Minnesota governor who would pardon Young and Schaefer. The FBI noted that "possibly $200,000 has been spent . . . trying to secure the release of these men from Stillwater."[107]

Young and Schaefer gained a measure of immortality when assistant district attorney Burton Turkus featured their killing of Abe Wagner (Loeb) prominently in his 1951 book, *Murder, Inc.: The Story of the Syndicate*, but even the efforts of Bugsy Siegel failed to get them out of prison. When they were paroled in the early 1960s they had outlived their benefactor, who was shot to death in Beverly Hills, California, in 1947. Siegel had once reassured a construction executive affiliated with the Flamingo Hotel that he and other civilians had nothing to fear from the mob. In the world of organized crime, Siegel said, "We only kill each other."[108]

3

ORGANIZED CRIME AT YOUR SERVICE

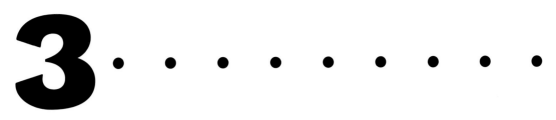

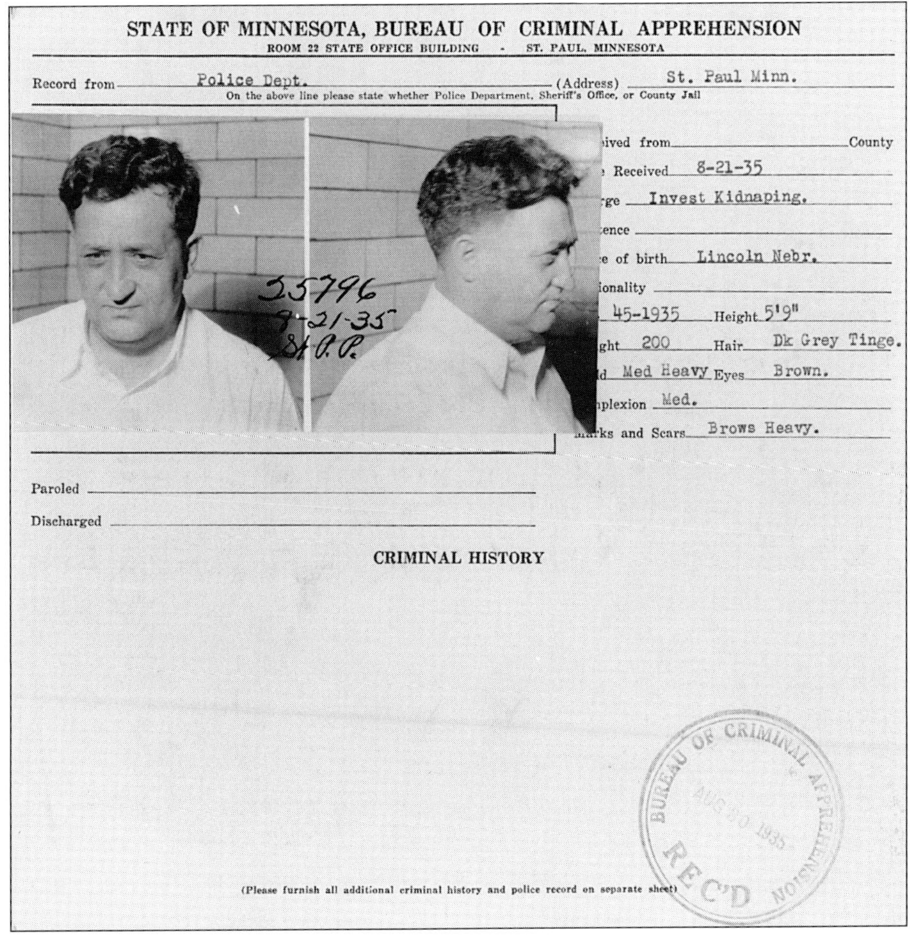
STATE OF MINNESOTA, BUREAU OF CRIMINAL APPREHENSION
ROOM 22 STATE OFFICE BUILDING - ST. PAUL, MINNESOTA

Record from Police Dept. (Address) St. Paul Minn.
On the above line please state whether Police Department, Sheriff's Office, or County Jail

...ived from ______ County
...Received 8-21-35
...rge Invest Kidnaping.
...ence
...e of birth Lincoln Nebr.
...ionality
... 45-1935 Height 5'9"
...ght 200 Hair Dk Grey Tinge.
...d Med Heavy Eyes Brown.
...nplexion Med.
...rks and Scars Brows Heavy.

35796
8-21-35
St. P. P.

Paroled
Discharged

CRIMINAL HISTORY

(Please furnish all additional criminal history and police record on separate sheet)

BUREAU OF CRIMINAL APPREHENSION
AUG 30 1935
REC'D

Green Lantern saloon proprietor Harry "Dutch" Sawyer, with his wife, Gladys; Sawyer's Bureau of Criminal Apprehension record

15 'The Fix Was in from Top to Bottom'

Harry "Dutch" Sawyer's Home
1878 Jefferson Avenue, St. Paul

Harry "Dutch" Sawyer—underworld banker and heir to Danny Hogan as supervisor of St. Paul's O'Connor system of collusion between police and gangsters—lived in a two-story home near the corner of Jefferson and Fairview Avenues. For the network of bank robbery gangs flourishing between 1930 and 1934—Dillinger out of Indiana, the Keating-Holden gang out of Chicago, and the Barker-Karpis, Frank Nash, and Harvey Bailey gangs out of Missouri and Oklahoma—men like Sawyer created a handful of safe havens, cities where they would not be picked up or prosecuted by local authorities.

"Criminals used to talk about 'safe cities,'" wrote bank robber and kidnapper Alvin Karpis. "They were places where the fix was in from top to bottom, and guys like me could relax. The chances were slim that in those cities we'd ever get arrested."[1]

In addition to St. Paul, "safe cities" included Kansas City, home of Thomas "Boss" Pendergast's political machine; Joplin, Missouri, where Herbert "Deafy" Farmer harbored Karpis and other outlaws; Reno, Nevada, treasured for its money-laundering facilities; Toledo, Ohio, where members of the Barker-Karpis gang went for plastic surgery on their faces and fingertips; Hot Springs, Arkansas, a vacation spot whose mud baths attracted Charles "Lucky" Luciano; and Cicero, Illinois, headquarters of the Capone syndicate and a city where many members of the Barker-Karpis gang obtained their automobiles.[2]

During an interrogation, Karpis confided to FBI agents that (in the words of an FBI report) if he "only had police officers to worry about he could live in Ohio, Oklahoma or Louisiana the rest of his life; that there is not a town in Ohio above 20,000 population that isn't fixed; that Tulsa and New Orleans are on the clout and Kansas City is a pushover." The safe cities were like "the imaginary bases used by children playing tag," wrote historian Michael Wallis in his biography of Oklahoma bank robber Charles Arthur "Pretty Boy" Floyd. "Once a criminal with local connections made it safely inside one of these cities, he was home free. He was 'on base' and could not be 'tagged' by the authorities."[3]

Under the O'Connor system—buttressed by ten years of payoffs from Sawyer to City Hall and the St. Paul police—detectives were unable to recognize the famous faces on the FBI's "wanted" posters, and authorities inexplicably failed to respond to extradition notices sent from other cities. If a raid was inevitable, Sawyer ensured that the police were courteous enough to call their targets half an hour before the invasion. When a new fugitive slipped off the train, Sawyer would dispatch his errand boy, former boxer William Albert "Pat" Reilly, to arrange a hotel room and introduce the felonious visitor to the local underworld.[4]

Bank robber Eddie Bentz recommended St. Paul as a base for criminal operations:

> Once you get planted in a town, the cops from every other city in the United States can wire your location, but nothing happens. For instance when Leon Gleckman had St. Paul, and Jack Peifer was running the Holly Hocks Inn, all a fellow had to do was to take care of Jack. . . . If a guy paid off, he didn't have any trouble. . . .
>
> If a fellow was going into the bank robbery business . . . I'd say the first thing to do would be to get a place to work from. That was always my system. . . . About the only way a fellow can really operate is to have his headquarters in some place where the police can't find you . . . for instance, there was St. Paul. . . .
>
> Most people think of a "right town" as some place where a yegg like myself walks in and calls up the Chief of Police and then meets him on a dark corner and gives him a wad of dough. Why, nine tenths of the time, you don't even know the Chief's name.[5]

By 1932 Sawyer had developed the O'Connor system into a citywide infrastructure of criminal services. Sawyer knew where gangsters could get a new car or repair a vehicle perforated with bullets, how to find an untraceable automatic weapon, how to launder stolen bonds, how to "finger" a kidnapping victim whose family had the financial resources for an appropriate ransom—and even how to ignite a romance with a new girlfriend. At Sawyer's Jefferson Avenue home, Karpis set up his first romantic rendezvous with Delores (Dolores) Delaney, whom he had met at the home of her brother-in-law Pat Reilly. "I knocked on Reilly's door and this beautiful young girl answered," recalled the smitten Karpis. "I could hardly speak. I just watched her. She was a brunette with brown eyes and a gorgeous figure. She was about sixteen."[6]

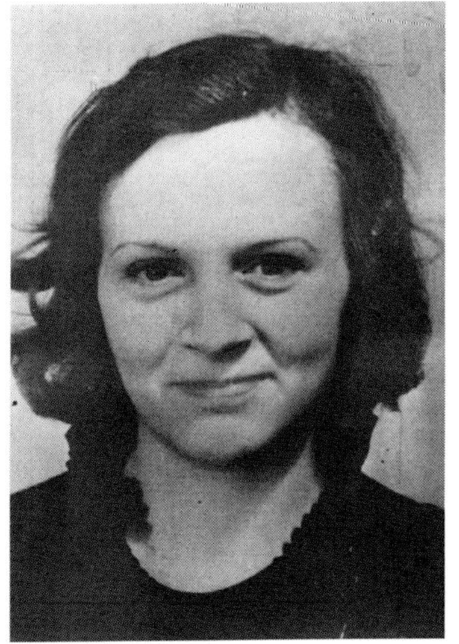

Delores Delaney, girlfriend of Alvin Karpis

Delaney was similarly smitten with Karpis, whom she had first glimpsed at Jack Peifer's Hollyhocks casino. (Karpis was not the first wanted man Delores had courted. In 1932 she had kept company with Clarence DeVol, brother of Barker-Karpis gang machine gunner Larry DeVol, and she served as an alibi witness when Clarence was arrested for a Minneapolis bank robbery.) In May 1933, Delaney decided to meet Karpis at Harry Sawyer's house so they could move into their own apartment. "As soon as I walked in, Dolores jumped up and planted a big, juicy kiss on my lips," recalled Karpis. "From then on, until the police finally separated us three years later, Dolores and I were a steady couple." Delaney eventually bore Karpis's only child.[7]

For a crime strategist like Karpis, St. Paul offered a support system matched by few cities. Available for hire were "jug marker" Eddie Green, an expert at identifying a vulnerable bank swollen with deposits; Frank Nash and Harvey Bailey, who provided expertise in escape maps, jailbreaks, and the timing of bank jobs; Dr. Clayton E. May, whose specialties included illegal abortions, sexually transmitted diseases, and gunshot wounds; defense attorneys Tommy McMeekin, Thomas Sullivan, and Tom Newman of St. Paul, and Archibald Cary of Minneapolis; and a rotating supply of freelance gunmen.

To stay in touch as they shifted from one St. Paul apartment to another, the gangsters created a system of telegram codes, mail drops, and safe houses, cloaking their messages to each other with multiple aliases. "All of it's done by word of mouth," said the dean of bank robbers, Harvey Bailey. "Writing is out—o-u-t. And telephone calls are out.... We never knew what the other's phone number was and we didn't want to." Instead, gangsters could call from anywhere in the country and leave word for one another through Harry Sawyer.[8]

Although the Dillinger gang was unhappy with Minnesota's climate, Harry Sawyer's valuable services more than made up for the grim weather. "The gang had frequently talked about leaving the Twin Cities," the FBI learned from Beth (Bessie) Skinner, who, as the girlfriend of Dillinger gang member Eddie Green, used the name Beth Green. But "because of Harry Sawyer's connections they decided that this was the safest place for them to be [since] Harry is always tipped off before a raid is made." "I don't know *how* he got connected," said former policeman Pat Lannon Sr., "but Sawyer *was* the connection with the underworld." Sawyer was often a shadowy presence at police headquarters. When newspaper reporter Fred Heaberlin bumped into him there one day, the racketeer warned: "Remember, you never saw me here."[9]

Born Harry Sandlovich into an Orthodox Jewish family in Russian-controlled Lithuania in 1890, Sawyer came to America in 1891 with his mother, Gertrude, and father, David, a cattle buyer. The family settled in Nebraska where Harry, the sixth of nine children, attended a religious school and had a traditional bar mitzvah at age thirteen. He later became a butcher, learning skills that would be useful in the kitchens at Alcatraz prison. Sawyer's criminal record began with a guilty plea in Lincoln, Nebraska, for the 1915 burglary of a Standard Oil office, followed by arrests for auto theft, robbery, and attempted grand larceny (each, notably, committed by Sawyer under a different alias).[10]

Sawyer had visited Minnesota before—under the alias Harry J. Porche, he was arrested by Minneapolis police for attempted grand larceny as early as 1918—and when he was arrested for theft in Lincoln in 1921, he jumped his $1,000 bond and fled permanently to St. Paul.[11]

By 1923 Sawyer had joined forces with underworld boss Danny Hogan at the Green Lantern saloon. "Sawyer handled . . . the disposal of jewelry and stolen goods for Hogan," Beth Green told the FBI. "Upon Hogan's death, the gangs naturally migrated to Sawyer." In addition to running the Green Lantern, Sawyer offered his police connections to a variety of Twin Cities gambling clubs. In Little Canada, six miles north of St. Paul, Sawyer owned part of the Owasso Tavern at Rice Street and Owasso Boulevard. "The gambling [at the tavern] was run on a pay-off basis to the Sheriff," the FBI learned from Sawyer's wife.[12]

Sawyer also provided protection services for the Gleckman liquor syndicate's Brown Derby nightclub at 340–380 Main Street in the Seven Corners section of downtown St. Paul, a favorite among visiting members of Bugsy Siegel's Murder Inc. squad of New York hit men. "The Brown Derby was a nightclub that was run for visiting criminals, sort of a Y.M.C.A. for criminals," recalled reporter Bill Greer, who dined there with Bonnie Parker of Bonnie and Clyde infamy. The FBI learned from a rival saloon keeper that "during the time [Tom] Brown was Chief of Police the Brown Derby . . . would not stand for any competition, and if any place opened . . . a gang of Jews, one of whom was Harry Sawyer, who were interested in the Brown Derby, would immediately go up and shoot up the competitor's place."[13]

The FBI placed Sawyer's home under surveillance during the search for fugitive bank robbers Tommy Holden and Jimmy Keating and again when the FBI was hunting for Barker-Karpis machine gunner Verne Miller. When Prohibition was repealed, Sawyer moved away from the liquor business and into more lucrative crimes; his home became a gathering place for the likes of bank robbers Frank Nash and Verne Miller. On Christmas Day 1933, the Sawyers entertained four of America's most-wanted fugitives: bank robber Fred Barker and his girlfriend, Paula Harmon, and Oklahoma burglar Harry "Limpy" Campbell and his companion Wynona Burdette.[14]

Questioned by FBI agents, more than a few of Sawyer's neighbors expressed anxiety about having an underworld power on the block. "Who knew if someone would bomb the Sawyer house, like they did with Danny

Hogan, or would fire a Thompson submachine gun?" said Jane Resler, who was ten years old when she lived at 1880 Jefferson, next door to Sawyer. One night, Resler's parents whispered, "Come here, come here," and pointed at Sawyer's house. There, through Sawyer's bedroom window, the Reslers could see a large pile of U.S. Post Office mailbags from a recent train robbery. Eventually, two of Sawyer's neighbors confronted St. Paul police official Tom Dahill, who lived nearby, with their suspicions about Sawyer's line of work. Dahill reportedly told them, "You just leave Harry Sawyer alone, and Sawyer will leave you alone." Once when he went hunting, Sawyer brought back ducks for his neighbors, and when he and his wife went to the state fair, he rewarded a neighbor's children with an odd toy monkey that shimmied up a cane.

The local children were fascinated by Sawyer. Resler recalled how Karpis's girlfriend, Delores Delaney, would park her Buick in front of Sawyer's home, usually in Sawyer's personal spot. Sawyer would arrive later, spy Delaney's car parked in his space, and cheerfully ram her automobile, inspiring a wave of obscenities from Delaney. The neighborhood youngsters sat eagerly on their front porches awaiting the spectacle, Resler said.[15]

During the 1933 hunt for gangster Verne Miller in the wake of the massacre of FBI agents and police in Kansas City, the FBI put a "mail cover" on every letter and package delivered to Sawyer's home, interrogated Sawyer's neighbors, and hid an agent in Resler's home for round-the-clock surveillance. The bureau discovered little, though, for Harry Sawyer used his home for gangland entertainment rather than business. Sawyer preferred to conduct the commerce of the underworld in the back rooms of his Green Lantern saloon.[16]

16 A Rogues Gallery of Crooks

The Green Lantern Saloon
545 North Wabasha Street, St. Paul

Bank robber and kidnapper Alvin Karpis described the Green Lantern saloon as "my personal headquarters in St. Paul. . . . Everyone had the same things in common—stealing, killing, and looting." Karpis had a weakness for the Green Lantern's hard-boiled eggs and often visited the saloon to relax, asking a cook to prepare a special milk drink to calm his sick stomach. Safe in his booth at the Lantern, Karpis could socialize with the best stickup men in America.[17]

"Sawyer ran the Green Lantern like a host at a great party," wrote Karpis in his memoirs. "The greatest blowout Sawyer threw in the place, in my experience, was on New Year's Eve, 1932. . . . There was probably never before as complete a gathering of criminals in one room in the United States as there was in the Green Lantern that night. There were escapees from every major U.S. penitentiary. I was dazzled. . . . For a kid like me it was great stuff. Rogues Gallery, or Hall of Fame. It depended on your point of view."[18]

Years later, Sawyer was asked during his kidnapping trial what kind of people frequented the Green Lantern. "All walks of life. State senators, attorneys, bootleggers, business men, lawyers," quipped Sawyer. "I forgot to mention newspapermen, quite a few of them, and printers." Pat Lannon Sr., the policeman who patrolled the beat that included the Green Lantern in 1928, disagreed: "Sure the rank and file could visit the Green Lantern, but they wouldn't get any service to speak of [because Sawyer] didn't want businesspeople in there. Anyone could walk into the Lantern, but everyone was not welcome. They wanted the *bad* boys at the Green Lantern!"[19]

And the bad boys came: racketeers Isadore "Kid Cann" Blumenfeld of Minneapolis; nationally known bank robbers John Dillinger, Verne Miller, and Frank Nash; Ma Barker's sons Fred and "Doc"; and reckless newcomers Volney Davis, Larry DeVol, and Earl Christman. Auto thief Claire Lucas admitted to a weakness for the Green Lantern's spaghetti, and bootlegger Isaac Goodman was partial to its fried pork chop sandwiches.[20]

Federal agents raided the saloon as early as 1923, discovering five barrels of spiked beer and arresting a bartender for violating Prohibition. Under Danny Hogan in the mid-1920s, the Green Lantern expanded both its clientele and its cuisine: a sign read "Dapper Dan, The Hot Dog Man," and hot dogs sizzled on a griddle in the front window. "I suppose some people even went in there for a wiener," said reporter Fred Heaberlin, who knew both Hogan and Sawyer. "But the Green Lantern was a front for bootlegging and whatever else, laundering and receiving stolen property." Behind a false wall was the Blue Room, a speakeasy where the underworld enjoyed liquor, piano music, slot machines, and nude dancers. Customers entered the Green Lantern by the back entrance, opening onto a deserted alley. The front door was locked and seldom used.[21]

From 1926 through 1933, Sawyer was able to offer illicit beer (sold as "near beer") to his Green Lantern customers through a secret arrangement with employees of the Schmidt Brewing Company. According to FBI interviews with his wife, Sawyer got the beer through a tunnel that ran from the Schmidt Brewery to the 339 Erie Street home of Schmidt plumber Carl Schoen. (The Schoen house, once located near the intersection of Erie Street and Jefferson Avenue, has since been razed.)[22]

The Green Lantern's resident professor of criminal techniques was Harvey Bailey, dean of American bank robbers. A safecracker of Scotch-Irish descent, born in West Virginia and raised in Missouri, Bailey discovered the comforts of Minnesota in the early 1920s while he was running bootleg whiskey from Canada into Minneapolis and St. Paul. When he graduated to major bank robberies, Bailey continued to seek rest and ancillary services in St. Paul. On September 17, 1930, Bailey's gang robbed the National Bank and Trust Company in Lincoln, Nebraska, of more than $2.6 million in securities and $24,000 cash, a heist described by the Associated Press as "the greatest bank robbery of all time." The responsibility for laundering the stolen bonds fell to Bailey, and he turned immediately to his fences in St. Paul. Bailey clucked his tongue when a bank robber of his acquaintance laundered some stolen bonds in New York. "I'd have dealt them out in St. Paul and Minneapolis," said Bailey. "I did pert near all my business with them people up there—they was good people."[23]

Camouflaged at the Green Lantern under the alias Tom Brennan, Bailey shared the secrets of his meticulous planning. He would explain to young thieves how to assess the size and financial worth of a town, pinpoint the lo-

Oklahoma's master bank robber Harvey Bailey, a frequent visitor to the Green Lantern

cation of traffic policemen, and figure the precise number of minutes the gang should be inside the bank, as well as how to determine the fastest getaway routes and precisely when a payroll deposit would swell the bank's store of cash. Who else but Harvey Bailey would think to obtain road maps from the county surveyor's office to ensure that the roads were adequate for a perfect getaway? Who else but Bailey would hide sawed-off shotguns in his banjo case and then joke with the landlady that he hoped his "practice" would not bother her? Bailey was also respected for his aversion to unnecessary bloodshed. After masterminding the 1933 Memorial Day prison break from the Kansas state penitentiary, Bailey prevented the escapees from killing the prison warden, to whom he gave five dollars and directions to the nearest bus station, ensuring that the hostage was released unharmed.[24]

If anything of value was stolen in St. Paul, someone in the Green Lantern was likely to know about it. FBI agents noted that racketeer Jack Peifer, owner of the Hollyhocks casino, confessed to FBI agents that whenever his liquor was hijacked, he went to the Green Lantern to arrange to buy it back. When the Barker-Karpis gang was tipped off that police were about to raid their Grand Avenue apartment in 1933, they knew where to meet before fleeing for Chicago: the Green Lantern was where criminals regrouped after a close call.[25]

The Green Lantern was a particular favorite with John Dillinger's gang. The FBI discovered that Pantorium Cleaners and Shoe Repair, next to the Green Lantern at 547 Wabasha Street, had been used by the Dillinger gang as a mail drop for the registration documents they filled out as they sold their getaway cars after each robbery. Visitors to the Green Lantern in fall 1933 included Dillinger's first lieutenant, Homer Van Meter; his partners, John Hamilton, Thomas L. "Tommy" Carroll, and Lester "Babyface Nelson" Gillis; and his errand boy, Pat Reilly, who often served as the Green Lantern's bartender.[26]

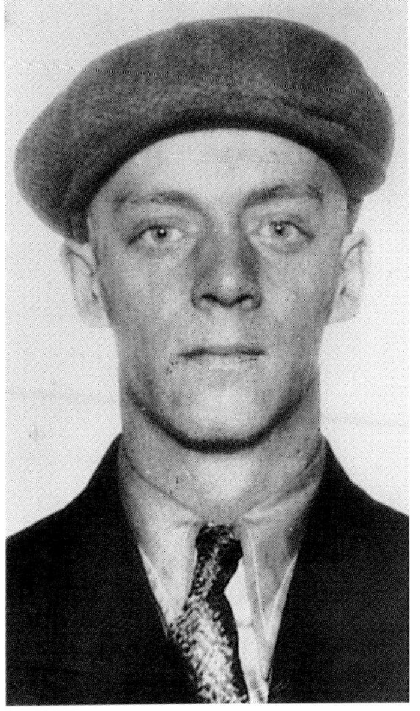

William Albert "Pat" Reilly, bartender at the Green Lantern saloon

George Hurley, a St. Cloud prison alumnus and former driver for the Gleeman brothers' bootlegging syndicate, managed the Green Lantern's restaurant for Sawyer. When Hurley was jailed for his bootlegging work with Sawyer and Dan Hogan, Sawyer gave Hurley's family $100 a week. "My father . . . kept his mouth shut," recalled Hurley's son Harold. "When my father was released from prison, Harry Sawyer took him into the Green Lantern and said, 'How do you like this place?' My father said, 'Fine.' And Sawyer said: 'Then, it's yours.'" Hurley was made manager "as a thank you for being true to the code of the underworld," his son said.[27]

By most accounts a meanspirited drunk with a violent temper, Hurley was acquitted of involvement in the murder of liquor hijacker Burt Stevens and then found not guilty of the 1930 shooting of St. Paul contractor William R. Bacheller, who died in a street brawl near the Green Lantern. Just before he was picked up for the Bacheller murder, Hurley threw the murder weapon into a snowbank near the old St. Paul Post Office. When his wife visited him in the Ramsey County jail, he asked her to get a message to Sawyer: "Tell Harry that the snow is melting." The murder weapon was never found.[28]

For many patrons, the air of gangland danger was one of the Green Lantern's attractions. Blanche Schude, who was then dating one of underworld fixer Tom Filben's employees, Horace "Red" Dupont, begged her boyfriend to take her to the Green Lantern: "All the gangsters hung around there, and I wanted to see it. Red said, 'No, I don't want to take you there.' "And I said: 'Red, if you don't take me there, someone *else* will." Reluctantly, Dupont took Schude into the Green Lantern. "We didn't even have a chance to have a drink," Schude continued, "before there was a fellow at the other end of the room pointing a gun at us! For no reason at all. Red threw me on the floor, threw himself down, and we crawled over to the stairs. His first words to me were, 'Well, are you satisfied?'"[29]

Reporter Fred Heaberlin, who during Prohibition often retired with his colleagues to the Green Lantern at two in the morning in search of beer, remembered another close call: "This fellow pulls out a pouch of jewels taken out of their settings, and wanted to sell them to us cheap. My companion started to make nasty remarks, so this guy carelessly let his suit jacket fall open, and displayed his pistol in a shoulder harness. My friend shut up! After all, the fellow in the Green Lantern was in the legitimate business of selling stolen goods!"[30]

On March 19, 1931, a twenty-seven-year-old cook named Frank Ventress stood up from his Green Lantern dinner and told his wife he would be right back. He walked to the rear door of the Lantern and was shot to death, forcing the temporary closing of the saloon. In another incident, gunmen Clarence Colton and William Weaver, later identified as a conspirator in the kidnapping of Edward Bremer, were arrested at the Lantern during a police raid in August 1932, but they jumped their bond and disappeared. [31]

The growing notoriety of the Green Lantern ultimately rendered it too dangerous for criminal get-togethers. When the FBI questioned Dillinger gang member Tommy Gannon about a meeting agents thought he had scheduled near the Green Lantern with robber Homer Van Meter, Gannon was surprised by the FBI's naiveté: this was "one of the 'hottest' blocks in town and it was not conceivable to him that such a spot could be used for a meeting," the FBI reported.[32]

The Green Lantern also served as a place where gangsters met with crooked police, many of whom befriended Harry Sawyer. FBI agents learned from the porter, Eddie Miller, that "it was not unusual for police officers to visit Sawyer's place from time to time to buy cigars."[33]

St. Paul police detective Tom Brown was a frequent visitor to the Green Lantern, where he chatted openly with gangsters. Years later, when detective Brown was assigned to investigate the William Hamm and Edward Bremer kidnappings, his relationships with the customers at the Green Lantern—many of whom were involved in the abductions—led J. Edgar Hoover to launch a fateful investigation into the corruption of the St. Paul Police Department.[34]

17 Tom Filben, Slot Machine King

The Hotel St. Francis

Old West Seventh between Wabasha and St. Peter Streets, St. Paul

The files of the Federal Bureau of Investigation contain transcripts of a series of remarkable 1936 interviews with half a dozen girlfriends of members of the Dillinger and Barker-Karpis gangs. The young women detail the drawbacks of being in love with a public enemy: physical abuse, furtive moving from city to city, sexual infidelity, venereal disease, abortions, false names, anxiety about capture by FBI agents—and, to top it all off, car trouble.

"The gang loses a car frequently for they are registered under fictitious names," the FBI learned from Beth Green of the Dillinger gang. "When they get a traffic ticket . . . they abandon the car and have to buy a new automobile." When they needed a new car, the gang often turned to Thomas Patrick Filben, the Irish slot machine king who, according to the FBI, was also a dealer in "hot" diamonds and was "considered to be a permanent guest at the St. Francis Hotel."[35]

The St. Francis was so popular with criminals that in 1934 the FBI recruited the hotel's telephone operator as a source. An agent noted that "this informant is located advantageously, in view of the fact that the St. Francis Hotel is looked upon as a gangster hotel." Dice games at the cigar counter in the lobby were a key attraction. Jack Ramaley, assistant manager of the St. Francis cafeteria in 1928, remembered a sharpie who was beating the cigar store clerk. "He was winning like crazy, and had the candy piled up," said Ramaley. Boxing promoter Jerk Doran saw her predicament and took over. He stripped off his jacket, picked up the dice, and won back all of the woman's candy along with all of the patron's money. Slipping his coat back on, Doran told the woman, "That guy was an amateur. He was only holding [concealing] one die. I was holding two!"[36]

Ramaley also recalled a New Year's Eve party at the St. Francis at which a gun dropped out of a gangster's pocket and bounced noisily three times on the floor. "The mobster just scooped the gun up and slipped it back into his coat," said Ramaley. So many underworld figures were visiting St. Paul then that a stray revolver was hardly enough to spark comment or elicit more than a passing glance.

Hotel St. Francis, a popular hostelry which served as headquarters for underworld fixer Tom Filben (inset)

The most powerful of the hoods who frequented the hotel was undoubtedly Thomas Filben—practical joker, slot machine czar, fence, underworld automobile financier, and the Dillinger gang's political campaign collector. Filben was questioned by the FBI during both the Bremer and Hamm kidnapping investigations, but he refused to talk about what he knew. The FBI recognized him as the Twin Cities contact for Lester "Babyface Nelson" Gillis and as a close friend of Fred "Shotgun George Ziegler" Goetz, hit man for Capone's syndicate.[37]

For a week in April 1934, Filben was a sensation when newspapers reported on his interrogation by the FBI for helping John Dillinger purchase getaway cars. The FBI had discovered that Filben, through his Federal Acceptance Corporation finance company, had negotiated the sale of the Hudson sedan used by Dillinger in his March 1934 escape from the FBI shootout at the Lincoln Court Apartments in St. Paul.[38]

Confronted with evidence of his dealings with Dillinger, Filben told the agents with refreshing candor that—in the words of an FBI summary—he "would not furnish the Government any information as he was not on the Government payroll and that was not his business; that he is in a racket and that he has to assist racketeers."[39]

Filben was born in St. Paul in 1890 to Irish parents, Delia and Patrick Filben, who ran a "man's saloon" at Eighth and Robert Streets. At the height of his power as an underworld fixer in the early 1930s, he lived in a two-story beige-and-cream stucco home (still standing at 2133 Fairmount Avenue, near the intersection with Finn Avenue) with his second wife. A Filben family yarn says that, in the wake of Danny Hogan's fiery demise, Filben always asked his first wife to start his car for him. According to family legend, when she discovered why, she divorced him.[40]

Filben's family was often ashamed of his notoriety, particularly when he was publicly identified with John Dillinger. "My father didn't want anything to do with Tom's connections. . . . [He] was a big embarrassment, there'd be these stories about his taxes," said Anita Vogelgesang, a relative of Filben. "My father used to get wild with him, angry with him. Tom's personality, well, some people just seem to enjoy that kind of thing, living on the edge."[41]

Gangsters knew they could find Filben at Patrick Novelty company, his slot machine operation at 518 St. Peter Street, a few blocks from the Hotel St. Francis in downtown St. Paul. The windows of Patrick Novelty (which is no longer standing) were filled with radios, none of which was for sale. Filben's slot machines were installed throughout the city, from the lounges of fine restaurants to the living room of Nina Clifford's brothel. Tom Filben's niece, Jean Preston, once visited Patrick Novelty with her mother. "He had this safe three feet high with drawers," recalled Preston. "Tom said, 'Now you and your mom pick out a ring, any ring in this safe.' He opened a drawer, and there [was] nothing but diamond rings in the safe!"[42]

Like Harry Sawyer, Filben acted as an underworld banker; whenever a St. Paul hoodlum was sent to prison, Filben was available to safeguard his bankroll until his release. "Tom's two safes were *crammed* with money," recalled former Patrick Novelty employee Horace Dupont, who said he helped Filben launder stolen currency through his slot machine company: "Jimmy Keating and Tom Holden would rob banks, and then they'd bring the stolen change to Filben at Patrick Novelty Company, stuffed in the canvas bags that we used to cover up our slot machines. My job was to take the bank identification wrappers off the rolls of stolen coins and reroll them into another wrapper, as if they were just our slot machine proceeds."[43]

According to an FBI informant close to the Dillinger gang, Filben also helped the gang fulfill its political responsibilities. He accepted cash contributions totaling $1,500 from Dillinger, Babyface Nelson, and five other mobsters to benefit police detective Tom Brown's campaign for sheriff.[44]

Filben was known throughout the underworld for his bizarre taste in cruel pranks. "Sit down, have a seat," Filben would say, directing a gangster to an upholstered armchair in his Patrick Novelty offices. Moments later, the thug would leap to his feet howling, for the chair was wired to give him a jolt of electricity. Filben once poured burning oil of mustard on the groin area of a sleeping bootlegger's pants. "Herman [the bootlegger] tore out of the place, yelling," recalled Dupont. "That was a joke, that was all."[45]

The joking Irishman may have been drawn into homicide as well. State crime files suggest that Filben was involved in the deaths of two women who were about to turn witness against the Barker-Karpis gang. It all began on January 5, 1932, when a half-dozen gangsters traveled fifty-five miles north of St. Paul to hold the little town of Cambridge, Minnesota, hostage. The gang stole goods worth $3,000 from Cambridge stores and took a Buick sedan from the Gillespie Auto Company but failed to crack open Gillespie's two-thousand-pound safe. (The safe, which is still owned by the Gillespie family, now sits in the front office of Peter Iten's Auto Center at 115 North Main Street in Cambridge.) The gang kidnapped the town marshal, pistol-whipped an elderly garage attendant, and fled for the Twin Cities.[46]

Two months later, the St. Paul police telephoned George Gillespie of Gillespie Auto in Cambridge and mayor Guy Runyan. Would they enjoy witnessing a double cross? According to Gillespie's son Eben, two women—Margaret "Indian Rose" Perry, an Ojibway from Virginia, Minnesota, and her girlfriend Sadie Carmacher of Duluth—were going to "turn tables and squeal on the boys" in the Barker-Karpis gang. The women never showed

Women's Murder Car Identified As Cambridge Terrorists' Loot

An automobile, stolen by bandits in a raid on Cambridge, Minn., three months ago, was found burning with the bodies of two slain women inside, near Turtle Lake, Wis., Saturday night. It is shown above. Insets are officials of Polk County, Wis., who are conducting the investigation of the double murder. Above left is Sheriff James Olson. Upper right is J. L. McGinnis, district attorney. The lower inset shows Coroner Willis C. Park. The bodies of the women were first disfigured with acid, before being burned in an effort to destroy clues to their identities.

The burned-out car in which police found the bodies of Margaret "Indian Rose" Perry and Sadie Carmacher

up, and on March 7, 1932, their bodies were found near Balsam Lake, Wisconsin, in a burned-out sedan—the Buick that had been stolen at Cambridge. The pair had been shot to death with a .38-caliber pistol, their features obscured by nitric acid, and their bodies burned in the car.[47]

Harry Sawyer told a farfetched story to explain the double homicide: a Twin Cities banker who had laundered the money stolen in December 1922 from the Denver branch of the Federal Reserve Bank of Kansas City had had them killed. (Perry was the girlfriend of "Denver Bobbie" Walker, a suspect in the $200,000 Denver robbery.) More convincing are FBI reports that Jack Peifer of the Hollyhocks casino "had them murdered as Indian Rose was making certain demands on Pfeiffer's friend, Thomas Filben and threatened to expose members of the Cambridge, Minnesota, burglary gang if she were not paid off." The state BCA came to the same conclusion: "Jack Peiffer had had some one kill these women for Thomas Filben." Filben, interviewed by the FBI, would say only that Perry was killed "because it was believed she was threatening certain people."[48]

One obstacle to determining whether Peifer and Filben were involved in the slayings was the fact that the police officer assigned to the murder investigation was none other than Thomas Brown, a friend of both Filben and Peifer. Filben and Brown often vacationed together in northern Minnesota, in a rustic mingling of law enforcement and crime. Filben's extravagantly furnished two-story wood frame summer cottage on Trout Lake, near Crane Lake and the U.S.-Canadian border, even contained a player piano that had been painstakingly transported through the wilderness. "Tom Filben would make one trip up to Crane Lake with his wife and the next trip up with his girlfriend," remembered Crane Lake resident John Bowser. "Tom and his wife came up to the place in a line of five cars, all Packards. Filben was a character."[49]

The Filben cabin on Trout Lake, once owned by post office robber William "Dutch" Canner, now stands abandoned in Voyageurs National Park; local residents inaccurately call it "the Capone cabin." The cottage is so remote that in order to reach it the gangsters had to drive to a fishing lodge, rent an inboard motorboat, travel thirty-five miles by water, and then portage to another boat. But the isolation was worth it: how could FBI agents possibly raid the cottage without being noticed? Near Filben's cottage was a twelve-and-a-half-acre vacation site on Crane Lake owned by Tom Brown. Neighbors told stories of underworld figures hunting wild game with Thompson submachine guns near Brown's cottage. A game warden told FBI agents that he ran into bank robber Harvey Bailey and Brown hunting deer together in 1930.[50]

Police detective Bill McMullen, an associate of bootlegger Leon Gleckman, ran six cottages on the west shore of Sand Point Lake. Crane Lake offered a resort run by Bill Randolph, whom the FBI described as "an underworld character . . . intimately acquainted and associated with Jack Peiffer, Harry Sawyer and Tom Filbin, and others of the St. Paul underworld [who act] as 'lookout' for members of the St. Paul 'mob' when they are at their cottages on Sand Point Lake and Trout Lake."[51]

At least one life was saved by the remote cabins of Tom Filben, Bill McMullen, and Tom Brown. Legendary crime reporter Nate Bomberg, equally trusted by gangsters and police, took time off to show the girlfriend of a Chicago mobster the sights of St. Paul one night. The grateful woman wrote two letters that week—one telling a girlfriend about the marvelous time she had with a handsome bachelor named Nate Bomberg and one to her mobster boyfriend—and accidentally switched them, mailing her breathless account of partying with Bomberg to the gangster.

"This hit man, a friend of Nate's . . . said: 'Nate, I've received a contract on you tomorrow, so make yourself scarce,'" recalled retired St. Paul police officer Ted Fahey. "Nate took off for Crane Lake [where] two St. Paul detectives had a resort. . . . After Nate was gone long enough, the whole thing died [down]."[52]

By June 1932, the nationwide hunt for fugitive bank robbers Jimmy Keating, Verne Miller, Tommy Holden, and Frank Nash led the FBI to recognize that the Trout and Sand Point Lakes area was a gathering place for gangsters. Agents recruited informants throughout the region, interviewing post office inspectors, game wardens, sheriffs, border patrol officers, customs agents, and even members of the Royal Canadian Mounted Police. The FBI was playing on Filben and Brown's territory, though, and was unable to capture any vacationing gangsters.[53]

The relationships between police and criminals—Tom Brown and Tom Filben were a classic pair—forged by the O'Connor system of bribes, became the foundation for the Barker-Karpis gang crime waves of 1933 and 1934.[54]

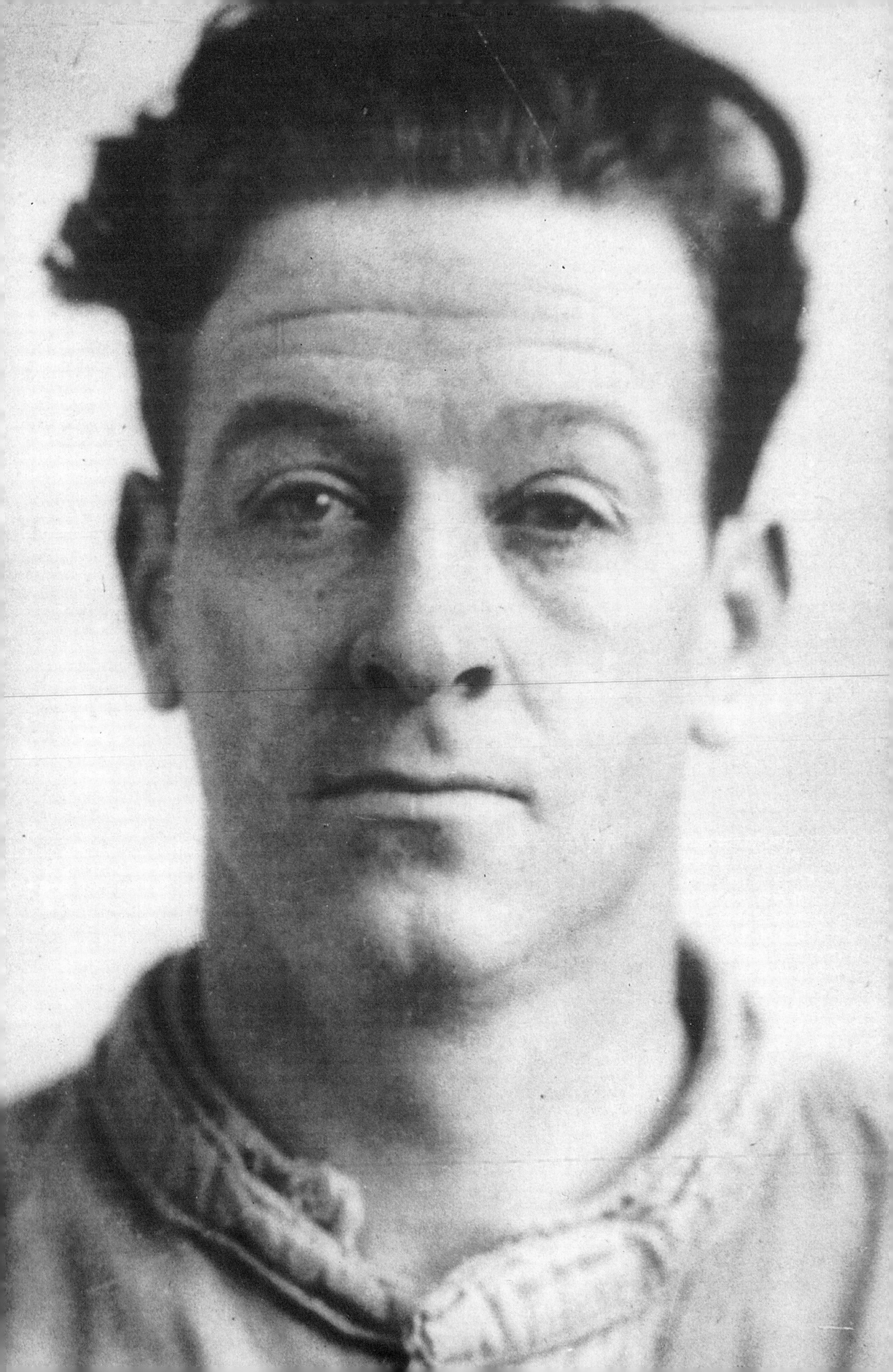

4

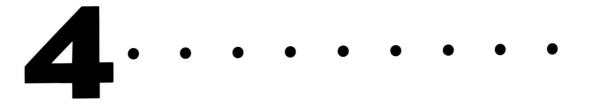

A BANK ROBBERS' HAVEN

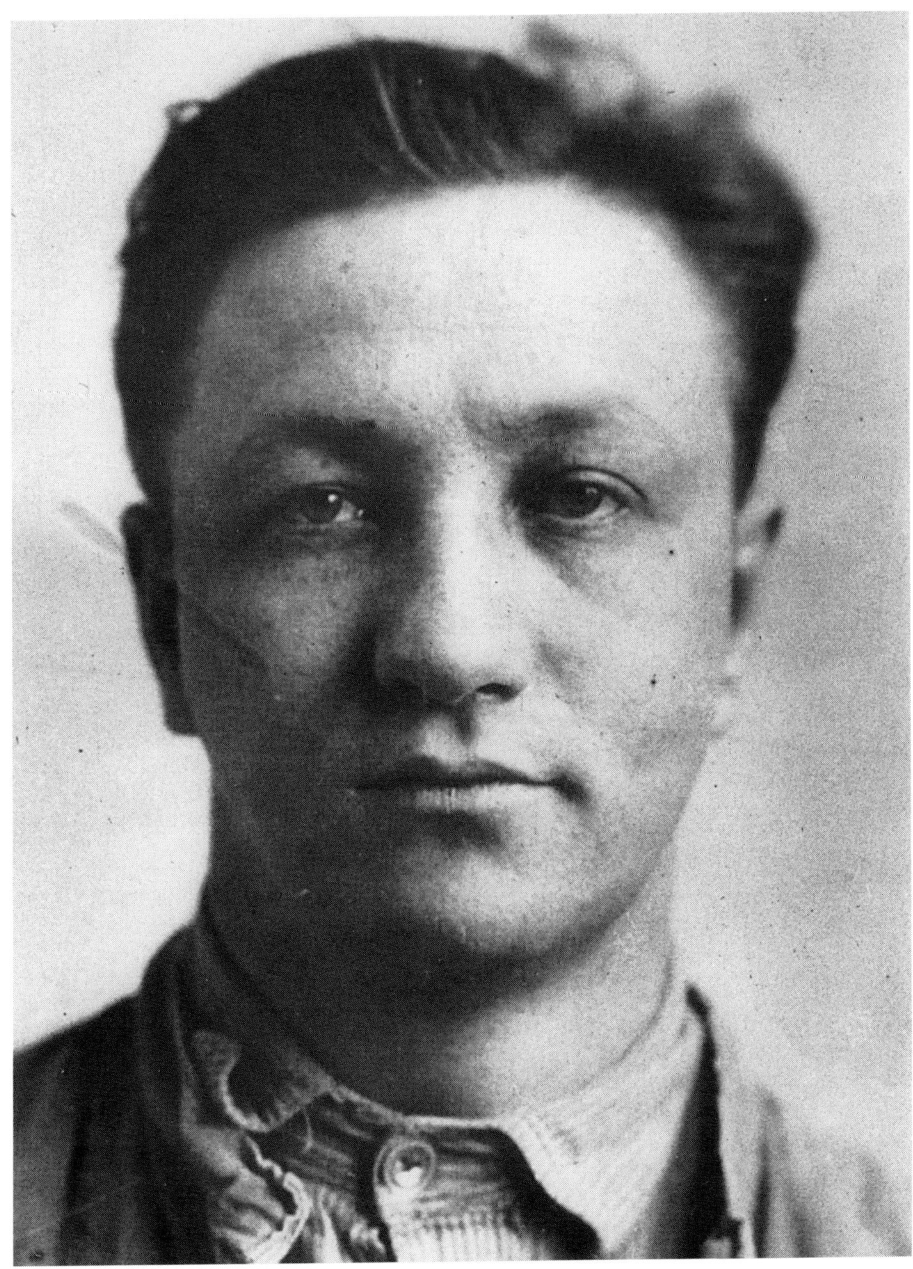

Thomas Holden (far left) and Francis L. "Jimmy" Keating (left), escapees from Leavenworth prison in 1930

18 The 'Lamsters' Hideout'

The Edgecumbe Court Apartments
1095 Osceola Avenue, St. Paul

The FBI was never able to determine why the Edgecumbe Court Apartments, at the northeast corner of Osceola Avenue and Lexington Parkway, attracted so many Leavenworth prison escapees, but they had no doubt that the building had become a "lamsters' hideout." From 1931 through 1933, the most skillful bank robbers in America paid $85 a month to live in what the FBI called "one of the best furnished apartment houses in the city." Among the Edgecumbe tenants were Oklahoma bank robber Frank "Jelly" Nash; machine gunner Verne Miller; Barker-Karpis gang members Arthur "Doc" Barker, Volney "Curly" Davis and his girlfriend, Edna "the Kissing Bandit" Murray, and con artist Earl Christman; bandit Charles Preston Harmon and his wife, Paula, (later to become Fred Barker's girlfriend); and the two "Evergreen bandits," train robbers Jimmy Keating and Tommy Holden.[1]

The Edgecumbe Court was operated by Henry P. Reed, a former banker from Hibbing, Minnesota, who had no inkling that he was renting to a convention of bank robbers. Reed's other tenants had no difficulty guessing the occupation of their odd neighbors. Robert Seng, who in 1931 lived in apartment 204, across from Frank Nash, recalled the day when another tenant, Esther Haybeck, responded to a knock on her door. "Hi, babe," grinned the visitor, whom Haybeck recognized as the infamous gangster Lester "Babyface Nelson" Gillis. For a moment, Haybeck was speechless, and then she screamed, sending Nelson running for cover. While the gangsters rested during the day, their cars were being polished outside. When night fell, their parties began, and Seng pounded on his apartment walls for respite from the noise.[2]

The influx of gangsters who were sworn under the O'Connor system not to commit crimes within the St. Paul city limits had sparked a wave of bank robberies in rural Minnesota towns such as Hugo, Sandstone, Elk River, Cushing, Savage, Shakopee, and Belle Plaine. In 1930 more than two dozen Minnesota banks were robbed of nearly $214,800; the small communities were not prepared for big-city bandits equipped with machine guns and high-speed cars. In May 1930, after banks in the small towns of Clements, Winthrop, and Bixby were robbed during a three-day period, the Minnesota Bankers Association urged its members to instruct their guards to shoot to kill robbers.[3]

A speaker at the Minnesota Bankers Association's 1933 annual convention noted that 21 percent of all bank holdups in the United States in 1932 occurred in the state of Minnesota—a total of forty-three daylight bank robberies netting $1.39 million.[4]

Just as devastating were the bank robberies in neighboring states. North Dakota banks lost more than $102,000 to robberies in 1930, and robbers struck five North Dakota banks in a thirteen-day span in September 1932. Wisconsin banks in Cameron, Cumberland, Milton Junction, Grantsburg, Stone Lake, Colfax, and other towns suffered similar fates in 1931. During an October 1931 robbery of $5,000 from a Stone Lake bank, four thieves carefully examined the bank's books and determined that there had to be more bonds worth stealing than those they had seized so far.[5]

Police found that some of the Upper Midwest bank robberies were committed by farm youths and desperate amateurs, but others—such as the October 1931 robbery of the Kraft State Bank in Menomonie, Wisconsin, and the Austin, Minnesota, mail robbery of August 1931—clearly involved professionals. Newspaper accounts often noted that the robbers were "last

The Edgecumbe Court Apartments, a hideout for the Barker-Karpis gang; bankrobber Frank "Jelly" Nash (inset)

Aftermath of a Good Thunder, Minnesota, bank robbery in which the safe was blown open with nitroglycerine

seen driving toward St. Paul" or "are believed to be heading toward the Twin Cities."

The most prominent career bank robber living at the Edgecumbe Court Apartments was Frank "Jelly" Nash from Hobart, Oklahoma. An FBI wanted poster listed his occupations as "cook, hotel worker, bank robber." FBI records indicate that Nash lived as "Frank Lee" in apartment 205, rented with his bank-robbing friend from Leavenworth, Charlie Harmon, from June 1 through August 28, 1931.[6]

Born in Indiana in 1887, Nash earned a reputation as a crime strategist with impeccable manners. Like Harvey Bailey, Nash was respected for his detailed planning and daring escapes. In 1913, he broke out of an Oklahoma jail, kidnapped a prosecution witness about to testify against him in a murder trial, and then returned to lock himself in his jail cell the next morning.[7]

"Frank Nash was, perhaps, the most successful bank robber in history . . . [whose] career of bank robbing [was] unparalleled by either old-time outlaw or modern day gangster," wrote his biographers, Clyde Callahan and Byron Jones. Nash, who had a record of more than a hundred successful robberies, was a transitional figure, "a new breed of criminal . . . [with] automobiles rather than horses, automatic pistols and sub-machine[gun]s taking the place of the old fashioned six-shooter [and] urban homes or resorts for hide-outs instead of a rough camp in the hills." In contrast to sociopaths like Fred Barker and Larry DeVol, Nash was intelligent and something of a literary aesthete: in prison, he read Dickens and Shakespeare.[8]

Nash was first arrested for a burglary at an Oklahoma store in May 1911. He was picked up for burglary again in June, July, August, September, October, and November of the same year, but none of the arrests led to a conviction. Though Nash generally was poor at evading capture, once he was caught he was adept at cutting his prison sentences short. In 1913, for example, he was sentenced to life in the state penitentiary in McAlester, Oklahoma, for shooting his partner. But in 1918 the governor of Oklahoma commuted his sentence to ten years because officials believed that Nash's victim "was a man of questionable character with a criminal record." Nash was pardoned and freed from prison in July to serve in the U.S. Army.[9]

Convicted in 1924 of an Oklahoma mail train robbery, Nash began to serve a twenty-five-year sentence in Leavenworth prison. He befriended his future partners in crime, bank robbers Jimmy Keating and Tommy Holden, whom he helped escape from Leavenworth in February 1930. In October 1930 Nash walked out of Leavenworth himself, slipping away from the home of the deputy warden, for whom he served as a housekeeper. Nash hid in Joplin, Missouri, vacationed in Hot Springs, Arkansas, and then joined Keating and Holden in Minnesota. When he arrived, Nash first stayed in Minneapolis at the Senator Hotel, run by St. Paul racketeer Jack Peifer and bootlegger Tommy Banks, and then moved to the Edgecumbe Court in St. Paul.[10]

"Since his escape, Nash is reported to have changed his appearance," warned an FBI wanted poster, "having gained approximately 50 pounds, now wears a wig-toupee and has had his nose reshaped by plastic operations." The forty-four-year-old Nash was a balding heavy drinker with an ill-fitting toupee. According to FBI memos, he "apparently did not have any regular woman companion, and was never seen by Mr. Reed [the landlord] in company with any woman other than Mrs. Ryan [Paula Harmon] and her friends."[11]

Then, in late 1931, Nash fell in love with a former schoolteacher and cook from Aurora, Minnesota, a twenty-eight-year-old divorcee named Frances Mikulich. Nash courted Frances using an alias, visiting her family in Aurora as "Mr. Harrison." When they were married in Hot Springs, the fugitive used another alias—George Miller. "After the marriage ceremony I asked

Frances Mikulich Nash, the Aurora schoolteacher who married Frank Nash

Frank why we were married under the name of Miller," Frances told the FBI, "when I thought his name was Frank Harrison."[12]

The residents of the Edgecumbe Court continued to plot new criminal ventures. On April 8, 1931, Nash and Harvey Bailey, using Verne Miller and George "Machine Gun Kelly" Barnes as getaway drivers, stole $40,000 from the Central State Bank of Sherman, Texas.[13]

The tension of the robberies, alternating with the anxiety of life as a fugitive, accelerated Nash's drinking. Miller, a close friend, tried to dry Nash out. "Frank was drinking heavily all during this time," Frances told the FBI, "and every time Verne would see him he would bawl Frank out, but Frank paid no attention, and continued to drink; in fact Frank was a heavy drinker, and indulged freely, and frequently, in intoxicating liquor all during the time I associated with him."[14]

Meanwhile, the FBI was examining every paper, telegram, and telephone call related to Nash's life with Keating, Holden, Miller, and Charlie Harmon. FBI agent Oscar Hall listed the FBI's methods: "surveillance of hangouts of St. Paul hoodlums, covering of their telephones and mail, and the establishing of reliable contacts at what are believed strategic points." During the summer of 1932, FBI agents interviewed dry cleaners, electric utility clerks, tailors, and milkmen who had served Nash and his gang members while they were living at the Edgecumbe Apartments. Agents relentlessly traced their movements through gas, electric, and water records, laundry delivery services, credit bureaus, and auto dealers and registrations. Agents compared the signatures of the gang's girlfriends on utility bills in painstaking efforts to trace forwarding addresses and track their movements from city to city.[15]

Right to the end, Nash lived up to his nickname, "the Gentleman Bandit." When he moved out of the Edgecumbe in August 1931, the FBI learned that Nash had congratulated his landlord "on the manner in which he conducted the apartment house and stated that he enjoyed living there very much."[16] Within two years, the polite bank robber was dead. Nash earned underworld immortality on June 17, 1933, when he was accidentally slain by his friend Verne Miller during the Kansas City Massacre—a botched escape attempt at Kansas City's Union Station.

Even after Nash's departure, crime figures continued to be drawn to the Edgecumbe Court. In mid-December 1933—during the pause between the kidnapping of William Hamm and the abduction of Edward Bremer—Barker-Karpis gang member Volney "Curley" Davis and his girlfriend, Edna Murray, drove into St. Paul from Reno and moved into an Edgecumbe apartment. When Davis met Murray, she was a struggling Oklahoma waitress with a teenage son from a previous marriage. Born in Marion, Kansas, in 1898, Murray was described by moll Beth Green as having a large mouth packed with gold fillings, "small through the back and built like a tent." Murray had an extraordinary history of romancing scoundrels. She fell in love with Davis shortly before he was sentenced to the Oklahoma State Penitentiary at McAlester in 1923 for murdering a night watchman with Doc Barker. While Davis was in prison, Murray lived with jewel thief Fred "Diamond Joe" Sullivan in Kansas City. But in 1924 Sullivan was imprisoned, and ultimately electrocuted, for murdering two Little Rock, Arkansas, police officers. After that, Edna moved in with Kansas City liquor hijacker Jack Murray, with whom she was arrested and convicted of a highway holdup; both received twenty-five-year sentences in the Missouri State Penitentiary in Jefferson City.[17]

Edna "the Kissing Bandit" Murray

The popular media nicknamed Murray "the Kissing Bandit." A 1937 issue of *Official Detective Stories* gave this explanation for her moniker: "It was her habit, in the midst of a hi-jacking job to rush up to the truck-driver or some other male victim and kiss him lustfully. . . . Edna was lavish with her kisses in underworld resorts. She often lulled the suspicions of future victims by this means. . . . While a robbery was in progress, she may have kissed with the idea of keeping the man occupied and blocking a counter-attack." To members of the Barker-Karpis gang, Murray was "Rabbits," a tribute to her ability to escape from prisons. She escaped from the Missouri State Penitentiary in 1927, returned to prison in September 1931, escaped from a Missouri prison farm in November 1931, was returned to prison the next day, and then escaped again by sawing through the bars of her cell in December 1932. Once more a fugitive, Murray arranged a rendezvous in Kansas City with gangster Volney Davis.[18]

Born in Tahlequah, Oklahoma, Davis was a slender man with light blue eyes and chestnut hair, marked by a scar on his forehead. Convicted of grand larceny in Tulsa at the age of seventeen, he was sent briefly to the state prison. In 1925 he escaped from McAlester and joined the Barker-Karpis gang. Murray told the FBI about always being broke, of Davis's having to borrow money from Fred Barker, and of quarreling frequently with Davis "on account of his chasing around with other women."[19]

Far from being a master criminal like Frank Nash, Davis stumbled along on the periphery of the gang. In 1933 he and Murray slipped away to Reno, where he promised to borrow money from his underworld contacts, but as he cruised the streets aimlessly, Murray realized that "he did not know where any of the boys were living." Murray later told FBI agents that Fred Barker's girlfriend, Paula Harmon, would "always bring up the subject that we were living off of Fred's money, which I did not like, and, as a result, I often wanted to get away from them, but Volney and I could not very well afford to do that as . . . we were low on money at that time." During the summer of 1934 Davis loaned Murray money for a cancer operation she urgently needed, but, Murray told the FBI, her doctor "wanted the record of my previous operation, and I could not furnish him with this record without revealing my true identity." She did not have the surgery.[20]

The end for Davis, Murray, and the Edgecumbe Court's lamsters' hideout came in late 1934. On December 26, detective Thomas Brown of the St. Paul police called fixer Harry Sawyer of the Green Lantern saloon with an urgent tip-off. The police were about to raid the Edgecumbe Court, warned detective Brown—were there any members of Sawyer's gang still living there who should be notified? Fred Barker drove to the apartments and warned Davis and Murray, who fled to gangster "Lapland Willie" Weaver's apartment above the Moonlight Gardens on Selby Avenue.[21]

Once again, an O'Connor-system tip had saved a member of the Barker-Karpis gang. But not even the police could save the unluckiest gangster in Minnesota, Charles Preston Harmon.

19 'Unlucky' Charlie Harmon

The Lincoln Oaks Apartments
572 Lincoln Avenue, St. Paul

When the couple calling themselves Thomas and Paula Ryan moved into the Edgecumbe Court Apartments, they told the landlord they were hotel owners from Arkansas. But Charles Preston Harmon, ex-convict and bank robber, and his wife, Paula, were lying. In August 1931 when they told the landlord they were going back to Arkansas, they were lying again: they were moving to the Lincoln Oaks, at 572 Lincoln Avenue.[22]

Texas-born Charlie Harmon was short, slight, scarred (from gunshot wounds in his right leg and abdomen), tattooed (with a bizarre illustration of a man straddling a hog), and unlucky. A U.S. Navy veteran and a carpenter by trade, Harmon was first arrested in 1921 for armed robbery and sent to the Huntsville, Texas, state prison. Released in October 1924, he was identified in prison records as having become a chronic nail-biter. In 1928 Harmon was incarcerated in Leavenworth for a post office robbery in Davenport, Iowa. Typical of his shambling criminal skills, the heist netted barely $174—not in cash, but in postage stamps and C.O.D. parcels. (Harmon later told the prison chaplain he committed the Iowa robbery to "get some clothes.") By the time he was paroled in 1930, Harmon already had been arrested by police in Dallas and Houston, Texas; Chicago and Rock Island, Illinois; and Council Bluffs, Iowa. His bad luck continued on a return stay in Leavenworth in July 1930, when he was injured playing sandlot baseball. A fellow convict's curve ball sailed across the field and struck his left ear; he was hospitalized and had to have stitches. Released again from Leavenworth in January 1931 and discharged to Chicago, Harmon made his way to St. Paul.[23]

The Barker-Karpis gang thought of Harmon as a grumpy hanger-on, wrote Frank Nash's biographers. He "was not considered good company in their leisure hours, was boastful and a poor loser on the golf course. . . . He was included in on bank jobs only because of his persistence and the fact he knew so much about their plans."[24]

Even Charlie's marriage was plagued with missteps. Paula Harmon was raised in Port Arthur, Texas, and educated at a girls' finishing school in Atlanta. She married Charlie in 1925, just after his release from a Huntsville, Texas, prison. According to Beth Green, Eddie Green's girlfriend, Paula was a strange-looking woman: she had false upper teeth, and her face looked flat as a result of automobile-accident injuries. In a 1929 telegram to her imprisoned husband, she cooed, "I just wanted to say I really love you and if I had to do over would be glad to do the same as one hour with you erases all

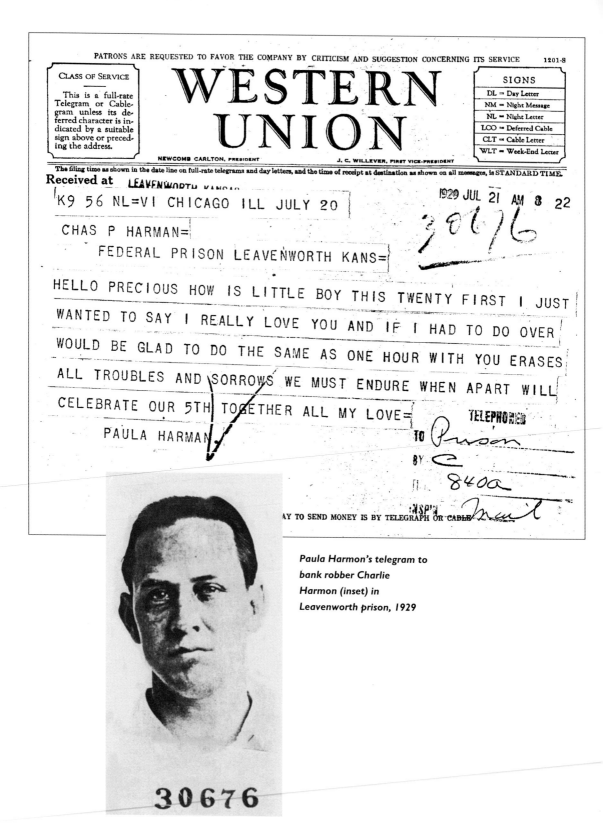

PATRONS ARE REQUESTED TO FAVOR THE COMPANY BY CRITICISM AND SUGGESTION CONCERNING ITS SERVICE 1201-S

CLASS OF SERVICE
This is a full-rate Telegram or Cablegram unless its deferred character is indicated by a suitable sign above or preceding the address.

WESTERN UNION

NEWCOMB CARLTON, PRESIDENT J. C. WILLEVER, FIRST VICE-PRESIDENT

SIGNS
DL = Day Letter
NM = Night Message
NL = Night Letter
LCO = Deferred Cable
CLT = Cable Letter
WLT = Week-End Letter

The filing time as shown in the date line on full-rate telegrams and day letters, and the time of receipt at destination as shown on all messages, is STANDARD TIME.

Received at LEAVENWORTH KANSAS

K9 56 NL=VI CHICAGO ILL JULY 20 1929 JUL 21 AM 8 22

30676

CHAS P HARMAN=

FEDERAL PRISON LEAVENWORTH KANS=

HELLO PRECIOUS HOW IS LITTLE BOY THIS TWENTY FIRST I JUST WANTED TO SAY I REALLY LOVE YOU AND IF I HAD TO DO OVER WOULD BE GLAD TO DO THE SAME AS ONE HOUR WITH YOU ERASES ALL TROUBLES AND SORROWS WE MUST ENDURE WHEN APART WILL CELEBRATE OUR 5TH TOGETHER ALL MY LOVE=

PAULA HARMAN.

TELEPHONED TO Prison BY C 840a

INSP'N Mail

AY TO SEND MONEY IS BY TELEGRAPH OR CABLE

30676

Paula Harmon's telegram to bank robber Charlie Harmon (inset) in Leavenworth prison, 1929

troubles and sorrows we must endure when apart . . . all my love—Paula Harman." But while Charlie was in prison, Paula opened what she termed a "call house" in Chicago; the FBI daintily referred to Paula's business as a "house of ill fame." The brothel became a source of growing tension between the Harmons, and Paula told the FBI that after her husband was released from Leavenworth in 1930, the couple never really got along.[25]

For his part, Charlie was squiring another woman around St. Paul during the summer of 1931. The FBI was later able to convince this woman to talk. When she met Harmon, noted an FBI report, she "did not know that he was a gangster and he conducted himself as a gentleman and always had lots of money and claimed to be an investigator for a nationally known concern. After she had been going with him several months she heard other members of the 'gang' and their sweethearts make comments which led her to believe that her sweetheart was an underworld character." When she confronted him, "he became very angry and denied he associated with any outlaw gang, but admitted that he was a 'fixture' for a liquor ring."[26]

In October 1931, Charlie Harmon made the worst decision of his life. He joined Tommy Holden, Jimmy Keating, and Frankie Webber in taking $130,000 (all but $10,000 in nonnegotiable securities) from the Kraft State Bank of Menomonie, Wisconsin—the thirty-fourth Wisconsin bank robbed in 1931 and the last bank Harmon ever robbed. The Menomonie job was a disaster from the start. Minutes after the robbers entered the bank, the burglar alarm was set off, attracting a swarm of townspeople who fired back at the robbers with deer rifles. Inside the bank, the gangsters were delayed by needless violence. When one of them demanded more money, bank official William Kraft replied, "You have all there is . . . you have every cent in the bank." The gangster yelled "I'll fix you" and fired a bullet into Kraft's chest as he lay helpless on the floor. Twenty-one-year-old cashier James Kraft, son of bank president Sam Kraft, was taken hostage by Harmon, who used him as a shield.

Minutes later, James Kraft was murdered during the getaway ride, his body left on a road just north of Menomonie. Nearby was the bullet-riddled body of the machine gunner who had protected the bank-robbing trio, Utah State Prison alumnus Frank Webber of Minneapolis. Two days later, officials found another body at Shell Lake, Wisconsin. It was Charlie Harmon, shot through the neck and knee—either by the townspeople or his partners. Harmon was buried with Webber in a potter's field grave.[27]

20 Hideout of 'A Very Fine Gentleman'

The Cretin Court Apartments
50 South Cretin Avenue, St. Paul

To the FBI agents hunting them across the United States, gangsters Thomas Holden and Francis L. "Jimmy" Keating were known as the "Evergreen bandits." Their notoriety grew from their robbery of $130,000 from a Port Huron and Chicago Railway train in Evergreen Park, Illinois, for which they had been sentenced in 1928 to serve twenty-five years in Leavenworth prison.[28]

Francis Keating, a muscular former Chicago cab driver and streetcar conductor, was the son of middle-class Irish parents and the youngest in a family of eight. His father died of tuberculosis in 1906, when Keating was just seven years old. Before his conviction, Keating, a U.S. Navy veteran, was married and had two young sons. Holden, two years older, two inches taller, and twenty pounds heavier than his partner, was a former Stutz auto salesman and steam fitter. Neither Keating nor Holden had been convicted of a crime before being apprehended for the train robbery. Keating insisted for decades that they were innocent, their conviction a case of mistaken identity.[29]

While they were in Leavenworth for the Evergreen robbery, Keating and Holden befriended George "Machine Gun Kelly" Barnes and robber Frank Nash. "Frank was deeply interested in what they had to say about crime methods under the Al Capone regime," wrote Nash's biographers, Clyde Callahan and Byron Jones. "They talked of big money, of plush hideouts in large cities . . . of big hauls, of big time bootlegging, bank jobs and gambling. . . . Both Keating and Holden were typical of the coterie that gravitated around Frank Nash. They were intelligent, pleasant, friendly, enjoyed good times, lived in excellent apartment houses and hotels, played golf on exclusive courses, wore good clothes and spent money freely."[30]

In February 1930, Keating and Holden escaped from Leavenworth. With the inside help of Nash, Harmon, and Machine Gun Kelly (who had been assigned to the Leavenworth records room, where fingerprints and photographs were stored), Keating and Holden obtained forged trustee passes. Minneapolis defense attorney Irv Nemerov, who represented Keating years later, recalled their prison-break stratagem: Keating "got himself a pass to get through the prison gate . . . but how was he going to get to the gate? Well, there were signs that said, 'Stay off the Grass.' So he'd run over and step on the grass. The guards would order him off the grass. And he moved off the grass toward the gate."[31]

After the escape, Keating and Holden traveled to Kansas City, Missouri, and Chicago. Bank robber Harvey Bailey suggested they seek haven at the Green Lantern saloon in St. Paul, and like so many gangsters before them, they plugged into fixer Harry Sawyer's contacts there. They stayed for a while in January 1931 at the Admiral Hotel in downtown Minneapolis (also known as the Senator Hotel), which was operated by St. Paul racketeer Jack Peifer and Minneapolis syndicate figure Tommy Banks.[32]

Unfortunately for the gangsters, the O'Connor system of protection did not extend to Minneapolis: an FBI memo noted that "Minneapolis soon became 'too hot' for the Fugitives and they moved to St. Paul and the suburbs near the lakes." By September 1930 Tommy Holden was living on St. Paul's prestigious Summit Avenue; Keating followed in May 1931.[33]

The fugitives were nearly captured early on, when a federal agent recognized them while they were eating in Nelson's Cafe in Minneapolis. Machine Gun Kelly told the FBI that the agent went to bootlegger Tommy Banks, whom Kelly identified as "the town fixer" in Minneapolis, and "told this individual that he had 'spotted' the two fugitives and asked him what it was worth if he took no action." The FBI learned that "through Tommy Banks . . . Keating and Holden paid $5,000 to an agent for protection. This agent . . . understood that he would be 'bumped off' if he double-crossed Keating and Holden on the payoff."[34]

Rescued from the threat of exposure in Minneapolis, Keating and his wife, calling themselves Mr. and Mrs. James Courtney, moved to St. Paul. He drove up to the Cretin Court Apartments in a maroon Buick coupe so fresh the dealer's stickers and tags were still attached. The "Courtneys" were rather fresh, too: an informant told the FBI that "when these people first came to the apartment, they left the impression that they had been recently married." The Keatings pretended to be "show people" performing at the Plantation nightclub in White Bear Lake.[35]

Barber Frank Doran styled Keating's hair every week in the Cretin Court basement. The bank robber "appeared to be a very fine gentleman," Doran told FBI agents. The barber "never saw him under the influence of liquor and he was of good manners and was very likable." Doran noticed that Keating did indulge himself with thick, expensive cigars—"probably they were La Unica cigars, [the] three for 50 cent[s] size." Jimmy Keating was also a terrific dresser. He would take as many as five suits—the finest $125 suits from Minneapolis tailor Ben Millman—to be pressed at Zolly Vetloff's dry cleaners across the street at 2166 Grand Avenue.[36]

The FBI uncovered more information on Keating's personal habits from the Orth family, who ran a delicatessen in the basement of the Cretin Court Apartments. "Keating and his girl would come into our store—we called it the Orth Grocery—and she'd always carry lots of gold coins in her purse," recalled Earl Orth, who managed the deli in the summer of 1931. Keating made long-distance calls from the pay phone to Kansas City—not to plan criminal activity but to make reservations at the golf course there.[37]

Throughout his life, Francis Keating preferred to be known as Jimmy. "I knew him as Jimmy," Charlie Reiter, a former St. Paul police officer who befriended Keating, remembered. "Francis Keating was his real name, but that sounds like a woman."[38] The aliases Keating used during his criminal career included Jimmy Courtney, Jimmy Olson, Jimmy Bates, Jimmy Larson, and Jimmy Stanley. As they searched the Twin Cities for some sign of Keating, the FBI knew that wherever he was hiding, his partner Tommy Holden would be secreted nearby.

21 'Dangerous Men' with Machine Guns

The Summit-Dale Apartments
616 Summit Avenue, St. Paul

"The search for these fugitives [Keating and Holden] led to St. Paul, Minnesota, where it was ascertained that they had taken up their residence and had become associated with the criminal underworld headed by Leon Gleckman," noted a 1934 FBI memo. "Thomas Holden, using the name William McCormick, with his wife, occupied a furnished apartment at 616 Summit Avenue, St. Paul, Minnesota, from September 2, 1930 to August 7, 1931."[39]

Holden lived with his wife in apartment 102 of the twenty-eight-unit apartment building still at the corner of Summit and Dale. Holden's wife Lillian tried to establish a semblance of domesticity in spite of the nationwide manhunt for her husband. She bought a $295 baby grand piano (later repossessed when they failed to keep up the payments) and a fur coat. (Unbeknownst to her, the FBI met with her furrier and piano company in their search for Keating and Holden.) The Holdens' existence was uneasy: Holden's maid told FBI agents that Lillian "had a sullen disposition" and "never appeared happy," and another informant said Jimmy Keating and his wife "quarrelled and cursed each other a great deal."[40]

Both Keating and Holden often left their wives at home to spend winter evenings at the Boulevards of Paris nightclub; during the summer, the pair would gamble at the Plantation nightclub in White Bear Lake. They ate frequently around the corner from the Holdens' Summit-Dale apartment in the French Cafe at 38 South Dale Street (today the site of La Cucaracha restaurant). Anxious about being spotted, Holden always held a hand on one side of his face.[41]

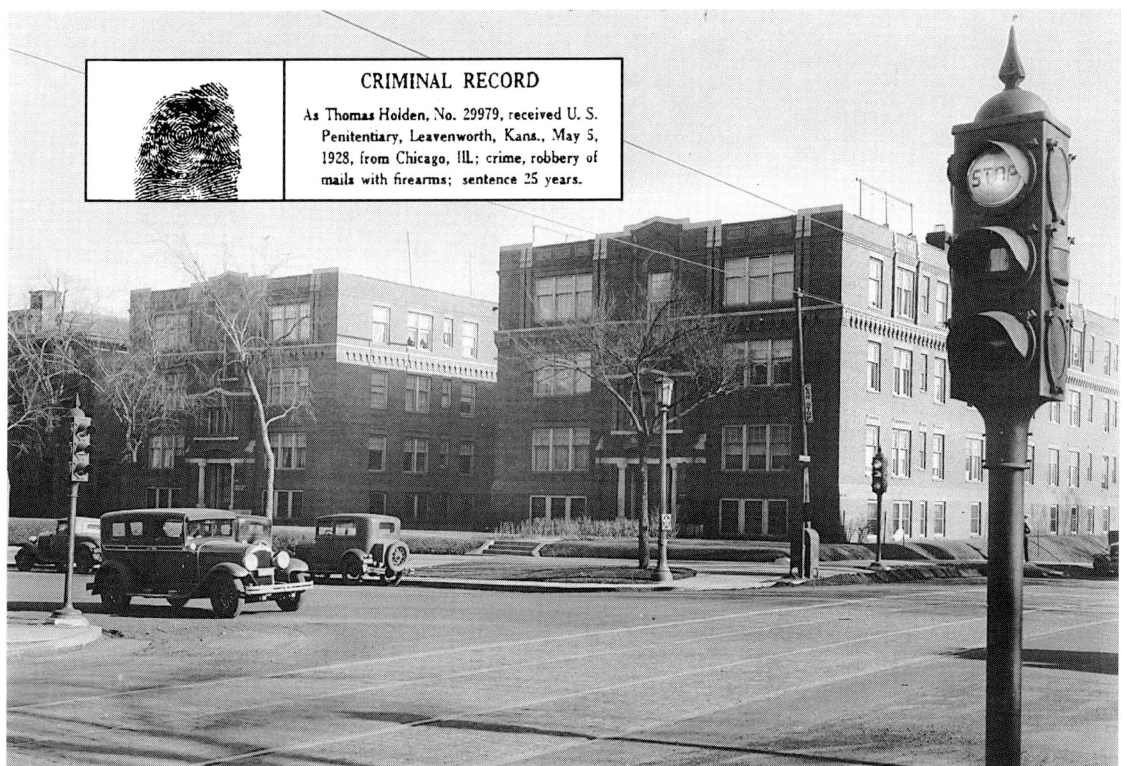

CRIMINAL RECORD

As Thomas Holden, No. 29979, received U. S. Penitentiary, Leavenworth, Kans., May 5, 1928, from Chicago, Ill.; crime, robbery of mails with firearms; sentence 25 years.

Summit-Dale Apartments, hideout for bank robber Tommy Holden (inset record), about 1932

Keating and Holden did not lead bank robberies themselves but were talented freelancers who collaborated with the Barker-Karpis or Frank Nash gangs for a cut of the proceeds. In September 1930 they joined Harvey Bailey, Larry DeVol, Fred Barker, Machine Gun Kelly, and Verne Miller in robbing a bank in Ottumwa, Iowa. The duo also helped Alvin Karpis, DeVol, Bailey, and Barker steal $32,000 from a Fort Scott, Kansas, bank in June 1932.[42]

The FBI did not underestimate the hazards of trying to bring Keating and Holden back to Leavenworth. "Keating and Holden . . . are now classed as dangerous men who are at all times armed, and also have a Thompson sub-machine gun in their possession," warned a 1932 FBI report." An FBI agent noted that

> during the stay of Keating, Holden, Nash and their gang in St. Paul, a number of gang murders occurred, but for some reason or another the victims were always dumped in the adjoining counties although every evidence indicated that the men had been murdered elsewhere. In some cases the St. Paul Police would rush to the scene of the "finding of the body," gather up all the evidence and depart before the authorities charged with the solution of the crime could get there. The neighboring County authorities have complained that the case became so garbled they could never solve it.[43]

During the summer of 1932 Jimmy Keating became a prime suspect in the killing of another ex-con from Leavenworth, St. Paul auto thief Eddie Harlow. In December 1931, Harlow's body—with five bullet wounds—had been found in a bullet-riddled convertible seven miles outside Farmington, Minnesota. Shortly before his demise, Harlow had complained to authorities that Keating was "gunning" for him. The Justice Department admitted that Harlow had served as a government informant. Keating, however, was never questioned about the slaying, and Eddie Harlow's murder remained unsolved.[44]

22 'Cold-Blooded Disregard of Human Life'

The Murder of Sammy Silverman
Near Wildwood and Katherine Abbott Parks, Mahtomedi

As the manhunt for bank robbers Jimmy Keating, Tommy Holden, Verne Miller, and Frank Nash accelerated, a number of clues pointed the FBI toward the Mahtomedi area, just fourteen miles northeast of St. Paul. Particularly mystifying to the bureau were the August 1930 murders of gangsters Sammy Silverman, Frank "Weanie" Coleman, and Michael Rusick on a gravel road that ran from Wildwood Road to Long Lake Road, half a mile southeast of Wildwood Park in Mahtomedi.[45]

Weeks earlier, Keating and Holden, grateful to George "Machine Gun Kelly" Barnes for helping them escape from Leavenworth, invited him to join them in robbing the Bank of Willmar, Minnesota. Accompanying the trio to Willmar, about a hundred miles west of St. Paul, were prowler Sammy Silverman, Robert "Frisco Dutch" Steinhardt of Chicago, veteran bank robber Harvey Bailey, and, according to some accounts, machine gunner Verne Miller. The *St. Paul Pioneer Press* called the July 1930 Willmar robbery "one of the most daring bank holdups in the Northwest since the days of the Younger Brothers and Jesse James gangs." W. F. Rhinow, head of the state BCA, said, "I can't remember a holdup in the history of the state since the raids of the Younger Brothers and Jesse James gangs which compares to the one at Willmar for daring and cold-blooded disregard of human life."[46]

During the eight-minute attack, the machine gun-toting bandits demanded that two dozen employees and bank customers lie on the bank floor. A member of the gang pistol-whipped a cashier, yelling, "Lay down or we will kill you. We mean business." A final fusillade of machine-gun fire aimed directly into the crowd of a hundred people surrounding the bank wounded two women, one of them cradling her two-year-old daughter.[47]

The gang left with $142,000 in cash and securities, forcing a man and a

WILLMAR TRIBUNE

Willmar, Minnesota, Wednesday, July 16, 1930 — 5c PER COP

# of Willmar Robbed of $7

Forcing the
Lie on the
Street are

man slumped over
elieved to have been
bandit was also
eported.

river Shift

saw the man, shot
over at the wheel.
jumped into the
ed the wounded
back seat and then
driver's place and
otion.

y Wounded.

were shot while
the robbery. They
the hospital. Mrs.
about 60 years old,
ous condition. She
the corner of Fifth
avenue, directly in
ed Owl store, with
rs. D. Gildea, about
A shot was fired
unger woman's leg,
afterward another
s. Johnson through
bullet came out of
Gildea picked her
carried her to the
al Bank corner. A
at the Red Owl
other shot at her
er in the hip. The
dged there. Physi-
will recover. Mrs.
ion is very serious.
also standing on
shot in the heel.

st Shot.

ove down Fifth St.
r of Becker avenue
elson of Albert Lea
the street. Think-
ial they shot. Mr.
down on the street
et spattered in the
He was uninjured.
cars, armed with
r the bandits, driv-
street to Limit ave.
however that the
st from Fifth street.
employe in the
heard the order to
nd lie down on the
into the basement.
not pursue her.

e Number.

ison, a bystander
license number as
The car was a 1930
with wire wheels.
nd in several cars
rner, several struck
ilding and Security
et struck into the
r of deeds at the

n, standing in the
he Security bank
pat and hid behind
the entrance. He
men shot down on
d bullets spattered

Here a Week.

n town claim they
well dressed men
s during the past

CROWD INSPECTS WHERE BULLETS FLEW

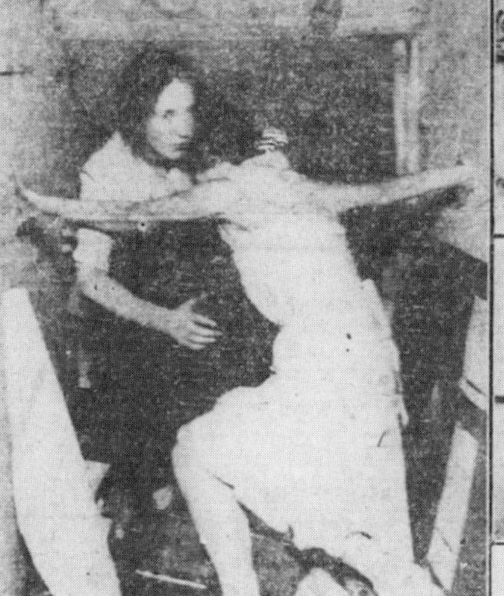

THE crowd which gathered about the Bank of Willmar after a machine-gun armed band of holdup men had robbed it Tuesday is shown here. Below, left, are Miss Alice Heltmann and Miss June Fladeboe, employes, who chanced the robbers' bullets by disobeying commands to lie on the floor and fled to the basement where they hid under a stairway. They are demonstrating how they hid. At the right of the girls are Sam Evans, top, who shot and is believed to have wounded the driver of the bandit car with a rifle he borrowed in a hardware store across the street. Below him is R. S. Paffrath, jeweler, who took a revolver from under his counter and fired at the bandits.

REHEARSALS OF PAGEANT ARE ON

that has already attracted much interest is the depiction of the important contributions made to our county's growth by the several ra-

Found Guil
Killing

Carl Dosch of La
ship was found g
pal court Wednesd
a charge of killing
was fined $10 and
He was arrested b
J. R. Hultgren.

BATHER
A FATA

Body Was Reco
Noon Frida
Long S

Alvin Erickson,
this city, was drown
east end of Green
clock Thursday ev
dove off a motor b
feet of water. He
ied by L. J. Rolan
city. The body wa
morning, shortly
by Geo. Martins, w
lake. A herring
the recovery.

Erickson and Ro
out to the lake aft
evening and had f
Hvam farm, on th
visit with Elmer H
borrowed the Hvam
ed out in the lake
suits. When abou
the southeast shor
into the water and
up. Rolander c
where Alvin had go
to see him, but w
called for help. S
of Willmar was not
immediately, with
grappling hooks th
recover the bodies
ers, who were drown
gonga last fall. A
last night they th
hooked the body a
it up, but it prove
log. Divers and ot
til after midnight
find the body, but
was resumed again
ing and over a hu
were aiding in the
not until ten o'clock
was recovered.

Surviving Alvin
Mr. and Mrs. Geo
of this city, two si
old Dahlheim and
son, both of this
brothers, Edwards,
and Roger, all of
this city.

For the past mo
been employed at th
Asylum and this w
ing for the Willma
Co.

Luther Leag
Progra

The Tripolis Lut
give a program at
eran church Wedn

A local newspaper account of the 1930 robbery of the Willmar bank

woman to serve as shields before releasing them. At least two of the robbers were wounded by Willmar residents who fired from nearby buildings, and the windshield and back window of the gang's four-door sedan was shattered by bullets. In what had become an underworld cliché, the *St. Paul Dispatch* reported that "following the robbery, the bandits drove to the Twin Cities." The getaway car was found abandoned in Minneapolis. The robbers switched the Willmar bank loot into another car, which was seen driving from Minneapolis to the safety of St. Paul.[48]

Harvey Bailey's recollections of the Willmar robbery, when he was interviewed some three decades later by biographer J. Evetts Haley, were uncharacteristically confused—he placed the Willmar robbery in "Williston" or "Wilburn":

> We was on a job up there [in Willmar]—this was a help out job, too. On our jobs that we cased, we never did have trouble, but every time we helped somebody else we had trouble. Because the place was not cased down and they didn't know just where they were at, you see. And this boy had got out and got into the car and he got shot right in the back of the neck. . . . They must have got a ring from inside; they must have got a buzzer from the inside that we didn't know about. [The assistant cashier had tripped an alarm bell under the cash drawer with his leg.] When we come out, they showered down on us. . . . The car got shot up pretty bad.[49]

After the Willmar robbery, Sammy Silverman hid in Big Lake, Minnesota, posing as a cattle businessman, and then masqueraded at Lake Minnetonka, just west of Minneapolis, as a Hollywood movie executive. "They lived a peaceful life, spending much of their time boating and swimming," reported the *St. Paul Dispatch* of Silverman and his gangland partners. They "were friendly to the children, buying them candy and ice cream, and intimated they desired seclusion to plan forthcoming motion picture productions."[50]

On August 14, a posse of agents from the BCA, searching for clues to the Willmar robbery, pulled up to examine three fresh bodies found near Wildwood Amusement Park. The agents immediately identified one body as that of Willmar bank robber Sammy Silverman, a former taxi driver known in Minneapolis variously as "the Ten Dollar Kid," "Sammy Stein," and Harry "Heckle" Silberman. Before the Willmar raid, Silverman had been suspected of killing a Kansas City policeman (and wounding four innocent bystanders) when he and four partners held up the Home Trust Company bank during the 1928 Republican National Convention. The FBI heard from informants that "Silverman got away from the [Kansas City] robbery with all of the money, and he was supposed to have been slain by members of the Bugs Moran gang."[51]

Minnesota Weather

Generally fair tonight and Friday; not much change in temperature.

St. Paul Dispatch

General telegraph, Northwest and local news. Radio.

Editorial page and its daily features.

VOL. 62. NO. 356. 24 PAGES Exclusive Service of the Associated Press. ST. PAUL, MINN., THURSDAY, AUGUST 14, 1930. HOME EDITION. ☆☆ PRICE TWO CENTS IN ST. PAUL.

3 GANGSTERS MURDERED ON ROAD NEAR WILDWOOD

MATSON FIGHTS PHONE TOLLS IN TWIN CITIES

Commissioner to Seek Abolition If State Approves Merger of Companies.

SEE OTHER REVISIONS

Combination Considered With Possibility of "Effect on Future Rate Schedules."

Commissioner Frank W. Matson of the Minnesota Railroad and Warehouse Commission announced today he will seek to have the Commission force abolition of telephone toll charges between St. Paul and Minneapolis if the Commission approves the sale of the Tri-State Telephone Co. of St. Paul to the Northwestern Bell Co. controlling the Minneapolis properties.

Commissioner Matson expressed the opinion there no longer is any excuse for the continuance of the 10-cent toll charge on intercities calls, which has been in effect for many years except in the Midway district of St. Paul.

He also said that savings, which may be effected by the combination of the properties in both cities under one direction, will be considered with a possibility of "having effect on the future rate schedules."

Under One Control Now.

Sale of the St. Paul and suburban holdings of the Tri-State Co. to the Northwestern Bell Co., placing all Twin Cities telephone properties under one control and ownership, was announced Wednesday by George W. Robinson, president of the Tri-State Co.

By a series of stock transfers, however, Theodore Gary & Co. of Kansas City, owners of 82 per cent of the stock of the Tri-State will continue to own and operate the present Tri-State and Dakota Central Telephone Co. properties in southern Minnesota and the Dakotas and the company's toll lines.

"I always have opposed the toll ...

Where Bullets Settled Feud of Gangsters

The spot where Sammy Stein, Minneapolis gangster, met his

ST. PAUL MAN BELIEVED ONE OF VICTIMS; MINNEAPOLIS RACKETEER IDENTIFIED; THIRD THOUGHT KANSAS CITY GAMBLER

4 Physicians Await Royal Child's Birth

Quartet Attending Duchess of York Includes Noted Caesarian Expert.

Glamis, Scotland, Aug. 14.—(AP)—Four physicians today were in attendance on the Duchess of York, whose second baby has been expected for several days. Among them was Sir Henry Simson, noted obstetrician and expert in Caesarian operations. For many hours one of the physicians has remained constantly on duty.

Today was the ninth day Home Secretary J. R. Clynes had been waiting at Glamis to attest to the birth of the royal child. This is in accordance with the ancient British law which decrees that the birth of a possible heir to the throne must be attested by a Secretary of State.

Sir Henry Simson is the chief surgeon of the group. He was in charge of the confinements of Princess Mary and also ushered into the world the little Princess Elizabeth, first child of the Duke and Duchess of York, in April, 1926.

ASPHALT TO REPLACE WOOD ON UNIVERSITY

Will Be Laid From Lexington to City Limits Within Two Months.

Asphalt pavement will replace the bumpy wooden block road on University avenue from Lexington avenue westward to the City limits within the next two months.

This was assured today when the City Council let contracts for resurfacing the street.

It also was brought out that the new Third street paving probably will not go farther west than St. ...

General Rhinow, Seeking Clues in Willmar Bank Robbery, Encounters One Corpse and Dying Man Late Wednesday Night Near Abandoned Sedan; Other Found by Passing Party Early This Morning.

QUARREL OVER LOOT OR REPRISAL IN GOLDEN SLAYING ADVANCED AS MOTIVES

Steel-jacketed death sped along a lonely road Wednesday night north of St. Paul near Wildwood and left three gangsters dead and dying.

The victims, obviously slain by gangster guns, have been identified partially as:

Sammy Stein, 25 years old, Minneapolis North Side gunman and racketeer, who was sought by Kansas City authorities for complicity in the murder of a policeman there for which three men recently were executed. Stein also was known as Sammy Heckle or Haeckle.

Frank Coleman, 25-year-old Kansas City racketeer, associate of a "big gambler" in that city.

Adolph (Butch) Myers of St. Paul or Sam Hessell of Minneapolis. Identification of this victim is the least complete.

Theories advanced today by General W. F. Rhinow,

> **CAPONE IN MILL CITY?**
>
> **Al Capone, Chicago gangster and bootleg "king," guarded by a motorcade of ten automobiles is reported to have passed through Minneapolis Wednesday bound for Winter Lake, Wis. He is said to have made a brief stop and confided to friends that he intends to spend a few weeks at that lake.**

director of the Minnesota Bureau of Criminal Apprehension, as to the motive for the triple slaying are:

That the victims participated in the robbery of the Bank of Willmar July 15 and were "put on the spot" after a disagreement with confederates as to splitting the loot.

Reprisal for the slaying last spring of Max Golden, Minneapolis bootlegger.

Double-crossing of the victims' accomplices in hi-...

Newspaper announcing the triple murders

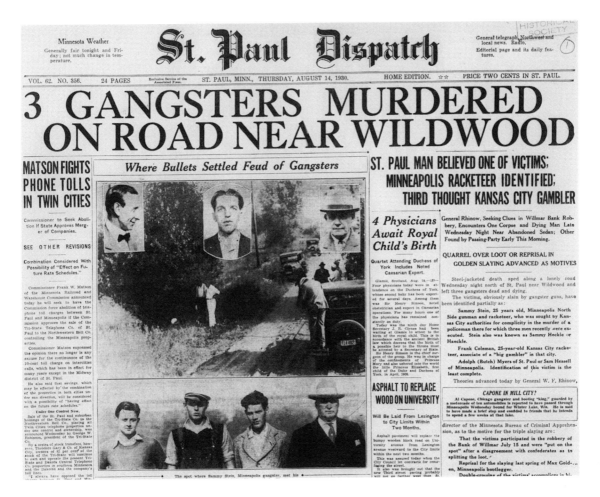

Silverman, his pockets full of unused .32-caliber bullets, had been shot in the head and neck. Killed along with him were Kansas City hoods Mike Rusick and Frank "Weanie" Coleman. The assailants left the three bloody bodies hanging from willow trees by a lovers' lane near Wildwood Park.[52]

They had left few clues. Police determined that a telephone call had been made from White Bear Lake to a Chicago gambling hall the night of the triple slaying. The FBI paid particular attention to suspicions that Chicago racketeer George "Bugs" Moran may have been involved in the murder. Although the murders were officially unsolved, an interview buried in Detroit police files on the murder of another gangster—Barker-Karpis gang machine gunner Verne Miller—offers the most likely answer. In a 1934 prison interview with police, Machine Gun Kelly identified Miller as the killer who committed the triple slaying near Wildwood Park. According to Kelly, Verne Miller had robbed the Willmar bank with Silverman and other gangsters. Foolishly, Silverman "double crossed Miller"; a few weeks later, "Miller saw this man [Sammy Silverman] with two friends at [White] Bear Lake, and killed all three of them."[53]

As the O'Connor system attracted more gangsters to St. Paul, multiple slayings between feuding criminals became more frequent, and it was not unusual for Minnesotans to stumble over stray corpses along the state's highways. Bank robber Harry "Slim Jones" Morris, for example, was found dead in August 1931 by a group of fishermen on Highway 3, four miles outside of Red Wing, Minnesota. Morris was believed to have robbed the Olmsted County Bank and Trust in Rochester, Minnesota, with Harvey Bailey in December 1926. His lifeless hand still clung to the barrel of a revolver. The FBI learned from Gladys Sawyer, wife of Harry Sawyer, that "the underworld understanding is that [Morris] was killed by 'Old Charlie' Fitzgerald following an argument at the Hollyhocks Inn" in St. Paul.[54]

In a 1966 interview, bank robber Harvey Bailey offered an opinion on how Morris ended up dead: "He was a funny guy, always on the rib. I said to him one time, 'Listen, Slim, you are just going to keep ribbing and somebody is going to shoot you right between the eyes sometime.' And sure enough, that is what happened. Ribbing somebody all the time. You know, it's all right to rib in fun, but when you get down to a man's own personal affairs, leave them alone, because that'll get you in trouble." Bailey's prediction was correct, though Morris was shot not between the eyes, but once in the heart.[55]

23 Ready Money and Riotous Nightlife

The Plantation Nightclub
Old White Bear Avenue, White Bear Lake

Nothing illustrates the prominence of White Bear Lake as a bank robber's playground better than a telegram sent to J. Edgar Hoover by a St. Paul FBI agent on April 1, 1934, the day after John Dillinger machine-gunned his way out of the Lincoln Court apartment house: "Checking each apartment house [in the] Twin Cities," the agent reported. "Also check all houses [in] White Bear Minnesota."[56]

Hoover was infuriated that the gangsters felt so safe they didn't bother to hide from his agents but lived openly in White Bear Lake, partying uproariously at local nightclubs. "With ready money and confidence in their power," said an official FBI summary, the gangs "relaxed vigilance and indulged in riotous nightlife" in White Bear Lake.[57]

The Plantation nightclub, once located at the intersection of Cottage Park Road and Old White Bear Avenue, at what is today Lion's Park, was the mobsters' White Bear Lake headquarters. Among the Plantation's patrons during the summers of 1931 and 1932 were local thugs like fixer Jack

THE PLANTATION

"The Plantation" White Bear's Beautiful Night Club, to be Formerly Opened Wednesday Night, July 2, 9 o'clock

White Bear is to have one of the most beautiful night clubs in the Middle West, and it is to open on Wednesday night, July 2. This is

Manager Harris has succeeded in securing the services of Chris. Gade, who eight years ago was chef at the White Bear Yacht Club, but who of recent years has delighted

Grand opening of the Plantation nightclub, 1930

Peifer and bootlegger Morris Roisner, nationally known bank robbers Jimmy Keating and Tommy Holden, and Capone gunman Fred Goetz.[58]

Frank Nash was also a fan of the Plantation during the summer of 1931, although an FBI informant noted that "Nash, when visiting the beach at White Bear with other members of the gang, could not go swimming because he wore a wig." Gladys Harrington, Holden's girlfriend, remembered that Nash had "a terrible looking" hairpiece. Nash rented the White Bear Lake cottage of Minnella Robertson, a cat fancier whose home was located just off what is today Highway 244 near Rose and Spruce Streets. Nash, who served as croupier at the Plantation, had won $6,000 in a single night's gambling there.[59]

Not everyone was distressed by the presence of mobsters in White Bear Lake. Minneapolis tailor Ben Millman, who provided Keating with his suits, told the FBI that he hung around the Plantation in order to get the gangsters' business and that Ben Harris, Jack Peifer, Tom Filben, and others had bought suits from him.[60]

"When the gangsters took over the Ramaleys' White Bear Castle, they renamed it the Plantation," recalled Walter "Buster" Johnson, a longtime White Bear resident. "They built a gambling hall, with every kind of gambling device available." The Plantation was condemned by White Bear Lake mayor Charles E. Buckbee in 1932 as a rendezvous for gangsters, but it was much more than that.[61]

The Plantation was managed for the underworld from 1930 to 1932 by Ben Harris, a Minneapolis gambling figure the FBI claimed "was directly connected with the Karpis-Barker gang, and with practically all of the well-known crooks in Minneapolis and St. Paul during the prohibition days." Harris told FBI agents he had taken over the Plantation nightclub in 1930 in partnership with impresario John Lane, owner of the Boulevards of Paris dance club.[62]

Robert "Frisco Dutch" Steinhardt was a bouncer and gambling consultant at the Plantation. A friend of the Barker-Karpis and Keating-Holden gangs, the florid-faced Steinhardt had participated in the Willmar bank robbery with Keating, Holden, and the unlucky Sammy Silverman. Steinhardt was a beefy pickpocket who had amassed a record of more than eighteen arrests for petty larceny, disorderly conduct, con-game operations, thievery, and pickpocketing—a series of swindles that took him from Cincinnati to St. Louis to Pittsburgh to Cleveland.[63]

"In the summer of 1931, Bennie Harris and John Lane opened the Plantation Club, a roadhouse at White Bear Lake," Steinhardt told the FBI. "Bob Hamilton and I opened up a gambling casino at the Plantation Club and became partners with Harris and Lane." In 1932 Steinhardt proposed to Harris that he run the gambling at the Plantation for 60 percent of the proceeds; Harris agreed and accepted the remaining 40 percent.[64]

In 1934, after the Plantation had closed, Ben Harris pleaded guilty to gambling violations for operating a roulette wheel at the club. The Plantation reopened as a legitimate restaurant and theater, and was later razed and replaced by a park.[65]

With the passing of the Plantation, its gambling manager, Frisco Dutch Steinhardt, predicted that the casino's underworld patrons—Frank Nash, Jimmy Keating, Tommy Holden—would also be closed down by the FBI. FBI agents learned from Steinhardt that "at the time Hamm was kidnapped, he remarked to his partner in the [Plantation] night club that he supposed they would have to get out of town before very long, because the authorities probably wouldn't let any of the old gang remain in town."[66]

He could not have guessed that one of the last chapters in the saga of Jimmy Keating and Tommy Holden would be played out not during a bank robbery or in a gambling hall but on a golf course.

24 The Golfing Gangsters

Keller Golf Course
2166 Maplewood Drive, Maplewood

Former caddies at the Keller Golf Course in Maplewood, now a St. Paul suburb, claimed that vacationing bank robbers carried two golf bags—one filled with golf clubs, the other with submachine guns and rifles. According to gangland legend, John Dillinger was playing the third hole at Keller in the early 1930s when he saw policemen approaching his party. Dillinger hopped aboard the train that ran adjacent to the links and escaped, leaving only his golf clubs behind.[67]

"It appears from past investigation that wherever [Jimmy] Keating may be he will be a regular patron of some golf course," predicted a 1932 FBI memo, "and . . . in St. Paul he will regularly play at the Keller Golf Course." The FBI considered devoting a full-time agent to the course—at least "on good golfing days between the hours of 11:00 A.M. and 4:00 P.M."—in an attempt to track down the bank-robbing fugitives. During 1931 and 1932, the FBI recruited Keller caddies, golf supply clerks, and a soda jerk in the locker room as informants to keep gangsters under surveillance.[68]

Melvin Passolt, superintendent of Minnesota's Bureau of Criminal Apprehension, knew that the gangsters, like birds, returned to old haunts during the summer. The FBI learned from Passolt that "Holden and Keating may re-appear in the Twin Cities when the weather becomes warmer, and . . . might then be found frequenting golf links." Agent Oscar G. Hall revealed that the FBI, acting on a tip from the doomed Eddie Harlow, once narrowly missed capturing Keating and Holden at Keller.[69]

One FBI agent wrote of the bureau's frustration over the political connections that Keating and Holden enjoyed through their mentor, Leon Gleckman, who in turn was friendly with the county commissioner in charge of the golf course. The agent recounted how Keating and Holden golfed at Keller while they acted as bodyguards for Gleckman. One afternoon, four telephone company employees were playing when a sudden rainstorm soaked them. Two of them decided to return to the clubhouse to change clothing and hitched a ride with a fellow golfer who, unbeknownst to them, was an underworld character. The mobster apparently mistook his passengers for hit men out to kill Gleckman, for a car pulled up and they were pulled out by St. Paul police detectives and Gleckman's bodyguards. The hapless pair was finally able to convince the policemen and the bodyguards that they "had no intention of taking Leon Gleckman for a ride."[70]

FBI surveillance at Keller was so thorough that the agents knew Keating played with Wilson irons purchased from gangster Verne Miller. An agent

Keller Golf Course, about 1932

noted disapprovingly that "Keating during the time he played at the Keller Golf Course played the eighteen holes with a score in the high 90's or between 100 and 112, and showed little improvement in his game."[71]

During the peak of the nationwide manhunt for them, the FBI noted that "Keating and Holden and their women played golf at the leading public golf course in St. Paul almost daily during the summer. . . . They all had expensive golf equipment and carried large rolls of money, tipped caddies liberally, drove large cars, and attracted considerable attention on the golf course." For his games, Jimmy Keating dressed in white linen golf knickers and a light blue sweater and golf socks, his face obscured behind octagonal eyeglasses.[72]

Keating and Holden were not the only gang members to court arrest by playing on a public golf course. An informant told the FBI that Charlie and Paula Harmon "had expensive clothing and expensive golf equipment and left the apartment to play golf almost every day." But Frank Nash was puzzled by their golfing. The FBI noted that Nash "did not play golf and chided the others for their interest in the game." In fact, Keating's and Holden's love of golf would lead to their capture.[73]

On October 2, 1931, two men (almost certainly Keating and Holden) robbed a pair of messengers from the First American National Bank of Duluth of $58,000 in front of the Duluth police building. Months later, a St. Paul bootlegger tried to cash some bonds stolen from the Duluth bank. The bootlegger identified Keating and Holden, calling themselves Jimmy Stanley and Bill McCormick, as the men who gave him the bonds. Simultaneously, the FBI identified Charlie Harmon's Edgecumbe Court apartment house and was able to trace a call that Harmon made from a St. Paul telephone to a golf equipment company in Kansas City. Within days, lawmen had the elusive Keating, now living in Kansas City, under surveillance.[74]

Four FBI agents and a police squad waited on July 7, 1932, at the Mission Hills Country Club golf course as Jimmy Keating, Tommy Holden, and bank robber Harvey Bailey walked toward them; mobster Bernard "Big Phil Courtney" Phillips was nearby. Bailey recalled later that he had expected to meet machine gunner Lawrence DeVol that day, so Bailey could deliver a $500 Liberty Bond that had been stolen during the June 17 Fort Scott bank robbery. When DeVol failed to show up, the gangsters decided instead to go golfing at Mission Hills. "When we got around to the 8th hole on the golf course," said Bailey, "up out of the ravine come eight men, Department of Justice and Deputy Sheriffs from Kansas City, Kansas, and Kansas City, Missouri."[75]

After being fugitives for 861 days, Keating and Holden returned to prison on July 8, 1932. Phillips, to the eternal suspicion of the underworld, slipped away without capture. The hapless Harvey Bailey, veteran of more than two dozen bank robberies without an arrest since 1922, was caught with the stolen Liberty Bond and sent to Kansas State Penitentiary at Lansing, convicted of a crime he did not commit.

A jailer reportedly turned down a $15,000 bribe offered by Keating and Holden, refusing to allow them to escape. The golf-loving convicts were finally placed in solitary confinement at an isolation camp, forbidden to talk or have visitors for the next eleven years. They were put to work in Leavenworth's underground rock quarry, locked together with other "incurables." Security precautions included three guards to watch every prisoner.[76] By the time they were released from Leavenworth decades later, the era of tommy guns, speakeasies, and golfing gangsters was long over.

$1,200.00 **REWARD** $1,200.0

Twelve Hundred Dollars.

WANTED

For the Murder of C. R. Kelly, Sheriff of Howell County, Missouri, on December 19, 1931

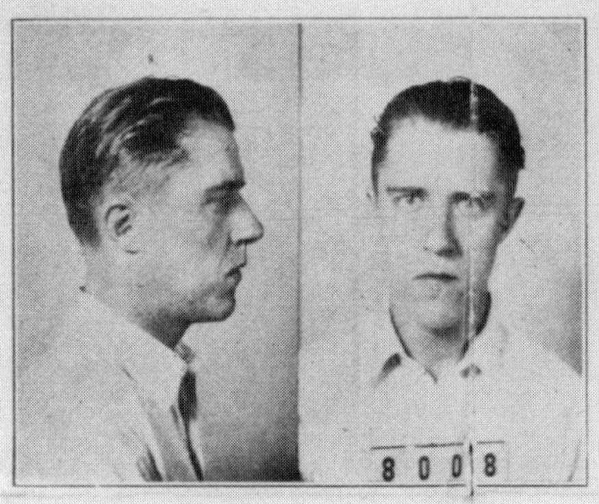

Gangsters of Kimes-Inman Gang of Oklahoma Missouri Kansas and Texas

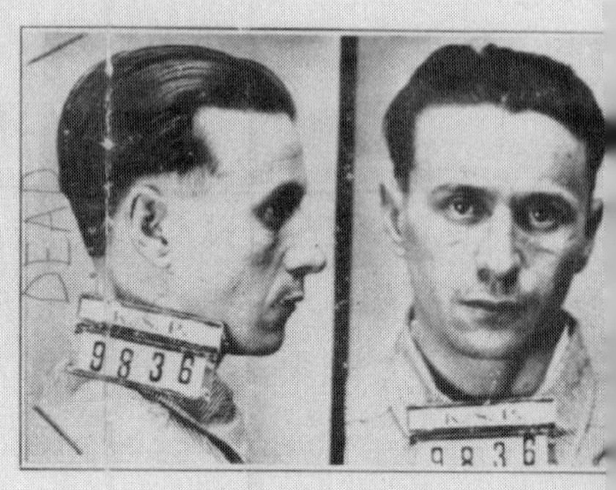

ALVIN KARPIS **FRED BARKER**

DESCRIPTION: ALVIN KARPIS, alias George Dunn, alias R. E. Hamilton, alias Ray Karpis, alias Raymond Hadl alias George Haller; Age 22; Height 5-9¾; Weight 130 lbs.; Hair-brown; Eyes-blue; Scars-cut SC base L. hand; Oc pation, Worked in bakery.

FPC 1-R-II-5
1-U-UU-8

Karpis is ex-convict having served State Reformatory Hutchinson, Kansas, 1926, No. 7071 Also State Penitenti Lansing, Kansas, May, 1930, Crime Burglary.

DESCRIPTION: FRED BARKER, alias F. G. Ward, alias Ted Murphy, alias J. Darrows; Age 28; Weight 120 l Height 5-4; Build-slim; Complexion-fair; Hair-sandy; Eyes-blue; Teeth-lower front gold, two upper front gold. Sente ed State Reformatory, Granite, Oklahoma. Robbery 1923. Sentenced State Penitentiary Lansing, Kan., March, 19

FPC 29-I-20
20-O-22

These men acting together murdered Sheriff C. R. Kelly, West Plains, Missouri in cold blood when he attempte question them.

The Chief of Police and Sheriff at West Plains, Missouri, will pay a reward of $300.00 each for the arrest and render of either of these men to Howell County, Missouri officers. $200.00 additional will be paid on conviction. will come after them any place.

An additional Reward of $100.00 each will be paid for the arrest and surrender to Howell County officers of A. Dunlop and Old Lady Arrie Barker, Mother of Fred Barker. Dunlop is about 65 years of age; slender, white hair, blood Irishman. Mrs. Barker is about 60 years of age. All may be found together on farm. We hold Felony Warra for each of these parties.

Police and other authorities: Keep this Poster before you at all times as we want these Fugitives. If further formation is desired Wire Collect Chief of Police or Sheriff at West Plains, Missouri.

James A. Bridges
Chief of Police

Mrs. C. R. Kell
Sheriff

West Plains, Missouri

JOURNAL PRINT, West Plains, Mo.

5

MURDERING FOR MA

Wanted poster for Alvin Karpis and Fred Barker, 1931; Kate "Ma" Barker

25 'A Vicious, Cold-Blooded Crew of Murderers'

Ma Barker's West St. Paul Hideout
1031 South Robert Street, West St. Paul

Nick Hannegraf recognized the three faces of evil.

They were there in black and white, printed in the pages of the April 1932 issue of *True Detective Mysteries*. The Barker-Karpis gang, a trio of killers from Tulsa, Oklahoma, were wanted for bank robbery and the murder of a Missouri sheriff. The magazine was offering a $100 reward for the apprehension of each member of the gang.

Hannegraf was closing up his Drover's Tavern on South St. Paul's Concord Street on April 25, 1932. It was 1:00 A.M. on a Monday night, Hannegraf's time to escape inside the pages of *True Detective*. As he read about the exploits of the Barker-Karpis gang, it dawned on Hannegraf that he had seen those faces somewhere before. Not in a magazine but in person, that very morning. Those lethal felons were living in his mother's house on South Robert Street. The Barker-Karpis gang, hunted by FBI agents and sheriffs across the country, was driving his children to school!

The gang had moved into Grandma Helen Hannegraf's rental home at 1031 South Robert (still standing near the intersection with Bernard Street) on February 1, 1932. They claimed to be musicians in a local orchestra and carried black violin cases to prove it. To add to the wholesome image, a blonde 5-foot, 4-inch woman in her late fifties accompanied the performers. They called her Mrs. Anderson or Ma, and she was often seen walking her bulldog down Robert Street. The gang was then at the midpoint of a larcenous career that would earn them about $3 million in bank robbery and kidnapping loot. Within months, FBI director J. Edgar Hoover would call them "the most vicious, cold-blooded crew of murderers, kidnappers and robbers in recent history."[1]

Among the "musicians" living in Hannegraf's home was Alvin Karpis, the blue-eyed son of two Lithuanian immigrants, painter John Karpovicz and his wife, Anna. Born Albin Francis Karpovicz in 1908 in Montreal, the slight, 130-pound Karpis spent his early adult years in Topeka, Kansas, working as a baker and shipping clerk. In 1925 his doctor noted a defective heart and advised Karpis to find a less stressful job. Within a year, Karpis had turned to safe blowing and jewel theft—what the FBI called "a career of plunder, pillage and despoilation."[2]

"Alvin was always upset because my grandpa lost his money during the Depression in 1929," recalled Karpis's nephew, Albert Grooms. "Alvin didn't think it was fair, he thought banks should have to be accountable. Alvin thought the banks sort of legally stole my grandpa's money. . . . It was a burr under Alvin's saddle for a long time."[3]

The hallmark of Karpis's career was the leniency of his sentences. In March 1929 he engineered an escape from the State Industrial Reformatory in Hutchinson, Kansas, where he had been serving the fourth year of a sentence for burglary. Karpis was apprehended by Kansas City police a year later and transferred to the state penitentiary in Lansing, Kansas, in May 1930. He was released a year later, only to be arrested in Tulsa in June 1931 and found guilty of burglary, sentenced to four years, and, incredibly, immediately paroled by order of the court.[4]

Karpis met Fred Barker in the Lansing penitentiary in 1930, where Barker was serving a sentence for bank burglary. Released early in May 1931 because of his "good time" effort in the Kansas coal mines, Karpis joined Barker in a string of jewel thefts and robberies in Oklahoma, Missouri, and Minnesota. By the time the twenty-three-year-old Karpis moved into the Hannegraf's house with Barker, his wanted poster warned: "Take no chances with this man. He is a killer."[5]

Sandy-haired Fred Barker was Ma Barker's favorite son. In 1932, Fred was a short (5 feet, 4 inches), slim (120 pounds) thirty-year-old with three

Prison escapees Larry DeVol (left) and Alvin Karpis (right), with guns and burglary tools found in their car in 1930

gold teeth and a scar on his left knee where he had been shot. He had just been released from prison, after nine arrests and convictions for burglary and robbery. "Freddie had a vicious streak," mused Karpis years later. "To be frank, I was sometimes slightly stunned by Freddie's free and easy way with a gun. He never seemed to mind gunning down anybody who stood in his way, whether it was a cop, or a hood or an ordinary guy on the street."

Karpis referred to Katherine "Ma" Barker (born Arizona Clark near Springfield, Missouri, in 1872) as "just an old-fashioned homebody from the Ozarks . . . superstitious, gullible, simple, cantankerous and, well, generally law abiding."[6]

While Ma Barker was married to gas station operator George Barker, their four young sons—Herman, Lloyd, Fred, and Arthur—played in Tulsa parks with junior toughs Harry Campbell and Volney Davis, future members of the Barker-Karpis gang. None of the Barker children was destined for a law-abiding career. Although only Fred and Arthur ("Doc") were active in the Barker-Karpis gang, the eldest son, Herman, killed a Kansas policeman in 1927 and then committed suicide. Lloyd was incarcerated in Leavenworth prison from 1922 to 1947 for a post office robbery and was killed in a domestic dispute in 1949.[7]

J. Edgar Hoover demonized Kate Barker in newspaper interviews and crime books, calling her "the most vicious, dangerous and resourceful criminal brain of the last decade" and claiming she represented "a monument to the evils of parental indulgence." (Hoover always harbored special fury for female criminals. Inspired by Kathryn "Kit" Kelly, wife of Machine Gun Kelly, Hoover declared: "When a woman does turn professional criminal, she is a hundred times more vicious and dangerous than a man.")[8]

Hoover attacked Ma Barker for her sexual immorality, as well; the FBI claimed that before her 1928 separation from her husband, she "became loose in her moral life. She was seen with a neighbor of hers who was having outside dates with other men and was known to have been generally in the company of other men in the vicinity of Tulsa, Oklahoma . . . and cast her lot with [her sons'] lawlessness and criminal activities."[9]

When Karpis defended Ma Barker's innocence in his autobiography, an internal FBI review of his book revealed Hoover's scathing opinion: "Karpis or/and his writer must be on dope." The official bureau line over the past half-century has been that Ma Barker, "an intuitive criminal, with her shrewd thinking and meticulous planning, was responsible for the gang's 'success.'" Oklahoma bank robber Harvey Bailey laughed at the idea of Ma Barker as a criminal mastermind: "The old woman couldn't plan breakfast," said Bailey. "When we'd sit down to plan a bank job, she'd go in the other room and listen to Amos and Andy or hillbilly music on the radio." A review of the FBI's internal files on the Barker-Karpis gang—particularly the confessions of gang members who attended crime-planning meetings—strongly suggests that the FBI knew that Kate Barker had no significant involvement in her sons' criminal activities.[10]

Accompanying Ma Barker to St. Paul was Arthur "Old Man" Dunlop; they masqueraded as "Mr. and Mrs. George Anderson." Ma Barker's seventy-three-year-old lover was described in the acid words of the FBI as a perfect boyfriend for her, since Dunlop "said little and thought less." When his tongue was loosened by alcohol, however, Dunlop could be dangerously talkative. Dunlop was "a pain in the ass," wrote Karpis. "He was a drunk and an ingrate . . . when he was loaded, he'd turn mean and abuse Ma." Ma Barker's daughter-in-law Carol Hamilton called Dunlop "too lazy to work and too scared to steal."[11]

Fred's thirty-two-year-old brother, Arthur "Doc" Barker, was missing from the St. Paul hideout in April 1932. A diminutive (5 feet, 4 inches and 119 pounds) auto thief and convicted murderer easily recognizable by the three moles on his face, Doc Barker was serving a life sentence for murder in the Oklahoma State Penitentiary at McAlester. "Doc was the problem. . . . When Doc got to drinkin', he thought he was king of the world," recalled Karpis's nephew, Albert Grooms. "Doc Barker didn't have all his marbles, he was a little light between the eyes, but Freddie was sharper than the devil."[12]

Kate "Ma" Barker, with boyfriend Arthur Dunlop

Compared to Fred and Doc Barker, whose violent instincts were easily triggered, Karpis demonstrated some restraint. When Gladys Sawyer, wife of St. Paul gangland banker Harry Sawyer, expressed concern that her adopted daughter might get hurt in an FBI raid on the gangsters' hideout, Fred Barker callously replied that "both she and the little girl would have to take their chances and if they got in the line of fire, it would be 'just too bad.'" But Karpis promised "that he would give himself up before he would let anything happen to the child." Sawyer told FBI agents that she thought highly of Karpis ever after.[13]

None of this was known to Helen Hannegraf when she rented out 1031 South Robert to the "Anderson family." Hannegraf lived next door at 1035 South Robert, where she made bootleg whiskey out of sauerkraut in her basement. Nick Hannegraf sold his mother's whiskey through the family's speakeasy, the Drover's Tavern. Eventually, Nick was forced to switch to the St. Paul Syndicate's liquor (with its built-in protection money) after he was raided several times by local police.[14]

The Barkers had been on the lam since December 19, 1931, when Fred Barker had robbed a West Plains, Missouri, store and murdered Sheriff C. Roy Kelly. (An indication of their inept planning at this stage of their career: the gang's take from the Missouri store included fifty neckties.) The Barkers were forced to flee from their hideout near Thayer, Missouri—a ten-acre farm with a cottage, a target practice area, a security fence, and alarms to warn them of police raids.[15]

"Alvin was down the street in Missouri when it [the shooting of Sheriff Kelly] happened," remembered Grooms. "Alvin said there were other ways of doing it—they didn't *have* to kill anyone, they could have dropped the sheriff off in the country without killing him. . . . Ma Barker wasn't too happy with that killing."[16]

According to the FBI, Ma Barker and her sons first fled to Herb Farmer's underworld hideout in Joplin, Missouri. Farmer counseled the Barkers to seek haven in St. Paul through his friend Harry Sawyer of the Green Lantern saloon. "With the assurance of his [Sawyer's] powerful protection," recounted the FBI, the Barker-Karpis gang next "took up residence in a little house in West St. Paul."[17]

While they were living in the Hannegraf home, the gang drove Helen Hannegraf's granddaughter Marian to Catholic school in the rumble seat of their car. When it was time to pick up the children after school, Hannegraf would snare one of her boarders and insist that the gangsters drive her grandchildren home.

Marian Johnson remembered the Barker-Karpis gang as "the nicest people. We'd hurry home from St. Matthews School because if we got home early, we could walk Mrs. Barker's curly-haired dog. Whoever got there first, you'd get a nickel or a candy bar!" The Barker boys would visit the Hannegraf home, sinking deep into Helen's leather rocking chair. But to the gang's growing irritation, Dunlop would drink bootleg whiskey with Nick's brother, Pete Hannegraf.[18]

Inevitably, there were a few suspicious moments. When Marian's ten-year-old cousin Bernice brought some doughnuts over to the Barker boys, they asked her to wait while they gathered up a half-dozen candy bars for her in return. Bernice noticed shotgun shells scattered across a couch. Whenever Dunlop walked Ma Barker's dog behind the Robert Street homes, he kept one hand plunged into his pocket, presumably on a gun.[19]

In the midst of this parody of domesticity, the gang continued to launch criminal forays from the sanctuary of the South Robert Street hideout. They focused on Minneapolis and other cities outside the protection of the O'Connor system. Karpis was particularly pleased when Fred Barker invited him to participate in the robbery of the Northwestern National Bank and Trust Company on March 29, 1932—a milestone the youthful Karpis referred to as "my first genuine major stickup."[20]

The bank, at 1223 North Washington Avenue near downtown Minneapolis (today the bank site, between Twelfth and Plymouth Avenues, is an open lot), was robbed by five men: Karpis, Fred Barker, Tommy Holden, trigger man Larry DeVol, and Bernard Phillips. "It was DeVol's idea to use a big car in honor [of] the big job," recalled Karpis years later. "So we stole a luxury Lincoln with a gorgeous interior and drove up to the Northwestern National." Holding twenty-eight customers and bank employees at gunpoint, the gang escaped safely out the back door into the waiting sedan just as police burst into the front of the bank. "Back at the house we'd rented in St. Paul, the five of us counted out the money," wrote Karpis. "It added up to more loot than I'd ever seen in my life—over $75,000 in paper money, another $6,500 in coins, and $185,000 in bonds."[21]

It is ironic that the Barker-Karpis gang's idyll on South Robert Street would be shattered by the *True Detective* photos of Barker and Karpis, for Karpis told the FBI he bought all the detective magazines, both to read about his activities and to find out which magazines published his photograph. When Karpis had his hair cut, he went to a barbershop in an outlying part of the city; as he entered, "he would glance around to see if a detective magazine containing his picture was in the place, and if he noticed such a publication, he would immediately leave."[22]

After recognizing the faces of his mother's tenants, Nick Hannegraf ran over to her house, rousing her at two o'clock in the morning to show her the photographs. "Nick, those are the boys next door!" she exclaimed. Helen crept into the garage with a flashlight to take down the license numbers of the gang's Chevrolets. Nick borrowed the family's Essex and drove to the central police station, eager to claim a reward. Instead, he drove straight into a demonstration of the O'Connor system's power, still effective twelve years after the death of its architect, police chief John O'Connor.[23]

Hannegraf first approached police inspector James P. Crumley, blurting out that men who looked just like Fred Barker and Alvin Karpis were asleep in his mother's house on Robert Street, just waiting to be arrested. "The police were protecting these gangsters at that time, so they didn't pay too much attention to my dad," recalled daughter Marian Johnson. "They said he was drinking." Impatient, Hannegraf showed detective Fred Raasch the *True Detective Mysteries* photos, but the police made him wait in the Bureau of Records room until eleven o'clock the next morning. "He sat on a bench in an outer office and they said, 'We'll get to you,'" recalled Johnson. "My grandmother called to the police department and said, 'You might as well come home, because they're gone.' They'd been tipped off by the police. My dad was very angry at the police, because he figured he had a good chance at the reward."[24]

Years later, the FBI learned how the tip-off was engineered. Inspector Crumley had buttonholed police chief Thomas Brown, bootlegger Leon Gleckman's old friend from the Cleveland liquor conspiracy days, and told him that a "sucker" had spotted the Barker-Karpis gang on Robert Street. "Jesus Christ," gasped Brown, dashing into his office to make a phone call. "Brown seemed to be greatly disturbed and his face turned white, and he left in a hurry for his office," the FBI learned from Crumley. "A few minutes later a woman called up and asked if her son was there . . . and when this party answered the telephone, he was advised by the woman, his mother, that the people whom he had reported as being next door had just left in a hurry and in fact left so fast that they left the radio turned on."[25]

In his memoirs, Karpis added that Harry Sawyer phoned Chief Brown's warning to the Barker-Karpis gang while "Sawyer's man on the police force was stalling the raid against our house long enough to allow Harry to tip us off." The FBI learned from Gladys Sawyer that "Jim Crumley called Harry Sawyer at the saloon and advised him 'heat' was on the boys and they had better move. Harry telephoned to one of the parties at 1031 Robert Street, with the result they immediately vacated the place."[26]

By eight o'clock that morning, Ma Barker and Karpis were running behind the Hannegraf house to retrieve their car. Fred Barker and Dunlop dashed out in front, jumping into a second car. They "left the door open, the gas on, and the radio running, and part of a cooked dinner on the table," BCA agents noted with palpable frustration.[27]

The gang fled St. Paul, leaving behind a suitcase containing twelve .45 automatic shells, four .16-gauge shotgun shells, and two pistol cleaners. They neglected to pay their final rent and utility bills, and they took Helen Hannegraf's fine silverware. But they left behind Ma Barker's brown fur coat, a pile of Fred Barker's new shoes, a fishing box, a radio, and a camera containing candid photos of Ma Barker. The Hannegrafs also found a closet full of clothes tailored in gangland style: all identifying tags were torn off. Under her rug, Mrs. Hannegraf discovered a final memento—a $500 bond stolen in March 1931 from the Farmers Savings Bank of Alden, Iowa.[28]

Back at the police station, Detective Raasch bumped into Harry Sawyer, who was walking out of Chief Brown's office. Sawyer brashly asked the detective, "Hey, you were sent over to the West Side, weren't you?" Raasch said he had indeed raided the Barker-Karpis hideout. "You found everything all right, didn't you?" Sawyer asked.

"We found everyone gone," Raasch reassured him. "There was nobody there." Sawyer was relieved, until Raasch mentioned that the gangsters had left some ammunition. Sawyer asked the officer for the shells, saying cryptically, "I want to show these guys that that thing was all right—I want to show them their own stuff."[29]

By that time, the gang was driving through Webster, Wisconsin, en route to Kansas City. Unfortunately for Dunlop, they believed that it was his liquor-loosened tongue, not pictures in a detective magazine, that had blown their cover.[30]

On April 25, 1932, the naked body of a 160-pound man with steel-gray hair, a neatly clipped mustache, and a .45-caliber bullet hole in his head was found along the shore of Frenstad Lake, north of Webster. It was Ma's lover, Arthur Dunlop. The BCA concluded that the assassin's car had stopped midway along a short road:

> Here was found a forty-five caliber bullet, together with some blood indicating that the victim had been shot at that point. The evidence further indicated that a body had been dragged from this point through the brush to the lake shore, a distance of about one hundred feet. It seems that they had taken him by the arms, one person on each side of him, and pulled him through the brush. Apparently, they had planned on tossing him into the lake and possibly weighting him down. However, when they reached the shore of the lake, they found it so boggy that it was not possible for them to get the body out into the lake and they dropped it where it was partly submerged on the shore.[31]

Near Dunlop's corpse, the BCA noted, was "a black woman's glove with white trimming, size about eight, covered with blood." Karpis claimed that neither he nor Fred Barker shot Dunlop. "There were plenty of people in St. Paul who wanted to kill him," said Karpis, identifying fixer Jack Peifer as the man who killed Dunlop as a courtesy to the Barker-Karpis gang.[32]

The successful escape of the gang from the Robert Street hideout stunned St. Paul. Mayoral candidate William J. Mahoney charged in a campaign speech that the incident proved that the city was ruled not by law but by the underworld: "Here is a case of fugitives from justice carrying on their nefarious activities in St. Paul for three months, and then, just before they are to be arrested, are mysteriously tipped off, and get away. . . . I cannot complain against the police officers themselves. We have in St. Paul a fine lot of policemen. They would enforce the law if ordered to do so, but they are told to lay off."[33]

On the defensive, Chief Tom Brown made much of the Hannegraf house's location in West St. Paul, part of neighboring Dakota County. "The charges of Mr. Mahoney that St. Paul police are protecting and tipping off criminals are ridiculous," snorted Brown. "It seems strange St. Paul police could offer protection to so-called murderers in another city, where we have no jurisdiction." Still, Brown's behavior during the failed raid was suspicious, and in June he was demoted to the rank of detective.[34]

A week after the Robert Street escape, Helen Hannegraf spied what appeared to be a familiar face in a Woolworth store; she was sure it was Ma Barker. The woman dashed out of the store and disappeared into a waiting automobile while Hannegraf was slowed by the crowds. Gangland history might have been altered dramatically had Hannegraf managed to stop Ma Barker in Woolworth's that day. "My grandmother was a tough old son of a gun," recalled Nick Hannegraf. "Tougher than Ma Barker!"[35]

26 Not the Athletic Type of Gangster

Summering at the John Lambert Cottage
148 Dellwood Avenue, Dellwood

"Mahtomedi is the place to spend your summers," the tourist literature said of the resort community fourteen miles northeast of St. Paul. With "none of the rough crowds found at other resorts [it is] the most beautiful spot in the state. Sundays [are] positively quiet and homelike, with preaching services and Sunday School."[36]

Outlaws Alvin Karpis and Fred and Ma Barker drove to this serene haven on July 9, 1932, and rented the eight-room home of eighty-year-old John Lambert, a retired grocery store owner. In the ten weeks since they fled St. Paul, the Barker-Karpis gang had first stopped in Kansas City, where the gang helped Tommy Holden and Harvey Bailey plan the robbery of the Citizens National Bank in Fort Scott, Kansas. On June 17, 1932, Karpis and Fred Barker joined Bailey, Holden, Bernie Phillips, and Larry DeVol in taking $47,000 from the Fort Scott vault, briefly kidnapping two female bystanders to deter a police shootout and hurling nails onto the road to puncture the tires of pursuing automobiles.[37]

It was to be the last bank robbery of Holden's and Bailey's careers. On July 7, 1932, they were captured—along with veteran bank robber Jimmy Keating—by FBI agents on a Kansas City golf course. Lagging behind on the greens, Phillips witnessed the arrests and warned Karpis and the Barkers, who were living in Kansas City as the "Hunter family." Within thirty minutes of Phillips's alert, the gang was on the run, driving their Auburn sedan toward Mahtomedi. "The gang could afford several hideouts," reported an official FBI summary. "They chose St. Paul, as well as a summer cottage on White Bear Lake, Minnesota."[38]

One of the most popular Mahtomedi gambling spots was the Silver Slipper roadhouse at 230 Warner Road, later known as the King's Horses, and today a private residence near the corner of Warner and Greenwood. The stucco exterior and winding stone walk camouflaged the revelry of the blackjack players inside. The Silver Slipper was considered to be "about the most famous of all speakeasies in this area," recalled Althea Rohlfing, a long-time Mahtomedi resident. "It had the reputation of catering to gangsters and bootleggers of every variety, more specifically, those who were big-time operators. When the state or federal law officers were looking for some nefarious characters and came in the front door, the patrons charged out the back door."[39]

Bootlegger Morris Rutman, kidnapped from his St. Paul home in October 1931, was held prisoner at the Silver Slipper for a $10,000 ransom. Dragged into the basement by a half dozen masked men led by gangster Jack Ferrick, Rutman was beaten and tortured (the kidnappers applied alcohol to his body and lighted it with a match) for three days before being freed. Such displays of violence were anathema to the public enemies relaxing in Mahtomedi, including Chicago robber Lester "Babyface Nelson" Gillis, who lived unobtrusively in the Bauman cottage, dining nearby on pizza and spaghetti at Vince Guarnera's Italian restaurant at 959 Mahtomedi Avenue (Highway 244).[40]

The Barker-Karpis gang, who drove up to the Lambert cottage determined to act the perfect tenants, were just as quiet. "John Lambert and his wife were taking a trip to Scotland, and they were very tight—very particular," remembered their neighbor Evelyn Deyo. "So the Lamberts rented their White Bear Lake home out to these wonderful people—the Ma Barker gang!" Ma Barker told the Lamberts that she was "Mrs. Hunter," and that Fred Barker and Alvin Karpis (posing as "Freddie and Raymond Hunter") were her sons. "When they moved in, we told them we never allowed liquor on the place or late parties or carousing, and there never was any," Mrs. Lambert told reporters. "They were always quiet and very expensively dressed and drove expensive autos."[41]

Neighbors saw the Hunters floating in a rowboat in the middle of White Bear Lake, talking among themselves. The criminals were not difficult to identify. "All of those gangsters were here for vacation," recalled Walter "Buster" Johnson of White Bear Lake. "You could spot them easily because they were pale and sickly looking. The gangsters weren't the athletic type. They wore hats in the summertime—no one wore hats."[42]

During their vacation at Lambert cottage, Alvin Karpis and Fred Barker ventured out to rob the Cloud County Bank in Concordia, Kansas, with machine gunner Larry DeVol, swindler Earl Christman, and Jess Doyle, a thief who had been released in June from the Kansas state penitentiary in Lansing.

Cottage of John Lambert on the east shore of White Bear Lake, headquarters of the Barker-Karpis gang in July 1932

The July 26, 1932, robbery in Concordia, which netted $240,000 in bonds and cash, was meticulously choreographed: the gang had stashed gasoline, coffee, and sandwiches along the getaway route for quick refueling.[43]

"The five of us were living with Ma Barker in a big house out at White Bear Lake . . . when we decided to take the Concordia bank," wrote Karpis. The gang brought $22,000 back to the Lambert cabin after getting lost on the long drive through Kansas and Missouri, during which Doyle and DeVol engaged in a debate on the constellation guiding them back to Mahtomedi.

"There's the Big Dipper," said Doyle. "As a night burglar I know what it looks like."

"You're crazy," argued DeVol. "I've been a night burglar too, and that's the Little Dipper you're pointing to."[44]

Helen Ferguson, Christman's girlfriend, described the gang's return from the Concordia heist: "Kate Barker and I stayed there [in Mahtomedi] while Fred Barker, Karpis and Christman went to Concordia, Kansas. . . . They were away for about five or six days. When they came back, they had a lot of money . . . and the men went into a room to divide it." Christman's share came to about $4,000.[45]

Once again, the O'Connor system's network of fences and money launderers proved valuable to the Barker-Karpis gang. An FBI report noted that many of the bonds stolen from the Cloud County Bank were recovered in St. Paul in August, "through peaceable negotiations by W. S. Gordon of the Burns Detective Agency with some unknown underworld boss in St. Paul." Newspapers reported that the detectives agreed to pay the gangsters a $15,000 ransom for the Concordia securities. Such an arrangement, of course, was safer for the gang than trying to fence the government securities through underworld bankers.[46]

With the burst of activity surrounding the Concordia robbery, neighbors began to notice the odd habits of the tenants in Lambert cottage. "During their stay at White Bear Lake they were visited by many persons in high-powered and expensive automobiles, who usually came very late at night and slept through the morning," reported the FBI. "People in White Bear Lake knew something was going on," said longtime resident Paul Cromer. "The St. Paul newspapers built things up as if everything happened here in White Bear, 'cause they wanted to keep their own name clean!"[47]

The gang's idyll in Mahtomedi ended abruptly on August 12, 1932, when neighbors saw two men park their car outside the Lambert cottage and speak urgently to Karpis. "Mrs. Hunter said they just had had a telegram about some sickness in the family, in the East, and they had to go," Mrs. Lambert told the *St. Paul Dispatch*. Just 48 hours later, agents of the Bureau of Criminal Apprehension burst into the empty cottage. Once again, the gang appeared to have been warned of an upcoming raid.[48]

Karpis and Barker had made sure that the iceman, paperboy, and garbage carrier were paid before they left. Fred Barker casually dropped by the East Side Ice Company in Mahtomedi to pay the gang's final ice bill in person. The inscription remained on the company's books for decades: "Fred Hunter (Lambert Cottage)." The gang had stolen tens of thousands of dollars from banks across the Midwest, yet Barker risked capture to pay a thirty-dollar ice bill.[49]

27 The Routine of Bank Robbery

The Third Northwestern National Bank Robbery
430 East Hennepin Avenue, Minneapolis

"Bank robbery, dangerous as it was, could get to be routine," wrote Alvin Karpis. On the afternoon of December 16, 1932, the Barker-Karpis gang robbed the Third Northwestern National Bank of Minneapolis. Although the bank has been razed, a triangular parking lot at Southeast Fifth Street

A. Wahpeton, N.D. Site of alleged Barker-Karpis gang robbery, Sept. 30, 1932

B. Redwood Falls, Minn. Site of Barker-Karpis gang robbery, Sept. 23, 1932

C. Sioux Falls, S.D. Site of Dillinger gang robbery, March 6, 1934

D. Willmar, Minn. Site of Keating-Holden gang robbery, July 15, 1930

E. Brainerd, Minn. Site of bank robbery by Babyface Nelson and allies, Oct. 23, 1933

F. Cambridge, Minn. Town held hostage by Barker-Karpis gang, Jan. 5, 1932

G. Wyoming, Minn. Site of release of kidnapped brewery executive William Hamm Jr., June 19, 1933

H. Rochester, Minn. Site of release of kidnapped banker Edward Bremer, Feb. 7, 1934

I. Waterloo, Iowa Site of police shooting of Dillinger gang member Tommy Carroll, June 7, 1934

J. Mason City, Iowa Site of Dillinger gang robbery, March 13, 1934

K. Menomonie, Wis. Site of Keating-Holden gang robbery and death of bank robber Charlie Harmon, Oct. 20, 1931

L. Rhinelander, Wis. Site of failed FBI raid on Dillinger gang hideout at Little Bohemia Lodge, Apr. 22–23, 1934

M. Hastings, Minn. Site of police roadblock attempt to stop Dillinger gang after their escape from Little Bohemia Lodge, April 23, 1934

N. Minnesota-Canadian border lakes Site of vacation cabins owned by Twin Cities mobsters and corrupt policemen between Central and Hennepin Avenues retains the distinctive shape that made the robbery so daring.

"You had to be pretty wild and not a little crazy to take a bank like the Third Northwestern National in Minneapolis," recalled Karpis. "It was a triangular building smack on one of the city's busiest streets, with a streetcar stop right in front of it, and practically the whole goddamn place was in glass. . . . We sometimes did things like that deliberately, maybe to inject some extra excitement into our work."[50]

The robbery was among the most violent of the Barker-Karpis gang's escapades, leaving two policemen and one bystander dead, and it proved that innocent citizens could be victims of the gangsters harbored in St. Paul.

During the three months preceding this robbery, the gang had regrouped—Karpis recruited a crack bank robbery team—and waited for Doc Barker to be released from prison in Oklahoma. To ensure that local police would not interfere with their heists, the gang solidified its political alliances. During the Minneapolis mayoral campaign, Karpis said, he loaned supporters of candidate Ralph Van Lear $4,000. Fred Barker kicked in $6,500, his personal contribution toward good government in Minneapolis.[51]

After the election, Karpis told the FBI, he and Fred Barker "were offered 'a piece' in a slot machine concession, but he laughingly refused it. Karpis said he told the syndicate that there was too much work connected with the operation of slot machines." A lifelong brothel customer, Karpis told the Minneapolis mob he preferred to control the "houses of ill fame." As for Barker, Karpis explained to the FBI that "Freddie told them that he wanted nothing but to be left alone while [he was] in the Twin Cities."[52]

On September 10, 1932, Doc Barker was released from prison after serving thirteen years of a life sentence for murdering a night watchman. The FBI suspected that the early release was facilitated by bribing Oklahoma officials. Interviewed by the FBI years later, Karpis suggested that he and Fred Barker had supplied the payoff money that freed Doc Barker.[53]

On September 23, the reunited gang robbed the State Bank and Trust Company of Redwood Falls, Minnesota, displaying the full range of Barker-Karpis techniques: they forced the bank staff to lie face down on the floor, kidnapped bystanders to perch on the running boards of their getaway car, and scattered roofing nails to stop police cars. Careful planning ensured that the robbery was launched on the day the bank contained the most possible currency—$35,000. A newspaper account noted that the "band of swaggering" crooks "snapped through the robbery as if it was so much routine."[54]

"My profession was robbing banks, knocking off payrolls and kidnapping rich men. I was good at it," wrote Karpis in his memoirs. "We were professionals at our work, and we figured out timing, escape routes, each guy's individual job, and all the other details of every robbery or kidnapping as if we were laying out the strategy for a combat attack in a war."[55]

A September 30 robbery of $6,900 from the Citizens National Bank of Wahpeton, North Dakota, also had the gang's signature. Once again, five robbers used machine guns to hold a crowd at bay, pistol-whipped a bank cashier (a Fred Barker trademark), used hostages as shields on the running board of the getaway car, and tossed roofing nails to puncture tires of the posse following them. Police lost the quintet as they left North Dakota at speeds up to sixty miles an hour.[56]

With the November 3 release from the Oklahoma State Penitentiary of convicted murderer Volney Davis, one of Doc Barker's boyhood pals, the gang had grown to nearly full strength. Davis drove to a meeting with Doc Barker in Kansas, then headed for St. Paul to join the rest of the gang.[57]

Curiously, the Barker-Karpis gang declined to work with bank robber John Dillinger. "Alvin told me that Dillinger had a wild idea to merge the [Dillinger and Barker-Karpis] gangs, go into a town and clean the whole damned town out . . . rob eight banks in one day," said Albert Grooms, Karpis's nephew. "Alvin and Freddie Barker said they wanted no part of that idea. It would cause too much heat. Alvin was the quiet type, so he and the Barkers didn't like Dillinger's boastful personality and braggadocio crap." But the Barker-Karpis gang might have benefited from Dillinger's ability to avoid unnecessary bloodshed.[58]

The Third Northwestern National Bank robbery involved Fred and Doc Barker, DeVol, Karpis, Verne Miller, William Weaver, and Jess Doyle. The gang was armed with machine guns and .45-caliber automatics equipped with large-capacity clips. Two of the men entered through the Minneapolis bank's Central Avenue doors, and two others went in on the Hennepin Avenue side. DeVol stayed outside the bank, holding his machine gun. Miller ordered everyone in the bank to lie on the floor face down.[59]

"These men worked so fast and were so professional," remembered Earl Patch, who was then a bookkeeper in the bank. "First thing I heard, a guy said, 'This is a stick-up.' All of a sudden, it became *deathly* quiet in the bank." The gangsters had taken few precautions to hide their identities during a daylight robbery in front of dozens of witnesses. "Freddie Barker was running the show," said Patch. "He had some false teeth stuck in his mouth, but he didn't look much better when he took them out . . . Freddie Barker started screaming, 'Open the vault!'"[60]

Bank teller Paul Hesselroth tried to delay the robbery, protesting that he could not open the door to the vault. Miller beat the teller with a revolver, but not before Patch and Hesselroth tripped silent alarms.[61]

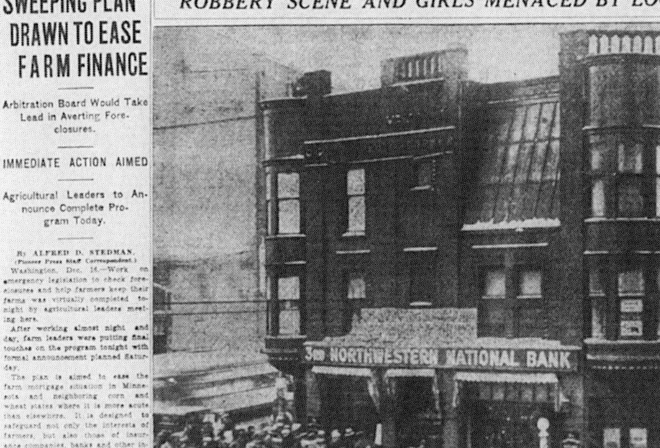

Minnesota Weather
Unsettled, probably snow east, colder west today; Sunday fair, colder east.
Detailed weather report on Page 17.

St. Paul Pioneer Press

A Lighted Christmas Tree
This Special Feature is Offered Juvenile Readers.
It Will Be Found in Sunday's Pioneer Press Magazine.

VOL. 79. NO. 352. ST. PAUL, MINN., SATURDAY, DECEMBER 17, 1932. PRICE THREE CENTS IN ST. PAUL

BANDITS KILL POLICEMAN IN MINNEAPOLIS

SWEEPING PLAN DRAWN TO EASE FARM FINANCE

Arbitration Board Would Take Lead in Averting Foreclosures.

IMMEDIATE ACTION AIMED

Agricultural Leaders to Announce Complete Program Today.

ROBBERY SCENE AND GIRLS MENACED BY LOOTERS

Killed

Ira Evans, Minneapolis patrolman, shown above, was killed by bullets of a bandit gang which robbed the Third Northwestern National Bank in Minneapolis Friday.

SECOND OFFICER AND ST. PAUL MAN NEAR DEATH; 5 ROBBERS ESCAPE WITH BANK'S $20,000

Patrolmen Answering Alarm Met at Door of Third Northwestern National by Withering Fire; Auto Driver Shot as He Watches Holdups Change Cars in Como Park When Machine Is Disabled.

MOTORIST FEARED KIDNAPED BY GANG TO ENABLE THEM TO GET SECOND AUTO

ST. PAUL POLICE ARREST SUSPECTS.

WARM WEATHER HOPE EXPRESSED BY SANTA

"I Don't Mind Cold," but Many Children Are Kept Away, He Says.

TODAY'S PROGRAM

ST. PAULITE TELLS OF DODGING BULLETS

Car Driver Shot as He Slowed

The Third Northwestern National bank in Minneapolis, where bandits shot down two policemen Friday afternoon, is shown at the top.

Headlines announcing the Third Northwestern National Bank robbery

Minneapolis policemen Ira Evans and Leo Gorski responded to the call. The officers drove immediately to the Third Northwestern National Bank, even though they had heard the report of the bank alarm going off just three minutes after they were to have quit for a 2:40 P.M. roll call. From a distance of fifteen feet, DeVol opened fired with his machine gun while the other thieves shot at the officers through the bank's plate glass windows. Ten of DeVol's bullets struck Evans, killing him instantly. The mortally wounded Gorski died forty-eight hours later.

"The squad car came down Central Avenue and the machine gunner sprayed them all the way down—ten to twelve bullet holes, each big enough to stick your thumb in, all over the police car," said Patch. "They were shooting from inside the bank and blew the windows away. For years, you could see [bullet] marks left on Arone's Bar across Central."[62]

The Barker-Karpis gang escaped with $22,000 in cash and close to $100,000 in securities. But one of the gang's own bullets had penetrated the front wheel of their getaway Lincoln. As the car pulled away from the bank, heading east on Fifth Street and then along East Hennepin and Larpenteur Avenues into St. Paul, the robbers knew they would have to switch tires soon. The tire change would have lethal consequences for Oscar Erickson, the twenty-nine-year-old son of Swedish immigrants.[63]

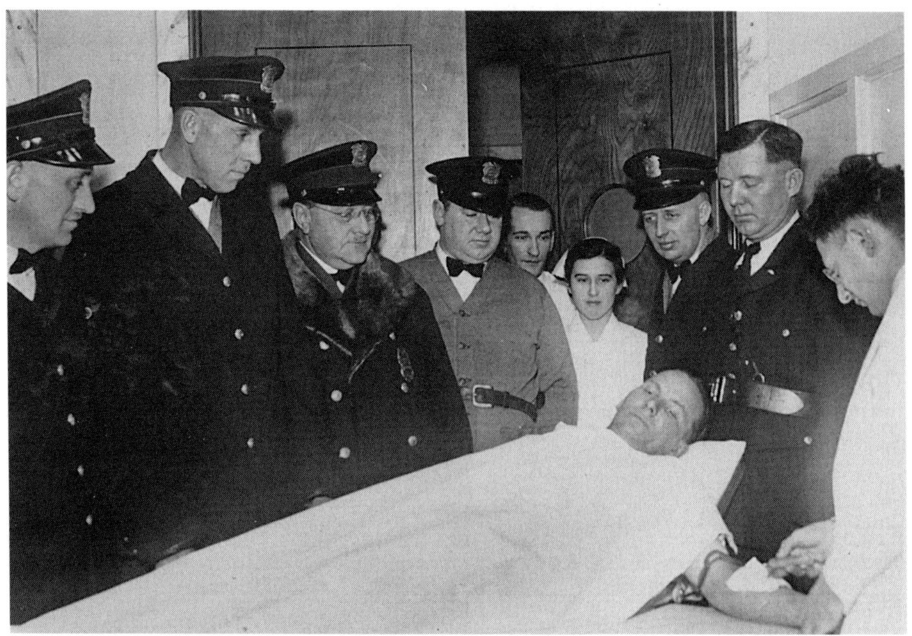

Minneapolis patrolman R. C. Lindvall (on bed) donating blood for Leo Gorski, the policeman mortally wounded in the December 1932 bank robbery

28 He 'Lost His Topper and Started to Fire'

The Como Park Slaying of Oscar Erickson

Near Como Zoo, St. Paul

The Barker-Karpis gang raced from the scene of the December 16 bank robbery to St. Paul's Como Park via "Bank Robber's Row," the route Karpis designed to avoid police roadblocks. The gang's Lincoln lost its tire on the east side of Snelling, just south of Larpenteur. Fortunately, they had left a green Chevrolet in Como Park in case of an emergency.[64]

Unaware of the bank robbers heading toward the "switch car" only blocks away, Oscar Erickson, accompanied by a twenty-two-year-old friend, Arthur Zachman, drove down Lexington to Como in his Chevrolet coupe. It was Erickson's first day selling Christmas wreaths in the neighborhood near the state fairgrounds. Searching for customers, Erickson and Zachman drove through Como Park, turning west past the monkey park and greenhouse. Just after three o'clock, Erickson saw a group of well-dressed men transferring objects from a Lincoln into a Chevy.[65]

"The tire and rim of the Lincoln's wheel were gone," recalled Alvin Karpis. "The Chevy had hot plates. These had to be taken off and the right ones put back on. Ignoring little details like that could result in capture. While this was being done, a jalopy came along with two fellows in it. The

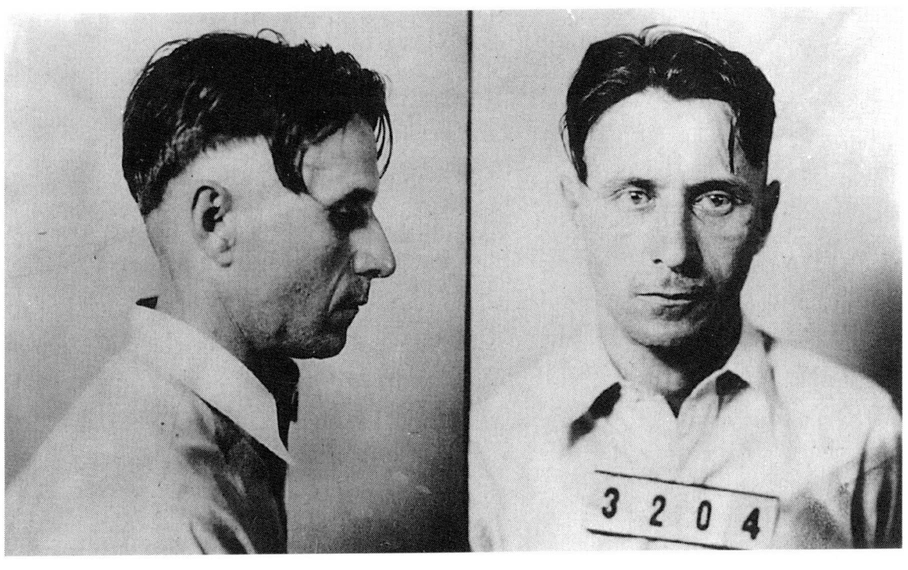

Fred Barker of the Barker-Karpis gang

driver stopped and damn near fell out of the car straining to get a look at the plates on the Chevy."[66]

"We were driving slowly through the park," Arthur Zachman told reporters, "when we noticed two cars standing alongside each other. As we went by, Oscar took his foot off the gas and we slowed down a little, looking out to see what was happening. Then all of a sudden there was a burst of gunfire and a lot of bullets went whistling by."[67]

According to the confession of gang member Jess Doyle, Barker mistakenly thought that Oscar Erickson was trying to catch a glimpse of the gang's license plates. Karpis recalled that Barker shouted, "Get going, or else!" "The guy ignored the warning and Freddie fired," wrote Karpis. "He got him right in the head and the blood streamed out over the side of the car."[68]

"Then Oscar slumped down in the driver's seat," Zachman recalled, "and his foot must have shoved up against the clutch, because the car started to coast." Zachman pulled Erickson onto the passenger side and, holding his bleeding friend with his right arm, drove down Lexington Parkway to the police station at University and St. Albans. Erickson was rushed to the hospital, where he died of a cerebral hemorrhage early the next morning. His wife of barely two years, Delvina Erickson, buried her husband in Roselawn Cemetery, mourning how happy Oscar had been on that first day of work.[69]

Bank robber Larry DeVol later told the St. Paul police that the man who shot Erickson in Como Park must have "been off his nut." Fred Barker just "lost his topper and started to fire," said DeVol. "I tried to stop him, but it was too late. The rest of the mob gave him hell," added DeVol. "That's one shooting that I didn't have a finger in."[70]

29 The Demise of the Incorrigible Larry DeVol

The Annbee Arms Apartments
928 Grand Avenue, St. Paul

Haskett Burton was a popular tenant at the Annbee Arms Apartments at 928 Grand Avenue. Because he was a telegraph operator for the Associated Press wire service, the friends gathered around his bridge table on Sunday morning, December 18, 1932, trusted his judgment when he predicted that the police would have difficulty finding the men who had robbed the Third Northwestern National Bank in Minneapolis two days earlier. "There doesn't seem to be much chance of catching this mob," Burton reportedly said. "Nobody knows who they are and I reckon they're plenty far away from here by now."[71]

Suddenly, a disheveled stranger wandered into the apartment, staggering and raving. Burton forced the drunk out of his home, which inspired the man to wave a pistol at Burton. Two St. Paul policemen, George Hammergren and Harley Kast, responded to the emergency call to disarm and arrest the drunkard. The officers were told that the man lived in apartment 206, where a search turned up packages of the money that had just been stolen from the Third Northwestern National Bank. Within hours, police identified the drunk in their custody as burglar Larry "the Chopper" DeVol, wanted for his role in killing police officers Evans and Gorski during the Minneapolis bank robbery. The police also found the .45-caliber automatic pistol used during the bank holdup.[72]

DeVol had been living for weeks in the Annbee Arms, a red-brick apartment building near the corner of Grand Avenue and Milton Street. The gang planned the robbery of the Third Northwestern National Bank there and returned to the Annbee hideaway to prepare the stolen bonds for laundering and distribution.[73]

Born in Ohio in 1905, DeVol had been sent to a Texas reformatory and an Oklahoma reform school by the time he was nine, at which time authorities labeled him "incorrigible." DeVol's first arrest was for a 1918 larceny charge in Tulsa, Oklahoma. The first of his three jail escapes occurred when he was fourteen, his first major arrest for burglary when he was sixteen.[74]

By the time the Barker-Karpis gang recruited DeVol, he had amassed a prodigious criminal résumé, including nearly forty safe-blowing jobs and imprisonment in Oklahoma and Kansas. DeVol was also being hunted for an array of homicides, including the double murder of a sheriff and a marshal in Washington, Iowa, in June 1930, a Tulsa murder in August 1930, and the murder of a Missouri policeman in November 1930.[75]

In prison photographs, DeVol's insolent stare overshadows his sunken

MPD-31

MINNEAPOLIS POLICE DEPARTMENT BUREAU OF IDENTIFICATION

23802
12-20-32
Mpls

Name LEONARD BARTON
Date of arrest 12/19/32
Charge BankRobber, Murder, Fugitiv
Disposition of case M. S. P. Life 1/10/33
Residence 928 Grand Ave., St. Pa
Place of birth ?
Nationality
Criminal specialty
Age 27 Build Med.
Height 5-8¼ Comp. Dark
Weight 157 Eyes Dk. Hazel
Hair Med. Dk. Ch.
Scars and marks

CRIMINAL HISTORY

With Robert Newbern - Clarence DeVol - Owen Lewis robbed the N. W branch bank on E. Henn ave Mpls. Minn - Eddie DeVol the fifth man was not arrested - He is wanted

12/27/35 Transfered to St. Peter Insane Asylum.

6-7-36, Escaped State Hosp. St. Peter, Minn.

DEAD

Barker-Karpis gang machine gunner Larry DeVol, alias Leonard Barton

cheeks and acne. His criminal career had left other marks: a scar over his eyebrows, a gunshot scar on his left hand, a deformed left ring finger, and a knife scar on his right elbow. As for his temperament, a wanted poster described DeVol as "a paranoid maniac [who] suffers from persecutory delusions and is apt to kill associates suddenly without warning."[76]

DeVol claimed in a Stillwater, Minnesota, prison interview that the bonds stolen from the Third Northwestern National bank were taken to Chicago by Verne Miller for "cleaning" and then divided six ways. The FBI heard rumors as late as 1948 that attempts were still being made to launder the stolen bonds. The rest of the Barker-Karpis gang—Alvin Karpis, Jess Doyle, and the Barker brothers—headed for Reno to celebrate another Christmas outside prison walls, fence what they had stolen in Minneapolis, and wait until the newspaper headlines cooled and the Minnesota weather warmed.[77]

DeVol pleaded guilty to the murder of officers Evans and Gorski and in January was sentenced to life in Stillwater Prison. After reviewing DeVol's extensive criminal record, Stillwater warden John J. Sullivan called his new inmate "probably the most cold blooded man that ever entered the prison." He wrote that "I have not the slightest doubt but that he would take any chance to make a break, and would not hesitate to kill anyone that might stand between him and his freedom." DeVol, restricted to detention, told fellow inmates that he "had friends on the outside and he would get out regardless of the Warden, his deputy or any of his God damn guards."[78]

Declared insane after he claimed that prison guards were attempting to inject poison gas into his cell, DeVol was later transferred to a hospital for the criminally insane in St. Peter, Minnesota, and in June 1936 led a mass escape of fifteen inmates. In attempting to rob three banks, DeVol wounded two police officers and killed a third. He was tracked down by police in Enid, Oklahoma, where he was chased into an alley and killed in July 1936.[79]

30 The Mystery of 'Big Phil' Phillips

The Cle-mar Apartments
2062 Marshall Avenue, St. Paul

After the St. Paul police discovered Larry DeVol's Grand Avenue hideout, they searched without success for the apartment where Karpis and Ma Barker's family had planned the Third Northwestern National Bank robbery. Not until 1936 did the FBI discover that the Barkers made their headquarters at the Cle-mar Apartments, at the southwest corner of Cleveland and Marshall Avenues, where tenants included Ma Barker, swindler Earl Christman, and a disloyal bank robber named Bernard Phillips.[80]

"The Barker gang lived on the third or fourth floor in the back," recalled Jim Lehman, whose mother, Erma, ran a beauty shop in the Cle-mar. "I had mixed feelings about the gangsters as a child. You thought of them as criminals. They were like bad movie stars. . . . [But it] was kind of thrilling, because that was the time when they broadcast radio serials like *Gangbusters*."[81]

Why did so many gangsters live at the Cle-mar? The FBI later uncovered a link between the apartment building and underworld fixer Jack Peifer, who helped many visiting mobsters get settled in their first apartments when they checked into the Twin Cities. Peifer had lived there with his first wife.[82]

Con man Earl Christman of the Barker-Karpis gang and his girlfriend, Helen Ferguson, also lived in the Cle-mar in 1933. But the FBI was most interested in tracking down Doc, Fred, and Ma Barker. FBI investigators interviewed Cle-mar janitor Ed Wiechman about the months when the Barkers lived as "the Gordons" in apartment 37. Wiechman reported that the Barkers "would go away from their apartment for weeks at a time." While they were gone, he found chauffeur caps in the apartment. Apparently these caps were the underworld rage: Jess Doyle wore one during the Third Northwestern robbery, as did Alvin Karpis when he drove the William Hamm kidnap car.[83]

Easily the most intriguing mobster to live in the Cle-mar was an auto thief and former Cicero, Illinois, police officer named Bernard Phillips, also known as Big Phil Courtney. Phillips lived at the Cle-mar as "Mr. Stewart" from October 1931 to January 1932, after his parole from Leavenworth prison. Although he was never considered a gang leader, Phillips participated in a variety of major crimes: he joined veterans Harvey Bailey and Fred Barker in robbing the Citizens National Bank of Fort Scott, Kansas, in June 1932 and helped the Barker-Karpis gang with the March 1932 robbery of Northwestern National Bank and Trust Company of Minneapolis.[84]

FBI files suggest that Phillips was held in low regard by the underworld. From Helen Ferguson the FBI learned that members of the Barker-Karpis gang had said that the reason "Big Phil left St. Paul and went East was because no one would work with him." Gladys Sawyer, wife of Harry Sawyer, was more specific: she told the FBI that the Barkers and Karpis refused to work with Phillips because he was once "an officer of the law."[85]

George "Machine Gun Kelly" Barnes gave Detroit police an idea of how inept a crook Phillips could be. During a 1930 Chicago kidnapping in which Kelly and Phillips were partners, one of the victims taken by Phillips was accidentally killed. Soon after, Phillips asked Kelly to join him in another kidnapping. Kelly declined, concluding that the proposed victim did not have enough money to come up with the ransom. Phillips went ahead with the abduction and discovered that Kelly's assessment had been correct. Phillips released the kidnap victim with the pathetic order to bring his own ransom to a meeting and then borrowed Kelly's Cadillac to collect the ransom. Kelly, now "hot" with police for a kidnapping he had refused to have anything to do with, had to load his coupe into a truck and flee with it to Chicago.[86]

Alvin Karpis was similarly disappointed with Phillips's criminal acumen. In 1931 Karpis loaned Phillips his Buick and was stunned when the burned wreckage of his car appeared on the front page of the St. Paul newspapers in March 1932. Inside were the mutilated bodies of Margaret "Indian Rose" Perry and Sadie Carmacher, whom the underworld had feared would talk about the Barker-Karpis gang's assault on stores in Cambridge, Minnesota. The car was easily recognizable as Karpis's.[87]

Phillips's habit of being the only participant to escape unscathed from a crime scene proved to be his downfall. (In 1932, for example, eyewitnesses identified him as the heavyset man who dashed out of the Green Dragon during the slaying of bootlegger Abe Wagner—just before killers George Young and Joey Schaefer were captured.) Few in the underworld could have been surprised when, during the summer of 1932, Phillips visited a hotel in New York with fellow bank robbers Frank Nash and Verne Miller, received a telephone call, walked out to meet someone, and disappeared.[88]

Years later, Machine Gun Kelly revealed to Detroit police that Phillips had been killed and secretly buried near the Twin Cities. Kelly said that he had heard the story from casino operator Jack Peifer. According to Peifer, the mob never forgot that Phillips was playing just one hole behind Harvey Bailey, Jimmy Keating, and Tommy Holden at the Mission Hills Golf Course in Kansas City when they were arrested by the FBI. The underworld concluded that Phillips had enjoyed more than a lucky break, that in fact he had been allowed to escape because he helped send Bailey, Keating, and Holden to prison.

Police reports and FBI interviews with Phillip's girlfriend, Winnie

Cle-mar Apartments at Cleveland and Marshall, a hideout for Bernard "Big Phil" Phillips (inset) and other members of the Barker-Karpis gang

Williams, indicate that he was stabbed to death with ice picks, covered with lime to prevent identification, and buried on a lonely road. His body was never found. Underworld legend holds that Bernie Phillips got a special treatment reserved for double-crossers: he was buried with his forearm jutting out of the ground. Visible on the exposed arm was a tattoo: a cross with flowers and the words "My Mother" etched in red, blue, and green.[89]

31 Gangland Tip-Off on Grand Avenue

The Barker-Karpis Gang's Grand Avenue Apartments
1290 Grand Avenue, St. Paul

"It was the custom of the gang to immediately install a telephone in their apartments," the FBI learned from Barker-Karpis gang member Jess Doyle. The purpose of the telephone was to receive "telephone calls from Harry Sawyer concerning tip-offs of police raids." But when the members of Ma Barker's gang moved in February 1933 into a four-story brick apartment building near the corner of Grand Avenue and Syndicate Street, they neglected this security precaution.[90]

Doc and Fred Barker rented three apartments; swindler Earl Christman and gunman Jess Doyle joined them. Gradually, other members of the Barker-Karpis gang, who had avoided the Minnesota winter by vacationing in Nevada, drifted back to St. Paul as well. Edna Murray had escaped in December from solitary confinement at the Missouri State Penitentiary and drove to St. Paul to keep company with her beau, Volney Davis.[91]

On March 4, 1933, underworld fixer Harry Sawyer received a tip from a source in the St. Paul Police Department that detectives were about to raid the 1290 Grand apartments. The gang did not yet have a telephone, so Sawyer sent his wife, Gladys, to "tell the boys the 'heat' was on," the FBI reported. Unaware of the unfolding drama, Jess Doyle drove up to the building at about eight o'clock that evening. Three policemen were parked in a squad car in front of the building, Doyle recalled. Gladys Sawyer had already arrived, warning Karpis, Davis, and Christman that the police were outside. Doyle brazenly packed his suitcases, then walked out the front door, sauntering past the police car. The officers courteously waited to raid the building until all of the Barker-Karpis gang had a chance to flee. Doyle, Karpis, and Fred Barker met at Sawyer's Green Lantern saloon, whereupon they all departed for Chicago.[92]

After that brush with capture, the Barker-Karpis gang bounced between the Kansas City, Missouri, and Chicago areas, planning their next major robbery. On April 4, 1933, they struck the First National Bank of Fairbury,

Nebraska. For the Fairbury job, Doyle later told the FBI, the gang consisted of a sprawling conglomeration of hoods: Karpis, Doyle, Volney Davis, Earl Christman, Fred and Doc Barker, Eddie Green (a St. Paul hoodlum then affiliated with Lester "Babyface Nelson" Gillis), and Frank Nash (who usually worked with the Keating-Holden gang).[93]

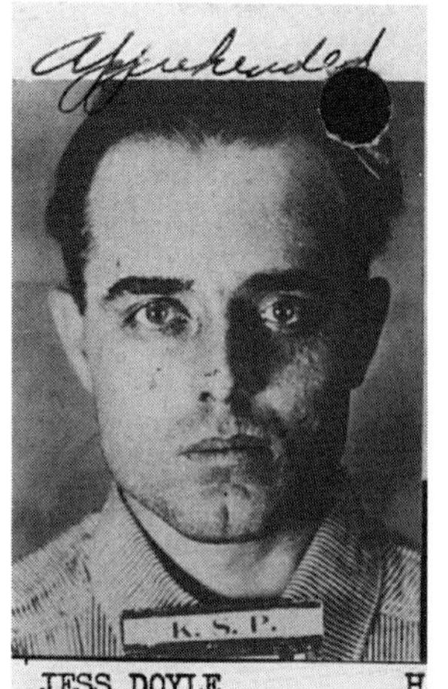

Jewel thief Jess Doyle of the Barker-Karpis gang

This gang took more than $151,000 worth of government bonds, coin, and silver from the bank vault, but when one of their machine guns jammed, they discovered they were outgunned by the people of Fairbury—and a visiting machine-gun salesman. The looting of the bank, which took just eight minutes, ended in a gory shootout between the gang and a squad of heavily armed townspeople.[94]

Christman, shot in the chest by a Fairbury deputy sheriff, was driven to Verne Miller's bungalow in Kansas City for treatment. Karpis and Eddie Green provided amateur medical care that consisted of injections of morphine and washing the wound with "drugstore prescription whiskey." According to Karpis's confession to the FBI, Christman was recovering so well from the wound that one day, when the doctor was about to lift him out of bed, he got up unaided, reopening the wound and causing a hemorrhage. The doctor said Christman would not live more than an hour, and he was right. Somewhere outside Kansas City, Christman was buried in an unmarked grave.[95]

Doc Barker and Jess Doyle returned to St. Paul, where Barker met with Harry Sawyer to plan the kidnapping of a prominent St. Paul businessman. Fred and Ma Barker drove from Chicago to join Doc in St. Paul in May, bringing Christman's girlfriend, Helen Ferguson, along to the Commodore Hotel. The Barkers told Ferguson that her lover had been wounded during the Fairbury raid—but not too seriously, they reassured her. Christman would have to recuperate in a Kansas City hideout for a few weeks.

Ferguson naively believed them; some of the gang women were hardened, but her background had not prepared her for a lifestyle that involved prison and shootouts. She was described unkindly in FBI files: "pointed nose, prominent big jaw, has dropsy." A former product demonstrator for the H. J. Heinz Company, Ferguson had been married to and divorced from a Prudential insurance salesman before she fell for Christman, a man she knew to be a con man.

Ferguson clearly loved Christman and stuck by him when he was charged with a Seattle mail robbery in 1930 (the charges were dismissed) and again when he was convicted in Michigan of running a confidence game. In the five years she lived with him, Ferguson traveled under a variety of assumed names from Kalamazoo, Michigan, to San Francisco and then to Toledo; Asheville, North Carolina; Hot Springs, Arkansas; Juarez, Mexico; Kirkwood, Missouri; and finally back to St. Paul. Ferguson said of her life as a bank robber's girlfriend: "We had plenty of money and neither Christman nor I ever did any work."

That April 14, Fred Barker took Ferguson aside and told her Christman was dead. His body had already been disposed of. "Fred refused to tell me where he [Christman] was buried," Ferguson bitterly told the FBI, "and refused to permit me to tell Christman's mother, stating that it would put too much 'heat' on the gang." She got $2,000 from Christman's share of the Fairbury money. It was as close to an underworld death benefit as the Barker-Karpis gang ever gave any woman.[96]

32 Ma Barker Meets the Girls

The Commodore Hotel
79 Western Avenue, St. Paul

The Commodore Hotel was widely known as a haven for novelist F. Scott Fitzgerald and his wife, Zelda, in 1921 and 1922. The anonymity cherished by the socialites who sipped at the Commodore's art deco bar also attracted more notorious tenants, Ma Barker and Al Capone among them.

When the Commodore Hotel opened in 1920, it was one of St. Paul's most elegant nightspots for dining and dancing. Patrons were enticed with descriptions of its spacious lobby and ballroom, its "home-like spirit," and its location in "the most aristocratic and quiet section of the city." A city directory ad boasted that "the Commodore has no equal in the Northwest."[97]

Chicago train robber Jimmy Keating, pursued by the FBI for his role in the Menomonie, Wisconsin, bank robbery, stayed at the Commodore in November 1931. Then, in May 1933, Ma Barker moved into the Commodore's apartments 215 to 221, using the alias Mrs. A. B. Gardner. Fred Barker, who was about to have his appendix removed at a Twin Cities hospital, joined her there as Fred E. Gardner. Helen Ferguson was secreted upstairs, in apartment 404. Ma Barker, jealous of any younger women living near her boys, made Ferguson's life miserable at the Commodore.

"Ma Barker was very jealous of her boys and did not wish to have them associate with girl friends," stated a 1936 FBI summary. "She would disclose the conversations had with various women members of the gang to her sons, particularly stressing the women's statements with reference to them. This . . . caused frequent evidence of dissension among the other women of the gang who, in most instances, made every effort to avoid the presence of Ma Barker."[98]

"After Christman died," Helen Ferguson told the FBI, "I was in Kate Barker's company considerably." Ferguson "gradually developed a strong dislike for her company."[99]

At the Commodore, Ma Barker endured her first and last meeting with Fred's new girlfriend, thirty-year-old Paula Harmon. Fred met Paula Harmon at Herb Farmer's gangland hideout in Joplin, Missouri, in the spring of 1931, during one of Paula's frequent marital spats with bank robber Charlie Harmon. When Charlie was shot to death during the robbery of the Kraft

The Commodore Hotel, a haven for Ma and Fred Barker in May 1933

Bank in Menomonie, Wisconsin, in October of that year, Paula was free to explore a relationship with Kate Barker's son.

"Girls liked Freddie and he didn't mind spending money on them," recalled Karpis. "But he wasn't always lucky in the type of broad who hooked him. Paula Harmon turned out to be a rotten choice, though you couldn't tell that to Freddie when he got stuck on her. . . . Paula was a drunk."[100]

On April 5, 1933, Fred Barker, flush with his share of the Fairbury National Bank loot, asked Verne Miller's girlfriend to call the young widow and invite her to meet him in Kansas City. The romance between Barker and Harmon blossomed in May, and Fred decided it was time to introduce Paula to his "Ma."[101]

Whether or not J. Edgar Hoover was correct in believing that Ma Barker "shuddered in jealous trepidation when a new gun moll threatened to steal the love of one of her boys," the first meeting between Ma Barker and Paula Harmon was not a pleasant experience. "The day Fred Barker was taken to the hospital I met his mother, who was living at the Commodore Apartments in St. Paul, under the name of Mrs. Gordon," Paula Harmon told the FBI. "Evidently, I did not make a favorable impression, as I have never seen her since."[102]

Not that it would have been easy for Ma Barker's sons to have found women who pleased their mother. "It was a rare time when she'd let us bring women to the house," mused Karpis. "Whenever Freddie or I got serious about a girl, we'd move out of Ma's place and keep the girls in another hotel or apartment." Doc Barker posed less of a problem for his mother in the arena of female companionship. "Doc Barker never at any time, to my knowledge, was accompanied by a girl," Gladys Sawyer told the FBI, "and apparently has been in the penitentiary so much he does not associate with women." Fred remained Ma's boy throughout his relationship with Harmon, who told the FBI that he kept leaving St. Paul to visit his mother in Chicago. Even though Fred was persuaded to spend New Year's with his girlfriend, he spent Christmas with his mother.[103]

According to legend, Chicago's most notorious gang leader also visited the Commodore Hotel. "Capone, when he came to town the two times that he did, [stayed] in the Commodore Hotel (incognito, of course)," said Bill Greer, veteran St. Paul crime reporter. The gangster era of Al Capone and Ma Barker was the Commodore's heyday, Greer said. "The place has deteriorated," he quipped, "since they've got politicians in there."[104]

Mr. Wm. Dunn

You're so god damed smart that you'll wind up getting both of you guys killed.It so happened that we taild that cab last night.

You better take advantage of the time before the papers get a hold of this.

Heres god news for you. Unless 199 the 100,000 dollars is delivered as per our instructions on Saturday the demand will be for 19979 150,000 thereafter.

Furthermore we demand that you personally deliver the money so that if there is any doble crossing we will have the pleasure of hitting you in the head.

Prepare to have the cash tomorrow. You will receive new instructions. If your not going to carry them out fully don't start. If the coppers succeed in following you it might prove fatal. You brought the coppers in to this now you get rid of the assholes.

Hamm is uncomfortable and dissapointed in the way you bungled this so far.

We won't continue to take these draws forever so dont spar to long. If we haddVent intended to go thru with this we would not have started.

I HEREBY AUTHORIZE THE ABOVE PAYMENT TO BE MADE AND REQUEST THAT ALL INSTRUCTIONS BE FULLY CARRIED OUT.

M;rWm. Dunn
1916 Summit Ave
St.Paul.

6

A VERY TROUBLING KIDNAPPING

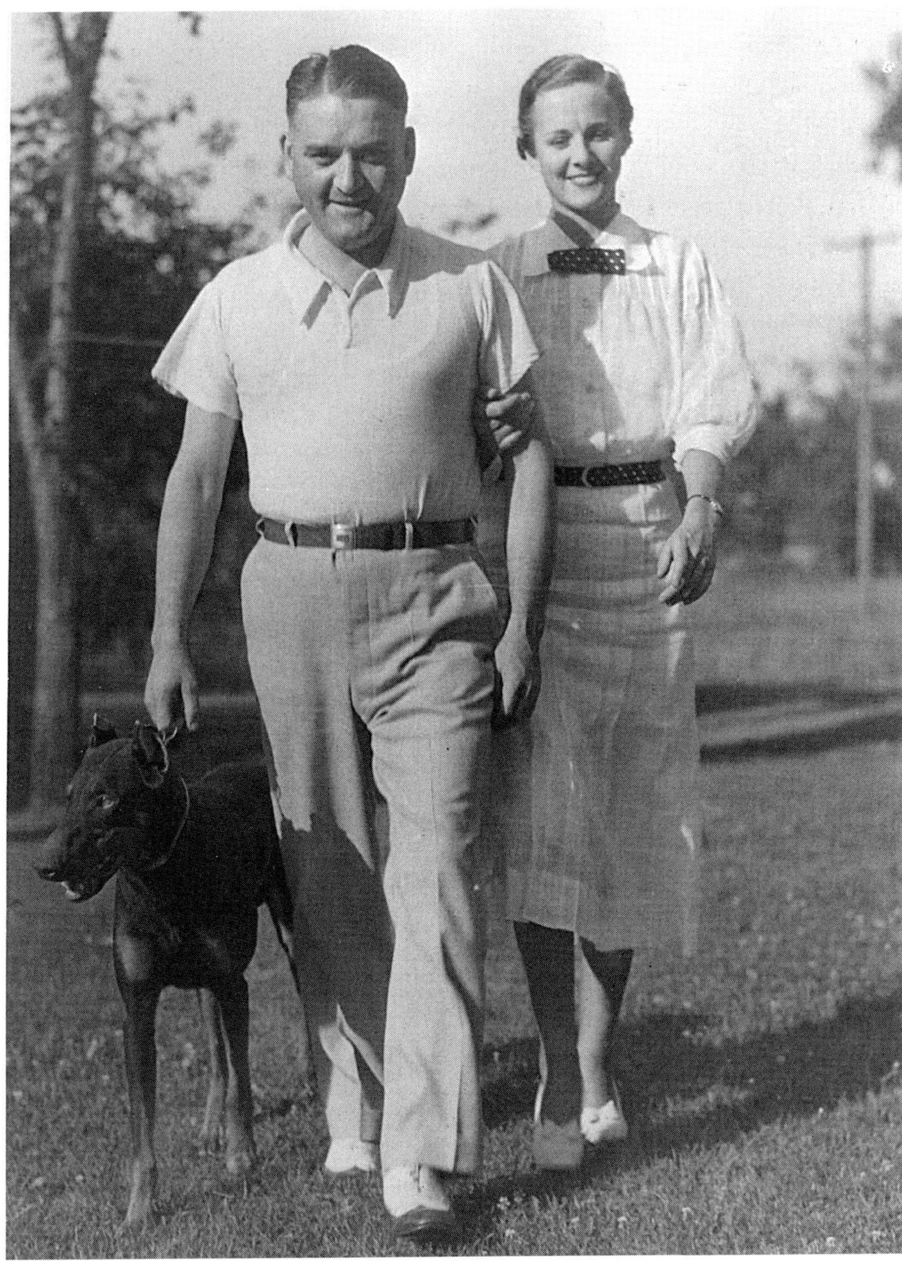

A Hamm ransom note, as retyped by FBI agents; family photo of fixer Jack Peifer and his wife, Violet, proprietors of the Hollyhocks Club

33 Gangland's Taj Mahal

The Hollyhocks Club Casino
1590 South Mississippi River Boulevard, St. Paul

During the early 1930s, a three-story mansion called the Hollyhocks was filled with tuxedo-clad businessmen and their wives sipping fine liqueurs and rubbing elbows with the most wanted gangsters in America. It was here that the Barker-Karpis gang met to plot the kidnapping that would elevate them to the top of J. Edgar Hoover's list of public enemies.[1]

The host of the Hollyhocks—and the "fingerman" who selected William Hamm as the gang's next victim—was John "Jack" Peifer, a former hotel bellhop and carnival worker turned underworld banker who, in the words of the FBI, "was always out of town whenever anything happen[ed]." A brown-haired, ruddy-skinned German-American from Litchfield, Minnesota, Peifer was 5 feet, 9 inches tall and weighed 189 pounds, with a mole in the center of his left cheek. He lived on the third floor of the Hollyhocks with his second wife, fashion model Violet Peifer, and their dog.[2]

Peifer had run other businesses on the fringes of the underworld, including a gambling operation on the seventh floor of the Radisson Hotel in Minneapolis; a St. Paul hotel (with future Barker-Karpis gang member Larry DeVol); the Senator Hotel in Minneapolis (with bootlegger Tommy Banks), a favorite of bank robbers Frank Nash and Charlie Harmon; and a cigar store/speakeasy on St. Peter Street.

Bank robbers who frequented the Hollyhocks were hesitant to keep their money in a traditional bank account—after all, who knew better how insecure the vaults were than the gangs who pried them open? Barker-Karpis gang members left their money with Peifer for safekeeping. He also made loans: "Some of the gang usually came to him for a 'touch,'" the FBI said. "Any time any hoodlum wanted a loan from him he usually complied with this request in order to keep the Hollyhocks from being held up, as he, Peifer, was operating gambling at the place."[3]

Not all gangsters in the underworld trusted Peifer to keep their money. Alvin Karpis recalled how he had once been forced to flee St. Paul and leave his money behind with a mob "banker" ("Karpis intimated that the man who was holding his money was Peifer," noted the FBI). While he was on the run, he needed the money and thought about going to St. Paul for it, but feared the "banker" might turn him in. Karpis considered kidnapping Peifer's wife to trade for his money but decided it would be too risky.[4]

Hollyhocks dinner guests, served by Japanese waiters on white tablecloths, included Alvin Karpis, Ma Barker and her boys Fred and Doc, bank robbers Verne Miller and Frank Nash, Chicago hoods Robert "Frisco

Dutch" Steinhardt and Fred "Shotgun George Ziegler" Goetz of Al Capone's syndicate, and members of the gangs operated by John Dillinger and Roger "the Terrible" Touhy. Karpis was especially fond of the Hollyhocks, and in May 1933 he romanced his teenaged lover, Delores Delaney, at the casino.[5]

The Hollyhocks site was originally developed by the wealthy family of Henry and Cornelia Boardman, who bought the land in 1904. In 1929 slot machine king Tom Filben, through his Federal Acceptance Corporation, backed the purchase of the property by Harry Silver and boxer Walter "Saph" McKenna, who transformed it into a gambling hall. Silver assured McKenna that the county attorney had told the chief of police to leave them alone, and McKenna told the FBI that 20 percent of the Hollyhocks's net profits were set aside as bribes for local police and politicians.[6]

In March 1931 Jack Peifer bought out McKenna's half share and took over the club with Filben. They named the Hollyhocks after the greenery surrounding the casino. McKenna stayed on to play two roles at the Hollyhocks: funneling weekly payoffs to the St. Paul police and managing the Hollyhocks dining room.[7]

Jack Peifer, manager of the Hollyhocks (below, seen from back), a favorite gangland casino

The Hollyhocks was a sizable operation. FBI agents noted that its garage could hold sixteen automobiles. "On the first floor [was] a large kitchen, butler's pantry, dance floor, semi-private dining rooms, bar, and store room," reported the FBI. "On the second floor . . . was a bedroom which was then occupied by the Japanese house man and a large gambling room." On the third floor were three bedrooms, one of them Peifer's private bedroom, equipped with a safe.[8]

Legend holds that a tunnel, entered through a hidden trap door, extended from the front porch to the Mississippi River below—a route for disposal of gangland victims—and of jewelry and cash stored in the club's walls. The current owners have searched and found no evidence of a tunnel.[9]

Peifer was the Minnesota contact for bank robber George "Machine Gun Kelly" Barnes, for whom he laundered the ransom paid for kidnapped Oklahoma oilman Charles Urschel. FBI agents uncovered Peifer's role in distributing the Urschel ransom through the Minneapolis syndicate of Isadore "Kid Cann" Blumenfeld when they found the Hollyhocks telephone number in the effects of Kelly's wife, Kathryn.

Peifer's menu of criminal services also included supplying alibis. When racketeer John Quinn murdered Frank Ventress at the Green Lantern saloon in 1931, homicide records show that Quinn dashed to the Hollyhocks to hammer out a bogus alibi. How could he have committed the murder, Quinn hoped to argue, if he and his wife were dining at the Hollyhocks at the time of the killing? Peifer's own criminal record was minor: a three-month jail term in 1924 for running illicit liquor out of a St. Paul "soft-drink bar" on St. Peter Street.[10]

Although FBI agents found a .38-caliber police-model revolver, a rusty .38 Colt automatic, and a Browning automatic shotgun when they raided the Hollyhocks, Peifer's value to the underworld was as a political fixer, not as a gunman. Friends claimed that Peifer was much more likely to hire a hit man than commit a murder himself, and in 1931 he demonstrated his incompetence with a gun in a firearms accident of an intimate nature. Precisely what happened is unclear from published reports. The St. Paul newspaper reported that "Peifer said a pistol discharged as he was removing it from his belt" and "a bullet grazed his abdomen," and FBI records showed that Peifer's body bore a scar from an abdominal bullet wound.[11]

Veteran newsman Fred Heaberlin was more explicit about the incident. "There was a telephone call to the St. Paul police one night about a shooting at the Hollyhocks Club," said Heaberlin. "The police detectives poured into their black Cadillac . . . and rushed out to the Hollyhocks. They were met at the door by Jack Peifer, who told them, 'It was nothing at all, boys. Just a scalp wound.' What had happened is that Peifer had a small-caliber pistol in his pocket, and when the derringer went off, the bullet creased the tip of his pecker!"[12]

Peifer's majordomo, Sam Tanaka (his real name was Shigematsu Yukimura), acted as the Hollyhocks chef and handled odd jobs. Peifer liked Japanese servants because, he told his mob associates, "they were very faithful and close-mouthed about what they saw or heard." No request was too unusual to be catered to at the Hollyhocks. When twenty guests asserted a desire for frog legs, Peifer said, "Well, just keep on drinking and I'll have my fellas go to Wisconsin and get frog's legs." Two hours later, Peifer's man "came back with the frog's legs and we ate like King Henry VIII!" recalled patron Blanche Schude. "Oh, the Hollyhocks was out of this world.... It was the elite!" The Hollyhocks food was so good, in fact, that Dillinger gang member Homer Van Meter was unable to resist braving a nationwide FBI manhunt to drive to the Hollyhocks with his girlfriend and devour his last Hollyhocks steak, which he ate in his car for security.[13]

"Dinner began at 6:00 P.M. on the first floor," recalled Martin Rohling, who was the Hollyhocks Club doorman during the early 1930s. "They gave food away at the Hollyhocks—you could get a porterhouse steak there for $1.50.... But we didn't have many diners at the Hollyhocks. They came to *gamble*... craps, roulette, and blackjack," said Rohling. "Once a week, we'd get a hundred women out to the Hollyhocks to play roulette for dimes!" Peifer and his associates "paid off the mayor and everyone else," added Rohling. Early one Sunday morning in July 1934, two policemen raided the club, confiscating two roulette wheels and detaining seven patrons and staff members, including Peifer. Because the roulette wheels were not operating at the time of the raid, the city promised not to charge Peifer with gambling and, Rohling said, two policemen returned the roulette wheels.[14]

In January 1931, the Hollyhocks had faced a crisis: With the election of Michael Kinkead as Ramsey County attorney, the club was temporarily forced to suspend operations, Walt McKenna reported. Interviewed by FBI agents, McKenna claimed that under Kinkead, bootlegger Leon Gleckman was able to tighten his control of gambling rackets. To keep the Hollyhocks gambling operations in business, Peifer would have to ally himself with Gleckman, "the Al Capone of St. Paul," who demanded about 20 percent of the net profits, McKenna told the FBI. The man who would collect Gleckman's $100 weekly payoffs was William W. Dunn, a sales manager for the Hamm Brewing Company. McKenna met Dunn in the lobby of the Hotel St. Paul to schedule payoffs. At the same time that Gleckman was securing his power over gambling payoffs, McKenna noticed another key player in the payoff schemes: St. Paul police chief Tom Brown was often seen speaking quietly with Jack Peifer in the front yard of the Hollyhocks. The payoff arrangement changed abruptly after Peifer negotiated Gleckman's return when the bootlegger was kidnapped in 1931. A grateful Gleckman canceled the Hollyhocks payoffs.[15]

A cast of scoundrels, petty thieves, and roustabouts enlivened the Hollyhocks's party atmosphere. Among them was a former carnival trick shooter nicknamed Tex. Alvin Karpis called Tex the biggest braggart he had ever met in his life, but Tex always lived up to his wildest boasts. He could slash a cigarette in two with a huge bullwhip, shoot six dimes with a gun at a distance of twenty-five yards, and balance six cups of steaming coffee on his arm at one time.[16]

During Christmas 1933 the Hollyhocks was particularly festive. Highway robber Harry Campbell, his girlfriend Wynona Burdette, Doc Barker, Volney Davis, and Edna Murray were all celebrating another holiday outside prison walls. "That [Christmas] night, we all went cabareting at Jack Pfeifer's Hollyhocks Inn," recalled Fred Barker's girlfriend Paula Harmon, "and we all stayed at Jack Peifer's place that night."[17]

Most Hollyhocks regulars were not mobsters. The club catered to businesspeople who enjoyed the thrill of dining and rolling dice in the company of notorious gangsters. "A customer visiting the Hollyhocks recognized as he approached the place that it was 'class' and that his billfold would need to be in a healthy condition," recalled *St. Paul Pioneer Press* crime reporter Nate Bomberg. "Going to the second floor after an excellent dinner, he found a gambling casino with the croupiers, also dressed formally, raking or pushing chips that represented thousands of dollars. If he lost, he knew at least that he had done so at the best illegal operation of its sort in St. Paul during the Prohibition era."[18]

Robert Brooks Hamilton, a white-haired gambling impresario, supervised the Hollyhocks casino with relentless honesty; his staff even supplied gamblers with calipers to test the dice. Hamilton considered it wise to let gamblers win every now and then. "They'll always come back when they win," Hamilton said, "and usually they lose all their winnings and plenty besides before they go home."[19]

Doorman Martin Rohling recalled one morning in 1933 or 1934 when William Mahoney, mayor of St. Paul, knocked at the Hollyhocks, curious to see its luxurious interior: "I had the chain on the door and he said, 'My wife has a headache, I'd like to get a glass of water.' I said, 'I'll bring it to you!' He said, '*I'm the mayor of St. Paul, let me in!*' And I *wouldn't*. The mayor wanted to see the inside of the place, but I never let him in."[20]

By 1932, during the nationwide manhunt for bank robbers Francis Keating and Tommy Holden, the FBI had begun to watch the Hollyhocks. FBI agents obtained a list of all long-distance telephone calls and telegrams charged to the club, documenting Peifer's contact with hoodlums in Miami Beach, Chicago, Montreal, and other cities. New reform-minded police officers—notably Chief Thomas E. Dahill—were now refusing to go along with the corrupt policies of the O'Connor era. In August 1932 he announced a police "drive against hoodlums" and "gun-toters," sparked by the public uproar over the murder of bootleggers Harry "Gorilla Kid" Davis and Abe Wagner by Murder Inc. "Gangsters and would-be gangsters are not wanted here," announced Dahill, "and we intend to do everything in our power to drive them out." A few days after that announcement, police were attracted by a fight outside the Green Lantern. Under Dahill's orders, officers arrested gunmen Clarence Colton, brother of Barker-Karpis gang member Larry DeVol, and William Weaver. Although both enforcers jumped their $500 bail bond and disappeared, a line had been crossed. If Dahill could violate the O'Connor agreement to leave crooks alone, was it time to violate O'Connor's prohibition against major crimes in St. Paul?[21]

The day after Colton's and Weaver's arrest, St. Paul police detective Fred Raasch saw underworld fixer Harry Sawyer sitting in a car across the street from the Public Safety Building on Tenth Street: "Sawyer said that he was in a jam because the police had picked up a couple of fellows in his place the night before. He said he wondered what was the matter with Dahill. . . . that when [Tom] Brown was Chief, he'd always get a call if they were going to come up to his place, and he said: 'If I had got a ring, I'd had those fellows out of there.'" Sawyer warned that he could "keep heat off a town, but he could put it on, too," Raasch told the FBI. "I wonder how Dahill would like a couple of snatches in this town," Sawyer said.[22]

Jack Peifer brought Fred Barker and Alvin Karpis to the Hollyhocks in April 1933 to initiate a "snatch" that would shatter the O'Connor system forever. "Whatever it was he had in mind, I figured it must be a bombshell," Karpis recalled. "Peifer leaned back with an extra-special important look and said, 'How would you boys like to work on a kidnapping?'" Once the kidnapping was set into motion, the Hollyhocks became an unofficial staging area for the abduction.[23]

The victim Peifer had chosen was William Hamm Jr., the young president of St. Paul's Hamm Brewing Company, who was also the president of a department store, a Minnesota Amusement Corporation officer, and a First National Bank board member. Peifer had met Hamm when he was a patron at the Hollyhocks in 1931. The ransom, Peifer said, would be $100,000 in unmarked bills.[24]

Karpis later wondered about the modest ransom amount; after all, Hamm was a brewer and Prohibition had just ended. Twin Cities liquor companies —forced for fourteen years to subsist on manufacturing near beer, malt syrup, and alcohol for industrial purposes—were now brewing money. Because "less money was demanded than the victim was able to pay," Karpis told the FBI years later, he speculated that the motive for the kidnapping was more complex: "[I] thought it was political and had something to do with [the] St. Paul police department and Ramsey County officials."[25]

Kidnapping someone as visible as Hamm was a far cry from kidnapping a racketeer like Leon Gleckman. "Before Prohibition was repealed, the people in rackets were out kidnapping the top bootleggers who were making lots of money," said Pat Lannon Sr., a former St. Paul policeman. "When Prohibition was repealed, those guys didn't have any money—and they had to snatch legitimate people, that's how the Bremer and Hamm kidnappings started."[26]

In the midst of the kidnapping, an act of violence in Kansas City shattered the complacency of every gangster dining at the Hollyhocks. On June 17, 1933, bank robber Verne Miller and two accomplices, armed with submachine guns, attempted to free their comrade Frank Nash from federal custody at Union Station. Instead, Miller slaughtered three policemen, an FBI agent, and Nash. "That damn thing with Frank Nash in Kansas City is going to be the worst thing that ever happened to guys like us," predicted Karpis.[27]

When the FBI launched its massive investigation into what was then dubbed the Kansas City Massacre, agents were curious why the Hollyhocks Club figured so prominently. Nash's wife, Frances, said that she and Frank had enjoyed lunch there in early June, days before the massacre. The agents also learned that gangsters had telephoned the Hollyhocks the morning before the Kansas City Massacre. Two additional phone calls were made to St. Paul from Union Station within hours after the massacre, one to Harry Sawyer's Green Lantern saloon and the other to the Hollyhocks.[28]

By July the FBI had authorized a mail cover on letters and packages delivered to the Hollyhocks and a covert wiretap on its telephone. The St. Paul FBI field office reassured J. Edgar Hoover that "the tapping of this telephone line was conducted entirely unbeknown to the telephone company." Working with a U.S. Army Signal Corps lieutenant at Fort Snelling, across the Mississippi River from the Hollyhocks, FBI agent Oscar Hall tapped Emerson 2121, a phone line at the club.[29]

Within two weeks, the agents learned that the Hollyhocks was far more than just a nightclub; it appeared to be the nerve center linking corrupt Twin Cities police with organized crime. In one wiretapped conversation, Peifer's wife, Violet, telephoned "Maxine," the girlfriend of Minneapolis bootlegger Tommy Banks. The FBI reported that Maxine "told Violet Peifer that their Minneapolis criminal defense attorney Archie Cary 'has been arranging the distribution of the rackets in Minneapolis since the change in police administration,' and proceeded to outline in detail how the rackets were to be divided." The wiretap proved that Peifer was helping mobsters with everything from repairing their getaway cars to dealing with wayward girlfriends.

Harry Sawyer was overheard on a Hollyhocks wiretap complaining to Peifer that criminal defense attorney Tom Newman had referred him to a Ramsey County child welfare agent who was "a bum steer." According to the FBI report, Sawyer said the adoption agent was "investigating more than Newman said she would" when the Sawyers adopted a little girl.[30]

The FBI understood that Peifer's chief value to the underworld was his access to police, judges, and grand juries. When agents raided Vi Peifer's third-floor bedroom at the Hollyhocks, they found a typewritten list titled "Grand Jurors—March-April" with the names of members of a Hennepin County grand jury.[31]

In the most revealing Hollyhocks wiretap, Peifer was overheard negotiating with Jack Lally, junior captain of Minneapolis detectives, precisely how many pickpockets would be allowed on the streets and determining how many pockets had been picked that day. "This is Jack Lally," the policeman said to the gangster. "Have you got any pickpockets working over here? If you have, you better call them off. Things are too hot."[32]

The combined investigations into the kidnapping of Hamm and banker Edward Bremer, and the Kansas City Massacre gradually drew a long shadow over Peifer and the Hollyhocks Club. The club was officially closed in 1934, just after Bremer was kidnapped. FBI agents searched the Hollyhocks for typewriters that might have been used to type the Hamm and Bremer kidnap ransom notes and interviewed a truculent Peifer to determine what he knew about the kidnappings. Peifer boldly claimed that he barely knew the Barkers, but agents retorted that they knew Peifer "was connected with practically every form of racketeering occurring in the Twin Cities."[33]

Although the ransom-note typewriters were never found, the FBI discovered months later that Peifer had not only selected William Hamm as the victim but had also chosen the White Bear Lake Township cottage from which the kidnapping would be launched.

34 Pennies from Gangster Heaven

The Barker-Karpis Gang at Idlewild Cottage
5500 East Bald Eagle Boulevard, White Bear Lake Township

Alvin Karpis and the Barker brothers initiated the June 1933 kidnapping of William Hamm from a Bald Eagle Lake cottage called Idlewild.

When Karpis visited the Hollyhocks Club with Fred Barker, he told Jack Peifer that he would move to Minnesota if he could find "a quiet place out on the lake someplace not too far from St. Paul." Peifer told Karpis to come back after he had had a chance to search the White Bear–Bald Eagle Lake area for a suitable cottage. "I kidded him [Peifer] about it being a racket coming around at dinner time so as I would buy my dinner there instead of some place else," recalled Karpis later. "He just laughed and said I should patronize his place if he was going to the trouble of finding a cottage for me."[34]

White Bear Lake was an ideal spot for the Barker-Karpis gang to blend in with vacationers during the first explosion of "heat" generated by the Hamm kidnapping. Remote from St. Paul and Minneapolis, encircled by winding tree-lined roads and anonymous beach cabins, the resort area was marketed as a place for "people of wealth and refinement"—F. Scott and Zelda Fitzgerald and others attracted by yacht regattas, lawn tennis, and "popular hops and musicales." In fact, it was the playground of the same well-to-do Twin Citians who became the Barker-Karpis gang's kidnapping targets.[35]

Peifer drove up to the Idlewild cottage in a La Salle coupe in May 1933 and paid the $250 cash deposit to rent the home from owner Alex Premo. When the landlord offered a receipt, Peifer declined, preferring that there be no record of the transaction. The Premos had the money, said Peifer, and he had the cottage, "so to hell with a receipt." At that time, Idlewild was a one-and-one-half-story white-and-green building with a thousand-gallon water tank, a screened porch, and a two-car garage where Fred Barker kept his Ford coupe and a Hudson sedan.[36]

Doc and Fred Barker joined Karpis at Idlewild, eager to hammer out the

Idlewild cottage, the Barker-Karpis gang's Bald Eagle Lake headquarters during the Hamm kidnapping

details of the kidnapping. Fred Barker and Karpis followed Hamm as he walked up the hill from the Hamm brewery to his Cable Avenue mansion. "We made almost daily trips into St. Paul to case Hamm's brewery and home," recalled Karpis. "We mastered every last detail of the layouts of both places and spent hours studying Hamm's habits. We got to know so much about the guy that I was sick of him long before the kidnapping."[37]

Meanwhile, the gangsters told their new neighbors that they were entertainers from the Plantation nightclub. "Ma Barker wanted me to mow her lawn with one of our hand mowers," remembered Clifford Lindholm, who lived opposite the Idlewild cottage in 1933. "So I attempted to mow her lawn, and she gave me five dollars. Well, it was the Depression. I didn't know what the hell money was. When my mother saw that, it was like pennies from heaven. . . . And I must have done a horrible job of mowing the Barker-Karpis gang's lawn!" Lindholm tasted his first cream soda pop on the Idlewild back porch with Ma Barker, and when he and other children were selling ten-cent tickets for a community fund raiser, they headed for Idlewild: "I knew [the Barkers] would be very generous. Ma Barker bought the whole roll from me!" She gave the roll of tickets back to Lindholm and let him keep the money. "We thought they were very nice people!"[38]

"They were the perfect neighbors," said Steve Tuttle, whose grandfather had a cottage directly across from Idlewild. "Ma Barker's boys used to hold ice cream socials for the neighborhood kids in the backyard. . . . If people did know who the Barkers were, no one cared—as long as they didn't commit any crimes in the Bald Eagle area!"[39]

Area residents are fond of telling Barker-Karpis stories. It is said that the gang indulged in target shooting at Bald Eagle Lake. Hearing the gunfire, a neighbor ran over to Idlewild and shouted angrily at the gangsters, "You cut this out . . . there are kids around here!" Sheepishly, the story goes, the gang stopped shooting. "Criminals had some kind of ethics in those days," said Lindholm, expressing the lenient view that many citizens of St. Paul and White Bear Lake shared. "Those people would never do things like the drive-by shootings they do today. . . . They'd go into a bar in White Bear and buy everyone a round—which was great, even if the money was stolen from some banker!"[40]

With the gang at Idlewild was a Japanese cook, Henry Kazo Maihori, who had worked for the Nankin Cafe in Minneapolis. A friend of Hollyhocks chef Sam Tanaka, Maihori loved to fish off the nearby dock. He planted radishes and lettuce in a garden outside Idlewild and prepared the vegetables and fruit—sweet corn, potatoes, and strawberries—that children delivered to the gang's back porch. Maihori was paid about fifteen dollars a week for his services, which included fixing breakfast for the gang.[41]

Neighbors interviewed later by FBI agents said that most of the gangsters relaxed in bathrobes and bathing suits, but one plump man sunbathed nude, hoping to heal a rash on his stomach. He was Fred "Shotgun George Ziegler" Goetz, an enforcer for Al Capone's Chicago mob.[42]

White Bear area residents told of hearing loud parties and occasional fights, often fueled by liquor, at Idlewild. Iceman Otto Krause said the Idlewild occupants were "very good beer customers": he "sold them five or six cases of beer at a time and also considerable ginger ale," the FBI reported.[43]

Gradually the gangsters began to attract notice. An FBI report noted that a neighbor said they were "mysterious, as they stayed indoors practically all of the time with the shades of the cottage drawn and did not go swimming as is the custom of the average lake resident." The night William Hamm was released, Idlewild neighbors saw a car light flashing across the lake, as if they were signaling. Three weeks after moving into Idlewild, the gang vanished, leaving Maihori to clean up the emptied cottage.[44]

Steve Tuttle's grandmother Virginia Tuttle had given Ma Barker twenty-five cents to pay the iceman on behalf of the Tuttle family. Suddenly the Barker family fled, FBI agents at their heels. Virginia "lamented how she had given this infamous gangster her quarter to pay the iceman. My gosh, now it won't get paid," Steve Tuttle recalled. She telephoned the iceman to explain her predicament and learned that Ma Barker had stopped on her way out of town to pay the Tuttles' bill. "That was a great relief on my grandmother's part, [because] during the Depression every penny was precious," said Tuttle. "Grandma laughed about Ma Barker, this terrible villain, stopping during her escape from White Bear Lake to pay off the ice bill!"[45]

35 'Like Getting Money from Home'

The Hamm Brewing Company
681 East Minnehaha Avenue, St. Paul

When Fred Barker proposed kidnapping Hamm Brewing Company president William Hamm Jr., Alvin Karpis agreed to participate, on one condition: "I told him as long as it wasn't a woman or child it sounded rather attractive," said Karpis later. To identify their quarry, Barker had Karpis drive by the brewery on Minnehaha Avenue. "Do you think a man that owned a place of that sort," asked Barker, "would be able to pay $100,000 ransom?"[46]

Indeed, the Hamm Brewing Company (today the Stroh Brewery, near Minnehaha and Payne Avenues) was one of the most profitable breweries in the United States. It was founded by Theodore Hamm of Herbolzheim, Germany, who came to St. Paul from Chicago in the 1840s and expanded the brewery dramatically in 1894. The founder's grandson was to be the gangsters' victim.[47]

For this complex kidnapping, Karpis and Barker agreed to call in an experienced strategist from Chicago. Fred Goetz, known to Al Capone's syndicate as "Shotgun George Ziegler," had participated in the 1929 St. Valentine's Day Massacre, which left seven men dead in a garage run by the Bugs Moran gang. ("The object of this wholesale killing was to eradicate 'Bugs' Moran and his mob, who at that time were threatening the dominance of the Capone criminal organization," the FBI learned from the widow of gangster Gus Winkler.) Alvin Karpis claimed that the florid-faced Goetz planned the massacre. Goetz already knew key members of the St. Paul underworld, in particular Harry Sawyer. After meeting Goetz at the Hollyhocks club, Harry and Gladys Sawyer had spent Thanksgiving 1932 with Fred and Irene Goetz at their lodge on Cranberry Lake near Hayward, Wisconsin.[48]

The Hamm Brewery, near which William Hamm Jr. was abducted, and family mansion (far right)

Unique among Capone's enforcers, Goetz freelanced for both the Barker-Karpis and Jimmy Keating–Tommy Holden bank robbery gangs. Other Capone syndicate killers began their careers as petty thugs or bootleggers, but Goetz was once an engineering student and a University of Illinois football player. He even undertook a correspondence course in landscape gardening in 1928. His legitimate career had evaporated in 1925 when, as a lifeguard at a Chicago beach, Goetz was arrested for attempting to rape a seven-year-old girl. He forfeited his $5,000 bond and never stood trial. By October he had resurfaced as a suspect in the killing of a chauffeur during the robbery of a Chicago physician, and then as a hit man of great ingenuity: he invented a time bomb with leather straps that could be bound to a victim, forcing him to give in to demands for money. An FBI agent found that Goetz also invented for himself a belt that contained six steel saws concealed within the leather.[49]

Fred Goetz as a Chicago lifeguard

"His character was one of infinite contradictions," wrote FBI agent Melvin Purvis of Goetz. "Well mannered, always polite, he was capable of generous kindness and conscienceless cruelty."[50]

Irene Dorsey met Fred Goetz, then posing as salesman George Siebert, in an Illinois restaurant in 1924 and married him two years later in Alexandria, Minnesota. "He was changing names constantly," FBI agents learned from Irene Goetz. "He used the moniker Von Ash, because Goetz got a big kick out of using such a high sounding name." To ensure that she did not inadvertently call him by the wrong alias, Goetz trained his wife to refer to him only as her husband. Irene guessed that while her husband was hiding his criminal activities from the FBI, he was also hiding an extramarital affair from her. They vacationed together at the Greenwood Lodge in northern Minnesota to try "to regain their old selves," an FBI report noted.[51]

Summoned by a telephone call from Jack Peifer, Goetz drove to St. Paul in May 1933 to help plan the Hamm kidnapping. He brought along his bodyguard, William Byron Bolton, a tubercular forty-year-old alumnus of Al Capone's syndicate. The nephew of an Illinois police chief and the father of two, Bolton had been a carpenter, auto salesman, and golf teacher; he was honorably discharged from the U.S. Navy in 1919.[52]

Under the alias Monty Carter, Bolton operated on the fringes of Capone's syndicate as a driver for hit man Fred Burke. Bank robber Charlie Fitzgerald told the FBI that Bolton had "messed up" as the lookout during the St. Valentine's Day Massacre by giving an early go-ahead to kill the gangsters, moments before the intended target, Bugs Moran, arrived at the garage. Because his bungling had enabled Moran to escape, Capone demanded that Bolton be killed, according to two FBI sources. Only Goetz's protection kept him alive. The FBI learned from Fitzgerald "that Fred Goetz had implicit faith in [Bolton] but that numerous persons associated with both Goetz and Bolton did not trust Bolton and often tried to persuade Goetz that he should get rid of him."[53]

Alvin Karpis was one of those who distrusted Bolton. Karpis had urged Goetz to abandon him, but Goetz was determined to stick by his ailing partner. (Bolton got tuberculosis during his stint with the navy, and then suffered double pneumonia in 1930.) Karpis's suspicions were confirmed in 1936, when Bolton turned government witness and testified against the Barker-Karpis gang.[54]

Goetz and Bolton visited the Hollyhocks on June 10, 1933, while Peifer was still asleep, so they sat down to breakfast in the dining room. Half an hour later, Peifer joined them, saying that "the rest of the fellows were already in town," recalled Bolton, and "as soon as he got dressed he would take us out to meet them." When they finished breakfast, Peifer, Goetz, and Bolton drove out to a cottage on Bald Eagle Lake. "At the cottage were Alvin Karpis and Fred and Doc Barker."[55]

The gang discussed when and where to snatch their victim, and they decided that Karpis would drive the kidnap car, wearing a chauffeur's cap so as not to alarm Hamm. They planned every detail, from a switch of license plates when they got to Illinois to the three five-gallon cans of gasoline they would carry so they could avoid stopping at a gas station. They determined that Hamm would be held far from St. Paul in Bensonville, Illinois. They would demand a $100,000 ransom payment, with $40,000 earmarked for Jack Peifer to distribute as payoff money in St. Paul. (Karpis had suggested a $250,000 ransom, and Fred Barker argued for at least $200,000, but Goetz overruled the higher figures.)[56]

In this conversation, Bolton learned an astonishing fact that reflected three decades of police corruption: "Peifer had introduced [Goetz] to a police officer of the St. Paul Police Department, who was on the Kidnap Detail . . . and it was the plan to pay him $25,000 of the ransom money; that in return . . . this officer was to keep us advised of the developments at the Police Department" while the victim was being held. Having a high-ranking police officer on the payroll was the fulcrum of the kidnapping plan; the gang would be warned of any mistakes that might lead to capture. "Goetz said that this officer had told him and [Peifer] that we should be careful in telephoning," recalled Bolton. "It took about two minutes to trace a telephone call. . . . Goetz was greatly pleased with this arrangement . . . [since] there was very little chance of a slip-up. . . . It was like getting money from home."

The role of "greeter"—someone who could stop Hamm on the street without alarming him—fell to bank robber Charles "Old Charlie" Fitzgerald, a fifty-seven-year-old native of Missouri. Fitzgerald was gray haired, bull necked, and an imposing six feet tall. "He is an old time criminal, having been first convicted in 1898" for burglarizing a Kansas store, said an FBI file. "He is one of the shrewdest bank burglars and robbers in the country." By the time he joined the Barker-Karpis gang, Fitzgerald had been imprisoned in Anamosa, Iowa; Hutchinson and Lansing, Kansas; and Atlanta.[57]

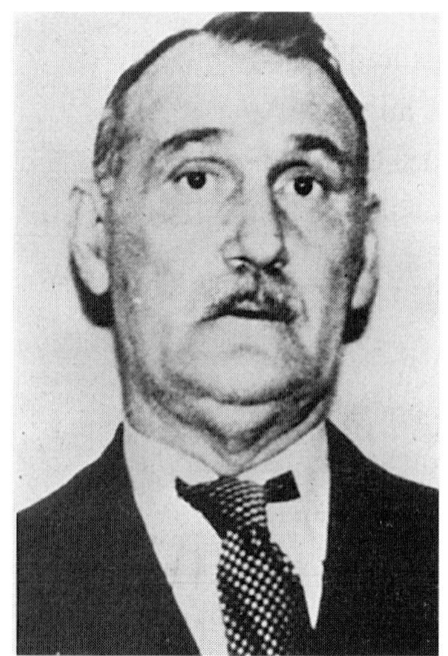

Charlie Fitzgerald, the Hamm kidnapping "greeter"

Fitzgerald's distinguished appearance in a banker's jacket and tie belied his thirty-five years of blowing bank safes with nitroglycerine. Gang member Jess Doyle told the FBI that Fitzgerald was "an outstanding bank stick-up man, especially good in 'casing' banks." After Fitzgerald agreed to Fred Barker's invitation to join the kidnapping for a cut of up to $8,000, he went to the Bald Eagle Lake cabin for the necessary rehearsals.[58]

At 12:45 P.M., on June 15, 1933, Hamm left his brewing company office to have lunch and crossed the street at the corner of Minnehaha and Greenbrier, walking toward his home at 671 Cable. Doc Barker raised his arm to signal that their victim was in view. Karpis was ready, having parked his black Hudson sedan half a block from the brewery. Charlie Fitzgerald stepped up to Hamm, reached out to shake his hand, and gripped Hamm's right elbow. "You are Mr. Hamm, are you not?" asked Fitzgerald. An FBI report documented Hamm's description of what happened next: "I said, 'Yes,' and took hold of [his hand] and he then took my right elbow with his left hand and tightened the grip on my right hand. I looked at him rather astonished and said, 'What is it you want?' The man on his right was then on my left taking hold of my left hand and arm and started pushing me to the curb. Just as we reached the curb, this car drew up right next to us. . . . The door was opened . . . [and] I was pushed into the car."[59]

Doc Barker forced Hamm into the rear seat, where he was sandwiched between Barker and Bolton. A white pillow case was dropped over his head and shoulders. Suddenly, Karpis worried that they had kidnapped the wrong man. With typical Minnesota good spirits, Hamm assured the gangsters that he was indeed William Hamm Jr.—which made Karpis even more suspicious. Fortunately for the gang, Hamm's name was found on the tailor's labels in his coat.[60]

During the drive, the gangsters talked about muskellunge fishing and shared drinks of ice water from a thermos. They told Hamm to be perfectly

Reporters and onlookers at the Hamm residence following the kidnapping

quiet and everything would be all right. "There wasn't much conversation on that trip; we didn't know each other well enough yet," Hamm later recalled. At one point, the hood was removed, and a gangster said, "You are awfully warm down there, aren't you?"[61]

The group traveled on gravel roads until, thirty miles outside St. Paul, they intercepted Fred Goetz and Fred Barker in a Chevrolet sedan. Hamm was given a handful of typewritten ransom notes to sign; one of the gangsters said, "I guess you know what this is all about." They reached the Bensonville, Illinois, hideout that evening. Hamm's blindfold was removed, and he was given a glass of milk and a pork sandwich before being locked in a second-floor bedroom. Fitzgerald, Goetz, and Fred Barker returned to St. Paul that night to begin negotiating the ransom.[62]

36 The Lovable Rogue

Home of Go-Between William W. Dunn
1916 Summit Avenue, St. Paul

With Hamm safely hidden away in Illinois, it was time for the Barker-Karpis gang to concentrate on securing the $100,000 ransom. Hamm was asked for the name of a contact with ties to his brewery, a man he trusted with his life, to serve as the intermediary between the kidnappers and the Hamm family. Hamm suggested William W. Dunn, the brewery's current sales manager.[63]

The gang was overjoyed that Hamm had chosen Dunn, who lived in a two-story white stucco home near the intersection of Prior and Summit Avenues. The FBI later learned from Alvin Karpis that Dunn was the man agreed upon by the gang prior to the kidnapping "because they knew he had contacts and had been the collector for the Police Department at St. Paul, so [he] would be forced to keep his mouth shut."[64]

Most previous accounts of the Hamm kidnapping accept the popular theory that the 1933 abduction was shocking because, for the first time, the "underworld" had dared to intrude upon the "overworld." Yet the FBI files detailing Dunn's career—which straddled the worlds of businessmen like William Hamm and underworld fixers like Harry Sawyer—reveal how permeable the walls were in St. Paul between "civilized" society and the gangsters. Far from holding gangland at arm's length, FBI records suggest, some St. Paul businessmen had profited from associations with underworld figures for decades. Dunn told FBI agents that in about 1920 William Hamm Sr. proposed that Dunn, who had sold billiard and bowling alley equipment for the Brunswick Company, operate the recreation end of his Hamm Building on St. Peter Street in downtown St. Paul. Dunn leased the basement for use as a billiard and pool room and bowling alley and ran the hall until 1929, when he joined Hamm Brewing Company.[65]

During the Hamm investigation, the FBI would learn that Hollyhocks Club manager Walt McKenna had used Dunn to deliver "'pay-off' money which ultimately went to the St. Paul Police Department. . . . Dunn was the contact man between the underworld and the St. Paul Police Department." Businessman Herb Benz, William Hamm's cousin, whose investment company held the mortgage for the Hollyhocks, told the FBI that Dunn was "the payoff between the underworld and the police department during the regime of Tom Brown as chief." (Under oath at Jack Peifer's trial for the Hamm kidnapping, Dunn would say only that he had been "a friend" of Peifer for fifteen years.)[66]

Police officials Charles Tierney and Thomas Dahill told the FBI that

The released William Hamm Jr. (at right) shaking hands with kidnap go-between William Dunn, his brewery sales manager. Hamm did not know that Dunn was also an intermediary between gangsters and corrupt police officers.

Dunn collected for Leon Gleckman, who controlled gambling in St. Paul, in exchange for a share of the proceeds. Gleckman himself was candid about Dunn's role in distributing underworld bribes. "Billy Dunn was very close to him, the reason being that Dunn had only recently entered the employ of the Hamm Brewing Company," the FBI reported after agents interviewed Gleckman in prison, "and was anxious to secure favorable license grants for customers of the company, and was active in having the police lay off of customers who operated their saloons after legal closing hours."[67]

William Figge, former president of the brewing company, remembered Dunn as a lovable rogue. "William Dunn was a refreshing personality," with "a million friends and no enemies," said Figge. "He knew *all* the underworld characters—many of them came to Dunn's pool hall. . . . When bootleggers and thugs came to town with a lot of money, Bill Dunn would put the cash in his safe for them over the weekend!"[68]

Interviewed by the FBI, Dunn denied that he was a payoff man, although "he admitted that he was acquainted with practically every underworld character in the Twin Cities, but claimed that he had met these people through his operation of the St. Paul Recreation Parlor." Dunn said that he had often visited Gleckman at the Hotel St. Paul and the Boulevards of Paris nightclub.[69]

This was the man who received the gang's ransom call at the Hamm brewery.[70]

"Is this W. W. Dunn?" asked the caller.

Dunn replied, "Yes, sir."

"I want to talk to you and I don't want you to say anything until I get all through. We have Mr. Hamm. We want you to get $100,000 in twent[ies], tens and fives."

"Hey, hey, what the hell is going on here?" Dunn blurted out.

"Now shut up and listen to what I have to say." After providing preliminary instructions on the delivery of the ransom, the caller continued, "If you tell a soul about this it will be just too bad for Hamm and you."[71]

Dunn called the St. Paul police; the FBI immediately installed wiretaps on Dunn's home telephone and on the phones at the brewery. Policemen Tom Brown and Charles Tierney of the kidnap squad were assigned to the Hamm case, meeting with Dunn at his Summit Avenue home.[72]

As if the kidnappers were following Dunn's every move—but were not upset by the presence of the police—they called again: "Well, Dunn, you're following instructions very well so far. Now, I have given you time to recover from the shock of the telephone call this afternoon and you must real ize that the call was not a joke as you thought. All you've got to do is follow instructions."[73]

The instructions were handed to a Yellow Cab driver by Fred Goetz at the Lowry Ramp Garage in downtown St. Paul. Police detective Tom Brown accepted the note at Dunn's house. "You know your boy friend is out of circulation," it said. "You are to pay off $100,000.00 in the manner explained to you this afternoon. . . . If you fail to comply with our demands, you will never see Hamm, Jr. again."[74]

In Bensonville, the gang promised Hamm that no harm would come to him. They told him to face the wall when they brought him food so that he would not recognize any of them. Hamm admitted later that he peeked at the gang's faces out of the corner of his eye. He also noticed the motto "Mother" on the top of the bed, a crayon sketch of flamingos on the wall, a broken faucet, the volume of traffic on nearby roads, the sounds of children playing, church bells, and the whistles of a nearby freight train. If he survived, William Hamm intended to bring his kidnappers to justice.[75]

37 'Get Away from the Coppers'

The Rosedale Pharmacy
1941 Grand Avenue, St. Paul

Late in the evening of June 16, another ransom demand was delivered, this time to a soda booth at Clarence J. Thomas's Rosedale Pharmacy at the corner of Prior and Grand Avenues. A potbellied, curly-haired blond man sauntered into the pharmacy to buy cigarettes and sulfur ointment, Thomas told the FBI. Based on interviews with kidnappers Charlie Fitzgerald and Byron Bolton, FBI agents were later able to identify the man as Fred Goetz. A few minutes after the shopper left, an unidentified telephone caller directed the Rosedale Pharmacy clerk to the ransom letter, which was delivered to Dunn's home around the corner.[76]

"You're so god dam[n]ed smart that you'll wind up getting both of you guys killed," the note read. "Furthermore we demand that *you* personally deliver the money so that if there is any doble crossing we will have the pleasure of hitting you in the head."[77]

The next day, yet another note was left on the back seat of a car owned by a Hamm Brewing employee. The gang offered precise instructions on how Dunn should deliver the ransom money and demonstrated an intimate knowledge of the Hamm family's contacts with St. Paul police. Dunn was told to drive to Highway 61 and look for five flashes of a headlight, the signal to drop the ransom at the side of the road. "If the coppers succeed in following you it might prove fatal. You brought the coppers in to this now you get rid of the assholes," read the first note. "Hamm is uncomfortable and diss-appointed in the way you bungled this so far."[78]

The FBI and the police considered setting a trap for the kidnappers: an armed policeman could be hidden inside a Hamm brewery truck, ready to ambush the kidnappers when they appeared to collect the ransom. Warned by the police officer of the proposed trap, the gang responded June 17 with a furious note: "If you are through with the bullshit and balyhoo, we'll give you your chance. . . . First of all, *get away from the coppers*. . . . If you try to out *s[m]art* us you only prolong the agony." The note demanded that Dunn remove the doors of his vehicle and hang a red lantern inside "so no one can be concealed."[79]

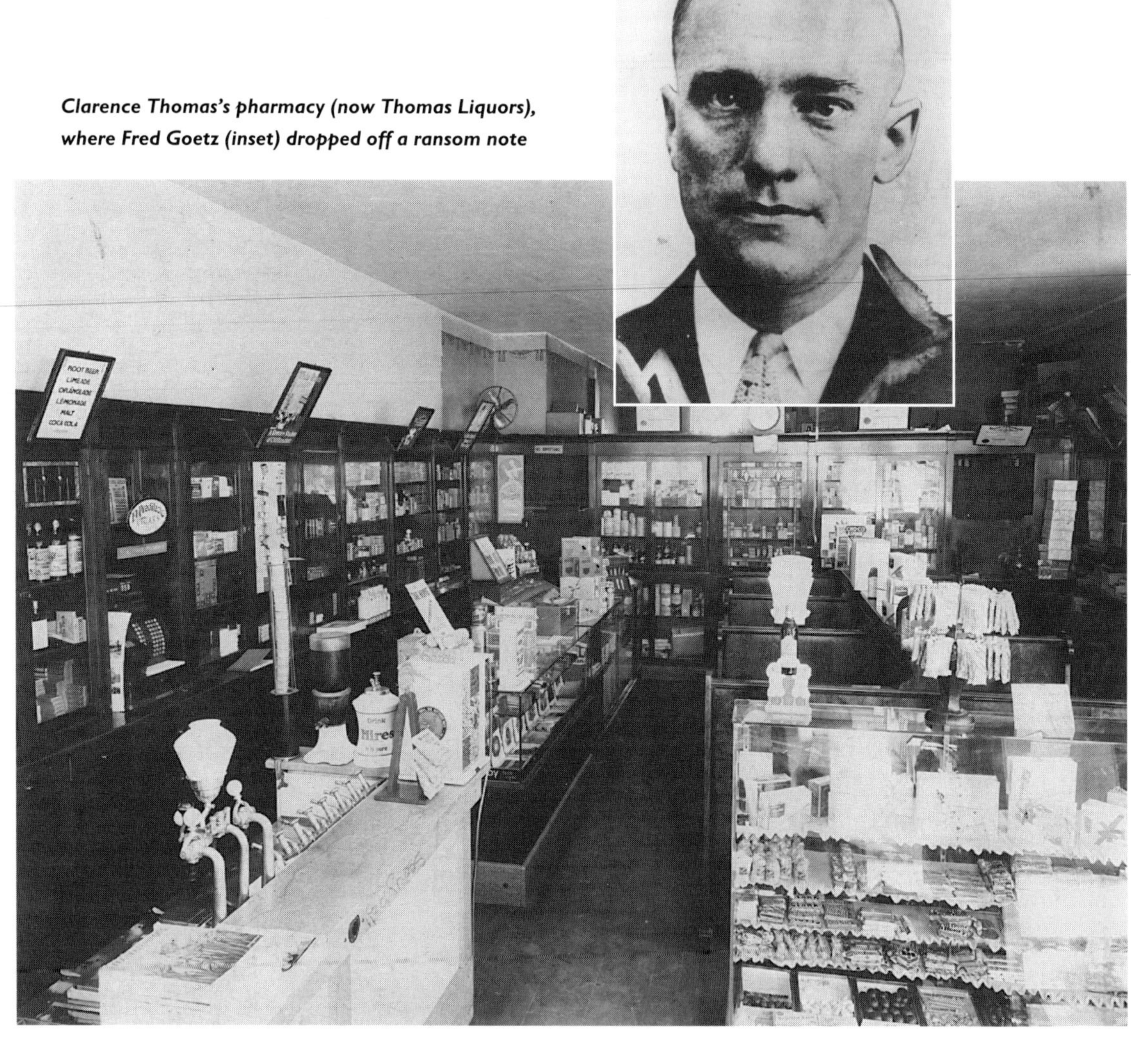

Clarence Thomas's pharmacy (now Thomas Liquors), where Fred Goetz (inset) dropped off a ransom note

Fred Goetz crowed to the gang that this warning alone made it worth paying the corrupt policeman $25,000, but the investment was about to pay additional dividends, once again saving the gang from virtually certain discovery.[80]

38 'There Goes the Ransom Money'

Hideout of the "Vernon Street Gang"
204 Vernon Street, St. Paul

The thumbprint was barely ½-by-2½-inches in size. Still, FBI headquarters in Washington, D.C., identified the smudge clinging to a beer bottle found at 204 Vernon Street as the print of Frank "Jelly" Nash, the ill-fated bank robber who died in a botched escape attempt that also left an FBI agent and three policemen dead in Kansas City. What had Nash been doing in St. Paul, days before the Kansas City Massacre?[81]

The two-story residence at 204 Vernon Street harbored a convention of public enemies from May 28 to June 19, 1933. Residents included Doc Barker, Fred Barker and his girlfriend Paula Harmon, and Alvin Karpis. Bank robbers Volney Davis, Charlie Fitzgerald, William Weaver, and Fred Goetz also came to do business.

Salesman James MacLaren and his wife, Gertrude, owned the home. They rented it out while summering with their children, Jack and Frances, at a vacation home on Bald Eagle Lake. Fred Barker and Paula Harmon, masquerading as Mr. and Mrs. Stanley Smith, responded to the MacLarens's newspaper ad. "Mrs. Smith . . . was very coy," recalled Frances MacLaren Paul. "'Oh, Mrs. MacLaren,' she told mother, 'I love to cook. Be sure to leave all these pans.' She was putting on an act!"[82]

The "Smiths" inspected the home and offered to rent it through August for forty-five dollars a month. Fred Barker pretended to be a salesman for Federated Metal Company of St. Louis. His "wife," Paula Harmon, was described by the MacLarens as a reddish-blonde with a Southern accent, a ring studded with eight diamonds, and a scarred nose that, in FBI parlance, gave "the appearance of once having been struck by a heavy instrument."[83]

As references, the Smiths offered the names of city health officer Dr. Nels Mortensen and attorney Tom Newman. Only later did the MacLarens learn that Mortensen was to be investigated for tending the bullet wounds of John Dillinger and that Newman was a criminal defense attorney who had represented a variety of underworld characters. The lawyer assured the MacLarens that J. Stanley Smith was "all right as far as [he] knew," the FBI reported. Satisfied with the character of their new tenants, the Mac-

Larens set off for Bald Eagle Lake while the Smiths drove up to 204 Vernon in their new Chevrolet sedan. The Barker-Karpis gang had a nearby drugstore deliver beer and ginger ale, over which they plotted the Hamm kidnapping. On June 15, the day that William Hamm was kidnapped, the Smiths of 204 Vernon ordered a case of Blatz beer to celebrate.[84]

Right away, neighbors noticed that the Smiths were different from most folks on Vernon. When a repairman arrived to fix the MacLarens's gas stove, Harmon refused to let him in until a neighbor intervened. And when a local teenager, John Miller of 211 Vernon, mowed the gang's lawn and trimmed the hedges, they paid him a very conspicuous three dollars—six times the going rate of fifty cents. Iceman Frank Lachowitzer complained that the drawn blinds made it too dark to find the ice box. One of the Smiths grudgingly raised the shade a little but put it down again right away, Lachowitzer recalled.[85]

On June 9 bank robber Frank Nash, accompanied by his wife, Frances, and her young daughter, Danella, drove to St. Paul and stayed overnight at 204 Vernon. During this last week of his life, Nash had dinner at the Hollyhocks Club and enjoyed a final meeting with Alvin Karpis and the Barker boys at the Green Lantern. Nash had intended to spend the night at Harry Sawyer's home, but when Barker and Harmon invited him to spend the night and drink some beer at 204 Vernon, Nash altered his plans.[86]

The girlfriends of the Barker-Karpis gang tried to maintain a semblance of normal family life, but they were always poised on the edge of exposure. Neighbor Helen Fullerton told the FBI that every time a car stopped or a door slammed, the woman at 204 Vernon Street looked out.[87]

Landlady Gertrude MacLaren returned one day for a surprise visit. "My mother was the bane of the existence of those gun molls," said her daughter, Frances MacLaren Paul. "She'd have Dad drive her to the 204 Vernon house, and knock on the door, saying she'd forgotten some bric-a-brac. She had no idea she was walking into a bee's nest." Paula Harmon remembered the shock of having Mrs. MacLaren walk in while Karpis had his gun lying on a chair; he quickly dropped a newspaper over it.[88]

But the gang's stay on Vernon Street was soon to end. Herbert Charles, head of the Hamm brewery's legal department, had brought the $100,000 ransom to the brewery's vaults. On June 17, Dunn drove along Highway 61, saw a car signal him with five flashes of its headlights near Pine City, and dropped the briefcase. In the car to pick up the money were Fred Barker, Fred Goetz, and Charlie Fitzgerald.[89]

In his memoirs, Karpis recalled the day that they returned to the Bensonville hideout with the $100,000 ransom. "You better round up some

Hamm's beer," Goetz told Karpis. "I got a feeling that it'll be my favorite brand for a long time to come."[90]

Hamm was outfitted in new clothes, fed a final ham sandwich, and released at daybreak on June 19 near Wyoming, Minnesota, about fifty miles north of St. Paul, in a vain attempt to convince officials that Hamm had never been taken out of Minnesota.[91]

After Hamm was freed, Fitzgerald and Fred Barker brought the ransom money to 204 Vernon and prepared to drive to Chicago to launder it. Onlookers watched as a Buick drove up to 204 Vernon and five men rushed into the house, one of them carrying a suitcase. Quipped one neighbor: "There goes the ransom money."[92]

The gang's timing was prudent, for a *St. Paul Dispatch–Pioneer Press* editor had informed police chief Tom Dahill and the FBI that a source was reporting strange activity at 204 Vernon. The tipster, according to FBI records, was Charles Bradley, a young man who was keeping company that summer with the niece of the Lester Quick family, then living at 210 Vernon. Intrigued by his girlfriend's stories about suspicious neighbors, Charles spoke to her aunt. Three men and a woman at 204 Vernon were "coming and going at all hours of the night," said the aunt, and she suspected that the small bags they carried with them contained guns. When a roadster drove up to 204 Vernon and a six-foot-tall man rushed out carrying suitcases, "it did enter her mind," the FBI noted, "that these grips might have contained the ransom money."[93]

Alerted to the commotion at 204 Vernon, Chief Dahill drove to police headquarters and asked the head of his kidnap squad, Tom Brown, to investigate the rumors about the occupants. Promising Dahill that he would take care of the situation, Brown left, returning half an hour later. Detective Brown assured Chief Dahill, straight-faced, that "the bunch at 204 Vernon Avenue have nothing to do with the Hamm case." Meanwhile, with all the lights blazing in the house, the Smith family ran upstairs and downstairs, frantically carrying suitcases out to two automobiles. By 2:00 A.M. on June 20, most traces of the gang had vanished.[94]

The FBI learned two weeks afterward "that Tom Brown, member of the St. Paul Police Department, Kidnap Squad, had tipped off the occupants at 204 Vernon Avenue to leave."[95]

Years later, the FBI found out what had really happened. According to Byron Bolton's confession, Tom Brown had called Jack Peifer and told him that the police were suspicious about the house. Peifer sped to 204 Vernon and took Barker and Fitzgerald to the Bald Eagle Lake cottage, then returned to the Vernon Street hideout to strip it of incriminating evidence.[96]

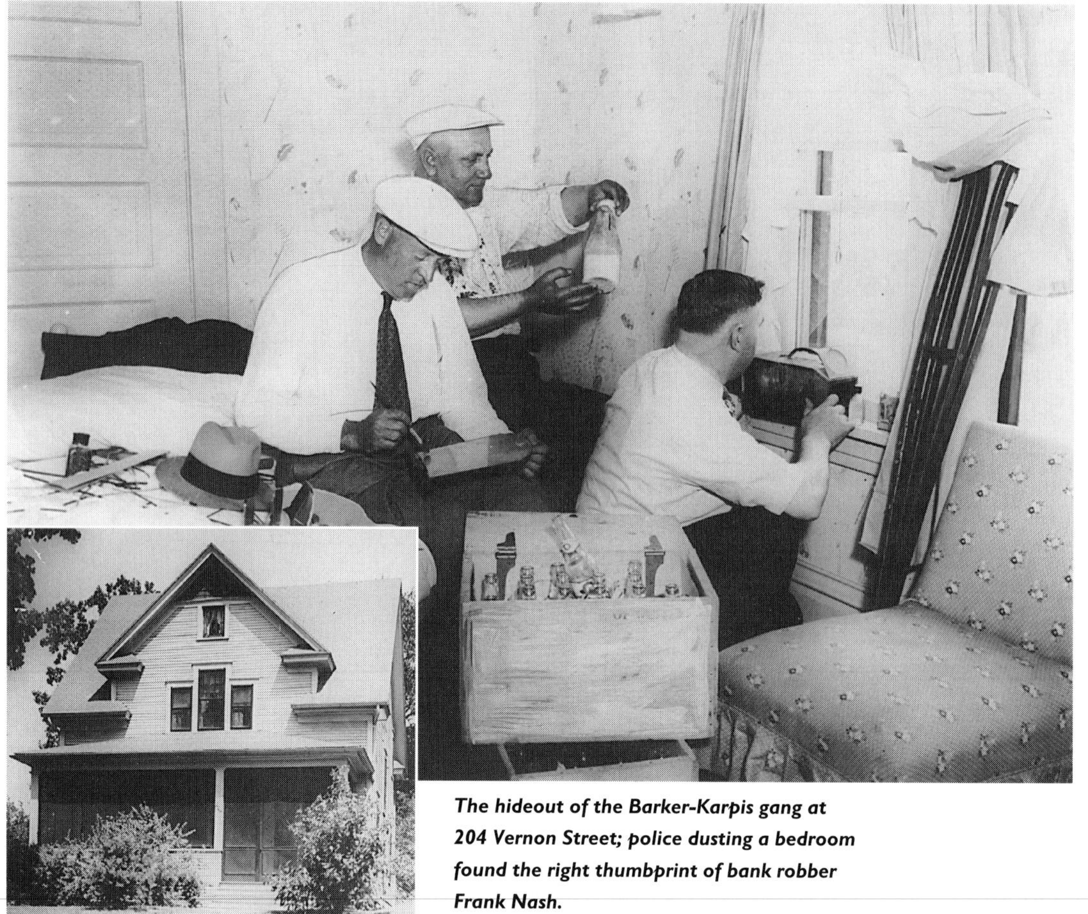

The hideout of the Barker-Karpis gang at 204 Vernon Street; police dusting a bedroom found the right thumbprint of bank robber Frank Nash.

Goaded by the *Pioneer Press* and the *Dispatch,* the police finally descended on the now-empty house, dusting it for fingerprints. True to the protocols of the O'Connor system, though, they did not manage to send the prints to FBI laboratories until eight months had passed.[97]

When the FBI finally searched the house on June 24, all they found was a slip of paper with a grocery list and Peifer's telephone number at the Hollyhocks Club.[98]

The debacle at 204 Vernon convinced the FBI special agent in charge, Werner Hanni, that efforts to apprehend the kidnappers had been thwarted by an inside source. He concluded that he was being betrayed by a police official who was "a close friend and associate of Leon Gleckman, alleged king of the underworld," and who had been tipping off gangsters for years."[99] As the FBI began to track down and arrest the Barker-Karpis gang's girlfriends and accomplices, a growing body of evidence supported Hanni's suspicions that a policeman at the highest level of command had been leaking law enforcement information to the underworld. The disloyal officer was the head of the St. Paul Police kidnap squad, detective Thomas Archibald Brown, the very man entrusted with protecting citizens from kidnappers.

39 'Big Tom' Brown's Kidnap Squad

Police Officer Tom Brown's Home
759 East Maryland Avenue, St. Paul

While he was waiting to divide the Hamm ransom, racketeer Jack Peifer invited the wife of mobster Gus Winkler to visit his casino. When Winkler's wife, Georgette, expressed concern over security, Peifer promised her: "You don't have to be afraid of that. *We've got police protection in St. Paul.*"[100]

That protection was personified by Thomas "Big Tom" Brown, a hulking 280-pound, 6-foot, 3-inch detective, who was forty-four when William Hamm was kidnapped in 1933. Brown lived with his wife, Mary, and five children in a two-story white-stucco home at 759 Maryland Avenue. A former Great Northern Railroad conductor, the West Virginia–born Brown had moved to St. Paul in 1910, joined the police as a traffic patrolman in 1914, rose to detective in 1919, and then served as chief of police from June 1930 to June 1932.[101]

"I'll never forget when my father was nominated to be police chief," said Brown's daughter Vera Peters. "He came home to tell my mother that he was going to get three hundred dollars a month—which was a big sum in those days. . . . My father was the first police chief in the new police station, [so] he took us to the station to have our photos taken like they did with criminals."[102]

Publicly, Chief Brown portrayed himself as a fearless gangbuster. In the summer of 1930, for instance, Brown declared war on Chicago gangsters who were exploring Minnesota's liquor and slot machine rackets: "St. Paul will not tolerate any gangsters. . . . This is an open statement. There is nothing concealed. To all gangsters who may be in St. Paul, get out and stay out."[103]

But Brown's ascent to the chief's office concealed a great deal. An informant, saloon keeper Frank Reilly, told the FBI about "a number of people who had contributed large sums to Brown's campaign," including, Reilly believed, a Dillinger machine gunner, Homer Van Meter, who donated $1,000. "It was understood that after he was appointed Chief of Police they were to be allotted certain rackets in St. Paul," the FBI reported. "During Brown's term it was impossible to run anything without paying off, and according to Reilly, it got to such a point where the various candy companies complained that they were not allowed even to install their merchandise boards in various stores without paying protection."[104]

At home, Brown was a fastidious man. A Baptist whose children were brought up Catholic by his wife, he was a strict disciplinarian. "We knew what was right and wrong in my family," said Peters. "When my brother Jim was engaged to be married, he still had to be home by eleven!" When Brown's daughters visited the state fair, using their father's complimentary tickets, they were free to roam the fairgrounds but forbidden to go to the midway, which was considered sleazy. "So we went to the midway to see the Fat Lady," Peters said. "When we came out of the Fat Lady's booth, there he was—my father, with police officer [Frank] Cullen. I never had such a ride home. Oh, he put us in his squad car. Oh, was he angry!"

Thomas Brown, chief of the St. Paul police, who fed police secrets to gangsters

The family heard stories of Tom Brown's generosity to down-on-their-luck criminals. One holiday—"it was either Thanksgiving or Christmas," Peters said—Brown came home late and told his family that he had let all the prisoners go free so they could be with their families for the night. Apart from tales like this, Brown was close-lipped about his police work. "Everything was kept from us kids," Peters said. "Dad was a private person . . . of the old German feeling that kids should be seen and not heard."[105]

Hints of Brown's intimacy with the St. Paul underworld surfaced early. In 1923, St. Paul police chief Frank Sommers was forced to resign in a vice scandal. The furor was sparked when then-detective Tom Brown, head of the "purity squad," raided a series of gambling spots and found no evidence of gambling. "Brown," snarled Mayor Arthur E. Nelson, "it's a remarkable thing that the only ones who look for gambling joints, moonshine parlors and disorderly houses and can't find them are certain St. Paul detectives."[106]

Three years later Brown was suspended for 30 days when a federal judge ordered that he be removed to Ohio to face federal charges that he had participated in the massive Cleveland liquor syndicate conspiracy involving bootlegger Leon Gleckman and the Gleeman brothers. The FBI concluded in 1932 that Brown was "known to be intimately associated with Leon Gleckman and to have been controlled by Leon Gleckman while in the St. Paul Police Department."[107]

When Brown's attorneys protested, District Court Judge John Sanborn noted that in his testimony, Brown (who had headed the purity squad from June 1922 to December 1923) swore that he had no idea what business Leon Gleckman was engaged in. The judge said he did not believe the vice chief's naiveté about the city's leading bootlegger and refused to intercede for Brown. Ultimately, the indictments against Brown were dismissed.[108]

In November 1930, Chief Brown—whose vice squad had seized more than 100 slot machines in five months—was called before a Ramsey County grand jury for questioning about his knowledge of a police protection racket involving illegal slot machines. Harold Heller, a slot machine hijacker, admitted that he had been told to steal some slot machines and "lay off" those with police protection. The Ramsey County attorney expressed concern that "profits from racketeering in St. Paul amount to about $1,000 a day and . . . the temptation for officials is considerable." Once again, no charges were filed against Brown.[109]

Previous police chiefs, notably John J. O'Connor and Frank Sommers, had looked the other way when criminals sought haven in St. Paul. According to testimony gathered by the FBI, Brown took the O'Connor system to new lows, actively supporting the criminal activities of gangsters Leon Gleckman, Harry Sawyer, and Jack Peifer.

Policeman Fred Raasch told the FBI that Brown asked him to commit perjury during the Gleeman brothers' trial for the murder of liquor hijacker Burt Stevens. "Brown asked me to testify that at the time that Stevens was shot, I was talking with the two Gleemans on the West Side at Tubby's place. I told him I would not do it, that I was home in bed at the time and that several witnesses had testified to seeing the Gleemans on St. Peter Street at the time of the murder, and I asked him why he didn't do it himself." Brown was angry at Raasch's refusal and threatened, "I'll get even with you." Raasch believed that when Brown became chief in 1930, he had Raasch demoted to squad car duty in retribution.[110]

Chief Brown himself was demoted to detective in the wake of the Barker-Karpis gang's 1932 escape from West St. Paul. Then, as head of the kidnap squad, Tom Brown led a heavily armed unit to Lake Minnetonka, Minnesota, in mid-June 1933 on a diversionary hunt for the Hamm kidnappers. At the time he knew the actual culprits were living in St. Paul and near White Bear.[111]

Several clues led the FBI to question Brown's integrity as they probed the Barker-Karpis gang. Chief Tom Dahill testified that when he was investigating the Hamm kidnapping, Brown had objected to giving the FBI any information on the grounds that "the government only wanted information and did not give anything in return, and that when the case did break the Federal Agents would get all the glory." During the Bremer kidnapping case in 1934, police officers were asked to supply their fingerprints so that the FBI could eliminate their prints from the ransom notes and identify the prints of the kidnappers. Curiously, Brown was the only one who refused.[112]

Even more revealing was the fact that throughout the Hamm and Bremer kidnappings the Barker-Karpis gang appeared to anticipate every move made by the police. At times, the kidnappers seemed to be playing bizarre games with the FBI, taunting them with information to which only a top police official like Brown had access. Dahill revealed to Brown his secret plan to hide a shotgun-wielding policeman in the truck that would deliver the Hamm ransom. A note from the gang the next day changed the ransom delivery instructions to prevent the involvement of a hidden policeman. When FBI agents displayed four Browning rifles to Dahill and Brown, Chief Dahill caressed the guns, murmuring of the Hamm kidnappers (as an agent later recorded it), "I would like to see one of those ______ now." The next Hamm ransom note teased Dahill: if he was so anxious to meet them, it said, he should come out with the "dough."[113]

During the Hamm kidnapping, "I had a constant feeling of uncertainty and fear of double crossing," FBI special agent in charge Werner Hanni told J. Edgar Hoover, mentioning what appeared to be shadowy friendships between certain police officers and underworld leaders. During the Bremer kidnapping, FBI assistant director Harold Nathan expressed his astonishment at the profusion of police leaks in St. Paul. Nathan noted that in January 1934 four of the Bremer ransom letters were turned over to the chief of police and the FBI and sent by airplane to Washington for laboratory analysis of fingerprints. Dahill told only two people, chief of detectives Charles Tierney and kidnap squad head Tom Brown, about the unusual manner in which the ransom communications had been delivered. Half an hour later, an extra edition of the *St. Paul Daily News* reported that a bottle thrown through the glass door of the vestibule of the house of Dr. R. T. Nippert a few days before contained two of the ransom notes. How could such a breach of secrecy have occurred, asked Nathan? Dahill replied that "there is only one man responsible and he knew it; that it was Tom Brown."[114]

When the Barker-Karpis gang met at Fred Barker's cottage in Illinois to split up the Hamm ransom, one of them asked outright about Tom Brown's share. "Who is Brown?" asked Byron Bolton, who later told the story to the FBI. Brown was the police officer who had given Jack Peifer information for the kidnappers, said one of the gang. Bolton gave a rough accounting for the division of the Hamm ransom money, including $25,000 to Tom Brown; $10,000 to Jack Peifer; $7,800 each to Fred Goetz, Alvin Karpis, Fred Barker, Doc Barker, Byron Bolton, and Charlie Fitzgerald; $2,500 to either Robert "Frisco Dutch" Steinhart or Tommy Banks; and $2,500 to bank robber Jack Davenport. Approximately $1,500 was earmarked for expenses (from gasoline to food), and $7,500 was spent to launder the ransom money in Reno.[115]

Gradually, a parade of FBI informants attested to Tom Brown's involvement in the Hamm kidnapping. Gladys Sawyer reported to the FBI that she overheard a conversation between her husband, Harry, and Jack Peifer, in

To the best of my recollection the division of the ransom money collected in this kidnaping was made in the following manner:

TOM BROWN	$25,000.00
JACK PFEIFFER	10,000.00
JACK DAVENPORT	2,500.00
TOM BANKS or "FRISCO DUTCH"	2,500.00
FRED GOETZ	7,800.00
ALVIN KARPIS	7,800.00
FRED BARKER	7,800.00
DOC BARKER	7,800.00
CHARLES FITZGERALD	7,800.00
BRYAN BOLTON	7,800.00
BARTHOLOMEW	650.00
VOLNEY DAVIS	700.00
HERBERT FARMER	2,500.00
EXPENSES	1,500.00
Cost of exchanging money in Reno, Nevada -	7,500.00

Kidnap conspirator Byron Bolton provided the FBI with this accounting of the split of the Hamm ransom between gang members and policeman Tom Brown.

which Peifer said that he and Brown split $36,000 in the Hamm case. She named Brown, James Crumley, and William McMullen as the sources of police information telephoned to Harry Sawyer and Jack Peifer who delivered it to "interested parties," and said that the tip-off at the Vernon Street house traveled this route.[116]

In 1935 the FBI learned from Barker-Karpis gang girlfriend Edna Murray, imprisoned in Missouri State Penitentiary, that while Bremer was being held by the gang, "Tom Brown was keeping the gang informed of the activities of the Bureau." In fact, the FBI discovered Brown brought to Harry Sawyer police pictures of Doc Barker and several other members of the gang suspected by the FBI. Even more startling was Murray's revelation that when imprisoned gang member Larry DeVol was to be transferred to testify as a witness at a bank robbery trial, Brown notified Karpis and "some of the other boys in Chicago" of the route that DeVol was to take from the Minnesota state prison to Minneapolis, so that they could make arrangements to release him. (The plans were changed, and DeVol remained in prison.)[117]

Next, the FBI learned from a convicted bank robber in the Wisconsin state prison that DeVol claimed he paid $100 each week to Harry Sawyer and that Sawyer then passed the bribe money to Brown and other police officers. DeVol said that 10 percent of the Barker-Karpis gang's robbery money was turned over to Brown for protection.[118]

ELECT
THOMAS A.
BROWN
SHERIFF
Prepared and issued for Thomas A. Brown, 759 E. Maryland St., by Vincent C. Jenny, 1594 Wellesley Ave., Secretary Brown-for-Sheriff Volunteer Committee.

Tom Brown's political campaign card

Finally, government informant Beth Green told the FBI that Dillinger gang members had contributed $1,500, "delivered in cash personally by Eddie Green to Tom Filben," to Tom Brown's campaign for sheriff.[119]

Alvin Karpis was amused by the FBI's shock at Brown's betrayal. "If you are a thief and are fortunate enough to find a copper that is also a thief, you'd be a chump if you didn't get together with him," Karpis told FBI agents in 1936, to which an FBI agent retorted: "Particularly if the thieving copper is head of the kidnap squad and you are in the snatch racket." Karpis, laughing, agreed.[120]

Chief Dahill was tormented by the discovery that his kidnap squad head had leaked the police department's secrets to the underworld. He attended the Bremer kidnapping trial in 1936 to see if testimony would prove Brown's involvement with the gangsters. An FBI memo noted in the same year that "Tom Dahill and Tom Brown are and have been for the past two years, at least, bitter enemies."[121]

Dahill's belief that Brown acted in part out of a desire to embarrass the chief became "an obsession with Dahill, who has spent much of his time in an endeavor to procure information from police officers whom he believes he can trust, which would lead to the prosecution of Brown," reported the FBI. "Neither Dahill nor anyone else has been able to furnish any concrete evidence of these rumors."[122]

With Brown exposed and isolated, the Barker-Karpis gang was forced to use other contacts to prevent Hamm from testifying against them. About a month after the kidnapping, William Hamm Jr. was invited to play golf with his cousin Herbert G. Benz, a liquor and real estate executive.

Peifer told the FBI that Benz's Jackson Investment Company held the mortgage for the Hollyhocks Club, where the Hamm kidnapping had been planned. The Ramsey County auditor confirmed that during the early 1930s Benz was paying taxes on the Hollyhocks, at its height as a gambling casino and underworld hangout, and rented the club out to Jack Peifer. Benz told the FBI that he had frequented the underworld's Plantation nightclub, where he met Peifer. According to the FBI, Benz was "on friendly terms with practically every underworld character in the Twin Cities." Now Benz told William Hamm that Jack Peifer and "the boys" had a message for him: Hamm should be careful about identifying Peifer as part of the Barker-Karpis kidnap gang or "harm might come to him."[123]

After Hamm was released, the Hamm Brewing Company became an informal loan institution for the periphery of the underworld. Gambling figure Ben Harris of the Plantation and Boulevards of Paris nightclubs told the FBI that in 1936 he borrowed $2,000 from the Hamm company through William Dunn, to be paid back in monthly installments.[124]

Dunn told the FBI that after Hamm's kidnapping, a high-ranking police officer had "borrowed $500 from the brewery on three separate occasions. . . . These loans have always been approved by William Hamm, Jr." The police officer was none other than Thomas A. Brown.[125]

The Hamm ransom money was flown to Reno and exchanged for laundered cash, although a conflicting account by Charlie Fitzgerald claimed that the Reno launderers shunned the money because of government interest in the case, and that the gang had to launder the money in Chicago through a mobster for a 10 percent handling fee. In any case, the "clean" money was split up in the bedroom of the Barkers's cottage in Illinois. "Fred Barker took the money out of the briefcase, put it on the bed, and started handing out $100 and $500 bills to each of us," recalled Bolton.[126]

Fitzgerald said that Verne Miller and two other gangsters suspected of involvement in the Kansas City Massacre each received $2,500 of the Hamm ransom as a courtesy to defray their legal costs. To celebrate, on July 4 the Barker-Karpis gang had a fireworks display on the lawn of their cottage.[127]

As late as 1940, the FBI was still hunting for the William Hamm ransom —based on rumors that a gangster had drawn maps showing where it was buried. None of the ransom money has ever been recovered.[128]

40 'Cool and Reckless, Not Giving a Dam[n] Who They Shot'

The South St. Paul Post Office Robbery
236 North Concord Street, South St. Paul

No criminal act illustrated how far the O'Connor system had eroded better than the August 30, 1933, payroll robbery at the South St. Paul Post

Office. In less than ten minutes, bullets from the Barker-Karpis gang's machine guns crashed through businesses in a three-block area, a $33,000 payroll was stolen, one policeman was severely wounded, and another police officer lay dead.

According to Fred Barker's girlfriend Paula Harmon, members of the Barker-Karpis gang returned to the Twin Cities in August 1933 after moving restlessly between Chicago and Long Lake, Illinois, to distribute the Hamm ransom money. Charlie Fitzgerald said his partners in the South St. Paul payroll robbery included Alvin Karpis, Fred Barker, and Chicago gunmen Byron Bolton and Fred Goetz. Karpis drove the heavily armored car with Fred Barker beside him in the front seat, reading the getaway map. Bolton was assigned the role of machine gunner if any policemen intruded during the robbery.[129]

The gang was waiting when a Great Western Railroad train brought the money bags from the Federal Reserve Bank of Minneapolis to South St. Paul. Two policemen were escorting the Swift and Company payroll that day: John Yeaman, father of three; and Leo Pavlak, father of two, who had joined the force in April.[130]

Two of the gangsters waited for the payroll delivery at "Bulldog Mike" Pappas's Depot Cafe on North Concord Street, drinking beer and watching from the window. "Freddie Barker with a machine gun wrapped in a newspaper carrying an account of the William Hamm kidnapping, stood in a beer parlor on the corner north of the post office," Dakota County attorney Harold Stassen told reporters.[131]

Two payroll carriers walked down the front steps of the South St. Paul Post Office at 9:45 A.M., and the robbery commenced. The gang drove up in a black sedan and unloaded Doc Barker, carrying a sawed-off shotgun, just south of the post office entrance. Shouting "Stick 'em up," Barker disarmed Pavlak, forced him to lift his hands above his head, and then shot him in the head, screaming "You dirty rat, son of a bitch!"[132]

"Fred shot Officer Yeaman as he sat in his squad car near the post office," Stassen said. "Doc Barker killed Officer Pavlak without any warning and then the signal man whipped out two .45 caliber pistols from his back pockets and started firing, too."[133]

Yeaman, who had been sitting quietly in his car in the alley between the post office and the Great Western Railway depot, was seriously injured. One bullet plunged through the bill of his cap, just above his right eyebrow. "Dad used to tell me that if that guy had just held his machine gun down, it would have taken Dad's head right off," recalled Jack Yeaman, the officer's son. "The gangsters opened up on my dad; they wanted to put him out of action first, because he had the machine gun."[134]

Weather Forecast

FAIR, SLIGHTLY WARMER TO-NIGHT; THURSDAY FAIR AND WARMER IN EAST AND SOUTH

SOUTH ST. PAUL DAILY REPORTER

The Only Daily Newspaper Published in Dakota County

TODAY'S CHUCKLE. "Your boy friend talks too much. He rattles on like a flivver. I'm afraid he's a flat tire." "I know Pa, but his clutch is grand."—Exchange.

VOL. XXXXIII. NO. 128. HOME EDITION SOUTH ST. PAUL, MINNESOTA, WEDNESDAY, AUGUST 30, 1933. SINGLE COPIES 3 CENTS — BY MAIL 5 CENTS BACK NUMBERS (except current month) 10 CENTS

Officer Slain, Another Wounded, In $30,000 Robbery Here Today

BANDITS KILL OFFICER PAVLIK, RIDDLE YEAMAN WITH BULLETS AND FLEE

A postmortem was conducted at 2 p. m. at the Meeker Funeral chapel, Dr. Tom Lowe and Dr. H .R. Tregilgas, performed the postmortem examination.

Blazing their way with death-dealing gunfire in the heart of South St. Paul's main district on Concord street at an hour in mid-forenoon today when the street was jammed with traffic, six bandits in a big black sedan escaped with $30,000 in cash taken from bank messengers in front of the postoffice building, leaving Officer Leo Pavlik of the South St. Paul police force dead on the sidewalk where they had shot him down and Officer John Yeaman seriously wounded in his car in the driveway between the postoffice and the Great Western depot. The bandits who apparently had been awaiting the arrival of the money on the train from St. Paul began firing as the bank messengers, Joe Hamilton and Herbert Cheyne, were intercepted and forced to deposit money bags on the postoffice steps and shot Officer Pavlik down after he had been surprised and forced to raise his hands. He sank as the withering fire of a sub-machine gun swept the front of the postoffice building. Officer Yeaman was also a target for the gunmen in their first fusillade and was shot while sitting in his car in the driveway between the postoffice and the depot. He was seriously wounded and later was taken to the West Side General hospital in St. Paul.

Hamilton and Cheyne set their bags of silver on the postoffice steps while Cheyne went into the postoffice to get the registered package of currency. As he came out he was ordered to place the package on the steps. The bandits slew Pavlik as Hamilton and Cheyne ducked under a truck. One of the bandits was shot in the back and crumpled up beside Pavlik's pros-

LATE NEWS BULLETINS

(By United Press)

St. Louis, Aug. 30.—A climbing death toll today faced baffled medical men, organized here in a determined fight against the rapidly spreading epidemic of encephalitis, or sleeping sickness. An additional death today—the 46th within a month—sent the ratio of fatalities among encephalitis victims here to one to six, or 14.2 per cent. Alarmed, leaders in the medical fraternity divided into many fields of research to seek some clue of the source of the epidemic.

Pleasantville, Ia., Aug. 30.—His feet seared by a hot poker used to torture him, Miles Galvin, farmer, told today how he and his wife were bound and injured by bandits who attempted to rob them. Galvin, who has been sick in bed for Two bandits forced their way past two weeks, retired early last night. Mrs. Galvin a few minutes later and entered his bedroom, demanding to know where his money was hidden.

Devils Lake, N. D., Aug. 30.—County authorities today sought the driver of an automobile believed to have struck and killed Adam Westbrook, elderly Columbus, Neb., harvest hand Sunday night. Westbrook was found on a little used road behind a garage. He was taken to a hospital where he died shortly after midnight. Police investigating the case said a witness had seen an automobile stop at the spot where Westbrook was found. He said that after its driver had investigated he reentered the automobile and drove away.

Kenosha, Wis., Aug. 30.—Mrs. Pearl Anderson, 38, was shot and killed by her husband, Otto, 45, as she lay in bed today with her three-year-old son beside her. Anderson then rushed into another

Victims of South St. Paul Bandit Raid and Witnesses at Scene of Shooting Today

The two South St. Paul policemen who were shot, one fatally, the two bank messengers who were forced to surrender their money bags, and a woman who sat in a truck cab in the thick of the gun fire in today's holdup are pictured herewith. Above, from left to right, are Patrolman John Yeaman, who was wounded, Mrs. Albin Metzger, Hancock, Minn., who sat in the cab of her husband's truck a few feet from the slaying, and Patrolman Leo Pavlik, who was killed. Below are the two bank messengers, Hery Cheyne, left, and Joe Hamilton, right.

(Picture Courtesy of St. Paul Daily News.)

ECHOES OF SOUTH ST. PAUL'S INVASION BY GANGSTERS

George Kreuger, proprietor of a restaurant across the street from the scene of the killing, was a target for one of the machine gun men, and just as he disappeared

NATURAL GAS FOR PLANTS IN CITY POSSIBLE

Packing plants here are reported

PATROLMAN YEAMAN MAY LOSE WOUNDED EYE BUT CONDITION IS GOOD

Officer John Yeaman, who was shot in the head by gangsters here today while in the squad car just north of the postoffice guarding the bank messengers and who was taken to the West Side General hospital may lose his right eye but has a fighting chance to live, it was said this afternoon. Several machine gun slugs were in his head, neck and shoulder and about 25 buckshot were found in his body. He was dragged from his car and disarmed and left riddled with bullets by two bandits who had been lying in wait in the Depot cafe. Despite his wounds his condition late this afternoon was reported as "good" considering the serious nature of his wounds. Barring complications, he was given a fighting chance to recover.

L. J. Ouradnik of Beron, Minn., who has been in South St. Paul several weeks, was at the Grand Concord corner in front of the Exchange building when the shooting started. He hurried and arrived as the bandit car pulled away, but he said he failed to get the number. He was one of the first to approach the fallen policeman Pavlik.

Francis McCormick, son of a former police chief of South St. Paul, was on the opposite side of the street north of the postoffice. He heard the shooting but was too far away to see exactly what was going on.

Truman P. Alcorn, former chief of police, was in the office and warehouse of the Dakota County Beverage company, 231 North Concord street, when a shot ripped through the window over his head and passed Allan Burt's head by inches. Burt was seated at his desk in the office. Others in the office included George Albrecht, former policeman, and his son. They flopped onto the floor or ran into the back room.

Another bullet crashed through the upper light of the Minneapolis shoe store south of the Beverage company place but did no great damage. Al. Robinson's garage, 100 feet farther along was struck by a bullet and Joe Althoff, trucker, who was talking to a friend three blocks south, heard bullets passing over his head. He jumped into his car and came to the scene.

John A. Waldhauser, Reporter employe, was in front of the postoffice when the gunplay started. He saw the big bandit who slew Pavlik draw two pistols. He also saw him swing his leg in a movement that looked like a signal

Newspaper headline after the South St. Paul robbery in August 1933

The choreography was evidence of the gang's careful planning. "The bandits undoubtedly had been watching delivery of that payroll every Wednesday for several weeks," said Melvin Passolt, BCA chief. "They had every movement timed perfectly and the whole thing was over so quickly that many bystanders hardly realized what was happening."[135]

It was, concluded Karpis, "a good day's work, even if it did cost one wounded crook [Charlie Fitzgerald had been shot in the leg] and, as we found out from the papers, one wounded and one dead cop."[136]

"The bandits put on a Jessie James exhibition by shooting up and down Concord St., shooting about a dozen shots into the Postal Building and across the street," noted a BCA report on the robbery. "These bandits used a Thompson machine gun and a sawed off shot gun with which they did their shooting, and it is a miracle that no one else was shot and wounded. They appeared to be cool and reckless, not giving a dam[n] who they shot."[137]

The robbery was so bloody that even Dillinger gang member Eddie Green condemned the assault. An FBI report noted that Green told his wife "how crazy the whole plan was, as they had apparently, without necessity, shot down individuals during the course of that robbery."[138]

South St. Paul Post Office, site of a 1933 stockyards payroll robbery; the Thompson submachine gun taken during the robbery and found in Doc Barker's Chicago apartment

There were rumors that the payroll robbery was an "inside job." James Crumley, former St. Paul inspector of detectives, told the FBI that "Truman Alcorn, former Chief of Police of South St. Paul, is very close to Tom Brown and . . . there is no question but Brown and Alcorn were in on the payroll robbery in South St. Paul."[139]

County attorney Stassen also believed that Alcorn—who had been just a few dozen yards down the street at the time of the robbery—was involved in the crime. "Dad was never bitter about being shot, because you go into police work with the idea that it could happen to you," said Jack Yeaman. But for years, the father and son investigated rumors that police knew in advance that a gang was in town to "make a payroll."[140]

When Doc Barker's Chicago apartment was raided in January 1935, the Thompson submachine gun taken from John Yeaman during the robbery was found. The gun was given to Stassen and then passed along to the South St. Paul police, who store it in the chief's office at police headquarters today.[141]

Robert Pavlak, who became a police officer himself, was nine years old when his father was murdered. Of the day of his father's death, Pavlak said, "I ran home. . . . That's all I remember. My mother was dying of cancer at the time—we had so much grief then." Pavlak knew that his father faced danger, and not just from the underworld. "There was so much criminality then, both within and without the department, that Lieutenant Jeff Dittrich used to tell me, 'You never went to take the garbage out at night without having a gun in your hand.'"[142]

In August 1993, the South St. Paul Police Department paid tribute, awarding the family Pavlak's posthumous Medal of Honor. A wreath was laid at the national law enforcement memorial in Washington, D. C., alongside the name of Leo Pavlak—the only South St. Paul policeman to be murdered while on duty.

Yeaman, despite having twenty-five bullet fragments lodged in his body, survived. When he died in 1971, a number of these fragments were still in his shoulder and neck.[143]

No one was ever charged with the robbery, or with shooting Yeaman and Pavlak. But within three years every outlaw who participated in the South St. Paul robbery was either dead or in federal prison.

7

VERNE MILLER'S KANSAS CITY MASSACRE

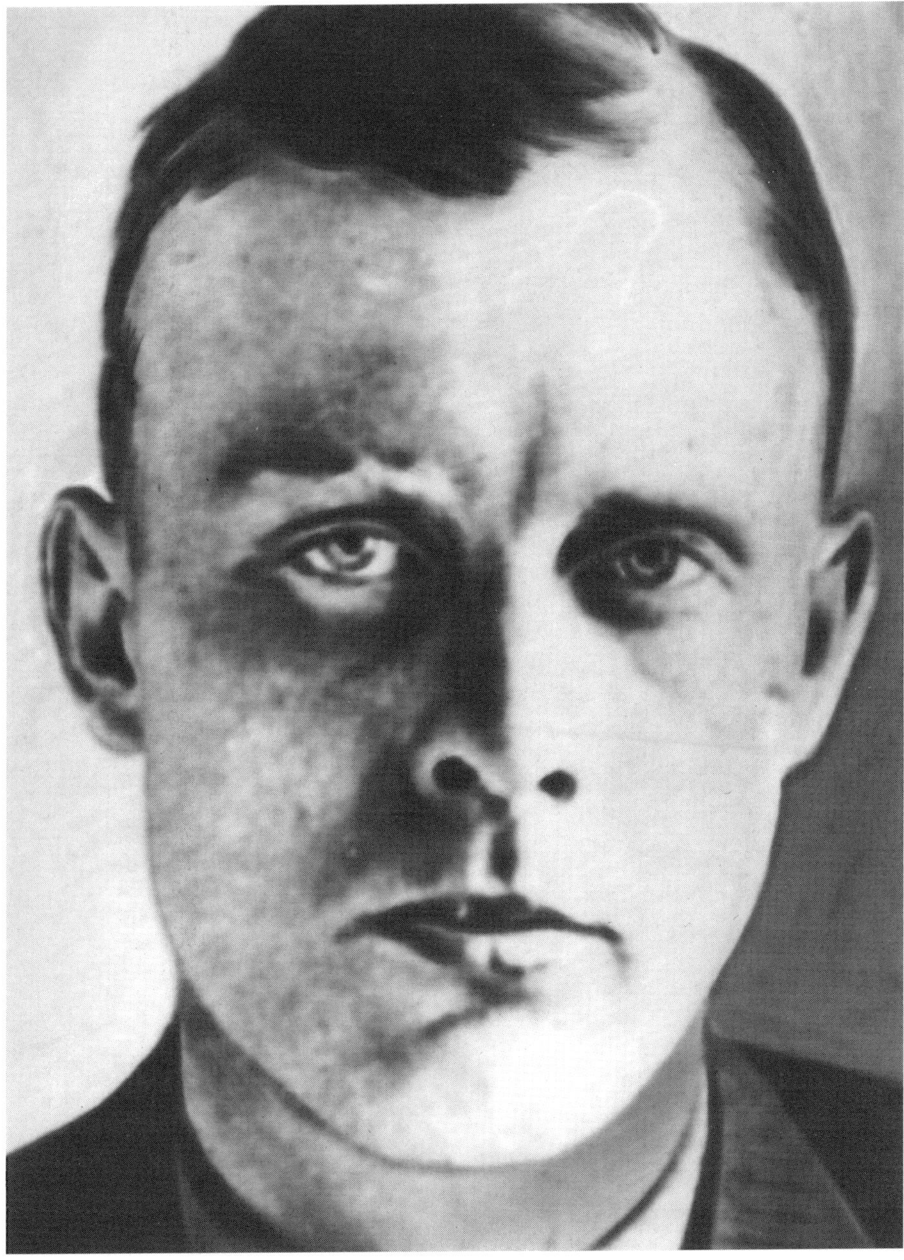

Verne Miller fishing with his girlfriend, Vivian Mathis, near Brainerd, Minnesota; Miller's FBI mug shot

A Gangster's Brainerd Hideaway

6111 Legionville Road, near Brainerd

Vivian Mathis, the daughter of a Brainerd, Minnesota, dairy farmer, was in love with a former South Dakota sheriff—a World War I veteran, boxer, and parachute jumper named Vernon C. Miller.[1]

Mathis told her family that she had been working a carnival concession in the Twin Cities when a belligerent customer refused to leave her booth. The customer hit her, knocking Mathis to the ground, and a stranger—Miller—rushed to her aid. His gallantry led to a friendship, then blossomed into a four-year romance.[2]

"Verne Miller first came to our farm in 1929," recalled Janet Gibson, Mathis's sister-in-law. "He was a very warm person. . . . [He] would take the kids shopping in Brainerd and to the Brainerd county fair." A handsome man of thirty-three, Miller had medium-blond hair and a trim 145-pound, 5-foot, 7-inch physique. His gray eyes had a slightly melancholy expression.[3]

Everything the former sheriff told the Mathis family was technically true. What the family could not know was the darker side of Miller's résumé. Miller—alias Vincent C. Moore—was also a convicted embezzler, bootlegger, and bank robber. His botched attempt to free his friend Frank Nash from FBI custody in June 1933 would result in what newspapers dubbed the Kansas City Massacre, a gangland killing that made Miller the most wanted man in America—by both the FBI and the underworld. But back in 1929, courting Mathis, Miller seemed to be an unlikely candidate to commit a bloodbath. While Fred Barker and other gang members drifted from city to city, restlessly committing petty crimes, Verne Miller relaxed between bank robberies with Vi's family at the Gibson dairy farm, eight miles from Brainerd on Legionville Road, at the south end of North Long Lake. (Today the farm—about three miles from Highway 25—is the Boy Scout's Legionville Camp.)[4]

Miller was born to Scotch-Irish parents in 1896 in Kimball, South Dakota. He left school in the fourth grade, became an auto mechanic, and married his first sweetheart, Mildred, in 1917. He served in the 164th Infantry in France in World War I, distinguishing himself with his machine-gun technique. (FBI special agent Melvin Purvis later claimed that Miller was so expert with a machine gun, he could shoot his initials into the gas tanks of fleeing bootleggers.)[5]

Basking in his wartime glory, Miller was elected policeman in 1920. The people of Huron, South Dakota, made him Beadle County sheriff in 1921 and, in the words of a state's attorney, Miller "made a fine record as a peace officer." But when he was caught embezzling nearly $2,600 in county funds, the disgraced lawman pleaded guilty and was sent to the South Dakota State Prison in April 1923. According to prison records, Miller lost little time in making connections with organized crime: within ninety days he was corresponding with St. Paul fixer Jack Peifer and his wife, the future proprietors of the underworld's Hollyhocks Club.[6]

In October 1925 Miller was indicted in Sioux Falls, South Dakota, for violating the Volstead Act, but he forfeited his bond and the case was dropped. As an ex-convict whose skills included exceptional dexterity with a machine gun, Miller advanced from minor bootlegging to major crimes. The FBI's Purvis claimed that Miller, determined to reassure the Keating-Holden gang that he was ruthless, asked for the name of someone of whom the gang disapproved. "Miller proved his worth by kidnapping the man, taking him out on a country road, and breaking all ten of his fingers," wrote Purvis.[7]

The first public mention of Miller's link to organized crime surfaced on February 3, 1928, when he was identified as a participant in a shooting involving gangster Isadore "Kid Cann" Blumenfeld. A scuffle at the Cotton Club in Minneapolis, incited by an ungentlemanly pass at a female entertainer, erupted into a shootout between bootleggers and policemen. One officer was wounded; another was paralyzed by (and later died from) bullets in his shoulder and stomach. The Minneapolis police quickly called off the search for Miller, claiming a case of "mistaken identity." But in a 1934 police interview in Leavenworth prison, George "Machine Gun Kelly" Barnes said that it was indeed Miller who pulled his gun at the Minneapolis club, adding that Miller had also murdered a police officer in Montreal.[8]

Moving up from bootlegging, Miller tried his hand at running gambling rackets in Montreal in 1930. He developed ties to labor racketeer Louis "Lepke" Buchalter, one of the founders of the national crime syndicate. At the same time, Vivian Mathis formed a close friendship with Lepke's wife, Betty Buchalter. FBI files contend that Miller became a hit man for Buchalter while he was still freelancing as an enforcer for Al Capone's gang in Chicago and the Purple Gang of Detroit. Miller's body bore evidence of his violent trade. Wanted posters identified him by a scar curving over his left eye and an irregular scar on the left side of his head; the end of the third finger on his left hand was missing.[9]

By 1931 Miller had begun to work with a husky Tennessee-born bootlegger who later earned notoriety as "Machine Gun Kelly." "The one man who had the most effect on George [Machine Gun Kelly] was Verne Miller, a machine gun toting desperado," wrote Bruce Barnes, Kelly's son. Miller and other gangsters taught him the intricacies of a successful bank robbery long before Kelly robbed his first bank. "It wasn't only the money" that appealed to his father, wrote Barnes in his book, *Machine Gun Kelly: To Right a Wrong*. "The picture of himself going into a bank, holding a gun and knowing that he had power over those he was robbing appealed to him."[10]

Verne Miller and Mathis lived with Kelly and his wife, Kathryn "Kit" Kelly, in Chicago, Kansas City, and the Twin Cities during the early 1930s. Gradually, Miller's cool under fire led to his involvement with both Kelly and Oklahoma's Harvey Bailey in a series of profitable robberies. Miller was identified as one of those who joined Charlie Fitzgerald and Harvey Bailey in robbing a bank in Lincoln, Nebraska, of $2 million in bonds in September 1930.[11]

"For a criminal, he [Miller] had a peculiar set of morals," mused crime historians Clyde Callahan and Byron Jones. "It was said he had done murder for hire, but at the same time disliked hearing anyone use foul or profane language. He would have nothing to do with kidnappers and dropped the Barkers when they became involved in this sort of business."[12]

In the underworld, Miller's history as a policeman and sheriff was a dirty secret. When Alvin Karpis, suspicious of Miller's background, questioned him about it, Miller denied that he had ever been a sheriff—it was his cousin, he said, who was the white sheep of the family. Karpis, unconvinced, refused to deal with Miller, explaining to the FBI that "he did not care to associate with an 'ex-copper.'"[13]

Miller's retired badge may also have fueled a long-standing feud with bank robber Harvey Bailey. Together, Miller and Bailey had robbed banks in Ottumwa, Iowa, Sherman, Texas, and other cities. But Bailey was perturbed when he found out that, in Kelly's words, "Miller had been the law and then had turned into the racket." Bailey decided that although Miller had "guts," he no longer wanted to work with him.[14]

In his memoirs, Bailey claimed that their falling out had little to do with Miller's law-abiding past. Rather, Bailey distrusted Miller's willingness to tell Mathis about his illegal doings. "If she's not good enough to tell," Miller responded, "she's not good enough to live with." Gradually, Miller grew to distrust Bailey, too. Kelly recounted to police how Bailey had been assigned the job of laundering the nearly $200,000 in bonds stolen by the Barker-Karpis gang in March 1932 from Northwestern National Bank and Trust Company of Minneapolis. Although he'd been advised to cash in the bonds for twenty-five cents on the dollar, Bailey returned to Minnesota, insisting that all he could get from his New York contacts was fifteen cents. With Miller's underworld contacts, it did not take long for him to discover that Bailey was lying: he had received the higher exchange rate for the bonds. Miller forced Bailey to flee to Chicago, and Bailey swore that he would kill Miller in revenge.[15]

Miller did not allow underworld tensions to restrict his increasingly warm relationships with Mathis, her ten-year-old daughter, Betty, and the rest of the family back in Brainerd. Surviving family members and FBI surveillance files confirm that he appeared to be genuinely fond of Betty, who told her grandfather that her "stepdaddy," as she called Miller, had measured her for a set of golf clubs.[16]

Mathis would show up in Brainerd wearing nice clothes, driving a new Cadillac, and bearing expensive gifts for her daughter. Miller went deer hunting at the Brainerd farm, fished for northern pike at North Long Lake, and took Betty golfing at a nearby golf course.[17]

"When I was seven years old I remember playing with one of my neighbors at my grandparents' house in Parkerville, and we were jumping around in Verne Miller's car and the seat came loose. Underneath the seat was an *arsenal*—it was just filled with guns!" recalled Mike Gibson, Vivian Mathis's nephew.

Miller bought the boy his first three-piece suit to wear during a Christmas play. "Verne used to put small coins in my vest pockets as a surprise for me," said Gibson. He "would always bring toys up for us—one time he brought me some toy guns and gave Betty a whole trunk full of doll clothes." When the Mathis family fixed Miller a meal one evening, he noticed that they had few dishes. The machine gunner surprised the family by buying dishes and a tablecloth for their home.[18]

"You could see two sides to Verne," recalled Janet Gibson, Mathis's sister-in-law. At times Miller was "jolly." But on other days, the Mathis family would see him gripped by depression, sitting silently in a lawn chair for hours, his face drawn with tension.[19]

Associating with gangsters, many of whom were emotionally unstable, had its drawbacks. Mathis told FBI agents later that although the Barker boys were "nice little fellows," she felt that Karpis was "a cold proposition" and "she had never felt at ease around him." She clearly loved Miller, whom she always called "Sugar." The FBI observed after he died that "it is apparent from her actions and the way she talks that she is still very much broken up over his death."[20]

Miller's demise was precipitated not by his enemies but by his own loyalty to his longtime friend, Frank Nash. Three years after Nash had escaped from Leavenworth, he was recaptured by FBI agents on June 16, 1933, in the "safe" city of Hot Springs, Arkansas. An underworld contact, "Doc" Stacci, telephoned Miller in Kansas City and alerted him to the arrest; the "feds" would be taking Nash through Kansas City's Union Station en route to prison.[21]

Miller is believed to have called the Dillinger gang's errand boy Pat

Reilly in St. Paul in an attempt to enlist Alvin Karpis and Arthur and Doc Barker to help spring Nash, but the Barker-Karpis gang had its hands full with the William Hamm kidnapping.[22]

On June 17, 1933, Miller and two associates drove up to Union Station minutes before Nash was to arrive. (The FBI insisted that Miller was accompanied by Charles "Pretty Boy" Floyd and Floyd's partner, Adam Richetti; Floyd biographer Michael Wallis believes that evidence of Floyd's involvement is slim.) It is clear from telephone records and other documentation that Miller watched outside Union Station as Nash was forced into the front seat of a police officer's Chevrolet, surrounded by FBI agents and police. Suddenly, Miller, armed with a submachine gun, leaped forward—shouting "Let 'em have it!"—and opened fire on the men guarding Frank Nash. Witnesses heard Nash howl, "For God's sake, don't kill me!" Within thirty seconds, Nash was dead. Other victims of what came to be known as the Kansas City Massacre were FBI agent Raymond Caffrey; Otto Reed, police chief of McAlester, Oklahoma; and two Kansas City police officers, William Grooms and Frank Hermanson.[23]

An alternate scenario for the massacre was posed by gangster Gus Winkler's widow, Georgette, who told the FBI that "Frank Nash and Verne Miller were the best of friends." But after Miller began firing at the guards, Nash exclaimed: "Verne, have you gone crazy?" The question aggravated Miller, who turned his gun on Nash and killed him, Winkler said.[24]

"We heard on the radio about the Kansas City Massacre," recalled Janet Gibson, who had had no hint of the extent of Miller's criminal life. "On the radio they said Verne Miller's gang had killed lots of police and an FBI agent and Frank Nash as well. Oh my, we were dumbfounded."[25]

J. Edgar Hoover said that "no time, money, or labor will be spared toward bringing about the apprehension of the individuals responsible for the cowardly and despicable act. . . . *They must be exterminated and must be exterminated by us, and to this end we are dedicating ourselves.*"[26]

FBI agents swarmed toward Brainerd in the search for Miller, obtaining a mail cover (observation of letters and packages) and telephone surveillance on Mathis's family. When a box of salt water taffy was mailed in July from Atlantic City to Vi Mathis's daughter, the FBI tracked down the clerk in New York who had sold the taffy to Miller. The FBI found that Miller had made two telephone calls to St. Paul on July 15: one to Jack Peifer's Hollyhocks casino, the other to Gladys Sawyer, a close friend of Mathis.[27]

After the massacre in Kansas City, Miller and Mathis fled to Chicago to meet with Volney Davis and Doc Barker and have Miller's hand bandaged. Mathis told her family that Miller intended to spirit her off to Europe. But the nationwide dragnet made escape impossible.[28]

Aftermath of the Kansas City Massacre in June 1933

By October, the FBI was hunting Miller with a vengeance, not only for his role in the Kansas City debacle but for nearly every other unsolved crime in the Midwest as well: the kidnapping of oilman Charles Urschel (actually committed by Machine Gun Kelly), the machine-gunning of Chicago policeman Miles Cunningham, the October 1933 robbery of a Brainerd bank (by Babyface Nelson), and the kidnapping of William Hamm. Miller fled first to New York and then shot his way out of a police trap in Chicago on Halloween.[29]

Miller was targeted by the underworld as well, because the furor over the massacre had made life miserable for every gangster in the country. The Detroit police learned from Louis Stacci, one of Miller's underworld contacts, that "any number of people were only too willing to kill Miller, as he was so hot from the law that he was dangerous to everyone." His money dwindling, Miller moved from New York to West Virginia; from Roaring Gap, North Carolina, back to Brooklyn; and then to Lima, Ohio, and Chicago.[30]

Detroit police learned from Machine Gun Kelly that "a number of people, from different gangs, in Chicago and Cicero, were sore at Miller. . . . Not many around Chicago would have much to do with Miller on account of him being so hot with the law and also the gangs." Many gangsters disliked him, Kelly said, because of his habit of avenging underworld assassinations. If a mobster killed a friend of Miller, he felt compelled to track the hit man down and kill him; he confessed to slaughtering three hoodlums in Fox Lake, Wisconsin, in 1930 because the trio had murdered the brother of a friend.[31]

Even Miller's mentor Lepke Buchalter told FBI agents that "no one will have anything to do with Miller now. If he shows up, you will know about it." When an agent asked if Miller was likely to be "bumped off," the mob chieftain "responded with a knowing look" and simply said, "I will have to look into that."[32]

The simultaneous FBI and underworld manhunts ended on November 29, 1933, when Miller's body, nude and mutilated, was found in a ditch along a highway near Detroit. His skull had been crushed by thirteen blows, and he had been strangled with a garrote, then wrapped in a cheap blanket with a fifty-foot sash cord. Miller was so severely beaten that the police could identify him only by his fingerprints. "We wanted Miller badly, but whoever killed him probably saved us from having to do it," the FBI's Werner Hanni told reporters.[33]

Who killed Verne Miller? Machine Gun Kelly suggested to police that he could have been killed only by people he trusted: "Miller never went any place without being armed and never let anyone he did not know real well get close to him on account of there being any number of people who would have taken him. . . . The ones who did get him were real close to him," the Detroit police reported.[34]

Whoever killed Miller, his death was a relief for both the mob and the FBI. "The underworld never forgave Miller for the Kansas City raid," wrote FBI agent Melvin Purvis. "Crime is a business and Verne Miller had become a debit; they wiped him off the ledger and the photograph of his mangled body, which I later saw, told a gruesome story of a cold and bloody murder."[35]

Vivian Mathis had been arrested by the FBI that October in Chicago, where she had been hiding under the alias Mrs. George Hayes. The Minnesota farmgirl pleaded guilty to harboring a criminal and conspiracy to obstruct justice. Mathis told the FBI that she planned to find out who killed Miller and "take care of them." After being released from the federal detention farm at Milan, Michigan, Mathis recuperated in Brainerd for seven months, grieving for Miller. She later married a hotel operator with a penchant for battering women and moved with him to Sioux Falls, South Dakota, where she died in 1940—from complications of domestic abuse, her family suspects.[36]

Verne Miller—ex-sheriff and bank robber, former policeman and assassin—was buried on December 6, 1933. His funeral in White Lake, South Dakota, incorporated the full military rituals of the American Legion: a color guard and an armed escort of Legionnaires.[37]

Mathis's niece Donna Eue recalled the shock her family felt when a detective magazine published photographs of Mathis on the witness stand testifying about Miller. To protect Mathis's daughter, Betty, Grandma Bertha Gibson went into town and bought every available issue of the lurid periodical, brought the magazines home to the farm where Miller had enjoyed dinners with the family, and burned them.[38]

J. Edgar Hoover called the Kansas City Massacre a "turning point in the nation's fight against crime." Indeed, public outrage over the Kansas murders—coupled with the FBI's capture of Machine Gun Kelly in September 1933 and John Dillinger's jail escapes and shootouts in 1934—helped catapult the FBI into national prominence and generated the strong support Hoover needed to overcome opposition to his creation of a federal police force. Agent Purvis wrote in his book, *American Agent*, that "the mad bravado and consummate insolence" of the Kansas City Massacre marked a shift in the public's opinion on gangsters, that it convinced citizens "it was

President Franklin Roosevelt signing new crime bill into law in 1934, watched (left to right) by Attorney General Homer Cummings, Hoover, a senator, and assistant attorney general Joseph Keenan

high time for a new deal on crime. . . . There was no telling who the next victim would be."[39]

Goaded by Hoover's publicity machine, Congress in 1934 passed a series of Justice Department–sponsored initiatives that expanded FBI powers to hunt down criminals. Congress finally made it a federal crime to kill an FBI agent and authorized federal intervention in kidnapping cases a week after the abduction, presuming that by then the victim would have been taken across state lines. The FBI was given the green light to hire two hundred additional agents and to arrest criminals without involving local police, who,

Poster for the 1936 film* You Can't Get Away with It *(left), which received J. Edgar Hoover's personal support; Hoover, posing on movie camera (above), films his assistant Clyde Tolson, for FBI publicity reels.

attorney general Homer Cummings widely complained, were "hopelessly corrupt."[40]

The attorney general, Hoover's ally, inaugurated a "public enemies" list of ten most-wanted criminals, including Charles "Pretty Boy" Floyd and John Dillinger—a master stroke of publicity that further elevated inept rural hoodlums to national celebrity. The Justice Department in August 1934 hired brilliant public relations man Henry Suydam, while the FBI hired former YMCA publicist Louis Nichols, both of whom promoted Hoover's hunt for the Barker-Karpis gang with a wave of media adulation. By spring 1935, the public was entranced with Jimmy Cagney's portrayal of an FBI agent in the Warner Bros. film *G-Men* and was reading about heroic agents in books like *Ten Thousand Public Enemies*, written by Hoover's ghostwriter Courtney Ryley Cooper.[41]

Hoover vilified gangsters with increased gusto, condemning them as "under-filth. . . . rats crawling from their hide-outs to gnaw at the vitals of our civilization."[42]

The *Chicago Tribune* marveled in 1936 that "in less than three years a tide of printer's ink, accompanied by a roar of sound films and radio programs, has given heroic stature to a relatively obscure burocrat [sic]. . . . Over the air and on the screen the fire was repeated, and out of the welter of dramatic gore Hoover emerged as the leading criminal chaser of all time."[43]

The American public, which Hoover believed had romanticized bank robbers like Pretty Boy Floyd and Dillinger as Dust Bowl Robin Hoods, began to accept the FBI director as a new hero. Now the FBI had to prove that it could destroy the targets it had so avidly pursued in the media—the Barker-Karpis and Dillinger gangs.

Minnesota Weather

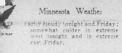

Partly cloudy tonight and Friday; somewhat colder in extreme west tonight and in extreme east Friday.

St. Paul Dispatch

Recognition

The unruly boy may have ideas; don't suppress him, Angelo Patri warns on Page 10 today.

66. NO. 112. 18 PAGES Exclusive Service of the Associated Press. ST. PAUL, MINN., THURSDAY, JANUARY 18, 1934. TWO CENTS IN ST.

The National Whirligig

Behind The News

WASHINGTON

EDW. G. BREMER KIDNAPED; $200,000 RANSOM ASKE

ABDUCTION VICTIM, KIN AND KIDNAP SQUAD

Edward G. Bremer, president of the Commercial State bank, and son of Adolph Bremer, part owner of the Schmidt Brewing Co., was kidnaped Wednesday morning. He is in the center above. Police received no official notification of the kidnaping and the family refused to discuss it. Reports were that Mr. Bremer is being held for $200,000 ransom. In the picture above are Walter Magee (upper left) who first was told of the kidnaping. Below is Adolph Bremer, father of the missing man. At the upper right is Charles Tierney, inspector of detectives, and below him is Detective Thomas A. Brown. These two officers comprise the St. Paul police kidnap squad. In the lower center is the Schmidt brewery on West Seventh street. Inset in the brewery picture is Edward Penschuck, who was with Mr. Magee when he was reported to have been notified of the kidnaping.

Secrecy Veil Second Maj Seizure He

Victim Member of One of St. Paul's Wealthiest Son of Adolph and Nephew of Otto Bremer, Manager of Home Owners Loan Corporatio Call Gave "Tip."

VANISHED AFTER TAKING HIS DAUGH TO SUMMIT SCHOOL ON GOODRICH

Edward G. Bremer, president of the Co State bank and a member of one of St. Paul's families, was kidnaped for $200,000 ransom W morning.

Police say they have received no official n of the crime and the family refused to discuss it. Dahill, chief of police, said he was investigati of the crime.

Mr. Bremer is 37 years old and resides at Mississippi River boulevard. It is known he Tuesday from a business trip to Chicago. Efforts his release are reported to have failed thus far.

SECOND MAJOR CASE IN 7 MONTHS.

It was the second big abduction in seven months o of a St. Paul brewing family. William Hamm Jr., pres Hamm Brewing Co., paid $100,000 for his release last

Mr. Bremer is the son of Adolph Bremer, 855 W street, part owner of the Jacob Schmidt Brewing Co. and of Otto Bremer, 1344 Summit avenue, a Democratic powe of the American National bank and Minnesota manager o

U.S. Agent on Way Here by

Dallas, Jan. 18.—(AP)—Frank J. Blake, Department agent who directed most of the search for the kidnapers F. Urschel, Oklahoma City oil millionaire, left by plane St. Paul.

Owners Loan corporation. He also is a nephew of Paul Amherst avenue.

Kidnapers are reported to have seized him between and 10 A. M. Wednesday, possibly on Summit avenue or St. Paul.

As was his custom, he drove his 8-year-old daughte Summit school, 1150 Goodrich avenue, where she is a third grade, and apparently continued on his way to Sixth and Washington streets to begin his day's work.

His route probably lay east on Summit avenue to and thence to the bank. Somewhere along this line th are believed to have forced his automobile to a halt and

He failed to show up at the bank.

According to reports, the next heard of Mr. Bremer telephone jingled in the office of Walter W. Magee, 118 W avenue, general contractor, an associate of the Bremers of the new state office building. Mr. Magee also said he k of the affair.

PHONE CALL TELLS WHERE TO FIND CA

A low voice is said to have told Mr. Magee he co Bremer car at the Highland park water tower, Snellin avenues, and a note on the back door step of his office.

The contractor, trying to prolong the conversation to have hastily instructed Ed Penschuck, former city missioner of public utilities, who was in the office, to get line to trace the call, but the kidnaper clicked his recei effort failed.

Magee found the note under a mat. It was addressed Magee," was written on a typewriter and signed in ink by The signature was shaky, indicating he was nervous.

The man who telephoned Magee is reported to have we've got your friend Bremer and if you are not damn c get you, too."

He was warned, it was reported, that any attempts cate with police or newspapers would result in the imme of Bremer.

The note found by Magee apparently had been writ folded and Mr. Bremer forced to sign it, probably witho its content.

IN SAFE PLACE, NOTE SAYS.

The note, it was reported, said Mr. Bremer had captive by the kidnap gang and that he was held in a sa was unharmed. A demand for $200,000 for his safe made. Again a threat of death for their victim was mad

4 OTHER KIDNAPINGS IN 30 MONTHS HERE

Obtained $128,400 of $310,000 Demanded; Eight of 20 Suspects in Prison.

St. Paul has been the scene of four other major kidnapings in the past two and one-half years. From their four victims the abductors obtained $128,400 of the $310,000 demanded as ransom. All of the victims suffered physical hardships, but are alive today. Of the approximately 20 suspects in the four abductions, eight have been convicted.

Here are details of the kidnapings in chronological order:

SEPTEMBER 24, 1931—Leon Gleckman, reputed political manipulator, kidnaped by four men. Held approximately a week in a Northern Wisconsin cabin. Ransom first demanded, $75,000; amount paid, $6,400, of which $3,500 was recovered. Five men serving terms in Stillwater for the abduction.

OCTOBER 5, 1931—Morris Roiman, dress shop owner, abducted from his home, 1079 Dayton avenue, by two men. Held for several days and tortured before released. Ransom asked, $100,000. Later reduced to $10,000. Reported to have been paid. Two men convicted and serving prison sentences. A third still sought for complicity in the case.

JUNE 30, 1932—Haskell Bohn, youthful son of a refrigerator manufacturer, kidnaped from garage at his home, 1466 Summit avenue and held until July 6 in a Minneapolis home. Abductors first demanded $35,000, but released Bohn for $12,000. One man convicted and serving sentence, and the wife of another suspect, whom police since have sought, acquitted of complicity.

JUNE 15, 1933—William Hamm Jr., millionaire brewer, kidnaped by two men as he left his office. Believed to have been taken to Wisconsin

COURT RESTRAINS BANCO STOCK SIFT

Molyneaux Signs Order Halting Action of State Commerce Commission.

Federal Judge Joseph W. Molyneaux of Minneapolis signed today an order temporarily restraining the Minnesota Commerce commission from proceeding with its investigation of sale of stock of the Northwest Bancorporation.

The order was issued at the request of officials of the corporation, and the matter is set for hearing in Federal District court in Minneapolis at 10 A. M., January 27.

At the same time the commission received a notice from the Bancorporation signed by J. C. Thompson, president, stating that the corporation "consents, requests and demands" that the exempt status of its securities be revoked and offering to surrender all rights and privileges under the exempt status.

The commission also temporarily revoked the exempt status which prevented general and open sales in

(Please Turn to Page 2, Col. 5.)

WARRANTS ISSUED FOR SINCLAIR, 24 OTHERS

Tulsa, Okla., Jan. 18.—(AP)—Warrants for the arrest of Harry F. Sinclair, oil magnate, and 24 other men

THE WEATHER

Women Tossed From Sinking Ship

8

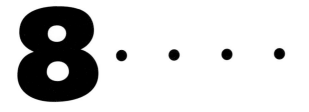

ONE KIDNAPPING TOO MANY

Newspaper announcing kidnap of Edward Bremer, with (clockwise from upper right) Inspector of Detectives Charles Tierney, Thomas Brown, Adolf Bremer, and intermediary Walter Magee; West Seventh Street home of Adolf Bremer Sr.

41 The Gang's All Here

Fred Barker's Dale Apartments
628 Grand Avenue, St. Paul

The Barker-Karpis gang gathered at the Dale Apartments in St. Paul in December 1933 and January 1934 to plot their next kidnapping. The men barricaded themselves in the living room of apartment 103 to debate the abduction of a member of what the FBI would term one of the wealthiest and "most prominent" families of the Twin Cities.[1]

Paula Harmon later told the FBI that she and Fred Barker had "rented an apartment on the corner of Dale and Grand Avenues, just off Summit Avenue, using the alias 'the Bergstroms.'" From January 1 to January 15, 1934, Harmon said, "all of the members of the gang were in St. Paul," having been called back to the Twin Cities from the warmth of Reno and Phoenix. "Several times . . . the gang would have meetings in my apartment," recalled Harmon, who sat with Wynona Burdette drinking beer in the kitchen "while the members of the gang talked. By 'members of the gang,' I mean George Ziegler, Alvin Karpis, Harry Campbell, Volney Davis, William Weaver, Fred Barker and Arthur R. Barker."[2]

At first, the gang considered robbing the Commercial State Bank of St. Paul, but fixer Harry Sawyer argued that kidnapping the bank's president, thirty-seven-year-old Edward Bremer, would be more profitable. Bremer was the son of Adolf Bremer, president of the Jacob Schmidt Brewing Company. The ransom was to be $200,000, double what the gang had demanded when they abducted William Hamm Jr.[3]

The decision to kidnap a second local businessman just seven months after Hamm was ransomed was audacious. The consequences of failure had increased dramatically since July 22, 1933, when Machine Gun Kelly and his wife, Kathryn, kidnapped Oklahoma oilman Charles F. Urschel. The Barker-Karpis gang knew all about the Urschel kidnapping—in fact, about $5,500 of the $200,000 Urschel ransom had been laundered in the Twin Cities. The twenty-dollar ransom bills were passed through the First National Bank and Trust Company and Hennepin State Bank by members of Isadore "Kid Cann" Blumenfeld's Minneapolis syndicate. George and Kathryn Kelly had also visited the offices of Minneapolis bootlegger Tommy Banks to have an additional $30,000 of the money exchanged for "clean" bills.[4]

The Kellys were captured on September 26, 1933, by police and FBI agents in Memphis, Tennessee; the FBI account had Kelly begging, "Don't shoot, G-men!" On October 12 they were convicted and sentenced to life in prison. Two members of Kid Cann's gang, Clifford Skelly and Ed "Barney"

Berman, were among the twenty-one people found guilty in the Urschel kidnapping case; both were sentenced to five years in prison.[5]

The Urschel trial was the first held under the new Lindbergh kidnapping law—federal legislation passed in the wake of the March 1932 kidnapping and slaying of the son of Charles A. Lindbergh Jr.—which allowed life sentences for abductions. After the Urschel verdict, assistant U.S. attorney general Joseph Keenan declared: "This is just the first skirmish. We are going right down the line and every criminal and gangster in the United States may well begin shaking in his boots. This law is a powerful weapon, and we are prepared and eager to wield it to the finish."[6]

The women in the Barker-Karpis gang knew something big was being planned; on January 13, Fred Barker asked Paula Harmon to move from

George "Machine Gun Kelly" Barnes, taken into FBI custody in 1933 for the kidnapping of oilman Charles Urschel

Grand Avenue into the underworld's favorite Edgecumbe Court Apartments with Wynona Burdette and Edna Murray.

When the FBI identified the Dale Apartments hideout during the search for Bremer's kidnappers, agents probed the identities of "Edwin Bergstrom" (actually Fred Barker) and his wife (Paula Harmon), who was described to the FBI as a sandy-haired thirty-year-old Irish woman with crossed eyes and a thick brogue.

The Bergstroms vanished from 628 Grand the evening after Edward Bremer was kidnapped. Their Grand Avenue neighbors extolled the sociability of the mysterious couple. "The people did a lot of drinking and always had friends in their apartment," the building manager told the *St. Paul Dispatch*, "although they never were noisy or troublesome." Apart from an occasional bank robbery or kidnapping, the Barker-Karpis gangsters were ideal neighbors.[7]

42 Beer, Banks, Politics, and Kidnapping

The Jacob Schmidt Brewery
882 West Seventh Street, St. Paul

After the shock of the Hamm kidnapping, the St. Paul Police Department took a decisive step to protect other prominent businessmen: it established a squad whose sole mission was to search out and protect likely kidnap vic-

The Bremer family's Jacob Schmidt Brewery, about 1905; (inset) a Schmidt beer ad shortly after repeal of Prohibition

tims. To head the Kidnap Detail, the police chose Thomas Brown, the officer who had secretly leaked confidential law enforcement information to the Barker-Karpis gang.

Inspector of detectives James Crumley, an ally of Brown's who was dismissed from the police force in 1935 for accepting bribes, revealed to the FBI that it was Brown who gave the Barker-Karpis gang information on the habits of Edward Bremer, as gathered by the Kidnap Detail.[8]

The gang knew that the Bremer family could easily pay the ransom. With the repeal of Prohibition in March 1933, the Schmidt Brewery had returned to night-and-day production of beer. It had been founded as the North Star Brewery in 1855, when Minnesota was a six-year-old territory. By 1872, a German immigrant named Jacob Schmidt was running the company. To ensure that Schmidt would not be hired away by one of North Star's eleven local competitors, he was made half-owner in 1884. With the 1896 marriage of Schmidt's daughter Maria to young Adolf Bremer, a stable family to lead the growing company was established. When a flash fire destroyed the original plant, Bremer purchased the old Stahlman brewery in 1900 and named his new empire the Jacob Schmidt Brewing Company.[9]

During Prohibition, the Bremers weathered the closing of U.S. breweries by producing soft drinks, root beer, and enormously popular malt-based near beer—which enterprising customers could simply spike with their own illicit alcohol. Schmidt's near beer was delivered to the area's private homes, to drug and grocery stores, and to Jack Peifer's Hollyhocks Club casino. "I delivered Schmidt's near beer to lots of bootleg places," recalled Schmidt driver Gordon "Curley" Merrick. "Some bootleg places on Summit Avenue had peepholes, and [they would] look at you, [and] once they knew you were the driver for Schmidt's, they'd open up."[10]

Harry Sawyer's selection of Edward Bremer as the Barker-Karpis gang's next target clearly was not a random choice. "I don't know what Sawyer's beef was," Alvin Karpis wrote in his memoirs, "but he sure didn't like Bremer." Sawyer's wife, Gladys, told gang members that Bremer and Sawyer "once had some differences over some alcohol." Even Bremer himself, interviewed when he was released, said "he knew plenty that he would never tell about banks and politics which caused the kidnapping," the FBI reported.[11]

Years later, Gladys Sawyer, bitter after her husband had been abandoned by the underworld, spoke freely to the FBI of the circumstances preceding the Bremer kidnapping. According to the FBI, "Mrs. Sawyer said that the beer sold by her husband in the Saint Paul [Green Lantern] saloon, during Prohibition Days, was not 'near beer,' but real beer and that it all came from the Schmidt Brewing Company."

From 1926 to 1933, said Gladys, Harry Sawyer had an arrangement with the Bremers' Schmidt Brewery to have real beer delivered for sale at the Green Lantern. The beer was transported through an underground tunnel to the house of brewery employee Carl Schoen on Erie Street. Sawyer sold this illicit Schmidt beer at the Green Lantern as if it were legal near beer. A rival bar owner, Andrew Rothmeyer, stopped handling the Schmidt real beer during Prohibition because of a dispute over money with the brewery. Harry Sawyer became the "exclusive agency for this beer in Saint Paul and bootlegged it through his place of business on Wabasha Street, where he was doing business through virtue of a cigar store license," the FBI reported.[12]

Gladys said that her husband's Green Lantern saloon properties at 545, 543, and 541 Wabasha Street were actually *owned* by the Schmidt Brewing Company. When the Green Lantern was closed in the mid-1930s, a Schmidt truck was dispatched to pick up the fixtures, tables, and chairs. The curious relationship between the Bremer family and Sawyer took its most unusual turn on August 3, 1932, when two gangsters were arrested at Sawyer's Green Lantern bar for possession of firearms. Adolf Bremer requested that a family friend, Walter W. Magee, personally intercede on behalf of the two criminals. "Harry Sawyer is a customer of ours," the elder Bremer told Magee, "and anything that can be done for them will be appreciated." As a result, the gunmen were freed by St. Paul police on $500 bail, after which they vanished. Compounding the irony, one of the two gangsters arrested at the Green Lantern was William Weaver, a Barker-Karpis gang member who was to play a key role in the kidnapping of Adolf's son Edward a year and a half later.[13]

The FBI also learned that the Sawyers banked with Ed Bremer's Commercial State Bank, as did bootlegger Leon Gleckman and slot machine czar Thomas Filben.[14]

In addition, an FBI report noted that while waiting for the kidnapped Bremer's return, the family talked with the FBI. "Reference was made from time to time . . . that Edward Bremer . . . had considerable contact with underworld characters during his business activities at the bank" and that Bremer said he was "perfectly willing to do business with them," noted the report.[15]

In his memoirs, Karpis claimed that during the long wait for the delivery of the ransom money, Bremer confided to his captors that "he was a good buddy of Harry Sawyer's and Jack Peifer's and that either guy would vouch for him." When Dillinger gang member Eddie Green was interrogated on his deathbed in 1934, he stated that Sawyer had fingered Ed Bremer to be kidnapped, remarking, "That's bad, Eddie [Bremer] was a friend of his [Sawyer]."[16]

As the kidnapping of Ed Bremer unfolded, the FBI struggled to uncover the secrets of the police officer who betrayed those he was sworn to protect, and the victim who may have done business with his kidnappers.

43 A Cinch for Two Hundred Grand

Myrtle Eaton's Haven at the Kennington
565 Portland Avenue, St. Paul

Fred and Doc Barker desperately wanted Fred Goetz of Al Capone's Chicago syndicate to help with this second kidnapping. After the Hamm kidnapping, however, Goetz had told the Barkers that he was "through with the kidnapping racket and absolutely would not participate in another as he did not approve of this way of making money," the FBI reported. The Barker brothers enticed Goetz with the promise that their target was "a 'cinch' who was good for two hundred grand." Goetz protested that the Barkers should stay away from St. Paul because another kidnapping there would ruin Jack Peifer and his business. But Goetz finally agreed to participate.[17]

With Goetz on board, the Barker-Karpis gang held final planning sessions in apartment 104 at the Kennington, hosted by kidnap conspirator William "Lapland Willie" Weaver and his girlfriend, Myrtle Eaton. According to the FBI, the meetings in Eaton's apartment involved Karpis, Weaver, Fred and Doc Barker, Volney Davis, Harry Campbell, Fred Goetz, and Harry Sawyer.[18]

Eaton, an Iowa native and the ex-wife of Stillwater Prison parolee Clarence Eaton, was a thirty-one-year-old shoplifter with a taste for fur coats. At the time of the Bremer kidnapping, she was dating Weaver, a Little Rock, Arkansas, gangster who had been paroled in 1931 from a life sentence at the Oklahoma state prison for murdering a member of a posse pursuing him after a bank robbery. Released from prison, Weaver lived in St. Paul in a flat over the Moonlight Gardens saloon at 777 Selby Avenue, a brick apartment building at the intersection of Selby and Avon.[19]

Neighbors noted that Karpis, Weaver, and Fred Barker met at 565 Portland more than a dozen times before the Bremer kidnapping. The FBI reported that Weaver told friends he "had a falling out with Karpis and Barker" after the kidnapping because "Fred Barker was a hot-headed ____; that Fred Barker tried to put him [Weaver] on the spot and bump him off." FBI files suggest that Weaver was finally ordered to leave the hideout where Bremer was being held because he walked back and forth in front of the house, consumed with nervousness over the delays in the delivery of the ransom.[20]

Tensions rose before the Bremer kidnapping. Fred Barker went to Jess Doyle's St. Paul apartment to air another gang dispute. Barker, who had served time in Kansas State Penitentiary with Doyle, told his former partner that he wanted Doyle to leave town. Edna Murray explained that by the fall of 1933 "none of the boys were on speaking terms" with Doyle because "they wanted him to break away from his sister Doris, and he would not do so." The FBI learned from Murray that the Barker brothers felt Doris was "far too outspoken in her manners and also that she knew too much of Jess' business, of which they likewise disapproved." Understanding that the alternative to following the gang's wishes could mean his body being identified by its fingerprints, Doyle left for Oklahoma.[21]

Two days before the Bremer kidnapping was to be carried out, with gang conflicts growing, a figure was seen outside the windows of Eaton's Ken-

Shoplifter Myrtle Eaton (inset) hosted the Barker-Karpis gang at the Kennington (below left); Mr. Cowin and friend Roy McCord in the Holly Falls Apartments (below right) mistook the gang for peeping toms.

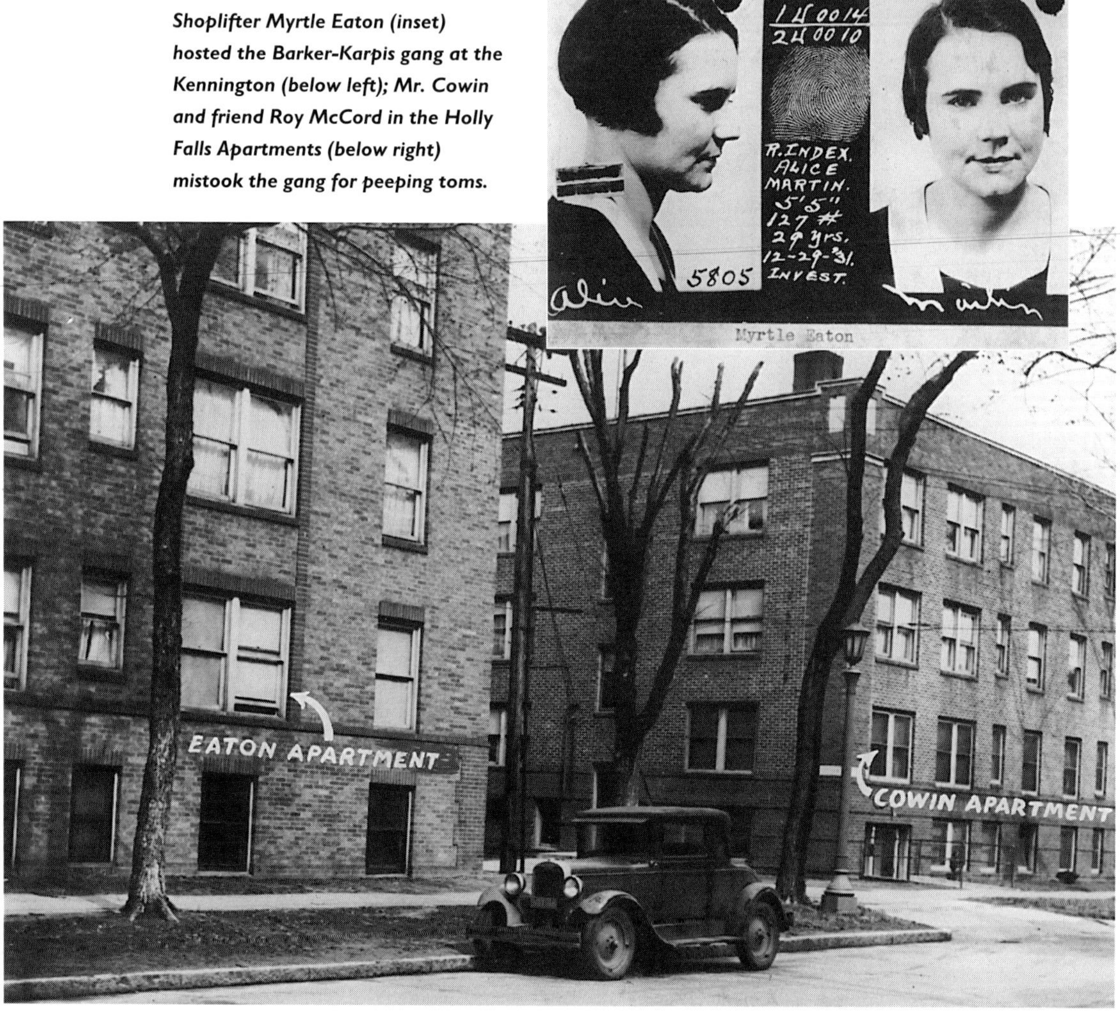

nington apartment—a uniformed man who looked very much like a St. Paul police officer to nervous gang members.

44 The Shooting of Roy McCord

The Holly Falls Apartments
562 Holly Avenue, St. Paul

For years, as the O'Connor system drew mobsters to their city, St. Paul citizens comforted themselves with the belief that the criminals would follow an underworld code of conduct: machine guns would be fired only at other gangsters, not at innocent bystanders. The FBI knew that the Barker-Karpis gang offered no such guarantees. After the 1934 shooting of Roy McCord, FBI agent Oscar Hall wrote that the Barker-Karpis gang members "are very reckless in their shooting and it has often been mentioned that they are 'blasters', that is, they shoot at the least provocation."[22]

Early in the morning on January 13, the gang's anxiety over plans to kidnap Bremer led to the shooting of a Northwest Airlines employee, a man who had the misfortune merely to *look* like a policeman. The previous evening, Northwest radio operator Roy McCord had been alerted by neighbors to peeping toms lurking at a friend's Holly Falls apartment, just behind the Kennington. Wearing his aviator's uniform, a peaked hat, and a dark jacket with brass buttons, McCord caught sight of three suspicious-looking men—strangers in a familiar neighborhood—and, just before 1:00 A.M., followed their Ford toward 562 Holly. McCord, accompanied by his friend, "saw a coupe drive down the alley near their home, followed it, and later drove abreast of the coupe," said a 1934 FBI memo. "As soon as their car was stopped, one or more occupants of the coupe fired into McCord's car with one or more machine guns, seriously injuring McCord."[23]

An underworld source told the FBI that "McCord was wearing a radio dispatcher's uniform of the Northwest Airways and was mistaken for a policeman." Karpis described the incident in his autobiography: "We were sitting around an apartment in St. Paul where Bill Weaver lived with a shoplifter named Myrtle Eaton, when someone noticed a guy peeping through the window of an apartment across the alley." Karpis and Fred Barker ran outside and climbed into their Chevrolet sedan, and Karpis pulled out a machine gun. "Freddie was at the wheel," wrote Karpis, "and I told him to pull around a corner and stop suddenly. He did, and I leaped out of the passenger side with a machine gun. I must have thrown twenty or thirty slugs into the cop car. When we drove away that time, nobody was trailing us."[24]

Karpis had fired nearly fifty .45-caliber bullets at McCord's car. "They weren't peeping toms—they were gangsters. . . . A gang like that is not going to be window peeping," said McCord's son Roy Norman McCord, who was then nine years old. "My brilliant father got out of the car with a .32 service revolver and they really let him have it. My dad had a peaked hat with a bill, dark blue suit, like the police."[25]

McCord's daughter Mary Johnson recalled that her father "walked into the hospital himself. Three of the bullets dropped out in the hospital room as they undressed him; these bullets had passed right through him. The doctors went in for the other three bullets."[26]

"I went to the hospital and saw him on the table," recalled Pat Lannon, a former police officer. "He was covered with blood. The doctors were working on him, and he looked up and said, 'Pat, can I have a cigarette?'"[27]

"Here's my first memory of *anything*," said McCord's daughter Colleen McCalla: "I was just two months short of four years old when dad was shot. . . . We drove to the hospital, and I was standing outside the door of my father's room. Then I remember this red bottle and a tube that ran down into his arm, which my father told me was *tomato juice*. Well, I never drank tomato juice until I was nineteen after that!"

Three decades later, McCord died of heart failure in Lancaster, California. "Now that's all ancient history, just a part of our growing up," said McCalla. "We used to go over the Bay Bridge when Alvin Karpis was at Alcatraz, and we'd wave at him."[28]

The uproar over the shooting of McCord proved to be only a minor setback for the gang. At Edna Murray's Edgecumbe Court apartment, Harry Sawyer and Fred Barker discussed a delay in the timing of the Bremer kidnapping: "The shooting of that radio man has made this town hot," Murray heard Sawyer say. "You'd better wait awhile."[29]

45 Threatening the 'Fat Boys'

The Edward Bremer Kidnapping
South Lexington Parkway and Goodrich Avenue, St. Paul

The Barker-Karpis gang was counting on Edward Bremer to follow his usual routine on January 17, 1934, so they could interrupt it. He did not disappoint them. After breakfast at his mansion at 92 North Mississippi River Boulevard, the banker started his Lincoln sedan, bundled his nine-year-old daughter, Betty, into the car, and drove the third-grader to the Summit School at 1150 Goodrich Avenue. Then Bremer began his drive to the Commercial State Bank at Washington and Sixth, braking for the stop sign at the corner of Lexington Parkway and Goodrich Avenue.[30]

Bremer's routine was so precise that students walking to Summit School along Goodrich could time their arrival for morning chapel by watching to see when his car turned onto their street.[31]

When Bremer stopped, Fred Barker and Harry Campbell blocked his car with their black sedan. In another car, Doc Barker, Alvin Karpis, and Volney Davis prevented Bremer's escape from behind. One man opened the front door of Bremer's sedan, stuck a gun in his stomach, and hissed: "Don't move or I'll kill you."

When Bremer began to struggle, the kidnappers bludgeoned him over the head with the butt of a revolver. Blood dripping over his eyes, Bremer attempted to block the closing of the car door with his legs. The kidnappers slammed the door anyway, severely injuring his knee. Forced down to the floor of his car, the banker thought there might still be hope when the gang was unable to start it. But "they continued to beat him over the head so furiously that he decided that he had best start the car, which he did with the starter button on the dash, which they were unable to locate," the FBI reported later.[32]

Veteran crime reporter Nate Bomberg, who covered the kidnapping, remembered how it shocked the ruling families of St. Paul. The abduction of William Hamm Jr. might have been excused as a one-time aberration, but after this second kidnapping, the city's wealthy families—many of whom had connections to the administration of President Franklin D. Roosevelt—demanded a crackdown before another millionaire businessman disappeared. "We had a lot of murders and gangster killings and kidnapping of minor

A reenactment of the January 1934 kidnapping of Edward Bremer at Lexington Parkway and Goodrich Avenue

hoodlums for ransom," recalled Bomberg. "Nobody paid any attention to it. . . . But when you started to pick on the fat boys, then people get alarmed. . . . When a fat boy or a rich man is threatened, he will get action."[33]

46 'A Very Desperate Undertaking'

Home of Go-Between Walter W. Magee
1295 Lincoln Avenue, St. Paul

The action began less than two hours after the gang seized Bremer when contractor Walter W. Magee received an unforgettable telephone call at his St. Paul office. "We've got your friend Bremer and if you are not damn careful, we'll get you too," the caller said. Magee was told to retrieve a ransom note left near the stairway at the office.[34]

"*You* are hereby *declared* in on a very *desperate* undertaking," said the note. "Don't try to cross us. . . . Police have never helped in such a spot, and wont this time either. You better take care of the *payoff first* and let *them do* the *detecting later*. Because the police usually butt in your friend isnt none too comfortable now so don't delay the payment." The payoff demands reflected Fred Goetz's criminal savvy: the $200,000 ransom was to be delivered in used five- and ten-dollar bills. ("*No new money—no consecutive numbers—large variety of issues*," the kidnappers warned.)

The Bremers were to place a personal advertisement ("We are ready Alice") in the *Minneapolis Tribune* to signal their ability to deliver the money. "Dont attempt to stall or outsmart us," read the note. "Dont try to bargain. Dont plead poverty we know how much they have in their banks. . . . Threats arent necessary—*you just do your part*—we *guarantee* to do ours."[35]

Magee notified the St. Paul police and the FBI, but the Barker-Karpis gang had again found a go-between with shadowy connections to the underworld. Magee—an old friend of Adolf Bremer—had risen from an apprentice bricklayer's helper during the construction of the Hotel St. Paul to found the Walter W. Magee Company. The FBI suspected that Magee had also enjoyed contacts with the underworld. A 1934 FBI investigative file claimed that after the Canadian-born Magee arrived in St. Paul in 1914, he had taken over the Tobin family saloon and after the passage of "prohibition, engaged in bootlegging on a large scale." In 1928, six trusted associates had served as pallbearers at the funeral of slain underworld leader Dan Hogan—among them was Magee. In short, concluded the FBI, Magee was "a rather shady character."[36]

As Magee scrambled to maintain contact with the kidnappers, it became clear that the gang had underestimated the firestorm that their abduction of Edward Bremer would ignite. President Roosevelt issued a formal statement deploring the kidnapping of the son of a friend. Governor Floyd B. Olson called the Bremer family to promise the aid of all Minnesota law enforcement agencies. J. Edgar Hoover announced that he was sending a special team of FBI agents. The American Legion offered tens of thousands of Legionnaires to help find their comrade. A thousand mail carriers were ordered to watch for suspicious activity on their routes.[37]

Within hours of Bremer's disappearance, the FBI had the first physical clue to his whereabouts: his blue Lincoln, its interior spattered with blood, was found one mile from St. Paul's Highland Park water tower on Snelling Avenue at Ford Parkway.[38]

47 Blood on the Steering Wheel

Bremer's Abandoned Automobile
1910 Edgecumbe Road, St. Paul

The kidnappers had discarded Bremer's Lincoln sedan here on Edgecumbe Road near the Highland Park golf course. An FBI report described what Walter Magee found in the car: "Bloodstains on the steering wheel, the gear shift lever, the doorsill, the back of the front seat and the floor of the car indicat[ing] . . . that a struggle had occurred." So that Adolf Bremer would not be alarmed, Magee quickly had the bloody Lincoln towed to his Third Street Garage. The FBI had to consider whether Bremer had already been killed. "I can't imagine what my mother felt when they found the car with the blood all over the inside," said Edward's daughter, Betty Bremer Johnson.[39]

Chief of police Tom Dahill confided to his Kidnap Detail supervisor, Tom Brown, his concern that the banker might already be dead. Curiously, the next three ransom notes contained samples of Bremer's handwriting—and Bremer's comment, "I suppose you are worrying about the blood in the car" —as if to reassure Dahill that the victim was still alive.[40]

Meanwhile, J. Edgar Hoover, who had read about the Bremer kidnapping in the Washington, D.C., newspapers, was not happy. He launched a scathing memo to Werner Hanni, the special agent in charge of the St. Paul FBI office: "It appears that it is necessary for me to rely upon the press for information concerning important cases being investigated by the Division under my supervision," Hoover wrote. "It is difficult for me to understand why you neglected, in a case of such significance as the present one, to fully advise me. . . . I must add that I am entirely dissatisfied with the manner in which you have handled this case."[41]

Hoover and the Justice Department were particularly obsessed with the intrusion of the news media into the Bremer case. Assistant attorney general Joseph Keenan confided in a memo that "we are experiencing difficulty in solving the Bremer kidnapping by reason of approximately one hundred newspapermen and photographers gathering in the City of St. Paul and literally pursuing agents of the Government, police and the prosecutor's office. . . . It is almost impossible to make any headway in the solution of the crime."[42]

48 'If That Cheese Moves, It's a Goner!'

The Edward G. Bremer Home
92 North Mississippi River Boulevard, St. Paul

"The telephones of all the relatives of the Bremer family have been tapped and are constantly under surveillance," reported an FBI memo. Indeed, FBI-monitored wiretaps were installed on the telephones at Walter Magee's home, at the Schmidt Brewing Company, and at the home of Edward's uncle, Otto Bremer, at 1344 Summit Avenue.[43]

But most of all, the FBI focused on Edward Bremer's home at 92 North Mississippi River Boulevard. "We had an FBI man living on our second floor

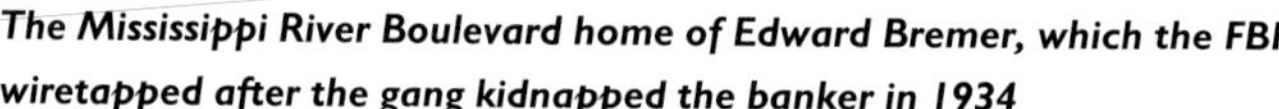

The Mississippi River Boulevard home of Edward Bremer, which the FBI wiretapped after the gang kidnapped the banker in 1934

throughout the time my father was kidnapped," recalled Betty Bremer Johnson. "I thought FBI agents were nice to have around! I thought it was a lark and the agents would play with me." Mike Malone, the Treasury Department agent who went undercover in Chicago to destroy Al Capone, virtually adopted the girl during the ordeal, and the FBI agents tried to amuse her. One night, Betty's grandfather brought some malodorous imported cheese to the house. "I can still see the FBI agent, Brennan, drawing his gun at it and saying: 'If that cheese moves, it's a goner!'" Johnson said.[44]

Although Isadore "Kid Cann" Blumenfeld and other local racketeers were investigated as possible suspects, Mel Harney of the Treasury Department's Alcoholic Beverage Unit in St. Paul guessed early on that "Bremer's kidnapping was not committed by any Twin City talent." Harney reasoned that both kidnapping victims, Hamm and Bremer, were influential and could command police attention, and "for that reason alone, it would indicate that outsiders have committed the crime. Mr. Harney believes that if they were local men they would not tackle families which would have at their disposal the entire police assistance of the Twin Cities."[45]

The day after the kidnapping, gangster Volney Davis took his girlfriend Edna Murray to a safe house, Harry Sawyer's Shoreview farm. "Boy, this town is hot; it's full of G-Men!" a worried Sawyer said to Davis. To reduce the possibility of capture, the gang sent three girlfriends—Murray, Paula Harmon, and Wynona Burdette—to Chicago. The men of the Barker-Karpis gang were forced to remain in St. Paul, even as the investigation intensified. After all, the gang still had Edward Bremer, and the Bremer family still had the ransom money.[46]

49 Delivery of the Bremer Ransom Note

The Home of Dr. Henry T. Nippert
706 Lincoln Avenue, St. Paul

Dr. Henry T. Nippert, the Bremer family's physician, was briefly awakened by a tinkling crash at 6:00 A.M. on January 20. A bottle had been thrown through the glass front door of his home. Although puzzled by the sound, the doctor drifted back to sleep. Then the telephone rang, and an impatient caller told the sixty-five-year-old physician to go downstairs. There, Nippert found the bottle, the shattered pieces of his plate-glass door, and a ransom note for go-between Walter Magee:

> You must be proud of yourself by now. If Bremer dont get back his family has you to thank. Youve made it almost impossible but were going to give

> one more chance—the *last*. First of all *all coppers must be pulled* off. Second *the dough must be ready* . . . the *money must not be hot* as it *will be examined* before bremer is released. If Dahill is so hot to meet us, you can send him out with the dough. Well try to be ready for any trickery if atempted. This is positively our LAST atempt. DONT duck it.[47]

The gang enclosed a letter from Bremer to his wife, Emily ("Patz"), and daughter, Betty ("Hertzy"), reproduced in an FBI memo:

> My dearest Patz and Hertzy:
>
> Oh, I've been thinking of you so much, day and night. I'm sure you could nearly feel it. I never knew I could miss you two so much. I can just see you waiting for me to come back—my dears—Dont loose courage, I'll be back with you before long & we'll never be apart again. I'm at a loss what to say—if I could only express my feeling you could understand.
>
> Now my dears pray hard and dont loose courage. I'll be holding you both in my arms before long and that is all that I want in this world is both of you—
>
> Your own, Daddy.[48]

To his sister Lill Bremer he wrote:

> I'm sure you'll do just as I ask you to. We always did understand each other. Its a living hell here and the time I've been here seems like ages. Please do your part and I'm assured I'll be home soon.[49]

Bremer was detained in Bensonville, Illinois, blindfolded and bound. The gang stripped him of his rosary, so Bremer said the rosary on his fingers throughout his captivity. "I would be so cramped that they would have to hold me when they bound me up at night to take me to the toilet when I went to bed," Bremer told the FBI. "I couldn't get my limbs apart."[50]

The gangsters fed the banker badly cooked oatmeal, chili, chop suey, and fried chicken, with desserts of strawberry shortcake and apple pie. The FBI reported later that "all of his food was too well seasoned, indicating to him that a man, who was inexperienced, did the seasoning."[51]

The gang quizzed Bremer about how much money was kept in his Commercial State Bank vault; he claimed there was never more than $50,000 in the bank at one time.[52]

On January 25, the Bremer family received another ransom note, this one stuffed inside a coffee can that had been left for the family at the home of John Miller, a pool hall proprietor.

"You better stop listening to those assholes this time do what *we* tell you," said this latest note. "The money *must be delivered tonight.* With all the conniving *we still got the boy. We* keep our word. Either *you* get him back tonight or the coppers bring him back *stiff.*" The Bremer family was to pick up a black zippered bag from St. Paul's Union Bus Depot. The ransom note ended with these words: "Its up to you—you *get* the boy *alive* or *dead.*"[53]

The bag contained yet another note with further instructions. On January 27, when Karpis learned that the Bremers were taking steps to obtain the money to pay the ransom, he prepared for the final act of the kidnapping. Wearing a dark wool jacket, high-topped leather boots, and a wool cap pulled down over his eyes, Karpis visited a St. Paul department store and bought some $3.12 worth of supplies—three flashlights, with bulbs and batteries.[54]

The banker's wife, Emily Elizabeth Bremer, and their daughter, Betty

The gang fed Bremer a final dinner of steak, mashed potatoes, and peas. "Eat hearty," they told him, "because this is going to be your last meal here." Throughout his captivity, Bremer had listened to and observed his captors. Interviewed later by the FBI, Bremer recalled the sounds of dogs barking and children playing nearby, the design on the gang's plates, the noise of a coal stove being filled, and even the look of the handle on the toilet: broken enamel over a metal screw. Most importantly, Bremer remembered every detail of the wallpaper pattern adorning the bedroom where he was imprisoned. It was a simple visual clue that—after the FBI sifted through 60,000 wallpaper patterns—would link several of the gangsters to the kidnapping and send them to prison for life.[55]

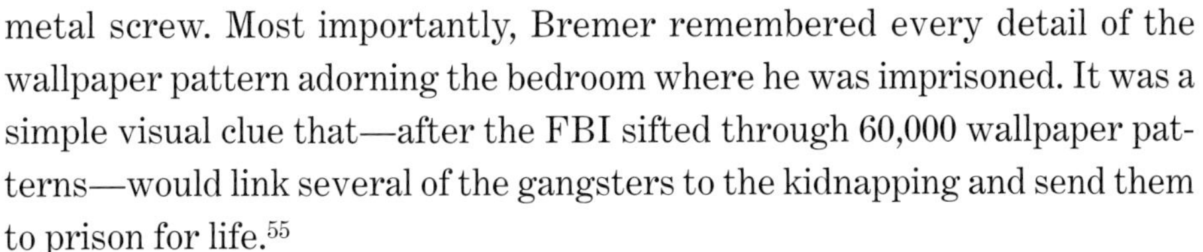

50 'Boys, I Am Counting on Your Honor'

The Home of Adolf Bremer Sr.
855 West Seventh Street, St. Paul

The $200,000 Bremer ransom was taken from a bank vault to the West Seventh Street home of Edward's father, Adolf. It was the same house where the newly freed Bremer would later be debriefed by officer Tom Brown after he was released by his kidnappers. The Bremer family later built a safety tunnel from Adolf Bremer's home to the basement of the Schmidt Brewery's Rathskeller bar.[56]

On February 6, 1934, Walter Magee drove a Ford sedan from the parking lot behind the Jacob Schmidt Brewing Company to the corner of St. Clair Avenue and West Seventh Street, where Adolph Bremer Jr., Edward's brother, helped him transfer the ransom money, packed in two suit boxes, to his car. Magee drove on to 969 University Avenue—the intersection of Chatsworth and University—where the gang said he would find a black Chevrolet coupe with Shell Oil signs on the door. Placing the $200,000 inside, Magee followed the instructions in a typewritten note ordering him to drive the Chevrolet to Farmington, Minnesota, and follow the Rochester bus until he saw five flashes of light.

Five miles outside of Zumbrota, at about 11:15 P.M., Magee saw the red lights on the left side of the road; behind him, a car flashed its lights five times. Magee left the ransom on the road, with a note from Adolf Bremer: "I have done my part and kept my word 100 percent, as I said I would. This money is not marked and you have the full amount asked for. Now, boys, I am counting on your honor."[57]

After twenty-one days in captivity, Bremer was released near Rochester, Minnesota, on February 7. His body still sore from being bound, he took a train and a bus to St. Paul, and walked onto the back porch of his father's home just after midnight. He was an apparition to his surprised sister Louise and to the FBI agent on guard. "My father had gone to bed, and suddenly I heard someone at the door," recalled Louise Benz, still moved by the memory nearly sixty years later. "And there was Ed. I had to look twice as he had quite a beard at that time. We brought him inside—and he was scared to death. . . . He was so shaken and . . . frightened."[58]

"When my dad returned he was ashen, very thin," recalled Betty Bremer Johnson. "We tried not to talk about [the kidnapping]. It made dad nervous and his knuckles would whiten."[59]

The FBI interviewed Bremer at his home on February 11 but found him a terrified and sometimes frustrating source of information. "I mentioned the duty which he owed the Government and to the American people," wrote one FBI agent, "whereupon, he remarked: 'To hell with the duty.'" The kidnappers had threatened to kill Bremer's daughter if he talked to the FBI.[60]

The bureau was unmoved by Bremer's distress. After speaking to both kidnap victims—William Hamm Jr. and Bremer—an FBI inspector wrote in May 1934 to J. Edgar Hoover that "I can readily understand why it is called '*kid*'naping."[61]

Magee returned with FBI agents to Zumbrota, where they found the three flashlights and a pocket lantern purchased by Alvin Karpis. The bureau's nationwide investigation was astonishingly detailed. Ten agents in New York alone searched through thousands of wallpaper samples to help identify the Bensonville hideout. Others searched for the Sears Roebuck store that sold the Barker-Karpis gang its red signal light. Agents even searched for the store where the gang bought the underwear given to Bremer as his final change of clothes.[62]

The bureau's breakthrough came on February 10, when a Wisconsin farmer discovered four gasoline cans and a tin funnel that had been used to refill the gang's car. The Washington, D.C., crime laboratory identified a fingerprint from a gas can as Doc Barker's. Two days later, an underworld informant told the FBI that the Bremer kidnapping involved "two brothers by the name of Dick and Freddy, who have an ugly old woman with them who poses as their mother"—a passable description of the Barker-Karpis gang. The informant said that the FBI telephones in St. Paul were not secure, warning "that at St. Paul everything is under the control of the syndicate and that it would probably be very unwise to use either the telephone or telegraph between Washington and St. Paul," the FBI noted.[63]

By then policeman Tom Brown, no longer head of the Kidnap Detail and under investigation by the FBI for leaks to the underworld, did not have access to information that could benefit the Barker-Karpis gang. For the first time since 1931, the gang had no inside contact in the police department to warn them of FBI and police raids. The FBI learned that Fred Goetz had revealed that "Harry Sawyer wanted to give Tom Brown his full split out of the Bremer Case, but some of them objected because he wasn't doing them any good, because the Federal officials wouldn't let him sit in on the conferences. And it was finally decided to give him $5,000."[64]

J. Edgar Hoover's public fury was aimed at Ma Barker, but FBI files make clear that it was Goetz, not Doc's and Fred's mother, who directed the Hamm and Bremer kidnappings. Unfortunately, Goetz loved to brag in Chicago pubs about his exploits back in the Twin Cities—regaling his drinking partners with hints about where the Bremer ransom was hidden and the names of his collaborators. On March 20, 1934, the thirty-nine-year-old Goetz walked out of the Minerva Cafe in Cicero, Illinois, and, in the words of FBI agent Melvin Purvis, was "shot directly in the face from close range with a shotgun, which caused considerable disfigurement, and any photographs will very likely be of doubtful value." Agents had to identify the body from the fingerprints.[65]

Newspapers guessed that Goetz was slain by the Barker-Karpis gang in a fight over the Bremer ransom money. Louis "Lefty Louie" Campagna, a Capone syndicate associate of Goetz, told friends that he was killed because "the St. Paul outfit put him on the spot." In his autobiography, Karpis insisted that the murder was a syndicate hit, although he acknowledged that Goetz had been "getting kind of gabby" and could easily have led the FBI to the Barkers. Irene Goetz told the FBI that immediately after her husband's death, Fred Barker heard her speaking of him and muttered, "To hell with George."[66]

Two days after Goetz was shot, the U.S. attorney general publicly

Deputy inspecting evidence for the Bremer trial, including gasoline can with Doc Barker's fingerprint

identified Karpis as one of the men who kidnapped Ed Bremer. The next day, the gang retrieved about $100,000 of the ransom money from Goetz's hiding place—wrapped in brown paper in the garage of Irene Goetz's relatives in Wilmington, Illinois—and distributed it to gang members.[67]

By then the gang had begun to splinter. The FBI later learned from Karpis, who had always been fond of Ma Barker, that "towards the last months of her life Kate Barker appeared to be endeavoring to cause trouble between the various members of the gangs, in that she would make statements to one member of the gang derogatory to the other, and that he believed that she was going insane from worry."[68]

In her confession, Edna Murray told the FBI that in July 1934, "I overheard a heated argument between Fred Barker and Volney [Davis]. From their conversation, I believed they were arguing about something that Fred's mother was supposed to have said about Volney, which Volney thought was a lie. I overheard him say, 'I am a man and I cover all the ground I stand on. I wouldn't bring my mother into an argument, you would be a ______ if you didn't hold up for your mother, but I still say she is a damn liar.'" Davis decided to leave the gang to avoid the friction caused by Ma Barker.[69]

While the gang members squabbled, the forensic evidence that would send them to prison was being collected by the FBI crime laboratory. "The Bremer case provided the ultimate justification of a federal police corps which transcends state lines and the rivalries and inefficiencies of local jurisdictions," wrote FBI agent Melvin Purvis.[70]

Many of the clues led directly to the Shoreview farm of Harry Sawyer, the Green Lantern operator, who had chosen Bremer as the gang's second kidnapping victim.

51 Secret Tunnels, Forgotten Dynamite, and Buried Bullets

Harry "Dutch" Sawyer's Farm
305 Snail Lake Road, Shoreview

During Harry Sawyer's trial for kidnapping Edward Bremer, government witness Edna Murray was asked for the name of the first person whom she saw when she and Volney Davis, Paula Harmon, and Fred Barker drove back to Minnesota in August 1933. "Harry Sawyer," answered Murray. "We saw him at this country home, about four or five miles from downtown St. Paul." Sawyer's Shoreview farm operated as a rustic hideout, overnight haven, message drop, and conference center for many of the most wanted gangsters of the 1930s.[71]

FBI files suggest that Sawyer's farm was purchased, in part, with money stolen on April 4, 1933, from the First National Bank of Fairbury, Nebraska. The Fairbury culprits—the Barker brothers and Alvin Karpis, along with Frank Nash, Jess Doyle, and Verne Miller—drove off with more than $151,000. "The money obtained in this robbery was turned over to Harry Sawyer to exchange for cool money," the FBI learned from Beth Green of the Dillinger gang. "Sawyer kept a much larger percentage than they planned for him to take and shortly afterwards bought a farm near the Twin Cities, and the boys frequently laughed about having bought this farm for Sawyer."[72]

Harry Sawyer, then proprietor of the Green Lantern saloon, purchased the ten-acre farm in 1933. He lived there with his wife, Gladys, and Francine, the five-year-old they hoped to adopt, until April 1934, when the Sawyers fled an FBI dragnet. As each of the Barker-Karpis gang's girlfriends was captured and interrogated, the FBI got a fuller picture of the role the farm played for the underworld. The guest list included bank robbers Frank Nash, Alvin Karpis, Fred and Doc Barker, Harry Campbell, Volney Davis, Jack Peifer, and William Weaver, along with Myrtle Eaton, Paula Harmon, and Edna Murray.[73]

The farm offered the mobsters two benefits: advance warnings of police raids and a location remote enough to frustrate surveillance. Immediately after the March 31, 1934, shootout between John Dillinger and St. Paul FBI agents, John "Three Fingered Jack" Hamilton hid at the farm. Hamilton was able to escape when a St. Paul policeman telephoned Sawyer, warning that his fellow officers were about to arrest the Dillinger gang member.[74]

"Dapper Dan" Hogan had succeeded in the 1920s by serving criminals; his protégé, Harry Sawyer, was the fulcrum between gangsters and corrupt policemen in the 1930s. Tom Brown was a frequent visitor to the farm, and other officers often dropped by to discuss the FBI's activities with Sawyer. Finally the FBI struck back, raiding the farm on July 26, 1934, and then again on September 7, 1934. The September raid netted three of Sawyer's helpers—housekeeper Marie McCarthy, handyman Frank Kirwin, and caretaker William Gray—who were wanted for harboring Dillinger gang member Homer Van Meter at a Leech Lake, Minnesota, resort.[75]

When Sawyer discovered that FBI agents were hunting him for questioning in the Bremer case, he fled the farm and met Karpis in Cleveland to retrieve his share of the ransom money. It was a testament to Sawyer's criminal standing that he was entrusted by the gang to launder the remaining $100,000 of the Bremer ransom money for "clean" bills and Cuban gold in Miami.[76]

On September 5, 1934, Gladys Sawyer and two of the farm's most frequent visitors—Wynona Burdette and Paula Harmon—got tipsy in a Cleveland hotel and were arrested by police on drunk and disorderly charges. The trio was nearly freed, but Sawyer's little girl innocently blurted out her mother's identity. The three wanted women were held in the Chicago FBI office and persuaded to provide lengthy confessions that exposed the inner workings of the Barker-Karpis gang. It was the breakthrough the FBI had been searching for.[77]

As the decades passed, the farm disgorged evidence of its gangland legacy. A new tenant, sausage company employee Fred Kohrt, was digging in the garden in May 1936 when he unearthed machine gun cartridges and sticks of dynamite buried in two-gallon pails. His six-year-old son found a pail of .45-caliber machine gun bullets in a nearby grove of trees.[78]

Virginia and Paul Comstock discovered two tunnels in the basement after they moved into the farmhouse in 1963. One tunnel crossed under Highway 49 (Hodgson Road), and the other led behind the barn. "The cement covering the tunnel was so honeycombed, when you tapped on it, it was clearly hollow," recalled Paul Comstock. "I went down with a pickax and broke through that cement. It was only two inches thick and it had been filled out with sand. The tunnel went straight down four or five feet to get under the footings and then veered out toward Hodgson Road."[79]

After purchasing the Sawyer farm in 1985, Dirk Boardsen, a residential contractor, was gutting the upstairs of the farmhouse when he made an odd discovery. "I was doing the upstairs bedroom, insulating the knee walls," he said. He was reaching down in the floor and discovered two pairs of prescription bifocal eyeglasses from the 1930s or 1940s. A few years later, he found three more pairs in the ceiling. "I don't know why they would have hid eyeglasses in the ceiling," Boardsen said, "unless the glasses were from the guys they killed."[80]

9

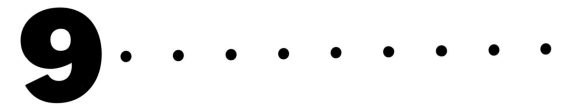

JOHN DILLINGER SLEPT HERE

Bank robber John Dillinger; FBI Director J. Edgar Hoover, aiming a submachine gun

52 A Dillinger Mob Reunion

Dillinger's Hideout at the Santa Monica Apartments
3252 South Girard Avenue, Minneapolis

The habits of the couple living in apartment 106 at the Santa Monica Apartments in Minneapolis were strange, all right. It wasn't just how Mrs. Olson paid the fifty-dollar advance deposit on the apartment from a roll of dollar bills. More sinister were the shades in the Olsons' apartment: janitor Silas Lancaster told the FBI that after the Olsons moved in on March 5, 1934, he found the shades wired shut to prevent any light from escaping outside.[1]

But then, the Olsons had good reason to be wary of daylight. Irvin Olson was actually outlaw John Dillinger, then evading a nationwide manhunt after his escape from the Lake County Jail in Crown Point, Indiana.

The thirty-one-year-old Dillinger, held on charges of murdering a police officer during his robbery of $20,000 from the First National Bank of East Chicago, Indiana, had bluffed his way out of the "escape-proof" Crown Point jail on March 3, 1934, with a fake gun he made with wood from a washboard, razor blades, and black shoe polish.[2]

Mrs. Olson was really Evelyn "Billie" Frechette, a twenty-six-year-old Wisconsinite raised on a Menominee Indian reservation, who had fallen in love with Dillinger when she met him in a Chicago nightclub in November 1933. FBI files noted Frechette's "use of a great deal of profanity," describing her as "of the 'hard-boiled' gangster moll type of woman . . . the thrill-seeking type."[3]

When Dillinger met Evelyn, he treated her "like a lady," though his dancing was terrible, she said later: "I didn't know he had been locked up in a prison for years and didn't have a chance to dance. We stepped all over each other's toes, but he said he liked to dance with me." Dillinger confessed to Evelyn, then working variously as a waitress, saleswoman, and nanny, the larcenous nature of his livelihood. The men accompanying them to Minnesota were more than friends, Dillinger admitted. They were thieves, bank robbers, and killers—the Dillinger gang. "What did Dillinger tell you his gang did for a living?" a federal prosecutor asked Frechette during her trial for harboring Dillinger. "Robbing banks, I suppose," she replied.[4]

After his May 1933 parole from Indiana State Prison in Michigan City, Dillinger had launched a career that left at least twelve men dead and at least seven wounded. His violent "withdrawal" of $500,000 from numerous banks resulted in the conviction of twenty-seven people for aiding the Dillinger gang and inspired J. Edgar Hoover to dub him "Public Enemy Number One."

The nation's most famous fugitive had picked up Frechette in Chicago on

Train robber Homer Van Meter, Dillinger's partner after meeting in an Indiana prison

March 4, 1934, and reunited with gang members Lester "Babyface Nelson" Gillis and John Hamilton. Dillinger drove his partners to the cities that boasted the safest haven in America for mobsters—St. Paul and Minneapolis. By stealing a car from an Indiana sheriff and driving it across state lines to Chicago (thus violating the National Motor Vehicle Theft Act), Dillinger gave the FBI its opportunity to launch a manhunt for his gang. His case was assigned the FBI designation JODIL.[5]

At the Santa Monica Apartments in south Minneapolis, Dillinger hosted a reunion of his gang, and they began plotting bank heists in Iowa and South Dakota. Like Dillinger, who started out as a machinist in Indianapolis, most of the gang gathered there had abandoned legal employment during the Depression, concluding that steady but slow bank deposits were less rewarding than a series of quick withdrawals. Dillinger had been forced to re-create his gang because his original partners—Harry Pierpont, Russell Clark, and Charles Makley—had been jailed in Tucson, Arizona, in early 1934.[6]

Closest to Dillinger was train robber Homer Van Meter, a former waiter from Fort Wayne, Indiana, who had befriended the bank robber while both were serving time in Indiana State Reformatory at Pendleton and the state prison at Michigan City. The twenty-nine-year-old Van Meter was a slender (just over 130 pounds and 5 feet, 10 inches tall), blue-eyed recluse with a scar in the middle of his forehead and "Hope" tattooed on his right forearm.[7]

"Homer Van Meter was more or less a lone wolf," recalled Bernice Clark, wife of Dillinger gang member Russell Clark. "He kept to himself as much as possible." Although Van Meter had a girlfriend, Clark said that "Van was afraid of women—I mean he figured that most of them couldn't be trusted. And I guess he was right. If he had just stuck to that idea maybe he wouldn't have got killed the way he did." An FBI informant who had eavesdropped on the gang recalled, "Van Meter seemed to dominate over Dillinger," who "would ask the advice of Van Meter about different things."[8]

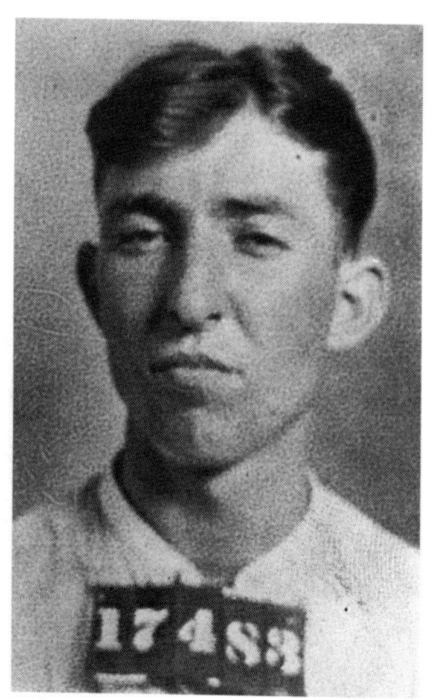

Harry Eugene "Eddie" Green, bank-robbery scout for Dillinger

Of special value to Dillinger was Harry Eugene "Eddie" Green, a St. Paul iron worker who served six months in a Milwaukee workhouse for grand larceny and a state prison term in St. Cloud and Stillwater in 1922 for robbing a cashier of a $2,000 payroll. While he was in St. Cloud, Green was repeatedly locked in solitary confinement for a variety of infractions, including striking an inmate during dinner and causing a disturbance when he returned from chapel "imitating the ladies singing." Describing Green's temperament as "mercurial," the St. Cloud physician's report said that "this is the type with criminal tendencies, selfish, impulsive and hard to manage."[9]

"They were two of the most unruly prisoners we have had any dealing with," said the chief of the Des Moines, Iowa, police, who arrested Green and a companion in 1922 on a charge of grand larceny. "They said they would return and get revenge. I informed them that I would be here when they came. . . . Unless they have changed their attitude wonderfully they would be a menace to society."[10]

Green was born in Pueblo, Colorado; his father died when he was just three. "His mother is a good woman," said Ramsey County judge J. B. Sanborn, "but the rest of the family prefer to live outside of the law." Green became a "jug marker"—a scout who evaluated banks as robbery targets for Dillinger and Babyface Nelson. "You've got to case a jug," advised bank robber Eddie Bentz, a contemporary of Green. "It's a lot like playing solitaire. You drive past the bank a few times and size up the surroundings, whether there are good getaway streets, whether the bank's got a squawker on the outside, whether there's a traffic cop on the corner. . . . Maybe you meet the bank manager. . . . maybe you'll throw out a few hints that you've heard the bank wasn't too solid, and half the time the guy will take you on a personal tour of inspection to show you what a swell lay-out he's got."[11]

Rounding out the Dillinger gang was a quiet but hot-tempered Michigan carpenter named John Hamilton, who received a twenty-five-year prison term for robbing an Indiana gas station. Hamilton was nicknamed "Three Fingered Jack," a reference to his having lost the index and middle fingers on his right hand. Family members attributed the missing digits variously to a factory accident or to an angry girlfriend with a butcher knife. Hamilton owed Dillinger and Van Meter for enabling him to escape from the Indiana State Prison in Michigan City on September 26, 1933, via revolvers hidden in barrels of thread. In turn, Hamilton had proven his worth by helping Dillinger take $74,728 from the Central National Bank of Greencastle, Indiana, and $27,789 from the American Bank and Trust Company of Racine, Wisconsin. Hamilton was also responsible for the brutal murder of Chicago police detective William T. Shanley, who was shot to death in Chicago on December 14, 1933, after he investigated reports that Hamilton's green auto had been seen in an Illinois garage.[12]

Apparently, Hamilton had one major flaw as a bank robber: "Somebody forgot to give John a memory," recalled Bernice Clark. "He'd forget addresses of the places we were staying and he'd even forget the aliases he was using. He'd stumble into trouble and stumble out of it somehow."[13]

Finally, there was jewel thief Lester Gillis, a veteran of Al Capone's syndicate. Just under 5 feet, 5 inches, and weighing barely 133 pounds, he preferred to be called "Big George" but was best known by the nickname he despised: Babyface Nelson. Famous for a near-psychopathic love of machine guns, Nelson was considered a reckless killer.[14]

Reportedly consumed with jealousy over Dillinger's fame, Nelson applied to Homer Van Meter to offer his services to the Dillinger gang. From the day he joined the gang, Nelson proved to be a magnet for violence. On March 4, 1934, a thirty-five-year-old paint salesman named Theodore Kidder had a streetside altercation involving a Hudson sedan at the intersection of Lake Street and Chicago Avenue in Minneapolis. In the Hudson was Nelson and his partner John Paul Chase, who followed the unsuspecting Kidder to his St. Louis Park home. There, as Kidder's wife watched, Nelson stepped out of the car and fired several .32-caliber bullets, killing Kidder. Police were able to identify the shooter's 1934 California license plate, which, according to the FBI, "was traced to James Rogers, the alias used by Gillis [Nelson] in purchasing the Hudson sedan." Not until 1941, when Nelson's partner Joseph "Fatso" Negri talked about his underworld adventures, was an inside account of Kidder's murder released—although Negri mistakenly believed the murder occurred at the scene of the car accident. Nelson had told him, "I and two or three of the boys were driving . . . in Minneapolis . . . and we happened to cut in ahead of another car. The driver, one of those fresh guys, cut right back in front of us. He stopped his car, got out and came back toward us and said to me: 'What the h[ell] do you mean? Get out of that car and I'll slap your face for you.' He had taken a step or two toward us when I leveled on him and hit him. Then we had to tear out of that place."[15]

Uniting the gang was John Dillinger himself, the baseball-loving son of an Indianapolis grocer. Dillinger graduated from car thievery, mugging, and

WANTED

LESTER M. GILLIS,

aliases GEORGE NELSON, "BABY FACE" NELSON, ALEX GILLIS, LESTER GILES, "BIG GEORGE" NELSON, "JIMMIE", "JIMMY" WILLIAMS .

On June 23, 1934, HOMER S. CUMMINGS, Attorney General of the United States, under the authority vested in him by an Act of Congress approved June 6, 1934, offered a reward of

$5,000.00

for the capture of Lester M. Gillis or a reward of

$2,500.00

for information leading to the arrest of Lester M. Gillis.

DESCRIPTION

Age, 25 years; Height, 5 feet 4-3/4 inches; Weight, 133 pounds; Build, medium; Eyes, yellow and grey slate; Hair, light chestnut; Complexion, light; Occupation, oiler.

All claims to any of the aforesaid rewards and all questions and disputes that may arise as among claimants to the foregoing rewards shall be passed upon by the Attorney General and his decisions shall be final and conclusive. The right is reserved to divide and allocate portions of any of said rewards as between several claimants. No part of the aforesaid rewards shall be paid to any official or employee of the Department of Justice.

If you are in possession of any information concerning the whereabouts of Lester M. Gillis, communicate immediately by telephone or telegraph collect to the nearest office of the Division of Investigation, United States Department of Justice, the local offices of which are set forth on the reverse side of this notice.

The apprehension of Lester M. Gillis is sought in connection with the murder of Special Agent W. C. Baum of the Division of Investigation near Rhinelander, Wisconsin on April 23, 1934.

JOHN EDGAR HOOVER, DIRECTOR,
DIVISION OF INVESTIGATION,
UNITED STATES DEPARTMENT OF JUSTICE,
WASHINGTON, D. C.

June 25, 1934

BUREAU OF CRIMINAL APPREHENSION
IDENTIFICATION DIVISION
488 WABASHA STREET
ST. PAUL 2, MINNESOTA

Wanted poster for Lester "Babyface Nelson" Gillis

stealing coal from railroads to become, in the words of *True Detective* magazine, "a by-word in every country of the civilized world. . . . His trail across the black vault of national notoriety has been as spectacular as the rocket-like course of a comet. A red comet!"[16]

Dillinger was embittered by a severe ten- to twenty-year sentence, which he served in the Pendleton, Indiana, reformatory and the state penitentiary in Michigan City, for mugging an elderly grocer. During his imprisonment, his wife, Beryl, filed for divorce. His stepmother died less than an hour before his May 1933 release from a nine-year stretch in prison. Just three weeks after his release, Dillinger robbed a New Carlisle, Ohio, bank of $10,600. During the next nine months, he was believed to have robbed nearly a dozen banks in Indiana, Illinois, Wisconsin, Ohio, and Michigan; escaped a police ambush in Chicago; and raided police stations in Auburn and Peru, Indiana, to acquire bulletproof vests and weapons. By March 1934, Dillinger found himself hiding in Minneapolis—hunted by county sheriffs, state and city police, the FBI, the National Guard, and a forty-member Chicago police "Dillinger Squad."[17]

Evelyn Frechette later told *Startling Detective Adventures* magazine how the gang's stay in the Santa Monica Apartments was cut short: "[John] Hamilton was taking off his coat one evening when he pulled his pistol from its shoulder holster," said Frechette. "The weapon clattered to the floor and discharged. We packed our clothes and were on our way in less than ten minutes."[18] Dillinger next surfaced at the Lincoln Court Apartments in St. Paul. It turned out to be among the most dangerous moves of his career.

53 John Dillinger's Safehouse

The Charlou and Josephine Apartments
3300 and 3310 South Fremont Avenue, Minneapolis

When the FBI raided the Charlou Apartments hideout of the Dillinger gang at 3300 Fremont Avenue in Minneapolis in April 1934, the usually grim bureau offered a glimpse of Justice Department humor. In tallying the armaments they found, the agents counted "one bullet-proof vest, one loaded 50-round machine-gun, one Thompson sub-machine gun and one .45 automatic pistol and one high-powered rifle (nice people)."[19]

Dillinger lieutenant Eddie Green, masquerading as shoe salesman Theodore J. Randall, had rented apartment 207 in the Charlou Apartments in September 1933 to store this weaponry.[20]

Homer Van Meter, newly paroled from Indiana State Prison, lived in the adjacent 3310 Fremont building—the Josephine Apartments. Van Meter stayed in apartment 201 with his twenty-year-old girlfriend Marie Conforti from January to early February 1934. Van Meter, posing as John L. Ober, told Marie that his real name was Ted Ancker, giving her an alias for his alias. "He never told me what his business was," Conforti later told the FBI. "He never told me the address of any business he was connected with, and never introduced me to any of his friends."[21]

From these Fremont Avenue apartment buildings, members of the Dillinger gang executed their March 6 robbery of $49,500 from the Security National Bank of Sioux Falls, South Dakota. On March 13 the gang took $52,000 from the First National Bank of Mason City, Iowa, where they held nearly fifty customers and employees at gunpoint, leaving two innocent bystanders wounded. A telegram from the FBI's Melvin Purvis to director J. Edgar Hoover reveals that the bureau learned from informant Bernice Clark of the Dillinger gang that the "mob now has plenty of money because of Mason City and Sioux Falls Bank jobs[,] also some of mob shot up a little in these jobs but not serious enough for medical attention."[22]

What inspired the gang's girlfriends to risk their lives to follow these armed men from state to state, hunted by police and deceived by their lovers? Conforti, a former department store clerk from Chicago, recalled how Van Meter asked her to leave Illinois and accompany the gang: "Van Meter told me at this time that he was glad to see me again and asked me if I would go with him. At first I was undecided, but later agreed to do so, inasmuch as I did not have any money, and further I did not care to hang around the house."[23]

In other cases, the gangsters may have used force. FBI agents learned from Beth Green, Eddie Green's girlfriend, that Myrtle Eaton, girlfriend of Barker-Karpis gang member William Weaver, "disliked Bill very much, but that Bill would on occasions kidnap her or force her to accompany him on trips at the point of a gun. . . . Myrtle Eaton would welcome Bill Weaver's apprehension [by the FBI] because she is desperately in fear of him."[24]

The lifestyle of the Dillinger gang girlfriends was hardly more glamorous than the tedious jobs they left behind. J. Edgar Hoover publicly reviled them, referring to them in his 1938 book, *Persons in Hiding*, as "dirty, filthy, diseased women." The mobsters often left their women infected with venereal disease (the FBI files are filled with references to treatment at Twin Cities hospitals for "abdominal and female trouble"), pregnant, battered, and betrayed.[25]

At times, gang members were more frightened of having their illicit affairs exposed than of being apprehended by the police. Bank robber Tommy Gannon confessed to FBI agents that he hung out at a root beer stand on Rice Street in St. Paul because he was attracted to a woman there. Having blurted out this admission, Gannon suddenly begged the FBI not to mention it "because it might cause some trouble if his wife found out."[26]

In the end, both Beth Green and Jean Delaney saw their lovers gunned down before their eyes; virtually all of the other Dillinger women were arrested, convicted, and imprisoned. Yet Frechette wrote, "I think I was happier with John Dillinger while we were living in the Twin Cities than I ever was before or since. It wasn't because we didn't have plenty to worry about, because we did. We went out a lot, but it didn't seem the same because—well, we all were getting the jitters. All except John. He was just a little more careful."[27]

The most likely place to spot a Dillinger gang member was not in a bank vault but in a Twin Cities movie house. Green told FBI agents that Dillinger "was crazy about motion pictures." He took in the film *Joe Palooka* in St. Paul and *Fashions of 1933* at a Minneapolis theater. Dillinger warned Eddie Green not to take Beth to see *Fashions* because it would put bad ideas into her head. Frechette wrote that Dillinger's favorite movie was a cartoon, Walt Disney's *The Three Little Pigs*. Tommy Carroll went to the movies about three times a week, and Marie Conforti told FBI agents that Homer Van Meter was particularly fond of Eddie Cantor films.[28]

St. Paul residents were not distressed when they saw John Dillinger and his gang in a Grand Avenue movie theater or in a nightclub like the Boulevards of Paris. "As kids, we thought gangsters were like football players—guys like Dillinger were *heroes* to us," said Charlie Reiter, a former police officer and Bureau of Criminal Apprehension executive. "Those gangsters were glamorized in the newspapers and the detective-story magazines. In those days, kids didn't have many people to admire—we had fighters, baseball players, and gangsters!"[29]

Reiter worked as a fry cook at Frank McCormick's Town Talk Sandwich Shop at 418 Wabasha in downtown St. Paul, a favorite spot for Homer Van Meter. "Three Fingered Jack" Hamilton hid in the Town Talk immediately after Dillinger's 1934 shootout in the Lincoln Court Apartments. "It was nothing in St. Paul to see John Dillinger's men in the Town Talk," said Reiter. "Van Meter would want the special center cut of the ham, the best. He'd tip me a quarter, which was an hour's wage!" As a boy, Reiter sold newspapers; he recalled gangsters who would "give you a quarter for a three-cent paper. They were great people as far as we were concerned!"[30]

Unlike the St. Paul citizens who romanticized the gangsters, the FBI considered Dillinger a "brutal thief and a cold-blooded murderer." He dismissed the threat of local police but viewed the FBI with respect born of fear. Dillinger "made the remark that he got a big kick out of filling station attendants asking him whether he had seen Dillinger," the FBI learned from an informant. He "expressed the utmost contempt for local police departments, calling them a 'lot of clucks,'" but admitted his fear of federal agents because they "had all the money they needed to keep up the search."[31]

On April 3, 1934, the FBI found the address of the Charlou Apartments on a fake driver's license in Beth Green's purse, but when detectives burst into the Charlou, the Dillinger gang was gone. Besides guns and ammunition, they had left behind a first aid kit (morphine, bandages, tape, and cat gut), and eleven notebooks filled with what the FBI called "get-away road charts, generally used in bank robberies."[32]

Those highway maps were vital to the success of Dillinger's vault-busting raids; he had taken to carrying an atlas with him to find the most suitable roads for high-speed getaways.[33]

54 Midnight Medicine

The Home of Dr. Nels Mortensen
2252 Fairmount Avenue, St. Paul

Just after midnight on March 14, 1934, St. Paul physician Nels Mortensen answered the doorbell at his Fairmount Avenue home and discovered four desperate men on his front steps. "I had no thought that these men were criminals or belonged to any gang or underworld group, until they were departing," said Dr. Mortensen in a statement later to authorities. "Then I caught sight of a machine gun under one of the men's coats."[34]

Wounded in the left shoulders by shots fired by a policeman during the Mason City bank job earlier in the day, Dillinger and John Hamilton had driven with Homer Van Meter to St. Paul, seeking emergency medical care. They decided to make an unannounced visit to Dr. Mortensen, an acquaintance of the Dillinger gang's driver, William Albert "Pat" Reilly.[35]

Born in Copenhagen, Denmark, in 1884, Mortensen was a 6-foot-tall war veteran with bushy gray hair. Far from being an underworld sawbones, he was a distinguished physician who had served as president of the state's Board of Health, as city health commissioner, and as a lieutenant colonel in the U.S. Army Reserve Medical Corps.[36]

The two robbers were escorted into the Mortensens' vestibule by Reilly, who was also a bartender at Harry Sawyer's Green Lantern saloon. Reilly was the official mascot and clubhouse boy for two teams, the local American Association baseball franchise and the Dillinger gang. A twenty-seven-year-old Irish American, he had been a petty gambler and bootlegger since 1928. Prison records described his florid face as "slightly pitted, slightly cleft chin, cut scar" and listed his bad habits: "smokes, drinks to excess, sex experience." Reilly "has for many years associated with underworld characters of the worst type," said a Leavenworth prison parole report. "He has never worked, except to sell alcohol. He has also at various times operated a soft drink parlor which has been a rendezvous for criminals and other under world characters." Although authorities admitted that Reilly himself was "not to be regarded as vicious," his association with the Dillinger gang led them to label him "a menace to society."[37]

Dr. Nels Mortensen, president of Minnesota's Board of Health, who tended John Dillinger's wounds

In 1927 Reilly married into what would become a family trio of gun molls when he wed Helen "Babe" Delaney, the wisecracking sister of Delores Delaney (girlfriend of Alvin Karpis) and Jean Delaney (girlfriend of Tommy Carroll). Reilly's mother-in-law, also named Helen Delaney, was not happy about the marriage. ("She utterly hates Pat Reilly," the FBI noted.) FBI files recorded an incident in which the mother personally served divorce papers for her daughter against Reilly; when the thug drew a pistol on his mother-in-law, she swore at him, walked up, and wrenched the revolver out of his hands.[38]

Reilly told Dr. Mortensen that Hamilton and Dillinger had been injured in a gunfight in Minneapolis. Dillinger stripped off his shirt and nearly fainted from the pain when Mortensen probed the wound. Because the doctor did not have his medical bag at home, he asked the quartet to visit his office during the next day. The men did not reappear, but FBI agents did—with a vengeance.[39]

When the FBI interrogated Beth Green, she revealed Mortensen's role in taking care of Dillinger. The FBI "invited" Mortensen, who claimed that he had been too frightened to report the Dillinger visit, to drop by the FBI office on April 20, 1934, for a chat. Mortensen had first come to the attention of the FBI in July 1933, when his name surfaced as a reference for Fred Barker, who rented the Barker-Karpis gang's hideout at 204 Vernon Street. A bottle of medicine for treating venereal disease that was found at 204 Vernon had been prescribed by Mortensen. He also admitted that he had received a contribution toward his campaign for Ramsey County coroner from underworld fixer Harry Sawyer and that he served as physician to both Sawyer and Pat Reilly. The FBI discovered that Alvin Karpis had used Mortensen as a reference when he leased an Illinois apartment in April 1933. Accordingly, the FBI placed the doctor's home under surveillance in the hope that Dillinger might return, but the bank robber had already gone underground on Lexington Parkway.[40]

"An example should be made of this physician," wrote a frustrated J. Edgar Hoover in April, when other FBI officials recommended leniency for the doctor, "particularly in view of his official status in the medical profession in St. Paul. . . . [Mortensen] should be publicly exposed and prosecuted for the action which he has indulged in." The bureau's desperation was reflected in an FBI official's comment that "Pat Reilly was the man to get, that frankly they had been informed that if they drug him in and knocked him in the head with something and waited until he came to and then started talking to him, that he would give them more information than anybody else possesses in the Twin Cities." When the bureau later arrested three Dillinger gang girlfriends at a Wisconsin resort, an FBI official privately advised special agent in charge Sam Hardy "not to give the girls anything to eat and not to let them sleep until they talked."[41]

The FBI knew that the U.S. attorney's office in St. Paul had declared "positively that they had no evidence" that Dr. Mortensen was aware of Dillinger's identity when he examined his wounds, and FBI officials privately admitted that "it would be hard to prove." Still, they recommended on April 24 that agents manufacture negative newspaper publicity against Mortensen through "a statement out of Washington blasting him," which "would no doubt ruin the doctor." One week later, the U.S. attorney general savaged Mortensen publicly: "Excuse me for getting so heated about it," Homer Cummings said to reporters, after he castigated "doctors and lawyers and political bosses [who were] co-operating with criminals."[42]

Mortensen died in 1971 at the age of eighty-seven, insisting to the last that he had no idea that his patients, the men with the poorly concealed machine guns, were public enemies.[43]

55 'I Am Not Going to Let These Cops in Here'

Shootout at the Lincoln Court Apartments
93 South Lexington Parkway, St. Paul

While his gunshot wounds were healing, John Dillinger moved with Evelyn Frechette on March 19, 1934, to the Lincoln Court Apartments, a block from gracious Grand Avenue. It was to be a brief but climactic stay.

Building owner Daisy Coffey noticed something odd about the couple, registered as Mr. and Mrs. Carl P. Hellman, shortly after they moved into apartment 303, and she reported them to the FBI's St. Paul office. "The Hellmans usually remained indoors and when they did go out, they used the rear entrance," the FBI reported. "They lowered their shades just after dusk each evening and kept them lowered until about 10:30 each morning. They

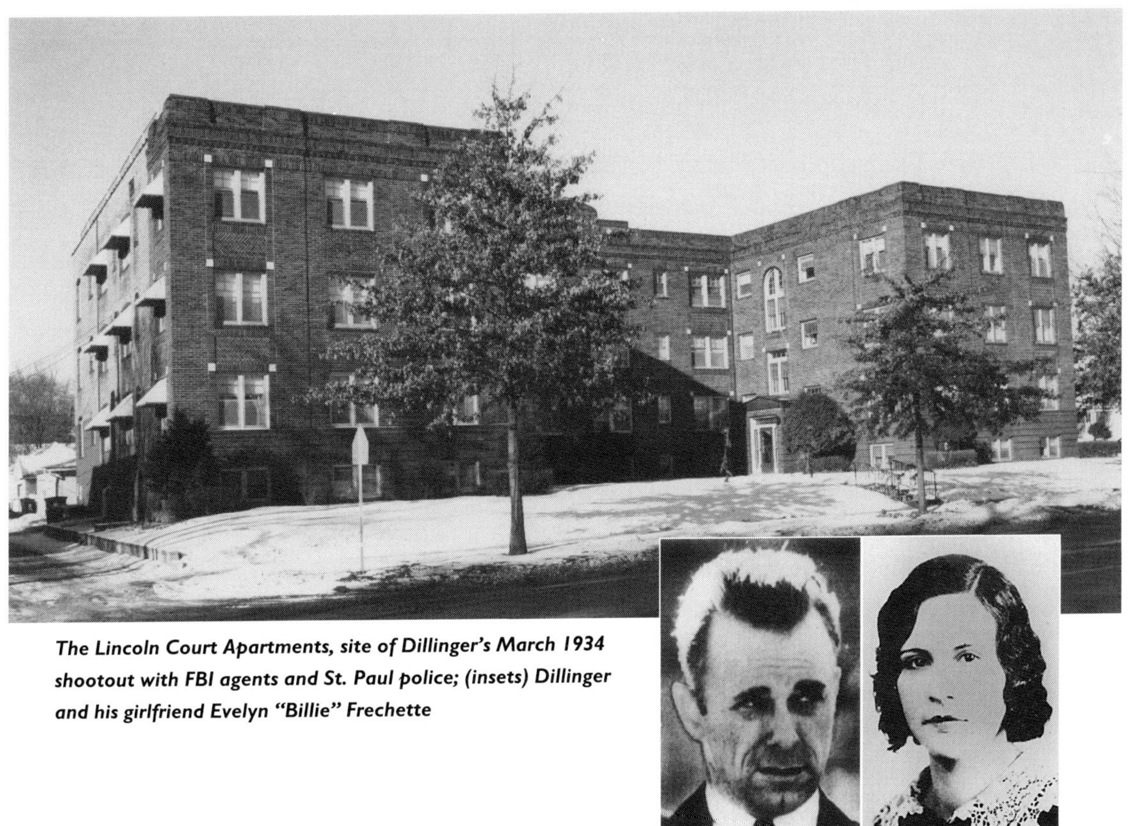

The Lincoln Court Apartments, site of Dillinger's March 1934 shootout with FBI agents and St. Paul police; (insets) Dillinger and his girlfriend Evelyn "Billie" Frechette

refused to allow the caretaker to enter the apartment on one occasion to replace a bathroom fixture, advising him that Mr. Hellman was bathing."[44]

Neighborhood boys also made a noteworthy discovery. "This Evelyn—she was an attractive woman," recalled Louis Schroth, then a fourteen-year-old living next to the Lincoln Court at 105 Lexington. He watched Frechette hang the wash on the clothesline behind her building. "She wore red shorts and a red halter [top] when she did the laundry. We kids in the neighborhood, we'd never *seen* women in shorts and halters before. So we'd whistle at Dillinger's girl from the distance."[45]

Dillinger wrote to his sister Audrey from St. Paul in March:

> Dear Sis, I thought I would write you a few lines and let you know I am still perculating, Dont worry about me honey, for that wont help any, and besides I am having a lot of fun. I am sending Emmett my wooden gun and I want him to allways keep it. I see that Deputy Blunk says I had a real forty five[.] Thats just a lot of hooey to cover up because they dont like to admit that I locked eight deputys and a dozen trustys up with my wooden gun before I got my hands on the two machine guns and you should have seen their faces Ha! Ha! Ha! . . .

I got shot a week ago but I am all right now just a little sore I bane one tough sweed Ha! Ha! Well honey I guess I'll close for the time give my love to all and I hope I can see you soon. Lots of love from Johnnie.[46]

Bank robberies and jail escapes may have been thrilling for Dillinger, but Frechette's life as his girlfriend was a bore. She later described her role at the Lincoln Court as "chief cook and bottlewasher" for the Dillinger gang; she also did the grocery shopping and ironed Dillinger's clothes. Her only fun during the two weeks of hiding on Lexington was going to a St. Paul movie theater.[47]

Her dreary existence changed dramatically on March 30, 1934, when the FBI responded to the landlady's tip. For backup, the bureau contacted St. Paul police chief Thomas Dahill, who, admitting that "I have found that I can not trust all my men," sent Henry Cummings, a twenty-seven-year veteran of the force, to accompany the agents. The FBI threw up a ring of overnight surveillance around the Lincoln Court. Two women and a man—later identified as John Hamilton and sisters Bernice Clark and Pat Charrington—walked by without drawing undue attention.[48]

At 10:15 A.M. on March 31, Rufus Coulter, a thirty-one-year-old Tennessee-born law school graduate turned FBI agent, and detective Cummings knocked on the door of apartment 303. Agent Rosser Nalls, Coulter's partner, waited outside the building. Inside, Dillinger and Frechette were in bed, talking. When they heard the police knock, Frechette opened the door the few inches allowed by the chain lock. The agent and the police officer asked to speak with Carl Hellman. "Carl? Carl who?" asked Frechette, who had forgotten Dillinger's alias. "My God, I know I am not going to let these damn cops in here," she thought.

"He's just left and won't be back until this afternoon. Come back then," she improvised.

Cummings asked if she was Mrs. Hellman, and when she answered that she was, said, "We will talk to you."

"I'm not dressed. Come back this afternoon," Frechette said.

Cummings responded, "We'll wait until you dress."

Frechette agreed and closed the door, snapping the night latch closed, and turned to Dillinger, who said calmly, "Keep your shirt on. Grab some clothes, put something in a bag and let's get out of here."[49]

Nalls watched outside as a green Ford coupe stopped by the Lincoln Court; the driver, Homer Van Meter, walked inside toward Dillinger's apartment. Simultaneously, Coulter left Cummings alone to guard apartment 303 and ran downstairs to call for reinforcements. Moments after Coulter rejoined Cummings, Van Meter wandered into the hallway, glibly explaining to the lawmen that he was a soap salesman. Challenged to prove his identity, Van Meter led Coulter down the stairs to see his "soap samples." As they reached the first floor, Van Meter pulled out an automatic pistol. "You want it. Here it is," yelled Van Meter, opening fire. Coulter hurled himself through the outside door, drew his gun, and returned fire as Van Meter chased him across the front lawn and toward the intersection of Lexington and Lincoln. When Nalls joined the gunfight, Van Meter retreated inside the Lincoln Court complex.[50]

Back in apartment 303, Frechette begged Dillinger, "My God, don't shoot. Don't shoot. Try and get out of here, but don't shoot!" The FBI described Dillinger's next actions in slow motion: "When the shooting began, the door of the Hellman apartment was opened slightly and the muzzle of a machine gun protruded and began spraying the hallway with bullets." Detective Cummings flattened himself in an alcove as Dillinger sent bursts of machine-gun fire toward him, splintering walls in a shower of flying plaster. "The bullets were scraping the wall where I had cover and going right past my nose," recalled Cummings, who fired back toward the apartment.[51]

Not a single FBI agent or police officer guarded the rear of the building or Dillinger's path to his getaway car, hidden in a garage just yards away.

56 'Something Very Serious Going On'

Dillinger's Getaway Garage
1123 Goodrich Avenue, St. Paul

"A man came out from behind the apartment, dressed in gray clothes," recalled George Schroth, who saw John Dillinger emerge from the Lincoln Court Apartments on March 31. "He was carrying a machine gun. He was not running, however. He was merely walking. . . . [He] took his time and walked up the alley very casually, always keeping a good look behind him as though covering his retreat. When I saw the man with the machine gun, I knew that there was of course something very serious going on."[52]

Moments after Dillinger's gunfire sent the FBI agents running, Evelyn Frechette sprinted to the Halbert family's three-car garage behind the home at 1123 Goodrich Avenue. She backed a black Hudson sedan out toward Dillinger.[53] Nearby, young Louis Schroth—who almost became The Teenager Who Killed John Dillinger—was watching.

"I am in my bedroom at this point, a fourteen-year-old kid with a lot of guns in my closet, and [I] saw a man coming out of the door—about fifteen yards from me—with a Thompson submachine gun in his hand," recalled Schroth nearly sixty years later. "I didn't know who he was. I just knew you're not supposed to openly carry a Thompson submachine gun in St. Paul. I was going to shoot Dillinger, but my mother grabbed me by the neck and stopped me! She was worried that if I shot, but hadn't gotten him, Dillinger would have sprayed the whole building with bullets."

Schroth watched from his bedroom window as Dillinger, carrying the machine gun in his right hand and a suitcase in his left, gave Frechette "holy hell" for backing out of the garage the wrong way. Dillinger demanded that she drive into the garage and back out again in the other direction. With a bullet wound in his leg leaving a trail of blood in the snow, Dillinger climbed into the auto, and he and Frechette drove up the alley toward a rendezvous with Eddie Green in Minneapolis.[54]

Van Meter's getaway was even more stylish—he hijacked a garbage collector's horse and, disguised under the hauler's cap, trotted his way to freedom along Lincoln Avenue. For residents of the area it was the finale to an extraordinary afternoon. "We had a quiet, well-to-do neighborhood," said Bob Geisenheyner, who at the time was a seventh grader living across the street from Dillinger's apartment building. "Except for the John Dillinger shootout and the kidnapping of [Edward] Bremer down the block."[55]

Dillinger's sedan resurfaced on April 2 at Clements Auto in Mankato, Minnesota, where it had been taken for repainting by a Mr. Holmes (almost certainly Dillinger gang member Tommy Carroll). The mobster had requested new taillights and license plates attached with wing nuts, for easy removal.[56]

Dillinger's escape stunned St. Paul. The *Pioneer Press* called the city "a happy hunting ground for kidnapers, thugs, thieves, and machine gunners: St. Paul has become a disgrace and a shame before the whole country, because gangsters have been given refuge here. . . . Who brought Dillinger to St. Paul? Let us have an answer to that question." The shootout was a rebuff to a probe into St. Paul's underworld by a Ramsey County grand jury, which had just announced that there was no crime wave in the capital city. It was an embarrassment for Mayor William Mahoney, who had expressed doubts that Dillinger had even visited St. Paul.[57]

But most of all, the escape was a humiliation for J. Edgar Hoover, who vowed that no "rat" would ever take aim at his agents without suffering the consequences. To Hoover's dismay, the newspaper coverage generated by the Lincoln Court shootout made his "Public Enemy Number One" a nationwide antihero.

In its subsequent search for Dillinger, the FBI sent nearly fifty agents to question virtually every underworld figure in the Twin Cities, bunking the agents in hotels and on cots in the Federal Courts Building. Agents stripped the apartment down to the floorboards and found a picture of Dillinger as a three-year-old and a twenty-page guide to getaway routes from an Iowa bank to St. Paul.[58]

Dillinger had left behind a staggering arsenal—including a Thompson submachine gun, two automatic rifles, a 100-round loaded machine gun drum, a .38-caliber Colt automatic with twenty-shot magazine clips, a vertical grip to convert the Colt into a small submachine gun, and two bulletproof vests. In addition, Van Meter's car disgorged a .351-caliber Winchester repeating rifle with thirteen loaded clips, a submachine gun, and a loaded 100-round magazine.[59]

"There is not a big-time gangster who comes to St. Paul but who has more modern, high-powered equipment than the entire St. Paul Police Department," said police chief Tom Dahill. Two St. Paul newspapers responded by raising more than $1,800 to buy machine guns for the police. The FBI privately discussed outfitting its agents with the very .38 Colt automatic pistols and bulletproof vests used by the Dillinger gang.[60]

After the shootout, newspapers were filled with reports of Dillinger sightings. Rose Menke told her family that in 1934 a car filled with steel boxes drove up to her cabin in Rapid River, Minnesota, about thirteen miles south of Baudette. Her husband, a state forestry service employee, was gone at the time. "The men [in the car] asked for a drink of water," recalled Menke's daughter Mary Charlton. "One of the men asked my mother, 'Aren't you afraid out here all by yourself?' And my mother said: 'No, the only thing I'm afraid of is John Dillinger.'" The men roared with laughter and drove away. Menke later discovered that Dillinger was thought to have driven through Rapid River that week. Sightings of Dillinger look-alikes became so frequent that FBI officials discussed the "extreme precaution which we must exercise to prevent any innocent persons being shot in the mistaken belief that they are Dillinger."[61]

At FBI headquarters in Washington, D.C., Hoover's fury was relentless. Publicly, he declared: "In the twenty-odd years of the existence of this division, no one ever has shot at any of our agents and got away with it. We run them to earth. . . . We are going to run down the entire gang." Privately, the director sent scalding memos to the St. Paul field office, expressing his "extreme displeasure" with the agents' handling of every facet of the Lincoln Court shootout, including their having allowed St. Paul police officers to process the fingerprints found in Dillinger's apartment. Hoover seemed to be particularly outraged that his agents allowed evidence to be seen by the police because of the impact on what Hoover termed "the publicity angle" of the case.[62]

In a conversation with agent Melvin Purvis, Hoover raged that the St. Paul office was incompetent, referring to the agents' "atrocious bungling" of the raid on Dillinger's apartment. He asked Purvis to focus all attention on Dillinger and ensure that a copy of any information supplied to the field office be sent to headquarters. Hoover was particularly contemptuous of his agents' decision to bring a police officer with them: "If in order to have some courage it was necessary to have a man in blue uniform along, to go ahead and take one, that if such was the case he, Mr. Hoover, was not going to lay down any rule to forbid it," said a memo documenting a telephone conversation with Hoover. "However, he would not do it and certainly he would not have used a St. Paul policeman."[63]

At the FBI's St. Paul field office—then located in room 203 of the Federal Courts Building at Fifth and Market Streets—the agents fought back against Hoover's condemnations. Special agent in charge Werner Hanni fired off a "personal and confidential memorandum" to headquarters, laying the blame for Dillinger's escape on FBI orders that its agents avoid working with local police officers. "It is not easy for me to make these statements; however, I must do so at this time, for the sake of the good name of the Division," wrote Hanni. "At 93 South Lexington Avenue, in particular, if we had sought the assistance which was readily ours for the asking, Dillinger, undoubtedly, would never have made his escape from that place."[64]

Ironically, the publicity generated by the FBI's failure to stop Dillinger's escape from the Lincoln Court Apartments, and his subsequent flight from Wisconsin's Little Bohemia resort, built support for the FBI as a national crime-fighting organization. During the Dillinger gang furor, U.S. attorney general Cummings recommended adding 270 new Justice Department agents, equipping the G-men with machine guns and faster vehicles, and expanding federal law enforcement powers to capture gangsters operating between states. Police chief Tom Dahill agreed that when "the criminals in question operate all over the country . . . it requires the aid of a national crime-fighting organization to catch them."[65]

Finally, Hoover laid down an order for his agents: they were to find Dillinger at any cost, even if it meant enlisting help from the underworld. "Get the leaders of the gangs," Hoover instructed his St. Paul agents, "and let them know that if they [don't] produce Dillinger, we [will] 'give them the works.'"[66]

57 'I Will Blow Your Head Off!'

The Dillinger Doctor's Clinic
1835 Park Avenue, Minneapolis

The man who limped through the back door of Dr. Clayton E. May's clinic on the morning of March 31, 1934, his arm resting around his girlfriend's shoulder, was no ordinary patient. But then, Dr. May was not operating an ordinary medical clinic.

May was told that his patient had been injured in the explosion of a still, but the doctor soon learned that his business was robbing banks, not bootlegging. The man on his couch, bleeding from an "in-and-out" bullet wound received hours earlier during the Lincoln Court shootout, was John Dillinger.[67]

May had his own secrets to keep. At 1835 Park Avenue, for fifty dollars, he discreetly treated venereal disease and performed abortions, surgery too illicit for his main office. May had cared for the family of Dillinger gang member Eddie Green for more than a decade and had served in 1922 as an alibi witness for Green during his trial for payroll robbery.[68]

From March 31 to April 4, May tended to Dillinger's bullet wound, injecting the gangster's leg with antitetanus serum and bandaging the leg with gauze. When May first met Dillinger, the physician told the mobster he needed full treatment at a hospital. Dillinger pulled out a submachine gun and responded, "To hell with that. You take me where you said you were going to take me to, some private place, or I will blow your head off."[69]

Once he was secure at May's clinic and soothed by nurse Augusta Salt, Dillinger calmed down. When Salt fluffed up his pillow and discovered a pistol there, he assured her that she need not be afraid of it. The nurse made dinner for him and gave Frechette gray thread to mend the holes in his overcoat; Dillinger gave her a hundred-dollar tip in damp five-dollar bills. "I am accused of committing every crime in the country from the East to the West coast," he quipped to Dr. May. "It's a wonder that they don't charge me with crimes in Europe."[70]

With that, Dillinger left the Park Avenue clinic in a Hudson sedan, heading toward a family reunion in Mooresville, Indiana. May had been promised five hundred dollars for helping Dillinger, but instead he got "two telephone calls threatening me with bodily violence . . . if I told about the treatments I had administered to this man."[71]

The FBI learned about Dr. May from the confessions bank robber Eddie Green would make on his deathbed. FBI agent Thomas Dodd (later a U.S. senator from Connecticut) located the doctor by masquerading as a man seeking an abortion for his girlfriend. The FBI put the Park Avenue clinic under surveillance; four agents armed with machine guns apprehended May on April 5. All May earned from his adventure was a two-year stint in Leavenworth prison, the revocation of his medical license, and lifelong notoriety as "the Dillinger doctor."[72]

For five days, Dillinger had enjoyed a rare respite from the FBI's manhunt. He had only three and a half months to live.

58–59 'Lovers Don't Talk about That Kind of Thing'

58. Tommy Carroll's St. Paul Hideout
35 West Isabel Street, St. Paul
59. The Dillinger Gang's Minneapolis Mail Drop
3242 South Sixteenth Avenue, Minneapolis

John Dillinger's front-page exploits in the spring of 1934 overshadowed the extraordinary career of his partner, automobile thief and bank robber Thomas L. Carroll. At 5 feet, 10 inches and a trim 166 pounds, the chestnut-haired, blue-eyed Chicagoan looked roughly handsome in his mug shots, despite what police described as a furrowed upper lip, scars on his jaw and neck, and a mouth that twisted distinctly to the right.[73]

Carroll, one of the few married men in Dillinger's gang, was known for juggling women friends and aliases—which included James Roy Brock, George McLarken, and Frank Sloane. Born in Red Lodge, Montana, Carroll lost his mother when he was two and his father when he was nine. Originally employed as a boilermaker and taxicab driver in Missouri, he was arrested for drunkenness and possession of stolen property, earning his first term in the state prison at Anamosa, Iowa. Two years later, he was returned to Anamosa for auto theft, and in 1927, he was sent to the state penitentiary at Jefferson City, Missouri, for robbery.[74]

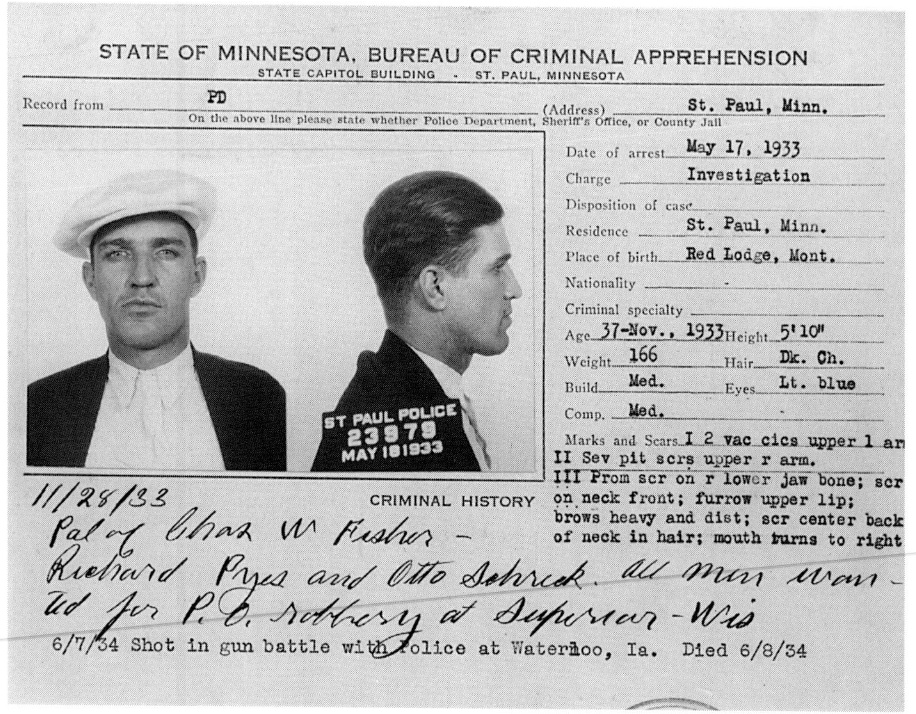

STATE OF MINNESOTA, BUREAU OF CRIMINAL APPREHENSION
STATE CAPITOL BUILDING - ST. PAUL, MINNESOTA

Record from PD (Address) St. Paul, Minn.
On the above line please state whether Police Department, Sheriff's Office, or County Jail

Date of arrest May 17, 1933
Charge Investigation
Disposition of case
Residence St. Paul, Minn.
Place of birth Red Lodge, Mont.
Nationality -
Criminal specialty
Age 37-Nov., 1933 Height 5'10"
Weight 166 Hair Dk. Ch.
Build Med. Eyes Lt. blue
Comp. Med. -
Marks and Scars I 2 vac cics upper l ar
II Sev pit scrs upper r arm.
III Prom scr on r lower jaw bone; scr on neck front; furrow upper lip; brows heavy and dist; scr center back of neck in hair; mouth turns to right

CRIMINAL HISTORY

11/28/33
Pal of Chas W Fisher — Richard Pryes and Otto Schreck. All men wanted for P.O. robbery at Superior - Wis
6/7/34 Shot in gun battle with Police at Waterhoo, Ia. Died 6/8/34

Post office burglar and auto thief Thomas L. Carroll

Finally, in May 1930, Carroll graduated to a twenty-one-month sentence at Leavenworth for transporting a stolen auto across state lines. While he was at Leavenworth, where he used his boilermaking skills as the prison plumber, Carroll was often reprimanded for breaking prison regulations. ("This man is continually loitering and visiting on the gallery," noted his prisoner file, "especially in some other cell. He has been repeatedly warned.") Released in October 1931, he would never again allow himself to be imprisoned.[75]

A 1933 wanted poster described Carroll: "Neat dresser; drives an automobile well; usually resides in an apartment; gambles and is addicted to the use of intoxicants; frequents night clubs; gives his occupation as salesman; is said to be wearing a derby and a reddish mustache."[76]

By that time he had been arrested on charges ranging from concealing weapons to grocery store robberies by police in Omaha, Nebraska; Council Bluffs, Iowa; Kansas City, St. Joseph, and St. Louis, Missouri; and Tulsa, Oklahoma. The U.S. Post Office was particularly eager to capture Carroll, who was suspected of engineering a wave of postal burglaries in Wisconsin, Iowa, and Minnesota.[77]

It is not surprising that when Carroll married his girlfriend, Viola, in 1925, they pledged their marital devotion using aliases: "Beaula Richard" married "Mr. McGuire." The couple moved to St. Paul in 1932, and for a time Carroll attempted to run a Mankato restaurant, briefly trading in his machine gun for a spatula. But that year he met and fell in love with "Radio Sally" Bennett, a twenty-year-old St. Paul nightclub singer, and abandoned his wife. "When I found him with this other girl naturally it was quite a shock to me," Viola told reporters. "After he left I took poison. I loved him. I always loved him."[78]

"Radio Sally" Bennett, girlfriend of Dillinger gang member Tommy Carroll

Bennett was a popular entertainer at John Lane's Boulevards of Paris nightclub. She sang Irish tunes like "Danny Boy," although her specialty was performing virtually any song requested on her ukulele ("like Arthur Godfrey, only she could sing," recalled her son, Kenneth Herschler). Interviewed by FBI agents later, Bennett recalled how Carroll had first walked into St. Paul's Green Gables nightclub with six other men and asked her to sing at his table. Utterly smitten, Carroll returned to the club each night for three weeks. He told Sally that he was a gambler and a bootlegger, and then asked her to marry him. Bennett answered that she could not marry him because of her religion, but she would live with him.[79]

For six months during the spring and summer of 1932, Bennett and Carroll lived in the second-floor apartment at 35 West Isabel Street. Their landlords, who lived on the first floor, were Pete and Mary Vogel, a foundry laborer and a schoolteacher.[80]

"Radio Sally lived with Tommy at our house," said their son Jim Vogel. "My mom referred to women who she didn't think much of, like Radio Sally, as 'frowsies'—let's say she was not the kind of girl you wanted to bring home to mother. . . . Well, that bothered my mother so much that she talked to the parish priest. The priest told mom, 'If you need the money for your income, it's not your problem!'"[81]

"My mom . . . knew Carroll was a criminal and a killer, which they didn't like," said Jim's brother, John Vogel. "But they still talked about the gangsters as refined people. The poor in those days looked up to the gangsters [because they had] money."[82]

Members of the Dillinger gang met regularly in the West Isabel apartment, smoking cigarettes and planning their banking activities. "The whole Dillinger gang . . . would meet in the front room," recalled Loretta Murphy, the Vogel brothers' aunt, who was thirty-one at the time. "They were respectful and wouldn't leave any ashes in the ashtrays—you'd think it was a board meeting for some business." Carroll was a relentless flirt, Murphy said: "He'd come to me and he'd say, 'Don't you think we should have a drink, you know, before you go to bed?'"[83]

Carroll often ate with the Vogels, simple food like potatoes and hamburgers, and always tipped them generously—as much as ten dollars per meal. He came across as a polished gentleman, well-dressed and mannered. Yet he always had to be on guard. When the Vogels' son John was robbed by neighborhood kids of ten dollars in grocery money, the Vogels called the police. Carroll looked out the window and saw the officers. Thinking they were coming for him, he leaped out the window. Later, he told the boy: "Next time that happens, you let me know and I'll just give you the money! We don't want the police here."

There were other clues to Carroll's real vocation. When Mary Vogel peeked inside a violin case in his room, she found it stuffed with hundreds of silver coins. Another day, Carroll left several newspapers open, with articles on local bank robberies underlined; a family member who opened one of his dresser drawers found it filled with U.S. postage stamps.[84]

Even with Bennett, Carroll was evasive about his line of work. She told FBI agents that she often asked about his activities and his friends, and that he always told her it was none of her business. Carroll rarely took Bennett anywhere but to a movie, to a cottage on Lake Owasso for gangster parties, or to the Green Lantern. When he finally brought her to Chicago in the summer of 1933 to enjoy the World's Fair, he was abruptly called back to St. Paul on criminal business.[85]

Carroll had two close calls with police in Minnesota. In May 1933 he was arrested in St. Paul for possession of burglar's tools, but he was released in June. The police, true to the O'Connor system, never pursued the charge. In September, after an auto accident at Rice Street and Wheelock Parkway in St. Paul, he was arrested when police discovered a loaded .45-caliber pistol in his car. Again he was released, despite the fact that he was then out of prison on $15,000 bond for a Wisconsin post office robbery. In October Carroll is believed to have joined Babyface Nelson for a final bank robbery.[86]

The crime may have been inspired by a dinner table conversation between Verne Miller, the Barker-Karpis gang's machine gunner, and the family of his girlfriend, Vivian Mathis, in Brainerd, Minnesota. In early October, the talk between Miller and Mathis's father, farmer John Gibson, turned to money and banks. "That was during the Depression and there were a lot of banks being held up," recalled Janet Gibson, the farmer's daughter-in-law. "John was talking about bank robberies with Verne . . . [and] said, 'I'm telling you, no one will *ever* break into the First National Bank of Brainerd, it's too well protected.' Verne had a snicker on his face. Verne just happened to go to the bank the next day. I think he was checking things out." A few days later, a *Brainerd Daily Dispatch* headline blared: "Daring Machine Gun Mob Robs First National Here," and the bank was $32,000 poorer.[87]

Although the identity of the five Brainerd bank robbers was never determined by police, Fatso Negri, a partner of Babyface Nelson, identified them as Nelson, Tommy Carroll, Homer Van Meter, John Paul Chase, and Charles Fisher.[88]

The Babyface Nelson–Tommy Carroll gang cased the Brainerd bank while they were staying in cabin two at the Sebago Resort, still operating fourteen miles from Brainerd on the north shore of Round Lake. Two black Buick sedans with North Dakota plates drove into the resort in mid-October 1933. "We like it quiet . . . real quiet," said one of the men, whom resort owner Lester Penney instantly recognized as Babyface Nelson. Their arrival pleased Penney: the post–Labor Day slump was on, and the strangers purchased his fresh vegetables and milk, paying him five dollars for fifty cents worth of milk and adding ten dollars extra to the twenty-dollar weekly rent. "They gave him to understand that he was not to even remember that they were there—that he wouldn't say anything about this if he knew what was good for him," recalled Don Fish, the current proprietor of Sebago Resort. "Penney didn't mention it until after Babyface Nelson died!"[89]

Nelson hired a Brainerd plumber to drive him around town, supposedly to look for real estate to purchase, but the tours often circled back to the First National Bank. The morning of the bank robbery, the gang packed up and left Sebago for good.[90]

The building that once housed the First National Bank at the corner of South Sixth and Front in downtown Brainerd now stands vacant, but eyewitnesses have not forgotten how well planned the robbery was. The five thieves, faces obscured by bandannas, knew the name of each bank employee. They methodically broke into the bank and forced everyone to the floor, waiting until the safe's time lock popped open at 8:45 A.M. Outside the bank were two bandits in hunting clothes, hiding a submachine gun under a bushel basket.[91]

One of the only surviving eyewitnesses to the October 23 robbery, Zane Smith, was then a seventeen-year-old collection clerk who had been on the job just twelve months. Arriving at 8:00 A.M., Smith let himself into the bank and headed for the president's office to deliver the day's mail, unaware that Babyface Nelson was crouching behind an ornamental pillar at the bank's main entrance.

"He jumped to his feet . . . took hold of the collar of my topcoat and swung me around and hit my jaw with his fist," recalled Smith. "He . . . dragged me across the bank lobby floor to an office where they had the bank guard and janitor."

Nelson quizzed the teenager on how much money was in the vault. "I didn't know, but he had the machine gun pointed at me. Nelson had the machine gun across his knees, and he'd turn it back and forth. I could hear the cartridges clicking, left and right, left and right. . . . I told them I didn't know. They threatened to put burning cigarettes in my ears to get better answers."

While they waited for the time lock, the gangsters set up a machine gun on a tripod—and then asked the bank employees if they wanted to smoke. The robbers passed out and lit the cigarettes so the hostages would not have to reach into their pockets. Once the money was stuffed into canvas bags, the staff was herded into the bathroom. The gang drove away in a Buick, firing machine gun bullets at the bank windows. "Banking was supposed to be a very tranquil business," said Smith. "It turned out quite differently for me."

"I think of the robbery often," added Smith, who eventually became vice president of the bank. "The strange part of it was, while the robbery was in progress . . . I wasn't frightened. I kept thinking, 'Won't it be fun to tell people this?' After it was over, I realized that those men had horrendous reputations as robbers and murderers. With three machine guns and two pistols, I thought about what *could* have happened that day!"[92]

After the robbery, Carroll hid in the duplex of Sally Bennett's brother, Joseph Bennett, at 3242 Sixteenth Avenue South in Minneapolis, which he used as a mail drop for submachine guns and other weaponry; visitors to the apartment included Homer Van Meter and Babyface Nelson.[93]

On November 11, 1933, two Minneapolis police officers attempted to arrest Carroll on suspicion of participating in the Brainerd robbery. Barefoot and cornered by the armed policemen, he escaped by kicking one officer in the face and punching the other and stealing his gun. Carroll left behind $1,600 in crisp bank notes, a rifle, a machine gun, and a shotgun.[94]

Later that month, Carroll returned to St. Paul, where he met his next lover, twenty-one-year-old waitress Jean Delaney, the sister of Alvin Karpis's girlfriend, Delores Delaney. She moved in with Carroll on Hennepin Avenue. "From the way Carroll talked," Delaney told the FBI, "I believed he was a gambler—he always seemed to have plenty of money." She avoided asking Carroll questions about the Dillinger gang "for fear that Tommy would slap her down," the FBI reported. Carroll told Delaney that one of the reasons he liked her was "because she did not ask questions." Delaney said that Carroll was jealous of her, threatening to "beat up college boys who would pass them in cars and holler, 'Hello, Blondie' and 'Hello, Cutie' at her."[95]

The violent pace of Carroll's life began to accelerate: he was suspected of killing Texas police officer H. C. Perrow on December 11, 1933, and the next year he joined Dillinger in robbing the Security National Bank of Sioux Falls, South Dakota, and the First National Bank of Mason City, Iowa. FBI interviews with Carroll's girlfriends revealed a tense life of incessant travel. On April 19, 1934, Carroll hid in Fox River Grove, Illinois, with Jean Delaney and Babyface Nelson and his wife, Helen. On April 20, 1934, the Dillinger gang moved en masse from Fox River Grove to the Little Bohemia Lodge near Rhinelander, Wisconsin. Three days later, Carroll escaped a shootout with the FBI at Little Bohemia that led to his being sought for the murder of FBI agent W. Carter Baum.[96]

FBI agents thought they came close to snaring Carroll in May 1934, when they received a tip that he was hiding in a lake cottage near Perham, Minnesota. The bureau costumed two of its agents as fishermen pretending to search Perham for a summer fishing cottage. But Carroll and Delaney never showed up; they were staying that month with Nelson at Lake Como in Wisconsin.[97]

Carroll's wanderings ended on June 7, 1934, when a gas station attendant near Waterloo, Iowa, noticed three license plates piled in the rear seat of Carroll's sedan. Two Waterloo detectives were waiting when Carroll and Delaney returned to the car. Delaney, who had been arrested and released by the FBI after the Little Bohemia raid, saw the detectives and volunteered to act as a decoy to climb into the auto to see if the men were police officers, she told the FBI. "But Carroll would not permit her to go alone, and stated that, if there were any danger, he wanted to share it with her," the FBI reported. Delaney added that Babyface Nelson's wife felt the same way about her husband, whom she lovingly called "Jimmy." "They were very devoted to each other and Helen wanted to die at the same time Jimmy died," recalled Delaney.[98]

As Waterloo detectives Paul E. Walker and Emil Steffen identified themselves, Carroll reached for his gun. Walker punched Carroll in the face, knocking him backward, and the officers fired five shots, hitting Carroll four times and mortally wounding him. "I was in love with him," wept Delaney later, explaining why she overlooked his criminal activities. "That was all that mattered to me. Lovers don't talk about that kind of thing." The police arrested Delaney, who was sent to the Alderson, West Virginia, reformatory for women.[99]

"The last thing we heard was that [Carroll] had been shot down in Iowa," recalled Loretta Murphy. Carroll's body was returned to Minnesota, where he was given a Catholic funeral at the Church of the Assumption in St. Paul. "Mary [Vogel] and I went there to be sure that it was our Tommy Carroll. And it was," sighed Murphy.[100]

Carroll and Eddie Green are the only two members of the Dillinger gang to have remained in Minnesota for eternity. Carroll's grave can be seen today in Oakland Cemetery at 927 Jackson. Its marker removed, the grave is located in Lot 279, Block 71.[101]

Startling Detective Adventures magazine offered a colorful eulogy, calling Carroll a "one-time taxi driver who shot himself into the big leagues as Dillinger's ace gunman, but finally was struck out by the great No Hit—No Run Pitcher," and predicted that "the message of blood spells the beginning of the end for John Dillinger and his mob!"[102]

60 Machine Guns for the Gang

The Dillinger Gang's Weapons Depot
2214 Marshall Avenue, St. Paul

John Dillinger's remarkable luck—three jailbreaks and his escape from the Lincoln Court Apartments shootout—began to collapse in April 1934, when the FBI identified his hideout on Marshall Avenue in St. Paul. He had left behind in his Lincoln Court suite a sheet of paper bearing a scribbled telephone number. It was Eddie Green's, traced by FBI agents to a three-story red-brick building in the Merriam Park neighborhood.[103]

The previous month, the Dillinger gang's black sedan ran out of gas a few hundred yards away from the Marshall Avenue safe house. The gangsters pushed the car into the Standard gas station at the intersection of Marshall and Cretin, now the Amoco station at 2178 Marshall. "All of a sudden these three or four guys are pushing a four-door black Pontiac or something into the gas station driveway," recalled Robert Wybest, who was then sixteen years old. "The men—real rugged-looking guys—didn't look like natives with their dark suits and hats, and they didn't smile much. One man got out. I saw that his vest was funny; it was stiff like a board inside his suitcoat."[104]

The gas station attendant, A. L. Martindale, noticed not only the bulletproof vest but also the submachine gun that one of the passengers was nervously covering in the rear seat. Martindale pulled Wybest aside and hissed, "Go across the street and you call the police! Go on!"

"I was trying to be really coy. . . . I put my hands in my pockets and walked across to the drugstore," recalled Wybest. "I should have run across to the drugstore, but then the guys would have blown my head off." By the time the police arrived, the Dillinger gang had refueled and driven away.

Eddie Green, Dillinger's thirty-four-year-old bank scout, rented the Marshall Avenue apartment under the name of D. A. Stevens for two weeks beginning March 15, 1934. Green and his girlfriend, Beth Green, were relieved to move away from Minneapolis, where Dillinger's apartment at Thirty-third and Girard, just one block from Green's Charlou Apartments on Fremont Avenue, was drawing too much attention in the neighborhood.[105]

Green turned the Marshall Avenue apartment over to Dillinger machine gunner Homer Van Meter. On April 3 St. Paul police chief Tom Dahill and a troop of FBI agents raided the apartment, which yielded shotgun shells, machine-gun clips, three notebooks marked "Get Away Charts," and a two-foot piece of dynamite fuse.[106]

While the agents were dusting the apartment for fingerprints, Lucy Jackson and Leona Goodman, sisters who had worked as maids for the Barker-Karpis gang, dropped by during lunch to pick up some baggage for Eddie Green. Greeted by FBI machine guns, the women explained that Green had asked them to clean up the apartment and bring the bags to a home at 778 Rondo. Could the women identify Green? the agents asked. Sure, they said. They had met him face to face in early March.[107]

The agents demanded that Jackson and Goodman carry out their mission —and accompanied them to the Rondo neighborhood where Eddie Green was scheduled to retrieve his suitcases.

61 'This Man Should Be Shot. . . . Kill Him!'

Eddie Green's Ambush House
778 Rondo Ave., St. Paul

Armed with automatic shotguns, rifles, and machine guns, a phalanx of FBI agents staked out the Rondo home on April 3. Backup agents were hidden nearby. The bureau's plan was simple. Leona Goodman was to hail Green at the side porch door and hand him the luggage from the Marshall Avenue hideout. An agent in the bedroom would then fire a .30-caliber rifle into the motor of Green's getaway car to disable it. After that, the instructions were simple. "This man should be shot. . . . Kill him."[108]

At 5:30 P.M., Eddie and Beth Green drove south down Avon and parked their Essex Terraplane across the street. Seeing nothing out of the ordinary, Eddie left Beth in the car and walked to the kitchen door, collected his suitcase from Goodman, and walked back toward the car. Somehow, the mobster then recognized the trap, made what agents later called a "threatening" or "menacing" gesture, and dashed back toward the Terraplane. FBI agent E. N. Notesteen yelled, "Let 'em have it!" Another agent fired at Green through the window of 778 Rondo. The bullets smashed into his shoulders and skull.[109]

Rushed by police ambulance to St. Paul's Ancker Hospital, Green was guarded around the clock by FBI agents. "Honey, back the car to the door," Green moaned wildly, "I've got the keys, he wants them. John . . . Dillinger!" With FBI agent Thomas Dodd transcribing his every delirious word, Green asked for guns and screamed, "Shoot that one!" Whenever Green began to talk, his mother attempted to drown out his confessions by reading from her prayer book, loudly interrupting her son's admissions and entreating, "Eddie, say your prayers." Green's brother Frank warned: "Don't talk, Eddie. Don't talk." The FBI had Frank temporarily barred from the hospital.[110]

When they were alone with Green, the agents' bedside interrogation called upon their acting skills: Green believed in his daze that he had been hit over the head during a robbery attempt, and "the agents played the part of doctors, other gangsters, etc.," in order to get him to talk, reported an FBI memo to J. Edgar Hoover. "Green couldn't see and was in a state of delirium and half the time subconscious and talking."[111]

Another agent reported that "Green did not have his eyes open and, apparently, was under the impression that the police officer was a doctor and . . . [was] advised that there were no police officers, or Agents of the Department of Justice, present." Green asked a police officer if he could perform plastic surgery on the telltale dimple on John Dillinger's chin. No prob-

The Rondo Street home where the FBI shot Dillinger gang member Eddie Green in April 1934. FBI agents fired through the circled windows, and Green was struck by their bullets at the X.

lem, the agent answered, but first Green would have to lead him to where Dillinger was hiding.[112]

"Doc, you sure are a nosey fellow. Give me a shot so I can sleep," begged Green. Promised an injection in exchange for information on Dillinger, Green blurted out the identity of his fellow gang members, the name of Dillinger doctor Clayton May, and the location of the Fremont Avenue safe-house in Minneapolis. His temperature soaring to 105 degrees, Green lived for a week before dying of meningitis on April 11, 1934. He was buried the next day in St. Peter's Cemetery in Mendota, Minnesota.[113]

By then, Dillinger had already left the Twin Cities. He visited his family for a chicken dinner in Indiana, robbed a Warsaw, Indiana, police station on April 3, and drove toward the peace of Little Bohemia Lodge, the setting for one of the bloodiest shootouts in FBI history.[114]

Relieved that the *St. Paul Pioneer Press* had "no unfavorable comment" about the Green shooting, the FBI noted that the newspaper "quote[d] verbatim the release which was furnished them." But *St. Paul Dispatch* reporter Tommy "Buck Tooth" Thompson demanded a Ramsey County coroner's inquest into the propriety of the ambush. The FBI peevishly noted in a memorandum that "Thompson is sometimes referred to as 'Horse Face.'"[115]

One FBI official suggested to J. Edgar Hoover that the bureau "bring pressure to bear to prevent any adverse publicity" and warned that the identity of the agents who participated in the Green shooting should not be disclosed so they could not be subpoenaed. Hoover wrote that an FBI executive had "suggested, in view of the fact that the St. Paul Dispatch has been exerting itself to try to embarrass us, that a confidential tip be given to the rival paper. . . . I approved this suggestion."[116]

Precisely what occurred during the Green shootout is unclear. An April 4, 1934, memo claimed that after agents demanded that he halt, Green made a "suspicious" gesture; "suspicious" was crossed out and changed to "threatening." It is certain from FBI memos that the bureau was determined to stop any investigation into Green's shooting. In a memo to Hoover, an agent noted newspaper coverage expressing "concern over the fact that a gangster was shot down, probably from the back," and reassured Hoover that if the inquest into Green's death were "not held until May 2, the date at which it is now set, it would be given very little consideration and it would probably be a mere formality; that there was a possibility that there would not even be one."[117]

The local police, held in contempt by Hoover, continued to tease the bureau for its inability to capture Dillinger. Hoover was informed after Green's shooting that a law enforcement official had "sarcastically asked if there was any danger of the man getting away from us at the hospital."[118]

Taking no chances, the FBI isolated Beth Green in Chicago for interrogation under the direction of Melvin Purvis. In a series of increasingly open confessions, Green provided many of the FBI's first tips on the Dillinger and Barker-Karpis gangs and the key role played by local fixers Harry Sawyer and Jack Peifer. "There appears to be some friction between this woman and Dillinger," an FBI memo reported happily, although the FBI also noted that her eighteen-year-old son could be "an imposing lever to hold over her head as a means of obtaining information." Through Green, the FBI first learned the identities of each member of the Dillinger gang and the names of the gangsters who had kidnapped Edward Bremer and who committed the Kansas City Massacre.[119]

When the FBI next caught up with Dillinger, Hoover's "shoot to kill" orders would ensure a fusillade of bullets.

John Hamilton's Last Ride

The Hastings Spiral Bridge Stakeout
Finch Drug Store Building
Second and Sibley Streets, Hastings

Dillinger's escape from the Lincoln Court Apartments in St. Paul may have been embarrassing for the FBI, but the Keystone Kops–style fiasco at the Little Bohemia Lodge sparked calls for J. Edgar Hoover's resignation. Had Dillinger's partner John Hamilton not been wounded during a shootout begun at the Hastings Spiral Bridge on the Minnesota-Wisconsin border, Dillinger's gang would once again have slipped away untouched.

On April 22, 1934, a planeload of FBI agents from St. Paul joined Melvin Purvis, then special agent in charge of the FBI's Chicago office, in a surprise raid on Little Bohemia. In the dark, the agents accidentally fired on three innocent visitors to the resort, killing one and wounding another in the belief that they were members of the Dillinger gang. Alerted by the gunfire, Dillinger and his gang slipped out a second-story window and shot their way out of the trap. Babyface Nelson's machine gun left one police officer and one FBI agent, W. Carter Baum, dead. Nelson reportedly sneered at Baum, "I know you have on bulletproof vests, so I will give it to you high and low."[120]

The gangsters got away, but three of their companions—Jean Delaney, girlfriend of Tommy Carroll; Helen Gillis, wife of Babyface Nelson; and Marie Conforti, girlfriend of Homer Van Meter—were arrested. "Three women and a much-shot-up house, which was later to prove of great financial benefit to its proprietors, were all we had to show for our efforts," wrote Purvis. "The raid had failed." The women were tried in Madison, Wisconsin, federal court for harboring Dillinger; they pled guilty and got eighteen months on probation.[121]

The debacle at Little Bohemia was particularly humiliating because Hoover, just before the raid, had boasted to the national news media that his agents had Dillinger surrounded. Distraught over the death of agent Baum, Purvis actually tendered his resignation, but it was refused.[122]

Senator Royal Copeland of New York savaged the FBI for bungling the raid, suggesting creation of a rival crime bureau made up of the best law enforcement officers from each state: "When Dillinger was hidden in the woods of Wisconsin, they brought up a lot of young lawyers from the Department of Justice and armed them and turned them loose. They should have called on local authorities in Wisconsin. . . . They fumbled it again."[123]

Perhaps worst of all, Hoover's men were ridiculed by humorist Will Rogers. "Well, they had Dillinger surrounded and was all ready to shoot him when he came out," quipped Rogers. "But another bunch of folks came out ahead, so they just shot them instead. Dillinger is going to accidentally get with some innocent bystanders some time [and] then he will get shot."[124]

The police figured Dillinger would head across the Mississippi River toward the safety of St. Paul. Alerted by the Justice Department, local sheriffs threw up an armed roadblock in Hastings, Minnesota, on April 23. Two policemen with rifles perched on the roof of the Finch Drug Store, awaiting a clear shot as Dillinger drove over the Hastings Spiral Bridge.[125]

(The magnificent Spiral Bridge, an engineering miracle dedicated in 1895, featured a remarkable 360-degree loop feeding into downtown Hastings. The wooden structure was destroyed in 1951.[126])

Just after 10:00 A.M., Dillinger, Homer Van Meter, and John Hamilton drove south over the bridge toward St. Paul. Recognizing Dillinger as the car crossed the north end of the bridge, the deputies chased it at speeds up to seventy miles an hour. The mobsters lobbed .45-caliber rounds into the police car's windshield; the police fired .30-.30 rifle bullets into the back of Dillinger's 1931 Ford coupe. The car wobbled but sped on, turning at Highway 3 near Newport at the railway station, and then off the highway onto a dirt road at St. Paul Park, eluding the police northwest of Cottage Grove. "The officers trailed this car, shooting at it at every opportunity, but the opportunities were rare because of the rolling land and the numerous curves," explained an FBI report.[127]

Dillinger and Van Meter reached the safe harbor of South St. Paul untouched; Pat Reilly and Tommy Carroll rejoined them there. John Hamilton was not so lucky. One Hastings police bullet had pierced the

A Hastings newspaper account of the gun battle that mortally wounded John Hamilton

HASTINGS GAZETTE

HASTINGS, MINNESOTA, FRIDAY, APRIL 27, 1934. HASTINGS OFFICIAL NEWSPAPER

Where Officer's Bullet Drew Blood

Pictured above is the blood soaked interior of the small Ford coupe in which three members of the notorious Dillinger gang staged a running gun fight with Deputy Sheriffs Joe Heinen, Norman Dieters and Larry Dunn, and Officer F. H. McArdle of the Hastings police force, Monday morning.

It was a 30-30 calibre bullet from McArdle's rifle, authorities believe, that tore through the back of the coupe and wounded one of the gangsters severely if not fatally.

The bullet hole in the back of the car seat indicates that a man sitting on that side of the coupe would have probably received the missile in the region of the kidneys, and the amount of blood lost by the wounded bandit is believed to be proof that his injuries were of a fatal nature. The blood-stained coupe was found a short distance outside of South St. Paul where it was abandoned for a faster car which the gangsters commandeered from a South St. Paul couple. One of the outlaw trio was wrapped in a blanket and apparently seriously injured when the gangsters abandoned the coupe and forced the So. St. Paul couple out of their Ford V-8 sedan.

At the right is a picture of F. H. McArdle, Hastings policeman who fired the bullet that is believed to have terminated the career of one of Dillinger's henchmen. The picture of the local officer was snapped at the South St. Paul police station by a Dispatch photographer shortly after the exciting bandit chase.

DILLINGER GANGSTERS IN RUNNING GUN BATTLE WITH LOCAL POSSE; 1 WOUNDED

Hastings Officer Scores In Gun Duel Although Gangsters Escape

A hazardous and exciting bandit chase, in which three Dakota county deputies and a Hastings policeman participated Monday morning, and in which one of a trio of fleeing Dillinger gangsters is thought to have been fatally wounded, came as a swift aftermath of the breaking up of a Dillinger rendezvous in the northern Wisconsin woods late Sunday night.

The bandit pursuit by the local posse culminated a six-hour vigil by Deputy Sheriffs Joe Heinen, Norman Dieters and Larry Dunn and Night Policeman F. H. McArdle, who had been assigned to guard the high bridge on the supposition that some of the Dillinger mob, fleeing from the Little Bohemia lodge from which they were routed by Federal agents Sunday, might try to gain access to the Twin Cities by crossing the river here.

Apprized of this possibility by a call from the Department of Justice in St. Paul at 3:40 Monday morning, Sheriff J. J. Dunn immediately summoned Deputy Sheriffs Heinen and Dieters, and the two officers, with Deputy Sheriff Larry Dunn and Officer McArdle, stationed themselves at the Finch drug store corner, in Heinen's car, to await developments. For six hours their vigil was fruitless, but shortly after ten o'clock, a coupe, containing there men and bearing a Wisconsin license plate, No. 92652, entered the city from the south on Highway No. 3, and turned the drug store corner to cross the high bridge, in the direction of St.

A. C. Bachman Passes on; Funeral to be Held Mon.

A. C. Bachman, passed away in St. Raphael's hospital Thursday noon from heart trouble and various complications. He had been a patient sufferer in the hospital since February 12.

The funeral obsequies will be held Monday morning from the St. Boniface church. A detailed account of his life will be published in next week's paper.

Petition Asks for Variable Closing Hours for 3.2 Beer

Police Ask City Council for Bullet-Proof Windshield

A petition signed by about 30 people was presented to the City Council at their adjourned meeting last Monday night, asking that the time of ending the sale or consumption of 3.2 per cent beer be extended from the 12 midnight hour to 1:00 o'clock on every night except Saturday and Sunday nights, and on any other nights on which there is a dance in the city which time shall be extended to 2 a. m.

The council received the petition

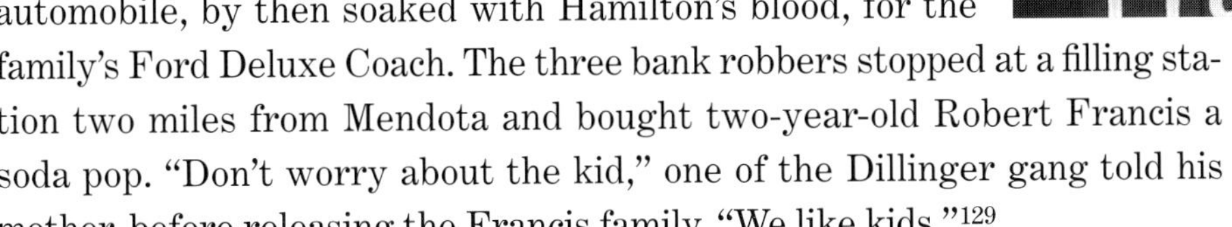

IDENTIFICATION ORDER NO. 1220
April 2, 1934.

DIVISION OF INVESTIGATION
U. S. DEPARTMENT OF JUSTICE
WASHINGTON, D. C.

Fingerprint Classification
12 29 W 0 13 AMP
19 W 0 12

WANTED
JOHN HAMILTON, with alias,
JOHN CAMPBELL.

MURDER - OBSTRUCTION OF JUSTICE.

	AMPUTATED SECOND JOINT	AMPUTATED SECOND JOINT		

John "Three Fingered Jack" Hamilton (right), mortally wounded as he and Dillinger drove through a police stakeout in Hastings, Minnesota; Hamilton's identification order (above), noting his two missing fingers

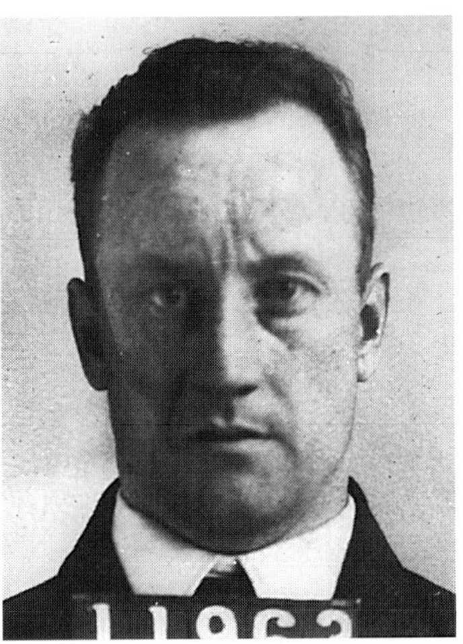

back of Dillinger's automobile, penetrated the rear seat cushion, and plunged into Hamilton's back, mortally wounding him.[128]

Desperate to evade the FBI long enough to find a doctor for Hamilton, Dillinger stopped a car carrying a South St. Paul utilities employee, Roy Francis, and his family at South Robert and Concord Streets. "We're sorry," said Dillinger, "but we have to have your car." Dillinger left his automobile, by then soaked with Hamilton's blood, for the family's Ford Deluxe Coach. The three bank robbers stopped at a filling station two miles from Mendota and bought two-year-old Robert Francis a soda pop. "Don't worry about the kid," one of the Dillinger gang told his mother, before releasing the Francis family. "We like kids."[129]

Hamilton was taken to the Aurora, Illinois, apartment of Barker-Karpis gang member Volney Davis, where he died ten days later. The FBI believed that Hamilton was buried by Davis, Dillinger, Van Meter, Doc Barker, William Weaver, and Harry Campbell in a rare case of cooperation between the Dillinger and Barker-Karpis gangs. The Francis family's car, its window shattered, .45 bullets on the floor, and stained with Hamilton's blood, was found abandoned in the Chicago area several days later. FBI agents searched swamps near Minneapolis for Hamilton's body but returned without a corpse.

In August 1935, more than a year later, the FBI found "Three Fingered Jack" Hamilton's body in a gravel pit in Oswego, Illinois, his face disfigured with lye to make identification difficult. His telltale right hand with its two amputated fingers had been cut off. Hamilton "sure was a hard-luck guy," said John Dillinger. "Whenever we went on a job he came back full of lead. They wounded him at East Chicago, they wounded him at Mason City, and then they killed him in St. Paul. He was a cinch to get it, sooner or later."[130]

62 Death in a Blind Alley

Homer Van Meter's Death Site

Intersection of University Avenue and Marion Street, St. Paul

Federal agents finally ambushed and killed John Dillinger in an alley outside Chicago's Biograph Theater on July 22, 1934. Bystanders dipped their handkerchiefs in his blood, and 15,000 gawkers walked through the morgue to view Dillinger's body.[131]

An exultant J. Edgar Hoover held a press conference to congratulate Melvin Purvis for leading the shootout, dined in triumph with President Roosevelt, and prominently exhibited a plaster death mask as a trophy at FBI headquarters. "I am glad that Dillinger was taken dead. . . . The only good criminal is a dead criminal," said Hoover.[132]

One month later, at an intersection just two blocks from the Minnesota State Capitol, Dillinger's partner Homer Van Meter met a similar end: he was shot to death by police in an alley, betrayed by the underworld. When they heard of Dillinger's death on the radio, Van Meter and his girlfriend Marie Conforti sought refuge in Minnesota. He first hid at Leech Lake Log Cabin Camp on Route 34 near Walker, Minnesota, sneaking into St. Paul for furtive "meets" with his colleagues at bars and bowling alleys along Rice Street.[133]

With the manhunt drawing closer, Van Meter met mob contact Frank Kirwin in St. Paul on August 3, and then hid from August 6 to 14 at Delia and James Coleman's Bear Island View Resort (known then as LeClaire's Resort) on Leech Lake in what is today Longville, Minnesota. Kirwin had recommended Bear Island for its splendid fishing. Visitors to the resort recalled the fugitive pair masquerading as Henry and Ruth Adams; Van Meter fished, Conforti swam, and both devoured the Coleman family's spaghetti.[134]

An FBI agent complained in a memo to Hoover that the search for Van Meter was hampered by "a serious handicap in that since the shootings, about 75 percent of the gangsters and mobsters of the underworld have scuttled out, had their telephones disconnected and have moved, that everybody is on the hideout, knowing that they would be brought in for questioning. There are numerous cottages and places up on the lakes where

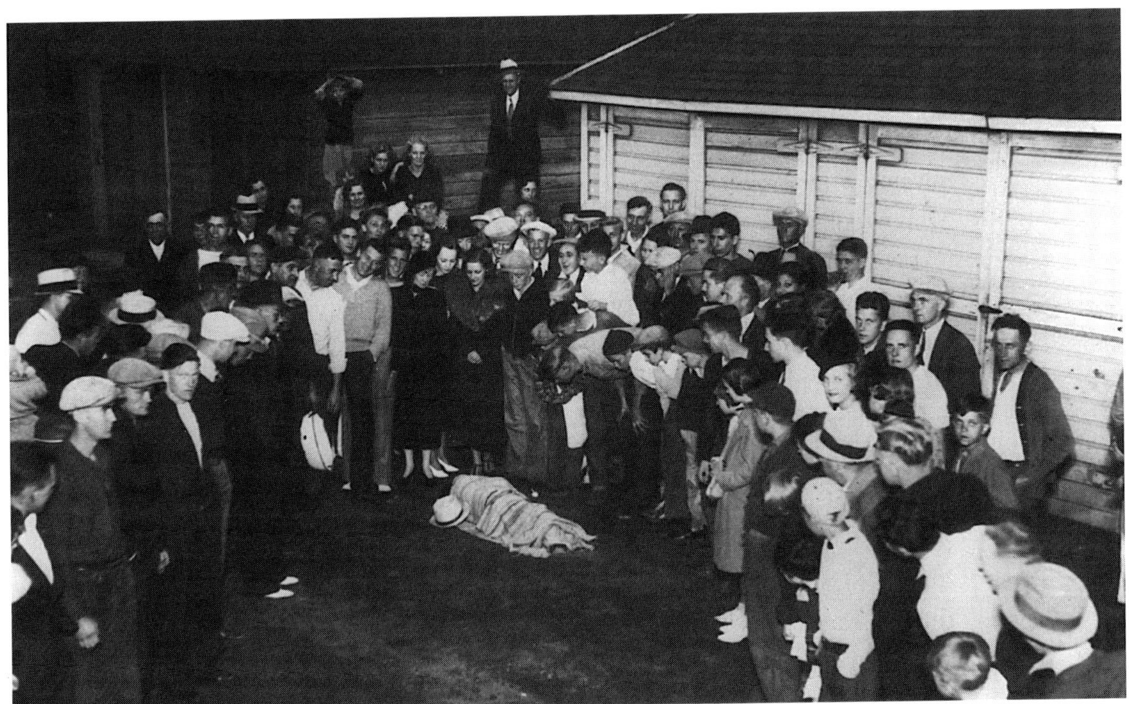

The body of Dillinger gang member Homer Van Meter, slain in an alley near University Avenue by St. Paul police; (below) newspaper account of Van Meter's betrayal by the underworld

THE ST. PAUL DAILY NEWS

Complete Wire Reports Of United Press, The Greatest World-Wide News Service

VOL. 35, NO. 178 ★ HOME EDITION — ST. PAUL, MINN., SATURDAY, AUGUST 25, 1934 — WEATHER: — PRICE TWO CENTS

GANG BETRAYED VAN METER

SOUGHT SHARE IN $46,000 BANK LOOT HELD FOR HIM BY UNDERWORLD LEADER HERE

Police Set Death Trap On Tip From Associates Of St. Paul "Fence" Now Fugitive.

(Copyright, 1934, St. Paul Daily News.)

Outlawed by the underworld of which he had been a "big shot," Homer Van Meter, Dillinger gang "tommy" expert, walked into the St. Paul police death trap Thursday because he tried to collect his share of the $46,000 loot of the Securities Bank & Trust Co. of Sioux Falls, S. D.

The money was being held for him by a St. Paul underworld leader who succeeded the late "Dapper Dan" Hogan as one of the leading "fences" for stolen goods throughout the middle west.

This man, who for several years operated a notorious bootleg establishment on Wabasha st., has been "on the lam" for about five months—since shortly after the daring raid on the Sioux Falls bank, March 6, by John Dillinger and five of his machine gun-armed mobsters.

Both federal agents and police have been searching for him, without warrants, for questioning, but have had no more success in finding him than had Van Meter.

The tip to police which resulted in Van Meter's slaying at University ave. and Marion st., by Police Chief Frank R. Cullen and Detectives Thomas A. Brown, Jeff Dittrich and Thomas McMahon came

GOV. OLSON WILL TAKE to radio Monday, and in a half-hour address from 8 p. m. to 8:30 p. m. will review the truck drivers' strike in Minneapolis.

* * *

EMIL OLSON, 60, 232 E. 10TH st., admitted in municipal court today that he set out last Sunday night to go into the liquor business with eight pints, but couldn't sell a pint." He was sentenced to 15

HELD IN VAN METER CASE

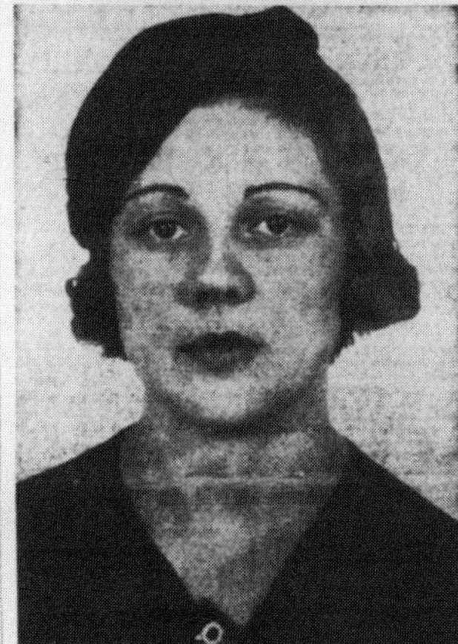

Held without charge at police headquarters following her arrest after the shooting of Homer Van Meter late Thursday is OPAL MULLIGAN, alias MILLIGAN, alias MELIGA, pretty 21-year-old brunet, whose home is at 295 W. Central ave. Police have refused to state in what connection with the Van Meter case she is held. She is a former girl friend of Albert W. (Pat) Reilly, now in the county jail awaiting trial as one who harbored John Dillinger.

Income Of Farms Best In 3 Years

Obtain 1.9 Per Cent Return On Capital, First Since 1930, U. S. Reports.

By United Press.

WASHINGTON, Aug. 25.—Farm owners obtained a 1.9 per cent return on their capital in 1933, the first gain for three years, the department of agriculture reported today.

In 1924 farmers obtained 5 per cent, the highest return in the last decade.

An analysis of farm incomes for 1933 by the bureau of agricultural economics said that the income available for return on capital and for the operator's labor and management in 1933 was $2,627,000,000. There remained only $366,000,000 as returns for capital and management after deducting for wages and unpaid family labor.

Net farm capital was placed at $19,079,000.

The gross income from farm production for 1933 was estimated at $5,985,000,000, including the value of products used on the farm. In addition, farm operators received $271,000,000 in AAA payments, making a total gross income of $6,256,000,000, compared with $5,331,000,000 in 1932.

Cash income of farmers in 1933 was placed at $2,525,00,000 after deducting total production expenses of $2,737,000,000. This was a gain of more than $1,000,000,000 over the previous year.

RIOTING CONVICTS SUBDUED BY MACHINE GUN TROOPS; SET FIRE TO 7 BUILDINGS

By United Press.

GRATERFORD, Pa., Aug. 25.—Rioting convicts in the new eastern penitentiary today caused thousands of dollars damage to machinery and equipment.

Before they were subdued by state troopers with machine guns they set fire to seven buildings.

Rioting began during the morning exercise period, when most of the inmates were in the prison yard.

Despite general confusion in the institution, no one was reported injured and no escapes were reported.

Two hundred and fifty of the 1,000 prisoners engaged in the riot. The trouble started in a kitchen and spread to the exercise yard.

A group of "bad actors" armed with clubs, stones and pieces of broken machinery ran to a hill and defied prison guards for two hours.

Finally 50 state troopers and a score of highway patrolmen trained submachine and riot guns on the rioters and threatened to fire if they did not surrender. Sullenly they submitted to capture and were at once placed in solitary confinement.

The fire which got out of control for a time damaged the new industrial plant, the canteen of a cell block, a barn, the prison kitchen and destroyed three abandoned wooden barracks.

Communists Are Freed After Tomato Brawl

Tomato seeds were still

Onion Strike Chief Beaten After Blas

Citizens Drive Out Weeders; Mayor's Home Bombed.

By United Press.

McGUFFEY, O., Aug. 25.—Striking onion weeders fled for the lives today before the wrath townspeople angered by the bombing of the home of Mayor Godfre Ott.

Mobs surged through the sho main street after having kidnape Okey O'Dell, militant leader of th ragged onion weeders who hav kept the region in a turmoil f three months with their demand for higher wages and shorter hour

O'Dell, seized while being questioned about the bombing, w beaten severely and taken to th Hardin county line. He was throw from a truck and released with stern warning to "stay out of th onion fields."

O'Dell, however, came back town, barricaded himself in h

they have friends or relatives . . . making it doubly hard in carrying out the investigation."[135]

Van Meter moved from Bear Island to the Birches Camp Resort near Grand Rapids for one evening and then to the Green Gables Tourist Camp outside Minneapolis for another night, before heading toward downtown Minneapolis on August 23.[136]

Precisely how the police traced Van Meter has never been determined. Police first claimed that they got a tip from the family of one of Van Meter's girlfriends, a twenty-one-year-old waitress named Opal Milligan. Two days later, they changed their story, insisting that a tip from an auto salesman had led them to ambush Van Meter.[137]

Pat Reilly, interrogated by FBI agents, suggested that the underworld had "fingered" Van Meter for police because he talked too much about upcoming bank robberies. The FBI learned from Reilly that "Van Meter returned to St. Paul and consequently brought heat on the underworld here; that he was advised by the underworld that if he did not keep under cover, he would cause trouble to the remaining members of the underworld. However, according to Reilly, Van Meter was not the type that would stay under cover and that his constant appearance on the streets in St. Paul angered the underworld."[138]

An employee of slot machine king Thomas Filben, a business contact of the Dillinger gang, suggested a very different story. Horace "Red" Dupont, who worked for Filben's Patrick Novelty Company, heard that Van Meter had asked the mob's banker, Harry Sawyer of the Green Lantern saloon, to safeguard $9,000. When Van Meter returned from Illinois and demanded his money back, Sawyer decided to keep it and called police with a tip on Van Meter's location. The *St. Paul Daily News* carried a similar rumor: Van Meter had been turned in by Sawyer's mob after Sawyer was hounded by Van Meter for his cut of the $49,500 stolen by the Dillinger gang from the Security National Bank of Sioux Falls, South Dakota.[139]

Five years after Van Meter's death, the FBI would hear a final hypothesis. An underworld informant told the bureau that Dillinger gang associate Tommy Gannon, a Twin Cities bank robber, had betrayed Van Meter in a conspiracy involving casino operator Jack Peifer. According to this theory, Peifer and members of the St. Paul Police Department divided up Van Meter's bank loot. As a reward, Tommy Gannon was given Van Meter's guns.[140]

The hunt for Van Meter ended at the corner of University Avenue and Marion Street on August 23, 1934. The FBI determined that he had an appointment with Frank Kirwin that day, followed by a meeting with Jack Peifer at the Hollyhocks Club.[141]

Disguised by a mustache, wearing a blue serge suit and a straw hat, Van Meter walked out of the St. Paul Motors auto dealership at 5:12 P.M., ready to hop into a car parked north of University on Marion.[142]

Without warning, Van Meter was confronted by detective Tom Brown, police chief Frank Cullen (who had served under Brown as assistant chief), and two other officers. The police were armed with two sawed-off shotguns, two machine guns, and three words: "Stick them up!" Firing two shots over his shoulder from a .38-caliber Colt automatic, Van Meter ran south on the east side of Marion across University, toward an alley near Aurora. He "either got rattled or didn't know the neighborhood when he turned into that alley, because it's a blind alley," recalled an eyewitness. "If he had turned right, he might have got away."[143]

A blast of buckshot from Brown's shotgun blew Van Meter two feet off the pavement. "As he lay on the ground, he tried to get his revolver up to fire another shot," recalled an eyewitness. "But his hand was mangled by a machine gun blast" that nearly severed his arm. By 5:30 P.M. Van Meter was dead, slumped against a garage wall between Aurora Avenue and Marion Street. He had fifty bullets in his body, $923 in his pocket, and a gold-filled Bulova watch on his wrist. A pistol lay ten feet from his hand.[144]

Paul Presby, the St. Paul beat reporter for the *Minneapolis Journal*, was tipped off that Homer Van Meter had just been shot to death. "Paul Presby was a man who would walk over his grandmother for a scoop. . . . He called the *Journal* office and told them to send a cameraman to University and

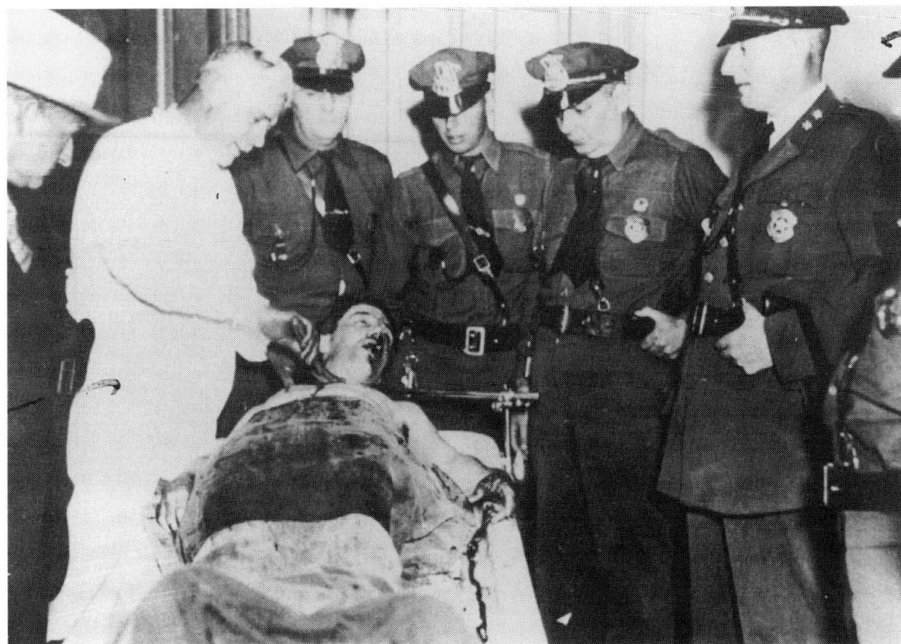

Homer Van Meter's body at the Ramsey County Morgue

Marion," recalled crime buff Woody Keljik. But when Presby arrived, the ward wagon had already come and picked up Van Meter's body. There was still blood in the gutter and a crowd of people there.

"Paul was disappointed he wasn't going to get a picture. He said to his cameraman, 'I'll lie in the gutter, turn up my collar and you take a picture—they won't know if it's Van Meter or Presby.'" He lay down in the gore-filled street and the *Journal* photographer grabbed his shot. "While Presby was lying on the street, a new woman joined the crowd who didn't know what was happening," said Keljik. "They just told her that Homer Van Meter had been shot to death. When the pictures are over, Paul Presby stands up—the woman thinks Van Meter has come back to life and she faints!"[145]

Van Meter's body gave evidence of the lengths to which he had gone to avoid capture. Wax injected under his skin to alter his appearance had begun to deteriorate, turning his face into a lumpy mask. FBI agents discovered scars on his fingertips (Van Meter had paid Chicago doctors $5,000 to obliterate his fingerprints with acid) and an attempt to remove a tattoo ("Hope") on his right arm.[146]

Instead of relishing the triumph, Hoover was furious that the St. Paul police had not notified the FBI until *after* they had killed Van Meter; the bureau learned of the shooting from an Associated Press employee. "The Director is very upset over the fact that that thing could take place in St. Paul without our knowing about it," confessed an FBI memo. The *Minneapolis Tribune* reported that "J. Edgar Hoover . . . had nothing to say about the gangster's death." Privately, Hoover raged at his agents. "I think our St. Paul office has shown utter lack of aggressiveness," he scrawled at the bottom of an August 24 memo. "The Director is rather discouraged about the whole thing," warned FBI executive E. A. Tamm. Although newspapers were reporting Van Meter was "fingered" for death by a girlfriend, "we did not know a thing as they [the police] would tell us nothing."[147]

Hoover's next discovery was even more outrageous: the police version of Van Meter's death, as told to the FBI, appeared to have been fabricated. The police had informed the bureau that they could not have alerted Hoover's men to the ambush because, chief Frank Cullen explained, they had received a tip that Van Meter was at University and Rice just five or ten minutes before the shooting. Yet the manager of the auto dealership at the corner of University and Marion said that plainclothes police officers had kept his garage under surveillance not for ten minutes but for ten *days* prior to the shooting of Van Meter. Even more intriguing, the manager told FBI agents that on the day of the shootout, a mystery man in a Chevrolet sedan had dropped the doomed Van Meter off a few feet from the police. Curiously, the officers allowed the Chevrolet to leave the ambush scene. What was going on under J. Edgar Hoover's nose?[148]

"In the estimation of the Manager, the person who placed Van Meter on the spot was the driver of the Chevrolet car, whom he classified as a 'stool pigeon,'" reported an FBI memo. "The police officers did not fire while the driver of the Chevrolet car was in the line of fire. . . . The whole episode had been put on more or less as a show for the benefit of the Police Department." The FBI believed the Chevrolet driver was Frank Kirwin, Van Meter's trusted mob emissary, but underworld rumor held that Tommy Gannon delivered Van Meter to University Avenue in exchange for protection against being arrested for some burglaries that he was suspected of committing.[149]

The FBI also discovered that detective Tom Brown had visited the manager of St. Paul Motors at 12:30 P.M. that day "and told him that a man would be in there that afternoon to buy an automobile and that they wanted the man. . . . Brown gave him a description of Van Meter." Had the police ambush been a police/underworld setup, with Van Meter as victim and the FBI as patsy?[150]

"A deal was made between some of the 'big shots' and Tom Brown of the Police Department," noted an FBI report of an interview with Pat Reilly, "whereby Van Meter was to be placed 'on the spot.' [Reilly] feels fairly certain that the police were notified of the fact that Van Meter was in town and that he would make his appearance at the corner of University Avenue and Marion Street on the date in question."[151]

Pat Lannon Sr., a patrolman who was present when Van Meter's body was brought to the morgue, asserted that "it was all of Brown's clique, they had Van Meter put on the spot." One FBI informant, a saloon keeper named Frank Reilly, said that "Van Meter was killed . . . to try to put Tom Brown back in a good light, because of certain rumors which had come to the front to the effect that he was a crooked police officer."[152]

Police did not welcome questions about Van Meter's death. "Was Van Meter put on the spot by fellow gangsters?" the *Dispatch* asked chief Cullen days later. "No," answered Cullen. "Is 'No' going to be the answer to all questions?" asked the reporter. "Yes," replied Cullen.[153]

Ironically, Van Meter, who was named by a Dillinger gang girlfriend as one of the gang members who made a donation toward Brown's campaign for sheriff, was shot by his candidate. Both Edna Murray and Byron Bolton of the Barker-Karpis gang told the FBI that Brown lost his $5,000 portion of the Bremer ransom as punishment for shooting Van Meter. The FBI learned that Murray had overheard Doc Barker say of Brown, "I guess you saw where that dirty _____ killed Van Meter." Murray added that "Brown was deprived of his share of the Bremer ransom money because he had double crossed Van Meter."[154]

When FBI agent Richard Pranke was informed that a gangster had been killed by police at University and Marion, he convinced special agent D. Milton "Mickey" Ladd to visit the police station for the first time. "Mickey had never been in the headquarters of the St. Paul police, because they were crooked," said Pranke. "The FBI couldn't trust the police." Of Tom Brown, Pranke said, "It was my ambition to get him indicted."[155]

In the battle between the police and the FBI, the bureau won a single skirmish. After examining Van Meter's body in the morgue, Pranke picked up the mobster's belt. "The belt was rather fat like a fat snake. . . . [I] found a zipper on it and pulled the zipper down and there was a very large bill, and I mean money," recalled Pranke. According to police, the belt contained barely $450. The money apparently was "overlooked by the St. Paul Police Department in their examination of the clothing," gloated an FBI memo. "Some of the members of the St. Paul Police Department hated my guts," wrote Pranke, because "a 'young squirt' like me found the money after the police had searched Van Meter's clothes."[156]

The FBI's satisfaction turned to shock when Van Meter's girlfriend insisted that he had been wearing a money belt containing $2,000 and had driven to the corner of University and Marion with a brown zipped bag containing $6,000—a bag that the manager of St. Paul Motors claimed was under Van Meter's arm just before he was slain. "Evidently the police had disposed of the money," mused J. Edgar Hoover; an agent reported that "the St. Paul Police probably have in their possession $7,000 or $8,000."[157]

Van Meter's body was returned to his birthplace, Fort Wayne, Indiana, and buried by his family in Lindenwood Cemetery.[158]

Three months after Van Meter's death, on November 27, 1934, the FBI caught up with Babyface Nelson on a highway near Fox River Grove, Illinois. Nelson died in a drainage ditch near a cemetery, perforated by seventeen FBI bullets after killing FBI agents Herman Hollis and Samuel Cowley.[159]

The deaths of Dillinger, Van Meter, and Nelson signaled the virtual extermination of the Dillinger gang, yet for years Hoover raged about the tenacity of the public's fascination with the Dillinger legend. "Well, wasn't he a rat?" said Hoover."Wasn't he everything that was low and vile? Didn't he hide behind women? Didn't he shoot from ambush? Wasn't his whole career as filthy as that of any rat that ever lived?" Dillinger continued to haunt Hoover as the media portrayed the bank robber as a gangland legend, a tommy gun–toting Robin Hood. *True Detective Mysteries* celebrated Dillinger as a "magician who got out of jails as easily as Houdini freed himself from handcuffs; [a] merchant of death who blasted himself and his pals out of one police trap after another."[160]

"Dillinger, who had been glorified by citizens having a distorted sense of values, met a fitting end," countered an FBI report. "And those to whom he had been an objective of hero worship, upon reconsideration, found that their misplaced admiration rightfully belonged with the law enforcement officer who daily risked his life to protect them from the violence of the Nation's Dillingers." The same report maintained that "the Dillinger case contributed greatly in earning for the FBI public confidence and support and caught the imagination of children of the day, many of whom are today devoted FBI employees."[161]

The *St. Paul Pioneer Press* welcomed the killing of Van Meter as "a first class serving of notice on the country at large and on the underworld in particular that St. Paul is really cleaning house and no longer deserves the evil reputation it acquired as a friendly harbor for gangsters." The *Minneapolis Tribune* asserted that "society is well rid of Van Meter. . . . The moral, we suppose, is that the trails of all criminals lead sooner or later to the inevitable 'blind alley' where Van Meter kept his rendezvous with justice."[162]

POLICE SHAKEUP FOLLOWS GRAFT R

Warren Tieups

roviding of most

Detective McGin-
department head
ent. Mr. Crum-
n under various
tment since Oct.
17 and McGinnis
ve youngster. He

the department
rved for a short

not fill the va-
public the possi-
ved.

F

s much specula-
Gus Barfus, now
the chief's office
manent. It was
he naming of a
Carr, in charge
Thomas Grace,
ead of the check
was believed.
progress for ap-
probably never

stalled in a pri-
sensitive instru-
dictograph con-
arks which offi-
e using the tele-
telephone calls

D

e are said to be

recorded every
was made by the
when suspicious
igators was de-
er engagements

may become in-
facilities which
mblers. A fed-
pplied these fa-

E

rs was Wallace
as brought from
police and crime
mie, former fed-
became head of
sible for ridding
oung Jamie was
University of

News indicated
tment were far
assistants were
an undercover

Policemen have
very of a dicta-
e several weeks
volcano.

s had been tap-
ntil the monitor
ths.
ayor Gehan, jus-
hat it is used in
cient police de-
d meritorious as
spicion could be

the alleged con-
idence collected
vidence is avail-

Commissioner Warren Inspects Recording Instruments

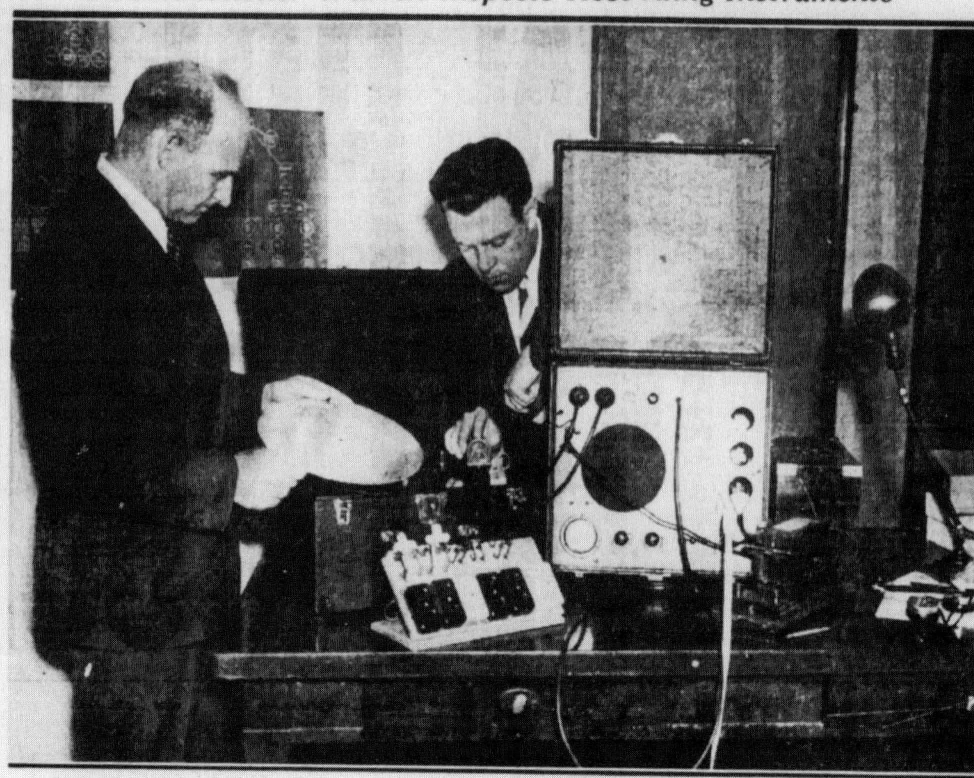

COMMISSIONER OF PUBLIC SAFETY H. E. WARREN, left, is shown above as he this morning inspected the modern scientific equipment which brought about the biggest shakeup in the history of St. Paul's police force. He is placing a record on the phonograph which recorded many of the incriminating conversations. At the rear is WALLACE JAMIE, Daily News investigator, who secured the facts which caused the shakeup.

Scientific Devices Trapped St. Paul Policemen

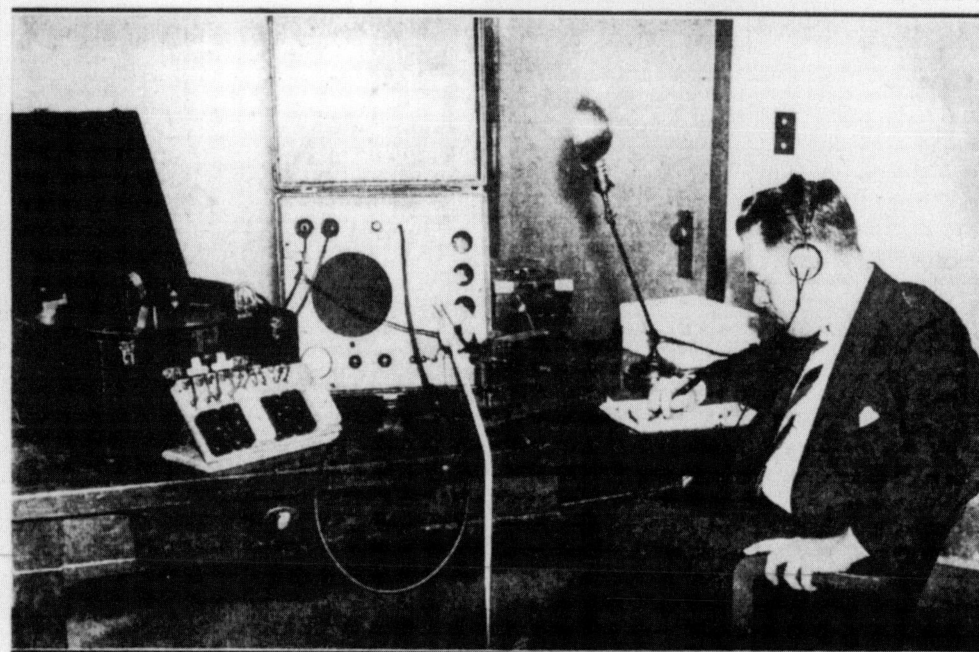

Equipment with which police were trapped through overheard conversations, is shown in the picture above. WALLACE JAMIE, investigator placed on the work by The Daily News, is pictured as he is listening to conversation coming to his office in the public safety building over a dictograph. At the left may be seen the recording phonograph on which much of the important information was recorded.

Autos Kill 1, 6 Are I[illegible]

Kin Knows Nothing Of Lindquist Surrender

Despite reports from Chicago that

Tries Jail Suicide

Man Under Life Sentence Slashes

Blames Bank For '29 Cr[illegible]

May B

tion in this
yours,

"The en
Mayor Geha
present it.
ren, and it
of the grand
"I don't
ney or myse
"These
ren's letter)
dicted or v
sound judgm
"I think
service. The

"If theis
should be se
earliest possi
service."
The may
be conducive
in any other

He imme
and John L.
but Mr. Kin
Warren lette
in determini
may be indic
Two me
adopted, the
grand jury
through com

HELD
ty jail, Iv
A. Wright,
charged
Wright wa
by Louis
secret servi
of St. Pau
that he fo
half dolla
which Wri
cast the m

GOV. OLS
ed a photo
Astor, founde
trading indu
dedication of
memorial a
Aug. 4, then
torical collec
came from W
on it a repre
trader's signa
ter he signed

UNHA
she fell f
window to
Elizabeth
old daugh
William M
st. The ch
ed upon a
screen, lea

STATE P
Carl Erickso
110,000 tons
various state
capitol durin
The bids w
Last year th
to $5.45 per

Randolp Plans On Ste

There will
steamer Cap
for the tardy
be any.
At least th
of the Rand

10

THE BIG CLEANUP

The electronic surveillance equipment (far left) that exposed police ties to the underworld also revealed gambling operations housed in the Hamm Building (left).

63 Sweeping the Police Clean

New St. Paul Police Headquarters
100 East Eleventh Street, St. Paul

St. Paul's new Public Safety Building, opened as the police department's headquarters in December 1930, was equipped with a garage, an Identification Division for fingerprints, "show-up" areas for lining up suspects, and three stories of Roman-Doric architecture. In the spring of 1935, the police station also harbored secret telephone wiretaps and microphones installed by the *St. Paul Daily News* and the public safety commissioner to capture corrupt policemen consorting with the underworld.[1]

By 1934 the public could no longer ignore the ties between police and the underworld. City officials were mortified when U.S. attorney general Homer Cummings said, "If there are two cities in America which need cleaning up, they are St. Paul and Minneapolis." Senator Royal Copeland of New York seconded the attorney general, condemning the Twin Cities as "the poison spots of American crime." Police-conducted "cleanup" campaigns had been closing down pinball games, gambling parlors, and brothels

St. Paul Police headquarters, from which investigator Wallace Jamie launched his probe into police corruption

since 1922, but no one had launched a campaign to clean up the St. Paul police themselves.[2]

Werner Hanni, the special agent in charge of the FBI's St. Paul office, reported to J. Edgar Hoover in February 1934 about the ballet the FBI had to dance with corrupt Twin Cities police. "In the Minneapolis Police Department there have always been a limited number that we know of in whom we have been able to place confidence.... It has been necessary for this Division, in the nature of investigations, to confine itself to those men of the department... whom we have found in the past that we could trust."[3]

Leading the charge for reform in St. Paul was Howard Kahn, the crusading editor of the *St. Paul Daily News,* located then at 55–65 East Fourth Street. A World War I hero who served in the U.S., French, and Italian armies, Kahn became a cub reporter at the *Daily News* in 1918 and rose to the post of managing editor by 1938.[4]

Howard Kahn, newspaper editor and relentless critic of police corruption

John Dillinger shot his way out of the Lincoln Court Apartments on March 31, 1934, the same day a Ramsey County grand jury report denied that the city was a magnet for gangsters. Kahn answered with the *News* headline, "Machine Guns Blaze as Jury Whitewashes Police." His editorial charged that the mayor "insulted the intelligence of St. Paul citizens" when he insisted that the city had no crime problem.[5]

St. Paul's Mayor William Mahoney angrily dismissed Kahn's relentless editorials. After one Kahn broadside, the mayor proclaimed, "There are no criminals here. They got Machine Gun Kelly in Memphis and Harvey Bailey in Oklahoma. These fellows just come here to visit our lakes. We have 10,000 lakes and a resort for every crook." "The newspapers of St. Paul are endeavoring to picture the Twin Cities as a Mecca for criminals," protested the director of the Minnesota tourist bureau, George Bradley. "Such publicity will irreparably injure the tourist business of this state."[6]

Kahn's *Daily News* answered that the public "will find it difficult to understand why such big-time gangsters as Harvey Bailey, Albert Bates, Machine Gun Kelly, Verne Miller, Verne Sankey and others were permitted to hide out in St. Paul.... Why shortly after Mr. Mahoney's election in 1932 perhaps the greatest conglomeration of national public enemies ever collected in one city gathered in St. Paul and remained here, unmolested by police."[7]

J. Edgar Hoover, still deeply suspicious of the St. Paul police, appeared reluctant to help the city change its image as a haven for criminals. Reform police chief Tom Dahill asked Hoover to compare street crime rates in

St. Paul to those of other cities. Within three days, the FBI had developed statistical tables of eight cities showing that—in spite of the highly publicized Hamm, Bremer, and Dillinger cases—the rates for everyday murder, assault, and larceny were indeed lower in St. Paul than in comparable cities.[8]

But FBI files show that Hoover lied to chief Dahill, responding that the FBI "has not prepared a compilation of data for individual cities, and that . . . due to the press of current work and limitations of personnel it will not be possible to do so." The FBI also refused requests to allow its agents to testify in the 1934 Ramsey County grand jury probe of civic corruption. Hoover declined to lend support in part because he distrusted the police and the grand jury system in St. Paul: "Within a few hours after any witness appears before the grand jury, the substance of his testimony appears in the local papers," wrote Hoover in a memo to the U.S. attorney general. "Obviously, this situation at St. Paul has degenerated into a publicity campaign and I do not believe that our Agents should become parties to any such spectacle."[9]

The *Daily News* kept up the pressure with a March 8, 1934, editorial headlined "Why Do Big Time Criminals Center Their Activities in St. Paul?" Noting that an Indiana highway patrol captain guessed that the men who robbed a Sioux Falls, South Dakota, bank were from the Twin Cities, the *News* asked: "Can it be mere coincidence that impels big-time criminals to make St. Paul their center of operations? . . . Or is it probable that the underworld knows the St. Paul police are helpless?"[10]

FBI agent Melvin Purvis condemned St. Paul in his 1936 book, *American Agent.* The city's reputation was such, wrote Purvis, "that when the wife of a prominent motion-picture producer was robbed in Chicago, police and federal agents assumed that the thieves would go to St. Paul to make contact with buyers of stolen goods." Tapping a few wires in St. Paul "led to the recovery of the jewels and the arrest of the robbers."[11]

Inside the St. Paul Police Department, Tom Brown and others tied to the O'Connor system battled reformers, among them Tom Dahill, Gustave H. Barfuss, and Clinton A. Hackert. One FBI agent noted that two of the reform policemen "are honest and sincere, but are being 'knifed' by the old outfit that under the civil service rules cannot be entirely eliminated." The agent suggested that the older police "for political and personal reasons, can, through their underworld connections, have crimes committed in this city to embarrass their successors."[12]

Clearly, though, the era of Harry Sawyer, Jack Peifer, and Tom Brown was coming to an end. "St. Paul has paid for its complacency under the O'Connor system, as all must pay who foul their own nest," editorialized the

Police reformers Thomas Dahill (left) and Clinton Hackert (right) , who battled the corrupt followers of former chiefs Tom Brown and John O'Connor

St. Paul Pioneer Press. "St. Paul pays in a vicious underworld that is notorious before the world and in the depredations of these criminals who, no longer under the iron hand of John O'Connor, have since then continually violated this rogues' compact."[13]

One thing was certain: the police could not clean house by themselves. In June 1934, the FBI was amused to hear that the police had created a new crime squad to raid St. Paul's gangster hideouts. The only problem, the FBI noted, was that "the head of this particular squad was Officer [Bill] McMullen, who, according to information furnished by Bessie [Beth] Green [of the Dillinger gang], is a friend of Harry Sawyer and a contact man between the police department and the underworld."[14]

Goaded into action, ten business leaders joined the *Daily News* in raising a $100,000 war chest to finance a campaign against corruption. Leading a team of investigators was a twenty-four-year-old criminologist named Wallace Ness Jamie, the third in a dynasty of gangster fighters. His father was Alexander Jamie of Chicago's "Secret Six," who had tackled Al Capone, and his uncle was Prohibition agent Eliot Ness, the famed head of the "Untouchables."[15]

Arriving in St. Paul in May 1934, Jamie worked with the full authority of public safety commissioner H. E. "Ned" Warren to install telephone taps in police offices to record conversations between officers and gangsters. Microphones were hidden in telephones, furniture, and air shafts throughout police headquarters. "In his preparatory investigations, [Jamie] had found

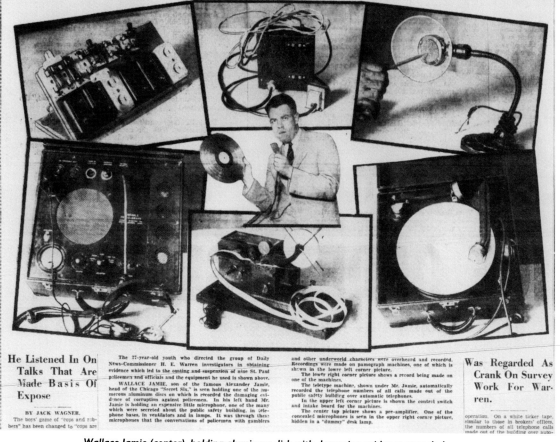

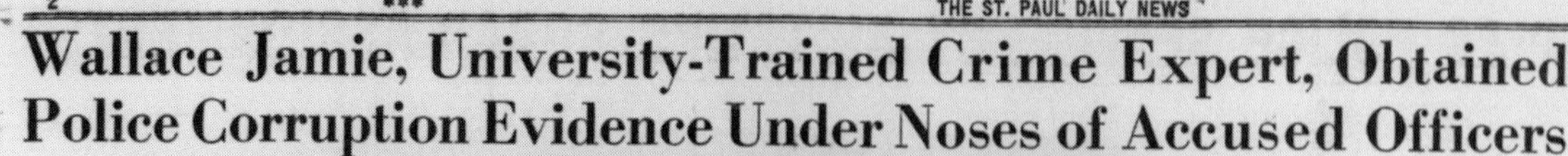

2 THE ST. PAUL DAILY NEWS

Wallace Jamie, University-Trained Crime Expert, Obtained Police Corruption Evidence Under Noses of Accused Officers

He Listened In On Talks That Are Made Basis Of Expose

BY JACK WAGNER.

The boys' game of "cops and robbers" has been changed to "cops are

The 27-year-old youth who directed the group of Daily News-Commissioner H. E. Warren investigators in obtaining evidence which led to the ousting and suspension of nine St. Paul policemen and officials and the equipment he used is shown above.

WALLACE JAMIE, son of the famous Alexander Jamie, head of the Chicago "Secret Six," is seen holding one of the numerous aluminum discs on which is recorded the damaging evidence of corruption against policemen. In his left hand Mr. Jamie is holding an expensive little microphone, one of the many which were secreted about the public safety building, in telephone bases, in ventilators and in lamps. It was through these microphones that the conversations of policemen with gamblers and other underworld characters were overheard and recorded. Recordings were made on pamograph machines, one of which is shown in the lower left corner picture.

The lower right corner picture shows a record being made on one of the machines.

The teletype machine, shown under Mr. Jamie, automatically recorded the telephone numbers of all calls made out of the public safety building over automatic telephones.

In the upper left corner picture is shown the control switch and intake board for the machines.

The center top picture shows a pre-amplifier. One of the concealed microphones is seen in the upper right corner picture, hidden in a "dummy" desk lamp.

Was Regarded As Crank On Survey Work For Warren.

operation. On a white ticker tape, similar to those in brokers' offices, the numbers of all telephone calls made out of the building over auto-

Wallace Jamie (center), holding aluminum disk with damaging evidence revealed by wiretaps on the St. Paul Police Department's telephones

that all the telephone wires at police headquarters entered the building through a single terminal box," one magazine writer recounted. "This box, fortunately, was in a remote corner of the building, and Jamie went to work on it without fear of discovery. Each wire had an identifying tag and, one after another, Jamie cut in on all the wires and led the connection into his own control room which he had set up in a cubby-hole in another deserted part of the building—room 201."[16]

Throughout the spring of 1935, Jamie recorded 2,500 police telephone calls on 400 aluminum pamograph discs. The wiretaps generated 3,000 pages of incriminating evidence, linking police officials to a $2,000-a-day racehorse wire operated out of St. Paul by gambler "Dutch" Otto Cameron and other mobsters with the full protection of police. Among those caught on the wiretaps was police detective Fred Raasch, who warned the

Riverview Commercial Club to hide its slot machines from an impending police raid: "Take the two slot machines down. This is Freddie Raasch. There's a couple of guys coming right over. . . . stick them away in the vault."[17]

Jamie and the *St. Paul Daily News* had finally exposed the ugliness of thirty years of police corruption to the stunned citizens of St. Paul. There on the front page of the *Daily News*, proud residents of Minnesota's capital city read proof of what they had ignored for so long: routine tip-offs to the underworld, payoffs to police officials, and unmistakable camaraderie between gangsters and the police officers the city had hired to stop them.

64 'When Are You Going to Play Santa?'

The Hamm Building Gambling Den
408 St. Peter Street, St. Paul

One of the most striking wiretaps in the 1935 *Daily News* corruption investigation involved conversations between a gambler and James P. Crumley, acting inspector of detectives, who had been a policeman since 1914 and once headed the morals squad. Crumley was heard openly soliciting bribes from Harry Reed, president of the St. Paul Recreation Company, which ran a gambling operation in the basement of St. Paul's Hamm Building.

"Say, when are you going to play Santa?" asked Crumley. "We're all broke up here!"

"Well, you know that there hasn't been anything for the last two weeks," apologized Reed.

"Two weeks, hell, it's been six weeks," roared Crumley, to which Reed replied, "I'll take care of it for you."[18]

The Hamm Building basement was leased by Hamm kidnap intermediary William W. Dunn, who ran a billiards hall, a cigar stand, and a gym with boxing rings and bowling alleys there. One wiretap caught Crumley warning Harry Reed to shut down the Hamm Building's gambling before a police raid. ("Close up that horse book," Crumley said. "Right away . . . no bets, see.") Another wiretap found Reed complaining to Crumley about the success of a rival gambling establishment, Dutch Otto's Royal Cigar Store at 443 St. Peter, which had been kept open while St. Paul Recreation had to lay low. "Did anybody down at the Royal get permission from anybody to open —to run their horse—behind closed doors up there that you know of?" asked Reed. "Well, I just got word that they said they got permission from somebody. I was wondering why the hell we should be closed and they should be open."

Reed agreed to close his gambling operation "tighter 'n a g[od] d[amned] clam," but he was bothered by the bettors gathered at the Royal Cigar Store. Reed asked the officer to assure him that it would be "just a couple days until it cools off and they [St. Paul Recreation] can take the bets in the front there like everybody else is doing. . . . I don't give a damn if they [the Royal Cigar Store] make a million dollars. . . . I aint gonna squawk unless somebody else does."[19]

In June 1935 the scandal exploded on the front pages of the *Daily News*. Public safety commissioner Ned Warren informed Mayor Mark Gehan that the Jamie tapes disclosed "surprising evidence of police ownership of slot machines, police connection with prostitution, police political activities . . . and a sensational connection between police and criminal lawyers." The Jamie investigation forced a Ramsey County grand jury investigation that resulted in twenty-one indictments against officers, detectives, and others. Ultimately, thirteen policemen were either discharged or suspended, and chief Michael J. Culligan was forced to resign.[20]

Crucial to the cleanup was disciplining Crumley, who was exposed in the wiretaps as the "brains" of the network between gangsters and police. The sixty-three-year-old Crumley had joined the force under chief John O'Connor, was appointed inspector of detectives by Tom Brown, and participated in the 1932 police tip-off that enabled the Barker-Karpis gang to escape capture. He was, in short, a living symbol of the corrupt old guard.[21]

During Crumley's 1936 Ramsey County trial for malfeasance in office, his lawyers mounted a spirited defense. The attorneys attacked prosecutors for their technical problems with the wiretaps ("I would like to have seen these amateurs, these investigators, sitting in Mr. Crumley's place at police headquarters, keeping this town clean of murderers, kidnappers and thieves," jeered his lawyer) and defended Crumley's unsavory methods of crime control ("A police station is not a Sunday School"). Although that jury cleared Crumley of criminal charges, he was dismissed from the force and then convicted in 1938 on unrelated charges of fixing a federal drug case. He died of heart disease one year later.[22]

There was still the matter of Thomas Brown, the crucial source of police tip-offs to the Barker-Karpis and Dillinger gangs. "While it is generally rumored in St. Paul that Brown is a crooked police officer," one FBI agent wrote in February 1936, "should he have participated in either the Hamm or Bremer kidnappings . . . he has apparently been smart enough to deal only through Harry Sawyer, as neither Dahill nor anyone else has been able to furnish any concrete evidence of these rumors."[23]

Brown was temporarily suspended during the 1935 trial of the Hamm kidnappers after government witness Byron Bolton testified that Brown had received a $25,000 cut of the ransom money.[24]

THE ST. PAUL DAILY NEWS

Complete Wire Reports of United Press and International News Service, the Greatest Worldwide Services.

HOME EDITION — ST. PAUL, MINN., MONDAY, JUNE 24, 1935 — PRICE THREE CENTS

TRAP NINE IN POLICE SIFT; 4 OUSTED, CHIEF SUSPENDED

Mayor Promises To Ask Jury Probe Of Police Dept. Graft

Commissioner Describes Scientific Equipment Used To Record Conversations With Graft Connections—Suspected Officers Discovered Surveillance Too Late—Many Other Changes In Department Predicted

Transmission by Commissioner of Public Safety H. E. Warren to Mayor Gehan of a letter telling of the scandal uncovered in the police department, brought an immediate pledge from the mayor of close co-operation and suggestion that a special grand jury be called to consider the case.

The mayor declared he would himself ask a special grand jury, if necessary. In the letter to the mayor, Commissioner Warren charged sensational police connivance with gamblers, underworld activities and alarming subversive tactics.

TEXT OF LETTER

June 24, 1935.

Dear Mayor Gehan: Last year I stated to you as well as to the public that I was concentrating on the detective division of the police department—in an effort to clean up a situation that was not only a black eye to the entire department of public safety, but the city as well.

Shortly after I became commissioner of public safety matters were brought to my attention which indicated that a number of police officers should be removed. At that time, however, I did not have sufficient evidence to sustain these removals if the men appealed for reinstatement before the civil service appeal board.

Because The Daily News had conducted a previous investigation into affairs of the police department, I decided to make the new inquiry with the co-operation and financial assistance of that paper.

Daily News investigators, working with me and under my direction, were given office space in the public safety building. Necessary authorization was given them to examine records and have the freedom of the building.

Men in the department under suspicion were placed in key positions where any illegitimate activities or particularly meritorious activities would be more easily discernible.

The greater part of this inquiry has been going on about a year.

INSTALL MONITOR UNIT

The investigators immediately started installing a monitor telephone unit—a clearing board on telephone conversations similar to that used in Milwaukee and other progressive police departments.

Supplementing this monitor system, Pamograph machines were installed. These machine make aluminum records of the actual conversations. Dictograph instruments also were placed in strategic points in the building. Phonographic records also were made of office conversations thus obtained.

RESULTS ASTOUNDING

HIT BY WARREN IN DAILY NEWS INQUIRY

CHARLES J. TIERNEY, inspector of detectives, started his police work as an alarm operator. He is 28 years old, has been on the force since March 22, 1921, is married and lives at 1639 Hoyt ave. He was suspended.

THOMAS E. DAHILL, former police chief with the present rank of assistant inspector of detectives, was suspended. He has been on the force since Sept. 1, 1914, is 46, married, and lives at 1859 Juliet st.

JAMES P. CRUMLEY, veteran policeman, was given 24 hours to resign "or be fired." With the rank of detective, he has been acting inspector of detectives in charge of the crime squad. He was appointed Oct. 1, 1914. He is 63, married, lives at 273 S. Saratoga ave.

POLICE CHIEF MICHAEL C. CULLIGAN today headed a list of five police officers suspended pending investigation. Appointed deputy commissioner of public safety June 5, 1934, he became chief in October. He is 38, married, and lives at North St. Paul.

PATROLMAN PATRICK RIDGE has been on the crime squad as a plainclothes man. He is 44, married, lives at 1322 Sargent ave., and has been on the police force since Dec. 16, 1913. He was suspended.

PATROLMAN MICHAEL McGINNIS, serving as a plainclothes man attached to the crime squad, was told to resign. On the force since June 16, 1920, he is 39, married, lives at 400 S. Warwick ave.

DETECTIVE FRED W. RAASCH, assigned to the crime squad, lives at 756 Oakdale ave. He is 41, has been a policeman since March 1, 1917, and is married. He was told to "quit or be fired."

JOHN McGOWAN, ranking as a police chauffeur, serving as a plainclothes man on the crime squad, was suspended. He is 41, has been on the force since May 12, 1921, is married, and lives at 236 N. Dunlap st.

"Nothing To Say," Declare All Fired And Suspended Officers

Daily News Assists Warren In Revealing Underworld Tieups

Crumley, Raasch, Flanagan, McGinnis Ordered To Resign; Dahill, Tierney, McGowan, Ridge Suspended With Culligan; Up-To-Date Devices Record Dealings With Race Gamblers, Slot Machine Owners, Vice Leaders

Months of intensive investigation of the affairs of the St. Paul police department culminated today in the most drastic shake-up in the city's history including the suspension of Police Chief M. J. Culligan.

Other heads fell right and left as Commissioner H. E. Warren made public the result of a sensational inquiry which involved the use of dictographs, telephone wire supervision, and a remarkable new invention which permitted the phonographic recording of conniving conversations between police executives and members of the underworld.

The Daily News, whose crime and police campaign about 18 months ago, aroused the interest of the whole nation, participated in the present investigation, co-operating with Mr. Warren and supplying the personnel and mechanical equipment.

Ordered to resign today with the alternative of being discharged within 24 hours were:

James P. Crumley, inspector of detectives.
Fred W. Raasch, detective.
Michael McGinnis, patrolman, working as detective.
Ray Flanagan, alarm lineman, working as detective.

Suspended for 30 days pending further developments are:

Michael J. Culligan, chief of police.
Thomas E. Dahill, detective lieutenant, former chief.
Charles J. Tierney, detective inspector.
John McGowan, chauffeur, working as detective.
Patrick Ridge, patrolman, working as detective.

Messrs. Dahill and Tierney are expected to be reinstated at the end of their suspension period with a lower rank. Commissioner Warren admitted that their case involved neglect of duty which they have admitted, rather than more serious irregularities or dishonesty.

The lightning which struck today is not the end of the storm, according to the public safety head. Other policemen will be removed as a study of the more-than-3,000 pages of phonographic record transcriptions is completed.

PERMITTED HORSE RACE BETTING

While scores of offenses are charged against some of the police executives mentioned, the case revolves around a

***The 1935 police cleanup, as announced by the* Daily News**

The FBI wrote that during the *St. Paul Daily News*'s wiretapping of police headquarters, "Thomas Brown was running things in St. Paul and it was hoped ultimately that . . . evidence enough would be secured on him to at least get him out of the Police Department. However, about that time Brown was transferred to some outside detail and had no occasion to make telephone contacts."[25]

Commissioner Warren summoned FBI special agent in charge Clinton Stein to Mayor Gehan's office on April 30, 1936. According to FBI records, Gehan brought up the charge that Brown had received a portion of the Hamm ransom. The commissioner reported that two policemen might be willing to speak out if Brown was removed from the force, but as long as he remained, "they are afraid of being killed if they talk." Dismissed by chief Clinton A. Hackert on July 17, 1936, Brown appealed to the Civil Service Commission, which upheld the dismissal for "breach of duty, misconduct, misfeasance and malfeasance." In a letter written to Brown on August 5, 1936, Warren savaged the detective for his participation in the kidnappings of William Hamm and Edward Bremer, for his role in the Barker-Karpis gang's 1933 escape from 204 Vernon Street, and for his leaks of police information to Harry Sawyer.[26]

The O'Connor system, born in 1900 when John O'Connor became police chief, died on October 9, 1936, when the discharge of Thomas Brown became

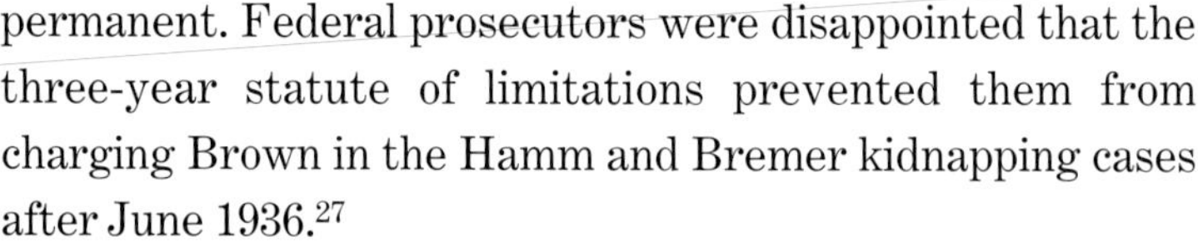

permanent. Federal prosecutors were disappointed that the three-year statute of limitations prevented them from charging Brown in the Hamm and Bremer kidnapping cases after June 1936.[27]

Public safety commissioner Gus Barfuss, who took bold steps to remove police corruption

Brown died of a heart attack in 1959, at the age of sixty-nine, in Ely, Minnesota, near where he had been running a liquor store. He insisted to the end that his dismissal was the result of political enmity between him and former chief Thomas Dahill.[28]

In a sweep of St. Paul's entire police establishment, reformer Gustave H. Barfuss—who had led the drive to suspend Tom Brown for consorting with gangsters—was installed as acting chief of police and then public safety commissioner. Barfuss then named Clinton Hackert chief of police, and Hackert in turn put detective lieutenant Tom Dahill in charge of five reorganized police districts.[29]

Together, Hackert and Barfuss lobbied successfully for city charter changes designed to depoliticize the job of police chief and cauterize the wounds of corruption. The reforms included changing the process for selecting the police chief to involve merit appointments and extending each chief's term to six years. Given the history of nearly one police chief every twelve months, this change alone was striking. "We had a comic saying in the St. Paul Police," former patrolman Joe Sherin recalled. "You didn't know who was chief until you went to work in the morning."[30] The reforms last to the present day: the St. Paul police chief can only be removed "for cause," and an independent committee selects a field of candidates from which a police chief is appointed.

St. Paul, "long known as a hideout for the nation's desperadoes, has cleaned house," the *Chicago Daily News* cheered. "The chief broom wielder has been—and is—Gus Barfuss, commissioner of public safety."[31]

In the wake of the reforms, Mayor Gehan wrote to Senator Royal Copeland in April 1937, asking that he give the city he had branded a "poison spot of crime" a clean bill of health: "I am very frank in saying that I think your comments at that time were substantially correct, but it did hurt our city a good deal," wrote Gehan. Summarizing the strides made in cleaning up St. Paul, the mayor suggested that "it would be only right now that some short comment be made by the same officials as to the improved conditions."[32]

J. Edgar Hoover, ever mistrustful of city administrations, warned the attorney general against allowing any federal official to satisfy the mayor's hopes: "I think it would be most unwise for you to give St. Paul a 'clean bill of health,'" wrote Hoover. "While I think some improvement has been made . . . it is my opinion that we should make certain that a continued effort will be made so far as crime conditions there are concerned."[33]

The St. Paul police force had been cleansed. Now the last members of the Dillinger and Barker-Karpis gangs had appointments to keep at the Federal Courts Building.

11

FINAL JUDGMENTS

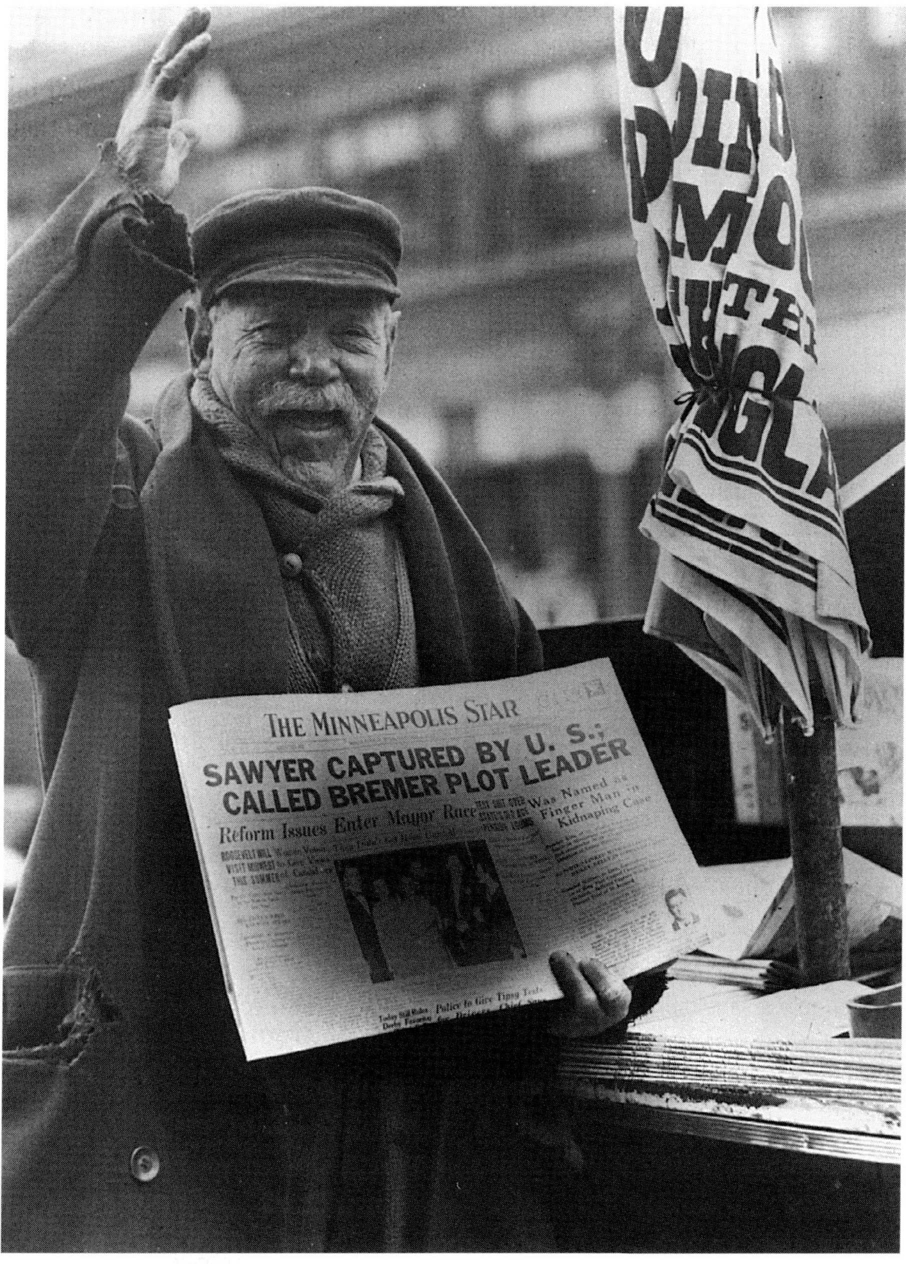

Alvin Karpis, being led by FBI agents into St. Paul's Federal Courts Building while crime reporter Nate Bomberg watches (far right, in profile); a "newsie" hails the **Minneapolis Star** *headlines announcing Harry Sawyer's capture.*

65 'We've Captured Alvin Karpis!'

Holman Municipal Airport
644 Bayfield Street, St. Paul

For members of the Dillinger and Barker-Karpis gangs, Holman Municipal Airport, just outside downtown St. Paul, was the gateway to a cell in the Ramsey County Jail, a trial in the Federal Courts Building, and then a train trip to a federal prison.

FBI agents brought William "Lapland Willie" Weaver and his girlfriend, Myrtle Eaton, to the airport after they were arrested for participating in the Bremer kidnapping. The couple had been hiding near Allendale, Florida, pretending to be chicken farmers. Weaver was apprehended on September 1, 1935, just after he awoke to feed his chickens—a chore that took him far from the two shotguns he stored in his house.[1]

Weaver's arrest was eclipsed by another, exactly eight months later: Alvin Karpis was seized in New Orleans on May 1, 1936. While most other members of the Barker-Karpis gang were being killed or jailed, Karpis—accompanied by Harry Campbell—was robbing jewelry stores, mail trucks, and even a railroad train. The FBI was infuriated that while Karpis was being hunted, he was indulging in "uninterrupted revelry" and "pleasureable activities," including a stay with a madam in Hot Springs, Arkansas, and fishing in the Gulf of Mexico. In January 1935 Campbell and Karpis machine-gunned their way out of a police raid in Atlantic City, New Jersey, but their girlfriends, Wynona Burdette and Delores Delaney, were arrested.[2]

Karpis was finally captured by the FBI, as he walked out of his apartment in New Orleans. "We've captured Alvin Karpis; generally known as Public Enemy No. 1—but not to us," chortled J. Edgar Hoover, who had traveled to New Orleans to participate in the arrest. "Karpis never had a chance." At 6:00 P.M. on May 1, Hoover informed special agent in charge Clinton Stein that Karpis had been seized and was being flown to St. Paul that night.[3]

Hoover ensured that his presence at Karpis's arrest was widely publicized. When the FBI director had testified before Congress in April 1934, he had been shamed by Senator Kenneth McKellar. The Tennessee Democrat had charged that the FBI was "running wild" and forced Hoover to admit he had never made an arrest. "I am talking about the actual arrests," the senator pressed Hoover. "You never arrested them, actually?" According to biographer Curt Gentry, Hoover left the Capitol after McKellar's inquisition and went directly to FBI headquarters, where he issued orders that he be notified the moment Karpis was found so that he could personally attend the arrest.[4]

As FBI publicity executive Louis Nichols told Gentry later, the capture of Karpis "pretty much ended the 'queer' talk"—widespread rumors that Hoover was hiding his life as a homosexual. Back in August 1933, for example, *Colliers* said the never-married Hoover walked "with mincing step." Magazines such as *True Detective* reported that during the arrest Karpis said to Hoover, "Go ahead—kill me. Get it over with." Karpis's nephew Albert Grooms told a different story. "Alvin told Hoover: 'You're a big brave S.O.B., you let these agents do all the work, and you take all the credit. What makes me mad is that the number one queer in the FBI captured me.' Hoover boiled, and told those guys to get Karpis up to St. Paul; Alvin had embarrassed Hoover in front of his own FBI crew!"[5]

J. Edgar Hoover, seen here in a 1942 photograph with his assistant Clyde Tolson, flew to St. Paul to supervise the interrogation of Karpis.

The bureau claimed that while Karpis was a fugitive, he sent a letter to Hoover in Washington, D.C., "threatening to come to FBI headquarters with a machine gun and kill the Director, thus striking a crippling blow to law enforcement." Grooms said that the message his uncle sent the director was of a very different character: "The letter said he knew that Hoover was as queer as a three-dollar bill. Alvin and Ma [Barker] laughed and laughed in my folks' kitchen about that letter. Alvin said, 'Just imagine how that queer blew his stack!'" Asked in 1994 to produce a copy of Karpis's death threat against Hoover, the FBI admitted that it could not find such a letter.[6]

Karpis got along well with members of organized crime, including the American Mafia, Grooms said: "It was a mutual admiration society—the Italians had their thing and Alvin knew people who could help the Italians out in various cities. . . . Alvin tipped off Lucky Luciano and Meyer Lansky while they were meeting in Toledo, Ohio . . . about J. Edgar Hoover being queer. Lansky, who was going to be deported, got the idea of getting a photograph of Hoover with his boyfriend, Clyde [Tolson, assistant director of the bureau]. After that, Hoover lost all interest in deporting Lansky."[7]

Grooms's account dovetails with the research of Hoover biographer Anthony Summers, who learned that two Nevada hoods had boasted that Lansky "nailed J. Edgar Hoover" with, according to writer Pete Hamill, "pictures of Hoover in some kind of gay situation with Clyde Tolson. . . . That was the reason, they said, that for a long time they had nothing to fear from the FBI."[8]

Karpis was flown 1,530 miles to St. Paul, accompanied by Hoover and Tolson. Remembering the Kansas City Massacre, the FBI took no chances with Karpis; he was bound hand and foot with fifteen-pound chains. Accounts of

Alvin Karpis (in white shirt) arriving at St. Paul's Holman Municipal Airport with Hoover and FBI agents from New Orleans

the words passed between Hoover and Karpis during the flight to St. Paul vary. The pilot told journalists that Hoover treated the gangster like "a little boy," saying, "Now come in here, Alvin." Karpis claimed that the FBI men played terrifying games with him, intimating that unless he cooperated they might toss him out of the airplane. At one point, Hoover said, Karpis talked about his life: "Everybody I knew had to work for a living," he told Hoover. "They didn't get much out of it. What I wanted was big automobiles like rich people had and everything like that. I didn't see how I was going to get them by making a fool of myself and working all my life. So I decided to take what I wanted."[9]

Hoover's publicist, Courtney Ryley Cooper, wrote that Karpis told Hoover, "I'm no hood, and I don't like to be called a hood. I'm a thief. . . . A thief is anybody who gets out and works for his living—like robbing a bank . . . or kidnapping somebody. He really gives some effort to it. A hoodlum is a pretty lousy sort of scum. He works for gangsters and bumps guys off." Hoover responded, "You're still a hoodlum."[10]

Karpis arrived at Holman Municipal Airport at 8:47 A.M. on May 2, 1936, surrounded by thirty FBI agents bristling with machine guns. *Daily News* reporter Nate Bomberg described the scene: "Finally the plane came in. It was the biggest plane I'd ever seen at that time. Gigantic. It pulled up to the administration building and finally the doors opened and down the ramp came a flock of FBI agents led by J. Edgar Hoover. . . . Karpis was wrapped in leg irons and arm irons and he was irons all over. Mr. Hoover was holding the irons and led Karpis to a waiting car."[11]

For the next half century, Karpis would argue that Hoover had been no hero—that the director had arrested him after Karpis was disarmed by other bureau agents. "That May day in 1936, I made Hoover's reputation as a fearless lawman," wrote Karpis. "It's a reputation he doesn't deserve. I have nothing but contempt for J. Edgar Hoover."[12]

66 'We Have the Right People, I Think'

St. Paul City Hall and Ramsey County Courthouse
15 Kellogg Boulevard West, St. Paul

For the November 1933 trial of the accused kidnappers of William Hamm Jr., the FBI had almost everything lined up—eyewitnesses, expert testimony, and forensic evidence. Only one thing was lacking—the right culprits.

The trial of Roger "the Terrible" Touhy, Chicago bootlegger and arch rival of Al Capone, unfolded on the eighth floor of the twenty-story St. Paul City Hall and Ramsey County Courthouse, a stunning Art Deco building that had just been completed the previous year. The Justice Department decided to use this courtroom, rather than the Federal Courts Building two blocks away, because the Touhy gang could be brought from the Ramsey County Jail to the courtroom via a tunnel.[13]

In addition to Touhy, the defendants were robber "Gloomy" Gus Schaefer, burglar Willie Sharkey, and Eddie "Father" McFadden, twice arrested for, but never convicted of, robbery. The four were arrested after an auto accident on July 19, 1933, in Elkhorn, Wisconsin. Police seeking a hit-and-run driver found in Touhy's Chrysler sedan extras that were not automotive standard equipment: three loaded .38 revolvers, a .45 pistol, a .38 automatic, and, concealed under a golf bag filled with bullets, an automatic rifle.[14]

The mobsters were indicted on August 12 in St. Paul because, an FBI memo concluded, "it is believed that public opinion would be more in favor of the prosecution in Hamm's home town [than in Wisconsin]." During the trial, which lasted from November 9 to 28, the gang was guarded by federal agents, police detectives, deputy sheriffs, and U.S. marshal's deputies equipped with machine guns. "Detectives and deputy sheriffs, armed with pistols, rifles and tear gas bombs, took their stations to prevent any last-minute breaks for freedom," reported the *Dispatch*. "Telegraphers sat at their keys, wires cleared, ready to flash to the world the word 'guilty' or 'not guilty'. . . . Machine guns were added to the armament to forestall violence." Kidnap conspirator Fred Goetz, the FBI learned from his wife, Irene, surfaced in the Twin Cities during the Touhy trial to help the gangsters get an acquittal, "not because he was friendly with them, but. . . [because] he did not wish to see them take a 'rap' for a crime they did not perform."[15]

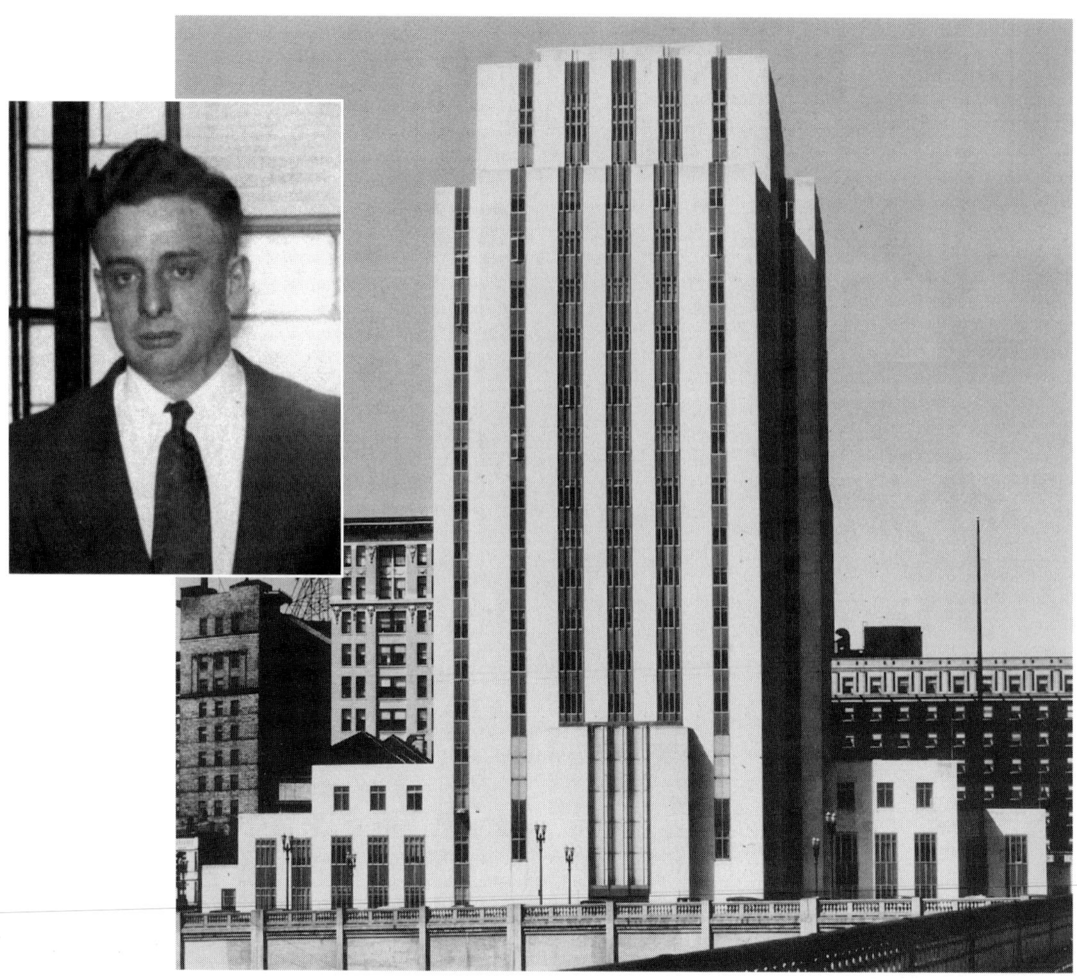

Ramsey County Courthouse and St. Paul City Hall, site of the 1933 trial of Roger "the Terrible" Touhy (inset) for the Hamm kidnapping

The FBI was under tremendous pressure to solve the Hamm kidnapping case quickly. Under its prodding, several witnesses to the abduction tentatively identified the Touhy gang, saying they resembled the men who had abducted Hamm and delivered the ransom notes. Privately, Justice Department officials knew the evidence was tenuous at best. It included white linen bandages found in Touhy's car that the FBI referred to as "appropriate for use in blindfolding kidnaped persons." When William Hamm was introduced to the Touhy gang, he admitted that they neither sounded nor looked like the men who had kidnapped him, but Hoover nevertheless determined to press on. In a confidential August 1933 memo regarding U.S. attorney Lewis Drill's doubts that the Touhy gang could be identified by witnesses, Hoover scrawled, "I don't like Drill's attitude. We have the right people, I think."[16]

After nineteen hours of deliberation, the jury disagreed, acquitting all four gangsters of any involvement in the kidnapping of William Hamm. The only bright spot for the law enforcement officers was Sharkey's hanging himself with a necktie in Ramsey County Jail on November 30. "By dying as he did, Sharkey has done a service to society," said Illinois state attorney Tom Courtney.[17]

To the FBI's credit, the subsequent detective work on the Bremer and Hamm kidnap cases was extraordinary. Their mistake with the Touhy gang behind them, the FBI tracked down the wallpaper Hamm remembered from the Bensonville hideout where he had been held and identified the siren he heard there. Agents researched the source of hundreds of socks to identify the ones given to Edward Bremer by his kidnappers. Within twenty-four months, the FBI would have identified and arrested more than a dozen conspirators for the Bremer and Hamm kidnappings.

Touhy, whom Al Capone believed to be an obstacle to his control of Chicago crime, had no similar run of good fortune. He was convicted in February 1934 of the "kidnapping" of con man Jake "the Barber" Factor, an ally of Capone. The FBI "assumed from the start, with no material evidence, that the Touhy gang was responsible" for kidnapping Factor, wrote FBI agent Melvin Purvis. "Every fact was fitted to the theory and the theory was correct." Touhy served two decades in prison for the kidnapping, until a federal judge declared him innocent, framed through perjured testimony, and freed the fifty-five-year-old bootlegger. In December 1959, less than a month after being released, Touhy was shot to death by Chicago crime figures. "I've been expecting it," moaned the dying Touhy, certain that Capone loyalists were behind the shotgun blasts. "The bastards never forget."[18]

67 'Before They Kill Me, I'll Kill Karpis'

Old Ramsey County Jail
St. Peter and Fourth Streets, St. Paul

Doc Barker, Alvin Karpis, Roger Touhy, and Edna "the Kissing Bandit" Murray were among the gangsters who were secured inside the Ramsey County Jail, a sandstone-and-granite structure built in 1903. Dillinger's girlfriend Evelyn Frechette, being held there on charges of harboring a fugitive, complained to reporters in April 1934 that the jail prevented her from practicing dances: "It's kind of close quarters for it in this cell," she quipped, "and besides, there isn't any music."[19]

Virginia Gibbons Schwietz, a secretary in the jail in 1935 for Sheriff Tommy Gibbons, her uncle, recalled the excitement as the nation's public enemies were brought to the jail in handcuffs: "It was a romantic time," said Schwietz. The gangsters "were like celebrities. Every time they came down the jail steps to go to federal court . . . shackled with FBI guys—oh, God, newsmen all over."[20]

A lower profile was sought for gangster Byron Bolton, the Bremer kidnap conspirator who turned government informant. Captured January 8, 1935, by Justice Department agents, he pleaded guilty to kidnapping and inspired some of the FBI's most cryptic public statements. Asked about Bolton's confession, FBI assistant director Harold Nathan explained, "I am not even admitting that there is such a man as Bolton or that he is in St. Paul. However, if there is, and if he is in St. Paul, I know nothing about any such confession."[21]

After his January 8 arrest in Chicago, Doc Barker was also installed in the Ramsey County Jail, locked alone in a cell block guarded by machine gun-equipped federal agents; when he was taken to the Federal Courts Building, he was chained and handcuffed to three different agents.

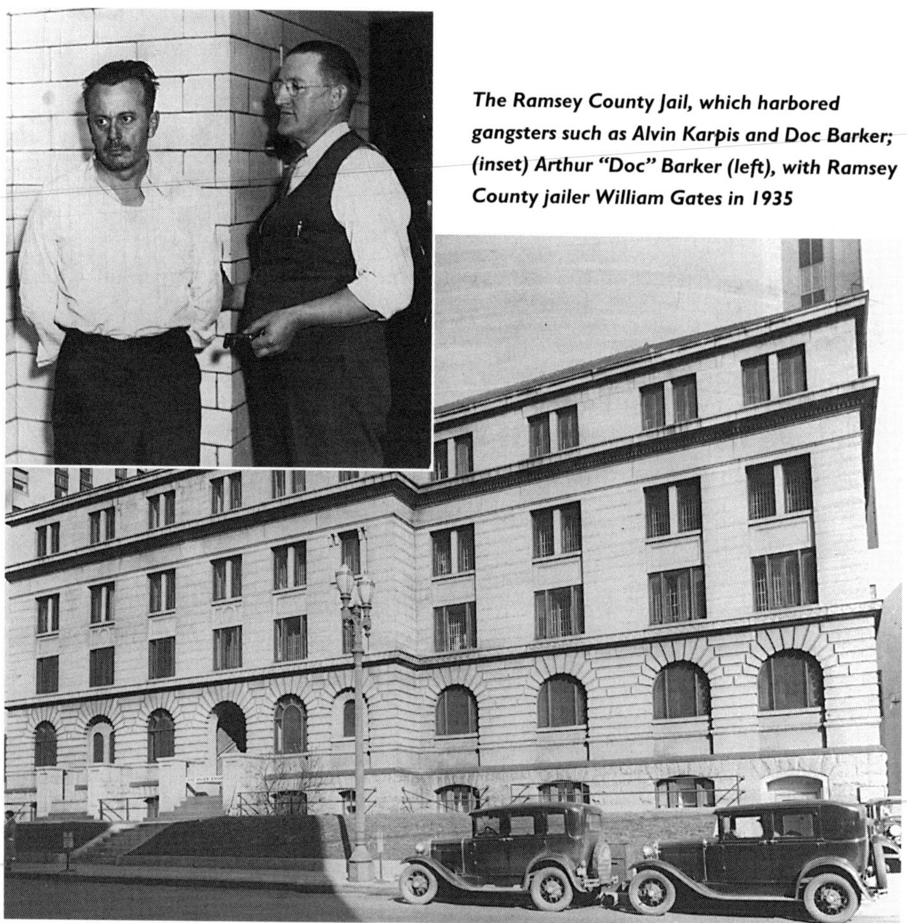

The Ramsey County Jail, which harbored gangsters such as Alvin Karpis and Doc Barker; (inset) Arthur "Doc" Barker (left), with Ramsey County jailer William Gates in 1935

Barker "slept . . . like a baby elephant—trumpeting," jailer William Gates told a newspaper. "He snored all night." Barker volunteered to teach Ramsey County sheriff Tommy Gibbons how to load and fire the new machine guns supplied to guard the Barker-Karpis gang, but the sheriff declined the offer.[22]

A talkative Karpis was brought to the jail on May 6, 1936. He told the FBI that he had turned down Al Capone's invitation to join the Chicago syndicate, which would have earned Karpis $250 a week for "strong arm work." When he asked to speak with defense attorney Archibald Cary, the FBI brought the lawyer to the jail and attempted to eavesdrop on the conversation. Before Cary arrived, "confidential arrangements were made to place a microphone near the place where the conference . . . was to take place. Special agent J. E. Brennan concealed himself in the adjoining cell tier." But Cary, the lawyer for Minneapolis gangster Isadore Blumenfeld, was no fool: he "began thumping on the table," reported the FBI, "and it was difficult for Agent Brennan to over hear the exact nature of the conversation." Later, when attorney Tom Newman conferred with Karpis, the FBI fussed that "efforts to overhear the conversation between Karpis and Newman were made by this office through the use of a dictaphone, but the results were not successful to any extent."[23]

J. Edgar Hoover personally ordered a guard be placed around Karpis, then held in solitary confinement, twenty-four hours a day. Hoover decreed that Karpis could not receive newspapers, have visitors, or even meet with his attorney without written permission from the prosecutors. "In view of the extremely dangerous character of this man, with a record of fifteen bank robberies, three kidnapings, four murders and three jail breaks," wrote Hoover to the U.S. attorney general, "I considered it imperative that every precaution be taken to prevent a possible escape."[24]

When Hoover learned that postal inspectors wished to interview Karpis without FBI agents monitoring the meeting, Hoover issued an ultimatum to the attorney general: let the agents remain or Hoover would withdraw them from the detail guarding "this extremely dangerous prisoner."[25]

Robert Schwietz, then a young deputy sheriff, recalled the rumor that Karpis might be sprung from his cell by the Barker-Karpis gang: "I received a phone call in the jail at around two in the morning, saying that they were going to break Alvin Karpis out. I got ahold of [jailer] Emory Clewett and Emory called the FBI. . . . Now I'm 21 years old and scared to death, shaking like a leaf. The FBI agent came into the jail at 2: 30 A.M. and told me 'If the gang comes in, they're going to come in shooting.' So the FBI agent puts a machine gun on my desk, aiming toward the door. I'd never *seen* a

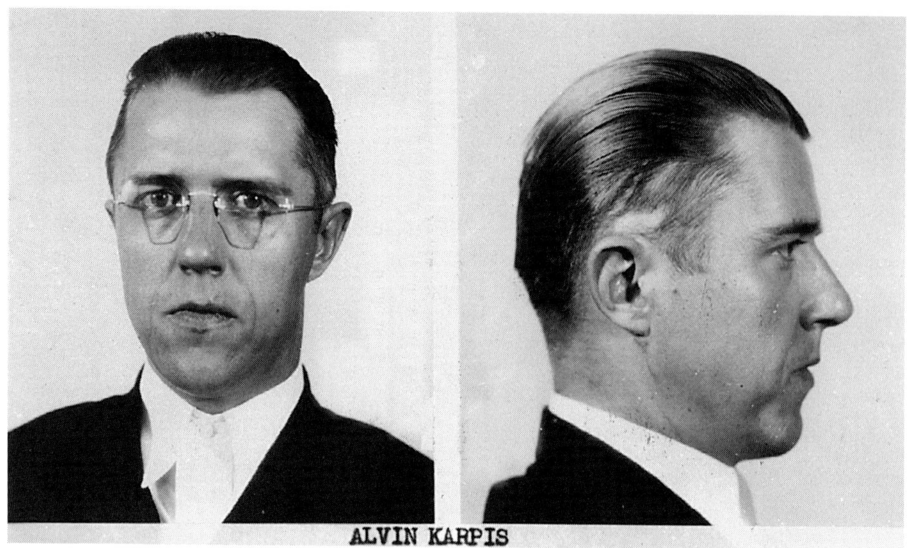

Alvin Karpis in custody, 1936

machine gun before. The FBI [agent] told me, 'If they come in, just aim at the door and keep pulling that trigger.'"

Schwietz knew that everyone who entered the jail had to check their guns, even FBI agents. "The agent asked for his pistol," and Schwietz asked, "What good is a pistol?" The agent answered, "If the gang comes in, they're going to kill me. But before they kill me, I'm going to kill Karpis."

"So I'm sitting there," said Schwietz, "thinking 'Oh, Jesus—they'd have to get by me first!' I signed up for vacation in Texas the next morning and got out of town!"[26]

Easily the most dramatic exit from the jail was that of Jack Peifer, the Hollyhocks Club proprietor who had first proposed kidnapping William Hamm. On April 17, 1936, two teams of FBI agents stationed themselves outside the Hollyhocks and arrested Peifer, "in a semi-intoxicated condition," for his part in the kidnapping. By April 22 he was in Ramsey County Jail, forced to put up the Hollyhocks, then worth an estimated $40,000, to secure the $100,000 bail bond that won his temporary release. Peifer was vigorously defended by lawyer Archie Cary and former Minnesota Supreme Court justice Samuel Wilson, who said his client was "an ordinary citizen from a typical good Minnesota family . . . a man about town, a gambler, a wet, if you will, whom the government of the United States is trying to send to prison by innuendo."[27]

Peifer's claim to being an "ordinary citizen" was undermined by his codefendants, many of whom identified him as the "fingerman" who selected William Hamm for kidnapping. After a ten-day trial, the jury declared Peifer guilty of kidnapping and he was sentenced to thirty years in prison.

"I am sorry for your relatives and friends," said the judge, as Peifer held his face, and Vi, his wife of one year, fell to the floor of the courtroom in shock.[28]

Awaiting the ride to Leavenworth, Peifer, according to the FBI, "is said to have walked into the cell, made some statement about it being pretty tough that he had gotten thirty years, and then walk[ed] over to get a drink. When he did not come right back, the others went over to him, and found that he had taken poison."[29]

"I put Jack in his cell the day he went to court," recalled Robert Schwietz. Peifer "scared the hell out of me. . . . I was walking through the cellblocks checking and someone said, 'Peifer fell asleep—but he looks like he's dead!' And I wasn't going into the cell. . . . I first called Emory Clewett and got the police department and they went in and found he was dead. Definitely, it was a suicide." After a forty-five minute effort to resuscitate him, Peifer was pronounced dead from the effects of a potassium cyanide pill on July 31, 1936.[30]

On hearing of his suicide, Vi Peifer told reporters, "I know Jack was innocent and he took his case to a higher court." According to at least one source, provided for his widow with a bundle of cash. Around the time of the Hamm kidnapping, Peifer told his wife that if anything happened to him, she should pull up a board in the floor of the Hollyhocks, where she would find some money so she could go on with her life. According to Vi's attorney, William Walsh, after Peifer's death she did just that, and she found $25,000 in cash hidden there.[31]

Not everyone accepts the official verdict that Peifer killed himself with poison just hours after defense lawyers had announced an appeal of his conviction. Clewett, the jailer, insisted that he had personally searched Peifer and found nothing that he could have used to kill himself. Could someone have assisted Peifer into the hereafter?[32]

The *Daily News* estimated that almost a thousand people jammed the service at Sunset Memorial Park, where Peifer was buried with military honors. Among the pallbearers were Minneapolis syndicate boss Tommy Banks, gambler Robert Hamilton from the Hollyhocks, bank robber John Davenport, and restaurant owner Charlie Saunders. Slot machine czar Tom Filben, liquor baron Frank McCormick, and nightclub owner Ben Harris were honorary pallbearers.[33]

"I've tried to figure out who could have smuggled that poison pill to Jack," said Martin Rohling, doorman for Peifer's Hollyhocks Club. "I was surprised when Jack committed suicide. He'd been laughing [just before], saying, 'I didn't do the kidnapping.'"[34]

'Hearts as Cold as Crystal'

Old Federal Courts Building (also site 5)
75 West Fifth Street, St. Paul

Two agents hid a microphone in the FBI's St. Paul field office, located on the second floor of what is now Landmark Center. They then left Hamm kidnapping suspect Charles Fitzgerald "alone" with racketeer Jack Peifer—before Peifer's suicide. Who knew what admissions of underworld skullduggery the pair might blurt out? As they bent over their surveillance apparatus, the agents were startled to hear an ear-splitting pounding. Peifer was rhythmically smashing the FBI's furniture with Fitzgerald's cane, completely obscuring the whispered conversations with his fellow gangster.[35]

At the old Federal Courts Building the last members of the Barker-Karpis and Dillinger gangs faced their victims, and, as some members turned into government informants, often faced each other. Suite 529 had been the headquarters of the Prohibition Bureau, which employed former Congressman Andrew Volstead, author of the Prohibition law. The federal grand jury investigating the Edward Bremer kidnapping in May 1934 met on the fourth floor; FBI inspector H. H. Clegg had to threaten reporters with contempt to keep them from loitering in search of a story. The U.S. marshal's office and the federal courtrooms, lush with marble and hand-carved cherry wood, were on the third floor. The most impressive space is courtroom 317, where Judge Matthew Joyce presided over the Hamm kidnapping trials. Room 203 was the St. Paul office of the FBI, where Alvin Karpis, Doc Barker, and other gangsters were interrogated.[36]

Most of the male associates of the John Dillinger gang—Homer Van Meter, John Hamilton, Tommy Carroll, and Eddie Green—were dead by spring 1934, when the FBI targeted the girlfriends, doctors, and errand boys who made the gang's stay in St. Paul so comfortable. Beth Green pleaded guilty to harboring a fugitive and was sentenced to fifteen months in the federal women's prison in Alderson, West Virginia. Dr. Clayton May, who had cared for Dillinger's gunshot wounds, was tried in St. Paul in May 1934 and sentenced to two years in Leavenworth. Evelyn Frechette was tried at the same time for harboring her boyfriend, John Dillinger. Attorney Louis Piquett, who defended Frechette, walked out of the courthouse and heard someone whisper his name. There, sitting in an automobile just a few dozen yards from the FBI's St. Paul offices, was Dillinger, smiling. "What the hell are you doing here?" Piquett asked. "Just thought I'd run up and see how the trial was coming along," quipped Dillinger—who then drove off.[37] Frechette received a two-year prison sentence.

In the spring of 1935, Judge Joyce presided over the first trial of the

The third-floor courtroom of the old Federal Courts Building, where surviving Dillinger and Karpis gang members were tried, with the assistance of gangster Byron Bolton (inset)

Bremer kidnapping conspirators, including Doc Barker and nine others. Fred Barker, however, did not live to face a jury. When they searched Doc Barker's Chicago apartment, agents found a map with a circle around Oklawaha, Florida, the site of Ma Barker's Lake Weir hideout. On January 16, 1935, FBI agents engaged in a six-hour machine-gun battle with Fred and his mother. The firing stopped after an estimated fifteen hundred rounds of ammunition had been fired at the Barkers. Fred Barker was found dead with a machine gun gripped in his left hand and a pistol in his right hand. "Close-by was 'Ma,'" claimed the FBI, "lying on her back, with a machine gun beside her lifeless body. The barrel was still smoking."[38]

After Kate Barker's death, the FBI took steps to convince the public that she had been the criminal mastermind behind the Barker-Karpis gang. In a *Chicago Tribune* series, Doris Lockerman, secretary to FBI special agent Melvin Purvis, wrote: "The Bremer kidnaping was Ma Barker's idea . . . [Fred] Goetz tried to talk her out of it . . . but Ma overruled him. . . . There were a hundred details to be arranged. Ma Barker and Goetz arranged them, planning the crime as carefully as a general staff ever planned a battle." Yet according to the FBI's internal files, the bureau knew all along that Goetz and Harry Sawyer, not Ma Barker, had planned the Bremer kidnapping. In fact, FBI interviews with surviving gang members and their girlfriends indicated that Ma Barker was not present at the key planning sessions before, during, or after Bremer's abduction. The files tend to support the claims of crime historians such as William J. Helmer, who suggest that the FBI—stunned to find a grandmotherly corpse on their hands—may have attempted to justify her death by transforming Kate Barker into a Medusa of gangland crime.[39]

The trial of Doc Barker and his accomplices began on April 15, 1935, at the Federal Courts Building. Government witness Bolton pleaded guilty to kidnapping and received four concurrent three-year prison sentences as a reward for betraying the gang. When Karpis heard that Bolton had informed against him, the FBI reported, Karpis said that he "would like to see Bolton run over by an automobile . . . and linger with a broken back for months and then die." Bolton was sent to a Milan, Michigan, prison in 1936 and released in December 1938.[40]

Kidnapping charges against gang members Jess Doyle and Edna Murray were dismissed on May 6, 1935, but Murray returned to Missouri State prison to continue her twenty-five-year sentence for robbery. Doyle, captured when his car got stuck in the mud in Kansas, was returned to the Nebraska state penitentiary for his role in the 1933 Fairbury National Bank robbery.

Assistant U.S. attorney George Heisey's final plea to the Bremer jury in mid-May 1935 was intense: "The kidnapping of Edward Bremer was not the crime of the century, but the crime of the ages. For every day of anguish and torture that Bremer went through, and for every day that his wife and daughter and father suffered, somebody ought to be made to suffer. And I think you know who it is!"[41]

On May 17, the jury issued guilty verdicts against Doc Barker and four others. Sentenced to spend the rest of his life in prison, Barker was sent to Leavenworth, and later transferred to Alcatraz. A few days earlier, Harry Campbell was arrested in Toledo, Ohio, and pleaded guilty to his part in the Bremer kidnapping; he, too, was sentenced to life and sent to Leavenworth. Pat Reilly received a twenty-one-month sentence in the El Reno, Oklahoma, reformatory for harboring a fugitive and for helping to set up medical care and other services for Dillinger.[42]

J. Edgar Hoover continued to campaign for longer prison sentences for the women who had harbored the public enemies, even those who had relatively little contact with the men's criminal activities. Helen Gillis, wife of Babyface Nelson, was sentenced to prison in Milan, Michigan. A 1934 FBI memo noted that "every method of attack has been used by agents in an effort to get this woman to talk, but without avail. It was thought that possibly her weak point would be her children . . . when discussing her children, she broke down and wept at length, but would not give in." Jean Delaney,

The Bremer kidnapping jury, guarded by deputy marshals, crosses Fifth Street on its return to the old Federal Courts Building after a break.

Tommy Carroll's lover, was found guilty of harboring Dillinger and sentenced to the women's prison in Alderson, West Virginia. Myrtle Eaton, whose Kennington apartment had been a planning center for the Bremer kidnapping, was found guilty in Jacksonville, Florida, in June 1936 and sentenced to six months in jail for harboring William Weaver.[43]

A second trial of Bremer kidnapping suspects began in St. Paul federal court on January 6, 1936: Edna Murray testified as a government witness against Harry Sawyer and William Weaver. The forty-four-year-old Sawyer, once the most powerful underworld fixer in Minnesota, had fled to Florida, Michigan, Wisconsin, Ohio, Nevada, Iowa, and finally to Mississippi, where he was arrested in Pass Christian on May 3, 1935.[44]

Pleading innocent, Sawyer enjoyed superb legal representation from former U.S. attorney Lewis L. Drill and lawyer Robert Rensch, but the evidence against him was overwhelming. Prosecutor George Heisey said that

Sawyer and Weaver had "hearts as cold as crystal and as hard as granite," that they were willing to commit "the most horrendous crime known to man." Building steam, Heisey roared that Bremer "still is suffering from his harrowing experience. Every day, every hour, every minute, while he was being held prisoner was a living hell. There was not a minute when he did not see death staring him in the face." The trial ended on January 24, when both Weaver and Sawyer were found guilty and sentenced to life imprisonment.[45]

Harry Sawyer's wife, Gladys, turned FBI informant against the Barker-Karpis gang in 1936. She told the FBI that, in the words of its report, "her husband is serving a life sentence . . . mainly because he was faithful to his friends and associates and because those friends deserted both him and her when they were needed." An FBI official wrote Hoover in July 1936 that Gladys Sawyer feared that gangsters would "knock her off." He suggested that the bureau "endeavor to instill a proper degree of confidence in this woman so that she will make a satisfactory witness. I don't believe, however, that we should waste any time attempting to protect Gladys Sawyer after the various attempts which she has made to embarrass the Bureau."[46]

Gladys begged Harry to blow the whistle on the St. Paul underworld in order to avoid a transfer from Leavenworth to Alcatraz: "With the deal that you got . . . why should we try any longer to protect some people," she wrote. "You know you shouldn't be there, so why stay if you can help yourself. . . . Life isn't worth living the way it is now. All my love. Gladys Sawyer." He refused to talk and was transferred.[47]

Alvin Karpis also refused to turn informer. During the airplane trip from New Orleans to St. Paul, he spoke freely about the shootouts he had participated in and other subjects, but drew the line at "ratting" on his friends. Karpis "frankly admits that this is the code of the underworld; that he has operated outside of the law since he was about fifteen years of age, and that he intends to abide by this code," the FBI reported.[48]

At the FBI's St. Paul field office, J. Edgar Hoover had him chained to a radiator, according to Karpis's account. Hoover reportedly demanded of his agents: "I want a signed confession from this man for every crime he ever committed in his life. I want to know the names of all the people who were in on his crimes. . . . If he starts to lie, kick his teeth in for him." In his autobiography, Karpis later described the experience: "They put handcuffs on me—real cuffs, not a necktie—and they chained shackles around my ankles and locked the other ends of the shackles to a steam radiator. I felt like an animal."[49]

Karpis told FBI agents that he would be willing to plead guilty to the Hamm kidnapping but might still testify to exonerate his friend Jack Peifer. "Karpis then laughingly remarked that he did not mind helping out anybody, and that 'a fellow can't get life for perjury.'" The FBI knew that Karpis's weak spot was the safety of his girlfriend, Delores Delaney, who had been captured in Atlantic City, New Jersey, and had been imprisoned in 1935 at Milan, Michigan. Karpis insisted that he had not told Delaney about his business and said he had considered offering the judge a $10,000 bribe to give Delaney a bench parole but was unable to figure out how to reach the jurist.[50]

Delaney gave birth to a son, named Raymond Alvin after Karpis's alias Raymond Hadley, in February 1935, while she was in federal custody. "I wish Al could see him," Delaney told reporters. "But I don't know where he is and if I found him, it would only mean Al's arrest. . . . My baby positively will never go inside a jail—no matter what happens to me." With his father and mother in prison, the boy was given to Karpis's parents to raise.[51]

"The FBI kept Karpis in a little detention room—still marked "U.S. Marshal"—on the third floor of the Federal Courts Building," reported Landmark Center tour guide Woody Keljik, and "when the trial was about to start, J. Edgar Hoover walked into the detention room and had Karpis handcuffed to him, so he could personally walk him the thirty feet to the trial!"[52]

On July 14, Karpis stood in the sweltering heat of judge Matthew Joyce's courtroom and pleaded guilty to the Hamm kidnapping. "I don't want to stay in that hot courtroom for three weeks," he joked, before being sentenced to life in prison. In the three-year span ending in the fall of 1936, with Karpis locked in Leavenworth, Hoover had succeeded in killing or imprisoning most members of the Barker-Karpis, Keating-Holden, Harvey Bailey, Frank Nash, and Dillinger gangs.

After Karpis was captured, he wrote to Delores Delaney:

> I received your letter and was certainly surprised as I realize that I am unworthy of any kind thoughts that you have of me. I don't know how to express my feelings toward you in words, but when I lost you the light just seemed to go out.
>
> As I slowly read your letter, it seemed as though I could see your laughing Irish eyes, but this time they didn't seem to be laughing. I can truthfully say that I have never received a letter in my life that has made me realize how selfish and inconsiderate I have been ever since I was a child.
>
> I am not getting religious, or crying the blues, but it woke me up quicker than all the time I will do if I live to be one hundred years old. If a person like myself is capable of loving any one or having any affection for another, I certainly feel that way about you. Alvin Karpis.[53]

EPILOGUE

Hit man Joey Schaefer, released from Stillwater Prison after serving thirty-one years; Alvin Karpis at McNeil Island prison in November 1968, about to be paroled

More than half a century has passed since the slaying of Dillinger gunman Homer Van Meter and the suicide of Jack Peifer, two deaths that capped what the *St. Paul Daily News* called "an unsavory, ugly epoch" in St. Paul stretching from 1920 to 1936. "We did it all ourselves," said the *Daily News* on July 25, 1934. "We brought on the era of high crime and we cut it off. . . . We tolerated slums, crooked politics, fixers of high and low degree, four-flushers and go-getters, we got just about what we asked for, and we had nobody to blame but ourselves."

While St. Paul struggled to bury its gangster past, the FBI's newsreels, television and radio shows, books, and tours have turned minor thugs with colorful nicknames into legends who eclipsed far more powerful organized-crime figures. So vivid were the FBI's larger-than-life images of Dillinger-era outlaws that people found it hard to believe that criminals who survived so many shootouts could actually be dead. Crime historian Jay Robert Nash, for example, claimed that inconsistencies in John Dillinger's autopsy report prove that he was not the man killed by the FBI outside Chicago's Biograph Theater in 1934.[1]

"I think about him every day," Dillinger's sister Audrey Hancock told a

John Dillinger Sr., the bank robber's seventy-year-old father, shown here (in dark suit) with family members, who toured vaudeville theaters after Dillinger Jr.'s death in 1934

reporter, "and I wonder what I would do if he came in that door. I dreamed about him one night. I heard him calling, 'Sis!' just so plain and I got out of bed and swung that door wide open, expecting to find my brother there. But it wasn't; it was a dream. I never have had a dream as real as that one."[2]

Bruce Hamilton of Shiprock, New Mexico, claimed that his uncle, Dillinger gang member John "Three Fingered Jack" Hamilton, did not die of the wounds he suffered during the Hastings Spiral Bridge shootout in April 1934. Rather, Hamilton was smuggled to Chicago and then into Canada for medical attention—said his nephew—and returned to his family in South Bend, Indiana, eighteen months later with his face altered by surgery. What of the mutilated body found in August 1935 in an Oswego, Illinois, gravel pit? What of Hamilton's teeth, displayed by the FBI at a 1939 Chicago Dental Society meeting? The Dillinger gang obtained a corpse of appropriate size, explained Bruce Hamilton, and poured lye over the body to disfigure identifying marks. "The FBI got my grandfather, William Hamilton, to identify my uncle's body," added Hamilton. But "everyone in my family knew that my uncle was alive and back in South Bend."[3]

In fact, John Hamilton had "died" and been resurrected once before. Dillinger told newspaper reporters in early 1934 that Hamilton had been killed during the robbery on January 15, 1934, of the First National Bank of East Chicago. "Poor Red . . . he died from the wounds he received in East Chicago," mourned Dillinger. "Caught a whole flock of bullets in his stomach. . . . They dumped his body in the Calumet River." Dillinger was lying to reduce police interest in apprehending Hamilton; although he was wounded in the robbery, Hamilton was very much alive at the time.[4]

There are clues that support Bruce Hamilton's story. In September 1934, the FBI interrogated thief Frank Kirwin, one of the Dillinger gang's contacts in Minnesota. He told the FBI that Hamilton had indeed been severely wounded during the Hastings shootout. But, Kirwin insisted, "Hamilton was not killed and buried as reported."[5]

In his autobiography, FBI agent Melvin Purvis added another note of support for the rumors. He wrote of a man who brought photographs to the FBI, claiming the gentleman pictured was a very much alive John Hamilton. "The amazing part of his story was that he had recently taken the photographs, had made Hamilton pose in various positions so that there could be no doubt as to the identity of the person in the picture," marveled Purvis. "He even had the man holding a cap in his hand so that it appeared that his fingers were amputated in the same way as were those of Hamilton. He told us that Hamilton was at that time fully recovered from his wounds and was hiding out in the country somewhere in Missouri." Yet Purvis spurned the

The body of Dillinger gang member John Hamilton being exhumed from a grave in Oswego, Illinois, in August 1935

account as "obviously false," based on "faked photographs," and thus "no action was taken by the government."[6]

What of the other members of the Dillinger and Barker-Karpis gangs—and their victims?

Arthur "Doc" Barker, serving a life sentence in Alcatraz for the Bremer kidnapping, was slain by prison guards in January 1939. He had scaled a wall and tried to reach San Francisco Bay. "I am crazy as hell," said Barker to a guard as he expired, "I should never have tried it." John Knutson, an Alcatraz guard, insisted that the felon took his own life: "Barker got depressed—his relatives were all gone—so when he was out on the yard he ran across, scaled the wall, and started climbing the fence," recalled Knutson. "The guards yelled at him to let go. He wouldn't and they shot him off. It was suicide.[7]

George "Machine Gun Kelly" Barnes died of coronary failure in Leavenworth prison in July 1954 after serving nearly two decades for the kidnapping of Charles Urschel. "My dad was something of a braggart. He didn't express any remorse," said Kelly's son Bruce Barnes. "My Dad was *proud* that he got away with so much and the police never knew he even existed. In fact, the police were blaming those bank jobs on someone else. Dad told me he never made less than $125,000 a year on bank jobs, and yet he wasn't even on the list of the bank robbers they were looking for!"[8]

Kelly's wife, Kathryn, was also sentenced to life imprisonment, chiefly on the basis of testimony by a government handwriting expert that she had written threatening letters to Charles Urschel. J. Edgar Hoover condemned her as the mastermind behind the kidnapping, pointing to the "feminine thought and psychology" in the ransom letters.[9]

George "Machine Gun Kelly" Barnes in front of his Alcatraz jail cell

In 1970, however, former FBI agent William Turner released the text of a suppressed 1933 FBI laboratory test that would have exonerated her. The agency's analyst admitted that "detailed analysis indicated that Mrs. Kelly did not write these letters." Turner also released a 1959 memo from the special agent in charge of the FBI's Oklahoma City field office that suggested the lab report not be released to the U.S. attorney because it could be "a source of embarrassment to the Bureau." Kelly, who had protested her innocence for decades, appealed her conviction and was released from prison in 1958. She moved to Oklahoma and is now living at an undisclosed location.[10]

Harvey Bailey, dean of the 1920s bank robbers and associate of St. Paul's "Dapper Dan" Hogan, survived thirty years of a life sentence in Alcatraz and Leavenworth. After the seventy-six year-old Bailey was paroled in 1964, he collaborated with author J. Evetts Haley on his memoir, *Robbing Banks Was My Business*, and became a woodworker in a furniture factory. He died of a kidney ailment in 1979 in Joplin, Missouri, at the age of ninety-one.[11]

George Young and Joey Schaefer, the Murder Inc. hit men who killed bootlegger Abe Wagner in 1932, remained locked in Stillwater Prison for more than thirty years. Schaefer, sixty-five, was paroled in December 1963, and Young, fifty-four, was paroled shortly afterward. Neither broke his vow of silence about who paid them to murder Wagner. "It was me or him," Schaefer told reporters as he was taken to the Minneapolis–St. Paul airport for a flight to Philadelphia. "Loeb [Wagner] was trying to kidnap me."

"These were tough guys. . . . Mentally and physically, they had toughness that even someone in law enforcement has to grudgingly admire," said captain Joseph O'Connor of the Philadelphia Police Department's Organized Crime Unit, which monitored Young and Schaefer's activities in Pennsylvania after their release. "Thirty years hard time. . . . He never talked," added O'Connor. "They don't make people like this anymore!" Young died in 1971, and Schaefer died in 1982, both in Philadelphia.[12]

Leon Gleckman, the liquor czar who dreamed of becoming mayor of St. Paul, died in a bizarre car accident in July 1941. En route to his home, contemplating yet another prison term, he drove his Chevrolet into an abutment at Kellogg Boulevard and Wacouta Street, adjacent to St. Paul's Depot Bar. He died of a fractured skull; his blood alcohol level was .23—the equivalent of drinking thirteen ounces of 90-proof liquor. The death certificate called Gleckman's death "probably accidental." "You can't prove it, but in my heart, as a policeman, I think [he] wanted to do himself in," said Joe Sherin, then a St. Paul patrolman. "We all think Leon killed himself. . . . He was due to go to federal prison. He was the king of the bootleggers and he didn't fancy sitting in the Can."[13]

Harry Sawyer, the Green Lantern saloon proprietor who chose Edward Bremer for kidnapping by the Barker-Karpis gang, was transferred in 1936 from Leavenworth to Alcatraz. He was returned to Leavenworth in 1943 for another twelve years of imprisonment. The U.S. attorney vigorously opposed parole for Sawyer, warning that he was a "confirmed public enemy and has devoted his entire life to the commission of crime." Yet prison authorities hailed his "remarkable conduct record"—not a single disciplinary action was taken against him while he was behind bars. Sawyer became as indispensable in prison as he had been at the Green Lantern. He worked seven days a week, eight to nine hours a day, as a baker, kitchen helper, and server in the Leavenworth cafeteria, even filling in for absent inmates and volunteering for extra duty.[14]

Harry and Gladys Sawyer had begun efforts to adopt Francine, the five-year-old girl who had inadvertently led authorities to the Barker-Karpis gang hideout in Cleveland. But in September 1934 the adoption was stopped, and the girl was taken from them by the Minnesota Children's Bureau. A heartbroken Gladys moved back to Nebraska, and then to Denver, Colorado, where she divorced her incarcerated husband.

Sam Sandlovich was one of the only members of the family to keep in touch with Harry Sawyer while he was in prison. "My mother said that the Sandlovich family disowned Harry," said Carole DeMoss, Sandlovich's daughter and Sawyer's niece. "First for running a saloon in St. Paul, and then when he became involved with the Barker-Karpis gang, they severed all ties with him. I didn't even know I *had* an uncle Harry until he died."[15]

Sawyer's wealthy family in Nebraska was mortified by his notoriety. Most of his relatives refused to visit him or answer his letters; one offered Gladys Sawyer a thousand dollars to keep quiet about her husband's prison sentence. "It is apparent that there has been a deep family pride," said a caseworker, "and Harry's behavior has wounded them greatly." In 1955, after Sawyer suffered through years of chronic liver disease and arthritis, doctors found cancer attacking his spinal cord. He was paroled in February 1955 and sent to a Chicago hospital, where he died in June; his body was taken for burial in Chicago's Westlawn Cemetery. Even in death, Sawyer remained an outcast from his family.[16]

Kidnap victim William Hamm Jr. led the Hamm Brewing Company as president and then chairman of the board until 1965. "Bill Hamm didn't talk a lot. He was not a very demonstrative man and held everything into himself," recalled William Figge, former president of the company. "But one time, I drove with him to a brewing convention in Duluth. Just outside St. Paul, Hamm started to tell me all the details of his kidnapping. He wanted to talk to someone about it."[17]

Hamm's cousin John Flanagan wrote that Hamm was perceived as being "gloomy and possibly a bit fearful of the future. He apparently had thought about the possibility of being kidnapped . . . before the dreaded event occurred. Undoubtedly the kidnapping affected his later life and [he] developed a tendency to brood and even to be laconic in business meetings. . . . My cousin avoided unnecessary travel and even employed bodyguards when he visited the homes of relatives in the Lake Minnetonka area." Hamm died in Minneapolis in August 1970.[18]

Edward Bremer, victim of the Barker-Karpis gang's second kidnapping, died of a heart attack in Pampano Beach, Florida, in 1965 at the age of sixty-seven. His daughter, Betty Bremer Johnson, said her father did not speak about the event that had so traumatized him. Still, the obituary of the Commercial State Bank president and chairman described him as "the central figure in St. Paul's most famous kidnapping case in the 1930s."[19]

Most of the Dillinger and Barker-Karpis gang girlfriends put their criminal past behind them, sinking into anonymity. Evelyn Frechette, who was released in 1936 after serving two years for harboring John Dillinger, died of cancer in 1969. As Evelyn Tic, she had lived with her husband, Art, a state game warden and barber, in Shawano, Wisconsin. "I got the impression that Evelyn was glad to get out of it, with the guns and all, that it wasn't an easy life," said Bernice Tic, widow of Evelyn's stepson. "She liked the peace and quiet, taking care of my four daughters and cooking fish and venison that Art caught. She didn't speak about Dillinger much, and we let it go at that."[20]

Delores Delaney, Alvin Karpis' girlfriend, was released from prison and returned in 1938 to her family in St. Paul. Raymond Karpovicz, her son by Karpis, was born while she was in FBI custody and raised by family members in Chicago.[21]

No other gangster of the public enemies era endured as many years in prison as Alvin Karpis. He was incarcerated for thirty-three years—first in Alcatraz and then in McNeil Island prison on Puget Sound. Minneapolis defense attorney Eugene Rerat met him in Alcatraz in 1937: "I had expected to find a savage, snarling brute, a man filled with hate, an illiterate animal, dangerous even in prison," Rerat recalled. "Instead, I talked with one who had all the poise and polish of a business executive. Karpis was soft-spoken, extremely intelligent, and completely dignified in his conduct. What a success he might have been if he had turned those talents to business instead of crime!"[22]

Karpis secretly delivered his portion of the bank robbery and kidnapping loot to his family during the 1930s, according to his nephew Albert Grooms. The ill-gotten gains were deposited, with full interest accruing during his imprisonment, in savings accounts in Des Moines, Kansas City, and Duluth. "Those banks were just tickled as hell to have the money," said Grooms. "You didn't need a Social Security number in those days."

After Karpis was paroled, Grooms met with him in Port Arthur, Canada, and handed him a large check—the principal and interest from the crimes he had committed nearly half a century before. "It was a bundle, you damned well bet it was," says Grooms. "It was all the money he'd squirreled away during the 1930s!"[23]

When Karpis's autobiography, *The Alvin Karpis Story,* was published in 1971, Thomas McDade, a retired FBI agent who had investigated the Barker-Karpis gang, wrote Karpis a friendly note: Would the aging gangster like to meet the elderly agent who had hunted him four decades earlier? From his home in Spain, Karpis agreed to the interview. "I was pleased by his readiness to accept my note in the spirit intended—the nostalgia of a long retired lawman," recalled McDade. To his surprise, Karpis's letter "exuded energy, intelligence, enterprise and imagination. . . . He welcomed correspondence and so between us began an international exchange of letters." When Karpis and McDade met in Spain, Karpis recalled how irritating it had been to guard Ed Bremer. ("Oh, that fellow Bremer. How tired I got of him. All he did was complain about the food.") Karpis displayed his printless fingers, a legacy from the operations of Dr. Moran years before.[24]

Karpis died from an overdose of sleeping pills in the summer of 1979 in Torremolinos, Spain, at the age of seventy-one. He had outlived his nemesis, J. Edgar Hoover, by seven years.[25]

The golf-loving, fugitive Evergreen bandits, Francis "Jimmy" Keating and Tommy Holden, who had been recaptured at the Mission Hills golf course in 1934, were transferred to Alcatraz, locked in solitary confinement, and put to work breaking rock in an underground quarry. Holden was only disciplined once—when he asked for two extra pieces of turkey from the prison steam table. Prison officials warned, however, that "since return from escape, he [Holden] has been a constant plotter," seeking a way to break out again. After being released from prison, he died awash in violence and despair. Driving home on June 5, 1949, after drinking beer in a Chicago tavern, the fifty-three-year-old Holden got into a quarrel with his wife, Lillian. He slapped her face and she dashed up to her apartment. Holden chased after her with a .38-caliber revolver and shot her and two others dead. Once again a federal fugitive, he was hunted by the FBI and captured in Oregon in 1951. He died of heart failure in 1953 at Stateville Hospital, after being sentenced to serve twenty-five years in the Illinois State Penitentiary for the triple murder.[26]

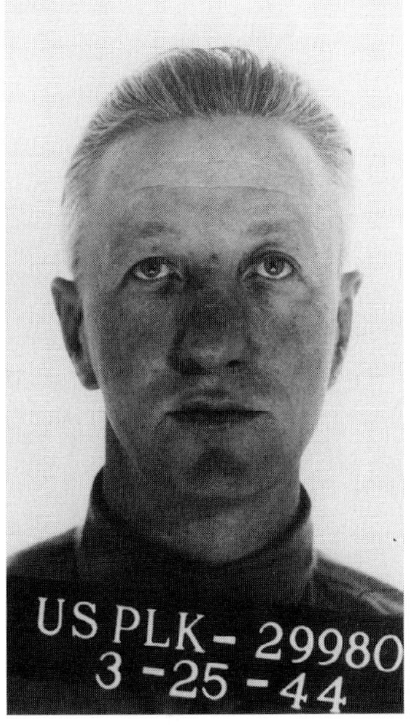

Veteran bank robber Jimmy Keating in 1944, twelve years after his return to custody

Jimmy Keating, in contrast, achieved a rare form of gangster redemption. Working in a prison brush factory as a bristle clerk, he received high marks from both Leavenworth and Alcatraz officials for his good nature and intelligence. Although Keating was punished for nine disciplinary violations, his infractions were pranks: taking an unauthorized bowl of ice cream, playing baseball in the prison yard, laughing too loudly in the mess hall, making faces at the prison guards. After being released from prison in the late 1940s, Keating retired to Minneapolis, where he befriended former prizefighter Ernie Fleigel, one of the founders of the 620 Club (its motto: "Where Turkey is King") on the downtown Hennepin Avenue strip.

Every Sunday, Keating had brunch at Fleigel's home with another guest, former FBI agent John Roberts. "Keating believed he'd paid his debt and Roberts. . . . knew of his background and had come to terms with it," said Robert Fleigel, Ernie's son. "Keating was a soft-spoken, white-haired gentlemanly fellow. What few people knew was that he was the most successful train robber of the '20s and '30s. . . . Dad cautioned me not to bring up [Keating's] past, and I never did. I knew him only as a kindly old gentleman who had a way with kids."[27]

During the 1950s, Keating tended a floral shop in the Calhoun Beach Club in Minneapolis. He befriended Charlie Reiter, a former St. Paul Police officer and Bureau of Criminal Apprehension agent. He spoke little of prison or of his years as a bank robber, simply confessing that as a young man he had hungered for excitement—and bank robbery was how he got it. "I made lots of money," Keating told Reiter. "But the lawyers got the money and I got the time."[28]

Through the 1960s and 1970s, Keating remarried, became a grandparent, and found success as an organizer for the machinists union based in St. Paul. "When Jimmy got out of prison . . . someone directed him back to the Twin Cities, where he hooked up with a union. . . . It was his chance to be legitimate," said his friend "Shy" Troupe. "Jimmy's specialty had been anything that was illegal, and that specialty was *over* with; so what's a guy to do?"[29]

"Jimmy would say to me, 'I always wanted to be a banker,'" recalled Charlie Reiter. "'But the bankers wouldn't hire me. So I took my own banks.'"[30]

Keating died of heart failure in July 1978 in a nursing home in St. Louis Park, Minnesota. He was seventy-nine and had outlived virtually every public enemy he had golfed with back in 1931.[31]

Before his death, Keating was introduced by Ernie Fleigel at the 620 Club to a prominent Republican financier. "I don't think you've met my friend . . . he's a banker up in North Dakota," said Fleigel to Keating.

"Oh, really?" said an amused Keating. "What bank is that?" The financier identified his institution as the Fargo National Bank and asked if Keating had been there.

"Oh, I think I've done some business up there," chuckled Keating. Fleigel later told the banker that the business Keating had undertaken decades before in Fargo had involved a getaway car, a submachine gun, and thousands of dollars in cash withdrawn hastily in canvas bags.[32]

With the benefit of hindsight, former FBI agent William Turner, crime historian Carl Sifakis, and others have questioned whether the FBI's obsession with criminals like John Dillinger and Ma Barker (who was never convicted of, nor even arrested for, any crime) distracted the bureau from tracking a far more insidious foe. "No one argues that the Dillinger-style criminals were not genuine desperadoes," wrote Turner, "but the G-men's quarry was, essentially, the 'few preying on a few.' While all eyes were riveted on the blazing chases of Prettyboy Floyd, Babyface Nelson, et al., the Mafia and its allies were quietly building a criminal cartel preying on the nation."[33]

In contrast to the manpower lavished in 1934 on chasing Dillinger (who was personally accused of killing only one man), FBI agents ignored syndicate leaders such as Al Capone, who directed hundreds of murders. It was, after all, the accountants in the Special Intelligence Unit of the Treasury Department, not the FBI, that sent Capone to Alcatraz. "Had the full energies of Hoover's agency been turned on the major menace of the Capone-Luciano-Lansky organizations," Sifakis wrote, "it has been argued by many crime experts [that] organized crime today would be far less effective and pervasive, if not totally eliminated."[34]

For years, J. Edgar Hoover denied that the Mafia existed. In choosing to target Dillinger rather than the Mafia, Hoover showed a canny sense of how newspapers would cover—and history books would remember—the crime fighters at the bureau. Few recall today the names of Treasury agents Frank Wilson or Elmer L. Irey, the men who successfully prosecuted Al

Capone. Yet Hoover and his Chicago agent Melvin Purvis were lauded in newsreels, films, and front-page headlines for slaying Dillinger.

The official tour of FBI headquarters in Washington, D.C., kept the Dillinger myth alive with a shrine containing his guns, bulletproof vest, eyeglasses, and straw hat, along with a death mask, molded from the bank robber's face.

A St. Paul policeman points to bullet holes in the door of the Lincoln Court's apartment 303.

In Wisconsin today, tourists visit the Little Bohemia resort to see the bullet holes, the bed that Dillinger slept in, a bullet-shattered tin can used by the gang for target practice, and the shirts, underwear, and suitcases the gang left behind when the FBI raided the Rhinelander lodge.

In Minnesota, many ask what has become of the Dillinger door, a slab of veneered mahogany removed from apartment 303 after the March 1934 shootout at the Lincoln Court Apartments.

Lincoln Court landlord Daisy Coffey presented the bullet-riddled door to the family that ran the Brigham Inn, a resort, country store, and gas station near Remer, Minnesota.[36]

For twenty years, tourists gawked at the door, stuck their fingers through the holes, and listened to stories of the day when Dillinger answered the FBI's knock with a fusillade of bullets.[35] Eventually, the door began to disintegrate and was abandoned behind the Remer resort, where the wooden panels from Dillinger's apartment crumbled into dust.

Sites are in St. Paul, unless otherwise noted.

1 Dan Hogan's home, 1607 W. Seventh St.
(near May St. and I-35W entrance), private residence. (Map A)
A bomb planted in Dan Hogan's Paige coupe in the white stucco garage behind this home exploded on December 4, 1928, killing St. Paul's Irish Godfather.

2 Old St. Paul police headquarters (demolished),
110 W. Third St. (Kellogg Blvd. W., near Washington St.),
across from the St. Paul Public Library. (Map C)
Police chief John J. "the Big Fellow" O'Connor supervised his "layover agreement" with the underworld from police headquarters. O'Connor lived nearby at 144 West Fourth St. (demolished)

3 Nina Clifford's brothel and home (both demolished),
147 and 145 S. Washington St.
(now Hill St. near Kellogg Blvd. W.). (Map C)
The two-story brick mansion that served as St. Paul's most elegant brothel was demolished in the late 1930s. The site of madam Nina Clifford's home, at the corner of Hill and Washington, was next to the old Ramsey County morgue (164 S. Washington St.). The brothel site is below the Kellogg Blvd. underpass. The entrance to the tunnel that may have run between Clifford's back door and the Minnesota Club (317 Washington St.) is visible on new Hill St. below Kellogg Blvd., near the medical examiner's office at 155 Hill St.

4 Dan Hogan's grave, Calvary Cemetery, 753 Front Ave.
(near N. Grotto St.). (Map A)
Gangster Dan Hogan's grave is marked with a red granite monument and footstone in lot A, block 6, section 59. Other architects of the O'Connor system are buried nearby: fixer William "Reddy" Griffin's red granite monument is in lot 15, block 19, section 51; police chief John O'Connor's family mausoleum is in lots 2–3, block 52, section 6.

5 Old Federal Courts Building (now Landmark Center),
75 W. Fifth St. (Map C)
A brown-granite Romanesque masterpiece that cost nearly $2.5 million, the Federal Courts building opened in 1902. The Prohibition Bureau, which employed former Congressman Andrew Volstead, author of federal

Prohibition legislation, had an office on the fifth floor in suites 528–529. The FBI pursued kidnappers and bank robbers from its second-floor field office in room 203. The Barker-Karpis gang's trials for kidnapping were held in Judge Matthew Joyce's federal courtroom, room 317, lush with marble and hard-carved cherry wood. Alvin Karpis was held during his trial in the third-floor detention center, room 323.

6 Dreis Brothers' Drug Store (demolished),
465 St. Peter St. (at W. Seventh St./Old W. Ninth);
the site is adjacent to Mickey's Diner. (Map C)
Liquor hijacker Burt Stevens was murdered by a "phantom gunman" at the southwest corner of this intersection in 1925, setting off a chain of events that would destroy one of the nation's biggest bootlegging rings.

7 Hotel St. Paul, 363 St. Peter St.
(southwest corner at Fifth St.). (Map C)
Built in 1910 (and reopened in 1989 after renovation), the hotel contained the third-floor headquarters of underworld figure Leon Gleckman, "the Al Capone of St. Paul."

8 Leon Gleckman's home, 2168 Sargent Ave. (near Cretin Ave.),
private residence. (Map A)
On September 24, 1931, gangsters kidnapped liquor czar Gleckman from this two-story residence, where he lived with his wife and three daughters.

9 Merchants Bank Building,
northwest corner of Fourth and Robert Sts.,
now First National Bank, St. Paul. (Map C)
The seventh floor of this white-brick skyscraper, built in 1915, provided a luxurious office for liquor baron Leon Gleckman and for the Justice Department agents determined to wiretap his suite 713.

10 Mystic Caverns nightclub (demolished), 676 Joy Ave.
(near the entrance to the former Twin City Brickyard),
now W. Water St. (Map A)
Built into a mushroom cave along the Mississippi River, the Mystic Caverns featured strippers, roulette wheels, and blackjack tables. Now abandoned (and known to cavers as Horseshoe Cave), the ruins of Mystic Caverns can be identified by the crumbling entrance .6 mile southwest of the new High Bridge, adjacent to the Lilydale Regional Park sign.

11 Castle Royal nightclub, 6 W. Channel St., now 215 S. Wabasha St. (near Plato Blvd.). (Map A)
With rich oriental carpets, crystal chandeliers, and seats for 300 revelers, the underground Castle Royal hosted performers like Cab Calloway, Harry James, and the Dorsey brothers in the front rooms and illicit gambling in the back rooms.

12 The Boulevards of Paris and the Coliseum Ballroom (both demolished), 1100 W. University Ave. (at N. Lexington Pkwy.). (Map A)
At the Boulevards of Paris, tuxedoed and gowned patrons could enjoy European cuisine, big-band jazz, and a full-scale reproduction of the American Bar in Paris, as well as the thrill of dancing side-by-side with notorious gangsters. The Coliseum, once an ice rink, claimed to have the largest dance floor in the world (100-by-250 feet).

13 The Green Dragon Cafe (demolished), 469 N. Snelling Ave. (at W. University Ave.), now site of the Spruce Tree Center. (Map A)
On July 25, 1932, two hit men from the Murder Inc. syndicate gunned down bootlegger Abe Wagner and his partner, Al Gordon, here in broad daylight.

14 Lowry Hotel, 339 N. Wabasha St. (between Fourth and Fifth Sts.), now Lowry Office Building. (Map C)
Opened in 1927, the Lowry had a long history of association with the underworld, providing a haven for Bugsy Siegel, Alvin Karpis, and other gangsters.

15 Harry "Dutch" Sawyer's home, 1878 Jefferson Ave. (near Fairview Ave.), private residence. (Map A)
Underworld banker Sawyer, who supervised St. Paul's O'Connor system after the murder of Danny Hogan, hosted underworld parties in this two-story house.

16 Green Lantern saloon (demolished), 545 N. Wabasha St. (between W. Tenth and W. Eleventh Sts.), now site of the Wabasha Street Apartments. (Map C)
The Green Lantern was St. Paul's premier criminal hangout—a saloon for safecrackers and bankrobbers which "Creepy" Karpis called "my personal headquarters." The Lantern was turned over to Dillinger gang members Tommy Gannon and Pat Reilly in 1933, closed in 1934, and became a photography studio and a beauty shop in the 1950s before being razed.

17 Hotel St. Francis, Old W. Seventh St. (between Wabasha and St. Peter Sts.), now 7th Place Residences, Francesca's restaurant, and the old Orpheum Theatre. (Map C)
Slot machine king and Dillinger gang patron Tom Filben used the St. Francis, built in 1916, as his base of operations. At the height of his power as an underworld fixer in the early 1930s, Filben lived in the two-story, stucco home at 2133 Fairmount Ave. (near S. Finn St.); his slot machine company, Patrick Novelty, was at 518 St. Peter St. (demolished), just a few blocks from the Hotel St. Francis.

18 Edgecumbe Court Apartments, 1095 Osceola Ave. (at S. Lexington Pkwy.). (Map B)
Known to the FBI as a "lamsters' hideout," these apartments were home to many of America's most-wanted bank robbers and prison escapees from 1931 to 1933.

19 Lincoln Oaks Apartments, 572 Lincoln Ave. (near Grand Ave.). (Map B)
The "unlucky" bank robber Charlie Harmon and his wife, Paula, lived in apartment 1 of this brown-brick building while on the run from the FBI.

20 Cretin Court Apartments, 50 S. Cretin Ave. (at Grand Ave.). (Map A)
This three-and-a-half story brick building was once the home of bank robber Francis "Jimmy" Keating, one of the "Evergreen bandits" hunted by the FBI.

21 Summit-Dale Apartments, 616 Summit Ave. (at Dale St.), now Hawthorne Apartments. (Map B)
Keating's bank robbing partner, Tommy Holden, hid under an alias in this handsome four-story red-brick structure.

22 Wildwood triple-murder site, near Wildwood and Katherine Abbott Parks, Mahtomedi. (Map D)
On August 13, 1930, authorities discovered the bodies of three Kansas City gangsters hanging from willow trees about a half-mile southeast of the entrance to Wildwood Park, located at the intersection of Highway 244 and Birchwood Rd. A few hundred yards away at 92 Mahtomedi Ave. (at Stillwater Rd./County Rd. 12) is Big Ben Restaurant, on the site of the original Picadilly, a favorite diner for the John Dillinger gang.

23 Plantation nightclub (demolished), Old White Bear Ave. (at Cottage Park Rd.), White Bear Lake; the site is now Lion's Park. (Map D)
The gangsters who vacationed around White Bear Lake—including Al Capone's gunman Fred "Shotgun George Ziegler" Goetz—spent their

evenings at the Plantation, where, in the words of the FBI, they indulged in a "riotous nightlife."

24 Keller Golf Course, 2166 Maplewood Dr. (near County Rd. B), Maplewood. (Map A)
Founded in 1929, this eighteen-hole course was so popular with bank robbers such as "Evergreen bandit" Jimmy Keating that the FBI used its golf caddies as informants.

25 Ma Barker's hideout, 1031 S. Robert St. (near Bernard St.), West St. Paul, private office. (Map A)
The Barker-Karpis gang, which rented this house from the Hannegraf family in February 1932, escaped a police raid after being tipped off by corrupt officers. Owner Helen Hannegraf lived next door at 1035 S. Robert.

26 John Lambert cottage, 148 Dellwood Ave., Dellwood, private residence. (Map D)
Located on the east shore of White Bear Lake near the intersection of Tamarack St. and Mahtomedi Ave./Highway 244, this eight-room cottage provided a vacation spot for the Barker-Karpis gang in the summer of 1932. The underworld gambled at the Silver Slipper roadhouse at 230 Warner Ave. in Mahtomedi, now a private residence near the corner of Warner and Greenwood, and socialized at Elsie's speakeasy at 159 Dahlia. Babyface Nelson and his wife lived in a Mahtomedi cottage and ate at Vince Guarnera's Italian restaurant at 959 Mahtomedi Ave.; bank robber Frank "Jelly" Nash lived in a Mahtomedi home near Rose and Spruce Sts.

27 Third Northwestern National Bank (demolished), 430 E. Hennepin Ave. (at S.E. Fifth St.), Minneapolis; the site is now a parking lot. (Map E)
The triangular bank building that stood at this spot was the scene of one of the most violent bank robberies in Minnesota history. On December 16, 1932, the Barker-Karpis gang took more than $120,000 from the bank and left two Minneapolis policemen dead.

28 Como Park Zoo (off N. Lexington Pkwy.). (Map A)
During the getaway from their December 16, 1932, bank robbery in Minneapolis, the Barker-Karpis gang stopped near this spot to switch cars. Unaware of the robbery, Christmas tree salesman Oscar Erickson slowed down to look and was shot to death by Fred Barker.

29 Annbee Arms Apartments, 928 Grand Ave. (near S. Milton St.), now Kensington Hall. (Map B)
Two days after the Third Northwestern National Bank robbery, police captured an intoxicated Larry DeVol at his apartment in this twenty-one-suite, red-brick building.

30 Cle-mar Apartments, 2062 Marshall Ave. (at N. Cleveland Ave.). (Map A)
This four-story red-brick apartment building was home to Katherine "Ma" Barker, con man Earl Christman, kidnapper Bernard "Big Phil" Phillips, and other members of the Barker-Karpis gang.

31 Grand Avenue Apartments, 1290 Grand Ave. (near S. Syndicate St.). (Map B)
In February 1933, the Barker-Karpis gang set up headquarters in this four-story brick apartment building—but were forced to flee in March after a tip-off of an impending police raid.

32 Commodore Hotel, 79 Western Ave. (at Holly Ave.). (Map B)
Opened in 1920, the hotel and its elegant art deco bar attracted literary figures F. Scott and Zelda Fitzgerald as well as gangsters Al Capone and Fred Barker. The hotel was renovated in the 1970s but still looks much like it did when Ma Barker met her son Fred's girlfriend here.

33 Hollyhocks Club casino, 1590 S. Mississippi River Blvd. (white home between 1606 and 1616 S. Mississippi River Blvd. near S. Cleveland Ave.), private residence. (Map A)
Hosted by fixer Jack Peifer, this club overlooking the river bluffs was a favorite haven for members of the Dillinger and Barker-Karpis gangs. The facade was significantly renovated in the early 1990s, but the circular driveway and expansive lawn still evoke its gangster-era splendor.

34 Idlewild cottage, 5500 E. Bald Eagle Blvd. (at Taylor Ave. near Highway 61), White Bear Lake Township, private residence. (Map D)
This one-and-a-half-story cottage provided an ideal hideout for the Barker-Karpis gang to plan the kidnapping of William Hamm Jr. in 1933.

35 Hamm Brewing Company, 681 E. Minnehaha Ave. (at Payne Ave.), now Stroh Brewery Company. (Map A)
On June 15, 1933, William Hamm Jr., grandson of the brewery's founder, was kidnapped near the brewery (at the corner of Minnehaha and Greenbrier, now obscured by the Stroh buildings) while he was walking toward his home at 671 Cable Ave. for lunch. The Hamm mansion at what is today the intersection of Greenbrier and Margaret Sts. was destroyed by fire in 1954; a nine-foot-high brick column on the site, overlooking the

entrance to Swede Hollow Park, marks the southeast corner of what was once the Hamm estate.

36 William W. Dunn home, 1916 Summit Ave. (near Prior Ave.), private residence. (Map A)
William Dunn, the intermediary between William Hamm's kidnappers and the Hamm family, lived in this two-story stucco home. Unbeknownst to Hamm, Dunn had also served as the conduit for underworld payoff money to corrupt policemen.

37 Rosedale Pharmacy, 1941 Grand Ave. (at Prior Ave.), now Thomas Liquors. (Map A)
On June 16, 1933, kidnapper Fred Goetz left a ransom note for the Hamm family at a soda booth in Clarence Thomas's drugstore. A portrait of Thomas now hangs at the back of the liquor store managed by his son.

38 Hideout of the Vernon Street Gang, 204 Vernon St. (near St. Clair Ave.), private residence. (Map A)
During the Hamm kidnapping, this two-story house near Macalester College housed a convention of public enemies, including Fred and Doc Barker, Frank "Jelly" Nash, and Alvin Karpis.

39 Tom Brown's home, 759 E. Maryland Ave. (near Weide St.), private residences. (Map A)
Former St. Paul police chief Tom Brown and his family resided in this two-story stucco house during the years when he used his position to aid some of the country's most notorious criminals.

40 South St. Paul Post Office, 236 N. Concord St. (near Grand Avenue), South St. Paul. (Map A)
On August 30, 1933, the Barker-Karpis gang stole $33,000 from a South St. Paul stockyards payroll brought by rail to this two-story brick building from the Federal Reserve Bank of Minneapolis. The bandits severely wounded one police officer and shot another dead.

41 Dale Apartments, 628 Grand Ave. (at S. Dale St.). (Map B)
In December 1933 and January 1934, the Barker-Karpis gang used this imposing three-story building as its headquarters for planning the Edward Bremer kidnapping.

42 Jacob Schmidt Brewery, 882 W. Seventh St. (at Webster St.), now Minnesota Brewing Company. (Map A)
Founded in 1855, this brewery helped make the Bremers one of Minnesota's wealthiest families—and a target for kidnappers. During

Prohibition, Schmidt beer was delivered to the underworld's Green Lantern saloon via a tunnel to a brewery employee's house on Erie St.

43 The Kennington, 565 Portland Ave. (at N. Kent St.). (Map B)
Shoplifter Myrtle Eaton offered her apartment 104 in this red brick building as a hideout for the Barker-Karpis gang before the Bremer kidnapping.

44 Holly Falls Apartments, 562 Holly Ave. (at N. Kent St.). (Map B)
On January 13, 1934, Roy McCord, wearing his Northwest Airlines radio operator's uniform, was mistaken for a police officer by Alvin Karpis and severely wounded near this four-story brick building in a hail of gunfire.

45 Bremer kidnapping site, intersection of S. Lexington Pkwy. and Goodrich Ave. (Map B)
On the morning of January 17, 1934, banker Edward Bremer, who had just dropped his daughter off at the Summit School at 1150 Goodrich, was seized here by the Barker-Karpis gang.

46 Walter W. Magee's home, 1295 Lincoln Ave. (near S. Syndicate St.), private residence. (Map B)
Magee, contacted by the Bremer kidnappers to act as intermediary between the gang and the Bremer family, had his two-story stucco home placed under police surveillance.

47 Bremer's abandoned automobile, outside 1910 Edgecumbe Rd. (near Montreal Ave.), private residence. (Map A)
Hours after he was kidnapped, Edward Bremer's Lincoln sedan was found here in the Highland Park neighborhood, its interior stained with blood.

48 Edward Bremer home, 92 N. Mississippi River Blvd. (near Otis Ave.), private residence. (Map A)
Protected by FBI agents, the Bremer family waited at their two-and-one-half-story brick mansion near the Lake St. bridge for word on the fate of Edward Bremer. The home of Edward's uncle, Otto Bremer, is at 1344 Summit Ave. (at Hamline Ave.).

49 Dr. Henry T. Nippert home, 706 Lincoln Ave. (near S. St. Albans St.), private residence. (Map B)
After abducting Edward Bremer, the kidnappers placed a ransom note in a bottle and threw it through the front-door window of the three-story red-brick home owned by the Bremer family doctor.

50 Adolf Bremer Sr. mansion, 855 W. Seventh St. (near Oneida St.), now a private social service agency. (Map A)
Before paying the $200,000 ransom, Adolf Bremer Sr. called reporters to his two-story home to appeal for the safe return of his kidnapped son. Later the family built a tunnel from the house to the basement of the Schmidt brewery's Rathskeller bar across the street. Visitors to the Rathskeller can identify the tunnel, now sealed off to protect children who might be attracted by the underground passage, by a six-foot-high wooden door.

51 Harry "Dutch" Sawyer's farm, 305 Snail Lake Rd., Shoreview, private residence. (Map D)
Surrounded by groves of cottonwood trees, this small farm—in part financed with loot stolen in 1933 from the First National Bank of Fairbury, Nebraska—served as a hideout and conference center for underworld friends of nightclub owner Harry Sawyer. The two-story home across from Sitzer Park harbored such gangsters as Fred Barker, Alvin Karpis, and Edna "the Kissing Bandit" Murray.

52 Santa Monica Apartments, 3252 S. Girard Ave., Minneapolis. (Map E)
Just after his March 1934 escape from an Indiana jail, John Dillinger and his lover, Evelyn Frechette, moved into apartment 106 of this four-story building. Babyface Nelson and other Dillinger gang members reunited here to plan a wave of bank robberies.

53 Charlou and Josephine Apartments, 3300 and 3310 S. Fremont Ave., Minneapolis, now Fremont Apartments. (Map E)
These two four-story apartment buildings were home to several Dillinger gang members in 1934. Gunman Homer Van Meter and his girlfriend Marie Conforti lived in apartment 201 of the Josephine Apartments, while bank scout Eddie Green used the Charlou's apartment 207 to stash machine guns and bulletproof vests.

54 Dr. Nels Mortensen's home, 2252 Fairmount Ave. (near Woodlawn Ave.), private residence. (Map A)
Just after midnight on March 13, 1934, Dr. Nels Mortensen answered his doorbell and found wounded gangsters John Dillinger and John Hamilton on his front steps.

55 Lincoln Court Apartments, 93 S. Lexington Pkwy. (at Lincoln Ave.). (Map B)
On the morning of March 31, 1934, FBI agents and police knocked on the door of Lincoln Court apartment 303 on a landlady's hunch—

inadvertently stumbling into a gun battle with John Dillinger and Homer Van Meter. Dillinger's third-floor apartment, where he lived with girlfriend Evelyn Frechette, overlooked Lexington Pkwy.

56 Dillinger's getaway garage, 1123 Goodrich Ave. (near S. Lexington Pkwy.), private. (Map B)
Evelyn Frechette—covered by the machine gun-wielding Dillinger—backed Dillinger's Hudson sedan out of this garage near the Lincoln Court shootout and drove the bank robber to safety.

57 The Dillinger doctor's clinic, 1835 Park Ave. (near E. Nineteenth St.), Minneapolis, private residence. (Map E)
Accompanied by girlfriend Frechette and fellow gang members, the wounded Dillinger sought help from underworld doctor Clayton May. The outlaw recuperated in apartment 1, on the south side of this two-story red-brick building.

58 Tommy Carroll's hideout (demolished), 35 W. Isabel St. (at Hall Ave.). (Map A)
Post office robber and auto thief Tommy Carroll rented the upper floor of this house from the Vogel family during the spring and summer of 1932. He lived there with singer "Radio Sally" Bennett.

59 The Dillinger gang's Minneapolis mail drop, 3242 S. Sixteenth Ave. (near E. Thirty-third St.), Minneapolis, private residence. (Map E)
Dillinger gang member Tommy Carroll received his mail-order submachine guns at this duplex, where the brother of his girlfriend Sally Bennett lived. The residence is opposite the Powderhorn Park Baptist Church. Carroll is buried at Oakland Cemetery, 927 Jackson St., St. Paul.

60 The Dillinger gang's weapons depot, 2214 Marshall Ave. (near N. Cretin Ave.). (Map A)
In his hasty escape from the Lincoln Court shootout, John Dillinger left behind a note with the telephone number of gang member Eddie Green, traced by FBI agents to this three-story red-brick building in the Merriam Park neighborhood. Green rented apartment 106, on the east side of the building, for two weeks in March 1934. The Dillinger gang sought automotive repairs at the nearby gas station at 2178 Marshall.

61 Eddie Green's ambush house (demolished), 778 Rondo Ave. (Concordia Ave. at S. Avon St.), today Interstate-94. (Map A)
FBI agents ambushed Dillinger gang member Green at this house, which was demolished—along with much of the Rondo neighborhood—for construction of I-94. Backup agents were hidden at Avon St. and

St. Anthony Ave., adjacent to what is today the baseball field at Maxfield Elementary School.

62 Homer Van Meter's death site, University Ave. and Marion St. (Map A)
Tipped off by underworld informants, St. Paul police officers surprised Dillinger gang member Van Meter at an auto dealership here on August 23, 1934. Van Meter, firing his .38 Colt automatic, was cut down by police gunfire when he ran into a blind alley between Aurora Ave. and Marion St., just two blocks from the state capitol.

63 New St. Paul police headquarters, 100 E. Eleventh St. (between Minnesota and Robert Sts.). (Map C)
The St. Paul police headquarters was renovated in the mid-1980s, but the facade is similar to that of the 1930s, when a St. Paul Daily News *wiretap of police telephone lines exposed ties between gangsters and law enforcers.*

64 Hamm Building, 408 St. Peter St. (between W. Sixth St. and Seventh Pl.). (Map C)
Fronted by the St. Paul Recreation Company—a billiard room, cigar stand, gym, boxing ring, and bowling alley—the basement of this Chicago-styled building housed one of the city's biggest illegal gambling operations. The gambling dens have long since been converted into offices.

65 Holman Municipal Airport, 644 Bayfield St., now St. Paul Downtown Airport. (Map A)
After his capture in New Orleans on May 1, 1936, Alvin Karpis, accompanied by FBI director J. Edgar Hoover and scores of special agents, was flown to St. Paul's Holman Airport to stand trial for the Hamm and Bremer kidnappings.

66 St. Paul City Hall and Ramsey County Courthouse, 15 Kellogg Blvd. W. (between Wabasha and St. Peter Sts.). (Map C)
Connected to the nearby Ramsey County jail by an underground tunnel, the Art Deco courthouse was the site of the 1933 trial of Roger Touhy, which took place on the eighth floor. The 1935 police corruption trials, sparked by wiretaps, occurred in the eleventh-floor courtrooms.

67 Old Ramsey County Jail (demolished), St. Peter and W. Fourth Sts. (Map C)
This sandstone-and-granite structure on the southeast corner of the intersection of Fourth and St. Peter, completed in 1903, had an Italian Renaissance exterior. It held some of the most wanted criminals of the gangster era, including Alvin Karpis, Doc Barker, Roger Touhy, and Edna "the Kissing Bandit" Murray.

A. ST. PAUL

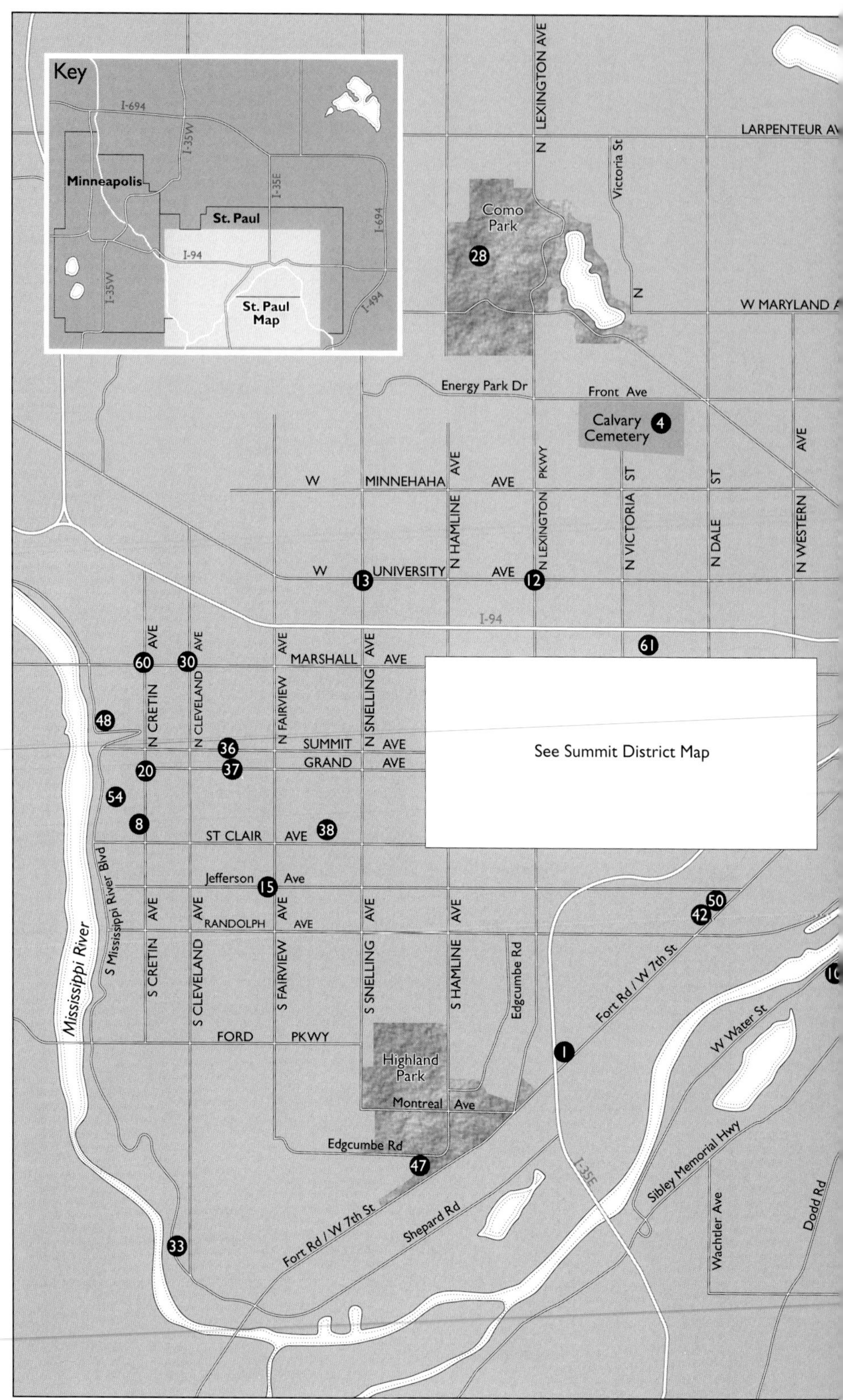

Key
I-694
I-35W
I-35E
Minneapolis
St. Paul
I-94
I-494
St. Paul Map
LARPENTEUR AV
N LEXINGTON AVE
Victoria St
Como Park
28
W MARYLAND A
Energy Park Dr
Front Ave
Calvary Cemetery
4
W MINNEHAHA AVE
N HAMLINE AVE
N LEXINGTON PKWY
N VICTORIA ST
N DALE ST
N WESTERN AVE
W UNIVERSITY AVE
13
12
I-94
61
60
30
MARSHALL AVE
N CRETIN AVE
N CLEVELAND AVE
N FAIRVIEW AVE
N SNELLING AVE
48
36
SUMMIT AVE
GRAND AVE
20
37
See Summit District Map
54
8
ST CLAIR AVE
38
Jefferson Ave
15
RANDOLPH AVE
50
42
Mississippi River
S Mississippi River Blvd
S CRETIN AVE
S CLEVELAND AVE
S FAIRVIEW AVE
S SNELLING AVE
S HAMLINE AVE
Edgcumbe Rd
Fort Rd / W 7th St
W Water St
FORD PKWY
1
Highland Park
Montreal Ave
Edgcumbe Rd
47
I-35E
Sibley Memorial Hwy
Shepard Rd
Fort Rd / W 7th St
33
Wachtler Ave
Dodd Rd

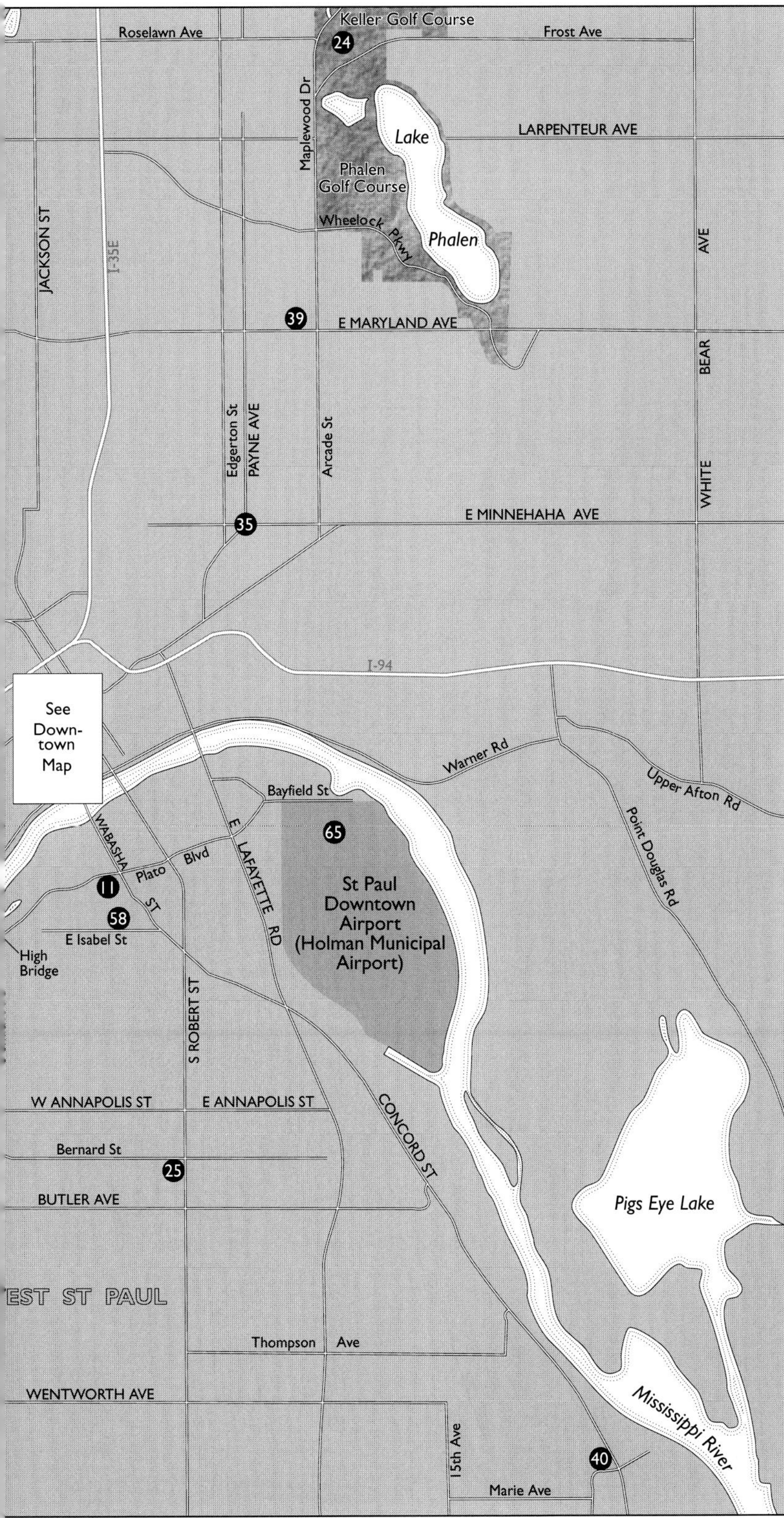
Roselawn Ave
Keller Golf Course
Frost Ave
Maplewood Dr
Lake
Phalen
LARPENTEUR AVE
Phalen
Golf Course
Wheelock Pkwy
JACKSON ST
I-35E
WHITE BEAR AVE
E MARYLAND AVE
Edgerton St
PAYNE AVE
Arcade St
E MINNEHAHA AVE
I-94
See Downtown Map
Warner Rd
Upper Afton Rd
Point Douglas Rd
Bayfield St
WABASHA ST
Plato Blvd
E LAFAYETTE RD
St Paul Downtown Airport (Holman Municipal Airport)
E Isabel St
High Bridge
S ROBERT ST
W ANNAPOLIS ST
E ANNAPOLIS ST
CONCORD ST
Bernard St
BUTLER AVE
Pigs Eye Lake
EST ST PAUL
Thompson Ave
WENTWORTH AVE
15th Ave
Mississippi River
Marie Ave
24
39
35
65
11
58
25
40

B. ST. PAUL'S SUMMIT DISTRICT

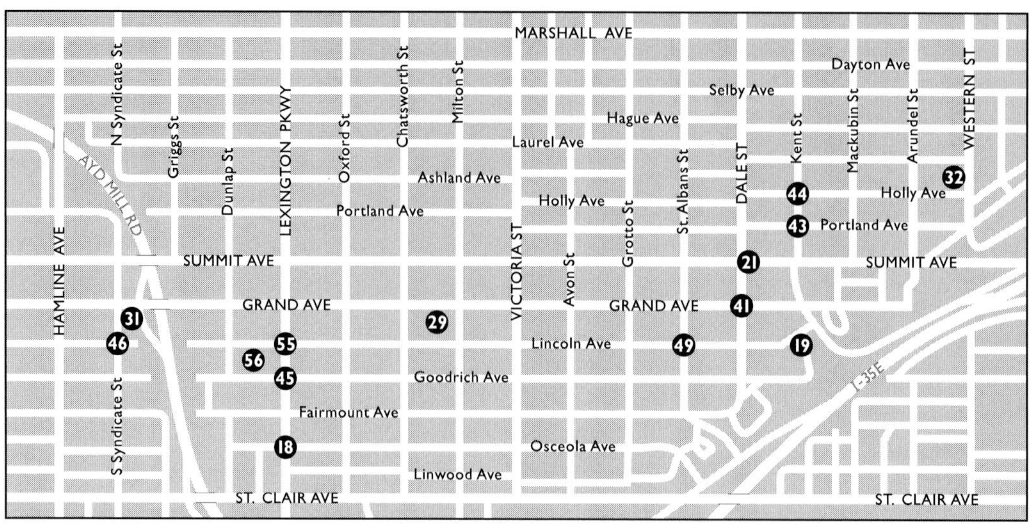

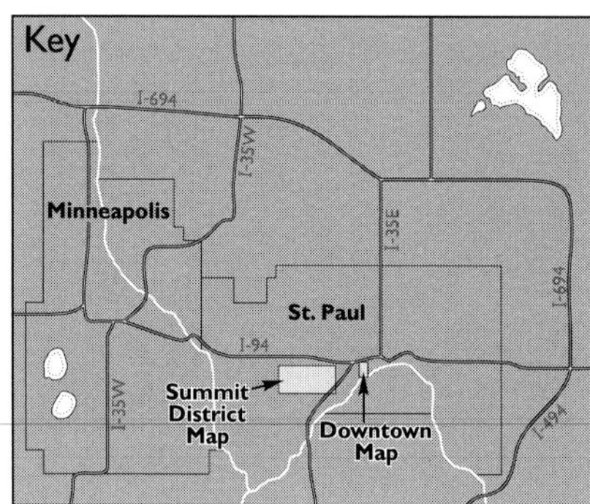

C. DOWNTOWN ST. PAUL

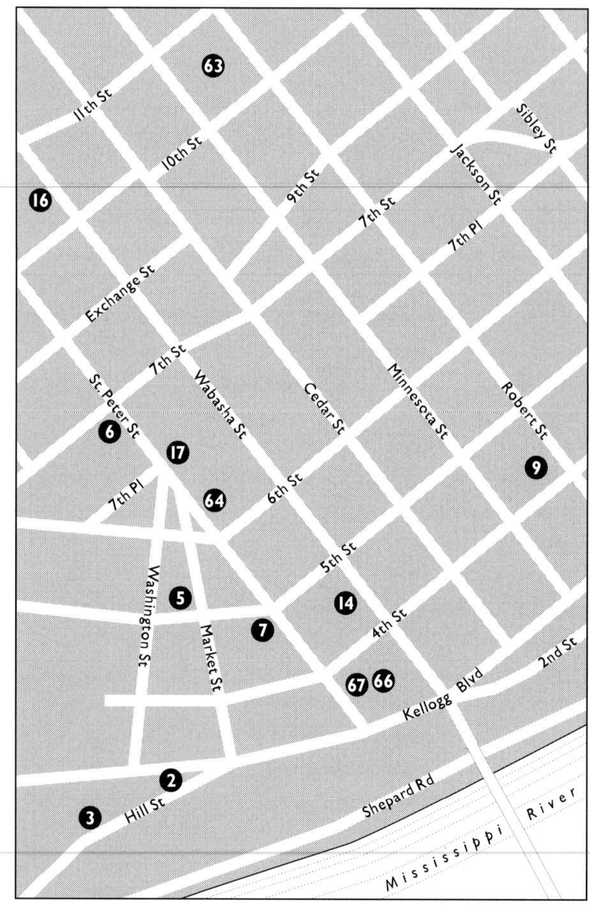

D. WHITE BEAR LAKE DISTRICT

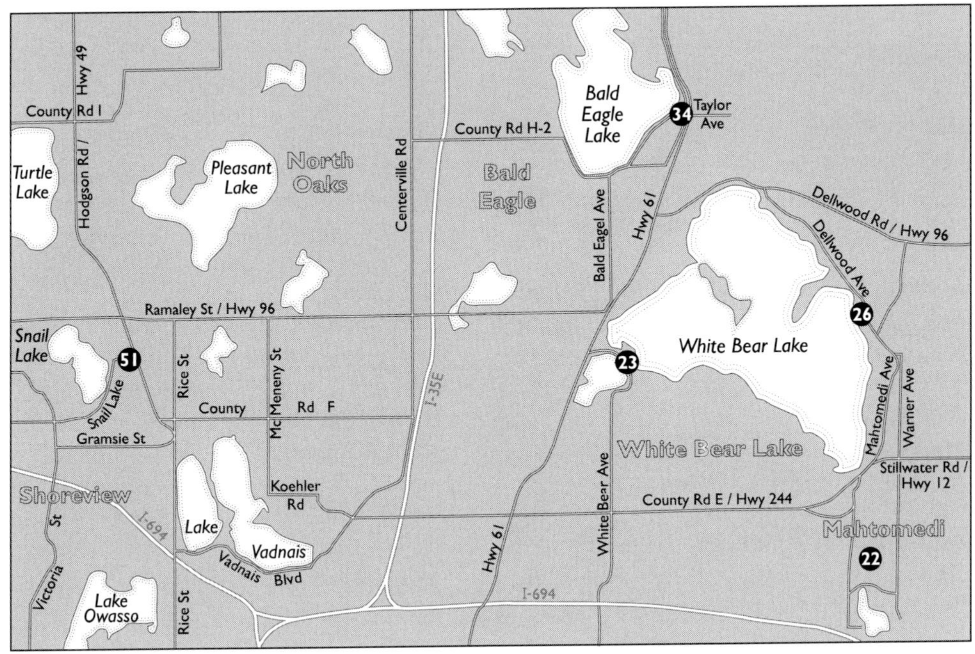

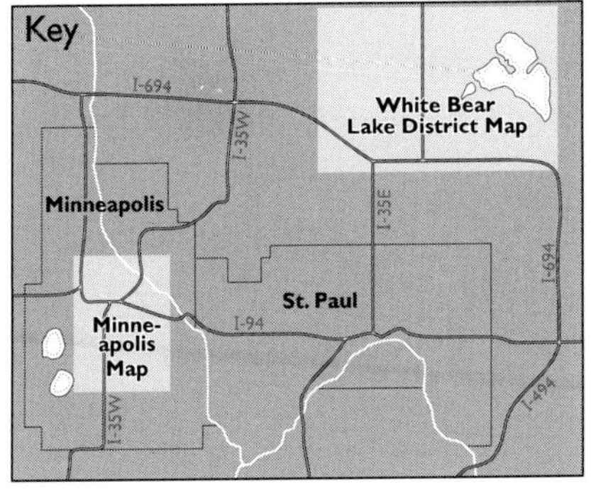

E. MINNEAPOLIS

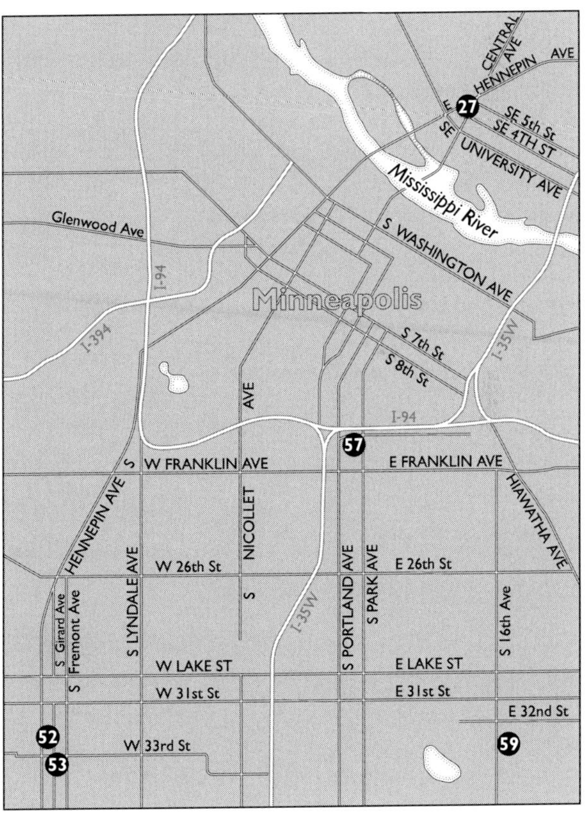

ROGUES AND REFORMERS GALLERY • • • •

ROGUES

Harvey Bailey Oklahoma bootlegger turned bank robber whose 1920s crime spree netted nearly $1 million in stolen cash and bonds, much of which was laundered through the St. Paul syndicate.

Arthur "Doc" Barker Convicted murderer and, as a member of the Barker-Karpis gang, a principal in the kidnappings of brewing company president William Hamm and bank president Edward Bremer.

Fred Barker Bank robber, jewel thief, and kidnapper from Tulsa, Oklahoma; founding member of Barker-Karpis gang.

Katherine "Ma" Barker Born Arizona "Donnie" Clark, mother of Fred and Arthur Barker; after her death named by J. Edgar Hoover as the mastermind of Barker-Karpis gang.

George "Machine Gun Kelly" Barnes Minor bootlegger and bank robber who earned notoriety as "Machine Gun Kelly" through publicity over his kidnapping of Oklahoma oilman Charles Urschel.

Sally "Radio Sally" Bennett St. Paul nightclub singer and girlfriend of Dillinger gang member Tommy Carroll.

Isadore "Kid Cann" Blumenfeld Romanian immigrant who headed the Minneapolis combination liquor syndicate; prosecuted but acquitted for laundering George "Machine Gun Kelly" Barnes's kidnapping money.

William Byron "Monty Carter" Bolton Driver for Al Capone's Chicago syndicate; partner of gunman Fred Goetz; took part in Hamm kidnapping and later turned government witness.

Thomas A. Brown St. Paul police chief from 1930 to 1932 and later head of elite police kidnap squad; suspected by FBI of leaking information to members of the Dillinger and Barker-Karpis gangs.

Alphonse "Scarface" Capone Legendary Chicago racketeer who reportedly stayed at St. Paul's Commodore Hotel.

Thomas L. Carroll Chicago-area auto thief, post office robber, and sometime Dillinger gang associate; suspected of joining Babyface Nelson and Homer Van Meter in the October 1933 robbery of the First National Bank of Brainerd, Minnesota.

Earl Christman Con man and freelance bank robber for Barker-Karpis gang; mortally wounded during 1933 robbery of First National Bank of Fairbury, Nebraska.

Nina Clifford St. Paul's most prominent madam, whose elegant brothel on Washington Street attracted the city's wealthiest businessmen and politicians.

Marie Conforti Girlfriend of Dillinger gang member Homer Van Meter.

James P. Crumley St. Paul police inspector and former head of the morals squad; onetime ally of police chief Thomas Brown; dismissed in 1935 after wiretaps exposed his tip-offs to the underworld.

Harry "Gorilla Kid" Davis Philadelphia hoodlum slain near St. Paul in 1932 by Murder Inc. assassins George Young and Joey Schaefer.

Volney "Curly" Davis Convicted murderer, Oklahoma prison escapee, burglar, and fringe member of Barker-Karpis gang.

Jean Delaney St. Paul girlfriend of Dillinger gang member Tommy Carroll; sister of Delores and Helen Delaney.

Delores Delaney Girlfriend of Alvin Karpis; sister of Jean and Helen Delaney.

Helen "Babe" Delaney Wife of Dillinger gang member William "Pat" Reilly; sister of Delores and Jean Delaney.

Lawrence "the Chopper" DeVol Mentally unstable bank robber, jail escapee, cop killer, and freelance machine gunner for the Barker-Karpis gang.

John Dillinger Indiana bank robber, jail escapee, and folk hero, named Public Enemy Number One by J. Edgar Hoover.

Jess Doyle Bank robber, auto thief, and minor member of Barker-Karpis gang; participant in 1933 robbery of First National Bank of Fairbury, Nebraska.

Arthur "Old Man" Dunlop Indiscreet boyfriend of Katherine "Ma" Barker; gangland murder victim.

William W. Dunn Hamm Brewing Company sales manager who served as intermediary during kidnapping of William Hamm Jr.; reported bribe collector for St. Paul police and friend of liquor czar Leon Gleckman.

Myrtle Eaton Shoplifter and girlfriend of Barker-Karpis gang member William Weaver.

Helen Ferguson Girlfriend of ill-fated Barker-Karpis gang member Earl Christman.

Thomas P. Filben Slot machine king and underworld fence working through his Patrick Novelty company; gangland supplier of automobiles, banking services, and political clout.

Charles "Old Charlie" Fitzgerald Veteran bank robber and burglar, employed as "greeter" by Barker-Karpis gang during William Hamm kidnapping.

Evelyn "Billie" Frechette Wisconsin-born girlfriend of bank robber John Dillinger.

Thomas E. Gannon St. Paul contact for Dillinger gang, one-time proprieter of underworld's Green Lantern Saloon.

Lester "Babyface Nelson" Gillis Bank robber, machine gun aficionado, and casual murderer who participated in crimes involving both Dillinger and Barker-Karpis gangs.

Leon Gleckman Liquor syndicate head and political fixer for St. Paul underworld with close ties to police chief Thomas Brown.

Benjamin and Abraham Gleeman St. Paul bootleggers wrongly convicted of killing hijacker Burt Stevens; their testimony helped expose the multimillion-dollar Cleveland liquor syndicate.

Fred "Shotgun George Ziegler" Goetz Chicago killer for Al Capone's syndicate, reputed triggerman at St. Valentine's Day Massacre, and freelancer with Barker-Karpis gang on St. Paul kidnappings.

Beth Green (aka Bessie Skinner) Government informant and girlfriend of Dillinger gang member Eddie Green.

Harry Eugene "Eddie" Green St. Paul contact man, convicted payroll robber, and "jug marker" (bank scout) for Dillinger gang.

John "Three Fingered Jack" Hamilton Indiana prison escapee and member of Dillinger gang; mortally wounded during 1934 Hastings shootout after FBI's Little Bohemia raid.

Robert B. Hamilton Gambling impresario who directed casino operations at the Hollyhocks Club, the Plantation nightclub, and the Boulevards of Paris.

Charles P. Harmon Unlucky bank and post office robber; friend of Frank Nash and hanger-on with Barker-Karpis gang until his death during the robbery of Wisconsin's Kraft State Bank in 1931.

Paula Harmon Widow of bank robber Charlie Harmon and girlfriend of Fred Barker.

Ben Harris Twin Cities gambling figure and operator of the Plantation nightclub, believed by FBI to be connected to the Barker-Karpis gang.

Daniel "Dapper Dan" Hogan Owner of underworld's Green Lantern saloon and fence of stolen merchandise; recognized as unofficial head of St. Paul underworld until his car-bomb murder.

Thomas Holden One of the Chicago-area "Evergreen bandits" who escaped with partner Jimmy Keating from Leavenworth prison in 1930, sparking a nationwide FBI manhunt focusing on golf courses.

Alvin "Creepy" Karpis Montreal-born bank robber, kidnapper, jewel thief, prison escapee, safe blower, and founding member of Barker-Karpis gang.

Francis L. "Jimmy" Keating Chicago-area railroad and bank robber and inveterate golfer, known for his 1930 escape from Leavenworth prison; he and partner Tommy Holden were known as the "Evergreen bandits."

Machine Gun Kelly—See George Barnes.

Vivian Mathis Girlfriend of Barker-Karpis gang machine gunner Verne Miller; lived near Brainerd, Minnesota .

Dr. Clayton E. May Minneapolis underworld physician for members of the Dillinger gang.

Morrie "the Phantom Gunman" Miller St. Paul liquor syndicate hit man and killer of hijacker Burt Stevens.

Vernon C. "Verne" Miller South Dakota sheriff who became a freelance machine gunner, embezzler, bootlegger, bank robber, and perpetrator of the June 1933 Kansas City Massacre.

Edward G. "Big Ed" Morgan Minneapolis slot machine czar and boss of the city's Irish liquor and gambling syndicate during the 1920s.

Edna "the Kissing Bandit" Murray Holdup artist, liquor hijacker, and Missouri prison escapee; girlfriend of Barker-Karpis gang member Volney Davis.

Frank "Jelly" Nash Oklahoma bank and train robber, burglar, and convicted murderer (nicknamed "the Gentleman Bandit"), whose capture precipitated the Kansas City Massacre.

Babyface Nelson See Lester Gillis.

John J. "the Big Fellow" O'Connor St. Paul police chief, 1900–12 and 1914–20; architect of the O'Connor system, or layover agreement, which guaranteed safe haven for gangsters.

John "Jack" Peifer Underworld banker and police fixer, operator of Hollyhocks Club casino, and key strategist for Barker-Karpis gang's kidnappings of Edward Bremer and William Hamm.

Bernard "Big Phil Courtney" Phillips Auto thief, kidnapper, bank robber, and ex-police officer; mistrusted by Barker-Karpis gang, Phillips disappeared in 1932.

William Albert "Pat" Reilly St. Paul gambler, bootlegger, and Green Lantern saloon bartender who served as an errand boy for John Dillinger.

Gladys Rita Sawyer Wife of underworld fixer Harry Sawyer and government informant against Barker-Karpis gang.

Harry "Dutch" Sawyer Bootlegger, fence, gangland banker, protégé of fixer Dan Hogan, and St. Paul contact for Dillinger and Barker-Karpis gangs.

Joseph Schaefer Murder Inc. hit man, formerly employed by Irving "Waxey Gordon" Wexler's mob, who killed bootlegger Abe Wagner in St. Paul.

Benjamin "Bugsy" Siegel Organized crime executive, murderer, and casino entrepreneur who lobbied in 1939 for release of two Murder Inc. killers from Minnesota's Stillwater Prison.

Sammy "Ten Dollar Kid" Silverman Minneapolis gangster slain near Mahtomedi, Minnesota, in August 1930.

Frank Sommers St. Paul police chief with ties to gangster Danny Hogan; forced to resign in 1920s over "vice investigation" scandal.

Robert "Frisco Dutch" Steinhardt Chicago pickpocket employed at St. Paul's Boulevards of Paris nightclub and the Plantation nightclub in White Bear Lake.

Burton Stevens Liquor hijacker whose 1925 murder in St. Paul led to exposure of a nationwide liquor conspiracy.

Roger "the Terrible" Touhy Chicago bootlegger and rival of Al Capone; tried and aquitted in St. Paul federal court for the kidnapping of William Hamm.

Homer Van Meter Train robber from Fort Wayne, Indiana, who served as lieutenant for Dillinger's bank robbery gang.

Abe Wagner (aka Abe Loeb) New York bootlegger; victim of 1932 Murder Inc. assassination in St. Paul's Midway district.

William "Lapland Willie" Weaver Arkansas bank robber, kidnapper, convicted murderer, and Bremer kidnapping conspirator with Barker-Karpis gang.

George Young Murder Inc. killer allied with syndicate chieftain Meyer Lansky; murdered bootlegger Abe Wagner in St. Paul.

REFORMERS

Gustave "Gus" H. Barfuss St. Paul policeman and public safety commissioner who lobbied to eliminate politics from police department.

Thomas E. Dahill Reformer and St. Paul police chief during investigation of John Dillinger's robberies; foe of former chief Thomas Brown.

Clinton A. Hackert St. Paul police chief and ally of reformer Thomas Dahill in fight against corrupt officers with ties to organized crime.

Wallace Ness Jamie Criminologist nephew of Eliot Ness (of "the Untouchables"), who was hired by the *St. Paul Daily News* to expose police-underworld corruption.

Howard Kahn Anticrime crusader and editor of *St. Paul Daily News*, who joined with investigator Wallace Jamie to expose police corruption in mid-1930s.

H.E. "Ned" Warren Public safety commissioner who joined editor Kahn and investigator Jamie in exposing police-underworld corruption.

TWIN CITIES CRIME CHRONOLOGY • • • •

June 11, 1900 John J. O'Connor becomes chief of St. Paul police; his "layover agreement" with visiting gangsters establishes the foundation for a crime wave based in St. Paul.

October 28, 1919 Eighteenth Amendment, the Prohibition initiative written by Minnesota congressman Andrew Volstead, passes, nurturing organized crime syndicates in all major U.S. cities.

September 28, 1922 Harvey Bailey gang robs the Hamilton County Bank in Cincinnati of $265,000; portions of the money later surface in St. Paul.

December 18, 1922 Harvey Bailey gang robs the Denver Mint of $200,000; the stolen Denver bonds are traced to St. Paul.

February 16, 1925 Murder of bootlegger Burt Stevens in downtown St. Paul leads to exposure of $140 million nationwide liquor syndicate.

November 4, 1928 Fixer Arnold "the Brain" Rothstein is murdered in New York; murder weapon is traced to St. Paul.

December 4, 1928 Crime kingpin Daniel Hogan is slain by car bomb; protégé Harry "Dutch" Sawyer takes over Hogan's Green Lantern saloon.

February 14, 1929 St. Valentine's Day Massacre in Chicago, in which seven members of George "Bugs" Moran's gang are murdered by members of Al Capone's gang.

January 18, 1930 Bootlegger Leon Gleckman moves into Hotel St. Paul, which becomes the city's headquarters for corruption and graft.

February 28, 1930 Bank robbers Thomas Holden and Francis "Jimmy" Keating, the "Evergreen bandits," escape from Leavenworth prison and hide out in Minnesota.

June 3, 1930 Thomas A. Brown, once a defendant in the Cleveland liquor syndicate case, is appointed chief of St. Paul police.

July 15, 1930 Bank of Willmar, Minnesota, is robbed by George "Machine Gun Kelly" Barnes and the Keating-Holden gang.

August 13, 1930 Three Kansas City mobsters, Sammy "Ten Dollar Kid" Silverman, Michael Rusick, and Frank "Weanie" Coleman, are slain near White Bear Lake, Minnesota.

September 17, 1930 Harvey Bailey robs $2.6 million from National Bank and Trust Company of Lincoln, Nebraska, laundering the stolen bonds in St. Paul.

May–September 1931 Jimmy Keating and Tommy Holden hide out in St. Paul during nationwide FBI manhunt.

May 2, 1931 Gangster Alvin "Creepy" Karpis is released from state penitentiary at Lansing, Kansas.

June 1, 1931 Legendary bank robber Frank "Jelly" Nash of Oklahoma moves to St. Paul with members of the Barker-Karpis gang.

August 17, 1931 Bank robber Harry "Slim Jones" Morris is found dead near Red Wing, Minnesota.

September 24, 1931 Liquor czar Leon Gleckman is kidnapped and held for ransom; he is released eight days later; his kidnappers are either imprisoned or killed.

October 20, 1931 Bank robber Charlie Harmon is slain during Keating-Holden gang's holdup of Kraft State Bank of Menomonie, Wisconsin.

October 1931–January 1932 Bank robber Bernard "Big Phil Courtney" Phillips hides in St. Paul's Merriam Park neighborhood.

December 19, 1931 Fred Barker murders Sheriff C. Roy Kelly in West Plains, Missouri, and flees to St. Paul.

January 5, 1932 Barker-Karpis gang holds town of Cambridge, Minnesota, hostage, stealing $3,000 in goods and kidnapping the town marshal.

March 7, 1932 Bodies of Margaret "Indian Rose" Perry and Sadie Carmacher are found in burned-out car near Balsam Lake, Wisconsin, just before they are to inform on Barker-Karpis gang.

March 29, 1932 Barker-Karpis gang robs the Northwestern National Bank and Trust Company in Minneapolis.

April 25, 1932 Barker-Karpis gang, tipped off by police, escapes from Hannegraf family home; body of Arthur Dunlop, companion of Katherine "Ma" Barker, is later found at Frenstad Lake in Wisconsin.

May 3, 1932 William Mahoney is elected mayor of St. Paul, promising to eliminate influence of "organized, sinister, and invisible" gangsters.

June 7, 1932 St. Paul police chief Thomas Brown is demoted to detective on suspicion of having warned Barker-Karpis gang of April raid.

June 17, 1932 Members of Barker-Karpis and Keating-Holden gangs rob the Citizens National Bank of Fort Scott, Kansas, of $47,000.

July 7, 1932 Bank robbers Jimmy Keating, Tommy Holden, and Harvey Bailey are arrested by FBI agents at a golf course in Kansas City.

July 25, 1932 Murder Inc. hit men George Young and Joey Schaefer hunt down and kill bootlegger Abe Wagner and his partner, Al Gordon, in St. Paul's Midway district.

July 26, 1932 Barker-Karpis gang robs Cloud County Bank of Concordia, Kansas, then escapes to White Bear Lake, Minnesota, to divide $240,000 in stolen bonds and cash.

August 5, 1932 New St. Paul police chief Thomas Dahill announces war against "hoodlums" and "gun-toters."

September 10, 1932 Arthur "Doc" Barker is freed from Oklahoma state prison and rejoins the Barker-Karpis gang in Minnesota.

September 23, 1932 Barker-Karpis gang robs State Bank and Trust Company of Redwood Falls, Minnesota, of $35,000.

September 30, 1932 Citizens National Bank of Wahpeton, North Dakota, is robbed of $6,900, allegedly by the Barker-Karpis gang.

November 3, 1932 Volney "Curley" Davis of Barker-Karpis gang is released from Oklahoma state prison and moves to St. Paul.

December 16, 1932 Barker-Karpis gang robs Third Northwestern National Bank of Minneapolis. Two policemen are killed; bystander Oscar Erickson is murdered by Fred Barker in St. Paul's Como Park.

December 18, 1932 Larry "the Chopper" DeVol of the Barker-Karpis gang is arrested by police in St. Paul for the December 16 bank robbery.

March 22, 1933 Volstead Act is repealed.

February–March 1933 Barker-Karpis gang hides out in Grand Avenue apartment, escaping after tip-off by St. Paul police.

April 4, 1933 Barker-Karpis gang robs First National Bank of Fairbury, Nebraska; gang member Earl Christman is mortally wounded during the getaway.

May 1933 Ma Barker moves into St. Paul's Commodore Hotel; John Dillinger is released on parole from Indiana state prison at Michigan City, Indiana.

May 28, 1933 Barker-Karpis gang members Fred Barker and Alvin Karpis move to 204 Vernon Street in St. Paul, making plans to kidnap a prominent businessman.

June 9, 1933 Bank robber Frank Nash of Oklahoma visits St. Paul for the last time.

June 15, 1933 Brewing company executive William Hamm Jr. is kidnapped by Barker-Karpis gang in St. Paul.

June 17, 1933 Bank robber Frank Nash, an FBI agent, and three police officers are killed by Verne Miller in Kansas City Massacre at Union Station.

June 19, 1933 Kidnap victim William Hamm is released near Wyoming, Minnesota, after payment of $100,000 ransom.

July 22, 1933 George "Machine Gun Kelly" Barnes kidnaps Oklahoma oilman Charles Urschel and demands $200,000; portions of ransom money are laundered through Minneapolis syndicate.

August 30, 1933 Barker-Karpis gang robs $33,000 from stockyards payroll delivered by train to South St. Paul Post Office, killing one policeman and seriously wounding another.

September 1933 Eddie Green rents Charlou Apartment suite as Minneapolis headquarters for John Dillinger's bank robbery gang.

September 4, 1933 Dillinger gang member Tommy Carroll is arrested after auto accident in St. Paul; police release Carroll, despite finding a loaded revolver in his car.

October 23, 1933 First National Bank of Brainerd, Minnesota, is robbed of $32,000 by a group believed to include Babyface Nelson, Tommy Carroll, and other members of the Dillinger gang.

November 9–28, 1933 Roger "the Terrible" Touhy and associates are tried in St. Paul for William Hamm kidnapping; they are acquitted of all the charges.

November 29, 1933 Verne Miller, hunted by both the FBI and organized crime figures for the Kansas City Massacre, is found murdered in Detroit.

December 7, 1933 Fred Barker of the Barker-Karpis gang moves to St. Paul's Grand Avenue to plan next kidnapping.

January 13, 1934 Northwest Airlines employee Roy McCord, wearing his radio operator's uniform, is mistaken for a policeman and shot by the Barker-Karpis gang in St. Paul.

January 17, 1934 Barker-Karpis gang kidnaps banker Edward Bremer in St. Paul; Bremer is released February 7 near Rochester, Minnesota, after payment of the $200,000 ransom.

March 4, 1934 Lester "Babyface Nelson" Gillis murders an innocent motorist, Theodore Kidder, in St. Louis Park, a Minneapolis suburb.

March 5, 1934 John Dillinger, with girlfriend Evelyn Frechette, moves to Minneapolis after escaping from jail in Crown Point, Indiana.

March 6, 1934 Dillinger robs Sioux Falls, South Dakota, bank of $49,500, leaving one policeman dead, and returns to Minneapolis.

March 13, 1934 Dillinger gang robs First National Bank of Mason City, Iowa, of $52,000, then flees to Minneapolis. Dillinger and John Hamilton seek medical care from Dr. Nels Mortensen of St. Paul.

March 19, 1934 Dillinger moves into Lincoln Court Apartments in St. Paul to recuperate from gunshot wounds suffered during the Mason City, Iowa, bank robbery.

March 20, 1934 Fred "Shotgun George Ziegler" Goetz of Al Capone's syndicate, a key participant in the Bremer kidnapping, is shot to death in Cicero, Illinois.

March 31, 1934 John Dillinger and Homer Van Meter evade capture by FBI and St. Paul police during a shootout at the Lincoln Court Apartments; Dillinger takes shelter at the Minneapolis clinic of Dr. Clayton May.

April 3, 1934 Dillinger gang member Eddie Green is mortally wounded by FBI agents in St. Paul; he dies April 11.

April 23–24, 1934 Dillinger gang escapes from FBI raid at resort in Little

Bohemia, Wisconsin, killing one agent; Dillinger evades police roadblock in Hastings, Minnesota, but John Hamilton is mortally wounded by police fire.

May 1934 Investigator Wallace Jamie arrives in St. Paul to explore police corruption at the invitation of the *St. Paul Daily News*; he installs telephone taps in police offices.

June 7, 1934 Dillinger gang member Tommy Carroll is killed by police detectives near Waterloo, Iowa.

July 22, 1934 Dillinger is shot to death by FBI agents outside Chicago's Biograph Theater.

August 23, 1934 Dillinger gang member Homer Van Meter is shot to death in a police ambush in St. Paul.

September 5, 1934 Three girlfriends of Barker-Karpis gang members, including Fred Barker's lover, Paula Harmon, are arrested by police in Cleveland, Ohio.

November 27, 1934 Babyface Nelson is shot to death by FBI agents near Fox River Grove, Illinois.

January 8, 1935 Doc Barker is captured by FBI agents in his Chicago apartment and taken to St. Paul for kidnapping trial.

January 16, 1935 Fred and Ma Barker are killed in a gun battle with the FBI at Lake Weir, Florida.

May 17, 1935 Doc Barker and four other gang members are convicted in St. Paul federal court of the kidnapping of Edward Bremer; Barker is incarcerated at Leavenworth prison.

June 7, 1935 Volney Davis and four others are convicted in St. Paul federal court of the kidnapping of Edward Bremer, receiving sentences ranging from five years to life.

August 28, 1935 Body of Dillinger gang member John Hamilton is discovered by the FBI in Oswego, Illinois.

January 24, 1936 Underworld fixer Harry Sawyer and William Weaver are convicted in St. Paul federal court of kidnapping Edward Bremer.

May 1, 1936 Alvin Karpis is arrested in New Orleans and brought by J. Edgar Hoover to St. Paul in chains for trial.

June 8, 1936 Larry DeVol of the Barker-Karpis gang escapes from the prison hospital at St. Peter, Minnesota, and is shot to death by police in Enid, Oklahoma, on July 8.

July 31, 1936 Fixer Jack Peifer commits suicide in St. Paul's Ramsey County jail after being convicted of participating in the William Hamm kidnapping.

October 9, 1936 Former St. Paul police chief Thomas Brown is permanently removed from the force after evidence of his corruption and contact with the Barker-Karpis gang is released.

SOURCES

Stacked on shelves in the J. Edgar Hoover Building's reading room in Washington, D.C., are the documents that form the core of *John Dillinger Slept Here*—the FBI's voluminous files on Hoover's crusade against gangsters in the 1930s.

The FBI files on the Barker-Karpis gang (76,159 pages), Alvin "Creepy" Karpis (2,360 pages), Charles "Pretty Boy" Floyd, Frank Nash, and the Kansas City Massacre (15,786 pages), and John Dillinger and his gang (36,795 pages) are of special value to historians. In addition, the FBI's Crime Conditions files, covering 1930s underworld activity in Minneapolis and St. Paul, proved helpful. The verbatim transcripts of FBI interviews (1934–1936) with girlfriends of Barker-Karpis and Dillinger gang members were particularly useful, as were interviews with eyewitnesses and, in some cases, the gangsters themselves.

U.S. Prohibition Bureau, Treasury Department/Internal Revenue Service, U.S. Post Office, U.S. Attorneys Office, and other federal records stored in the National Archives in Washington, D.C., helped reconstruct the Leon Gleckman, Dan Hogan, Frank Nash/Kansas City Massacre, and Cleveland Syndicate cases.

Notes from the author's interviews and photocopies of documents from the FBI, the National Archives, and many other sources that were used in researching this work are held in the Paul Maccabee St. Paul Gangster History Research Collection at the Minnesota Historical Society (MHS), St. Paul.

GOVERNMENT PAPERS AND REPORTS

Federal

Department of Justice. Bureau of Prisons. Escaped Prisoners file, 1932–33. RG 129, National Archives, Washington, D. C.

———.Bureau of Prisons. Inmate Records. Inmate Locator Service, Department of Justice, Washington, D.C.

———. Bureau of Prohibition. Records, 1920–1933. RG 60, National Archives, Washington, D. C.

———. Federal Bureau of Investigation. Bremer Kidnap files, 1934–84; Dillinger files, 1934, 1954; Hamm Kidnap files, 1933–64; Kansas City Massacre files, 1933–34. Freedom of Information Act Reading Room, FBI Headquarters, Washington, D.C.

———. Federal Bureau of Investigation. Crime Conditions files, 1934–45; Leon Gleckman files. Paul Maccabee St. Paul Gangster History Research Collection, MHS.

———. Mail and Files Division. Postal Service Investigation Records, 1921–35. RG 60, National Archives, Washington, D. C.

National Commission on Law Observance and Enforcement. *Enforcement of the Prohibition Laws.* 71st Cong., 3d sess. Washington, D.C.: Government Printing Office, 1931.

U.S. District Court, Third Division. *U.S.A. v. Clayton E. May, Evelyn Frechette et al.*, 1934. MHS.

U.S. District Court, Third Division. *U.S.A. v. Albert (Pat) Reilly*, 1934.

U.S. District Court, Third Division. *U.S.A. v. Alvin Karpavicz*, 1935.

State

Michigan Department of Health. Death Certificates.

Minnesota Bureau of Criminal Apprehension. Homicide and Investigation files, 1930–36.

Minnesota Bureau of Prisons. Stillwater State Prison Inmate files. MHS.

Minnesota Manuscript Census Schedules, St. Paul, 1895, 1905.

Minnesota Department of Health. Death Certificates.

South Dakota, State Penitentiary. Prison Inmate files. South Dakota State Archives.

Wisconsin Department of Health and Social Services. Death Certificates.

Local

Detroit Police Department. Homicide files.

Hennepin County, Minnesota. Probate records.

Lancaster County, Nebraska. Probate records.

Minneapolis Police Department. Homicide files.
Philadelphia Police Department. Organized Crime Intelligence files.
Ramsey County, Minnesota. Minnesota Medical Examiner's records.
Ramsey County, Minnesota. Probate records.
Ramsey County, Minnesota, District Court. Indictment records.
Ramsey County, Minnesota, District Court. *State of Minnesota v. James Crumley et al.*, 1935. MHS.
St. Paul City Water Department. Sewer maps.
St. Paul Police Department. Homicide and accident files.

NEWSPAPERS

Brainerd Daily Dispatch, Oct. 1933.
Brainerd Journal Press, Oct. 1933.
Hastings Gazette, Apr. 1934.
Minneapolis Journal, 1919–40.
Minneapolis Tribune, 1919–60.
St. Paul Daily News, 1929–39.
St. Paul Dispatch, 1914–93 (merged with *Pioneer Press* in 1985).
St. Paul Pioneer Press, 1919–93 (merged with *Dispatch* in 1985).
St. Paul Pioneer Press-Dispatch morgue file, 1914– . St. Paul Public Library.
South St. Paul Daily Reporter, Aug.–Sept. 1933.
Willmar Tribune, July 1930.

SPEECHES AND MEMOIRS

Hoover, J. Edgar. "Patriotism and the War Against Crime." Speech before the Daughters of the American Revolution, Apr. 23, 1936. Washington, D.C.: Government Printing Office, 1936 (SUDOC J1.14/2:P27).
Minnesota Bankers Association. Speeches at the 44th Annual Convention, June 13–14, 1933, Minneapolis.
Pranke, Richard N. "Autobiography of Richard N. Pranke." Pranke Family Records, MHS.
Rohlfing, Althea. Speech at the Mahtomedi Club, Mar. 1984, copy in author's possession.

PRIMARY INTERVIEWS (partial list)

Interviews are by the author unless otherwise noted.

Bailey, Harvey. Interviews by J. Evetts Haley, Oct. 31, 1965, May 16, 1966, Sept. 18, 1966, and May 23, 1967. Nita Stewart Haley Memorial Library, Midland, Texas.
Barnes, Bruce. Jan. 11, 1994.
Benz, Louise. Oct. 30, 1992.
Bergaus, Mercia. May 1993.
Boardsen, Dirk. Sept. 5, 1992.
Bomberg, Nate. Interview by Ms. Cherry, ca. 1975. Ramsey County Historical Society, St. Paul.
Bowser, John. May 5, 1989, May 19, 1989.
Bremer, Donna. Dec. 29, 1993.
Brigham, Christine. N.d.
Bullert, Bernie. Dec. 17, 1993.
Cardozo, Ted. Dec. 29, 1993.
Charlton, Mary. Jan. 23, 1993, May 15, 1993.
Coleman, Jim. Apr. 24, 1992.
Comstock, Paul G. Sept. 4, 1992, Sept. 6, 1992.
Comstock, Virginia. Sept. 21, 1992.
Cravath, Calvert. June 1991, Aug. 7, 1991.
Delaney, Thomas. May 9, 1992.
DeMoss, Carole. Dec. 16, 1993.
Deyo, Evelyn M. May 1993.
DuPont, Horace. Oct. 31, 1992, Jan. 7, 1994.
Ehrlich, Max. Oct. 30, 1992.
Eue, Donna. Apr. 15, 1993.
Fahey, Ted. July 19, 1991.
Fenn, Ralph. N.d.
Figge, William. Jan. 6, 1994.
Filben, Bill. June 13, 1992.
Fish, Donald. Jan. 23, 1993.
Fleigel, Robert. Dec. 10, 1991.
Geisenheyner, Bob. N.d.
Gibson, Janet. Aug. 27, 1993.
Gibson, Michael. Apr. 9, 1993.
Gillespie, Eben. Jan. 15, 1992, Jan. 6, 1994.
Graves, Mary. May 28, 1992, Jan. 22, 1994.
Grooms, Albert. June 18, 1993.
Grossman, Bernice. May 30, 1992.
Guarnera, Marge. Apr. 1993.
Hamilton, Bruce. Dec. 17, 1993.
Hannegraf, Nick Jr. Dec. 19, 1991.
Harrington, Gladys. June 1993.
Heaberlin, Fred. Jan. 6, 1994.
Herschler, Kenneth. May 21, 1993.
Hesse, Howard. Interview by Tim Albright, Mar. 27, 1992.
Hiebert, Gareth. Dec. 3, 1993.
Holsapple, Janice. Apr. 9, 1993.
Hornig, David. N.d.

Horton, Norman Sr. May 15, 1991.
Hurley, George Jr. June 11, 1994.
Hurley, Harold. Aug. 27, 1993, June 10, 1994.
Jamie, Louise. Mar. 12, 1992.
Johnson, Betty Bremer. Jan. 27, 1992.
Johnson, Marien. Dec. 19, 1991, May 30, 1992.
Johnson, Mary. May 12, 1993.
Johnson, Walter "Buster." N.d.
Junterman, Marguerite. Aug. 8, 1993.
Keljik, Woody. Jan. 22, 1993.
Kohrt, Bonnie. Jan. 1993.
Koontz, Hope Healy. Dec. 3, 1993.
Knox, Jep. Dec. 3, 1993.
Knutson, John. Mar. 1993.
Lannon, Pat Sr. May 13, 1993, June 14, 1993, Aug. 27, 1993.
Lehman, Jim. N.d.
Lindholm, Clifford Allen. Dec. 1992.
McBride, Irene. N.d.
McCalla, Colleen. July 9, 1993.
Macey, John W. Jan. 3, 1992.
McCord, Roy Norman Jr. Dec. 23, 1992.
McGree, Aloysius. Apr. 11, 1992.
McLaughlin, J. T. N.d.
McLean, Ellie (Halberg). Apr. 15, 1993.
McMahon, Marie. Mar. 1993.
McNamara, Sally. Apr. 30, 1993.
Magine, Julio. July 1993.
Mattlin, Carroll. May 21, 1992.
Merrick, Gordon L. Dec. 11, 1992.
Merrill, Ralph. Oct. 10, 1990.
Michaud, Ann. Nov. 20, 1993.
Miller, Fred Jr. May 14, 1993.
Morgan, David J. June 8, 1993.
Murphy, Lorretta. Interview by relative, Apr. 1985. In the posession of Jim Vogel, Anoka, Minnesota.
Nemerov, Irving. May 17, 1991.
O'Connor, Joseph. Feb. 26, 1991.
Opsahl, Ross. N.d.
Orth, Earl. Mar. 14, 1993.
Patch, Earl A. July 20, 1993.
Paul, Francis MacLaren. April 13, 1993.
Pavlak, Robert. Feb. 6, 1993.
Peters, Vera. Mar. 27, 1993.
Phillips, Vern. Apr. 30, 1993.
Pranke, Richard N. Mar. 23, 1985, Oct. 23, 1992.
Preston, Jean. June 6, 1992.
Purcell, Tom. Apr. 1992.
Ramaley, Jack. May 22, 1992.
Rautenberg, Bunny. May 14, 1993.
Reiter, Charlie. May 2, 1991, Sept. 24, 1993, Oct. 12, 1993, Sept. 1, 1994.
Resler, Jane. Sept. 9, 1994.
Rohlfing, Althea. Apr. 16, 1993.
Rohling, Martin. June 16, 1991, May 22, 1992.
Roy, Elizabeth. Dec. 17, 1994.
Scarlett, Vicenta Donnelly. May 14, 1994.
Schroth, Louis. Apr. 2, 1993.
Schude, Blanche Carter. May 5, 1992.
Schwietz, Robert. Dec. 30, 1992.
Schwietz, Virginia Gibbons. Dec. 30, 1992.
Senesac, Peggy. Nov. 20, 1992.
Seng, Robert J. and Barbara. Sept. 24, 1993, Oct. 30, 1993.
Sherin, Joe. 1992.
Sinykin, Beverly. Apr. 12, 1992.
Smith, Zane. Apr. 1993.
Thomas, James. July 16, 1993, Jan. 14, 1994.
Tic, Bernice. Feb. 1994.
Tiemann, Tony. Nov. 20, 1992.
Troupe, "Shy." Nov. 3, 1993.
Tuttle, Steve. Jan. 30, 1993.
Vogel, Jim. Mar. 1993.
Vogel, John. May 14, 1993.
Vogelgesang, Anita. May 5, 1992.
Walsh, William. Jan. 6, 1995.
Wybest, Robert H. Oct. 10, 1993.
Yeaman, Jack. Aug. 24, 1993.

AUDIO AND VIDEO SOURCES

Brede, Neil. "St. Paul Gangster Days." Video documentary. First broadcast on public access television, St. Paul, 1987.
Heistad, Mark. "A Story of Crime, Criminals, and Corruption." Minnesota Public Radio. Broadcast Nov. 8, 1985.
"John Dillinger." *Biography.* Arts and Entertainment Channel. Broadcast April 4, 1995.

BOOKS

Barnes, Bruce. *Machine Gun Kelly: To Right a Wrong.* Perris, Calif: Tipper Publications, 1991.
Bergreen, Laurence. *Capone: The Man and the Era.* New York: Simon and Schuster, 1994.
Callahan, Clyde C. and Byron B. Jones. *Heritage of an Outlaw: The Story of Frank Nash.* Hobart, Okla.: Schoonmaker Publishers, 1979.

Cooper, Courtney Ryley. *Here's to Crime.* Boston: Little, Brown and Company, 1937.
———. *Ten Thousand Public Enemies.* Foreword by J. Edgar Hoover. Boston: Little, Brown and Company, 1935.
Cromie, Robert and Joseph Pinkston. *Dillinger: A Short and Violent Life.* Evanston, Ill.: Chicago Historical Bookworks, 1990; reprint of 1962.
Edge, L. L. *Run the Cat Roads: True Story of Bank Robbers in the 30s.* New York: Dembner Books, 1981.
Empson, Donald. *On the Street Where You Live.* St. Paul: Witsend Press, 1975.
Enright, Richard T. with Ray Cowdery. *Capone's Chicago.* Lakeville, Minn.: Northstar-Maschek Books, 1987.
Fenwick, A. R., ed. *Sturdy Sons of Saint Paul.* St. Paul: Junior Pioneer Association, n.d. [1899].
Fish, Donald E. *The Dillinger Connection: What Part Did John Dillinger Play in the Brainerd Bank Robbery?* St. Paul: Bywords Printing, 1986.
Flanagan, John T. *Theodore Hamm in Minnesota: His Family and Brewery.* St. Paul: Pogo Press, 1989.
Fox, Stephen R. *Blood and Power: Organized Crime in Twentieth-Century America.* New York: William Morrow, 1989.
Gentry, Curt. *J. Edgar Hoover: The Man and the Secrets.* New York: Norton, 1991.
Girardin, G. Russell, with William J. Helmer. *Dillinger: The Untold Story.* Bloomington: Indiana University Press, 1994.
Guilford, H[oward]. A. *Holies of Holies of the White Slave Worshipper.* [St. Paul,] Minn.: By the author, n.d. [ca. 1915].
———. *A Tale of Two Cities: Memoirs of 16 Years Behind a Pencil.* Robbinsdale, Minn.: By the author, 1929.
Haley, J. Evetts. *Robbing Banks Was My Business: The Story of J. Harvey Bailey.* Canyon, Texas: Palo Duro Press, 1973.
Hollatz, Tom. *Gangster Holidays: The Lore and Legends of the Bad Guys.* St. Cloud, Minn.: North Star Press, 1989.
Hoover, J. Edgar. *Persons in Hiding.* Boston: Little, Brown and Company, 1938.
Jennings, Dean. *We Only Kill Each Other: The Life and Bad Times of Bugsy Siegel.* Englewood Cliffs, N.J.: Prentice-Hall, 1967.
Karpis, Alvin, with Bill Trent. *The Alvin Karpis Story.* New York: Coward, McCann and Geoghegan, 1971.
Koblas, John J. *F. Scott Fitzgerald in Minnesota: His Homes and Haunts.* St. Paul: Minnesota Historical Society Press, 1978.
Kobler, John. *Capone: The Life and World of Al Capone.* New York: G. P. Putnam and Sons, 1971.
Koeper, H. F. *Historic St. Paul Buildings.* St. Paul: St. Paul City Planning Commission, 1964.
Kunz, Virginia Brainerd. *Saint Paul: The First 150 Years.* St. Paul: St. Paul Foundation, 1991.
———. *The Mississippi and St. Paul: A Short History of the City's 150-year Love Affair with Its River.* St. Paul: Ramsey County Historical Society, 1987.
Lacey, Robert. *Little Man: Meyer Lansky and the Gangster Life.* Boston: Little, Brown and Company, 1991.
Michels, Eileen, with Nate Bomberg. *A Landmark Reclaimed.* St. Paul: Minnesota Landmarks, 1977.
Millet, Larry. *Lost Twin Cities.* St. Paul: Minnesota Historical Society Press, 1992.
Nash, Jay Robert. *Almanac of World Crime.* Garden City, N.Y.: Anchor Press/Doubleday, 1981.
———. *Bloodletters and Badmen: A Narrative Encyclopedia of American Criminals from the Pilgrims to the Present.* New York: M. Evans and Company, 1973.
———. *The Dillinger Dossier.* Highland Park, Ill.: December Press, 1983.
Perkins, A. H. S. *All About White Bear Lake: Minnesota's Popular Summer Resort.* White Bear Lake, Minn.: n.p., 1890.
Powers, Richard G. *Secrecy and Power: The Life of J. Edgar Hoover.* New York: Free Press, 1987.
Purvis, Melvin. *American Agent.* Garden City, N.Y.: Doubleday, Doran and Company, 1936.
Schoenburg, Robert J. *Mr. Capone.* New York: William Morrow and Company, 1992.
Sevareid, Paul A. *The People's Lawyer: The Life of Eugene A. Rerat.* Minneapolis: Ross and Haines, 1963.

Sifakis, Carl. *The Mafia Encyclopedia.* New York: Facts on File, 1987.

Smith, Alice R., Sharon F. Wright, and Judy Kaiser. *Mahtomedi Memories.* [Mahtomedi?]: n.p., 1976.

Spiering, Frank. *The Man Who Got Capone.* Indianapolis: Bobbs-Merrill Company, 1976.

Summers, Anthony. *Official and Confidential: The Secret Life of J. Edgar Hoover.* New York: G. P. Putnam's Sons, 1993.

Thayer, Steve. *Saint Mudd: A Novel of Gangsters and Saints.* St. Paul: Birchwood Page Publishing, 1988.

Theoharis, Athan G. and John Stuart Cox. *The Boss: J. Edgar Hoover and the Great American Inquisition.* Philadelphia: Temple University Press, 1988.

Toland, John. *Dillinger Days.* New York: Random House, 1963.

Touhy, Roger and Ray Brennan. *The Stolen Years.* Cleveland: Pennington Press, 1959.

Turkus, Burton B. and Sid Feder. *Murder Inc.: The Story of "the Syndicate".* New York: Farrar, Straus and Young, 1951.

Turner, William W. *Hoover's FBI: The Men and the Myth.* New York: Dell Publishing Co., 1971; reprint of 1970.

Wallis, Michael. *Pretty Boy: The Life and Times of Charles Arthur Floyd.* New York: St. Martin's Press, 1992.

Weir, William. *Written with Lead: Legendary American Gunfights and Gunfighters.* Hamden, Conn.: Archon Books, 1992.

Wing, Frank. *Brewers Handbook of the U.S. and Canada.* New York: J. M. Wing Co., 1887.

Woolworth, Nancy L. *The White Bear Lake Story.* White Bear Lake, Minn.: White Bear Avenue Chamber of Commerce, 1968.

ARTICLES

Allenspach, Kevin. "It Was No Gangster Movie." *Brainerd Daily Dispatch,* Dec. 4, 1988, p. 1C.

Baker, Robert Orr. "The Minnesota Club: St. Paul's Enterprising Leaders and Their 'Gentlemen's Social Club.'" *Ramsey County History* 19, no. 2 (1984–85): 3–21.

Bellville, Lance. "Nina." *Minnesota Monthly,* October 1981, p. 15–17.

Best, Joel E. "Long Kate, Dutch Henriette and Mother Robinson: Three Madames in Post-Civil War St. Paul." *Ramsey County History* 15, no. 2 (1979–80): 3–10.

Bomberg, Nate. "The Day Karpis Returned." *Capital: St. Paul Pioneer Press and Dispatch Sunday Magazine,* Mar. 28, 1971, p. 6, 10.

Brueggemann, Gary J. "Beer Capital of the State—St. Paul's Historic Family Breweries." *Ramsey County History* 16, no. 2 (1980–81): 3–15.

Clark, Bernice. "My Adventures with the Dillinger Gang." *Chicago Herald and Examiner,* Sept. 10, 1934.

Dahill, Thomas E. and J. O. Myers. "When St. Paul Silenced New Jersey's Hired Guns." *Startling Detective Adventures* 10, no. 60 (July 1933): 40–43, 54.

"The Dillinger Man-Hunt." *True Detective,* July 1934, p. 65–66.

Ernst, Robert R. "The Last Days of Lawrence DeVol." *OklahombreS,* Winter 1991, p. 10–12.

Ex-Operative 48. "Sterilization: Preston Paden, Whelp of a Gun Moll," *Official Detective Stories,* Apr. 1, 1937.

Ferris, Joseph A. "How Barton 'The Chopper' Was Captured." *True Detective Mysteries* 20, no. 4 (July 1933): 20–25, 104–107.

Frechette, Evelyn. "Evelyn Tells Life with Dillinger." *Chicago Herald and Examiner,* Aug. 28, 29, 1934.

———. "What I Knew About Dillinger." *Chicago Herald and Examiner,* Aug. 30, 31, 1934.

"Gangsters: An Interview with Will Greer." *Scattered Seeds* (Central High School, St. Paul) 8 (1976): 2–9.

Hale, Avery, "The Inside Story of Dillinger at Last." *True Detective Mysteries* Dec. 1934, p. 6–13, 86–89; and Jan. 1935, p. 4, 54–57, 112–116, 118.

High, Stanley. "St. Paul Wins a War." *Current History* 49, no. 1 (1938): 18–20.

Kahlstrom, Jonathan. "Renovating the First National Bank Building." *Minnesota Real Estate Journal,* Dec. 23, 1991 (supplement), p. 2.

Karpis, Alvin. "Karpis Recalls St. Paul." *Capital: St. Paul Pioneer Press and Dispatch Sunday Magazine,* Mar. 27, 1971, p. 4–6, 9.

Liggett, Walter W. "Minneapolis and Vice in Volsteadland." *Plain Talk,* Apr. 1930, p. 385–399.

McDade, Thomas M. "Karpis Recalls His Crime Spree of the 1930s in Talks with McDade." *Grapevine,* May 1980, p. 36–38.

Nash, Alanna. "Memories of John Dillinger." *Chicago Reader,* July 20, 1984, p. 9, 32–38.

Negri, "Fatso," with Bennett Williams. "In the Hinges of Hell: How G-Men Ended Crime's Reddest Chapter." *True Detective Mysteries,* Dec. 1940, p. 14–19, 90–91; Jan. 1941, p. 16–19, 108–10; Feb. 1941, p. 30–32, 112–15; Mar. 1941, p. 66–69, 87–89; Apr. 1941, p. 30–32, 114–16; May 1941, p. 30–32, 102–105; July 1941, p. 30–32, 104–107; Aug. 1941, p. 30–32, 74–76.

Nienaber, Craig. "Gangsterland in the '30s." *Hennepin County History* 36, no. 4 (Winter 1977–78): 3–9; and 37, no. 1 (Spring 1978): 15–19.

Opsahl, Ross. "South St. Paul, Minnesota, Machine Gun Raid," *Thompson Collectors News* 10 (Aug. 15, 1991); and 12 (Oct. 15, 1991).

Pegler, Westbrook. "Fair Enough." *New York World-Telegram,* Feb. 19, 1934.

Pfleger, Helen Warren, as told to George A. Rea. "Volstead and Prohibition: A Roaring '20's Memoir." *Ramsey County History* 12, no. 1 (Spring–Summer 1975): 19–22.

Powner, John. "On the Scarlet Trail of the Twin City Terrorists." *Startling Detective Adventures,* July 1935, p. 28–35, 71–75.

Price, Mollie. "Swede Hollow: Sheltered Society for Immigrants to St. Paul." *Ramsey County History* 17, no. 2 (1981–82): 12–22.

"Rufus C. Coulter." *Grapevine,* Nov. 1975, p. 28.

Russell, John M. "Scenes from Yesteryear," *Dunn County News* (Menomonie, Wis.), Apr. 25, 1985.

Snider, John. "The Great Denver Mint Robbery." *Denver Post,* Aug. 18, 23, and 30, 1959.

Trohan, Walter. "J. Edgar Hoover, the One-Man Scotland Yard." *Chicago Tribune,* June 21, 1936, pt. 7, p. 1, 8, 11.

Yandle, Jim. "The Bloody End to Ma Barker's Crime Spree." *Orlando Sentinel,* Jan. 19, 1988, p. 4.

NOTES

Abbreviations:

BCA Bureau of Criminal Apprehension (Minnesota)
FBI Federal Bureau of Investigation (includes Bureau of Investigation, U.S. Bureau of Investigation, and Division of Investigation)
MHS Minnesota Historical Society
NARG National Archives Record Group
SPPD St. Paul Police Department

Many FBI documents are held in the FBI's Freedom of Information Act Reading Room in named file sets. The abbreviations listed below stand for the name of the set and the prefix that is common to all documents in the set. Most documents also have file numbers; many have both file and section numbers. Citations in the notes below use the given abbreviation for file set and prefix, as well as any file and section numbers available.

BKF Bremer Kidnap file 7–576–
CCF Crime Conditions file 62–30930–
DF Dillinger file 62–29777–
HKF Hamm Kidnap file 7–77–
KCMF Kansas City Massacre file 62–28915–

Notes from the author's interviews and photocopies of documents from the FBI, the National Archives, and many other sources that were used in researching this work are held in the Paul Maccabee St. Paul Gangster History Research Collection, MHS.

The *St. Paul Pioneer Press* and the *St. Paul Dispatch* are cited as *Pioneer Press* and *Dispatch* respectively.

Notes for Preface

1. Alvin Karpis with Bill Trent, *The Alvin Karpis Story* (New York: Coward, McCann, and Geoghegan, 1971), 100.

2. Avery Hale, "The Inside Story of Dillinger at Last," *True Detective Mysteries*, Dec. 1934, p. 9.

3. Anthony Summers, *Official and Confidential: The Secret Life of J. Edgar Hoover* (New York: G. P. Putnam's Sons, 1993), 43–44, 65–66, 225–34; Curt Gentry, *J. Edgar Hoover: The Man and the Secrets* (New York: Norton, 1991), 327–32.

4. Errol Stuart, Chicago police records officer, and Dennis Bingham, Chicago police executive, interviews by author, July 22, 1994.

5. Johnny "Dollar" Douthit, BCA agent, interview by author, May 14, 1993; Marcia Cummings, BCA staff member, interview by author, Feb. 1991.

6. Federal Bureau of Prisons archivist, to author, Anne Diestel, July 25, 1994; Mike Robar, Federal Bureau of Prisons staff member, interview by author, n.d.

Notes for Chapter 1

1. William Schader, deputy fire inspector, Division of Fire Prevention report, Dec. 4, 1928, Re: Danny Hogan, SPPD.

2. *Dispatch*, Dec. 6, 1928, p. 1; *Minneapolis Morning Tribune*, Dec. 7, 1928, p. 1.

3. Danny Hogan homicide report, Dec. 11, 1928, p. 1, SPPD. See also, Daniel Hogan death certificate, no. 2881, Dec. 5, 1928, City of St. Paul.

4. Daniel Hogan, San Quentin Prison record, California State Archives, Sacramento; FBI memo, May 31, 1927, p. 7, file 48–39–10, NARG 60.

5. Special assistant to Attorney General Pratt, to Assistant Attorney General Luhring, Justice Dept. memo, May 4, 1927, p. 3–4, 7–8, file 48–39–10, NARG 60.

6. Mark Heisted, "A Story of Crime, Criminals, and Corruption," Minnesota Public Radio documentary, Nov. 8, 1985.

7. Max F. Burger, FBI report, June 25, 1926, p. 9, FBI file 62–11743–13, file 48–39–10, NARG 60.

8. Here and preceding paragraph, see Burger report, June 25, 1926, file 48–39–10, NARG 60.

9. Office of the Inspector, Post Office Dept. memo, July 8, 1926, file 48–39–10, NARG 60.

10. John Pratt to Assistant Attorney General Lurhing, Justice Dept. memo, May 4, 1927, p. 18, file 48–39–10, NARG 60.

11. L. L. Edge, *Run the Cat Roads: The True Story of Bank Robbers in the 30s* (New York: Dembner Books, 1981), 35; J. Evetts Haley, *Robbing Banks Was My Business: The Story of J. Harvey Bailey, America's Most Successful Bank Robber* (Canyon, Tex.: Palo Duro Press, 1973), 48–50.

12. L. B. Reed, FBI report, May 31, 1927, p. 4, FBI file 62–14440–4, file 48–39–10, NARG 60; John Snider, "The Great Denver Mint Robbery," *Denver Post,* Aug. 18, 23, 30, 1959, quoted in Haley, *Robbing Banks,* 39; Dow Helmars, "The Denver Mint Robbery, 1927," *Denver Post Empire,* Dec. 7, 1975.

13. Edge, *Run the Cat Roads,* 37; Haley, *Robbing Banks,* 47 (quote), 48, 63–65; Reed report, May 31, 1927, p. 4, file 48–39–10, NARG 60.

14. Harvey Bailey, interview by J. Evetts Haley, Oct. 31, 1965, p. 7, 16–17, and Sept. 18, 1966, p. 4, J. Evetts Haley Collection, Nita Haley Library, Midland, Tex. (cited hereafter as Haley Collection); Haley, *Robbing Banks,* 50–51.

15. Pratt to Luhring memo, May 4, 1927, p. 4–5, file 48–39–10, NARG 60.

16. "Application for Reducing Hogan Bond is Denied," newspaper clipping dated Jan. 29, 1929, *St. Paul Pioneer Press* morgue file, St. Paul Public Library; *Minneapolis Morning Tribune,* Feb. 2, 1927, p. 2; *Dispatch,* July 5, 1927, p. 1.

17. Reed report, May 31, 1927, p. 1, 3, file 48–39–10, NARG 60.

18. E. L. Dole, FBI memos, Jan. 4, 1928, July 20, 1927, p. 12, file 48–39–10, NARG 60; FBI report, Apr. 7, 1928, FBI file 62–14440–21, file 48–39–10, NARG 60; John L. Talty, Statement to St. Paul Police, July 8, 1927, Ann Grenville and Teddy DuBois homicide file, SPPD.

19. Luhring to attorney general, Justice Dept. memo, July 12, 1926, p. 1–2, file 48–39–10–2, and Pratt to Luhring memo, May 4, 1927, p. 18, file 48–39–10, both NARG 60.

20. Ann Michaud, interview by author, Nov. 20, 1993.

21. *Minneapolis Journal,* Dec. 5, 1928, p. 1, 4; Michaud interview, Dec. 7, 1993.

22. *Pioneer Press,* Dec. 5, 1928, p. 1.

23. Special agent ____, St. Paul, to Werner Hanni, FBI memo, Feb. 19, 1934, p. 2, CCF 16, vol. 1. See also Nate Bomberg, interview transcript, Council of Arts and Sciences, Ramsey County Historical Society, St. Paul.

24. "Gangsters: An Interview with Will Greer," *Scattered Seeds* (Central High School, St. Paul) 8 (1976): 3–4.

25. *St. Paul City Directory, 1915,* 89; Maurice E. Doran, *History of the St. Paul Police Department* (St. Paul: Police Benevolent Society, 1912), viii, 29, 37, 45–50; A. R. Fenwick, *Sturdy Sons of St. Paul* (St. Paul: Junior Pioneer Association, 1899), 142–43; *St. Paul Daily News,* Jan. 17, 1922, p. 1.

26. *St. Paul Daily News,* July 4, 1924, p. 2; *Souvenir Book of the St. Paul Police Department* (St. Paul: Perkins-Thomas Printing Co., 1904), p. 3.

27. George C. Rogers, "Life of Dick O'Connor (Chapter 2)," *St. Paul Daily News,* Jan. 10, 1933, p. 1.

28. *Dispatch,* Mar. 21, 1913, p. 1; William H. Griffin death certificate, Mar. 20, 1913, Minnesota Department of Health; Ramsey County, William H. Griffin probate file, no. 20903, St. Paul City Hall; *St. Paul City Directory, 1912,* 727.

29. Paul Light (pseud. Howard Kahn), "So What," *Pioneer Press,* Sept. 7, 1943.

30. *Pioneer Press,* Nov. 27, 1912, p. 1.

31. "Long Career of Famous Sleuth Closes on Coast," newspaper clipping [ca. July 1924], *St. Paul Pioneer Press* morgue files; *Minneapolis Journal,* July 4, 1924, p. 1.

32. David J. Morgan, interview by author, June 8, 1993.

33. *Pioneer Press,* Feb. 24, 1910, p. 1 (dice), Dec. 14, 1916, p. 1 (haven); *Dispatch,* Mar. 3, 1910, p. 1 (liquor).

34. Westbrook Pegler, "Fair Enough," *New York World-Telegram,* Feb. 19, 1934; J. Edgar Hoover to Mr. Clegg, FBI memo, Feb. 28, 1934, CCF 26, vol. 1.

35. Heisted, "A Story of Crime."

36. Morgan interview, June 8, 1993.

37. *Pioneer Press*, July 5, 1924, p. 6.

38. *Pioneer Press*, May 21, 1922, p. 1; Luhring memo, July 12, 1926, p. 8, file 48–39–10–2, NARG 60. See also *Dispatch*, Dec. 15, 1923, p. 1; "Sommer Sketch," unpublished notes from *Pioneer Press* newspaper morgue file.

39. *Pioneer Press*, Dec. 5, 1928, p. 10.

40. Fred Heaberlin, interview by author, Jan. 6, 1994.

41. Pat Lannon Sr., interviews by author, June 14, Aug. 27, 1993.

42. Hanna Steinbracker [sic] death certificate, no. 10485, July 14, 1929, Wayne County (Detroit, Mich.); U.S. Manuscript Census Schedules, 1900, 1920, Precinct 1, St. Paul; Minnesota Manuscript Census Schedule, 1895, 1905, St. Paul, Precinct 1, Ward 4; Map of Mt. Elliott Cemetery Plots, lot 266N.

43. *St. Paul City Directories, 1889–1929;* St. Paul, "Detailed Statement of Specifications for New Buildings, 147 Washington Street South, June 9, 1888."

44. Joel E. Best, "Long Kate, Dutch Henriette and Mother Robinson: Three Madames in Post-Civil War St. Paul," *Ramsey County History* 15 (1979–80): 3–10.

45. *St. Paul City Directories, 1899–1931;* Oliver Towne column, "Fabulous Hill Street," *Dispatch*, Aug. 11, 1958.

46. U.S. Manuscript Census Schedule, 1900, Precinct 1, St. Paul.

47. Morgan interview, June 8, 1993.

48. Oliver Towne, "Madame of Madames," *Dispatch*, Dec. 1, 1973.

49. *Pioneer Press*, Dec. 18, 1923, p. 2.

50. Oliver Towne, "Nina Clifford's Legacy," *Dispatch*, July 4, 1963.

51. H. A. Guilford, *Holy of Holies of the White Slave Worshipper* (St. Paul: n.p., n.d. [ca. 1915]), 5, 8.

52. Horace Dupont, interview by author, Jan. 7, 1994.

53. Hanna Steinbracker death certificate, July 14, 1929; Map of Mt. Elliott Cemetery Plots, lot 266N.

54. *St. Paul Daily News*, July 17, 1929, p. 1; *Pioneer Press*, July 18, 1929, p. 16; Death notice for Hanna Steinbrecher, *Detroit News*, July 16, 1929.

55. Ramsey County, Hannah Steinbrecher probate file, no. 44961, July 1929; Wayne County, Hanna Steinbrecher Probate Court record (reviewed by Sal Giacona); Gareth Hiebert, interview by author, Nov. 17, 1993.

56. Heaberlin interview, Jan. 6, 1994.

57. Dupont interview; *St. Paul City Directories, 1931–1934*.

58. City of St. Paul, Div. of Building Inspection, Permit Application, May 3, 1933, 147 S. Washington; Oliver Towne, "Ode to Nina Clifford," *Dispatch*, Jan. 9, 1960; *Dispatch*, June 7, 1933, p. 1.

59. Bernie Bullert, St. Paul Water Utility general manager, interview by author, Dec. 17, 1993, quoting from *City Water Utility Standard Mains Book*, 1934, 239–240.

60. Robert O. Baker, "The Minnesota Club: St. Paul's Enterprising Leaders and their 'Gentlemen's Social Club' " *Ramsey County History* 19, no. 2 (1984): 15–16; author's interviews with Gareth Hiebert and Jep Knox, Dec. 3, 1993.

61. Donald Empson, *The Street Where You Live: A Guide to the Street Names of St. Paul* (St. Paul: Witsend Press, 1975), 158–59; Virginia Brainerd Kunz, *St. Paul: The First 150 Years* (St. Paul: St. Paul Foundation, 1991), 62–63; *St. Paul City Directory, 1887, 1889;* Charles Reiter, former police officer, interview by author, Sept. 24, 1993.

62. *Dispatch*, Dec. 8, 1928, p. 1, Dec. 7, 1928, p. 1.

63. Heaberlin interview, Jan. 6, 1994; *Minneapolis Morning Tribune*, Dec. 8, 1928, p. 15.

64. *Minneapolis Morning Tribune*, Dec. 6, 1928, p. 1–2.

65. *Dispatch*, Dec. 5, 1928, p. 1; Michaud interview, Dec. 7, 1993.

66. Gene DiMartino, Calvary Cemetery superintendent, interview by author, Oct. 8, 1993.

67. Lannon interview, June 14, 1993.

68. "Scores of Friends Offer Selves for Blood Transfusion," newspaper clipping dated Dec. 4, 1928, *Pioneer Press* morgue file; *Minneapolis Morning Tribune*, Dec. 6, 1928, p. 1–2.

69. "Hogan-Rothstein Link is Revived," newspaper clipping dated Dec. 19, 1928, *Pioneer Press* morgue file.

70. Michaud interviews, Nov. 20 and Dec. 7, 1993.

71. S. K. McKee, FBI report, May 20, 1936, p. 10, HKF 732, sec. 8.

72. McKee report, May 20, 1936, p. 10, HKF 732.

73. Woody Keljik, interview by author, Jan. 22, 1993.

Notes for Chapter 2

1. *Pioneer Press,* June 29, 1919, sec. 2, p. 4.

2. Dean Jennings, *We Only Kill Each Other: The Life and Bad Times of Bugsy Siegel* (Englewood Cliffs, N.J.: Prentice-Hall, 1967), 35.

3. Helen Warren Pfleger as told to George A. Rea, "Volstead and Prohibition: A Roaring '20s' Memoir," *Ramsey County History* 12 (Spring/Summer 1975): 21.

4. *Dispatch,* Nov. 25, 1920, p. 1–2; *Dispatch,* Nov. 26, 1920, p. 1; *Dispatch,* Nov. 27, 1920, p. 1.

5. Frank Wing, *Brewers Handbook of the U.S. and Canada* (New York: J. M. Wing Co., 1887), 67–73, cited in Gary J. Brueggemann, "Beer Capital of the State—St. Paul's Historic Family Breweries," *Ramsey County History* 16 (1980–81): 3; McKee report, May 20, 1936, p. 9, HKF 732. *Pioneer Press,* Jan. 17, 1926, p. 1.

6. Bomberg interview, Ramsey County Historical Society.

7. *Dispatch,* Mar. 21, 1922, p. 1; *Pioneer Press,* Dec. 23, 1926, p. 1.

8. Frank Buckley, "Prohibition Survey of Minnesota," in *Enforcement of the Prohibition Laws,* Official Records of the National Commission on Law Observance and Enforcement, 71st Cong., 3d sess. (Washington, D.C.: Government Printing Office, 1931), 4:598–99.

9. C. W. Hitsman and Ray J. Casserly, Bureau of Prohibition report, Dec. 6, 1932, p. 3, file 23–39–140, NARG 60.

10. *Pioneer Press,* Oct. 20, 1921, p. 1, Aug. 8, 1930, p. 1.

11. Judge John F. McGee, Minneapolis, to U.S. attorney general, Mar. 4, 1924, p. 2–3, file 23–05–39–46, NARG 60.

12. *Pioneer Press,* May 8, 1921, p. 1, Oct. 20, 1921, p. 1; *Dispatch,* Sept. 14, 1927, p. 1, Dec. 9, 1922, p. 1.

13. *Pioneer Press,* Mar. 21, 1922, p. 1, Aug. 3, 1923, p. 1, Apr. 13, 1924, p. 1; *Dispatch,* Feb. 1, 1922, p. 1.

14. Walter W. Liggett, "Minneapolis and Vice in Volsteadland," *Plain Talk,* Apr. 1930, p. 390, in possession of Marda Woodbury, daughter of Walter Liggett; Heisted, "A Story of Crime."

15. Bomberg interview, Ramsey County Historical Society; Liggett, "Minneapolis and Vice in Volsteadland," 389.

16. *Dispatch,* Sept. 16, 1922, p. 1; *Pioneer Press,* Sept. 3, 1922, p. 1.

17. Lafayette French Jr., U.S. attorney, St. Paul, to U.S. attorney general, Justice Dept. memo, Nov. 27, 1925, file 23–39–51, NARG 60.

18. *Pioneer Press,* June 27, 1925, p. 1, Oct. 22, 1925, p. 1.

19. *Dispatch,* Sept. 13, 1920, p. 1; H. H. Clegg to director, FBI memo, May 8, 1934, p. 5, DF 1310, sec. 25.

20. *Dispatch,* Sept. 26, 1925, p. 4.

21. Affidavit of Abe Gleeman, Ramsey County Court, Sept. 15, 1925, sec. 1–6, Dispatch-Pioneer Press Papers, MHS. This affidavit also appears in full in the *Pioneer Press,* Sept. 26, 1925, p. 1.

22. *Pioneer Press,* Mar. 16, 1926, p. 1; Affidavit of Bennie Gleeman, Ramsey County Court, Sept. 15, 1925, sec. 1–3, Dispatch-Pioneer Press Papers, MHS; Burger report, June 25, 1926, p. 6, file 48–39–10, NARG 60. The Gleeman affidavit also appears in full in the *Pioneer Press,* Sept. 26, 1925, p. 1.

23. Max F. Burger, Justice Dept. report, July 23, 1926, p. 16–21, file 48–39–10, NARG 60.

24. P. W. to director, FBI memo, July 29, 1926, p. 3–5, file 23–39–50, NARG 60; Burger report, June 25, 1926, p. 1–7, July 23, 1926, p. 19, file 48–39–10, NARG 60.

25. Bennie Gleeman affidavit, sec. 6, 14–16; *Pioneer Press,* Sept. 26, 1925, p. 2.

26. Bennie Gleeman affidavit, sec. 26; Burton Stevens death certificate, no. 6257, Feb. 18, 1925, Minnesota Department of Health.

27. Bennie Gleeman affidavit, sec. 21.

28. Bennie Gleeman affidavit, sec. 22–24.

29. Bennie Gleeman affidavit, sec. 24–27, 31; Abe Gleeman affidavit, sec. 34–37, 40, 44.

30. *Pioneer Press*, Sept. 26, 1925, p. 1, Sept. 28, 1929, p. 10.

31. *Pioneer Press*, Sept. 26, 1925, p. 1.

32. *Pioneer Press*, Feb. 17, 1926, p. 1–2.

33. *Pioneer Press*, Mar. 23, 1926, p. 2; *Dispatch*, Feb. 19, 1926, p. 1; *Pioneer Press*, Feb. 24, 1926, p. 1, 3.

34. *Dispatch*, Sept. 26, 1925, p. 4.

35. *Pioneer Press*, Sept. 28, 1925, p. 1, June 20, 1923, p. 1 (McGee); Buckley, "Prohibition Survey of Minnesota," 4:595–97.

36. Liggett, "Minneapolis and Vice in Volsteadland," 388.

37. *Pioneer Press*, Sept. 28, 1929, p. 1.

38. *Pioneer Press*, Oct. 1, 1929, p. 10, July 8, 1933, p. 3; *Dispatch*, Jan. 14, 1930, p. 1.

39. M. E. Evans (Ohio), assistant U.S. attorney, to M. D. Kiefer, special assistant U.S. attorney general, Justice Dept. memo, May 4, 1926, file 23–57–142–57, NARG 60.

40. Morris Roisner, Prison Admission Summary, file 51308–1, Leavenworth, Kans., July 2, 1937, Federal Bureau of Prisons; *Pioneer Press*, Nov. 16, 1927, p. 1, Sept. 13, 1935, p. 1.

41. C. W. Stein to J. Edgar Hoover, FBI memo, Mar. 18, 1936, HKF 444, sec. 6; *Dispatch*, Mar. 10, 1926, p. 1.

42. J. D. Glass, FBI report, June 28, 1932, p. 6, file 4–2–11–0, NARG 129.

43. Drill to U.S. attorney general, Justice Dept. memo, Mar. 15, 1933, p. 1–2, NARG 60; *Pioneer Press*, May 5, 1934, p. 1; Rep. Einar Hoidale to U.S. Attorney General Homer Cummings, letter, Sept. 17, 1934, file 5–39–54, and Hoidale to Cummings, telegram, Oct. 4, 1934, file 5–39–52, both in NARG 60.

44. "In re: Leon Gleckman, St. Paul, Minnesota," IRS memo, Feb. 9, 1933, Chicago, SI-8369-F, NARG 60; Leon Gleckman, Prison Admission Summary, file 48710–L, Leavenworth, Kans., Apr. 22, 1936, p. 2, Federal Bureau of Prisons.

45. Gleckman admission summary, p. 4–5.

46. "Raid Yields 13 Stills, 1,000 Gallons Liquor," newspaper clipping, ca. Aug. 1922, *Pioneer Press* morgue file; *Dispatch*, Nov. 6, 1922, p. 5; *U.S. v. Leon Gleckman*, Federal district court, Minneapolis, 1922.

47. FBI memo for the director, July 29, 1926, p. 1–2, FBI file 62–11743, file 23–39–50, NARG 60; *Leon Gleckman v. U.S.A.*, Affidavit for Withdrawal of Confession of Error, no. 6506 (8th Cir. 1923).

48. FBI memo, July 29, 1926, p. 1, file 23–39–50; Gleckman admission summary, p. 1.

49. L. B. Nichols to Clyde Tolson, FBI memo, July 17, 1939, containing Treasury Dept. report of Elmer Irey on Leon Gleckman, p. 4, file 51–39–2, NARG 60; H. M. Slater, FBI report, Mar. 11, 1932, p. 3, and R. J. Caffrey, FBI report, July 29, 1932, p. 30 (quote), both in file 4–2–11–0, NARG 129; Frank Spiering, *The Man Who Got Capone* (Indianapolis: Bobbs-Merrill, 1976), 85.

50. S. K. McKee, FBI report, June 3, 1936, p. 3, HKF 776, sec. 9; Stein to director, FBI teletype, May 1, 1936, HKF 629.

51. R. T. Noonan, FBI report, May 27, 1936, p. 5, HKF 759, sec. 9; K. R. McIntire to director, FBI memo, June 15, 1936, HKF 834, sec. 10. The relationship between Gleckman and Brown is confirmed by the author's interview with retired St. Paul Police Lt. Ralph Merrill, Oct. 10, 1990.

52. McKee report, June 3, 1936, p. 3, HKF 776.

53. Calvert Cravath, interviews by author, June 1991 and Aug. 7, 1991; Calvert Cravath to Ann DeJoy of the Hotel St. Paul, July 5, 1985, letter in author's possession.

54. Cravath interviews, June 1991 and Aug. 7, 1991; Cravath to DeJoy, July 5, 1985; John S. Hurley, assistant director, Bureau of Prohibition report, Feb. 28, 1934, p. 6–9, NARG 60.

55. R. T. Noonan, report, June 18, 1936, p. 43, HKF 880, sec. 10; *Pioneer Press*, Oct. 3, 1931, p. 1, 6.

56. Noonan report, June 18, 1936, p. 40–41, 44, HKF 880.

57. Noonan report, June 18, 1936, p. 50, HKF 880; McKee report, June 3, 1936, p. 4–5, HKF 776.

58. Frank LaPre death certificate, Oct. 7, 1931, Minnesota Department of Health; Ramsey County Medical Examiner, Frank LaPre

autopsy report, file 9536, Oct. 3, 1931; *Pioneer Press*, Oct. 5, 1931, p. 1–2.

59. Noonan report, June 18, 1936, p. 41, HKF 880, and Lannon interview, May 13, 1993 (Tallerico information); anonymous former St. Paul police officer, interview by author, June 1993.

60. Noonan report, June 18, 1936, p. 47, 51, HKF 880.

61. *Dispatch*, June 29, 1932, p. 1.

62. Special agent ____, St. Paul, to Werner Hanni, FBI memo, Feb. 19, 1934, p. 3, CCF 16, vol. 1.

63. McKee report, June 3, 1936, p. 5, HKF 776.

64. Gertrude Sletner, interview by author, July 30, 1993.

65. Director A. W. W. Woodcock to Mr. Youngquist, Bureau of Prohibition memo, July 22, 1932, p. 1–2, file 23–39–140, NARG 60.

66. Max Ehrlich, interview by author, Oct. 30, 1992.

67. *Dispatch*, Jan. 29, 1932, p. 1; Nichols to Tolson, July 17, 1939, p. 1–2, file 51–39–2, NARG 60.

68. Leo E. Owens, *Dispatch* publisher, to U.S. Attorney General William D. Mitchell, Oct. 6, 1931, file 5–39–52, NARG 60.

69. Heisey to L. L. Drill, U.S. attorney, Justice Dept. memo, May 18, 1933, p. 2, file 5–39–52, NARG 60.

70. Norman J. Morrison, special assistant, to attorney general, St. Paul, Justice Dept. memo, Nov. 11, 1933, NARG 60.

71. E. C. Crouter to Mr. Key, Justice Dept. memo, Mar. 27, 1933, p. 2–3, file 5–39–52, NARG 60.

72. *St. Paul City Directory, 1932*, 10.

73. Noonan report, May 27, 1936, p. 6, HKF 759; Reiter interview, Sept. 24, 1993; D. P. Sullivan, FBI report, June 11, 1936, p. 5, HKF 823, sec. 10.

74. Sarah Knutson, interview by author, Nov. 1993; *State of Minnesota v. Doc Jones et al.*, Jan. 11, 1935, Ramsey County District Court Indictment Record, MHS.

75. Donna Bremer, interview by author, Dec. 29, 1993; *Pioneer Press*, Feb. 8, 1994, p. 1C, 4C; Jim George, "Castle Royal: In the Spotlight Again," *Dispatch*, July 20, 1977, p. 33–34.

76. Lannon interview, June 14, 1993.

77. Castle Royal advertisement, *Dispatch*, Oct. 27, 1933, sec. 2, p. 5.

78. Marguerite Junterman, interview by author, Aug. 8, 1993.

79. Junterman interview; *Dispatch*, July 23, 1958, p. 38.

80. Boulevards of Paris advertisement, *St. Paul Daily News*, Sept. 8, 1929, rotogravure section, p. 4–5.

81. Sullivan report, June 11, 1936, p. 5, HKF 832; Junterman interview; McKee report, May 20, 1936, p. 8, HKF 732.

82. Junterman interview; Noonan report, June 18, 1936, p. 49–50, HKF 880.

83. *Pioneer Press*, Oct. 31, 1926, p. 1; *Dispatch*, Dec. 25, 1926, p. 1; Junterman interview; Marie McMahon, John Lane's granddaughter, interview with author, Mar. 1993.

84. Junterman interview; *Dispatch*, July 23, 1958, p. 38.

85. Noonan report, May 27, 1936, p. 8, HKF 759; *Pioneer Press*, Jan. 21, 1936, p. 1; Statement of Thomas E. Gannon, undated, p. 3, Walter Liggett homicide file, BCA.

86. McMahon interview; Junterman interview; *Dispatch*, Sept. 18, 1929, p. 1.

87. John E. Brennan, FBI report, Feb. 15, 1936, p. 7, HKF 423, sec. 5; Noonan report, May 27, 1936, p. 6, HKF 759; St. Paul Street Address Index, MHS; *Dispatch*, June 2, 1952, July 23, 1958, p. 38.

88. *Pioneer Press*, Nov. 4, 1932, p. 1–2.

89. William Weir, *Written with Lead: Legendary American Gunfights and Gunfighters* (Hamden, Conn.: Archon Books, 1992), 200–201.

90. Abe Loeb death certificate, no. 1752, July 29, 1932, Minnesota Department of Health; Burton B. Turkus and Sid Feder, *Murder, Inc.: The Story of "the Syndicate"* (New York: Da Capo Press, 1992, reprint of 1951), 16–18.

91. Excerpts from Philadelphia Police Dept. intelligence files, supplied by Capt. Joseph O'Connor, interview by author, Feb. 26, 1991.

92. R. E. Newby to director, FBI memo, July 15, 1935, p. 3–4, BKF 240x, sec. 3; *Dispatch*, Nov. 9, 1932, sec. 2, p. 1; Statement of

Gustav Enaas, Sept. 2, 1932, Abe Loeb, Al Gordon homicide file 6970, SPPD.

93. Harry Davis murder file, no. 1193, July 21, 1932, BCA; Richard N. Pranke, "Autobiography: Travels and Genealogy," p. 173, Pranke Family Records, MHS; R. E. Newby to M. Nathan, FBI memo, Feb. 26, 1934, p. 13, CCF 46, vol. 1.

94. Statement of Lila Danz, July 26, 1932, Loeb and Gordon homicide file, SPPD; Thomas E. Dahill and J. O. Meyer, "When St. Paul Silenced New Jersey's Hired Guns," *Startling Detective Adventures* 10, no. 60 (July 1933): 40–43, 54.

95. Ellie (Hallberg) McLean, interview by author, Apr. 15, 1993.

96. Dahill and Meyer, "When St. Paul Silenced," 40, 43; Statement of Mrs. Helen Schultz, July 26, 1932, and Report of Officer Kahler, July 25, 1932, Loeb and Gordon homicide file, SPPD; Ramsey County coronor, Abe Loeb file, no. 9950, Ancker Hospital autopsy record, July 26, 1932; Thomas Delaney, interview by author, May 9, 1992.

97. Richard N. Pranke, former FBI special agent, interview by author, Oct. 23, 1992.

98. Statements of Pauline Poetz, Sept. 17, 1932, Dr. Henry H. Hall, Aug. 13, 1932, Mrs. T. W. Edwards, Aug. 24, 1932, Mrs. Hortense Nickolaus, Aug. 24, 1932, Loeb and Gordon homicide file, SPPD.

99. Dupont interview, Oct. 31, 1992; *Dispatch*, Nov. 3, 1932, p. 1, 3.

100. *Pioneer Press*, Nov. 11, 1932, p. 1, 3; Turkus and Feder, *Murder, Inc.*, 20.

101. Special agent in charge, St. Paul, to director, FBI memo, June 15, 1949, BKF 1528, sec. 273.

102. Special agent in charge to director memo, June 15, 1949, p. 2, BKF 1528; Roy Farnham, retired head of Stillwater Records and Identification, interview by author, 1985; statement of Thomas E. Gannon, undated, p. 2, Liggett homicide file, BCA; Philadelphia Police Dept. intelligence files, quoted in O'Connor interview, Feb. 26, 1991. These files included the 1956 letter from Stillwater Warden Douglas C. Rigg to Senator Hubert H. Humphrey.

103. M. B. Rhodes to director, FBI memo, Sept. 12, 1944, p. 6, BKF 15266, sec. 272; special agent in charge to director, FBI memo June 15, 1949, p. 3. See also transcription of letter from Stillwater inmate Tommy Gannon, Liggett homicide file, BCA.

104. Special agent in charge to director memo, June 15, 1949, p. 2; Rhodes to director memo, Sept. 12, 1934, p. 1, 7–8, BKF 15266; Jennings, *We Only Kill Each Other*, 36.

105. Karpis with Trent, *Karpis Story*, 243; S. W. Hardy, FBI report, Apr. 6, 1932, p. 6, file 4–2–11–0, NARG 129.

106. Jay Robert Nash, *Bloodletters and Badmen: A Narrative Encyclopedia of American Criminals from the Pilgrims to the Present* (New York: M. Evans and Co., 1991; reprint of 1973), 500–501; "Vice Conditions—Minneapolis and St. Paul, Minnesota," FBI report, July 19, 1943, p. 84, CCF 315, vol. 6.

107. Rhodes to director memo, Sept. 12, 1944, p. 8, BKF 15266; "Vice Conditions—Minneapolis and St. Paul," July 19, 1943, p. 78; Joe Sherin, former St. Paul police officer, interview by author, 1992.

108. Jennings, *We Only Kill Each Other*, 4.

Notes for Chapter 3

1. Karpis with Trent, *Karpis Story*, 98.

2. Karpis with Trent, *Karpis Story*, 99–100; Michael Wallis, *Pretty Boy: The Life and Times of Charles Arthur Floyd* (New York: St. Martin's Press, 1992), 170–71; FBI interview with Edna Murray, Feb. 12, 1935, p. 10–11, BKF 4546, sec. 69; R. C. Suran, FBI report, May 18, 1936, p. 2, BKF 11653, sec. 203.

3. John E. Brennan, FBI report, May 22, 1936, p. 3, BKF 11766, sec. 204; Wallis, *Pretty Boy*, 171.

4. Special agent ____ to Werner Hanni memo, Feb. 19, 1934, CCF vol. 1; Lannon interview, June 14, 1993; S. P. Cowley to director, FBI memo, Apr. 24, 1934, p. 5, DF 1010, sec. 19.

5. Courtney Riley Cooper, *Here's to Crime* (Boston: Little, Brown and Co., 1937), 81–82.

6. Cowley to director memo, Apr. 24, 1934, p. 5, DF 1010; Karpis with Trent, *Karpis Story*, 101, 110–11.

7. Statement of Delores Delaney to FBI, Jan. 22, 1934, p. 1–3, BKF, NR Bulky Box 3,

pt. 1; Karpis with Trent, *Karpis Story,* 110–11, 113.

8. Haley, interview with Harvey Bailey, Sept. 18, 1966, p. 18, Haley Collection.

9. Clegg to director memo, May 8, 1934, p. 4, DF 1310; Lannon interview, June 14, 1993; Heaberlin interview, Jan. 6, 1994.

10. Harry Sawyer, FBI wanted poster, Feb. 12, 1935, identification order 1240; Carole J. DeMoss, Harry Sawyer's niece, interview by author, Jan. 19, 1994; "Aunt Billie," DeMoss family letter, n.d., copy in author's possession; *Pioneer Press,* Jan. 25, 1936, p. 3; Harry Sawyer, Leavenworth and Alcatraz prison files, Federal Bureau of Prisons.

11. Harry Sawyer, FBI file, fingerprint record, R44401, Feb. 28, 1958; *Pioneer Press,* Jan. 25, 1936, p. 3.

12. Clegg to director memo, May 8, 1934, p. 1, DF 1310; *Pioneer Press,* Jan. 21, 1936, p. 1, 7; McKee report, May 20, 1936, p. 8, HKF 732.

13. Hardy report, Apr. 6, 1932, p. 6, file 4–2–11–0, NARG 129; *Pioneer Press,* Nov. 4, 1932, p. 1; *Dispatch,* Nov. 4, 1932, p. 1; "Gangsters: An Interview with Will Greer," p. 3–4; Noonan report, June 18, 1936, p. 50, HKF 880.

14. J. D. Glass, FBI report, June 28, 1932, p. 4, file 4–2–11–0, NARG 129; R. C. Suran, FBI report, Oct. 6, 1934, p. 40–41, 48, KCMF 2655, sec. 63; R. C. Suran, FBI report, Sept. 1, 1934, p. 30, KCMF 2366, sec. 57.

15. Jane Resler, interview by author, Sept. 9, 1993.

16. O. G. Hall, FBI report, Dec. 7, 1933, p. 2, KCMF 950, sec. 28; Resler interview.

17. Karpis with Trent, *Karpis Story,* 101–2; Earl Van Wagoner, FBI report, Apr. 11, 1934, p. 9, DF 538, sec. 11.

18. Karpis with Trent, *Karpis Story,* 101–3.

19. *Pioneer Press,* Jan. 21, 1936, p. 1, 7; Lannon interview, June 14, 1993.

20. Harold J. Hurley, son of Green Lantern manager George Hurley, interview by author, June 10, 1994; McKee report, May 20, 1936, p. 3, HKF 732; Statement of Claire Lucas, Mar. 21, 1931, and statement of Isaac Goodman, Mar. 20, 1931, Frank Ventress homicide file, SPPD.

21. *Pioneer Press,* Nov. 4, 1923, p. 1, 8; Heaberlin interview, Jan. 6, 1994; Heisted, "A Story of Crime"; George Hurley, interview by author, June 11, 1994; Hardy report, Apr. 6, 1932, p. 6, file 4–2–11–0, NARG 129.

22. K. R. McIntire to director, FBI memo, May 26, 1936, p. 2, HKF 769, sec. 9; McKee report, May 20, 1936, p. 9, HKF 732.

23. Edge, *Run the Cat Roads,* 39–40; Haley, interview with Harvey Bailey, Oct. 31, 1965, p. 3–4, 16, Haley Collection. See also Haley, *Robbing Banks,* 81.

24. Haley, *Robbing Banks,* 8, 24, 107–14.

25. S. K. McKee, FBI report, Apr. 27, 1936, p. 14, HKF 647; K. R. McIntire, FBI report, Apr. 10, 1935, p. 96, BKF, sec. 96.

26. D. L. Nicholson, FBI report, June 27, 1934, p. 18, DF 2274, sec. 40; D. L. Nicholson, FBI report, Sept. 19, 1934, p. 2, St. Paul file 26–2434, in Albert Reilly Leavenworth prison file, no. 48037, Federal Bureau of Prisons; Van Wagoner report, Apr. 11, 1934, p. 4, DF 538.

27. Harold Hurley interview, Aug. 27, 1993.

28. *Dispatch,* June 21, 1926, p. 1; *Pioneer Press,* Mar. 14, 1930, p. 1, 2; Harold Hurley interview, Aug. 27, 1993.

29. Blanche Schude Carter, interview by author, May 5, 1992.

30. Heaberlin interview, Jan. 6, 1994.

31. Frank Ventress file 9250, Mar. 23, 1931, Ramsey County coroner; statement of Mrs. Dorothy Van [Ventress], Mar. 21, 1931, and statement of Harry Kramer, Mar. 26, 1931, Ventress homicide file, SPPD; *Pioneer Press,* May 29, 1931, p. 1, 2; *Dispatch,* Mar. 20, 1931, p. 1, 2; O. G. Hall to Werner Hanni, FBI memo, Feb. 12, 1934, p. 1, BKF 334, sec. 4.

32. D. L. Nicholson, FBI report, Sept. 22, 1934, p. 6, 8, DF 4004, sec. 66.

33. Noonan report, June 18, 1936, p. 21, HKF 880.

34. FBI memo on Thomas A. Brown, Nov. 10, 1936, p. 16, HKF 1082, sec. 11.

35. Clegg to director memo, May 8, 1934, p. 4, DF 1310; R. L. Nalls to Werner Hanni, FBI memo, Jan. 31, 1934, BKF 143, sec. 2.

36. H. H. Clegg to director, FBI memo, June 9, 1934, p. 5, DF 1956, sec. 35; Jack Ramaley, interview by author, May 22, 1992.

37. Special agent in charge ____, Minneapolis, to director, FBI memo, May 22,

1950, FBI file 62–32578–1087; R. C. Coulter, FBI report, Aug. 31, 1934, p. 1, 7–8, KCMF 2355, sec. 57.

38. Coulter report, Aug. 31, 1934, p. 4, KCMF 2355; special agent in charge to director memo, May 22, 1950, FBI file 62–32578–1087; *Dispatch*, Apr. 3, 1934, p. 1, 4; Dupont interview, Oct. 31, 1992.

39. Coulter report, Aug. 31, 1934, p. 10, KCMF 2355.

40. Thomas Patrick Filben death certificate, no. 3397, Sept. 13, 1973, State of California; Jean Preston, niece of Tom Filben, interview by author, June 6, 1992; Dupont interview, Oct. 31, 1992; Bill Filben, nephew of Tom Filben, interview by author, June 13, 1992.

41. Vogelgesang, interview by author, May 5, 1992.

42. Preston interview.

43. Dupont interviews, Oct. 31, 1992, and Jan. 7, 1994.

44. Clegg to director memo, May 8, 1934, p. 4, DF 1310; Clegg to Purvis, FBI teletype, May 6, 1934, HKF 318, sec. 4.

45. Dupont interviews, May 1991 and Oct. 31, 1992; Filben interview.

46. Eben Gillespie, son of George Gillespie, interviews by author, Jan. 15, 1992, and Jan. 6, 1994; S. W. Hardy, FBI report, Jan. 17, 1940, p. 2, BKF 1542, sec. 270; *Dispatch*, Jan. 5, 1932, p. 1, 2.

47. Gillespie interview, Jan. 6, 1994; Hardy report, Jan. 17, 1940, p. 2–3, BKF 1542.

48. Karpis with Trent, *Karpis Story*, 162; Hardy report, Jan. 17, 1940, p. 1, 6–7, BKF 1542; Dupont interview, Oct. 31, 1992; Noonan report, May 27, 1936, p. 10, HKF 759.

49. Hardy report, Jan. 17, 1940, p. 4–5, BKF 1542; Preston interview; John Bowser, interviews by author, May 5 and 19, 1989, May 28, 1992.

50. Bowser interview, May 5, 1989; Filben interview; Mary Graves, historian at Voyageurs National Park, interview by author, May 28, 1992; O. G. Hall, FBI report, July 27, 1933, p. 28, KCMF 401, sec. 13.

51. Glass report, June 28, 1932, p. 6, file 4–2–11–0, NARG 129.

52. Ted Fahey, former St. Paul police officer, interview by author, July 19, 1991.

53. Glass report, June 28, 1932, p. 6–8, file 4–2–11–0, NARG 129.

54. Noonan report, May 27, 1936, p. 9–11, HKF 759; Dupont interview, Oct. 31, 1992.

Notes for Chapter 4

1. H. H. Clegg to special agent in charge, Kansas City, FBI memo, May 31, 1934, DF 1733, sec. 32; J. D. Glass, FBI report, June 27, 1932, p. 3, file 4–2–11–0, NARG 129; R. C. Suran, FBI report, Sept. 22, 1934, p. 4, KCMF 2502, sec. 60; W. R. Ramsey Jr., FBI report, Aug. 8, 1934, p. 12, KCMF 2178, sec. 53.

2. Glass report, June 27, 1932, p. 3, file 4–2–11–0, NARG 129; Robert J. Seng and daughter Barbara Seng, interviews by author, Sept. 24 and Oct. 30, 1993.

3. *Dispatch*, Sept. 22, 1930, p. 1, May 8, 1930, p. 1.

4. V. A. Batzner (National Citizens Bank, Mankato), speech to Minnesota Bankers Association 44th annual convention, Minneapolis, June 13–14, 1933, Minnesota Bankers Association files, Minneapolis.

5. *Pioneer Press*, Sept. 17, 1932, p. 2, Oct. 13, 1931, p. 1.

6. Glass report, June 27, 1932, p. 1, 3–5, file 4–2–11–0, NARG 129.

7. Clyde C. Callahan and Byron B. Jones, *Heritage of an Outlaw: The Story of Frank Nash* (Hobart, Okla.: Schoonmaker Publishers, 1979), 19, 29.

8. Callahan and Jones, *Heritage of an Outlaw*, v, 1, 135 (quote from Hobart, Oklahoma, *Republican*).

9. Callahan and Jones, *Heritage of an Outlaw*, 27, 28–29, 34; D. O. Smith, FBI report, Aug. 18, 1932, file 4–2–11–0, NARG 129.

10. Kansas City Massacre, FBI Case Summary, revised May 1984, p. 1.

11. Frank Nash, FBI wanted poster, Mar. 21, 1932, identification order 1166, KCMF 542, sec. 18; Glass report, June 27, 1932, p. 4, file 4–2–11–0, NARG 129.

12. Suran report, Oct. 6, 1934, p. 39, 47, KCMF 2655; Callahan and Jones, *Heritage of an Outlaw*, 23.

13. Callahan and Jones, *Heritage of an Outlaw*, 56.

14. Glass report, June 27, 1932, p. 5, file

4-2-11-0, NARG 129; Suran report, Oct. 6, 1934, p. 47, KCMF 2655.

15. Hall report, July 27, 1933, p. 31, KCMF 401; Glass report, June 27, 1932, p. 5–9, and J. D. Glass, FBI report, June 8, 1932, p. 9, both in file 4-2-11-0, NARG 129.

16. Glass report, June 27, 1932, p. 5, file 4-2-11-0, NARG 129.

17. *Pioneer Press*, Jan. 10, 1936, p. 1–2; Murray, Statement to FBI, Feb. 12, 1935, p. 1, BKF 4546; H. H. Clegg to director, FBI memo, Apr. 16, 1934, p. 1, DF 601, sec. 13.

18. Ex-Operative 48, "Sterilization: Preston Paden, Whelp of a Gun Moll," *Official Detective Stories*, Apr. 1, 1937, p. 42; Barker-Karpis gang—Bremer Kidnapping, FBI case summary, Nov. 19, 1936, p. 12, BKF.

19. Murray statement to FBI, Feb. 12, 1935, p. 3, 5, BKF 4546.

20. Murray statement to FBI, Feb. 12, 1935, p. 4, 5, 11, BKF 4546.

21. FBI memo on Thomas A. Brown, Nov. 10, 1936, p. 11, HKF 1082.

22. Glass report, June 27, 1932, p. 4–5, file 4-2-11-0, NARG 129.

23. Charles P. Harmon, U.S. Penitentiary, Leavenworth, Kansas, prison inmate file, no. 30676, Federal Bureau of Prisons.

24. Callahan and Jones, *Heritage of an Outlaw*, 149.

25. Suran report, Sept. 22, 1934, p. 13, KCMF 2502; H. H. Clegg to director, FBI letter, May 4, 1934, p. 2, DF 1177, sec. 22; Paula Harman to Chas. P. Harman [*sic*], telegram, July 20, 1929, Harmon prison file, Federal Bureau of Prisons; Callahan and Jones, *Heritage of an Outlaw*, 149–50.

26. J. D. Glass, FBI report, June 10, 1932, p. 3, file 4-2-11-0, NARG 129.

27. Special agent ____, St. Paul, to special agent in charge Werner Hanni, FBI memo, Feb. 19, 1934, p. 3, CCF 16, vol. 1; Paul A. Sevareid, *The People's Lawyer: The Life of Eugene A. Rerat* (Minneapolis: Ross and Haines, 1963), 79–81; John M. Russell, "Scenes from Yesteryear," *Dunn County News* (Menomonie, Wis.), Apr. 25, 1985.

28. J. J. Keating, FBI report, Feb. 24, 1932, p. 10–11, file 4-2-11-0, NARG 129.

29. Glass report, June 27, 1932, p. 8, file 4-2-11-0, NARG 129; Francis Keating and Thomas Holden, prison inmate files, Federal Bureau of Prisons.

30. Callahan and Jones, *Heritage of an Outlaw*, 47, 152.

31. S. W. Hardy, FBI report, Apr. 6, 1932, p. 10, and Keating report, Feb. 24, 1932, p. 10, both file 4-2-11-0, NARG 129; Callahan and Jones, *Heritage of an Outlaw*, 144; Irving Nemerov, interview by author, May 17, 1991.

32. Haley, *Robbing Banks*, 77; R. J. Caffrey, FBI report, Aug. 1, 1932, p. 2–3, 8, file 4-2-11-0, NARG 129; D. P. Sullivan, FBI report, May 19, 1936, p. 5, HKF 723, sec. 8; Glass report, June 27, 1932, p. 8, file 4-2-11-0, NARG 129.

33. Special agent to Hanni memo, Feb. 19, 1934, p. 2, CCF 16, vol. 1; Glass report, June 8, 1932, p. 7, file 4-2-11-0, NARG 129.

34. E. E. Conroy to director, Apr. 4, 1934, p. 3, KCMF 1523, sec. 40; H. E. Anderson to director, FBI letter, Mar. 7, 1934, p. 3, KCMF 1374, sec. 38.

35. J. D. Glass, FBI report, May 11, 1932, p. 23–25, file 4-2-11-0, NARG 129.

36. Glass reports, June 8, 1932, p. 5, May 11, 1932, p. 26, file 4-2-11-0, NARG 129.

37. Earl Orth, interview by author, Mar. 14, 1993.

38. Reiter interview, Sept. 24, 1993.

39. Newby to Nathan memo, Feb. 26, 1934, CCF 46, vol. 1.

40. J. D. Glass, FBI report, June 2, 1932, p. 5–6, 7–10, file 4-2-11-0, NARG 129.

41. Special agent to Hanni memo, Feb. 20, 1934, p. 1, CCF 16, vol. 1; Hardy report, Apr. 6, 1932, p. 7, file 4-2-11-0, NARG 129.

42. Haley, *Robbing Banks*, 81–82; Wm. Larson to special agent in charge, St. Paul, FBI letter, Feb. 9, 1934, p. 7, BKF 206, sec. 3; McIntire report, Apr. 10, 1935, p. 95, BKF sec. 96.

43. Keating report, Feb, 24, 1932, p. 11, file 4-2-11-0, NARG 129; special agent to Hanni memo, Feb. 19, 1934, p. 2, CCF 16, vol. 1.

44. *Pioneer Press*, Dec. 3, 1931, p. 1–2, July 15, 1932, p. 18.

45. Ray Cowdery, *Capone's Chicago* (Küsnacht, Switzerland: Northstar-Maschek, 1987), 68.

46. Edge, *Run the Cat Roads*, 39; *Pioneer Press*, July 16, 1930, p. 1, 3.

47. *Pioneer Press,* July 16, 1930, p. 1, 3; *Dispatch,* July 15, 1930, p. 1–2.

48. *Dispatch,* July 15, 1930, p. 1–2.

49. Bailey interview, Sept. 18, 1966, p. 16–17, Haley Collection; Haley, *Robbing Banks,* 77–79.

50. *Dispatch,* Aug. 28, 1930, p. 2.

51. St. Paul agent, FBI report, Apr. 2, 1938, p. 11–12, FBI file 60–1501–1556.

52. Althea Rohlfing, transcript of speech given to Mahtomedi Club, 1984, copy in author's possession; *Pioneer Press,* Aug. 15, 1930, p. 1–2; *Dispatch,* Aug. 14, 1930, p. 1.

53. Earl Switzer to John I. Navarre, Detroit Police Dept. memo, Feb. 21, 1934, p. 3, Verne Miller homicide file, Detroit Police Dept.

54. *Dispatch,* Jan. 6, 1932, p. 1, Aug. 17, 1931, p. 1; Bailey interview, Sept. 18, 1966, p. 15, Haley Collection; McKee report, May 20, 1936, p. 9, HKF 732.

55. Bailey interview, Sept. 18, 1966, p. 15, Haley Collection; *Dispatch,* Aug. 17, 1931, p. 1.

56. Rorer to director, FBI telegram, Apr. 1, 1934, DF 386, sec. 9.

57. Barker-Karpis gang, FBI case summary, revised Apr. 1984, p. 5, FBI file IC 7–579.

58. Glass report, June 27, 1932, p. 4, file 4–2–11–0, NARG 129.

59. Glass report, June 10, 1932, p. 2, June 27, 1932, p. 4–5, file 4–2–11–0, NARG 129; Gladys Harrington, interview by author, June 1993; S. K. McKee, FBI report, Mar. 5, 1936, p. 15, HKF 400, sec. 5.

60. Glass report, June 8, 1932, p. 6, file 4–2–11–0, NARG 129.

61. Walter "Buster" Johnson, interview by author, n.d.; Glass report, June 27, 1932, p. 2, file 4–2–11–0, NARG 129.

62. ____, FBI report, July 19, 1943, p. 50, CCF 315, vol. 6; Noonan report, May 27, 1936, p. 6, HKF 759.

63. Robert Schmidt ("Frisco Dutch" Steinhardt) criminal history file, July 1, 1934, BCA; Joseph Wokrol homicide file C–5813, Chicago Police Dept. (contains information on Steinhardt).

64. D. P. Sullivan, FBI report, June 11, 1936, p. 5, HKF 823, sec. 10; *Dispatch,* Apr. 20, 1934, p. 1, 4.

65. Noonan report, May 27, 1936, p. 6, HKF 759; *Dispatch,* Apr. 14, 1934, p. 1.

66. E. A. Tamm to director, FBI report, June 5, 1936, HKF 794, sec. 9.

67. John W. Macey, Keller Golf Course caddy, interview by author, Jan. 3, 1992; crime buff Tim Albright, interview with Dillinger caddy Howard Hesse, Mar. 27, 1992, notes in author's possession; Tom Purcell, Keller Golf Course professional, interview by author, Apr. 1992.

68. Glass report, May 11, 1932, p. 42, file 4–2–11–0, NARG 129.

69. Hardy report, Apr. 6, 1932, p. 10, file 4–2–11–0, NARG 129; *Pioneer Press,* July 15, 1932, p. 18.

70. Special agent to Hanni memo, Feb. 19, 1934, p. 2, CCF 16, vol. 1.

71. Glass report, June 2, 1932, p. 20–24, file 4–2–11–0, NARG 129.

72. Glass report, June 27, 1932, p. 8, file 4–2–11–0, NARG 129.

73. Glass report, June 27, 1932, p. 4, file 4–2–11–0, NARG 129.

74. Callahan and Jones, *Heritage of an Outlaw,* 65–66, 142; Cooper, *Here's to Crime,* 241–42.

75. Harvey Bailey interview, May 23, 1967, p. 1, Haley Collection.

76. *Pioneer Press,* July 9, 1932, p. 1; *Minneapolis Journal,* July 19, 1932, p. 1.

Notes for Chapter 5

1. Interviews by author with Marian Johnson, Dec. 19, 1991, and May 30, 1992, Bernice Grossman, May 30, 1992, and Nick Hannegraf Jr., Dec. 19, 1991; J. Edgar Hoover, *Persons in Hiding* (Boston: Little, Brown, and Co., 1938), 8.

2. [Unsigned, untitled] FBI memo, Apr. 24, 1936, p. 1, BKF 11635, sec. 202; Karpis with Trent, *Karpis Story,* 26–30; Alvin Karpis file, May 10, 1932, BCA.

3. Albert Grooms, interview by author, June 18, 1993.

4. FBI memo, Apr. 24, 1936, p. 2–3, BKF 11635.

5. S. K. McKee, FBI report, June 9, 1936,

p. 198, HKF 810, sec. 9; Karpis file, BCA; Karpis with Trent, *Karpis Story*, 39–44.

6. Fred Barker file, May 10, 1932, BCA; Karpis with Trent, *Karpis Story*, 56, 81–82; Barker-Karpis gang, FBI summary, Apr. 1984, p. 1.

7. Bremer kidnap, FBI summary, Nov. 19, 1936, p. 1–2; Nash, *Bloodletters and Badmen*, 33–35.

8. Anthony Summers, *Official and Confidential: The Secret Life of J. Edgar Hoover* (New York: G. P. Putnam and Sons, 1993), 74–75.

9. Bremer kidnap, FBI summary, Nov. 19, 1936, p. 2.

10. M. A. Jones to Mr. Bishop, FBI memo, Mar. 5, 1971, p. 4, BKF 15562, sec. 277; Barker-Karpis gang, FBI summary, Apr. 1984, p. 1; Edge, *Run the Cat Roads*, 21.

11. Barker-Karpis gang, FBI summary, Apr. 1984, p. 3; Arthur W. Dunlop file, May 2, 1932, BCA; Karpis with Trent, *Karpis Story*, 84, 87–88.

12. Arthur R. Barker, FBI wanted poster, Mar. 23, 1934, identification order 1219; Grooms interview.

13. McKee report, May 20, 1936, p. 7, HKF 732.

14. Marian Johnson interview; Hannegraf interview.

15. Karpis with Trent, *Karpis Story*, 85–87; Bremer kidnap, FBI summary, p. 5; undated newspaper clipping, *West Plains Daily Quill*, Karpis file, BCA.

16. Grooms interview.

17. McKee report, May 20, 1936, p. 3, HKF 732; Barker-Karpis gang, FBI summary, Apr. 1984, p. 4.

18. Marian Johnson interview; Grossman interview.

19. Grossmann interview.

20. Karpis with Trent, *Karpis Story*, 44–45.

21. Hardy report, Apr. 6, 1932, p. 2, file 4–2–11–0, NARG 129; Karpis with Trent, *Karpis Story*, 45–46.

22. S. K. McKee, FBI report, May 8, 1936, p. 20–21, BKF 11529, sec. 200.

23. Marian Johnson interview.

24. Memo for the director, FBI memo, Feb. 21, 1934, p. 4, BKF 706, sec. 8; Marian Johnson interview; C. W. Stein to director, FBI memo (Raasch statement), Aug. 18, 1936, p. 1, HKF 1037, sec. 11.

25. Stein to director memo (Raasch statement), Aug. 18, 1936, p. 5, HKF 1037; Noonan report, May 27, 1936, p. 20, HKF 759.

26. Karpis with Trent, *Karpis Story*, 88–89; McKee report, May 20, 1935, p. 4, HKF 732.

27. Agents Vall and Mallette to Melvin Passolt, BCA memo, Apr. 30, 1932 (a), Arthur Dunlop file, BCA; Noonan report, May 27, 1936, p. 25–26, HKF 759.

28. Agents Vall and Mallette to Melvin Passolt, Apr. 30, 1932 (b), and Irie Mallette to Melvin Passolt, BCA memo, May 14, 1932, memos in Dunlop file, BCA; Grossman interview; Hannegraf interview.

29. Stein to director memo (Raasch statement), p. 2–3, HKF 1037.

30. Karpis with Trent, *Karpis Story*, 89.

31. Agent Mallette to Melvin Passolt, BCA memo, Apr. 30, 1932, Dunlop file, BCA.

32. Mallette to Passolt, Apr. 30, 1932, BCA; McKee report, May 27, 1936, p. 27, HKF 759; Karpis with Trent, *Karpis Story*, 89.

33. *Pioneer Press*, Apr. 28, 1932, p. 1, 3.

34. *Dispatch*, Apr. 28, 1932, p. 1; Thomas A. Brown, personnel file, SPPD.

35. Marian Johnson interview; Hannegraf interview.

36. A. H. S. Perkins, *All About White Bear Lake: Minnesota's Popular Summer Resort*, (White Bear: n.p., 1890), 50.

37. McKee report, Mar. 5, 1936, p. 15, HKF 400; Hope Healy Koontz, former Mahtomedi neighbor of John Lambert, interview by author, Dec. 3, 1993; *Dispatch*, Apr. 22, 1936, p. 1; McIntire report, Apr. 10, 1935, p. 95, BKF sec. 96; Karpis with Trent, *Karpis Story*, 47.

38. McIntire report, Apr. 10, 1935, p. 95, BKF sec. 96; Barker-Karpis gang, FBI summary, Apr. 1984, p. 5.

39. Interviews by author of Vern Phillips, Lincoln Township constable and White Bear Police Dept. employee, Apr. 30, 1993, and Fred Miller Jr., Mahtomedi resident, May 14, 1993; Rohlfing speech, Oct. 1, 1984.

40. "General Crime Survey: Semi-Annual Report," FBI report, Oct. 15, 1944 to Apr. 15,

1945, p. 127, CCF 62–75147–43, vol. 2; *Dispatch*, Oct. 8, 1931, p. 1–2; Oct. 9, 1931, p. 1–2; Rohlfing speech, Oct. 1, 1984; Rohlfing interview, Apr. 16, 1993; Marge Guarnera, co-owner of Guarnera's restaurant, interview by author, Spring 1993.

41. Evelyn M. Deyo, interview by author, May 1993; *Dispatch*, Apr. 22, 1936, p. 1, 3.

42. Walter Johnson interview.

43. McIntire report, Apr. 10, 1935, p. 95, BKF sec. 96; Karpis with Trent, *Karpis Story*, 19, 45–46; Ramsey report, Aug. 8, 1934, p. 12, KCMF 2178; Barker-Karpis gang, FBI summary, Apr. 1984, p. 5.

44. Karpis with Trent, *Karpis Story*, 18, 24.

45. Ramsey report, Aug. 8, 1934, p. 12, KCMF 2178.

46. M. F. Trainor, FBI report, Feb. 20, 1934, p. 14, BKF 676, sec. 7; *Pioneer Press*, Jan. 1, 1933, p. 1–2.

47. Memo for director, Feb. 21, 1934, p. 5, BKF 706; Paul Cromer, interview by author, Mar. 12, 1993.

48. *Dispatch*, Apr. 22, 1936, p. 1, 3.

49. Rohlfing interview.

50. Karpis with Trent, *Karpis Story*, 63.

51. C. W. Stein to director, FBI memo, June 13, 1936, p. 4–5, HKF 853, sec. 10.

52. S. K. McKee, FBI report, July 30, 1936, p. 6, HKF 1002, sec. 11.

53. McIntire report, Apr. 10, 1935, p. 96, BKF sec. 96; McKee report, May 8, 1936, p. 4, BKF 11529.

54. *Dispatch*, Sept. 23, 1932, p. 1–2.

55. Karpis with Trent, *Karpis Story*, 15, 16–17.

56. *Dispatch*, Sept. 30, 1932, p. 1.

57. Bremer kidnap, FBI summary, Nov. 19, 1936, p. 10–11.

58. Grooms interview.

59. M. A. Jones to L. B. Nichols, FBI memo, May 9, 1950, p. 1, BKF, sec. 273; Lawrence DeVol to L. F. Utecht et al., Stillwater prison statement, Dec. 13, 1934, Lawrence DeVol Stillwater prison file, MHS; Followup report on William Weaver, Jan. 27, 1936, Leo Gorski homicide file, Minneapolis Police Dept.; John Powner, "On the Scarlet Trail of the Twin City Terrorists," *Startling Detective Adventures*, July 1935, p. 28–33, 71–75.

60. Earl A. Patch, interview by author, July 20, 1993.

61. Patch interview; *Pioneer Press*, Dec. 17, 1932, p. 1–2.

62. Gorski homicide file, Dec. 18, 1932, Minneapolis Police Dept.; Joseph A. Ferris, "How Barton 'The Chopper' Was Captured," *True Detective Mysteries* 20, no. 4 (July 1933): 20–25, 104–107; Patch interview.

63. Karpis with Trent, *Karpis Story*, 64–66; Minneapolis Police Dept. reward poster, Apr. 8, 1932; *Pioneer Press*, Dec. 17, 1932, p. 1–2.

64. Karpis with Trent, *Karpis Story*, 64–65; *Pioneer Press*, Dec. 17, 1932, p. 1–2; Oscar Erickson homicide file 10132, Dec. 16, 1932, SPPD.

65. Arthur Zachman statement, Erickson homicide file, SPPD; *Pioneer Press*, Dec. 17, 1932, p. 1–2.

66. Karpis with Trent, *Karpis Story*, 65.

67. Zachman statement, Erickson homicide file, SPPD; *Pioneer Press*, Dec. 17, 1932, p. 1–2.

68. Jack Mackay, "State Lifer Is Termed Innocent," *Minneapolis Tribune*, Apr. 7, 1950, p. 1, 9; Karpis with Trent, *Karpis Story*, 64–65.

69. *Pioneer Press*, Dec. 17, 1932, p. 1–2; Ancker Hospital autopsy report, Dec. 17, 1932, Offense Report 8656, Erickson homicide file, SPPD.

70. Ferris, "How Barton 'The Chopper' Was Captured," 105.

71. Powner, "On the Scarlet Trail," 32–33.

72. Powner, "On the Scarlet Trail," 33, 71; Hammgren, Kast, Soderburg, and Kane reports, Dec. 18, 1932, Erickson homicide file, SPPD.

73. Ferris, "How Barton 'The Chopper' Was Captured," 104; *Minnesota v. Lawrence Barton*, Jan. 9, 1933, p. 3.

74. Lawrence M. DeVol, deputy warden's examination sheet, Stillwater prison file, MHS; Lawrence DeVol, FBI fingerprint file, July 16, 1936, BCA.

75. J. E. Risden, Des Moines, Iowa, to Minneapolis Police Dept. chief of detectives, Justice Dept. letter, Dec. 24, 1932, Gorski homicide file, Minneapolis Police Dept.; DeVol fingerprint file, BCA.

76. Lawrence DeVol criminal history file, BCA; Lawrence DeVol, St. Peter State Hospital wanted poster, Larry DeVol, Stillwater prison file, MHS.

77. DeVol, Stillwater prison statement; special agent in charge, St. Paul, to director, FBI memo, Dec. 31, 1948, p. 1, BKF 15287, sec. 273; McIntire report, Apr. 10, 1935, p. 96, BKF sec. 96.

78. Sevareid, *The People's Lawyer*, 40–41; John J. Sullivan, warden, to C. R. Carlgren, Stillwater prison letter, July 25, 1935, DeVol Stillwater prison file, MHS.

79. *Minneapolis Journal*, June 11, 1936, p. 1, 11, June 8, 1936, p. 1, 6; Robert R. Ernst, "The Last Days of Lawrence DeVol," *OklahombreS*, Winter 1991, p. 10–12.

80. R. T. Noonan, FBI report, Mar. 20, 1936, p. 25, HKF 431, sec. 5.

81. Jim Lehman, interview by author, 1992.

82. McKee report, July 30, 1936, p. 3, HKF 1002; S. K. McKee, FBI report, July 13, 1936, p. 2, HKF 922, sec. 10.

83. Ramsey report, Aug. 8, 1934, p. 13, KCMF 2178; J. Edgar Hoover to special agent in charge, St. Paul, FBI letter, June 17, 1936, HKF 845, sec. 10.

84. Anne Diestel (Federal Bureau of Prisons) to author, June 13, 1994, letter in author's possession; Edwin Wiechman statement, Dec. 19, 1932, Erickson homicide file, SPPD; R. J. Caffrey, FBI report, July 29, 1932, p. 2–3, file 4–2–11–0, NARG 129; Switzer to Navarre, Feb. 21, 1934, p. 1, Miller homicide file, Detroit Police Dept.; McIntire report, Apr. 10, 1935, p. 95, BKF sec. 96.

85. Ramsey report, Aug. 8, 1934, p. 29, KCMF 2178; Suran report, Sept. 22, 1934, p. 11, KCMF 2502.

86. Switzer to Navarre, Feb. 21, 1934, p. 2, Miller homicide file, Detroit Police Dept.

87. Karpis with Trent, *Karpis Story*, 161–162.

88. C. O. Lawrence, FBI report, Sept. 27, 1934, p. 1–2, KCMF 2548, sec. 61; McKee report, May 20, 1936, p. 11, HKF 732.

89. Switzer to Navarre, Feb. 21, 1934, p. 2, May 7, 1935, p. 3, Miller homicide file, Detroit Police Dept.; Ramsey report, Aug. 8, 1934, p. 28–29, KCMF 2178; Bernard Phillips, FBI wanted poster, July 13, 1933, identification order 1196.

90. A. Rosen to director, FBI memo, Apr. 3, 1936, p. 3, HKF 469x, sec. 6.

91. Murray statement, Feb. 12, 1935, p. 2, BKF 4546.

92. McKee report, May 20, 1936, p. 3, HKF 732; McIntire report, Apr. 10, 1935, p. 96, BKF sec. 96.

93. McIntire report, Apr. 10, 1935, p. 96, BKF sec. 96.

94. J. R. Green and R. B. Smith, FBI report, Sept. 21, 1934, p. 1–3, BKF 2932, sec. 36.

95. Karpis with Trent, *Karpis Story*, 79; Suran report, May 22, 1936, p. 4, BKF 11766; Suran report, Oct. 6, 1934, p. 12, KCMF 2655. See also Ramsey report, Aug. 8, 1934, p. 4, KCMF 2178.

96. Ramsey report, Aug. 8, 1934, p. 10–15, KCMF 2178.

97. *St. Paul City Directory, 1920*, p. 6.

98. Glass report, May 11, 1932, p. 21, file 4–2–11–0, NARG 129 (Keating): Bremer kidnap, FBI summary, Nov. 19, 1936, p. 3. See also R. D. Brown, FBI report, Sept. 19, 1934, p. 49, BKF 2919, sec. 36.

99. R. C. Suran, FBI report, Mar. 3, 1936, p. 11, HKF 401, sec. 5.

100. S. K. McKee, FBI report, Apr. 14, 1936, p. 5, HKF 520, sec. 6; Karpis with Trent, *Karpis Story*, 59.

101. Suran report, Sept. 22, 1934, p. 15, KCMF 2502.

102. Hoover, *Persons in Hiding*, 9; Suran report, Sept. 22, 1934, p. 15–16, KCMF 2502;

103. Karpis with Trent, *Karpis Story*, 90; Suran report, Sept. 22, 1934, p. 10, KCMF 2502; R. C. Suran, FBI report, Sept. 1, 1934, p. 19, KCMF 2366. See also Brown report, Sept. 19, 1934, p. 40, BKF 2919.

104. "Gangsters: An Interview with Will Greer," p. 9.

Notes for Chapter 6

1. McKee report, Apr. 27, 1936, p. 65–66, HKF 647.

2. Director to special agent in charge, St. Paul, FBI memo, Feb. 12, 1934, p. 1, file 62–30819–3; Jack Peifer file, 1936, BCA; *Dispatch*, Aug. 5, 1936, p. 1.

3. S. K. McKee, FBI report, Apr. 3, 1936, p. 2, HKF 468, sec. 6; Sullivan report, May 19, 1936, p. 5, HKF 723; Sullivan report, June 11, 1936, p. 6, HKF 823; McKee reports, July 30, 1936, p. 2–3, HKF 1002, and June 9, 1936, p. 206, HKF 810.

4. McKee report, July 30, 1936, p. 6–7, HKF 1002.

5. McKee report, Apr. 27, 1936, p. 67, HKF 647; Delaney statement, Jan. 22, 1934, p. 2, BKF NR Bulky Box 3, pt. 1.

6. R. T. Noonan, FBI report, May 14, 1936, p. 9–10, HKF 761, sec. 9.

7. Ramsey County Probate Court, Petition for General Administration, John P. Peifer, Decedent, July 21, 1937 (see also McKee report, Apr. 27, 1936, p. 65, HKF 647); C. W. Stein to director, FBI letter, Apr. 30, 1936, p. 1, BKF 11564, sec. 201 (see also Noonan report, May 14, 1936, p. 8, HKF 761).

8. McKee report, Apr. 27, 1936, p. 6–7, HKF 647.

9. Elizabeth Roy, interview by author, Dec. 17, 1994.

10. McKee report, July 30, 1936, p. 2, 4, HKF 1002; Harry Kramer statement, Mar. 26, 1931, Ventress homicide file, SPPD; C. W. Stein to director memo, June 13, 1936, p. 7, HKF 853.

11. *Pioneer Press*, May 17, 1931, p. 1; McKee report, Apr. 27, 1936, p. 6, 10, 17, HKF 647.

12. Fred Heaberlin interview, Jan. 6, 1994.

13. Bryan [Byron] Bolton, statement to FBI, Jan. 27, 1936, p. 30, HKF 365x, sec. 4; McKee report, June 9, 1936, p. 90, HKF 810; Schude interview; Nicholson report, Sept. 22, 1934, p. 4, DF 4004.

14. Martin Rohling, interviews by author, June 16, 1991, and May 22, 1992; *Pioneer Press*, July 23, 1934, p. 1. A 1936 FBI letter noted that in July 1934 "the Hollyhocks Inn was raided and numerous gambling devices seized by the police, but later returned to the Hollyhocks presumably to Peifer for some unknown reason." See C. W. Stein to George F. Sullivan, U.S. attorney, FBI letter, p. 2, HKF 613.

15. Noonan report, May 14, 1936, p. 10, HKF 761.

16. Stein to Director memo, June 13, 1936, p. 7–8, HKF 853.

17. R. C. Suran, FBI report, May 15, 1936, p. 10–11, BKF 11619, sec. 202.

18. Nate Bomberg, "St. Paul and the Federal Building in the Twenties and Thirties," in Eileen Michaels, *A Landmark Reclaimed* (St. Paul: Minnesota Landmarks, 1977), 55.

19. *Minneapolis Journal*, Nov. 23, 1936, p. 1.

20. Rohling interviews.

21. Glass report, May 11, 1932, p. 31, file 4–2–11–0, NARG 129; *Dispatch*, Aug. 5, 1932, p. 1, Aug. 9, 1932, p. 1; Stein to director memo (Raasch statement), Aug. 18, 1936, p. 3, HKF 1037.

22. Stein to director memo (Raasch statement), Aug. 18, 1936, p. 3, HKF 1037.

23. Karpis with Trent, *Karpis Story*, 127, 130; J. Edgar Hoover to assistant attorney general McMahon, FBI memo, May 13, 1936, p. 2–3, HKF 724, sec. 8; *Pioneer Press*, Aug. 8, 1936, p. 1–2.

24. John T. Flanangan, *Theodore Hamm in Minnesota* (St. Paul: Pogo Press, 1989), 108–22; "Denials Stand Unaltered by Grilling," newspaper clipping dated July 23, 1936, *Pioneer Press* morgue file.

25. *Dispatch*, July 31, 1936, p. 1, 8.

26. Lannon interview.

27. *St. Paul Daily News*, June 17, 1933, p. 1–2; Karpis with Trent, *Karpis Story*, 159.

28. Suran reports, Oct. 6, 1934, p. 48, KCMF 2655, Sept. 22, 1934, p. 59, KCMF 2502; Harold Nathan, FBI report, Feb. 21, 1934, p. 17, BKF 721, sec. 8.

29. Werner Hanni to director, FBI memo, Feb. 21, 1934, FBI file 62–12114–66; Hall report, July 27, 1933, p. 32, KCMF 401.

30. Hall report, July 27, 1933, p. 33–34, KCMF 401.

31. McKee report, Apr. 27, 1936, p. 7, HKF 647.

32. Special agent to Hanni memo, Feb. 19, 1934, CCF 16, vol. 1.

33. Nathan report, Feb. 21, 1934, p. 17, BKF 7210.

34. *Pioneer Press*, Aug. 8, 1936, p. 1–2.

35. Perkins, *All About White Bear Lake*, 3, 5, 9; John J. Koblas, *F. Scott Fitzgerald in Minnesota: His Homes and Haunts* (St. Paul:

Minnesota Historical Society, 1, 3, 25–26, 35, 39–41.

36. McKee reports, June 9, 1936, p. 93–94, HKF 810, and Mar. 5, 1936, p. 18, HKF 400.

37. Karpis with Trent, *Karpis Story*, 134.

38. Clifford Allen Lindholm, interview by author, Dec. 1992.

39. Steve Tuttle, interview by author, Jan. 30, 1993.

40. Sally McNamara, interview by author, Apr. 30, 1993; Lindholm interview.

41. McKee report, June 9, 1936, p. 90–92, 99, HKF 810; S. K. McKee, FBI report, Mar. 30, 1936, p. 7–8, HKF 458, sec. 6.

42. McKee reports, Apr. 27, 1936, p. 70–71, HKF 647, and June 9, 1936, p. 92, HKF 810.

43. McKee report, June 9, 1936, p. 99, 105, HKF 810.

44. McKee reports, Mar. 5, 1936, p. 21, HKF 400, and June 9, 1936, p. 92, HKF 810; Noonan report, May 14, 1936, p. 19, HKF 761.

45. Tuttle interview.

46. *Pioneer Press*, Aug. 8, 1936, p. 1–2.

47. Brueggeman, "Beer Capitol of the State," 12–13.

48. McIntire report, Apr. 10, 1935, p. 179; John L. Madala, FBI report, May 19, 1936, p. 10, HKF 738, sec. 9 (quote; see also Nash, *Bloodletters and Badmen*, 520–22); Schoenberg, *Mr. Capone*, 227; Brown report, Sept. 19, 1934, p. 51, BKF 2919; Suran report, Sept. 22, 1934, p. 5, KCMF 2502; Bilek, Arthur J., "St. Valentine's Day Massacre, Part II," *Real Crime Book Digest*, Spring 1995, p. 4–7.

49. Ramsey report, Aug. 8, 1934, p. 2, KCMF 2178; Melvin Purvis, *American Agent* (Garden City, N.Y.: Doubleday, Doran and Co., 1936), 151; Callahan and Jones, *Heritage of an Outlaw*, 155–56; M. H. Purvis to director, FBI memo, Mar. 21, 1934, KCMF 1475, sec. 40; McIntire report, Apr. 10, 1935, p. 177; M. H. Purvis to director, FBI memo, Mar. 23, 1934, KCMF, sec. 40.

50. Purvis, *American Agent*, 151–52.

51. E. P. Guinane, FBI report, July 21, 1934, p. 4, KCMF 2037, sec. 50 (quote); Ramsey report, Aug. 8, 1934, p. 2, KCMF 2178; Suran report, Sept. 22, 1934, p. 8, KCMF 2502.

52. Hoover to McMahon memo, May 13, 1936, p. 2, HKF 738; John W. Anderson, FBI report, Aug. 31, 1936, p. 5, HKF 1053, sec. 11.

53. S. K. McKee, FBI report, July 8, 1936, p. 6, HKF 913, sec. 10; Madala report, May 19, 1936, p. 11, HKF 738.

54. McKee report, May 8, 1936, p. 5, BKF 11529.

55. Bolton statement, Jan. 27, 1936, p. 3–4, HKF 365x.

56. McKee report, June 9, 1936, p. 9, HKF 810; Hoover to McMahon memo, May 13, 1936, p. 2–4, HKF 724; Stein to director memo, June 13, 1936, p. 1, HKF 853.

57. Bolton statement, Jan. 27, 1936, p. 5–6, HKF 365x; FBI memo, May 4, 1936, p. 2, HKF 650x; S. K. McKee, FBI report, July 28, 1936, p. 2–3; HKF 989, sec. 11; Charles Fitzgerald file, May 1936, BCA.

58. A. Rosen to director memo, Apr. 3, 1936, p. 6, HKF 469x, sec. 6; McKee report, July 8, 1936, p. 2, HKF 913.

59. Hoover to McMahon memo, May 13, 1936, p. 3, HKF 724; Werner Hanni, FBI report, June 26, 1933, p. 21, HKF 20, sec. 1.

60. McKee reports, July 8, 1936, p. 3, HKF 913 and June 9, 1936, p. 13, HKF 810; Hoover to McMahon memo, May 13, 1936, p. 3–4, HKF 724; S. K. McKee, FBI report, July 1, 1936, p. 7, HKF 891, sec. 10.

61. R. T. Noonan, FBI report, Oct. 10, 1933, p. 4, HKF 176, sec. 2; Hanni report, June 26, 1933, p. 22, 26, HKF 20.

62. Hoover to McMahon memo, May 13, 1936, p. 4, HKF 724; Hanni report, June 26, 1933, p. 22, 23, HKF 20; McKee reports, June 9, 1936, p. 14, HKF 810, and July 8, 1936, p. 3, HKF 913.

63. V. W. Hughes, FBI report, Aug. 10, 1933, p. 2, HKF 127, sec. 2.

64. Stein to director memo, June 13, 1936, p. 2, HKF 853. See also Noonan report, June 18, 1936, p. 49, HKF 880.

65. Noonan report, May 27, 1936, p. 3, HKF 759.

66. Stein to director memo, Apr. 30, 1936, p. 1, BKF 11564; K. R. McIntire to director, FBI memo, June 3, 1936, p. 1, HKF 800, sec. 9. See also Stein to director, FBI telegram, May 4, 1936, HKF 657, sec. 8; Noonan report, May 27, 1936, p. 9, HKF 759; "Peifer Named as Visitor to Karpis' House," newspaper clip-

ping dated July 16, 1936, *Pioneer Press* morgue file.

67. Noonan report, May 27, 1936, p. 5, 17, HKF 759; McKee report, June 3, 1936, p. 3, HKF 776 (quote). See also Stein to director teletype, May 1, 1936, HKF 629.

68. William C. Figge, interview by author, Jan. 6, 1994.

69. Noonan report, May 27, 1936, p. 4, HKF 759.

70. Hughes report, Aug. 10, 1933, p. 2, HKF 127.

71. Hanni report, June 26, 1933, p. 3–4, HKF 20.

72. FBI memo on Thomas Brown, Nov. 10, 1936, p. 7, HKF 1082; McKee report, June 9, 1936, p. 47, HKF 810.

73. Hanni report, June 26, 1933, p. 5, HKF 20.

74. Hughes report, Aug. 10, 1933, p. 2, HKF 127; R. L. Walls, FBI report, June 29, 1933, p. 2–3, HKF 30, sec. 1.

75. McKee report, June 9, 1936, p. 32–34, HKF 810; Hanni report, June 26, 1933, p. 30–32, HKF 20.

76. Hoover to McMahon memo, May 13, 1936, p. 5, HKF 724; McKee reports, June 9, 1936, p. 54, HKF 810, July 8, 1936, p. 3, HKF 913, June 9, 1936, p. 16, HKF 810, and Apr. 27, 1936, p. 86, HKF 759.

77. FBI reproduction of ransom note, HKF 1131, sec. 12.

78. FBI reproduction of ransom note, HKF 1131.

79. McKee report, June 9, 1936, p. 15, HKF 810; Hoover to McMahon memo, May 13, 1936, p. 6, HKF 724; McKee report, June 9, 1936, p. 50, HKF 810.

80. Bolton statement, Jan. 27, 1936, p. 11, HKF 365x.

81. McKee report, June 9, 1936, p. 83–87, HKF 810.

82. McKee report, June 9, 1936, p. 61, HKF 810; Frances MacLaren Paul, interview by author, Apr. 3, 1993.

83. Hall report, July 27, 1933, p. 4–6, KCMF 401.

84. Hall report, July 27, 1933, p. 3–4, KCMF 401; McKee report, July 8, 1936, p. 3, HKF 913.

85. Noonan report, May 14, 1936, p. 26–27, HKF 761; McKee report, June 9, 1936, p. 67, HKF 810.

86. E. E. Conroy to director, FBI letter, Mar. 13, 1934, p. 1, HKF 302, sec. 4; McKee reports, June 9, 1936, p. 69, HKF 810, and Mar. 5, 1936, p. 13, HKF 400. See also Suran report, Oct. 6, 1934, p. 48, KCMF 2655.

87. Hall report, July 27, 1933, p. 13, KCMF 401.

88. Paul interview; McKee report, Mar. 5, 1936, p. 7, HKF 400.

89. McKee report, June 9, 1936, p. 1, 56, HKF 810; Hoover to McMahon memo, May 13, 1936, p. 6, HKF 724.

90. Karpis with Trent, *Karpis Story,* 141.

91. McKee report, June 9, 1936, p. 17, 34–36, HKF 810.

92. Noonan report, June 18, 1936, p. 34, HKF 880.

93. Noonan report, May 14, 1936, p. 21, 24, HKF 761.

94. McKee report, Apr. 27, 1936, p. 29, HKF 647; Noonan report, June 18, 1936, p. 5, HKF 880. See also FBI memo on Brown, Nov. 10, 1936, HKF 1082.

95. O. G. Hall to W. A. Rorer, FBI memo, Mar. 7, 1934, p. 2, KCMF, sec. 39. See also Hall report, July 27, 1933, p. 13–14, KCMF 401.

96. McKee report, June 9, 1936, p. 23, HKF 810.

97. W. A. Rorer to director, FBI letter, Mar. 27, 1934, p. 2–3, KCMF, sec. 40. See also Noonan report, May 27, 1936, p. 16, HKF 759.

98. Hall report, July 27, 1933, p. 9, KCMF 401.

99. Hanni to Hoover memo, Feb. 20, 1934, p. 2, CCF 16, vol. 1.

100. *Dispatch,* July 21, 1936, p. 1, italics in original.

101. FBI memo on Brown, Nov. 10, 1936, p. 1, HKF 1082; Thomas A. Brown personnel file, SPPD; Thomas Archibald Brown death certificate, no. 16132, Jan. 8, 1959, Minnesota Department of Health.

102. Vera Peters, interview by author, Mar. 27, 1993.

103. *Dispatch,* June 10, 1930, p. 1.

104. Noonan report, June 18, 1936, p. 48, HKF 880.

105. Peters interview.

106. *Pioneer Press*, Dec. 15, 1923, p. 5.

107. Glass report, June 28, 1932, p. 6, file 4–2–11–0, NARG 129.

108. Stein to director memo, Mar. 18, 1936, HKF 444 (containing district court document dated July 23, 1926).

109. *Dispatch*, Nov. 6, 1930, p. 1, 4; *Dispatch*, Nov. 20, 1930, p. 1–2.

110. Stein to director memo (Raasch statement), Aug. 10, 1936, p. 3–4, HKF 1037.

111. *Dispatch*, June 24, 1933, p. 1.

112. FBI memo on Brown, Nov. 10, 1936, p. 7, HKF 1082; Noonan report, May 27, 1936, p. 5, HKF 759.

113. FBI memo on Brown, Nov. 10, 1936, p. 5, 10, HKF 1082.

114. Hanni to Hoover memo, Feb. 20, 1934, p. 2, CCF 16, vol. 1; Harold Nathan to director, FBI letter, Feb. 20, 1934, p. 1, BKF, sec. 7.

115. McKee report, June 9, 1936, p. 21, 22, HKF 810.

116. John Edgar Hoover to Mr. Tamm, FBI memo, May 16, 1936, BKF 11575x, sec. 201; McKee to director, FBI teletype, May 15, 1936, HKF 726, sec. 8.

117. Rosen to director memo, Apr. 3, 1936, p. 7, 8, HKF 469x.

118. T. G. Melvin, FBI report, June 16, 1936, p. 2, HKF 864, sec. 10.

119. Clegg to director memo, May 8, 1934, p. 4, DF 1310.

120. Suran report, May 22, 1936, p. 3, BKF 11766.

121. C. W. Stein to director, FBI memo, Mar. 16, 1936, p. 1–3, HKF 414, sec. 5.

122. Brennan report, Feb. 15, 1936, p. 4, HKF 423.

123. Stein to director memo, Apr. 30, 1936, p. 3, BKF 11564; Noonan report, June 18, 1936, p. 4, HKF 880; Stein to director telegram, May 4, 1936, HKF 657. See also Ramsey County Real Estate records, title and abstract for the Hollyhocks Club; McKee report, June 9, 1936, p. 57–58, HKF 810. Walt McKenna informed the FBI that Peifer told him to tell Benz to warn Hamm. Benz also admitted to the conversation.

124. Noonan report, May 27, 1936, p. 7, HKF 759.

125. Noonan report, May 27, 1936, p. 4, HKF 759.

126. Galen M. Willis to E. A. Tamm, FBI memo, Mar. 18, 1940, p. 2–3, HKF 1125, sec. 12; McKee report, July 8, 1936, p. 4, HKF 913; McKee report, June 9, 1936, p. 21, HKF 810.

127. McKee report, July 8, 1936, p. 5, HKF 913; *Dispatch*, July 21, 1936, p. 1–2.

128. Willis to Tamm memo, Mar. 18, 1940, p. 2, HKF 1125.

129. McKee report, July 8, 1936, p. 6, HKF 913.

130. *South St. Paul Daily Reporter*, Aug. 30, 1933, p. 1, 3.

131. Ross Opsahl, "South St. Paul, Minnesota Machine Gun Raid," *Thompson Collectors News* 10 (Aug. 15, 1991): 3; *Pioneer Press*, Apr. 22, 1936, p. 1, 2.

132. Irie Mallette and Herman Vall to Melvin Passolt, memo, "South St. Paul Hold-Up," Aug. 30, 1933, p. 2, BCA.

133. *Pioneer Press*, Apr. 22, 1936, p. 1, 2.

134. Jack Yeaman, interview by author, Aug. 24, 1993.

135. *Pioneer Press*, Aug. 31, 1933, p. 1.

136. Karpis with Trent, *Karpis Story*, 149.

137. Mallette and Vall to Passolt memo, Aug. 30, 1933, p. 1.

138. Clegg to director, Apr. 16, 1934, p. 5, DF 601.

139. Noonan report, May 27, 1936, p. 11, 18, HKF 759.

140. O. G. Hall to Werner Hanni, FBI memo, Feb. 20, 1934, p. 7, BKF, sec. 9; Yeaman interview.

141. Ross M. Opsahl, "South St. Paul Machine Gun Raid, Part II, Epilogue," *Thompson Collectors News* 12 (Oct. 15, 1991).

142. Robert Pavlak, interview by author, Feb. 6, 1993.

143. *South-West Review*, Aug. 15, 1993, p. 1; Yeaman interview.

Notes for Chapter 7

1. Callahan and Jones, *Heritage of an Outlaw*, 152.

2. Janet Gibson, interview by author, Aug. 27, 1993.

3. Janet Gibson interview; Verne Miller, FBI wanted poster, July 11, 1933, Identification Order 1195.

4. Michael Gibson, interview by author,

Apr. 9, 1993; Janice Holsapple, interview by author, Apr. 9, 1993.

5. Verne Miller, South Dakota State Prison file, Apr. 1923, State Archives, Pierre, S.D; Purvis, *American Agent*, 37.

6. Verne Miller, South Dakota State Prison file.

7. Miller, FBI wanted poster, July 11, 1933; Purvis, *American Agent*, 38.

8. *Dispatch*, Feb. 3, 1928, p. 1; *Minneapolis Journal*, Feb. 3, 1928, p. 1, 18, Feb. 5, 1928, p. 1; Switzer to Navarre, Feb. 21, 1934, p. 1, Miller homicide file, Detroit Police Dept.

9. Suran report, Oct. 6, 1934, p. 10, KCMF 2655; Callahan and Jones, *Heritage of an Outlaw*, 92, 152; Warden of the South Dakota Penitentiary to Melvin Passolt, letter, Sept. 5, 1933, in South St. Paul Payroll file, BCA.

10. Barnes, *Machine Gun Kelly*, 191–92.

11. Madala report, May 19, 1936, p. 11–12, Hamm 738.

12. Callahan and Jones, *Heritage of an Outlaw*, 54–55.

13. McKee report, May 8, 1936, p. 31, BKF 11529.

14. Switzer to Navarre, Feb. 21, 1934, p. 3, Miller homicide file, Detroit Police Dept.

15. Haley, *Robbing Banks*, 117; Switzer to Navarre, Feb. 21, 1934, p. 1, Miller homicide file, Detroit Police Dept.

16. Hall report, July 27, 1933, p. 25, KCMF 401.

17. Glass report, June 28, 1932, p. 3, file 4–2–11–0, NARG 129; Hall report, July 27, 1933, p. 25–26, KCMF 401; Michael Gibson interview.

18. Michael Gibson interview; Holsapple interview.

19. Janet Gibson interview.

20. Suran report, Oct. 6, 1934, p. 14–15, KCMF 2655.

21. Wallis, *Pretty Boy*, 312–14; Earl C. Switzer to inspector, May 7, 1935, p. 1, Miller homicide file, Detroit Police Dept.

22. Callahan and Jones, *Heritage of an Outlaw*, 76–78.

23. Kansas City Massacre, FBI case summary, revised May 1984, KCMF; Wallis, *Pretty Boy*, 314–17.

24. Madala report, May 19, 1936, p. 13, HKF 738.

25. Janet Gibson interview.

26. Wallis, *Pretty Boy*, 322.

27. Hall report, July 27, 1933, p. 30–31, KCMF 401.

28. McKee report, June 9, 1936, p. 42, HKF 810; Donna Eue, niece of Vivian Mathis, interview by author, Apr. 15, 1933.

29. William H. Schoemaker to Fred W. Frahm, Chicago Police Dept. letter, Jan. 6, 1934, Miller homicide file, Detroit Police Dept.; *Pioneer Press*, Nov. 2, 1933, p. 1, Nov. 30, 1933, p. 1–2.

30. Switzer to inspector, May 7, 1935, p. 1, and handwritten notes on Miller homicide, Dec. 14, 1933, p. 166–72, both in Miller homicide file, Detroit Police Dept.

31. Switzer to Navarre, Feb. 21, 1934, p. 1–2, Miller homicide file, Detroit Police Dept.

32. Louis Buchalter, interview by FBI, Nov. 29, 1933, p. 57, handwritten notes in Miller homicide file, Detroit Police Dept.

33. Wayne County, autopsy report on Verne Miller, Dec. 1, 1933, p. 188, and handwritten notes on Miller homicide, Dec. 14, 1933, p. 168, both in Miller homicide file, Detroit Police Dept.

34. Switzer to Navarre, Feb. 21, 1934, p. 3, Miller homicide file, Detroit Police Dept.

35. Purvis, *American Agent*, 40–43.

36. Kansas City Massacre, FBI summary, May 1984, p. 5; Suran report, Oct. 6, 1934, p. 1, KCMF 2655; Janet Gibson, letter to author, Apr. 28, 1994; Janet Gibson interview; Mike Gibson interview; Holsapple interview.

37. *Pioneer Press*, Dec. 7, 1933, p. 10; *Pioneer Press*, Dec. 4, 1933, p. 11.

38. Eue interview; Janet Gibson interview.

39. Athan G. Theoharis and John Stuart Cox, *The Boss: J. Edgar Hoover and the Great American Inquisition* (Philadelphia: Temple University Press, 1988), 123; Cooper, *Ten Thousand Public Enemies*, 270–72; Gentry, *Hoover*, 168–69; Purvis, *American Agent*, 35–36.

40. Purvis, *American Agent*, 45, 58–59; Theoharis and Cox, *The Boss*, 128–30; Gentry, *Hoover*, 168–69.

41. Theoharis and Cox, *The Boss*, 123–30.

42. J. Edgar Hoover, "Patriotism and the War Against Crime," speech to the Daughters of the American Revolution, Apr. 23, 1936, p. 6, Government Printing Office, JI.14/2:P27.

43. Walter Trohan, "J. Edgar Hoover, the One-Man Scotland Yard," *Chicago Tribune*, June 21, 1936, pt. 7, p. 1, 8, 11.

Notes for Chapter 8

1. Suran report, Sept. 1, 1934, p. 20, KCMF 2366; Director to attorney general, FBI memo, Jan. 20, 1934, BKF 13, sec. 1.

2. Suran report, Sept. 1, 1934, p. 19–20, KCMF 2366.

3. Bremer kidnapping, FBI summary, Nov. 9, 1936, p. 19–20.

4. George "Machine Gun Kelly" Barnes et al., kidnapping of Charles F. Urschel, FBI case summary, Oct. 15, 1935, revised July 1989; H.E. Anderson to director, FBI memo, Mar. 7, 1934, p. 2, KCMF 1374, sec. 38.

5. "Machine Gun Kelly" et al., FBI summary, July 1989.

6. *Dispatch*, Sept. 30, 1933, p. 1, 5.

7. R. C. Coulter, FBI report, Feb. 24, 1934, 2–4, BKF 771, sec. 9; *Pioneer Press*, Feb. 11, 1934, p. 1–2; *Dispatch*, Feb. 10, 1934, p. 1, 3.

8. Noonan report, May 27, 1936, p. 20, HKF 759.

9. *Your Visit to the Jacob Schmidt Brewing Company* ([St. Paul]: Jacob Schmidt Brewing Company, 1950), 3–5. See also Brueggemann, "Beer Capital of the State," p. 11.

10. Gordon L. Merrick, interview by author, Dec. 11, 1992.

11. Karpis with Trent, *Karpis Story*, 163; Suran report, Sept. 1, 1934, p. 23–24, KCMF 2366; Director to all field offices, FBI memo, Feb. 21, 1934, p. 49, BKF 711, sec. 8.

12. McKee report, May 20, 1936, p. 9, HKF 732.

13. Brown report, Sept. 19, 1934, p. 50, BKF 2919; Merrick interview; *St. Paul Daily News*, Sept. 23, 1936, p. 1.

14. Brown report, Sept. 19, 1934, p. 51, BKF 2919; Glass report, May 11, 1932, p. 22, file 4-2-11-0, NARG 129; Brennan report, Feb. 15, 1936, p. 6, HKF 423.

15. Director to field offices memo, Feb. 21, 1934, p. 16, BKF 711.

16. Karpis with Trent, *Karpis Story*, 167–68; D. L. Nicholson, FBI report, Apr. 14, 1934, p. 15, DF 688, sec. 14.

17. McIntire report, Apr. 10, 1935, p. 173, BKF sec. 96.

18. McIntire report, Apr. 10, 1935, p. 82, 173, BKF sec. 96.

19. Bremer kidnapping, FBI summary, Nov. 19, 1936, p. 18–19; Clegg to special agent in charge memo, May 31, 1934, DF 1733; *St. Paul City Directory, 1932*, 347; William Weaver, FBI wanted poster, Feb. 12, 1935, order no. 1238, BKF 4582, sec. 69; Bremer kidnapping, FBI summary, Nov. 19, 1936, p. 5–6; McIntire report, Apr. 10, 1935, p. 82, BKF sec. 96.

20. McIntire report, Apr. 10, 1935, p. 82–83, BKF sec. 96; Bremer kidnapping, FBI summary, Nov. 19, 1936, p. 51.

21. McIntire report, Apr. 10, 1935, p. 97, BKF sec. 96. Murray statement, Feb. 12, 1935, p. 4, BKF 4546.

22. Hall to Hanni memo, Jan. 27, 1936, p. 1, BKF 104.

23. *Pioneer Press*, Apr. 24, 1935, p. 1, 5; Roy Norman McCord Jr., interview by author, Dec. 23, 1992; Mary Johnson, interview by author, May 12, 1993; O. G. Hall to Werner Hanni, FBI memo, Feb. 6, 1934, p. 3, BKF 264, sec. 3.

24. Hall to Hanni memo, Feb. 6, 1934, p. 4; Karpis with Trent, *Karpis Story*, 165.

25. McCord interview.

26. Mary Johnson interview.

27. Lannon interview.

28. Colleen McCalla, interview by author, July 9, 1993.

29. *Pioneer Press*, Jan. 10, 1936, p. 1–2.

30. Director to field offices memo, Feb. 21, 1934, p. 23–24, 47, BKF 711.

31. Vicenta Donnelly Scarlett, interview by author, May 14, 1994.

32. Director to field offices memo, Feb. 21, 1934, p. 23–24, 47, BKF 711.

33. Bomberg interview, Ramsey County Historical Society.

34. *Minneapolis Journal,* Jan. 18, 1934, p. 1–2.

35. McIntire report, Apr. 10, 1935, p. 32–33, BKF sec. 96.

36. *Pioneer Press,* Apr. 5, 1952, p. 4; Director to field offices, Feb. 21, 1934, p. 16, BKF 711.

37. *Dispatch,* Jan. 19, 1934, p. 1, 7; *Dispatch,* Jan. 20, 1934, p. 1, 5; *Dispatch,* Jan. 25, 1934, p. 1–2, BKF sec. 96.

38. McIntire report, Apr. 10, 1935, p. 34–35, BKF sec. 96; Bremer kidnapping, FBI summary, Nov. 19, 1936, p. 21–22.

39. McIntire report, Apr. 10, 1935, p. 34–35, BKF sec. 96; Bremer kidnapping, FBI summary, Nov. 19, 1936, p. 21–22; Betty Bremer Johnson, interview by author, Jan. 27, 1992. See also *Dispatch,* Jan. 19, 1934, p. 1, 7.

40. Bremer kidnapping, FBI summary, Nov. 19, 1936, p. 23.

41. Director to Hanni memo, Jan. 19, 1934, BKF 10.

42. Joseph B. Keenan to attorney general, Justice Dept. memo in FBI files, Jan. 22, 1934, BKF 100, sec. 2.

43. Memo to Werner Hanni, FBI memo, Jan. 19, 1934, p. 1–2, BKF, sec. 1.

44. Bremer Johnson interview.

45. Werner Hanni to St. Paul office, FBI memo, Jan. 27, 1934, BKF, sec. 2.

46. *Pioneer Press,* Jan. 10, 1936, p. 1–2.

47. McIntire report, Apr. 10, 1935, p. 36–37, BKF sec. 96; *St. Paul Dispatch,* Feb. 8, 1934.

48. Director to field offices memo, Feb. 21, 1934, p. 26–27, BKF 711.

49. Director to field offices memo, Feb. 21, 1934, p. 31, BKF 711.

50. Edward G. Bremer, statement to FBI, Feb. 8, 1934, p. 2, BKF, sec. 3; Bremer Johnson interview.

51. Bremer statement, Feb. 8, 1934, p. 2, BKF sec. 3.

52. Director to field offices memo, Feb. 21, 1934, p. 23, BKF 711.

53. McIntire report, Apr. 10, 1935, p. 41–42, BKF sec. 96.

54. McIntire report, Apr. 10, 1935, p. 65, BKF sec. 96.

55. Bremer kidnapping, FBI summary, Nov. 19, 1936, p. 28; Purvis, *American Agent,* 149.

56. Tony Tiemann, interview by author, Nov. 20, 1992.

57. McIntire report, Apr. 10, 1935, p. 34–35, BKF sec. 96; *Dispatch,* Feb. 8, 1934, p. 1.

58. J. Edgar Hoover to attorney general, FBI memo, Feb. 8, 1934, BKF 212, sec. 3; S. L. Fortenberry to Werner Hanni, FBI memo, n.d., p. 1, BKF 310, sec. 4; Louise Benz, interview by author, Oct. 30, 1992.

59. Bremer Johnson interview.

60. Hoover to field offices memo, Feb. 21, 1934, p. 11/2, BKF 711.

61. H. H. Clegg to Director, FBI memo, May 8, 1934, HKF 317, sec. 4.

62. McIntire report, Apr. 10, 1935, p. 35, BKF sec. 96; R. G. Harvey to director, FBI memo, Feb. 11, 1934 (with enclosed memo dated Feb. 10, 1934), BKF 281, sec. 3; Nathan report, Feb. 21, 1934, p. 1, BKF 721.

63. Barker-Karpis gang, FBI summary, Apr. 1984, p. 8; Bremer kidnapping, FBI summary, Nov. 19, 1936, p. 29; Director to special agent in charge, St. Paul, FBI memo, Feb. 12, 1934, p. 2, BKF 310, sec. 4; R. E. Newby to director, FBI memo, Mar. 29, 1934, p. 3, BKF 1558.

64. Stein to director memo (enclosing statement of Byron Bolton to FBI), Aug. 18, 1936, p. 1, HKF 1037.

65. Callahan and Jones, *Heritage of an Outlaw,* 156; Purvis to director letter, Mar. 21, 1934, KCMF 1475.

66. Madala report, May 19, 1936, p. 15, HKF 738; Karpis with Trent, *Karpis Story,* 173–74; McIntire report, Apr. 10, 1935, p. 178, BKF sec. 96.

67. FBI memo, Apr. 24, 1936, p. 2, BKF 11635; McIntire report, Apr. 10, 1935, p. 175–77, BKF sec. 96.

68. McKee report, May 8, 1936, p. 8, BKF 11529.

69. Murray statement, Feb. 12, 1935, p. 12–13, BKF 4546.

70. Purvis, *American Agent,* 138.

71. *Pioneer Press,* Jan. 10, 1936, p. 1–2.

72. H. H. Clegg to director memo, May 8, 1934, p. 1, DF 1310.

73. D. L. Nicholson, FBI report, Sept. 11, 1934, p. 3, DF 3813, sec. 64; Ramsey County Register of Deeds, Abstract of Title, Lot 23, Eisenmenger's Lake Villas, since July 29,

1929; FBI memo on Thomas Brown, Nov. 10, 1936, p. 11, HKF 1082;; S. P. Cowley to Director, FBI memo, Apr. 11, 1934, DF 514, sec. 11; Suran report, Oct. 6, 1934, p. 48, KCMF 2655.

74. H. H. Clegg to Director, FBI memo, Apr. 13, 1934, p. 6, DF 560, sec. 12.

75. FBI memo on Thomas Brown, Nov. 10, 1936, p. 10, HKF 1082; R. E. Newby to Director, FBI memo, Sept. 12, 1934, and D. L. Nicholson, FBI report, Sept. 13, 1934, p. 2–3, both in DF 3904, sec. 65.

76. Gladys Sawyer, statement to FBI, Sept. 13, 1934, p. 5, BKF 2869, sec. 35; Bremer kidnapping, FBI summary, Nov. 19, 1936, p. 38–40.

77. Karpis with Trent, *Karpis Story*, 178; D. M. Ladd to special agent in charge, Detroit, FBI memo, Sept. 29, 1934, BKF 3029, sec. 37; McKee report, May 20, 1936, p. 2, 6, HKF 732; Bremer Kidnapping, FBI summary, Nov. 19, 1936, p. 37–40.

78. *Pioneer Press*, May 9, 1936, p. 2; Bonnie Kohrt, interview by author, Jan. 1993.

79. Paul G. Comstock, interviews by author, Sept. 4 and Sept. 6, 1992.

80. Dirk Boardsen, interview by author, Sept. 5, 1992.

Notes for Chapter 9

1. *U.S.A. v. Clayton E. May, Evelyn Frechette et al.*, 129–30 (U.S. 3d Dist., 1934), MHS; Clegg to director memo, Apr. 13, 1934, p. 8, DF 568.

2. Robert Cromie and Joseph Pinkston, *Dillinger: A Short and Violent Life* (Evanston, Ill.: Chicago Historical Bookworks, 1990; reprint of 1962), 133–35, 159–62; Evelyn Frechette, "Evelyn Tells Life with Dillinger" (part 3), *Chicago Herald and Examiner*, Aug. 29, 1934.

3. H. H. Clegg, FBI report, May 25, 1934, p. 4, DF 1712, sec. 32.

4. Evelyn Frechette, "Evelyn Tells Life with Dillinger" (part 2), *Chicago Herald and Examiner*, Aug. 28, 1934; *USA v. Clayton E. May et al.*, 581, 613–15.

5. H. H. Reinecke, FBI report, Apr. 20, 1934, p. 2 DF 672, sec. 14; Evelyn Frechette, "My Wild Flight with Dillinger," *Startling Detective Adventures*, 1934, p. 60, in DF 3771x, sec. 62; Cromie and Pinkston, *Dillinger*, 163–64, 170–72, 175.

6. Cromie and Pinkston, *Dillinger*, 5, 8, 172–74, 136–41, 176.

7. Homer Van Meter, FBI wanted poster, Apr. 11, 1934, DF 473, sec. 11; Russell G. Girardin with William J. Helmer, *Dillinger: The Untold Story* (Bloomington: Indiana University Press, 1994), 19.

8. Bernice Clark, "My Adventures with the Dillinger Gang," *Chicago Herald and Examiner*, Sept. 10, 1934, pt. 2, p. 1, 6; V. W. Peterson, FBI report, May 17, 1934, p. 3–4, DF 1478, sec. 28.

9. Eddie Green, St. Cloud State Reformatory file 5774, MHS.

10. Green, St. Cloud State Reformatory file.

11. Green, St. Cloud State Reformatory file; Cooper, *Here's to Crime*, 85–87.

12. Bruce Hamilton, nephew of John Hamilton, interview by author, Dec. 17, 1993; Girardin with Helmer, *Dillinger*, p. 26, 45; Cromie and Pinkston, *Dillinger*, 59–60, 83–84, 105–11.

13. Clark, "My Adventures with the Dillinger Gang," p. 6.

14. Lester M. Gillis, FBI wanted poster, Apr. 25, 1934, no. 1223, DF 1340, sec. 25; Nash, *Bloodletters and Badmen*, 402.

15. Nash, *Bloodletters and Badmen*, 403; John Herbert Dillinger, FBI case summary, July 12, 1954, 18; *Dispatch*, Mar. 5, 1934, p. 1, 9; *Pioneer Press*, Mar. 5, 1934, p. 1; Fatso Negri with Bennett Williams, "In the Hinges of Hell: How G-Men Ended Crime's Reddest Chapter" (part 6), *True Detective Mysteries*, May 1941, p. 102.

16. Cromie and Pinkston, *Dillinger*, 9–14; "The Dillinger Man-hunt," *True Detective*, July 1934, p. 66.

17. Girardin with Helmer, *Dillinger*, 271–74.

18. Frechette, "My Wild Flight with Dillinger," p. 60, DF 3771x.

19. H. H. Clegg to director, FBI memo, Apr. 4, 1934, p. 2, DF 402, sec. 9.

20. Clegg to director, FBI memo, Apr. 19, 1934, p. 1, DF 662, sec. 14.

21. Marie Marion Conforti, statement to FBI, Apr. 26, 1934, p. 1–2, DF 948, sec. 19.

22. John Herbert Dillinger, FBI summary, p. 6; *Pioneer Press,* Mar. 14, 1934, p. 1; Purvis to director, FBI teletype, Apr. 8, 1934, DF 393, sec. 9.

23. Marie Conforti, statement to FBI, Aug. 29, 1934, p. 1, DF 3702, sec. 61.

24. Clegg to director memo, Apr. 13, 1934, p. 12, DF 560.

25. Hoover, *Persons in Hiding,* p. 36. See also Suran report, Sept. 1, 1934, p. 36–37.

26. Nicholson report, Sept. 22, 1934, p. 9, DF 4004.

27. Evelyn Frechette, "What I Knew about Dillinger," *Chicago Herald and Examiner,* Aug. 30, 1934.

28. Clegg to director memo, Apr. 13, 1934, p. 5; Frechette, "Evelyn Tells Life with Dillinger" (part 1); D. L. Nicholson, FBI report, May 29, 1934, p. 3, DF 1714, sec. 32.

29. Reiter interviews, Sept. 1 and 24, 1994; V. W. Peterson, FBI report, June 23, 1934, p. 45–46, DF 2211, sec. 39.

30. Reiter interviews, May 2, 1991 and Sept. 24, 1993; Cowley to director memo, Apr. 11, 1934, DF 514.

31. John Herbert Dillinger, FBI case summary (revised), Feb. 1, 1984, p. 1; Peterson report, May 17, 1934, p. 5, DF 1478.

32. D. L. Nicholson, FBI report, Apr. 9, 1934, p. 33–34, DF 466, sec. 10.

33. Peterson report, May 17, 1934, p. 6, DF 1478.

34. *Dispatch,* Apr. 26, 1934, p. 1–2.

35. H. H. Clegg, FBI report, Apr. 21, 1934, p. 1, DF 670, sec. 14; D. L. Nicholson, FBI report, Sept. 19, 1934, p. 1–2, DF.

36. Clegg report, Apr. 21, 1934, p. 5–6, DF 670; Nels George Mortensen death certificate, no. 3146, Oct. 23, 1971, Minnesota Department of Health; *Pioneer Press,* Jan. 17, 1934, p. 8; *Pioneer Press,* Apr. 10, 1934, p. 1.

37. Nicholson report, Sept. 11, 1934, p. 1–2, DF 3813; *Dispatch,* July 19, 1934, p. 1; Albert Reilly, Leavenworth prison file 48037, Federal Bureau of Prisons; Pat Reilly, Minnesota Prison file 17141, MHS.

38. H. H. Clegg to special agent in charge, Cincinnati, FBI memo, June 9, 1934, p. 4, DF 1880, sec. 35.

39. Clegg report, Apr. 21, 1934, p. 3, DF 670.

40. Clegg report, Apr. 21, 1934, p. 2–3, 4, DF 670; Hall report, July 27, 1933, p. 17, KCMF 401; Suran report, Mar. 3, 1936, p. 16–17, HKF 401. See also Cowley to director memo, Apr. 24, 1934, p. 4, DF 1010.

41. Director to S. P. Cowley, FBI memo, Apr. 24, 1934, DF 754, sec. 16; Cowley to director memo, Apr. 24, 1934, p. 5, 6, DF 1010.

42. Cowley to director memo, Apr. 24, 1934, p. 3, 4–5, DF 1010; *Dispatch,* May 3, 1934, p. 1, 6.

43. Nels Mortensen death certificate, Oct. 23, 1971.

44. John Herbert Dillinger, FBI summary, July 12, 1954, p. 4.

45. Louis Schroth, interview by author, Apr. 2, 1993.

46. Letter of Mar. 1934 quoted in Alanna Nash, "Memories of John Dillinger," *Chicago Reader,* July 20, 1984, p. 33–34.

47. *USA v. Clayton E. May et al.,* 292; Cromie and Pinkston, *Dillinger,* 186.

48. J. T. McLaughlin, Lincoln Court Apts. caretaker, interview by author; D. L. Nicholson, FBI report, Apr. 2, 1934, p. 5–7, 10, DF 299, sec. 8.

49. Obituary of Rufus C. Coulter, *Grapevine,* Nov. 1975, p. 28; Nicholson report, Apr. 2, 1934, p. 11–13, DF 299; *USA v. Clayton E. May et al.,* 187. See also H. H. Reinecke report, Apr. 20, 1934, p. 2, DF 672.

50. *USA v. Clayton E. May et al.,* 177–79.

51. *USA v. Clayton E. May et al.,* 594; John Herbert Dillinger, FBI summary, July 12, 1954, p. 5; *Dispatch,* Mar. 31, 1934, p. 1.

52. *USA v. Clayton E. May et al.,* 95.

53. *USA v. Clayton E. May et al.,* 95–96; Bob Geisenheyner, interview by author, n.d.

54. Schroth interview; *USA v. Clayton E. May et al.,* 595; Cromie and Pinkston, *Dillinger,* 188.

55. Geisenheyner interview.

56. D. L. Nicholson, FBI report, Apr. 28, 1934, p. 5–7, DF 1144, sec. 22.

57. *Pioneer Press,* Apr. 2, 1934, p. 10, Apr. 3, 1934, p. 4; *St. Paul Daily News,* Mar. 31, 1934, p. 1.

58. *Dispatch,* Apr. 5, 1934, p. 12, Apr. 4, 1934, p. 1, 12, Apr. 2, 1934, p. 1; Cromie and Pinkston, *Dillinger,* 188.

59. *U.S.A. v. Clayton E. May et al,*

227–241; Cromie and Pinkston, *Dillinger,* 188; Nicholson report, Apr. 2, 1934, p. 9, DF 299.

60. *Dispatch,* Apr. 6, 1934, p. 1–2; *Dispatch,* Apr. 30, 1934, p. 1; Director to S. P. Cowley, FBI memo, Apr. 4, 1934, p. 4, DF 325, sec. 8.

61. Mary Charlton, interview by author, Jan. 23, 1993; F. A. Tamm to director, FBI memo, June 13, 1934, p. 1, DF 2072, sec. 37.

62. *Dispatch,* Apr. 4, 1934, p. 1, 12; Director to H. H. Clegg, FBI memo, Mar. 31, 1934, p. 2, DF 323, sec. 8.

63. Memoranda of conversations between Mr. Hoover and Mr. Purvis and between Mr. Hoover and Mr. Rorer, both Apr. 1, 1934, DF 264, sec. 7.

64. Werner Hanni to H. H. Clegg, FBI memo, May 1, 1934, p. 6, DF 1513, sec. 29.

65. *Dispatch,* Apr. 31, 1934, p. 1; *Dispatch,* May 3, 1934, p. 1, 6.

66. Director to Mr. Cowley, FBI memo, Apr. 2, 1934, DF 324, sec. 8.

67. *USA v. Clayton E. May et al.,* 475, 486.

68. *USA v. Clayton E. May et al.,* 352. See also *Pioneer Press,* Apr. 21, 1938, p. 1; H. H. Clegg, FBI report, Apr. 21, 1934, p. 3–4, DF 677, sec. 14.

69. *USA v. Clayton E. May et al.,* 479–82, 486–87.

70. *USA v. Clayton E. May et al.,* 545; *Pioneer Press,* Apr. 27, 1934, p. 1–2.

71. Clayton E. May, statement to FBI, Apr. 17, 1934, DF 673, sec. 14.

72. Clegg report, Apr. 21, 1934, p. 2–4, DF 677; *Pioneer Press,* Apr. 21, 1938, p. 1.

73. Thomas Leonard Carroll, FBI wanted poster, Apr. 25, 1934, Identification Order 1224.

74. Thomas L. Carroll, Ramsey County Probate file 53032, 1934; Thomas L. Carroll, Leavenworth prison file 36697, Federal Bureau of Prisons.

75. Carroll prison file.

76. Thomas Carroll, wanted poster, Post Office Dept., Dec. 1, 1933, BCA.

77. Carroll, FBI wanted poster.

78. Dan Lambert, "How Iowa 'Rubbed Out' Dillinger's Ace Gunman," *Startling Detective Adventures,* 1934, p. 9–10, in DF 3771x, sec. 62; *Dispatch,* June 8, 1934, p. 1–3.

79. Peterson report, June 23, 1934, p. 45, DF 2211; Kenneth Herschler, interview by author, May 21, 1993; Mercia Bergaus, who raised Kenneth, son of "Radio Sally" Bennett, interview by author, May 1993.

80. Interviews by author with Jim Vogel, Mar. 1993, and John Vogel, May 14, 1993.

81. Jim Vogel interview.

82. John Vogel interview.

83. Loretta Murphy, interview by relative, Apr. 1985, audiotape in the possession of Jim Vogel, Anoka, Minn.

84. Jim Vogel interview.

85. Peterson report, June 23, 1934, p. 46–47, DF 2211.

86. Carroll, FBI wanted poster, Apr. 25, 1934; *Pioneer Press,* June 8, 1934, p. 1, 3; Lambert, "How Iowa 'Rubbed Out' Dillinger's Ace Gunman," p. 11, DF 3771x.

87. Janet Gibson interview; *Brainerd Daily Dispatch,* Oct. 23, 1933, p. 1.

88. Fatso Negri with Bennett Williams, "In the Hinges of Hell: How G-Men Ended Crime's Reddest Chapter" (part 4), *True Detective Mysteries,* Mar. 1941, p. 89.

89. Donald Fish, interview by author, Jan. 23, 1993; Donald Fish, *The Dillinger Connection* (St. Paul: ByWords Printing, 1986), 3–4.

90. Fish interview.

91. *Brainerd Journal Press,* Oct. 27, 1933, p. 1.

92. Zane Smith, interview by author, Apr. 1993; Kevin Allenspach, "It Was No Gangster Movie," *Brainerd Daily Dispatch,* Dec. 4, 1988, p. 1C.

93. FBI memo, May 13, 1934, p. 11, DF 1415, sec. 27.

94. H. H. Clegg, FBI report, May 3, 1934, p. 3, DF 1219, sec. 23; *Dispatch,* Nov. 11, 1933, p. 1.

95. D. L. Nicholson, FBI report, May 14, 1934, p. 9, 30 DF 1410; R. C. Coulter to H. H. Clegg, FBI memo, June 10, 1934, p. 3, DF 1410, sec. 38.

96. Carroll, FBI wanted poster; *Pioneer Press,* June 8, 1934, p. 1, 3; D. L. Nicholson, FBI report, Sept. 28, 1934, p. 1, DF 4027, sec. 67; H. H. Clegg to director, FBI memo, June 20, 1934, p. 1–2, DF 2144, sec. 38.

97. Clegg to Purvis teletype, May 6, 1934, HKF 318.

98. R. C. Coulter to H. H. Clegg, FBI memo, June 10, 1934, p. 1, DF 2097, sec. 38; Clegg to director memo, June 20, 1934, p. 2, DF 2144.

99. Coulter to Clegg memo, June 10, 1934, p. 1, DF 2097; *Pioneer Press,* June 8, 1934, p. 1, 3.

100. Loretta Murphy interview.

101. June Bock, secretary, Oakland Cemetery, to Robert E. Bates, Sept. 17, 1987, letter in author's possession.

102. Lambert, "How Iowa 'Rubbed Out' Dillinger's Ace Gunman," p. 670, DF 3771x.

103. Clegg to Director memo, Apr. 4, 1934, p. 1, DF 402.

104. *Dispatch,* Mar. 13, 1934, p. 1; Robert H. Wybest, interview by author, Oct. 10, 1993.

105. Wybest interview; *Dispatch,* Mar. 13, 1934; Clegg to director memo, Apr. 13, 1934, p. 8, DF 560.

106. S. P. Cowley to director, FBI memo, Apr. 8, 1934, p. 1, DF 468, sec. 11; W. A. Rorer, FBI report, Apr. 9, 1934, p. 10, DF 491, sec. 11; S. P. Cowley, FBI memo, Apr. 4, 1934, p. 1, DF 294, sec. 7; Clegg to director memo, Apr. 19, 1934, DF 662; Nicholson report, Apr. 9, 1934, p. 28, DF 446.

107. H. H. Clegg to director, FBI memo, Apr. 4, 1934, p. 1–5, DF 467, sec. 10.

108. E. N. Notesteen to H. H. Clegg, FBI memo, Apr. 3, 1934, p. 1–2, DF 467, sec. 10.

109. Clegg to director memo, Apr. 4, 1934, p. 2, DF 402; Notesteen to Clegg memo, Apr. 3, 1934, p. 2–3, DF 467; *Pioneer Press,* Apr. 4, 1934, p. 1, 5.

110. Lannon interview; Thomas Delaney, an acquaintance of Eddie Green's brother, interview by author, May 9, 1992; H. H. Clegg to director, FBI memo, Apr. 17, 1934, p. 3, DF 664, sec. 14.

111. Cowley to director memo, Apr. 8, 1934, p. 5, DF 468; S. P. Cowley to director, FBI memo, Apr. 19, 1934, p. 4, DF 1584, sec. 30.

112. Nicholson report, Apr. 28, 1934, p. 50, DF 1144.

113. *Pioneer Press,* Apr. 8, 1934, p. 1; John Herbert Dillinger, FBI summary, July 12, 1954, p. 6; Harry Eugene Green file 10819–N, Apr. 11, 1934, Ramsey County coroner.

114. Cromie and Pinkston, *Dillinger,* 192–97, 206–7.

115. Clegg to director memo, Apr. 4, 1934, p. 3, DF 402; FBI memo, Apr. 16, 1934, p. 3, DF 1524, sec. 29.

116. S. P. Cowley to director, FBI memo, Apr. 19, 1934, DF 689, sec. 14; Director to S. P. Cowley, FBI memo, Apr. 18, 1934, DF 1537, sec. 29.

117. Cowley memo, Apr. 4, 1934, p. 1, DF 294; Cowley to director memo, Apr. 19, 1934, DF 689.

118. S. P. Cowley to director, FBI memo, Apr. 3, 1934, DF 292, sec. 7.

119. L. J. Rauber, FBI memo, Apr. 7, 1934, DF 407, sec. 9; Erik G. Peterson to director, FBI memo, Apr. 6, 1934, p. 2, DF 341, sec. 8.

120. Purvis, *American Agent,* 1, 10–14.

121. Purvis, *American Agent,* 15–18; Director to attorney general, FBI memo, June 27, 1934, DF 2224, sec. 40.

122. Purvis, *American Agent,* 16–19.

123. *Pioneer Press,* June 21, 1934, p. 1.

124. Gentry, *Hoover,* 172.

125. Aloysius "Ollie" McGree, Hastings resident, interview by author, Apr. 11, 1992.

126. Larry H. Johns, "The Hastings Spiral Bridge: Gone But Not Forgotten," *Minnesota Calls* 5, no. 3 (May/June 1992): 10.

127. *Hastings Gazette,* Apr. 27, 1934, p. 1; D. L. Nicholson, FBI report, May 11, 1934, p. 13, DF 1356, sec. 26.

128. Edwin J. Riege, "The Dillinger Case" (part 2), *The Investigator,* Dec. 1988, p. 3; John Herbert Dillinger, FBI summary, July 12, 1954, p. 10; *Hastings Gazette,* Apr. 27, 1934, p. 1.

129. *Minneapolis Journal,* Apr. 24, 1934, p. 1–2.

130. Bremer kidnapping, FBI summary, Nov. 19, 1936, p. 36; John Herbert Dillinger, FBI summary, July 12, 1954, p. 27; Cromie and Pinkston, *Dillinger,* 265; Girardin with Helmer, *Dillinger,* 156.

131. Cromie and Pinkston, *Dillinger,* 1–4, 250–56. Crime historian Jay Robert Nash, it should be noted, has argued that coroner's records suggest a "patsy" substitute, and not John Dillinger, was killed at the Biograph that day. See Nash, *Bloodletters and Badmen,* 176–78.

132. Summers, *Official and Confidential,* 72–73.

133. D. L. Nicholson, FBI report, Sept. 6, 1934, p. 3–4, DF 3788, sec. 62.

134. Jim Coleman, interview by author, Apr. 24, 1992; Nicholson report, Sept. 11, 1934, p. 7–8, 12, DF 3813.

135. Cowley to director memo, Apr. 8, 1934, p. 4, DF 468.

136. S. P. Cowley to special agent in charge, St. Paul, FBI memo, Sept. 5, 1934, DF 3786, sec. 62.

137. E. A. Tamm to director, FBI memo, Aug. 24, 1934, p. 1–2, DF 3630, sec. 59.

138. Nicholson report, Sept. 6, 1934, p. 19, DF 3788.

139. Dupont interview, May 1991; *St. Paul Daily News*, Aug. 25, 1934, p. 1–2. This version of Van Meter's death was also cited in Cromie and Pinkston, *Dillinger*, 263. See also Keljik interview.

140. Girardin with Helmer, *Dillinger*, 321.

141. S. P. Cowley to special agent in charge, St. Paul, FBI memo, Sept. 10, 1934, DF, sec. 64.

142. D. M. Ladd to director, FBI letter, Aug. 24, 1934, p. 3, DF 3595, sec. 59.

143. *Pioneer Press*, Aug. 24, 1934, p. 1.

144. Van Meter file 11023E, Aug. 23, 1934, Ramsey County coroner; *Minneapolis Tribune*, Aug. 24, 1934, p. 1–2; *Pioneer Press*, Aug. 24, 1934, p. 1.

145. Keljik interview.

146. St. Paul resident Norm Horton Sr., interview by author, May 15, 1991; *Dispatch*, Aug. 24, 1934, p. 1; Cromie and Pinkston, *Dillinger*, 239–40.

147. D. L. Nicholson, FBI report, Aug. 28, 1934, p. 1, DF 3676, sec. 61; E. A. Tamm to director, FBI memo, Aug. 24, 1934, p. 2, DF 3639, sec. 60; *Minneapolis Tribune*, Aug. 24, 1934, p. 1–2; Tamm to director memo, Aug. 24, 1934, p. 1–2, DF 3630.

148. Ladd to director memo, Aug. 24, 1934, 1–2, DF 3595; Nicholson report, Aug. 28, 1934, p. 6, DF 3676.

149. Nicholson report, Aug. 28, 1934, p. 6–7, DF 3676; Noonan report, June 18, 1936, p. 48, HKF 880.

150. Nicholson report, Aug. 28, 1934, p. 8, DF 3676.

151. Nicholson report, Sept. 6, 1934, p. 19.

152. Lannon interview; Noonan report, June 18, 1936, p. 48, HKF 880.

153. *Dispatch*, Aug. 27, 1934, p. 1.

154. Clegg to director memo, May 8, 1934, p. 4, DF 1310; Rosen to director memo, Apr. 3, 1936, p. 7, HKF 469x; Stein to director memo (Bolton statement), Aug. 18, 1936, p. 1, HKF 1037.

155. Pranke interview, Oct. 23, 1992.

156. Pranke, "Autobiography," 277; Nicholson report, Aug. 28, 1934, p. 3–4, DF 3676.

157. Nicholson report, Aug. 28, 1934, p. 2, DF 3676; J. Edgar Hoover to E. A. Tamm, FBI memo, Sept. 6, 1934, DF 3783, sec. 62.

158. *Pioneer Press*, Aug. 25, 1934, p. 1.

159. Nash, *Bloodletters and Badmen*, 404–5.

160. Hoover, *Persons in Hiding*, xvii; Avery Hale, "The Inside Story of Dillinger at Last," *True Detective Mysteries*, Dec. 1934, p. 7–8.

161. John Herbert Dillinger, FBI summary, July 12, 1954, p. 1, 12.

162. *Pioneer Press*, Aug. 24, 1934, p. 1; *Minneapolis Tribune*, Aug. 25, 1934, p. 8.

Notes for Chapter 10

1. Pranke, "Autobiography" 138–42.

2. *Pioneer Press*, Feb. 16, 1934, p. 1–2. On cleanup campaigns, see, for example, *Dispatch*, Nov. 7, 1922, p. 1, Nov. 22, 1929, p. 1, Dec. 9, 1929, p. 1.

3. Hanni to director memo, Feb. 20, 1934, p. 1, CCF 16, vol. 1.

4. *Dispatch*, Mar. 28, 1951, p. 25.

5. *St. Paul Daily News*, Mar. 31, 1934, p. 1.

6. *St. Paul Daily News*, Feb. 16, 1934, p. 1, and Feb. 24, 1934, p. 1.

7. *St. Paul Daily News*, Feb. 23, 1934, p. 1.

8. Thomas E. Dahill to John Edgar Hoover, SPPD letter, Feb. 17, 1934, CCF 20, vol. 1; R. T. Harbo to Mr. Tolson, FBI memo, Feb. 20, 1934, CCF 20, vol. 1.

9. J. Edgar Hoover to Thomas E. Dahill, FBI letter, Feb. 28, 1934, CCF 20, vol. 1; J. Edgar Hoover to William Stanley, FBI memo, Mar. 9, 1934, CCF 37, vol. 1.

10. *St. Paul Daily News*, Mar. 8, 1934, p. 1.

11. Purvis, *American Agent*, 140.

12. Lannon interview; Reiter interview; special agent ____ to Hanni memo, Feb. 19, 1934, p. 4, CCF 16, vol. 1.

13. *Pioneer Press*, June 27, 1934, p. 4.

14. H. H. Clegg to director, FBI memo, June 22, 1934, HKF 326, sec. 4.

15. C. W. Stein to director, FBI memo, June 12, 1936, p. 1, HKF 824, sec. 10; Louise Jamie, widow of Wallace Jamie, interview by author, Mar. 12, 1992. See also Stanley High, "St. Paul Wins a War," *Current History* 49, no. 1 (1938): 18–20.

16. High, "St. Paul Wins a War," 19.

17. *St. Paul Daily News*, June 27, 1935, p. 1, 5, June 29, 1935, p. 1–2; *Minnesota v. James P. Crumley et al.*, 344–45; *Pioneer Press*, June 26, 1935, p. 1. Although the present location of the wire recordings is unknown, transcripts of many of the wiretaps are contained *Minnesota v. James P. Crumley et al.*, Ramsey County District Court, Dec. 1935, MHS. Other excerpts appeared in the *St. Paul Daily News* in June 1935.

18. *Minnesota v. James P. Crumley et al.*, 369; *Dispatch*, Feb. 7, 1939, p. 1.

19. Noonan report, May 27, 1936, p. 3, HKF 759; *Minnesota v. James P. Crumley et al.*, 369, 373–76.

20. *St. Paul Daily News*, June 27, 1935, p. 1–3; *St. Paul Daily News*, June 24, 1935, p. 1–2.

21. *Dispatch*, Feb. 7, 1939, p. 1; Minnesota Police Association Official Bulletin, vol. 4, no. 8 (Mar. 1931).

22. Stein to director and Sal Connelly, FBI teletype, May 18, 1936, HKF 710, sec. 8; *Pioneer Press*, Apr. 23, 1936, p. 1–2, Apr. 25, 1935, p. 1, 3; *Dispatch*, Feb. 7, 1939, p. 1.

23. Brennan report, Feb. 15, 1936, p. 4, HKF 423.

24. Wills to Tamm memo, Mar. 18, 1940, p. 3–4, HKF 1125. See also John L. Connolly to J. Edgar Hoover, city of St. Paul letter, July 25, 1936, HKF 972, sec. 10.

25. Stein to director memo, June 12, 1936, p. 1–2, HKF 842.

26. T. D. Quinn to Mr. Tolson, FBI memo, Apr. 30, 1936, HKF 664, sec. 8; C. A. Hackert to G. H. Barfuss, SPPD letter, July 17, 1936, and H. E. Warren to Thomas A. Brown, City of St. Paul letter, Aug. 5, 1936, both in Thomas Brown file, SPPD.

27. C. A. Hackert to Personnel Division, memo, Nov. 4, 1936, Thomas Brown file, SPPD. S. W. Hardy, FBI report, Jan. 17, 1940, p. 4, BKF 15142, sec. 270.

28. Peters interview; Thomas A. Brown death certificate, Jan. 8, 1959, Minnesota Department of Health; *St. Paul Daily News*, Sept. 29, 1936, p. 1, 10.

29. *St. Paul Daily News*, June 3, 1936, p. 1, Aug. 1, 1936, p. 1; *Pioneer Press*, June 7, 1936, p. 1.

30. Sherin interview.

31. *Chicago Daily News*, Apr. 16, 1940, p. 1.

32. Mayor Mark E. Gehan to Senator Royal Copeland, city of St. Paul letter, Apr. 27, 1937, CCF 238, vol. 4.

33. J. Edgar Hoover to attorney general, FBI memo, May 7, 1937, CCF 238, vol. 4.

Notes for Chapter 11

1. *Pioneer Press*, Sept. 3, 1935, p. 1, 4.

2. Hoover to McMahon memo, May 13, 1936, p. 7, HKF 724; E. J. Connelley, FBI report, May 18, 1936, p. 1–3, BKF 11665, sec. 203; Karpis with Trent, *Karpis Story*, 190–98, 202–19, 223.

3. Karpis with Trent, *Karpis Story*, 230–33; *Pioneer Press*, May 2, 1936, p. 1–2; Gentry, *Hoover*, 185–87.

4. Gentry, *Hoover*, 185–87, 188.

5. Gentry, *Hoover*, 179–80; Ray Tucker, "Hist! Who's That?" *Colliers* 92, no. 8 (Aug. 19, 1933): 15, 48; Grooms interview.

6. Barker-Karpis gang, FBI summary, Apr. 1984, p. 10; Richard G. Powers, *Secrecy and Power: The Life of J. Edgar Hoover* (New York: Free Press, 1987), 208; Grooms interview; J. Kevin O'Brien, chief, FBI Freedom of Information section, to author, Oct. 24, 1994, letter in author's possession.

7. Grooms interview.

8. Summers, *Official and Confidential;* 241–42.

9. Connelley report, May 18, 1936, p. 9, BKF 11665; *Dispatch.*, May 2, 1936, p. 1, 3; Karpis with Trent, *Karpis Story*, 240; Hoover, *Persons in Hiding*, 45.

10. Cooper, *Here's to Crime*, 112–113.

11. *Dispatch*, May 2, 1936, p. 1, 3; Nate Bomberg, "The Day Karpis Returned," *Capital: St. Paul Pioneer Press and Dispatch Sunday Magazine*, Mar. 28, 1971, p. 6, 10.

12. Karpis with Trent, *Karpis Story*, 256.

13. *Dispatch*, Nov. 10, 1935, p. 3; Larry Millett, *Lost Twin Cities* (St. Paul: Minnesota Historical Society, 1992), 258.

14. Hughes report, Aug. 10, 1933, p. 1, HKF 127; Noonan report, Oct. 10, 1933, p. 7, HKF 176.

15. Hughes memo, Aug. 10, 1933, p. 2, HKF 127; Noonan report, Oct. 10, 1933, p. 4, HKF 176; *Dispatch*, Nov. 10, 1933, p. 3, Nov. 28, 1933, p. 1–2; McIntire report, Apr. 10, 1935, p. 173, 178, BKF sec. 96.

16. Noonan report, Oct. 10, 1933, p. 7, HKF 127; Parrish to Hoover, FBI memo, Aug. 3, 1933, HKF 89, sec. 1.

17. *Pioneer Press*, Dec. 2, 1933, p. 1.

18. Nash, *Bloodletters and Badmen*, 561–65; Purvis, *American Agent*, 74; Carl Sifakis, *The Mafia Encyclopedia* (New York: Facts on File, 1987), 325; Nash, *Bloodletters and Badmen*, 564–65.

19. *Dispatch*, Apr. 28, 1934, p. 1, 5.

20. Virginia Gibbons Schwietz, interview by author, Dec. 30, 1992.

21. Bremer kidnapping, FBI summary, Nov. 19, 1936, p. 43, 52; *Dispatch*, Jan. 23, 1935, p. 1–2.

22. *Dispatch*, Jan. 19, 1935, p. 1, 3; *Pioneer Press*, Oct. 17, 1935, p. 8.

23. McKee report, May 8, 1936, p. 25, BKF 11529; Suran report, May 18, 1936, p. 3, BKF 11653; C. W. Stein to director, FBI memo, May 22, 1936, p. 2, BKF 11755, sec. 204.

24. C. W. Stein to director, FBI memo, May 11, 1936, BKF 11541, sec. 201; J. Edgar Hoover to attorney general, FBI memo, June 29, 1936, HKF 885, sec. 10.

25. Hoover to attorney general memo, June 29, 1936, HKF 885.

26. Robert Schwietz interview.

27. *Dispatch*, Apr. 17, 1936, p. 1, 5, Apr. 28, 1936, p. 1–2; *Minneapolis Tribune*, July 25, 1936, p. 1, 4.

28. McKee report, July 28, 1936, HKF 991: *Dispatch*, July 31, 1936, p. 1–2.

29. E. A. Tamm to director, FBI memo, July 31, 1936, HKF 1013, sec. 11.

30. Robert Schwietz interview; Dr. Raymond Bieter, M.D., to coroner C. A. Ingerson, Aug. 7, 1936, University of Minnesota letter, John Peter Peifer file 12127, July 31, 1936, Ramsey County coroner.

31. *St. Paul Daily News*, July 31, 1936, p. 1; William Walsh, interview by author, Jan. 6, 1995.

32. S. K. McKee, FBI report, Aug. 1, 1936, p. 2, HKF 1005, sec. 11.

33. *St. Paul Daily News*, Aug. 3, 1936, p. 2; *Minneapolis Journal*, Aug. 3, 1936, p. 1–2.

34. Martin Rohling interview, June 1991.

35. McKee report, Apr. 27, 1936, p. 63, HKF 647.

36. Eileen Michels, "Old Federal Courts Building—Beautiful, Unique—Its Style of Architecture Faces Extinction," *Ramsey County History* 9, no. 1 (Spring 1972): 3–9.

37. Director to attorney general memo, June 27, 1934, DF sec. 40; Girardin with Helmer, *Dillinger*, 161.

38. Barker-Karpis gang, FBI summary, Apr. 1984, p. 9–10; Jim Yandle, "The Bloody End to Ma Barker's Crime Spree," *Orlando Sentinel*, Jan. 19, 1988, p. 4.

39. Doris Lockerman, "G-Men on the Trail of the Desperadoes," *Chicago Tribune*, Oct. 18, 1935; Helmer, *Dillinger*, 268.

40. *New York Times*, Aug. 26, 1936, p. 11; McKee report, July 10, 1936, p. 10, HKF 891; Anne Diestel to author, July 25, 1994, in author's possession.

41. *Dispatch*, May 14, 1935, p. 1–2; Ex-Operative 48, "Sterilization," 42.

42. Anderson report, Aug. 31, 1936, p. 3, HKF 1053; *Dispatch*, May 25, 1935, p. 1; Bremer kidnapping, FBI summary, Nov. 19, 1936, p. 63–64; Nicholson report, Sept. 28, 1934, p. 1–2, DF 4027.

43. Nicholson report, May 14, 1934, p. 12, DF 1410; Director to attorney general memo, June 27, 1934, DF sec. 40; *Pioneer Press*, June 4, 1936, p. 4.

44. *Dispatch*, May 4, 1935, p. 1, 3.

45. Anderson report, Aug. 31, 1936, p. 3, HKF 1053.

46. McKee report, May 20, 1936, p. 2, HKF

732; E. A. Tamm to director, July 15, 1936, HKF 941, sec. 10.

47. McKee report, May 20, 1936, p. 13–14, HKF 732.

48. McKee report, May 8, 1936, p. 12, BKF 11529.

49. Karpis with Trent, *Karpis Story,* 241–43.

50. S. K. McKee reports, July 30, 1936, p. 8, HKF 1002, and May 8, 1936, p. 8, 31, BKF 11529.

51. *Pioneer Press,* Feb. 2, 1935, p. 3.

52. Keljik interview.

53. McKee report, July 28, 1936, p. 1, HKF 989; *St. Paul Daily News,* July 14, 1936, p. 1; Richard Hirsch, "Killers Call Him 'Creepy'," *True Detective,* June 1940, p. 111.

Notes for Epilogue

1. *St. Paul Daily News,* July 25, 1934, p. 1; Nash, *Bloodletters and Badmen,* 176–78.

2. Nash, "Memories of John Dillinger," p. 38.

3. Hamilton interviews; Girardin with Helmer, *Dillinger,* 298.

4. Girardin with Helmer, *Dillinger,* 63.

5. Nicholson report, Sept. 11, 1934, p. 23, DF 3813.

6. Purvis, *American Agent,* 264.

7. Barker-Karpis gang, FBI summary, Nov. 19, 1936, p. 10; John Knutson, interview by author, Mar. 1993.

8. Bruce Barnes, interview by author, Jan. 11, 1994.

9. Hoover, *Persons in Hiding,* 143; William W. Turner, *Hoover's FBI: The Men and the Myth* (New York: Dell Publishing Co., 1970), 21.

10. Turner, *Hoover's FBI,* 21–23, Appendix.

11. Haley, *Robbing Banks,* 176–202.

12. *Minneapolis Tribune,* Dec. 27, 1963, p. 1; Joseph O'Connor interview; Social Security Administration locator service, 1995.

13. Minnesota Department of Health, Leon Gleckman death certificate, July 14, 1941, no. 14784; St. Paul police report on death of Leon Gleckman, July 15, 1941, Ramsey County medical examiner's files; Sherin interview.

14. Harry Sawyer, Leavenworth/Alcatraz prison file, Federal Bureau of Prisons.

15. DeMoss interview.

16. Inmate Locator Service, Harry Sawyer file; Carole J. DeMoss to author, Jan. 4, 1994, letter in author's possession; Sawyer prison file.

17. Figge interview.

18. Flanagan, *Theodore Hamm in Minnesota,* 108, 122.

19. *Pioneer Press,* May 5, 1965, p. 1–2; Bremer Johnson interview.

20. Evelyn Tic death certificate, Jan. 13, 1969, Wisconsin Department of Health and Social Services; Bernice Tic, interview by author, Feb. 1994.

21. *Chicago Tribune,* Jan. 6, 1961, p. F2, Oct. 7, 1973, p. F4.

22. Sevareid, *The People's Lawyer,* 107.

23. Grooms interview.

24. Thomas M. McDade, "Karpis Recalls His Crime Spree of 1930s in Talks with McDade," *Grapevine,* May 1980, p. 36–38.

25. Barker-Karpis gang, FBI summary, Apr. 1984, p. 12.

26. Thomas Holden, Leavenworth/Alcatraz prison file, Special Progress report, Dec. 1946, Federal Bureau of Prisons; Lillian Holden homicide report, June 1949, Chicago Police Dept.; Thomas Holden file, n.d., Illinois Dept. of Corrections.

27. Francis Keating, Leavenworth/Alcatraz prison file, Federal Bureau of Prisons; Robert Fleigel, interview by author, Dec. 10, 1991; Robert Fleigel to author, Nov. 19, 1991, letter in author's possession.

28. Fleigel letter; Reiter interview.

29. "Shy" Troupe, interview by author, Nov. 3, 1993.

30. Reiter interview.

31. State of Minnesota, Francis Keating death certificate, July 25, 1978.

32. Fleigel interview.

33. Turner, *Hoover's FBI,* 147.

34. Sifakis, *Mafia Encyclopedia,* 268.

35. Interviews by author with Christine Brigham and Irene McBride, n.d.

INDEX

Geographic places are in Minnesota unless otherwise noted. Italicized page numbers indicate photographs.

PICTURE CREDITS

Photographs and other illustrations used in this book appear through the courtesy of the institutions or persons listed below. The name of the photographer, when known, is given in parentheses, as is additional information about the source and location of the item. Donors of photographs now at the Minnesota Historical Society are individually identified.

Minnesota Historical Society (MHS) collections, St. Paul—pages i, ii–iii (Peter Latner), vi (Northwest Photographic Studio), 1, 8, 14 (A. F. Raymond), 28, 37 (Kenneth Wright), 52 *top* (Arthur Lund), 56 (C. P. Gibson), 70 (Gibson), 79 (Gibson), 80, 91 (Wright), 130 (Gibson), 148, 149, 168 *top*, 168 *bottom* (Phillip Hutchens; South St. Paul Police Dept.), 183, 186, 193, 196, 212, 217, 219 (Hutchens), 243 (Richard Pranke Papers), 249, 250, 253 left, 260, 261, 266, 278; cover: gun (Latner), building (Hutchens)
Associated Press/Wide World—pages x, 179, 202, 264, 273 *inset*, 279
Barfuss Family—pages 164, 253 *right*, 258 (all MHS)
Jane Bonne—page 133 (MHS)
Chicago Tribune—pages 146, 282 (AP/Wide World)
Federal Bureau of Investigation, Washington, D.C.—pages xv, 56 *inset*, 58, 79 *inset*, 91 *inset*, 121, 130 *inset*, 132, 135 *inset*, 163, 206, 207, 219 *left inset*, 239 top, 270; cover: Dillinger poster, face
Federal Bureau of Prisons, Washington, D.C.—pages 86, 91 *inset*, 287
Janet Gibson—page 170 (MHS)
Hastings Gazette—page 238 (Apr. 27, 1934)
Kenneth Herschlar—page 227 (MHS)
Keller Golf Course, Maplewood—page 100
Kansas City Star—pages 171, 177
Landmark Center, St. Paul—page 273
Lane Family—page *47*, 47 *inset* (MHS)
Library of Congress, Washington, D.C.—page 154 *inset* (AP/Wide World)
Ann Michaud—page 6 (MHS)
Minneapolis Public Library, Minneapolis Collection—pages 37 *inset*, 42, 103, 120 (*Star Tribune*), 151, 158 *inset*, 199, 251, 275
Minnesota Bureau of Criminal Apprehension, St. Paul—pages *59*, 102, 123, 209, 219 *right inset*, 226 (all MHS)
Sue Mollner—page 126 (MHS)
National Archives, Washington, D.C.—pages 180, 180 *inset*
Jean Preston—page 70 *inset* (MHS)

Ramsey County Historical Society, St. Paul—pages 23, 83, 128, 145, 190 *inset*

St. Paul Daily News—pages *21* (St. Paul Police Dept.), 22, *32*, 45, 241 bottom (Aug. 25, 1934), 248 (June 24, 1935), 254 (June 27, 1935), 257 (June 24, 1935), 266 *inset*, 268, 268 *inset* (all MHS)

St. Paul Dispatch—pages 45 *inset* (Oct. 27, 1933), 95 (Aug. 14, 1930), 182 (Jan. 18, 1934)

St. Paul Health Department—page 20

St. Paul Pioneer Press—pages vi *inset*, xxii (Dec. 5, 1928), 19, 50, 73 (Mar. 8, 1932), 114, 119 (Dec. 17, 1932), 158, 190

St. Paul Police Department—pages 8 *inset*, *21*

South St.Paul Daily Reporter—page 167 (Aug. 30, 1933)

Star Tribune/Minneapolis-St. Paul—pages 17, 53, 120, 126, 135, 142, 160, 280, 289

Startling Detective Adventures—page 52 *bottom* (July 1933)

James Thomas—page 154 (MHS)

University of Oklahoma Library, Western History Collections, Norman—page 185

UPI/Bettman—pages 61, 66, 67, 76, 77, 82, 105, 107, 126 *inset*, 210, 235, 239 *bottom*, 241 top, 263, 283

White Bear Press—page 97 (June 26, 1930)

Willmar Tribune—page 93 (July 16, 1930)

Maps by Mui D. Le and Alan J. Willis, University of Minnnesota Cartography Laboratory, Minneapolis

great speeches of our time

great speeches of our time

Hywel Williams

Quercus

Contents

Introduction

The oratory contained and discussed in this book reflects the currents of thought and alignments of power which created our contemporary world. Most of these speeches were delivered by politicians, national leaders who were intent on communicating the urgency of their message and the accuracy of their truth. Very many of them gained authority by democratic means and their words, spoken by and large at the very apex of their influence, reflect a career-long training in the art of eloquent persuasion. The speeches of Fidel Castro, Nikita Khrushchev and Chairman Mao reveal that dictatorial power may also seek to impress by demonstrating verbal skill – a technique which supplements the despot's habitual reliance on force. Generals MacArthur and Marshall show the military mind's analysis of geopolitics, while Eleanor Roosevelt and Martin Luther King, Jr display the commitment of the activist who gains moral authority and practical influence through dedication to a cause. The tide of events in war and peace, within nations and across frontiers, shapes the individual mind as well as the collective consciousness. Seamus Heaney and Orhan Pamuk show how literary art can reflect and also affect the conflicts within an individual artist's homeland, and their words track the impulsion of a writer's conscience towards the public domain.

This is therefore a book of many voices, one whose themes extend from the postwar era of reconstruction to the resurgence of a politicized Islam in the early 21st century. Many of these orators have been drawn to the question of national identity. Ben-Gurion in Israel, Nehru in India, Nyerere in Tanzania, and de Valera in Ireland: all were state-builders working in a culture whose origins were ancient. Thatcher's Britain and de Gaulle's France, by contrast, exemplify countries whose strong sense of a national culture was closely related to a long history of organized government. American political oratory, however, owes much of its zest to the feeling that the US is a civilization in the making rather than one whose history is behind it. Pierre Trudeau sought to ground Canadian national sentiment in a new constitution which respected diversity while also aspiring towards unity. Kevin Rudd's apology to Australia's indigenous peoples goes beyond introspection and invites a country to embark on a new phase of self-discovery. In all these instances, whether the nation-state was old or newer, oratory could pluck at the heart strings as well as appeal to the intellect when speaking of the roots of identity.

Nonetheless, the period which started in 1945, as Richard von Weizsäcker points out, records both victory and defeat for the notion of national self-determination. Western European nations were liberated from occupation, just as central and eastern European countries were to regain their freedom after 1989. But the past two generations have also recorded a rapid growth in the number of international organizations, such as the European Union, the United Nations, the Organization of African Unity, and the World Trade Organization. Their competence has often been tested and their authority criticized, but their existence is testimony to an ever-widening dimension in ethics, politics and economics. International issues involving human rights, disarmament, globalized capitalism and terrorism have given a new range to the oratory of those who seek to change the world by influencing our opinions. Anita Roddick's anger at multi-national companies, Tony Blair's aspiration to a renewed world order, and Nelson Mandela's message of multi-racial tolerance all touch on these wider themes which transcend the narrower lives of nations.

By the end of our period few public figures buttressed their speeches with quotations from the ancients, as Harold Macmillan liked to do. Attention was now gained by pithier means. But the elements that go to make a great speech hardly change at all, as the history of rhetoric shows. It was first formalised as a subject in classical Rome during the first centuries BC and AD, and from the middle ages to the renaissance a study of rhetoric was basic to the educational curriculum. Rote-learning led to an emphasis on mere technique, and 'rhetorical' acquired its pejorative modern meaning. Nowadays, we like our speakers to show authenticity rather than just follow the rules about how to vary pitch and tone. But without such skills a speaker can lose an audience and, thereby, the argument. The appeal to mind and heart through the order of thought and the clarification of feeling is the basis of great oratory. One person stands alone before the many, experiences the anticipation, and starts to speak. This is the grand continuity, and these are the voices that mattered in our time.

HYWEL WILLIAMS, 2008

'It is, indeed, hard for the strong to be just to the weak'

Éamon de Valera

(1882–1975)

IRELAND'S PRIME MINISTER EXPLAINS HIS GOVERNMENT'S POLICY OF NEUTRALITY; ADDRESS ON RADIO ÉIREANN, 16 MAY 1945

Winston Churchill's attack on the Irish government's neutrality during the Second World War formed part of a speech marking 'Victory in Europe' and had been broadcast across the world. In it he contrasted 'the action of Mr de Valera' with the 'instinct of thousands of Southern Irishmen who hastened to the battle-front to prove their ancient valour'. Irish neutrality, he maintained, had exposed Britain to additional danger during the Battle of the Atlantic, when German U-boats attacked the convoys travelling from North America to the UK. The inability to use Irish ports or to benefit from their refuelling facilities had reduced the range and effectiveness of British ships escorting the transatlantic convoys: 'if it had not been for the loyalty and friendship of Northern Ireland, we would have been forced to come to close quarters with Mr de Valera or perish forever from the earth.'

The ports in question were the deep-water bases at Cobh (Queenstown) and Berehaven on Ireland's southern coast, and Lough Swilly in the northwest. Known previously as the 'Treaty Ports', they had been retained as sovereign bases by the UK government following Ireland's 1922 partition and the creation of the Irish Free State. Neville Chamberlain returned the bases to Ireland in 1938, a move Churchill regarded as characteristically short-sighted, but which the Irish government regarded as vital to protect its neutrality in the event of war. Britain's exclusion from the two southern port facilities was especially significant since they were some 200 miles (320 km) further out into the Atlantic than any other naval bases available to its forces. Losses in this theatre of war were especially heavy

ÉAMON DE VALERA (1882–1975)

1913 Joins Irish Volunteers, a military organization backing Home Rule.

1916 Participates in Easter Rising against British rule and sentenced to death before a stay of execution.

1917 Becomes president of Sinn Féin.

1918 Sinn Féin wins majority of Irish seats in the British general election.

Jan 1919 An Irish parliament (Dáil) is formed but not recognized by the British.

1919–21 Irish War of Independence.

Oct–Dec 1921 Treaty negotiations in London, not attended by de Valera, agree to independence for 26 of Ireland's 32 counties.

1922–37 Constitution of the Irish Free State.

1922–3 Supports the anti-Treaty IRA in Irish Civil War; arrested and interned until 1924.

1926 Founds republican party, Fianna Fáil.

1932 Forms his first Free State government.

1937 New Irish constitution enacted.

1937 Becomes Ireland's first taoiseach (prime minister); in office 1937–48, 1951–4, 1957–9.

1949 Ireland becomes a republic and leaves the British Commonwealth.

for the British, with 245 vessels sunk by German U-boats between July and October 1940. Britain's occupation of Iceland in the same year, however, provided the Allies with additional bases for their Atlantic operations.

De Valera's dignified response is no less powerful for being so subtle. He hints that Britain's espousal of the rights of smaller nations is hypocritical, and Churchill is treated with a delicate irony. The imaginative shift portraying a German-occupied England, and the anticipated English reaction to being partitioned, is exquisitely done. As de Valera concedes, his reaction would have been less poised in earlier years, and the speech expresses a veiled regret at his own role in shedding blood. He had dissociated himself from the Anglo-Irish Treaty agreed in 1921 largely because it granted Ireland dominion status within the British Commonwealth, rather than full independence as a republic. The arrangements concerning the Treaty Ports formed part of a constitutional settlement which, for de Valera, limited Ireland's ability to pursue an independent foreign policy. As Colonial Secretary in 1921–2, Churchill had been one of the treaty's chief negotiators, so the issue he had now chosen to disinter was one with which he was very familiar.

Certain newspapers have been very persistent in looking for my answer to Mr Churchill's recent broadcast. I know the kind of answer I am expected to make . . .

I know the reply I would have given a quarter of a century ago. But I have deliberately decided that that is not the reply I shall make tonight. I shall strive not to be guilty of adding any fuel to the flames of hatred or passion which, if continued to be fed, promise to burn up whatever is left by the war of decent human feeling in Europe.

'I shall strive not to be guilty of adding any fuel to the flames of hatred or passion'

Allowances can be made for Mr Churchill's statement, however unworthy, in the first flush of his victory. No such excuse could be found for me in this quieter atmosphere. There are, however, some things which it is my duty to say . . .

Mr Churchill makes it clear that, in certain circumstances, he would have violated our neutrality and that he would justify his actions by Britain's necessity. It seems strange to me that Mr Churchill does not see that this, if accepted, would mean that Britain's necessity would become a moral code and that when this necessity became sufficiently great, other people's rights were not to count.

It is quite true that other great powers believe in this same code – in their own regard – and have behaved in accordance with it. That is precisely why we have the disastrous succession of wars – World War no. 1 and World War no. 2 – and shall it be World War no. 3?

Surely Mr Churchill must see that, if his contention be admitted in our regard, a like justification can be framed for similar acts of aggression elsewhere and no small nation adjoining a great power could ever hope to be permitted to go its own way in peace.

It is, indeed, fortunate that Britain's necessity did not reach the point when Mr Churchill would have acted. All credit to him that he successfully resisted the temptation . . . It is, indeed, hard for the strong to be just to the weak, but acting justly always has its rewards.

By resisting his temptation in this instance, Mr Churchill, instead of adding another horrid chapter to the already bloodstained record of the relations between England and this country, has advanced the cause of international morality . . .

'No small nation adjoining a great power could ever hope to be permitted to go its own way in peace'

That Mr Churchill should be irritated when our neutrality stood in the way of what he thought he vitally needed, I understand, but that he or any thinking person in Britain or elsewhere should fail to see the reason for our neutrality, I find it hard to conceive.

I would like to put a hypothetical question . . . Suppose Germany had won the war, had invaded and occupied England, and that after a long lapse of time and many bitter struggles she was finally brought to acquiesce in admitting England's right to freedom, and let England go, but not the whole of England, all but, let us say, the six southern counties.

These six southern counties, those, let us suppose, commanding the entrance to the narrow seas, Germany had singled out and insisted on holding herself with a view to weakening England as a whole and maintaining the security of her own communications through the Straits of Dover.

Let us suppose, further, that after all this had happened Germany was engaged in a great war in which she could show that she was on the side of the freedom of a number of small nations. Would Mr Churchill as an Englishman who believed that his own nation had as good a right to freedom as any other – not freedom for a part merely, but freedom for the whole – would he, whilst Germany still maintained the partition of his country and occupied six counties of it, would he lead this partitioned England to join with Germany in a crusade? I do not think Mr Churchill would.

Would he think the people of partitioned England an object of shame if they stood neutral in such circumstances? I do not think Mr Churchill would.

Mr Churchill is proud of Britain's stand alone, after France had fallen and before America entered the war. Could he not find in his heart the generosity to acknowledge that there is a small nation that stood alone, not for one year or two, but for several hundred years against aggression; that endured spoliations, famines, massacres in endless succession; that was clubbed many times into insensibility, but that each time on returning consciousness, took up the fight anew; a small nation that could never be got to accept defeat and has never surrendered her soul?

'A small nation that stood alone, not for one year or two, but for several hundred years against aggression'

Mr Churchill is justly proud of his nation's perseverance against heavy odds. But we in this island are still prouder of our people's perseverance for freedom through all the centuries. We of our time have played our part in that perseverance, and we have pledged ourselves to the dead generations who have preserved intact for us this glorious heritage, that we too will strive to be faithful to the end, and pass on this tradition unblemished.

Many a time in the past there appeared little hope except that hope to which Mr Churchill referred, that by standing fast a time would come when, to quote his own words, 'the tyrant would make some ghastly mistake which would alter the whole balance of the struggle.'

'I have had a vision of a nobler and better ending, better for both our peoples and for the future of mankind'

I sincerely trust, however, that it is not thus our ultimate unity and freedom will be achieved, though as a younger man I confess I prayed even for that . . .

In latter years I have had a vision of a nobler and better ending, better for both our peoples and for the future of mankind. For that I have now been long working. I regret that it is not to this nobler purpose that Mr Churchill is lending his hand rather than by the abuse of a people who have done him no wrong, trying to find in a crisis like the present excuse for continuing the injustice of the mutilation of our country . . . '

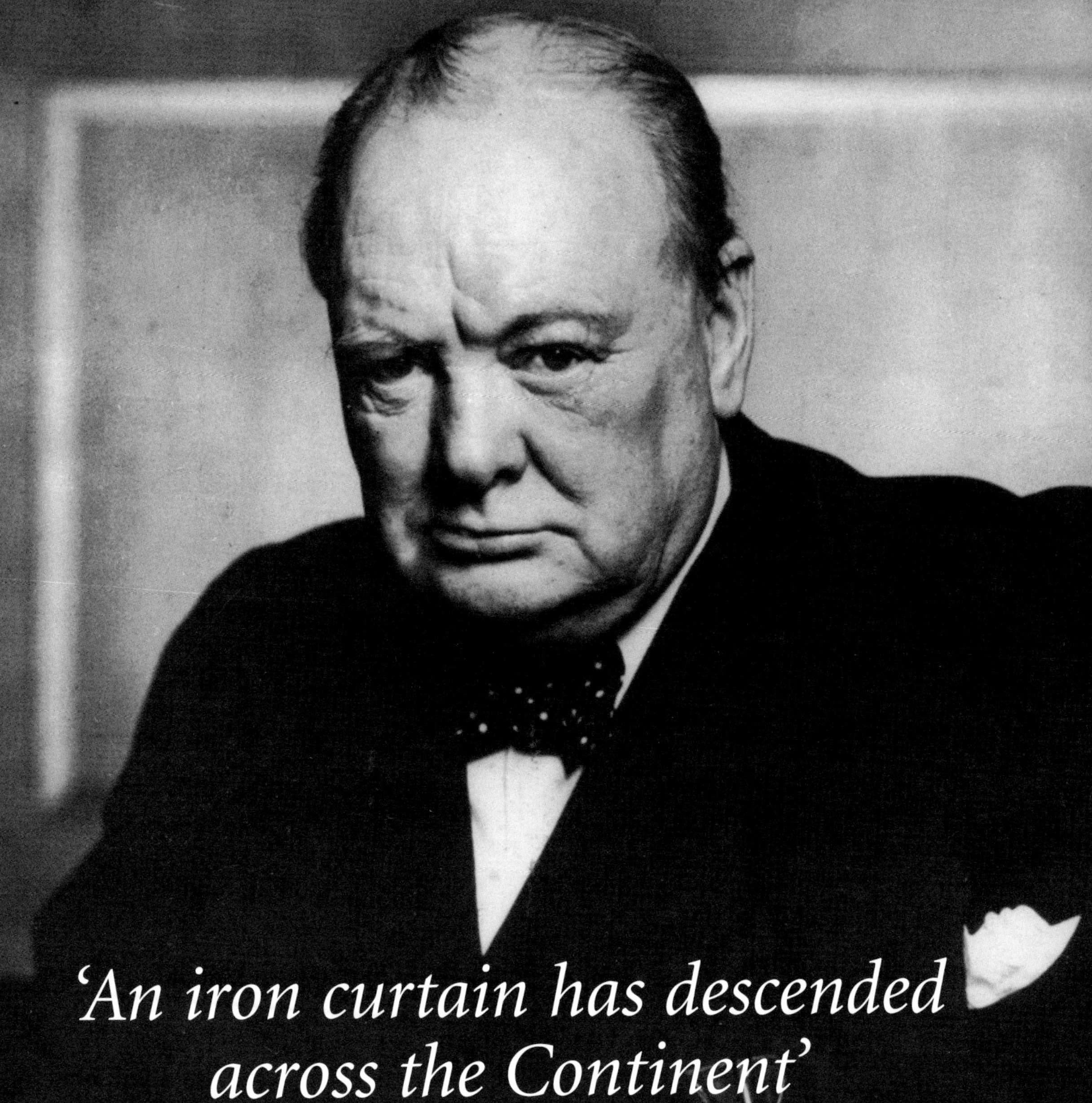

'An iron curtain has descended across the Continent'

Winston Churchill

(1874–1965)

BRITAIN'S WARTIME PRIME MINISTER WARNS OF THE DANGERS OF A DIVIDED EUROPE; LECTURE AT WESTMINSTER COLLEGE, FULTON, MISSOURI, 5 MARCH 1946

At the time of delivering this speech, Britain's wartime prime minister, Winston Churchill, was serving as leader of the opposition following the Conservative Party's defeat in the 1945 general election. The sonorous phraseology and broad historical sweep which had typified Churchill's wartime oratory remained undimmed and his speech marked the effective beginning of the Cold War. Broadcast by newsreel across the English-speaking world, the delivery of these words crystallized the significance of what was happening in Europe. The continent's division into two armed camps whose ethical and political values were fundamentally opposed to each other is described graphically, and the phrase 'iron curtain', here introduced for the first time, entered into common currency as a result. The man who had warned his country against appeasement of fascism in the 1930s was now resuming his role as prophet. Churchill is describing not just the reality of communist power in Europe but also the range of its totalitarian ambitions and the effectiveness of its subversive methods. The vision is a global one and the need to enrol the United States in what would be an Asian as well as a European struggle explains why Churchill deemed the American Midwest a good place in which to sound this particular trumpet.

Evocation of threat, however, is not the speech's sole keynote. Political imaginativeness, audacious planning and generosity of spirit are also present. Churchill the social progressive advocates welfare and government action to protect individuals and families from need and starvation. Democracy, he recognizes, has to prove its superiority to communism in this regard. Success in this area was needed to strengthen what Churchill

WINSTON CHURCHILL (1874-1965)

1900 Elected MP (Conservative) for Oldham, Lancashire.

1904 Joins Liberal Party.

1906 Elected MP (Liberal) for Manchester North-West.

1908 Appointed president of the Board of Trade; elected MP (Liberal) for Dundee.

1910 Appointed home secretary.

1911–15 Serves as first lord of the Admiralty.

1917–19 Minister of munitions.

1919–21 Secretary of state for war and air.

1921–2 Secretary of state for the colonies.

1922 Loses Dundee seat in the general election which returns a Conservative government.

1924 Elected MP for Epping, sitting initially as an independent, then as a Conservative.

1924–9 Chancellor of the exchequer.

1939 First Lord of the admiralty.

1940–5, 1951–5 Prime minister.

called 'the sinews of peace' and to consolidate thereby the wider political freedoms enjoyed in the democratic West.

In 1946 Churchill was still clinging to his ardent belief in the British empire, despite the obviousness of its imminent dissolution. Formed in the high noon of his country's late Victorian imperialism, he found it inconceivable that Britain should be anything other than an independent power. But his political education as an imperial statesman also meant that he thought naturally in terms that went beyond the confines of the nation state. It was this experience that equipped him to describe so imaginatively the immediate need of the postwar world: supranational institutions which transcended narrowly exclusive definitions of sovereignty and citizenship. After the fall of France in May 1940 he had proposed a joint Franco-British citizenship, and this speech's contemplation of British-American citizenship was similarly audacious. Speaking in Zurich in September 1946, Churchill would advocate 'a kind of United States of Europe', an entity that he thought should exist alongside the British empire and the Commonwealth. Security needs, as described in Fulton, Missouri, dictated large power blocs as a counterpoise to the USSR, and the idea of a balance of power exercised between a number of independent states was deemed obsolete and dangerous. At the beginning of his eighth decade Winston Churchill remained both a visionary and a realist.

The United States stands at this time at the pinnacle of world power. It is a solemn moment for the American democracy. For with primacy in power is also joined an awe-inspiring accountability to the future . . . Opportunity is here now, clear and shining for both our countries . . . It is necessary that constancy of mind, persistency of purpose, and the grand simplicity of decision shall guide and rule the conduct of the English-speaking peoples in peace as they did in war . . .

What then is the overall strategic concept which we should inscribe today? It is nothing less than the safety and welfare, the freedom and progress, of all the homes and families of all the men and women in all the lands . . . To give security to these countless homes, they must be shielded from the two giant marauders, war and tyranny . . . The awful ruin of Europe, with all its vanished glories, and of large parts of Asia, glares us in the eyes . . .

'Opportunity is here now, clear and shining for both our countries'

When I stand here this quiet afternoon I shudder to visualize what is actually happening to millions now and what is going to happen in this period when famine stalks the earth . . .

The United Nations Organization must immediately begin to be equipped with an international armed force . . . I propose that each of the Powers and States should be invited to delegate a certain number of air squadrons to the service of the world organization. These squadrons would be trained and prepared in their own countries, but would move around in rotation from one country to another . . . They would not be required to act against their own nation, but in other respects they would be directed by the world organization . . .

We cannot be blind to the fact that the liberties enjoyed by individual citizens throughout the British Empire are not valid in a considerable number of countries . . . In these states . . . power is exercised without restraint, either by dictators or by compact oligarchies operating through a privileged party and a political police . . .

'Eventually there may come – I feel eventually there will come – the principle of common citizenship'

Neither the sure prevention of war, nor the continuous rise of world organization, will be gained without . . . the fraternal association of the English-speaking peoples. This means a special relationship between the British Commonwealth and Empire and the United States. Fraternal association requires . . . the continuance of the intimate relationship between our military advisers, leading to common study of potential dangers, the similarity of weapons and manuals of instruction, and to the interchange of officers and cadets at technical colleges. The United States has already a Permanent Defence Agreement with the Dominion of Canada . . . This principle should be extended to all British Commonwealths with full reciprocity . . . Eventually there may come – I feel eventually there will come – the principle of common citizenship . . .

A shadow has fallen upon the scenes so lately lighted by the Allied victory . . . From Stettin in the Baltic to Trieste in the Adriatic, an iron curtain has descended across the Continent. Behind that line lie all the capitals of the ancient states of Central and Eastern Europe. Warsaw, Berlin, Prague, Vienna, Budapest, Belgrade, Bucharest and Sofia, all these famous cities and the populations around them lie in what I must call the Soviet sphere, and all are subject in one form or another, not only to Soviet influence but to a very high and, in many cases, increasing measure of control from Moscow. An attempt is being made by the Russians in Berlin to build up a quasi-Communist Party in their zone of Occupied Germany by showing special favours to groups of left-wing German leaders. This is certainly not the Liberated Europe we fought to build up. Nor is it one which contains the essentials of permanent peace.

'The old doctrine of the balance of power is unsound'

The safety of the world requires a new unity in Europe, from which no nation should be permanently outcast. It is from the quarrels of the strong parent races in Europe that the world wars we have witnessed, or which occurred in former times, have sprung. Surely we should work with conscious purpose for a grand pacification of Europe.

In front of the iron curtain which lies across Europe are other causes of anxiety. In a great number of countries . . . communist fifth columns are established and work in complete unity and absolute obedience to the decisions they receive from the communist centre.

I do not believe that Soviet Russia desires war. What they desire is the fruits of war and the indefinite expansion of their power and doctrines. From what I have seen of our Russian friends and Allies during the war, I am convinced that there is nothing they admire so much as strength, and there is nothing for which they have less respect than weakness, especially military weakness. For that reason the old doctrine of the balance of power is unsound. We cannot afford . . . to work on narrow margins, offering temptations to a trial of strength. If the Western Democracies stand together in strict adherence to the principles of the United Nations Charter, their influence for furthering those principles will be immense . . . If however they become divided . . . and if these all-important years are allowed to slip away then indeed catastrophe may overwhelm us all.

'I have had a vision of a nobler and better ending, better for both our peoples and for the future of mankind'

Let no man underrate the abiding power of the British Empire and Commonwealth. Because you see the 46 millions in our island harassed about their food supply . . . or because we have difficulty in restarting our industry and export trade . . . do not suppose that we shall not come through these dark years of privation as we have come through the glorious years of agony, or that half a century from now, you will not see 70 or 80 millions of Britons . . . united in defence of our traditions, our way of life, and of the world causes which you and we espouse. If we adhere faithfully to the Charter of the United Nations and walk forward in sedate and sober strength . . . if all British moral and material forces and convictions are joined with your own in fraternal association, the high-roads of the future will be clear, not only for us but for all, not only for our time, but for a century to come. ’

'Our policy is directed not against any country or doctrine but against hunger, poverty, desperation and chaos'

George Marshall

(1880–1959)

THE US SECRETARY OF STATE OUTLINES THE EUROPEAN RECOVERY PROGRAMME; SPEECH DELIVERED AT HARVARD UNIVERSITY, 5 JUNE 1947

'Our policy is directed not against any country or doctrine but against hunger, poverty, desperation and chaos'

The Marshall Plan was the brain-child of the US State Department. Dean Acheson, then under-secretary of state, was a major influence on the policy, as were two officials, Charles Bohlen, who wrote Marshall's speech, and George Kennan. During the four years of its operation until 1952 a total of 13 billion dollars' worth of economic aid and technical assistance was made available by the US to the participating countries: Austria, Belgium, Denmark, France, West Germany, the UK, Greece, Iceland, Ireland, Italy, Luxembourg, the Netherlands, Norway, Sweden, Switzerland and Turkey. The USSR and its satellite states in Central and Eastern Europe refused to participate, seeing the programme as an American ruse to exert control over their internal affairs. Western Europe's economic integration, however, was advanced by the Plan's removal of national tariff barriers, and the Organization for European Economic Cooperation, the institution devised to allocate the aid money, influenced the thinking of Europe's political integrationists.

Northwestern Europe's harsh winter in 1946–7 aggravated an already acute situation. Roads, railways and bridges, as well as most urban centres, had suffered aerial bombardment. Damage to infrastructure meant that smaller towns were isolated, and Eastern Europe's food surpluses were trapped behind the Iron Curtain. Germany's industrial base in coal and steel, vital for the entire European economy, was wrecked, and the Allies had imposed postwar restrictions on West Germany's heavy industrial capacity. Some of these constraints would be lifted, but the dismantling of German manufacturing businesses, including steel plants, would continue into the late 1940s.

With the US now alert to French and Italian communist threats, the Plan formed part of the State Department's newly embraced doctrine of 'containment', a policy which tried to stop

GEORGE MARSHALL (1880-1959)

1901 Graduates from Virginia Military Institute.

1917 Serves in France with the 1st Infantry Division during the the First World War.

1918 Joins headquarters of American Expeditionary Forces, the US's military force in Europe.

1936 Promoted to rank of brigadier-general.

1939 Promoted to full general; becomes US Army's chief of staff.

1944 Promoted to 5-star rank as general of the army, the US Army's highest rank.

1944–5 Coordinates Allied operations in Europe and the Pacific.

1945–7 Sent by President Truman to China: attempts unsuccessfully to broker peace in the country's civil war.

1947 Appointed US secretary of state.

1950–1 Secretary of defence.

1953 Awarded Nobel Peace Prize for the Marshall Plan.

the spread of Soviet influence to non-communist countries. Greece and Turkey, both exposed to communist aggression, were already receiving US economic and military assistance under the terms of the so-called Truman Doctrine, announced by President Harry S. Truman on 12 March 1947.

The aid money was mostly used to buy US goods, especially food, fuel and materiel for infrastructure development. This met a real American need for export-led demand. Geared to a war economy from 1942 to 1945, American factories had produced the fastest economic growth in US history. Peacetime required new markets and the Plan boosted postwar American consumerism.

By the early 1950s, the aggregate Gross National Product of countries participating in the Plan had risen by more than 30 per cent compared to pre-war levels; industrial production by 40 per cent. West Germany took longer to recover, and sceptics of the Marshall Plan adduced the country's reduction in economic regulations as the reason for its eventual phenomenal success.

The Plan's example encouraged the growth of an entire aid industry from the 1950s onwards. International organizations administering aid would also attract criticism of waste and corruption. But the principle outlined by Marshall in his speech had by then entered into the mainstream thinking of Western leaders: 'hunger, poverty, desperation and chaos' required the intervention of the powerful and prosperous.

I need not tell you, gentlemen, that the world situation is very serious. I think one difficulty is that the problem is one of such enormous complexity that the very mass of facts presented to the public by press and radio make it exceedingly difficult for the man in the street to reach a clear appraisement of the situation.

Furthermore, the people of this country are distant from the troubled areas of the earth and it is hard for them to comprehend the plight and consequent reactions of the long-suffering peoples, and the effect of those reactions on their governments in connection with our efforts to promote peace in the world.

'The rehabilitation of the economic structure of Europe quite evidently will require a much longer time and greater effort than had been foreseen'

In considering the requirements for the rehabilitation of Europe, the physical loss of life, the visible destruction of cities, factories, mines and railroads was correctly estimated. But it has become obvious during recent months that this visible destruction was probably less serious than the dislocation of the entire fabric of the European economy. Machinery has fallen into disrepair or is entirely obsolete. Under the arbitrary and destructive Nazi rule, virtually every possible enterprise was geared into the German war machine. Long-standing commercial ties, private institutions, banks, insurance companies and shipping companies disappeared, through loss of capital, absorption through nationalization or by simple destruction. In many countries, confidence in the local currency has been severely shaken. The rehabilitation of the economic structure of Europe quite evidently will require a much longer time and greater effort than had been foreseen.

There is a phase of this matter which is both interesting and serious. The farmer has always produced the foodstuffs to exchange with the city dweller for the other necessities of life. This division of labour is the basis of modern civilization. At the present time it is threatened with breakdown.

'A very serious situation is rapidly developing which bodes no good for the world'

The town and city industries are not producing adequate goods to exchange with the food-producing farmer. Raw materials and fuel are in short supply. Machinery is lacking or worn out. The farmer or the peasant cannot find the goods for sale which he desires to purchase. So the sale of his farm produce for money which he cannot use seems to him an unprofitable transaction. He, therefore, has withdrawn many fields from crop cultivation and is using them for grazing. He feeds more grain to stock and finds for himself and his family an ample supply of food, however short he may be on clothing and the other ordinary gadgets of civilization.

Meanwhile, people in the cities are short of food and fuel. So the governments are forced to use their foreign money and credits to procure these necessities abroad. This process exhausts funds which are urgently needed for reconstruction. Thus a very serious situation is rapidly developing which bodes no good for the world. The modern system of the division of labour upon which the exchange of products is based is in danger of breaking down.

The truth of the matter is that Europe's requirements for the next three or four years of foreign food and other essential products – principally from America – are so much greater than her present ability to pay that she must have additional help or face economic, social and political deterioration of a very grave character.

The remedy lies in breaking the vicious circle and restoring the confidence of the European people in the economic future of their own countries and of Europe as a whole. The manufacturer and the farmer . . . must be able and willing to exchange their products for currencies the continuing value of which is not open to question.

Aside from the demoralizing effect on the world at large and the possibilities of disturbances arising as a result of the desperation of the people concerned, the consequences to the economy of the United States should be apparent to all. It is logical that the United States should do whatever it is able to do to assist in the return of normal economic health in the world, without which there can be no political stability and no assured peace.

'The United States should do whatever it is able to do to assist in the return of normal economic health in the world'

Our policy is directed not against any country or doctrine but against hunger, poverty, desperation and chaos. Its purpose should be the revival of a working economy in the world so as to permit the emergence of political and social conditions in which free institutions can exist. Such assistance, I am convinced, must not be on a piecemeal basis as various crises develop.

Any government that is willing to assist in the task of recovery will find cooperation, I am sure, on the part of the United States government. Any government which manoeuvres to block the recovery of other countries cannot expect help from us. Furthermore, governments, political parties or groups which seek to perpetuate human misery in order to profit therefrom politically or otherwise will encounter the opposition of the United States.

It is already evident that, before the United States government can proceed much further in its efforts to alleviate the situation . . . there must be some agreement among the countries of Europe. It would be neither fitting nor efficacious for this government to undertake to draw up unilaterally a programme designed to place Europe on its feet economically. This is the business of the Europeans. The role of this country should consist of friendly aid in the drafting of a European programme and of later support of such a programme so far as it may be practical for us to do so. The programme should be a joint one, agreed to by a number, if not all European nations.

'Political passion and prejudice should have no part'

An essential part of any successful action on the part of the United States is an understanding on the part of the people of America of the character of the problem and the remedies to be applied. Political passion and prejudice should have no part. With foresight, and a willingness on the part of our people to face up to the vast responsibility which history has clearly placed upon our country, the difficulties I have outlined can and will be overcome. '

'A new star rises, the star of freedom in the east'

Jawaharlal Nehru

(1889–1964)

INDIA'S FIRST PRIME MINISTER MARKS HIS COUNTRY'S INDEPENDENCE; SPEECH TO THE CONSTITUENT ASSEMBLY, NEW DELHI, 14 AUGUST 1947

The influence of his English education is clearly evident in the speech delivered by Jawaharlal Nehru, India's first prime minister. Phrases such as 'tryst with destiny' and 'the stroke of the midnight hour' show a familiarity with the cadences of the language and a capacity to use it to poetic as well as dramatic effect. Born the son of a rich lawyer, Nehru wrote and spoke as the member of an Anglophone elite, and he had learnt English, as well as Hindi and Sanskrit, while growing up at the family home in Allahabad. Nehru's Westernization was not just a matter of speech and manner. The insurgent style of anti-colonialism he adopted in the 1920s owed much to the revolutionary agitation of contemporary Europe. Like his great mentor Mahatma Gandhi, he espoused India's self-reliance and attached himself to her native customs, practising yoga and reading the *Bhagavad Gita*. But the adoption of these cultural practices coexisted uneasily with his attachment to socialism, a European creed and one which showed the profound impact of the West on his intellectual development.

Part of the speech's fascination lies in the way it reveals these different aspects of Nehru's mind and personality. These are the words of a leader who was born to command, a patrician who enjoins his people to 'incessant striving' in order to be worthy of India. Nehru's father was an influential figure within the Indian National Congress, the political party which provided the country with its new establishment. Family patronage helped his early political career and, although he distrusted dynasticism, Nehru's successors among India's prime ministers include his daughter Indira and grandson Rajiv. Nonetheless, long periods of imprisonment by the British authorities, from 1931 to 1935 and again from 1942 to 1945, on account of his incitement to mass rebellion, earned Nehru the right to lead and gained him the adulation of the Congress masses.

JAWAHARLAL NEHRU (1889–1964)

1905 Leaves India for England and an education at Harrow, Trinity College, Cambridge, and the Inner Temple, London.

1924–6 President of the Municipal Corporation, Allahabad; pioneers schemes to improve education, health, sanitation and employment rates.

1928 Rejects his father's 'Nehru Report' which urges India's 'dominion status' within the British empire.

1929 Elected president of the Indian National Congress (INC), with the party now committed to full independence.

1936 Re-elected president of the INC; urges the party's adoption of socialism.

1942–5 Imprisoned by the British after urging rebellion in support of the Congress call for the British to 'quit India' in an immediate transfer of power.

1947–64 Prime minister of India.

'The greatest man of our generation' and 'father of our nation' Nehru alludes to is Gandhi, and the account of India's 'trackless centuries' echoes the Mahatma's tradition-based nationalism. But this is also a call to progressive politics issued by a secular-minded man to a deeply religious society. Nehru, quite significantly, makes no reference to India's gods. It was the Muslim–Hindu divide which explained why the pledge to achieve India's independence was redeemed only 'substantially'. The plan to partition India, released by the departing British on 3 June 1947, had been rushed through, and by August a Muslim-dominated state of Pakistan had been created, a country of two wings separated by more than 1000 miles (1600 km) of Indian territory. History's greatest population transfer involved some 18 million Muslims, Hindus and Sikhs, and the interreligious strife which spread through the Punjab, Bengal and Delhi claimed the lives of hundreds of thousands. This was the bloodiest inauguration possible. But in the decades following independence, and despite the persistence of religious violence, Nehru's words still stood as a reference point and a reminder of what India might yet become.

'Long years ago we made a tryst with destiny, and now the time comes when we shall redeem our pledge, not wholly or in full measure, but very substantially.

At the stroke of the midnight hour, when the world sleeps, India will awake to life and freedom. A moment comes, which comes but rarely in history, when we step out from the old to the new, when an age ends, and when the soul of a nation, long suppressed, finds utterance.

It is fitting that at this solemn moment we take the pledge of dedication to the service of India and her people and to the still larger cause of humanity.

'At the stroke of the midnight hour, when the world sleeps, India will awake to life and freedom'

At the dawn of history India started on her unending quest, and trackless centuries are filled with her striving and the grandeur of her successes and her failures. Through good and ill fortune alike she has never lost sight of that quest or forgotten the ideals which gave her strength. We end today a period of ill fortune and India discovers herself again . . .

Freedom and power bring responsibility. The responsibility rests upon this assembly, a sovereign body representing the sovereign people of India. Before the birth of freedom we have endured all the pains of labour and our hearts are heavy with the memory of this sorrow. Some of those pains continue even now. Nevertheless, the past is over and it is the future that beckons to us now.

That future is not one of ease or resting but of incessant striving so that we may fulfil the pledges we have so often taken and the one we shall take today. The service of India means the service of the millions who suffer. It means the ending of poverty and ignorance and disease and inequality of opportunity.

The ambition of the greatest man of our generation has been to wipe every tear from every eye. That may be beyond us, but as long as there are tears and suffering . . . our work will not be over.

And so we have to labour and to work, and work hard, to give reality to our dreams. Those dreams are for India, but they are also for the world, for all the nations and peoples are too closely knit together today for anyone of them to imagine that it can live apart.

'As long as there are tears and suffering, our work will not be over'

Peace has been said to be indivisible; so is freedom, so is prosperity now, and so also is disaster in this one world that can no longer be split into isolated fragments.

To the people of India, whose representatives we are, we make an appeal to join us with faith and confidence in this great adventure. This is no time for petty and destructive criticism, no time for ill will or blaming others. We have to build the noble mansion of free India where all her children may dwell.

The appointed day has come – the day appointed by destiny – and India stands forth again, after long slumber and struggle, awake, vital, free and independent. The past clings on to us still in some measure and we have to do much before we redeem the pledges we have so often taken. Yet the turning point is past, and history begins anew for us, the history which we shall live and act and others will write about.

'We have to build the noble mansion of free India where all her children may dwell'

It is a fateful moment for us in India, for all Asia and for the world. A new star rises, the star of freedom in the east, a new hope comes into being, a vision long cherished materializes. May the star never set and that hope never be betrayed! . . .

On this day our first thoughts go to the architect of this freedom, the father of our nation, who, embodying the old spirit of India, held aloft the torch of freedom and lighted up the darkness that surrounded us. We have often been unworthy followers of his and have strayed from his message, but not only we but succeeding generations will remember this message and bear the imprint in their hearts of this great son of India, magnificent in his faith and strength and courage and humility. We shall never allow that torch of freedom to be blown out, however high the wind or stormy the tempest.

Our next thoughts must be of the unknown volunteers and soldiers of freedom who, without praise or reward, have served India even unto death.

We think also of our brothers and sisters who have been cut off from us by political boundaries and who unhappily cannot share at present in the freedom that has come. They are of us and will remain of us whatever may happen, and we shall be sharers in their good and ill fortune alike.

'We shall never allow that torch of freedom to be blown out'

The future beckons to us. Whither do we go and what shall be our endeavour? To bring freedom and opportunity to the common man, to the peasants and workers of India; to fight and end poverty and ignorance and disease; to build up a prosperous, democratic and progressive nation, and to create social, economic and political institutions which will ensure justice and fullness of life to every man and woman.

We have hard work ahead. There is no resting for any one of us till we redeem our pledge in full, till we make all the people of India what destiny intended them to be.

We are citizens of a great country, on the verge of bold advance, and we have to live up to that high standard. All of us, to whatever religion we may belong, are equally the children of India with equal rights, privileges and obligations. We cannot encourage communalism or narrow-mindedness, for no nation can be great whose people are narrow in thought or action.

To the nations and peoples of the world we send greetings and pledge ourselves to cooperate with them in furthering peace, freedom and democracy.

And to India, our much-loved motherland, the ancient, the eternal and the ever-new, we pay our reverent homage and we bind ourselves afresh to her service. '

'This is our native land; it is not as birds of passage that we return to it'

David Ben-Gurion

(1886–1973)

ISRAEL'S SOON-TO-BE FIRST PRIME MINISTER ADDRESSES THE ELECTED ASSEMBLY OF PALESTINE JEWRY, JERUSALEM, 2 OCTOBER 1947

'This is our native land; it is not as birds of passage that we return to it'

The Mandate for Palestine was granted to Britain by the League of Nations after the Treaty of Sèvres (10 August 1920) split up the Middle Eastern territories of the Ottoman empire following its defeat in the First World War. The area for which Britain became responsible extended eastwards as far as the boundary of Britain's equivalent Mandate for Mesopotamia (Iraq). The Mandates for Lebanon to the north and for Syria to the northeast were administered by France. Britain's 'Palestine' included Transjordan, which it effectively ran as a separate area, while it recognized the territory to the west of the River Jordan as Palestine proper. The Balfour Declaration (2 November 1917), issued by the British foreign secretary A.J. Balfour, stated that the UK government favoured the establishment in Palestine of 'a national home for the Jewish people' and the clauses of Britain's Mandate empowered it to facilitate Jewish immigration to the region.

The Jewish Agency for Palestine, here addressed by Ben-Gurion, administered the local Jewish community and was officially recognized by the British. That community's numbers increased greatly as Jews fled European fascism, but the British government's 'white paper' of 1939 introduced controversial immigration quotas. Discontent with the Mandate led to the formation of militant Jewish organizations such as Irgun, which in 1946 blew up the King David Hotel in Jerusalem, the British administration's headquarters. By the time this speech was delivered, Britain had announced that it wanted to end the Mandate. Despite Ben-Gurion's fears that the British might be dilatory, the withdrawal of their 100,000 troops was effective by May 1948. The UN's partition plan, which created an independent state of Israel, was approved by the General Assembly on 29 November 1947, with 33 members voting for the proposal, 13 opposing it and 10 abstaining. Jordan and Egypt occupied those territories of the former British Mandate in Palestine which had been assigned by the UN plan to a Palestinian Arab state, an entity which therefore did not come into being. Over

DAVID BEN-GURION (1886–1973)

1906 Emigrates to Palestine, then part of the Ottoman empire, from Plonsk, Poland, then ruled as part of tsarist Russia.

1912 Studies law at Istanbul University.

1915 Expelled from Palestine by Ottoman Turkish authorities on account of his political activities and moves to New York City.

1918 Joins British army as part of 38th Battalion, Jewish Legion; returns to Palestine after First World War.

1920 Assists in formation of Palestine's Zionist Labour Federation, subsequently becoming its general secretary.

1930 Mapai, precursor of Israel's later Labour Party, is formed under Ben-Gurion's leadership.

1935–48 Chairman of executive committee of the Jewish Agency for Palestine.

1948 Becomes Israel's first prime minister (serves 1948–53, 1955–63).

half of the indigenous Palestinian population in Israel's new national territory either fled or were expelled, and the state defended its borders successfully during the Arab–Israeli war of 1948–9.

'Our movement', as Ben-Gurion calls it, was Zionism and its aspiration became a reality when the 'destined Jewish state' was proclaimed on 14 May 1948. The reference to 'the last eighteen hundred years' underlines the claim to legitimacy. Repressive measures were imposed by the Roman imperial authorities in Judaea following the second major Jewish rebellion (AD 132–5) against their rule in the province. The Jews were expelled from Jerusalem and, in an attempt at erasing the region's Jewish identity, the Romans renamed Judaea 'Syria Palaestina'. Centuries of Jewish diaspora (dispersal) across the world followed. But Ben-Gurion's idealistic claim to Israeli modernity also matters. He suggests that the Arab masses will wish to emulate his people's literacy and prosperity, and that this will emancipate them from their leaders' hostility to Israel. Subsequent history would test this optimism.

'

Politics, predominantly, abhor a vacuum. If we do not fill it, others will. Let us, once and for all, slough the fancy that others may run our errand, as Britain promised 27 years ago. The polemics which agitated our movement this last decade – the 'to be or not to be' of the Mandate – are meaningless now.

Now final judgement is passed by the United Nations and the Mandatory. The Mandate is to end. There is neither prospect nor proposal that Britain be replaced as Mandatory by another power. There is one vivid conclusion we must draw – if governance has to be in Palestine, for the sake of the immigration and settlement which are unthinkable in a void, it will be our very own, or not at all.

'Perhaps we are unready, immature – but events will not wait on us'

It is hard to guess when the British will actually leave – three months, three years, or thirty, there is no telling. We know of 'provisional' occupations that lasted sixty. So let us be neither over-sanguine nor cast down. We are vitally concerned that Britain should not keep on implementing the policy of the white paper. What we want is mass immigration. There is an account to settle with Britain for shutting out thousands of Jews since the white paper appeared, and we may let history make that settlement. But a new chapter is opening – the instant chapter of what is to befall in immigration now.

No more protests and clamour, not another day of a vacuum in theory, jurisdiction and ethics. We shall bear the grave responsibility ourselves, untried though we have been in the arts and burdens of sovereignty for the last eighteen hundred years. The strain will be terrific. Between acquiescing in the white paper, with its locked gates and racial discrimination, and the assumption of sovereign power, there can, in truth, only be one choice. Perhaps we are unready, immature – but events will not wait on us. The international calendar will not synchronize itself to ours. We are set the problem and must solve it . . . supervised by the United Nations, helped by the United Nations, but in our own name, answerable to ourselves, with our own resources.

'As Jews, and more so as Zionists, we must forego facile optimism and barren despondency'

To establish a Jewish government will not be enough. Defence incalculably stronger and more up to date than anything improvised in the past 70 years . . . even that will not be enough. The British episode was important, but transient: intrinsically, and from the outset, short-lived. But we cannot look upon our dealings with the Arabs in that way.

This is our native land; it is not as birds of passage that we return to it. But it is situated in an area engulfed by Arabic-speaking peoples, mainly followers of Islam. Now, if ever, we must do more than make peace with them; we must achieve collaboration and alliance on equal terms. Remembering what Arab delegations from Palestine and its neighbours say in the General Assembly and in other places, talk of Arab–Jewish amity sounds fantastic, for the Arabs do not wish it. This is the attitude officially proclaimed, and it is not to be scoffed at. Neither should we overrate it, or be panicked by it. As Jews, and more so as Zionists, we must forego facile optimism and barren despondency. Basic facts are our allies: the tragedy of the Jews, the desolation of the Land, our unbreakable bond with it, our creativity – they have brought us thus far.

There are basic facts in the Arab realm also . . . and understanding of them should blow away our pessimism. They are the historical needs of the Arabs and of their states. A people's needs are not always articulate . . . but they cannot be stifled for long, eventually they force their swelling way into expression and satisfaction.

'The tragedy of the Jews, the desolation of the Land, our unbreakable bond with it, our creativity – they have brought us thus far'

History has been harsh to us, perhaps, setting burdensome conditions which complicate our homecoming, but it has set conditions too which . . . will not only allow but will compel Arab and Jew to work together because they need and complement each other.

Just two examples. Egypt is the biggest country in the Arab world. More than three-quarters of its population are *fellahin* [peasants] with an average monthly income of a pound sterling; nine-tenths of the fellahin are disease-ridden, all but five per cent illiterate. You cannot go on forever feeding this people on anti-Jewish incitement.

Iraq is thrice as large as Britain . . . after 25 years of independence, 85 per cent of the population are illiterate, half are infected and there is one doctor for every 8500 persons. And this is among the richest countries in the world. An anti-Jewish diet will not do indefinitely in Iraq either. I will not discuss ostensibly independent Transjordan, its poverty and neglect, many of us have visited it and know.

'If they do not learn from us and labour with us, it is with strangers, potent and tyrannous, that they will find themselves partnered'

From our work in Palestine, from the society we are constructing, our economy and science, our culture and humanity, our social and fiscal order, and from no other source, must enlightenment come to our neighbours. If they do not learn from us and labour with us, it is with strangers, potent and tyrannous, that they will find themselves partnered.

They in turn have much to give us, they are blessed with what we lack. Great territories, ample for themselves and their children's children. We do not covet their expanses nor will we penetrate them – for we shall fight to end Diaspora in Arab lands as fiercely as we fought to end it in Europe, we want to be assembled wholly in our own Land. But if this region is to expand to the full, there must be reciprocity, there can be mutual aid – economic, political and cultural – between Jew and Arab. That is the necessity which will prevail, and the daily fulminations of their leaders should not alarm us unduly – they do not echo the real interests of the Arab peoples.

'There must be reciprocity, there can be mutual aid – economic, political and cultural – between Jew and Arab'

It is now, here and now, from Jerusalem itself, that a call must go out to the Arab nations to join forces with Jewry and the destined Jewish state, and work shoulder to shoulder for our common good, for the peace and progress of sovereign equals. ’

'The basic problem confronting the world today . . . is the preservation of human freedom'

Eleanor Roosevelt

(1884–1962)

AMERICA'S FORMER FIRST LADY ADDRESSES THE UN GENERAL ASSEMBLY, PARIS, 9 DECEMBER 1948

The Universal Declaration of Human Rights was formally adopted by the United Nations General Assembly, meeting in Paris, on the day after Eleanor Roosevelt delivered this speech. It built on Western political thought's long tradition of defining constitutional rights and defending them against the encroachment of executive power – most notably so in England's Bill of Rights (1689) and the US Declaration of Independence (1776). The Declaration of the Rights of Man and of the Citizen, adopted by the French National Assembly in 1789, marked a further stage by universalizing the notions of human equality and freedom. The UN document, however, was a radical development since it included economic, social and cultural rights, as well as those civil and political liberties which had been the focus of previous definitions. The rights to form and join a trade union, to social security and to equal pay were now recognized alongside such traditional goals as freedom of assembly and equality before the law.

Like the UN itself, the Declaration's preoccupations were shaped by the recent world war as well as by the continuing threat of totalitarianism. Roosevelt's lively attack on the abuse of language by Soviet communism signified a general awareness of totalitarianism's deliberate obfuscation of words – a technique which George Orwell's novel *Nineteen Eighty-Four* (1949) would term 'Newspeak'. The USSR was among the eight abstentions when the Assembly voted on the Declaration.

Eleanor Roosevelt's upbringing, like that of her distant cousin and husband, Franklin Delano Roosevelt, was one of patrician privilege, and this speech was delivered in the distinctive accent she acquired at a finishing school in England. The paralysis of FDR's legs

ELEANOR ROOSEVELT (1884–1962)

1899–1902 Allenswood Academy, England.

1905 Marries Franklin Delano Roosevelt ('FDR').

1928 FDR (Democrat) elected governor of New York.

1932 FDR wins presidential election; re-elected 1936, 1940 and 1944.

1933–45 US first lady.

1941 Co-founder of Freedom House, an organization advocating international democratic freedoms and human rights.

1943 Founds the UN Association of the US, which lobbies for the UN's formation.

April 1945 President Roosevelt dies.

Jan 1946 First meeting of UN General Assembly in London.

1946–52 Serves as US delegate to UN General Assembly.

1961–2 Chair of Presidential Commission on Status of Women.

after contracting a high fever in 1921 meant that she had to be an unusually prominent first lady, frequently standing in for the president on public occasions and supporting with characteristic eloquence her particular causes of civil rights for African-Americans and relief for the unemployed who were the Great Depression's chief casualties. By this stage, however, she was already a veteran activist and, possibly impelled by the discovery in 1918 of FDR's long-term affair with her social secretary, she had thrown herself into the work of the Women's Trade Union League, which campaigned for its members' rights in the workplace. National admiration for her candour, energy and seriousness led President Truman to nominate her a delegate to the UN General Assembly, where, as chair of its Commission on Human Rights, she played a major role in drafting the Declaration. Roosevelt herself expressed the hope that this non-binding statement of customary law would become an 'international Magna Carta' and the Declaration's regular invocation by nation states has helped it fulfil that role. In 1988 the Council of Europe moved to apply its own document, the European Convention on Human Rights (1950), by establishing a Court of Human Rights. Forty-seven states scattered across the continent and adhering to the Council of Europe would give legal depth to the nobility of Eleanor Roosevelt's work.

We must not be confused about what freedom is. Basic human rights are simple and easily understood: freedom of speech and a free press; freedom of religion and worship; freedom of assembly and the right of petition; the right of men to be secure in their homes and free from unreasonable search and seizure and from arbitrary arrest and punishment . . .

Democracy, freedom, human rights have come to have a definite meaning to the people of the world which we must not allow any nation to so change that they are made synonymous with suppression and dictatorship. There are basic differences that show up even in the use of words between a democratic and a totalitarian country . . .

'Certain rights can never be granted to the government, but must be kept in the hands of the people'

The USSR representatives assert that they already have achieved many things which we, in what they call the 'bourgeois democracies', cannot achieve . . . Our government seems powerless to them because, in the last analysis, it is controlled by the people . . . they would say that the people of the USSR control their government by allowing [it] to have certain absolute rights. We, on the other hand, feel that certain rights can never be granted to the government, but must be kept in the hands of the people . . .

In the totalitarian state a trade union is an instrument used by the government to enforce duties, not to assert rights . . . Our trades unions, on the other hand, are solely the instrument of the workers themselves . . .

The right to work in the Soviet Union means the assignment of workers to do whatever task is given to them by the government . . . A society in which everyone works is not necessarily a free society and may indeed be a slave society; on the other hand, a society in which there is widespread economic insecurity can turn freedom into a barren and vapid right . . .

We in the United States have come to realize . . . that people have a right to demand that their government will not allow them to starve because . . . they cannot find work of the kind they are accustomed to doing . . . But we would not consider . . . that we had gained any freedom if we were compelled to follow a dictatorial assignment to work where and when we were told . . .

'A society in which everyone works is not necessarily a free society and may indeed be a slave society'

The basic problem confronting the world today . . . is the preservation of human freedom for the individual and consequently for the society of which he is a part. We are fighting this battle again today as it was fought at the time of the French Revolution and . . . of the American Revolution . . .

Freedom for our peoples is not only a right, but also a tool. Freedom of speech, freedom of the press, freedom of information, freedom of assembly – these are not just abstract ideals to us; they are tools with which we create . . . a way of life in which we can enjoy freedom . . . Basic decisions of our society are made through the expressed will of the people. That is why when we see these liberties threatened, instead of falling apart, our nation becomes unified and our democracies come together . . . in spite of our varied backgrounds and many racial strains.

'Basic decisions of our society are made through the expressed will of the people'

In the United States we have a capitalist economy. That is because public opinion favours that type of economy under the conditions in which we live. But we have imposed certain restraints; for instance, we have anti-trust laws. These are the legal evidence of the determination of the American people to maintain an economy of free competition and not to allow monopolies to take away the people's freedom . . .

The USSR claims it has reached a point where all races within her borders are officially considered equal . . . and they insist that they have no discrimination where minorities are considered. This is a laudable objective but there are other aspects of the development of freedom . . . which are essential before the mere absence of discrimination is worth much . . . It is these other freedoms – the basic freedoms of speech, of the press, of religion and conscience, of assembly, of fair trial and freedom from arbitrary arrest and punishment – which a totalitarian government cannot safely give to its people and which give meaning to freedom from discrimination . . .

Among free men the end cannot justify the means. We know the patterns of totalitarianism – the single political party, the control of schools, press, radio, the arts, the sciences and the church to support autocratic authority; these are the age-old patterns against which men have struggled for three thousand years. These are the signs of reaction, retreat and retrogression . . .

The field of human rights is not one in which compromise on fundamental principles is possible . . . The future must see the broadening of human rights throughout the world. People who have glimpsed freedom will never be content until they have secured it for themselves. In a truest sense, human rights are a fundamental object of law and government in a just society. Human rights exist to the degree that they are respected by people in relations with each other and by governments in relations with their citizens . . .

'I pray Almighty God that we may win another victory here for the rights and freedoms of all men'

The propaganda we have witnessed in the recent past, like that we perceive in these days, seeks to impugn, to undermine and to destroy the liberty and independence of peoples. Such propaganda poses to all peoples the issue whether to doubt their heritage of rights . . . or to accept the challenge . . . and stand steadfast in the struggle to maintain and enlarge human freedoms . . . The immediate test is not only . . . the extent to which human rights and freedoms have already been achieved, but the direction in which the world is moving . . .

The place to discuss the issue of human rights is in the forum of the United Nations . . . where we can consider together our mutual problems and take advantage of our differences in experience. It is inherent in our firm attachment to democracy and freedom that we stand always ready to use the fundamental democratic procedures of honest discussion and negotiation . . . I pray Almighty God that we may win another victory here for the rights and freedoms of all men.

'Old soldiers never die; they just fade away'

Douglas MacArthur

(1880–1964)

ONE OF THE US'S GREATEST MILITARY HEROES DELIVERS HIS FAREWELL ADDRESS TO CONGRESS, WASHINGTON, 19 APRIL 1951

'We have heard God speak here today!' Congressman Dewey Short of Missouri's reaction was extreme, but Douglas MacArthur's address confirmed his high standing. Throughout his career he had cultivated public opinion, and MacArthur's personal flair as well as his gift for the memorable phrase had helped him to communicate his thoughts on military strategy to US citizens. In the 1930s he had criticized US isolationism and opposed pacifism, postures which enjoyed popularity in America at the time. MacArthur's personality was a towering one, but the qualities that were inspirational to some also seemed egotistical to others. On 11 April 1951 he paid the price and was dismissed as Supreme Commander of the Allied Powers by President Harry S. Truman. The title was the one he had held during the occupation of Japan following the Second World War, and by virtue of that command MacArthur had led the United Nations force authorized by the Security Council to defend democratic South Korea after the communist North launched an invasion force on 25 June 1950. MacArthur's public statements, and his many written ones, had expressed disagreement with the president on the conduct of the Korean War. Chinese involvement in the conflict, he thought, had to be punished and he urged aerial strikes on military bases in Manchuria, northern China. Truman thought such an escalation of the war would lead to Soviet involvement and possible nuclear conflict. MacArthur's gamble failed. He might have been personally popular but the president was nonetheless commander-in-chief and Truman rid himself of an insubordinate general. A subsequent Senate committee of inquiry into the dismissal vindicated the president.

MacArthur's address to Congress was a glorious last hurrah, and one punctuated by some 30 enthused ovations. The concluding image of the 'old soldier' is exquisitely calculated in

DOUGLAS MACARTHUR (1880–1964)

1903 Graduates from US Military Academy, West Point.

1918 Division commander, 84th Infantry Brigade, serving in France.

1919–22 Superintendent at West Point.

1928–30 Military commander of the Philippine Department.

1937–41 Field marshal of the Philippine army.

1941 Appointed commander of US armed forces in the Far East.

1942 Awarded the Medal of Honour for the gallantry of his defence of the Philippines in the face of the Japanese invasion.

1942 Appointed Supreme Commander of Allied Forces in the Southwest Pacific Area.

2 Sept 1945 Accepts the formal Japanese surrender on board the USS *Missouri*.

1945–51 Supreme Commander of the Allied Powers in Japan.

1950–1 Commands UN forces resisting North Korea's attempted invasion of South Korea.

its tug at the heart strings. But it is the speech's substance which impresses with its superb account of the Far East's impact on America's destiny and its evaluation of the country's stature as a great Pacific power. The geopolitical details are brought to life with immense flair and an acute strategic sense, and subsequent 20th-century history would show the US's role in the Pacific Rim supplementing her status as an Atlantic power.

By 1951 MacArthur had been away from the US for 11 years, but even before then the circumstances of high command had encouraged his independence of mind. When the Commonwealth of the Philippines attained semi-autonomy from the US in 1935, he had supervised the subsequent creation of the country's national army. MacArthur was Japan's effective ruler in the immediate postwar period and the country's constitution, effective from 1947 onwards, was drafted by his staff. The sight of a general exercising civilian power encouraged comparisons with the shoguns of Japan's past. But the man who stood before Congress, though imperious, was visibly no autocrat. It was rather the unique range of his experiences and responsibilities which lent authority to MacArthur's insights and earned him the plaudits of the people's representatives.

I address you with neither rancour nor bitterness in the fading twilight of life. The issues are global and so interlocked that to consider the problems of one sector, oblivious to those of another, is but to court disaster for the whole.

While Asia is commonly referred to as the Gateway to Europe, it is no less true that Europe is the Gateway to Asia, and the broad influence of the one cannot fail to have its impact upon the other. The communist threat is a global one. You cannot appease or otherwise surrender to communism in Asia without simultaneously undermining our efforts to halt its advance in Europe.

'The communist threat is a global one'

The peoples of Asia found their opportunity in the war just past to throw off the shackles of colonialism and now see the dawn of new opportunity, a heretofore unfelt dignity, and the self-respect of political freedom. Mustering half the world's population and 60 per cent of its natural resources, these peoples are rapidly consolidating a new force, both moral and material. This is the direction of Asian progress and it may not be stopped. It is a corollary to the shift of the world economic frontiers as the whole epicentre of world affairs rotates back towards the area whence it started.

The Asian peoples covet the right to shape their own free destiny. What they seek now is the dignity of equality and not the shame of subjugation. These political–social conditions . . . form a backdrop to contemporary planning which must be thoughtfully considered if we are to avoid the pitfalls of unrealism.

Of more direct . . . bearing upon our national security are the changes wrought in the strategic potential of the Pacific Ocean in the course of the past war. Prior thereto the western strategic frontier of the United States lay on the littoral line of the Americas. The Pacific was a potential area of advance for any predatory force intent upon striking at the bordering land areas.

All this was changed by our Pacific victory. Our strategic frontier then shifted to embrace the entire Pacific Ocean, which became a vast moat to protect us as long as we held it. We control it to the shores of Asia by a chain of islands extending in an arc from the Aleutians to the Marianas held by us and our free allies. From this island chain we can dominate with sea and air power every Asiatic port from Vladivostok to Singapore.

The holding of this littoral defence line in the western Pacific is entirely dependent upon holding all segments thereof. For that reason, I have strongly recommended . . . that under no circumstances must Formosa fall under communist control. Such an eventuality . . . might well force our western frontier back to the coast of California, Oregon and Washington.

'The Asian peoples covet the right to shape their own free destiny'

China, up to 50 years ago, was compartmented into groups divided against each other. At the turn of the century . . . efforts towards greater homogeneity produced the start of a nationalist urge. This . . . has been brought to its greatest fruition under the present regime. Through these past 50 years the Chinese people have thus become militarized in their concepts and in their ideals . . . with a lust for expansion and increased power.

The Japanese people, since the war, have undergone the greatest reformation recorded in modern history. Politically, economically and socially, Japan is now abreast of many free nations. I know of no nation more serene, orderly and industrious.

Of our former ward, the Philippines, we can look forward in confidence that . . . a healthy nation will grow. In our hour of need they did not fail us. The Philippines stand as a mighty bulwark of Christianity in the Far East, and its capacity for high moral leadership in Asia is unlimited.

I now turn to the Korean conflict. Our victory was complete, and our objectives within reach, when Red China intervened. This created a new war and . . . a situation which called for new decisions in the diplomatic sphere to permit the realistic adjustment of military strategy. Such decisions have not been forthcoming.

I felt that military necessity in the conduct of the war made necessary: first, the intensification of our economic blockade against China; two, the imposition of a naval blockade against the China coast; three, removal of restrictions on air reconnaissance of China's coastal areas; four, removal of restrictions on the forces of the Republic of China on Formosa . . .

We could hold in Korea by constant manoeuvre . . . but we could hope at best for only an indecisive campaign . . . if the enemy utilized its full military potential.

'The Japanese people, since the war, have undergone the greatest reformation recorded in modern history'

It has been said, in effect, that I was a warmonger. Nothing could be further from the truth. I know war as few other men now living know it, and nothing to me is more revolting. I have long advocated its complete abolition, as its very destructiveness on both friend and foe has rendered it useless as a means of settling international disputes. But once war is forced upon us, there is no other alternative than . . . to bring it to a swift end. War's every object is victory, not prolonged indecision.

The tragedy of Korea is further heightened by the fact that its military action is confined to its territorial limits. It condemns that nation . . . to suffer the devastating impact of full naval and air bombardment while the enemy's sanctuaries are fully protected from such attack.

The magnificence of the courage and fortitude of the Korean people defies description. They have chosen death rather than slavery. Their last words to me were: 'Don't scuttle the Pacific!'

'War's every object is victory, not prolonged indecision'

I am closing my 52 years of military service. When I joined the army . . . it was the fulfilment of all my boyish hopes and dreams. The world has turned over many times since I took the oath on the plain at West Point, and the hopes and dreams have long since vanished, but I still remember the refrain of one of the most popular barrack ballads of that day which proclaimed most proudly that 'old soldiers never die; they just fade away'.

And like the old soldier of that ballad, I now close my military career and just fade away, an old soldier who tried to do his duty as God gave him the light to see that duty.

'The cult of the individual brought about rude violation of party democracy'

Nikita Khrushchev

(1894–1971)

THE SOVIET PRESIDENT DENOUNCES STALIN AT THE 20TH CONGRESS OF THE SOVIET COMMUNIST PARTY, MOSCOW, 25 FEBRUARY 1956

The 20th Congress was the first one to be held after Stalin's death in 1953 and his successor, Nikita Khrushchev, was promoting liberalization. Greater freedom of information, foreign cultural links, the freeing of some eight million political prisoners: all constituted a 'Khrushchev thaw'. It took some four hours to deliver the entire speech and its content caused some delegates to suffer heart attacks. Others, similarly disabused, committed suicide afterwards. The idealized account of Lenin was tactically astute and intended to show that Stalin had betrayed the revolutionary legacy. The Congress was meeting in closed session when Khrushchev addressed it and the speech was sent to regional party secretaries who briefed party members on its contents. Emphasis on its secrecy contributed to the speech's celebrity and Khrushchev's aides ensured that copies were obtained by Western newspapers, whose publication of the text caused an international sensation.

The speech's background is one of rivalry within the Soviet leadership and Khrushchev was intent on consolidating his position. He had deposed Lavrenti Beria, the state security chief, who was executed in December 1953. Other rivals included Vyacheslav Molotov and Georgi Malenkov, both influential members of the Politburo (or Presidium), which administered the USSR's Communist Party and formulated its policies. These old-style Stalinists interpreted the speech, correctly, as a personal attack. The plot they proceeded to plan was exposed in May 1957 and Khrushchev subsequently expelled them from the party. Despite his attack on Stalinist methods of government, Khrushchev's speech did not criticize past economic policies – including the collectivization of agriculture which had caused the deaths of an officially estimated 12 million. The denunciation was cleverly selective for two

NIKITA KHRUSHCHEV (1894–1971)

1918 Joins Bolshevik Party.

1934 Appointed first secretary of the Moscow City Committee; impresses with work overseeing construction of the city's subway system.

1934 Elected to Central Committee of the Communist Party of the Soviet Union.

1938 Appointed first secretary of Ukrainian Central Committee.

1939 Becomes full member of the Politburo.

1941–5 Serves as a political commissar, with the rank of lieutenant general.

Sept 1953 Becomes first secretary of the Communist Party.

March 1958 Becomes chairman of the Council of Ministers of the USSR.

Oct 1964 Removed from office by the Soviet Presidium, a decision subsequently approved by the Communist Party's Central Committee.

reasons: the party's authority needed to be maintained, and Khrushchev was implicated in the Stalinist past – which is why his tirade struck many as hypocritical.

Fears that the thaw was getting out of hand came to a head in the autumn of 1956, when Hungary erupted in anti-communist rebellion and the premier Imre Nagy abolished the single-party system. The Presidium reacted by sending in Soviet troops to re-establish Hungarian communist control. In October workers rioted in the Polish city of Poznan, and the government there had to introduce liberalizing measures in order to survive. These insurgencies seemed to be a direct consequence of hopes aroused by Khrushchev's speech and therefore provided ammunition for his critics. He continued nonetheless with his critique of the past and a symbolic dénouement arrived in 1961, when Stalin's body was removed from public view and buried outside the Kremlin wall.

Having embraced 'peaceful coexistence' with the West, Khrushchev's position was then undermined by the Cuban Missile Crisis of October 1962. He had to agree to the US demand that the Soviets remove the weapons they had sent to Cuba, and the loss of face was the prelude to his ejection from office. There was, however, an important Khrushchev legacy. His speech influenced many younger communist officials, including Mikhail Gorbachev, whose aspirations as general secretary (1985–91) often mirrored those of Khrushchev.

'

After Stalin's death the central committee began explaining that it is foreign to the spirit of Marxism–Leninism to elevate one person, to transform him into a superman. Such a belief about a man, and specifically about Stalin, was cultivated among us for many years.

At present we are concerned with how the cult of Stalin became the source of a whole series of exceedingly serious perversions of party principles, of party democracy, of revolutionary legality.

'The cult of Stalin became the source of a whole series of exceedingly serious perversions of party principles'

The great modesty of the genius of the revolution, Vladimir Ilyich Lenin, is known. Lenin always stressed the role of the people as the creator of history. Lenin mercilessly stigmatized every manifestation of the cult of the individual. He patiently explained his opinions to others.

Lenin detected in Stalin those negative characteristics which resulted later in grave consequences. Fearing the future fate of the Soviet nation, Lenin pointed out that it was necessary to consider transferring Stalin from the position of general secretary because

Stalin did not have a proper attitude towards his comrades. As later events have proven, Lenin's anxiety was justified.

Stalin, who absolutely did not tolerate collegiality in leadership and in work, acted not through persuasion, but by imposing his concepts. Stalin originated the concept 'enemy of the people'. This term made possible the use of the cruellest repression against anyone who disagreed with Stalin, against those who were only suspected of hostile intent. 'Confessions' were acquired through physical pressures. Innocent individuals became victims. Mass arrests and deportations of many thousands of people, execution without trial, created conditions of insecurity, fear and even desperation.

Vladimir Ilyich demanded uncompromising dealings with the enemies of the revolution. Lenin used such methods, however, only against actual class enemies and not against those who blunder. Stalin, on the other hand, used extreme methods and mass repressions at a time when the revolution was already victorious.

'Stalin trampled on the principle of collective party leadership'

Lenin considered it absolutely necessary that the party discuss at length all questions bearing on the development of government. After Lenin's death, Stalin trampled on the principle of collective party leadership. Of the 139 members and candidates of the central committee who were elected at the 17th Congress, 98 persons, 70 per cent, were arrested and shot. It is inconceivable that a congress so composed could have elected a central committee in which a majority would prove to be enemies of the party. Delegates were active participants in the building of our socialist state; many of them suffered and fought during the pre-revolutionary years; they fought their enemies valiantly and often looked into the face of death. How, then, can we believe that such people had joined the camps of the enemies of socialism?

Lenin taught that the application of revolutionary violence is necessitated by the resistance of the exploiting classes, and this referred to the era when the exploiting classes existed and were powerful. As soon as the nation's political situation had improved, Lenin gave instructions to stop mass terror and to abolish the death penalty. Stalin deviated from these precepts. Terror was actually directed against the honest workers of the party; lying, slanderous and absurd accusations were made against them.

Stalin was a very distrustful man. He could look at a man and say: 'Why are your eyes so shifty today?' The sickly suspicion created in him a general distrust. Everywhere and in everything he saw 'enemies', 'two-facers' and 'spies'.

The power accumulated in the hands of one person, Stalin, led to serious consequences during the great patriotic war. When we look at many of our novels, films and historical–scientific studies, the role of Stalin in the patriotic war appears to be entirely improbable. Stalin had foreseen everything. The epic victory is ascribed as being completely due to the strategic genius of Stalin.

Stalin advanced the thesis that our nation experienced an 'unexpected' attack by the Germans. But, comrades, this is completely untrue. As soon as Hitler came to power, he assigned to himself the task of liquidating communism. The fascists were saying this openly. Despite grave warnings, the necessary steps were not taken to prepare. We paid with great losses – until our generals succeeded in altering the situation. Stalin tried to inculcate the notion that the victories gained by the Soviet nation were all due to the genius of Stalin and of no one else. Let us take our military films. They make us feel sick. Let us recall *The Fall of Berlin*. Here only Stalin acts. He does not reckon with anyone. He asks no one for advice. Everything is shown to the people in this false light. Not Stalin, but the party as a whole, the Soviet government, our heroic army, its talented leaders and brave soldiers, the whole Soviet nation – these are the ones who assured victory in the great patriotic war.

Comrades! The cult of the individual brought about rude violation of party democracy, sterile administration, deviations, cover-ups of shortcomings, and varnishings of reality.

Why did not members of the politburo assert themselves in time? Initially, many backed Stalin because he was one of the strongest Marxists and his logic, his strength and his will greatly influenced party work. After Lenin's death Stalin actively fought against those who deviated from the correct Leninist path. This fight was indispensable. Later, however, Stalin began to fight honest Soviet people.

'Everywhere and in everything he saw "enemies", "two-facers" and "spies"'

Comrades! Lenin had often stressed that modesty is an absolutely integral part of a real Bolshevik. We cannot say that we have been following this Leninist example in all respects. We must correct this. But this should be done calmly. We cannot let this matter get out of the party, especially not to the press.

Comrades! We must abolish the cult of the individual once and for all.

The fact that we present in all their ramifications the basic problems of overcoming the cult of the individual is evidence of the great moral and political strength of our party. We are absolutely certain that our party, armed with the historical resolutions of the 20th Congress, will lead the Soviet people to new successes.

Long live the victorious banner of our party – Leninism! '

'The government resorted to epic weapons for squalid and trivial ends'

Aneurin Bevan

(1897–1960)

THE SHADOW FOREIGN SECRETARY ATTACKS THE GOVERNMENT'S POLICY IN THE MIDDLE EAST; HOUSE OF COMMONS, LONDON, 5 DECEMBER 1956

'The government resorted to epic weapons for squalid and trivial ends'

On 26 July 1956 President Gamal Abdel Nasser of Egypt announced that his government would nationalize the Suez Canal Company which operated the waterway linking Port Said on the Mediterranean with Suez on the Red Sea. Britain and France, the company's shareholders, reacted by colluding with Israel and encouraging it to invade Egypt. A Franco-British force could then intervene, using as a pretext the need to separate the combatants. Forcing the Israeli and Egyptian armies apart on either side of the canal, the French and British could then resume control of its management. The US was not informed of these plans.

British radicals had always decried secret diplomacy, and Aneurin Bevan's combination of verbal mischief with oratorical passion had made him the star of the Labour Party's left-wing faction. His speech teases out inconsistencies in the government's public position, contradictions which resulted from its dishonesty about the campaign's motives. The mockery had a steely edge. Bevan, helped by the slight stutter he used to dramatic effect, was inveighing against the reactionary attitudes he regarded as an imbecilic brake on human progress.

The canal had played an important British strategic role as a communications link with the country's Asian colonies, and it had recently assumed a novel economic significance as a conduit for oil tankers. By July 1956 the last British troops guarding the canal had been withdrawn following Nasser's repudiation five years earlier of the Anglo-Egyptian Treaty (1936), which had confirmed the canal's status as a neutral zone under British protection. Charges to be levied on canal traffic were now earmarked by Nasser to help finance the Aswan Dam's construction. Britain and the US had withdrawn an earlier offer to meet the scheme's costs.

ANEURIN BEVAN (1897–1960)

1929 Elected member of Parliament (Labour) for Ebbw Vale, South Wales.

1945–51 Minister of health in Britain's Labour government; oversees introduction (1948) of the National Health Service.

1951 Minister of labour, but resigns over introduction of prescription charges for dental care and spectacles.

1951 Labour is voted out of office in the general election; Bevan initiates a left–right split within his party and leads opposition to high defence expenditure.

1955 Defeated in contest for leadership of the Labour Party.

1956–9 Shadow foreign secretary.

1957 Rejects unilateral nuclear disarmament in a speech to the Labour Party conference.

Canal nationalization was also a way of promoting Nasser as a hero of 'the Arab world'. The anti-colonial spirit he represented was a popular Egyptian sentiment, especially since Britain's influence on the country's government and army had survived Egypt's formal independence from the British in 1922 and lasted until the 1952 coup which brought Nasser to power. He also discomfited France with his profound influence on Arab nationalists in its north African colonies.

Initially, the plan worked. Israel invaded the Sinai on 29 October 1956. Franco-British forces stormed northwestern Sinai's beaches on 5 and 6 November. Port Said suffered heavy damage. The canal area was seized. But the US demanded an immediate ceasefire. In early November it was condemning the Soviet invasion which suppressed Hungary's national rebellion. Consistency, and irritation, dictated US opposition to the Suez expedition as another instance of a country's sovereign territory being invaded. Eisenhower threatened to sell the US treasury's sterling assets and thereby cause a run on the pound unless Britain withdrew. The Franco-British force left Egypt within weeks and Anthony Eden resigned as prime minister on 10 January 1957.

Bevan's speech marks Britain's enforced recognition of the limits to her power. Postcolonial realism, however, had unexpected consequences. Within a year Bevan was arguing that Britain needed its own nuclear deterrent – a policy reversal which dismayed erstwhile 'Bevanites'.

I have been looking through the various objectives and reasons that the government have given to the House of Commons for making war on Egypt, and it really is desirable that when a nation makes war upon another nation, it should be quite clear why it does so. There is, in fact, no correspondence whatsoever between the reasons given today and the reasons set out by the prime minister at the beginning.

On 30 October, the prime minister said that the purpose was, first, 'to seek to separate the combatants'; second, 'to remove the risk to free passage through the canal'. The speech we have heard today is the first speech in which that subject has been dropped . . . The right honourable and learned gentleman . . . has said that when we landed in Port Said there was already every reason to believe that both Egypt and Israel had agreed to a ceasefire.

'Our ambitions soar the further away we are from realizing them'

We are telling the nation and the world that having decided upon the course, we went on with it despite the fact that the objective we had set ourselves had already been achieved, namely, the separation of the combatants. As to the objective of removing the risk to free passage through the canal, I must confess that I have been astonished at this also. We sent an ultimatum to Egypt by which we told her that unless she agreed to our landing in Ismailia, Suez and Port Said, we should make war upon her. Did we really believe that Nasser was going to give in at once? He did what anybody would have thought he would do. He sank ships in the canal, the wicked man. The result is that the first objective realized was the opposite of the one we set out to achieve; the canal was blocked, and it is still blocked.

On 1 November, we were told the reason was 'to stop hostilities' and 'prevent a resumption of them'. But hostilities had already been practically stopped. On 3 November, our objectives became much more ambitious – 'to deal with all the outstanding problems in the Middle East' . . .

Our ambitions soar the further away we are from realizing them. After having insulted the United States, . . . after having driven the whole of the Arab world into one solid phalanx behind Nasser, we were then going to deal with all the outstanding problems in the Middle East.

'We cannot run the processes of modern society by attempting to impose our will upon nations by armed force'

The next objective of which we were told was to ensure that the Israeli forces withdrew from Egyptian territory. That is a remarkable war aim, is it not? To establish our case before the eyes of the world, Israel being the wicked invader, we being the nice friend of Egypt, went to protect her from the Israelis, but, unfortunately, we had to bomb the Egyptians first . . .

We started this operation in order to give Nasser a black eye – if we could, to overthrow him – but, in any case, to secure control of the canal . . .

In fact, very few of the activities at the beginning of October are credible except upon the assumption that the French and British governments knew that something was going to happen in Egypt . . .

These were objectives . . . that were not realizable by the means that we adopted. These civil, social and political objectives in modern society are not attainable by armed force. It is clear . . . that there is such bitter feeling against Western imperialism . . . among millions of people that they are not prepared to keep the arteries of European commerce alive and intact if they themselves want to cut them.

We cannot run the processes of modern society by attempting to impose our will upon nations by armed force. Therefore . . . whatever may have been the morality of the government's action, there is no doubt about its imbecility. There is not the slightest shadow of doubt that we have attempted to use methods which were bound to destroy the objectives we had . . .

How on earth do honourable members opposite imagine that hundreds of miles of pipeline can be kept open if the Arabs do not want it to be kept open? It is not enough to say that there are large numbers of Arabs who want the pipeline to be kept open because they live by it. It has been proved over and over again now in the modern world that men and women are often prepared to put up with material losses for things that they really think worthwhile. It has been shown in Budapest, and it could be shown in the Middle East . . .

It may be that the dead in Port Said are 100, 200 or 300. If it is only one, we had no business to take it . . . With eight million here in London, the biggest single civilian target in the world, with our crowded island exposed . . . to the barbarism of modern weapons – we ourselves set the example. We ourselves conscript our boys and put guns and aeroplanes in their hands and say, 'Bomb there.'

The government resorted to epic weapons for squalid and trivial ends, and that is why . . . ministers, all of them, have spoken and argued and debated well below their proper form – because they have been synthetic villains. They are not really villains. They have only set off on a villainous course, and they cannot even use the language of villainy . . .

'It will take us very many years to live down what we have done'

It is no use honourable members consoling themselves that they have more support in the country than many of them feared they might have . . . They have support among many of the unthinking and unreflective who still react to traditional values, who still think that we can solve all these problems in the old ways. Of course they have. Not all the human race has grown to adult state yet. But do not let them take comfort in that thought.

It will take us very many years to live down what we have done. It will take us many years to pay the price. I know that tomorrow evening honourable and right honourable members will probably . . . give the government a vote of confidence, but they know in their heart that it is a vote which the government do not deserve. ’

'Let a hundred flowers blossom. Let a hundred schools of thought contend'

Mao Zedong

(1893–1976)

CHINA'S LEADER ENCOURAGES OPENNESS AND FREEDOM OF EXPRESSION; THE 11TH SESSION OF THE SUPREME STATE CONFERENCE, BEIJING, 27 FEBRUARY 1957

Some half a million Chinese suffered in various ways because they acted on the recommendations Mao gives in this speech. The injunction to 'let a hundred flowers blossom and a hundred schools of thought contend' was an allusion to the Warring States period of Chinese history, between the fifth and third centuries BC, when numerous philosophical schools competed for predominance. In 1956–7 the leadership of the Communist Party of China (CPC) seemed to be urging a similar diversity of opinion.

The initial plan – associated with premier Zhou Enlai – was to encourage self-expression by those local bureaucrats who were not party members. Progress was slow in the first months of the campaign, but Mao's speech made the difference and it was subsequently published in *The People's Daily* – the official organ of the CPC's Central Committee. Posters expressing dissident views were posted on university campuses and many hundreds of thousands of letters criticizing the government were sent to the prime minister. The signatories' complaints included Chinese officialdom's economic corruption, privileges enjoyed by CPC members, and the harsh punishments meted out to supposed 'counter-revolutionaries'. Recommendations for action included the Communist Party's removal from power.

The impact of Khrushchev's denunciation of Stalin and the example of Hungary's anti-communist revolt in the autumn of 1956 may have aroused Mao's fears that Chinese rebels, heartened by these external events, were plotting against him. He therefore launched the 'Anti-Rightist Movement' in July 1957 – a government campaign which showed how, despite this speech's assertions, 'crude coercion' rather than 'painstaking reasoning' was indeed the

MAO ZEDONG (1893–1976)

1923 Elected a commissar of the Central Committee of the Communist Party of China (CPC).

1927 Kuomintang (Chinese Nationalists) purge their movement of communist influence; Chinese civil war starts.

1931–4 Establishes Soviet Republic of China within Jiangxi province, which becomes the base of the Workers' and Peasants' Red Army.

1934–5 The 'Long March'; Kuomintang army forces Red Army to retreat to northwest China.

Jan 1935 Becomes CPC leader and Red Army's military commander.

1937–45 Nationalist and communist forces resist, separately, Japanese invasion during Sino-Japanese war.

1946 Civil war resumes.

1945–76 Chairman of CPC.

1949 Red Army expels Kuomintang from mainland China and People's Republic is proclaimed (1 October).

1954–9 Chairman of People's Republic of China.

essence of Chinese communism. Those who had taken him at his previous word were subjected to a range of punishments including imprisonment, demotion, sacking, periods in labour and 're-education' camps, torture and murder. The fact that their critical letters were signed meant that dissidents could be easily discovered, and it is possible that Mao's encouragement of the 'Hundred Flowers' programme was a ploy enabling him to identify and punish his opponents.

Mao's command of Marxist–Leninism's pseudoscientific terminology is the chief feature of this speech, with its talk of 'contradiction' resolved through 'struggle', a 'law of development' leading to 'socialist transformation'. But the reality of recent Chinese history's 'twists and turns' had been savage and bloody. The years from 1949 to 1953 witnessed systematic state terror, with the implementation of land reform and suppression of internal opposition accounting for the deaths of anything between two and five million people. In 1958 Mao would launch the 'Great Leap Forward', a programme banning private food production and enforcing the merger of smaller agricultural collectives within 'people's communes'. The policy resulted in history's biggest famine claiming, on Chinese official statistics, the lives of at least 20 million, though the total number of deaths may well be up to three times that number. Mao lost some prestige as a result but retained his power base as CPC chairman. The Cultural Revolution, which he launched in 1966 and personally directed, was meant to safeguard his position and resulted in further persecution, the murder of opponents and a sustained attack on Chinese cultural and educational institutions.

Our state is a people's democratic dictatorship . . . What is this dictatorship for? Its first function is internal, namely, to suppress the reactionary classes . . . or in other words, to resolve the contradictions between ourselves and the internal enemy . . . The second function of this dictatorship is . . . to resolve the contradictions between ourselves and the external enemy.

The several million intellectuals who worked for the old society have come to serve the new society . . . China needs the service of as many intellectuals as possible for the colossal task of building socialism . . . Many of our comrades are not good at uniting with intellectuals. They are stiff in their attitude towards them . . . and interfere in certain scientific and cultural matters where interference is unwarranted.

'Not to have a correct political orientation is like not having a soul'

Although large numbers of intellectuals have made progress, they should not be complacent. They must continue to remould themselves, gradually shed their bourgeois world outlook and acquire the proletarian, communist world outlook so that they can fully fit in with the needs of the new society . . .

Among students and intellectuals there has recently been a falling-off in ideological and political work . . . It seems as if Marxism, once all the rage, is currently not so much in fashion. To counter these tendencies, we must strengthen our ideological and political work . . . Not to have a correct political orientation is like not having a soul.

Letting a hundred flowers blossom and a hundred schools of thought contend is the policy for promoting progress in the arts and sciences and a flourishing socialist culture in our land. Different forms and styles in art should develop freely and different schools in science should contend freely. We think that it is harmful . . . if administrative measures are used to impose one particular style of art or school of thought and to ban another.

Questions of right and wrong in the arts and science should be settled through free discussion . . . and through practical work in these fields. They should not be settled in an over-simple manner. A period of trial is often needed to determine whether something is right or wrong.

Throughout history at the outset new and correct things often failed to win recognition from the majority of people and had to develop by twists and turns through struggle. Often, correct and good things were first regarded not as fragrant flowers but as poisonous weeds. Copernicus's theory of the solar system and Darwin's theory of evolution were once dismissed as erroneous and had to win out over bitter opposition . . .

'Often, correct and good things were first regarded not as fragrant flowers but as poisonous weeds'

In a socialist society, the conditions for the growth of the new are . . . far superior to those in the old society. Nevertheless, it often happens that new, rising forces are held back and sound ideas stifled. Besides even in the absence of their deliberate suppression, the growth of new things may be hindered simply through lack of discernment. It is therefore necessary . . . to encourage free discussion and avoid hasty conclusions.

Marxism, too, has developed through struggle . . . In China the remoulding of the petty bourgeoisie has only just started. Class struggle is by no means over. The proletariat seeks to transform the world according to its own world outlook, and so does the bourgeoisie . . . the question of which will win out, socialism or capitalism, is not really settled yet . . . Therefore Marxism must continue to develop through struggle . . . What is correct inevitably develops in the course of struggle with what is wrong. The true, the good and the beautiful always exist by contrast with the false, the evil and the ugly, and grow in struggle with them. As soon as something erroneous is rejected and a particular truth accepted by mankind, new truths begin to struggle with new errors. Such struggles will never end. This is the law of development of truth and, naturally, of Marxism.

'The question of which will win out, socialism or capitalism, is not really settled yet'

It will take a fairly long period of time to decide the issue in the ideological struggle between socialism and capitalism in our country . . . Ideological struggle differs from other forms of struggle, since the only method used is painstaking reasoning, and not crude coercion . . . Although there are defects and mistakes in our work, every fair-minded person can see . . . that we have already achieved great success and will achieve still greater ones. The vast majority of the bourgeoisie and the intellectuals who come from the old society are patriotic . . . they know they will have nothing to fall back on and their future cannot possibly be bright if they turn away from the socialist cause and from the working people led by the Communist Party . . .

Marxists should not be afraid of criticism from any quarter . . . Fighting against wrong ideas is like being vaccinated – a man develops greater immunity . . . Plants raised in hothouses are unlikely to be hardy. Carrying out the policy of letting a hundred flowers bloom and a hundred schools of thought contend will . . . strengthen the leading position of Marxism in the ideological field.

What should our policy be towards non-Marxist ideas? . . . Will it do to ban such ideas . . . ? Certainly not. It is not only futile but very harmful to use crude methods in dealing with . . . questions about man's mental world. You may ban the expression of wrong ideas, but the ideas will still be there . . . Therefore, it is only by employing the method of discussion, criticism and reasoning . . . that we can really settle issues . . . Mistakes must be criticized and poisonous weeds fought wherever they crop up. However, such criticism should not be dogmatic . . . we must carefully distinguish between what is really a poisonous weed and what is really a fragrant flower . . .

In their political activities, how should our people judge whether a person's words and deeds are right or wrong? . . . we consider that words and deeds should be beneficial to socialist transformation. They should help to strengthen . . . the leadership of the Communist Party. These political criteria are applicable to all activities in the arts and sciences. In a socialist country like ours, can there possibly be any useful or scientific or artistic activity which runs counter to these political criteria? ’

'The wind of change is blowing through this continent'

Harold Macmillan

(1894–1986)

BRITAIN'S PRIME MINISTER SPEAKS TO THE SOUTH AFRICAN PARLIAMENT ON THIRD WORLD NATIONALISM; CAPE TOWN, 3 FEBRUARY 1960

In 1960, one year after leading the Conservative Party to general-election victory, Harold Macmillan stood at the height of his authority. The Suez episode (1956) had dented the government's reputation for competence and probity, and Macmillan, then chancellor of the exchequer, had shared collective cabinet responsibility for that disaster. But his cultivation of a languid manner concealed an adroit, even cynical, political opportunism. He replaced Eden as premier but in circumstances which ensured he could never forget Suez's lessons: Britain's foreign policy could never again be independent of the US, and that policy had to be sensitive to Third World nationalism.

The speech was delivered to a legislature which had embarked on a rigid application of apartheid, or separate development of blacks and whites. Britain's first properly post-imperial prime minister was informing Africa's most resolutely colonialist power that this policy was both wrong and stupid. The Union, whose 'golden wedding' is described in the speech, was formed during the second Boer War (1899–1902), when the Dutch settlers of the Transvaal and the Orange Free State attempted to resist absorption within the British empire. Britain's new-found anti-colonialism was therefore vulnerable to South African charges of hypocrisy. Delivering the speech took some courage, and Macmillan, never much of an orator, was physically sick moments before he spoke – as often happened just before his major speeches. But he knew how to construct an argument and was a past master at roping in the kind of historical allusions which could impart an elevated tone to a speech.

HAROLD MACMILLAN (1894–1986)

1924 Elected MP (Conservative) for Stockton-on-Tees.

1929 Loses his seat in the general election, but regains it in subsequent election (1931).

1938 Publishes *The Middle Way*, advocating greater government involvement in economic and business affairs.

1942 Sent to North Africa as British government representative to the Allies in the Mediterranean.

Nov 1945 Elected MP for Bromley at a by-election, having lost his seat at the general election (July).

1951–4 Minister of housing.

1954–5 Minister of defence.

1955 Foreign secretary.

1955–7 Chancellor of the Exchequer.

1957 Becomes prime minister.

Oct 1959 Leads Conservative Party to general-election victory with an increased majority.

1963 Resigns office amidst fears for his health.

1984 Created Earl of Stockton and Viscount Macmillan of Ovenden.

Mannered self-parody – as so often – helped to conceal his nerves and Macmillan survived the ordeal.

Neither the elegant tributes to South Africa's achievements nor his placing of the country in a historical context extending back to the Roman empire could, however, obscure Macmillan's message. Earlier in his tour he had visited Ghana, independent of Britain since 1957, and Nigeria, which would become independent in October 1960. Somalia, Sierra Leone and Tanzania were British colonies which would attain independence by the end of 1961. Before the parliament assembled in Cape Town, Macmillan explained the logic of Britain's policy. This was no ad-hoc process but a principled endorsement of black Africa's struggle for political self-expression. The British government was now committed to supporting the creation of societies in which all human rights were upheld, regardless of colour. The speech also contained a delicately veiled, but real enough, threat, one which owed as much to Cold War realpolitik as to anti-racist principle. If the West did not support these new states, they might well turn communist. It is unsurprising that his reception was unenthusiastic. Fearing British intervention in its domestic affairs, South Africa resolved to leave the Commonwealth and on 31 May 1961 the country became an independent republic. A gulf grew between the prime minister and the more reactionary element within the Conservative Party. But the greater gulf was that between South Africa's white ruling class and its black subjects, one which persisted for almost three decades after Macmillan spoke.

‘

It is a special privilege for me to be here in 1960 when you are celebrating what I might call the golden wedding of the Union. At such a time it is natural and right that you should pause to take stock of your position, to look back at what you have achieved, to look forward to what lies ahead. In the 50 years of their nationhood the people of South Africa have built a strong economy founded upon a healthy agriculture and thriving and resilient industries.

No one could fail to be impressed with the immense material progress which has been achieved. That all this has been accomplished in so short a time is a striking testimony to the skill, energy and initiative of your people. We in Britain are proud of the contribution we have made to this remarkable achievement. Much of it has been financed by British capital.

As I've travelled around the Union I have found everywhere, as I expected, a deep preoccupation with what is happening in the rest of the African continent. I understand and sympathize with your interests in these events and your anxiety about them.

Ever since the break-up of the Roman empire one of the constant facts of political life in Europe has been the emergence of independent nations. They have come into existence over the centuries in different forms, different kinds of government, but all have been inspired by a deep, keen feeling of nationalism, which has grown as the nations have grown.

In the 20th century, and especially since the end of the war, the processes which gave birth to the nation states of Europe have been repeated all over the world. We have seen the awakening of national consciousness in peoples who have for centuries lived in dependence upon some other power. Fifteen years ago this movement spread through Asia. Many countries there, of different races and civilizations, pressed their claims to an independent national life.

'The processes which gave birth to the nation states of Europe have been repeated all over the world'

Today the same thing is happening in Africa, and the most striking of all the impressions I have formed since I left London a month ago is of the strength of this African national consciousness. In different places it takes different forms, but it is happening everywhere.

The wind of change is blowing through this continent, and whether we like it or not, this growth of national consciousness is a political fact. We must accept it as a fact, and our national policies must take account of it.

You understand this better than anyone, you are sprung from Europe, the home of nationalism, here in Africa you have yourselves created a free nation. A new nation. Indeed, in the history of our times yours will be recorded as the first of the African nationalists. This tide of national consciousness which is now rising in Africa is a fact, for which both you and we and the other nations of the Western world are ultimately responsible.

For its causes are to be found in the achievements of Western civilization, in the pushing forwards of the frontiers of knowledge, the applying of science to the service of human needs, in the expanding of food production, in the speeding and multiplying of the means of communication, and perhaps above all and more than anything else in the spread of education.

As I have said, the growth of national consciousness in Africa is a political fact, and we must accept it as such. That means, I would judge, that we have got to come to terms with it. I sincerely believe that if we cannot do so we may imperil the precarious balance between the East and West on which the peace of the world depends.

The world today is divided into three main groups. First there are what we call the Western powers. You in South Africa and we in Britain belong to this group, together with our friends and allies in other parts of the Commonwealth. In the United States of America and in Europe we call it the Free World. Secondly there are the communists – Russia and her satellites in Europe and China whose population will rise by the end of the next ten years to the staggering total of 800 million. Thirdly, there are those parts of the world whose people are at present uncommitted either to communism or to our Western ideas. In this context we think first of Asia and then of Africa.

As I see it, the great issue in this second half of the 20th century is whether the uncommitted peoples of Asia and Africa will swing to the East or to the West. Will they be drawn into the communist camp? Or will the great experiments in self-government that are now being made in Asia and Africa, especially within the Commonwealth, prove so successful, and by their example so compelling, that the balance will come down in favour of freedom and order and justice?

The struggle is joined, and it is a struggle for the minds of men. What is now on trial is much more than our military strength or our diplomatic and administrative skill. It is our way of life. The uncommitted nations want to see before they choose.

'The great issue in this second half of the 20th century is whether the uncommitted peoples of Asia and Africa will swing to the East or to the West'

Our duty is to see [our differences] in perspective against the background of our long association. Of this at any rate I am certain – those of us who by grace of the electorate are temporarily in charge of affairs in your country and mine, we fleeting transient phantoms on the great stage of history, we have no right to sweep aside on this account the friendship that exists between our countries, for that is the legacy of history. It is not ours alone to deal with as we wish. To adapt a famous phrase, it belongs to those who are living, but it also belongs to those who are dead and to those who are yet unborn. ’

'We stand today on the edge of a New Frontier'

John F. Kennedy

(1917–63)

A YOUTHFUL DEMOCRATIC SENATOR ACCEPTS HIS PARTY'S NOMINATION FOR THE PRESIDENCY; DEMOCRATIC NATIONAL CONVENTION, LOS ANGELES, 15 JULY 1960

The senator from Massachusetts had consistently emphasized his comparative youth while campaigning to gain the Democrats' nomination to contest the 1960 US presidential election. Success in that election would confirm the appeal of his emphasis on novelty, freshness and vigour – themes which would therefore also typify JFK's speeches as president. Theodore (Ted) C. Sorensen was invariably by his side, first as senatorial assistant and then as special counsel to the president. Jack Kennedy had a literary side to him and in the young lawyer from Nebraska he found a staffer with a similar feel for language. The speeches they wrote together came to define a new era in American life, an era when the country was enjoined to turn its back on the immediate past of the 1950s as a time of 'drugged and fitful sleep'.

President Eisenhower, Kennedy's predecessor, had ended the war in Korea and warned against the development of a 'military–industrial complex' within US big business. But Kennedy campaigned for the presidency as a Cold War partisan, hence his reference here to the 'single-minded advance of the communist system'. A lazy American administration, he claimed, had allowed the Soviets to acquire a superiority in nuclear-armed missiles. There was a 'missile gap' and the US had to catch up. The campaign promise was more than fulfilled. By October 1962 the US had more than 25,000 nuclear weapons, while the USSR had less than half that number.

Kennedy was the first Catholic to be elected president, and the widespread American suspicion of his church as a foreign institution obliged him to assert his independence of the papacy's political influence. His own poor health was another drawback to the candidacy, and Kennedy's puffy expression was attributable to the steroids he took as treatment for Addison's disease, an endocrine disorder. A tan masked the sickness – and so

JOHN F. KENNEDY (1917–63)

June 1940 Graduates from Harvard University.

June 1944 Awarded Purple Heart for wartime bravery.

Nov 1952 Elected senator for Massachusetts (re-elected 1958).

July 1960 Wins Democratic presidential nomination.

Nov 1960 Narrowly defeats Richard Nixon to become 35th president of the USA.

Jan 1961 Inauguration as president.

April 1961 Bay of Pigs invasion of Cuba fails.

Oct 1962 Cuban Missile Crisis.

Aug 1963 Signs Partial Test Ban Treaty in Moscow.

22 Nov 1963 Assassinated in Dallas, Texas.

did the speeches. Those listening to a man committed to 'strong, creative . . . leadership' and to the provision of 'intellectual and moral strength' assumed that he was himself healthy.

California was a good place to explore the metaphor of a 'New Frontier' since it was the westward expansion of the US which had produced the 'pioneer spirit'. Subliminal imagery involving cowboys and stage-coaches was now enrolled to describe the 1960 frontier whose opportunities and perils were both intellectual and practical. Space had to be conquered and ignorance abolished, peace ought to be attained and poverty alleviated. Not all young men, however, were equally qualified to join the new pioneers, and Kennedy's patronizing reference to his Republican opponent, Richard Nixon, was calculated to wound. *Poor Richard's Almanack*, an annual publication written by Benjamin Franklin, enjoyed success in mid-18th-century America, with its collection of homely proverbs and traditional sayings appealing especially to the self-educated. Nonetheless, the oratory of this Harvard-educated politician also invoked the American tradition of self-help. FDR's New Deal had 'promised security and succour'. But JFK's New Frontier required the American people to supply their own frontier spirit. If the US was to endure as a democracy, its people had work to do.

'

I hope that no American . . . will waste his franchise by voting either for me or against me solely on account of my religious affiliation. It is not relevant . . . I am telling you now what you are entitled to know: that my decisions on any public policy will be my own – as an American, a Democrat and a free man . . .

After eight years of drugged and fitful sleep, this nation needs strong, creative Democratic leadership in the White House . . . the American people expect more from us than cries of indignation and attack. The times are too grave, the challenge too urgent, and the stakes too high to permit the customary passions of political debate . . .

For the world is changing. The old era is ending. The old ways will not do.

There are new and more terrible weapons, new and uncertain nations, new pressures of population and deprivation. One-third of the world, it has been said, may be free, but one-third is the victim of cruel repression – and the other one-third is rocked by the pangs of poverty, hunger and envy. More energy is released by the awakening of these new nations than by the fission of the atom itself. For the world is changing.

Meanwhile, communist influence has penetrated further into Asia, stood astride the Middle East and now festers some 90 miles off the coast of Florida.

The world has been close to war before, but now man, who has survived all previous threats to his existence, has taken into his mortal hands the power to exterminate the entire species some seven times over.

'For the world is changing. The old era is ending. The old ways will not do'

Here at home, the changing face of the future is equally revolutionary . . .

An urban population explosion has overcrowded our schools, cluttered up our suburbs and increased the squalor of our slums.

A peaceful revolution for human rights, demanding an end to racial discrimination, has strained at the leashes imposed by timid executive leadership . . .

And a revolution of automation finds machines replacing men in the mines and mills of America, without replacing their incomes or their training . . .

There has also been a change – a slippage – in our intellectual and moral strength. Seven lean years of drought and famine have withered a field of ideas. Blight has descended . . . and a dry rot, beginning in Washington, is seeping into every corner of America – in the expense account way of life, the confusion between what is legal and what is right. Too many Americans have lost their way, their will and their sense of historic purpose.

It is a time, in short, for a new generation of leadership – new men to cope with new problems and new opportunities.

All over the world, particularly in the newer nations, young men are coming to power – men who are not bound by the traditions of the past, men who are not blinded by the old fears and hates and rivalries, young men who can cast off the old slogans and delusions and suspicions.

'It is a time, in short, for a new generation of leadership – new men to cope with new problems and new opportunities'

The Republican nominee-to-be, of course, is also a young man. But . . . his party is the party of the past. His speeches are generalities from *Poor Richard's Almanack* . . . Their pledge is a pledge to the status quo – and today there can be no status quo.

For I stand tonight facing west on what was once the last frontier. From the lands that stretch 3000 miles behind me, the pioneers of old gave up their safety, their comfort and sometimes their lives to build a new world here in the west. They were not the captives of their own doubts . . . Their motto was not 'every man for himself' but 'all for the common cause'. They were determined to make that new world strong and free, to overcome its hazards and its hardships, to conquer the enemies that threatened from without and within. Today some would say . . . that all the battles have been won – that there is no longer an American frontier. But . . . we stand today on the edge of a New Frontier – the frontier of the 1960s, a frontier of unknown opportunities and perils, a frontier of unfulfilled hopes and threats . . .

Franklin Roosevelt's New Deal promised security and succour to those in need. But the New Frontier of which I speak is not a set of promises – it is a set of challenges. It sums up not what I intend to offer the American people, but what I intend to ask of them . . .

But I tell you the New Frontier is here, whether we seek it or not. Beyond that frontier are the uncharted areas of science and space, unsolved problems of peace and war, unconquered pockets of ignorance and prejudice, unanswered questions of poverty and surplus . . .

But I believe the times demand new invention, innovation, imagination, decision. I am asking each of you to be pioneers on that New Frontier . . .

'The New Frontier of which I speak is not a set of promises – it is a set of challenges'

We must prove all over again whether this nation – or any nation so conceived – can long endure; whether our society – with its freedom of choice, its breadth of opportunity, its range of alternatives – can compare with the single-minded advance of the communist system.

Can a nation organized and governed such as ours endure? That is the real question. Have we the nerve and the will?

That is the question of the New Frontier. That is the choice our nation must make – a choice that lies not merely between two men or two parties, but between the public interest and private comfort; between national greatness and national decline; between the fresh air of progress and the stale, dank atmosphere of 'normalcy'; between determined dedication and creeping democracy.

All mankind waits upon our decision. A whole world looks to see what we will do. We cannot fail their trust, we cannot fail to try . . .

Recall with me the words of Isaiah: 'They that wait upon the Lord shall renew their strength; they shall mount up with wings as eagles; they shall run and not be weary.'

As we face the coming challenge, we too shall wait upon the Lord and ask that He renew our strength. Then shall we be equal to the test. Then we shall not be weary. And then we shall prevail.

'Ask not what your country can do for you; ask what you can do for your country'

John F. Kennedy

(1917–63)

THE 35TH PRESIDENT OF THE USA DELIVERS HIS INAUGURAL ADDRESS; WASHINGTON, 20 JANUARY 1961

Ask not what your country can do for you; ask what you can do for your country'

John F. Kennedy's inaugural address as president displayed both clarity of thought and concision of expression. Its celebrity was immediate and has proved to be lasting. That this should be so owes much to the fact that the speech is a classically fine example of English prose at its unadorned best. The vocabulary is simple, the sentence construction is well balanced, relative clauses are kept under control. Similes and metaphors do not, on the whole, overreach themselves. The excessively elaborate 'beachhead of cooperation' and 'jungle of suspicion' contrast with the elegant lucidity which is this speech's predominant tone. Kennedy knew what he wanted to say and how to say it.

'New Frontier' themes of dangerous threats and hopeful opportunities continue to be balanced against each other. The famously unlimited commitment to liberty's survival and success was an important Cold War moment and owed much to the need that Kennedy felt to assert himself as a serious and knowledgeable statesman. At 43 he was the youngest president ever elected, and the international stage at that time was still dominated by the older generation of Nikita Khrushchev, Harold Macmillan, Charles de Gaulle and Konrad Adenauer. The inaugural address therefore turns youth and energy into qualifications for high office, and the idea of a briskly scene-setting first '100 days' in power captivated political practitioners and commentators alike. Kennedy's spare literary style was the perfect medium to express this business-like commitment to the job in hand. He belonged to a period when politicians were not expected to express their inner emotions or to empathize with the electorate by offering suitably edited highlights from their personal experiences. This is a strikingly dispassionate speech. But by avoiding the ponderous Kennedy achieved a sparse lyricism, and the constitutional truths of the late 18th century are re-expressed with a contemporary freshness and relevance.

The remarks addressed to 'our sister republics south of our border' had a special relevance for Cuba, then two years into its government by Fidel Castro's regime, as well as for the USSR, whose close Cuban involvement was now well documented. But Kennedy also outlined his government's commitment to the principle of negotiation and cooperation in order to reduce international tensions with the Soviets and their allies. There is a clear recognition of the link between political stability and economic progress, and an eloquent understanding of the dangers posed by the persistence of Third World poverty. The enterprise to which the new president had summoned his fellow citizens was undeniably grand – as well as one couched in terms of a traditional American trust in the individualizing virtues of self-reliance. But this was also a truly international moment, an assertion of America's leadership in both ethical and political terms, and a rejection of the idea that the US could be either isolationist or unilateralist when responding to the urgency of the present.

We observe today not a victory of party, but a celebration of freedom – symbolizing an end as well as a beginning, signifying renewal as well as change. For I have sworn before you and almighty God the same solemn oath our forebears prescribed nearly a century and three-quarters ago.

The world is very different now. For man holds in his mortal hands the power to abolish all forms of human poverty and all forms of human life. And yet the same revolutionary beliefs for which our forebears fought are still at issue around the globe – the belief that the rights of man come not from the generosity of the state but from the hand of God.

'Man holds in his mortal hands the power to abolish all forms of human poverty and all forms of human life'

We dare not forget today that we are the heirs of that first revolution. Let the word go forth from this time and place, to friend and foe alike, that the torch has been passed to a new generation of Americans – born in this century, tempered by war, disciplined by a hard and bitter peace, proud of our ancient heritage, and unwilling to witness or permit the slow undoing of those human rights to which this nation has always been committed, and to which we are committed today at home and around the world. Let every nation know, whether it wishes us well or ill, that we shall pay any price, bear any burden, meet any hardship, support any friend, oppose any foe, to assure the survival and the success of liberty . . .

To those old allies whose cultural and spiritual origins we share, we pledge the loyalty of faithful friends . . .

To those new states whom we welcome to the ranks of the free, we pledge our word that one form of colonial control shall not have passed away merely to be replaced by a far more iron tyranny . . .

'Let the word go forth from this time and place, to friend and foe alike, that the torch has been passed to a new generation of Americans'

To those people in the huts and villages of half the globe struggling to break the bonds of mass misery, we pledge our best efforts to help them help themselves, for whatever period is required – not because the communists may be doing it, not because we seek their votes, but because it is right . . .

To our sister republics south of our border, we offer a special pledge: to convert our good words into good deeds in a new alliance for progress, to assist free men and free governments in casting off the chains of poverty. But this peaceful revolution of hope cannot become the prey of hostile powers. Let all our neighbours know that we shall join with them to oppose aggression or subversion anywhere in the Americas. And let every other power know that this hemisphere intends to remain the master of its own house.

To that world assembly of sovereign states, the United Nations . . . we renew our pledge of support – to prevent it from becoming merely a forum for invective, to strengthen its shield of the new and the weak, and to enlarge the area in which its writ may run.

Finally, to those nations who would make themselves our adversary, we offer not a pledge but a request: that both sides begin anew the quest for peace . . . Only when our arms are sufficient beyond doubt can we be certain beyond doubt that they will never be employed.

But neither can two great and powerful groups of nations take comfort from our present course – both sides overburdened by the cost of modern weapons, both rightly alarmed by the steady spread of the deadly atom . . .

'Together let us explore the stars, conquer the deserts, eradicate disease, tap the ocean depths, and encourage the arts and commerce'

So let us begin anew – remembering on both sides that civility is not a sign of weakness, and sincerity is always subject to proof. Let us never negotiate out of fear, but let us never fear to negotiate . . .

Let both sides, for the first time, formulate serious and precise proposals for the inspection and control of arms, and bring the absolute power to destroy other nations under the absolute control of all nations . . .

Together let us explore the stars, conquer the deserts, eradicate disease, tap the ocean depths, and encourage the arts and commerce. Let both sides unite to heed, in all corners of the earth, the command of Isaiah – to 'undo the heavy burdens, and let the oppressed go free'. And if a beachhead of cooperation may push back the jungle of suspicion, let both sides join in creating . . . a new world of law, where the strong are just and the weak secure and the peace preserved.

All this will not be finished in the first 100 days. Nor will it be finished in the first 1000 days, nor in the life of this administration, nor even perhaps in our lifetime on this planet. But let us begin.

In your hands, my fellow citizens, more than mine, will rest the final success or failure of our course. Since this country was founded, each generation of Americans has been summoned to give testimony to its national loyalty . . . Now the trumpet summons us again – not as a call to arms, though arms we need; not as a call to battle, though embattled we are; but a call to bear the burden of a long twilight struggle, year in and year out . . . a struggle against the common enemies of man: tyranny, poverty, disease and war itself . . .

'Ask not . . . what America will do for you, but what, together, we can do for the freedom of man'

In the long history of the world, only a few generations have been granted the role of defending freedom in its hour of maximum danger. I do not shrink from this responsibility – I welcome it. I do not believe that any of us would exchange places with any other people or any other generation . . . And so, my fellow Americans, ask not what your country can do for you; ask what you can do for your country. My fellow citizens of the world, ask not what America will do for you, but what, together, we can do for the freedom of man . . .

With a good conscience our only sure reward, with history the final judge of our deeds, let us go forth to lead the land we love, asking His blessing and His help, but knowing that here on earth God's work must truly be our own.'

'Mankind must put an end to war – or war will put an end to mankind'

John F. Kennedy

(1917–63)

THE US PRESIDENT STRESSES THE URGENCY OF LIMITING NUCLEAR TESTING; UN GENERAL ASSEMBLY, NEW YORK CITY, 25 SEPTEMBER 1961

Kennedy was addressing an institution in crisis, a week after the death of Dag Hammarskjöld, a figure of unique authority in UN history. The general secretary had been killed in a plane crash while attempting mediation in the Congolese civil war, and in the ensuing vacuum doubts were raised about the UN's rationale. Kennedy's speech boosted its self-confidence and recalled the UN to urgent work on the control of nuclear testing as part of the more general goal of slowing down the arms race.

The US's successful test on 1 November 1952 of a hydrogen bomb – one based on the principle of staged radiation implosion – led to widespread fears about the effect of nuclear fallout on the planet's atmosphere. Western nuclear powers and the USSR therefore started to negotiate a test ban, but by 1961 these talks, presided over by the UN Disarmament Commission, had stalled. Kennedy's speech highlighted the issue's importance, and subsequent progress involved separating the question of nuclear disarmament from that of nuclear testing.

US, UK and Soviet government representatives signed the Partial Test Ban Treaty in Moscow on 5 August 1963, after which other countries could decide whether to follow suit. Most did so, though France and China were important exceptions. The treaty prohibits its signatories from conducting nuclear testing on the ground, in the atmosphere and underwater. Britain and the US maintained, however, that underground testing, to be effective, needed a neutral system of inspection based within the country concerned. The USSR disagreed, but in July 1963 President Khrushchev accepted that the treaty would have to exclude a ban on underground testing.

Kennedy remained the Cold War politician who in his inaugural address in January 1961 committed the US to 'pay any price . . . to assure the survival and the success of liberty'. In this speech he still thought his country should send arms and 'join free men in standing up to their responsibilities'. But his words here are tempered by experience of office and by a novel fear of the abyss, with the Bay of Pigs expedition (April 1961) providing a recent revelation of defects in US intelligence and military planning. A force of Cuban exiles, armed by the US, had hoped to oust Castro but were mown down when they landed in the bay. Ahead lay the Cuban Missile Crisis and its demonstration of how irrationality, fear and ignorance might upset the nuclear balancing act.

The speech expresses a major theme of the presidency: peace was 'primarily a problem of politics and people', and it therefore involved the human skills of negotiation. A federally funded Peace Corps composed of US civilian volunteers had been established just days before Kennedy spoke, and its provision of trained manpower working on Third World development projects formed an important part of his global vision. Kennedy's precisely formulated goals in this speech helped set the agenda for disarmament talks in the next quarter of a century, a time of intermittent hope that the great powers might be able to negotiate themselves out of a world crisis.

Unconditional war can no longer lead to unconditional victory. It can no longer serve to settle disputes . . . Mankind must put an end to war – or war will put an end to mankind . . .

Today, every inhabitant of the planet must contemplate the day when this planet may no longer be habitable . . . Men may no longer pretend that the quest for disarmament is a sign of weakness – for in a spiralling arms race, a nation's security may well be shrinking even as its arms increase . . .

'In a spiralling arms race, a nation's security may well be shrinking even as its arms increase'

It is therefore our intention to challenge the Soviet Union, not to an arms race, but to a peace race – to advance together step by step, stage by stage, until general and complete disarmament has been achieved.

The programme . . . would place the final responsibility for verification and control . . . in an international organization within the framework of the United Nations. It would assure . . . true inspection and apply it in stages proportionate to the stage of disarmament. It would cover delivery systems as well as weapons. It would ultimately halt their production as well as their testing, their transfer as well as their possession . . .

Such a plan would not bring a world free from conflict and greed, but it would bring a world free from the terrors of mass destruction. It would not usher in the era of the super state, but it would usher in an era in which no state could annihilate or be annihilated by another . . .

To halt the spread of these terrible weapons, to halt the contamination of the air, to halt the spiralling nuclear arms race, our new Disarmament Programme thus includes the following proposals:

– First, signing the test-ban treaty by all nations.

– Second, stopping the production of fissionable materials for use in weapons, and preventing their transfer to any nation now lacking in nuclear weapons.

– Third, prohibiting the transfer of control over nuclear weapons to states that do not own them.

– Fourth, keeping nuclear weapons from seeding new battlegrounds in outer space.

– Fifth, gradually destroying existing nuclear weapons and converting their materials to peaceful uses; and

– Finally, halting the unlimited testing and production of strategic nuclear delivery vehicles, and gradually destroying them as well.

To destroy arms, however, is not enough. We must create even as we destroy – creating worldwide law and law enforcement as we outlaw worldwide war and weapons . . .

Therefore, the United States recommends that all member nations earmark special peace-keeping units in their armed forces – to be on call of the United Nations . . . and with advanced provision for financial and logistic support . . .

For peace is not solely a matter of military or technical problems – it is primarily a problem of politics and people. And unless man can match his strides in weaponry and technology with equal strides in social and political development, our great strength, like that of the dinosaur, will become incapable of proper control – and like the dinosaur vanish from the earth.

As we extend the rule of law on earth, so must we also extend it to man's new domain – outer space . . . The cold reaches of the universe must not become the new arena of an even colder war.

To this end, we shall urge proposals . . . reserving outer space for peaceful use, prohibiting weapons of mass destruction in space or on celestial bodies, and opening the mysteries and benefits of space to every nation. We shall propose . . . a global system of communication satellites linking the whole world in telegraph and telephone and radio and television . . .

'My nation was once a colony, and we know what colonialism means'

Political sovereignty is but a mockery without the means of meeting poverty and illiteracy and disease. Self-determination is but a slogan if the future holds no hope . . . New research, technical assistance and pilot projects can unlock the wealth of less developed lands and untapped waters. And development can become a cooperative and not a competitive enterprise – to enable all nations . . . to become in fact as well as in law free and equal . . .

I do not ignore the remaining problems of traditional colonialism which still confront this body. But colonialism in its harshest forms is not only the exploitation of new nations by old, of dark skins by light, or the subjugation of the poor by the rich. My nation was once a colony, and we know what colonialism means; the exploitation and subjugation of the weak by the powerful, of the many by the few, of the governed who have given no consent to be governed . . .

And that is why there is no ignoring the fact that the tide of self-determination has not reached the communist empire where a population lives under governments installed by foreign troops . . . under a system which knows only one party . . . and which builds a wall to keep truth a stranger and its own citizens prisoners . . .

'The United States has both the will and the weapons to join free men in standing up to their responsibilities.'

Terror is not a new weapon. Throughout history it has been used by those who could not prevail, either by persuasion or example. But inevitably they fail, either because men are not afraid to die for a life worth living, or because the terrorists themselves came to realize that free men cannot be frightened by threats and that aggression would meet its own response. And it is in the light of that history that every nation today should know, be he friend or foe, that the United States has both the will and the weapons to join free men in standing up to their responsibilities . . .

We in this hall shall be remembered either as part of the generation that turned this planet into a flaming pyre or the generation that met its vow 'to save succeeding generations from the scourge of war'. In the endeavour to meet that vow, I pledge you . . . that we shall never negotiate out of fear, we shall never fear to negotiate . . .

'Together we shall save our planet, or together we shall perish in its flames'

Never have the nations of the world had so much to lose, or so much to gain. Together we shall save our planet, or together we shall perish in its flames. Save it we can – and save it we must – and then we shall earn the eternal thanks of mankind and, as peacemakers, the eternal blessing of God. ’

'There is no independence imaginable for a country that does not have its own nuclear weapon'

Charles de Gaulle

(1890–1970)

THE FRENCH PRESIDENT INSISTS ON FRANCE'S NEED FOR ITS OWN NUCLEAR WEAPONS; ÉCOLE MILITAIRE, PARIS, 15 FEBRUARY 1963

'There is no independence imaginable for a country that does not have its own nuclear weapon'

In 1963 the wounds inflicted on France's authority and reputation during the Algerian War of Independence remained raw. The French colony witnessed atrocities committed on both sides following the rebellion's outbreak in 1954, and four years later French officers based in Algiers led a military insurrection. Condemning their government for irresolute handling of the war, the dissidents called for de Gaulle's return to power. France's Fourth Republic was dissolved and the new constitution strengthened the authority of the presidency – the office to which de Gaulle was elected in November 1958 after exercising emergency powers as premier in the preceding six months. Having decided that suppression of Algerian nationalism was not feasible politically, de Gaulle changed tack and the national referendum of French voters held in January 1961 approved his plan for an independent Algeria. Right-wing elements within France and Algerian colonists were equally outraged. In an effort to reverse the policy, four retired generals organized a putsch which attempted the seizure of Paris and of Algeria's major cities in April 1961. Although it failed and Algeria became independent in 1962, the conspiracy showed a depth of feeling against de Gaulle within the army, and his critics associated the general's volte-face with a subversion of French national honour.

De Gaulle was speaking at France's elite military academy, and it was important that he should both inspire a demoralized army and move the national agenda on. The emphases are typically Gaullist: the invocation of France's destiny, nationality and independence, and the assertion of a personal link between the general and his country's fortunes. His instinct for the big historical picture – with France firmly in the foreground – is evident in his remarks on the evolution of weaponry and its relationship to differing forms of state power.

CHARLES DE GAULLE (1890–1970)

1912 Graduates from St-Cyr Military Academy; commissioned as an officer in the 33rd Infantry Regiment of the French army.

March 1916 Wounded at Battle of Verdun and taken prisoner.

1934 Publishes *The Army of the Future*, urging mechanization of the army and more mobile strategies in warfare.

18 June 1940 Broadcasts from London his 'Appeal' urging the French people to resist the German army's occupation.

1940–4 Leader of the Free French.

1944–6 Prime minister, French provisional government.

June 1958 Returns as premier, exercising emergency powers.

Jan 1959 Takes office as elected president of France.

May 1968 Student demonstrators disrupt central Paris.

April 1969 Resigns the presidency.

France became the world's fourth nuclear power in 1960 after detonating an atomic bomb in the Algerian desert, and de Gaulle's pursuit of an independent defence policy was designed to bolster French prestige and self-belief. This strenuous programme also had the political advantage of keeping the French military so busy that it had little time to dwell on Algeria and nurse grudges. Suspicion of the close links between the US and the UK determined de Gaulle's scepticism about NATO – an organization he considered subservient to the two allies' interests – and in 1966 France's armed forces were withdrawn from NATO's integrated command structure, though the country retained its membership of the military alliance. West Germany's membership of NATO was a further problem, in his view, since it made the country especially vulnerable to invasion from the communist powers to its east. This was the possible 'battle of Germany' here referred to and de Gaulle feared that France would then be drawn into a global war between NATO and Warsaw Pact forces. In that eventuality, he wished to maintain the option of concluding a separate peace between France and the Eastern bloc, a possibility strengthened by advertising his disagreement with NATO. French independence was basic to his vision of a 'free Europe', a third power bloc acting as a counterweight to the US and the USSR.

There is no point concealing from you the emotion I feel at finding myself, once more in my life, here where in the past I have had so many occasions to encounter ideas, participate in work, engage in reflections which have undoubtedly contributed in great measure to the tasks I have subsequently been called upon to perform in the service of France . . .

Nor do I wish to conceal from you the satisfaction I have felt in meeting you all, that is to say all the various branches of staff college training and the National Defence Institute . . .

Wherever I have passed among you, I have encountered in your work and in your concerns the overwhelming issue of the day, by which I mean nuclear weapons . . . It is only natural that I should explain to you . . . the underlying conceptions guiding the head of state and the government in the matter of defence as they see it, and as they are responsible for organizing and, potentially, directing it.Long ago, the emergence of metal weapons gave birth to the great hegemonies of antiquity. After them came the barbarian invasions and the feudal system that followed. Then the advent of fire-arms made possible the rebirth of centralized states. This resulted in the great wars, the wars of Europe, where each of the great powers of the period sought to dominate in turn: Spain, England, France, Turkey, Germany, Russia. The emergence of fire-arms also sparked off and made possible colonization, in other words the conquest of vast regions: America, India, the East, Africa.

Finally, the power of the motor emerged as a factor in combat, by sea, air and land. It was this that made it possible to bring the First World War to an end. It was this that furnished the conquering ambition of Nazi Germany with an instrument. It was this that also gave the free world what was required to crush that ambition.

Today, the development of nuclear weapons has in its turn brought about a complete upheaval in terms of security, and hence the policies, of states, even in times of peace. The upheaval would be all the greater in time of war. Imagination itself cannot encompass what might be the consequences of the use of nuclear weapons, except to realize that, in any event, such a use would lead to a total subversion in human society . . .

'Imagination itself cannot encompass what might be the consequences of the use of nuclear weapons'

Under such circumstances it is clear that there is no independence imaginable for a country that does not have its own nuclear weapon, because if it does not have such a weapon it will be forced to rely for its security, and consequently for its policy, on another country which does. It is true that certain countries of the world imagine that they can wrap themselves in neutrality . . . believing that in this way they will be overlooked by destiny. In reality, however, they will only be able to await their fate without being in any way able to alter it.

For France, whose geographical situation, whose historical raison d'être and political nature all rule out neutrality, for France which has no intention of handing over responsibility for her own fate to a foreign nation, no matter how friendly, it is absolutely necessary that she should have the wherewithal to act in any war, in other words that she should have nuclear arms.

The question of whether the total power of those arms will be equal to the total power of the arms of any adversary, and the question of whether our country could prosecute a global conflict without alliances – and, clearly, the answer to both those questions must be negative – in no way alters the elementary need for us to have our own nuclear weapons, to employ them, if necessary, as we see fit and, equally naturally, to combine the use of such weapons with the analogous weapons of our allies as part of a common effort.

These are the principles. How might they be applied?

The existence of nuclear weapons . . . causes an immense uncertainty to hover over all battles, over their nature, their rhythm, their development. If an exchange of strategic nuclear weapons between two camps . . . is capable of causing the destruction of those two states, it follows that . . . there is absolutely no way to predict if, why, where, when, how or to what extent the two nations, assured of mutual destruction, might wish to trigger such an exchange . . .

'We are resolved . . . not to be annihilated as a state and as a nation without having defended our homeland'

If the battle of Germany, the first battle in the war, went badly, whether it were to any degree a nuclear battle or not at all, the immediate consequence would be the destruction or the invasion of France and, at the same time, the loss of any bridgehead for the free world in Europe. We, however, are resolved, whatever may happen, not to be annihilated as a state and as a nation without having defended our homeland, body and soul, on the ground, and we are further convinced that in so doing we would create a chance of final victory.

All of these considerations therefore prompt us to possess our own nuclear arms at our own disposal for any nuclear strike. They prompt us also to possess the means of intervening, on land, sea and in the air, wherever circumstances would appear to us to dictate, and to possess the means of offering national resistance to the invader on our own territory . . .

'All of these considerations therefore prompt us to possess our own nuclear arms'

Such are the conceptions which have led the head of state and the government to draw up the defence plan, the organization plan and the arms plan currently in force or in preparation . . . These necessities are imposing on the French command structure a new era of initiative, authority and responsibility. For those who would have the honour of commanding in the midst of cataclysm . . . the role and duty of staff college training are essential . . . in holding themselves ready intellectually, morally and technically.

I have confidence in you, gentlemen, and in the commanders responsible for leading you, to fulfil this role and accomplish this duty.

Gentlemen, I have the honour to salute you. ’

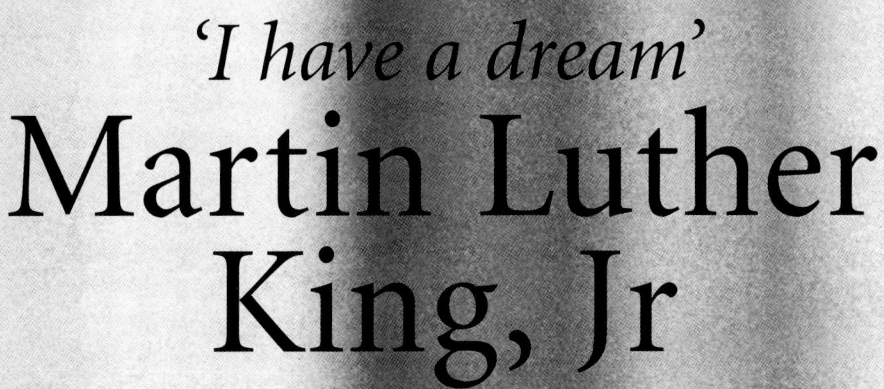

'I have a dream'

Martin Luther King, Jr

(1929–68)

THE GREAT CIVIL RIGHTS CHAMPION SPEAKS AT THE MARCH ON WASHINGTON FOR JOBS AND FREEDOM; LINCOLN MEMORIAL, WASHINGTON, 28 AUGUST 1963

Over 200,000 people had gathered in the damp savannah heat of a Washington summer's day to hear Dr Martin Luther King, Jr speak of the conquest of prejudice and the fulfilment of prophecy. The year 1963 was the centenary of the Emancipation Declaration, the edict which had been signed by Abraham Lincoln and whose provisions had freed the slaves of the Confederate states during their rebellion against the Union. The civil rights movement against racial prejudice had now broadened into a campaign against black poverty and unemployment, which is why the crowds addressed by King in the capital were part of a 'March on Washington for Jobs and Freedom'.

Assembled before the memorial to Lincoln, the marchers stood in his 'symbolic shadow' since black Americans, though emancipated in law, were still subjected to 'the chains of discrimination' in areas such as education, housing and employment. King's analogy with a bounced cheque was typically deft. The founding fathers of the US had signed the equivalent of a 'promissory note' when approving the text of the original Constitution and Declaration of Independence. But America had defaulted on this note 'in so far as her citizens of colour are concerned'. King suggests that the country's wealth is spiritual and intellectual as well as material, and that the bankruptcy of her 'bank of justice' is therefore a notion defying credibility. America was being reminded of her own best self and of the need to live up to her proclaimed goals of freedom and opportunity. King spoke therefore as an American whose own personal dream for his family and people was grounded in the reality of the 'American dream' as a whole. Much of the speech's impact was due to its emphasis on this collective experience of the nation and the shared destiny of its people.

King also spoke here as a Baptist minister intellectually grounded in biblical theology, in the protests of Old Testament prophets against unjust rulers and in the New Testament account of redemption through forgiveness. And the cadences of his delivery owed everything to his training in the technique of the Protestant sermon, with its emphasis on argument and its use of the illustrative example drawn from personal

MARTIN LUTHER KING (1929–68)

1955 Receives PhD in theology from Boston University.

1955–6 Leads Montgomery bus boycott in protest against racial segregation.

Aug 1963 Co-leader of March on Washington for Jobs and Freedom.

1964 Wins Nobel Peace Prize.

April 1967 Delivers 'Beyond Vietnam' speech in protest against US involvement in Vietnam.

April 1968 Assassinated in Memphis, Tennessee.

experience. Although approaching sublimity in content and delivery, King's oratory was never remote from his audience or congregation. In this speech he describes the journey which will take black Americans out of the ghetto and at the end of which 'justice rolls down like waters and righteousness like a mighty stream'. The imagery is biblical and exalted but the passage is introduced by a fact of daily life: the colour bar which frustrated the travels of black Americans by excluding them from certain motels and hotels. The urgency of the present crisis is captured by King's typical emphasis on heightened contrasts. Segregation's darkness in states such as Alabama and Mississippi, Georgia and Tennessee is defined by its remoteness from 'the sunlit path of racial justice'. But the concluding peroration offers an inclusive message, one which transcends the old and rings in the new.

Five score years ago, a great American, in whose symbolic shadow we stand, signed the Emancipation Proclamation. This momentous decree came as a great beacon light of hope to millions of Negro slaves who had been seared in the flames of withering injustice . . .

But one hundred years later, we must face the tragic fact that the Negro is still not free. One hundred years later, the life of the Negro is still sadly crippled by the manacles of segregation and the chains of discrimination. One hundred years later, the Negro lives on a lonely island of poverty in the midst of a vast ocean of material prosperity. One hundred years later, the Negro . . . finds himself an exile in his own land . . .

'The life of the Negro is still sadly crippled by the manacles of segregation and the chains of discrimination'

When the architects of our republic wrote the magnificent words of the Constitution and the Declaration of Independence, they were signing a promissory note to which every American was to fall heir. This note was a promise that all men would be guaranteed the inalienable rights of life, liberty and the pursuit of happiness.

It is obvious today that America has defaulted on this promissory note in so far as her citizens of colour are concerned. But we refuse to believe that the bank of justice is bankrupt. We refuse to believe that there are insufficient funds in the great vaults of opportunity of this nation . . .

Now is the time to rise from the dark and desolate valley of segregation to the sunlit path of racial justice. Now is the time to lift our nation from the quicksands of racial injustice to the solid rock of brotherhood . . .

'Now is the time to rise from the dark and desolate valley of segregation to the sunlit path of racial justice'

There will be neither rest nor tranquillity in America until the Negro is granted his citizenship rights . . .

We must forever conduct our struggle on the high plane of dignity and discipline. Again and again we must rise to the majestic heights of meeting physical force with soul force. The marvellous new militancy which has engulfed the Negro community must not lead us to distrust of all white people, for many of our white brothers . . . have come to realize that their destiny is tied up with our destiny and their freedom is inextricably bound to our freedom. We cannot walk alone.

We can never be satisfied as long as our bodies, heavy with the fatigue of travel, cannot gain lodging in the motels of the highways and the hotels of the cities. We cannot be satisfied as long as the Negro's basic mobility is from a smaller ghetto to a larger one. We cannot be satisfied as long as a Negro in Mississippi cannot vote and a Negro in New York believes he has nothing for which to vote. No, no, we are not satisfied, and we will not be satisfied until justice rolls down like waters and righteousness like a mighty stream . . .

'We will not be satisfied until justice rolls down like waters and righteousness like a mighty stream'

I still have a dream. It is a dream deeply rooted in the American dream.

I have a dream that one day this nation will rise up and live out the true meaning of its creed: 'We hold these truths to be self-evident: that all men are created equal.'

I have a dream that one day on the red hills of Georgia the sons of former slaves and the sons of former slave owners will be able to sit down together at the table of brotherhood.

I have a dream that one day even the state of Mississippi, a desert state, sweltering with the heat of injustice and oppression, will be transformed into an oasis of freedom and justice.

I have a dream that my four children will one day live in a nation where they will not be judged by the colour of their skin but by the content of their character.

I have a dream today.

I have a dream that one day the state of Alabama, whose governor's lips are presently dripping with the words of interposition and nullification, will be transformed into a situation where little black boys and black girls will be able to join hands with little white boys and girls and walk together as sisters and brothers.

I have a dream today.

I have a dream that one day every valley shall be exalted, every hill and mountain shall be made low, the rough places will be made plain, and the crooked places will be made straight, and the glory of the Lord shall be revealed, and all flesh shall see it together.

This is our hope . . . With this faith we will be able to hew out of the mountain of despair a stone of hope. With this faith we will be able to transform the jangling discords of our nation into a beautiful symphony of brotherhood. With this faith we will be able to work together, to pray together, to struggle together, to go to jail together, to stand up for freedom together, knowing that we will be free one day.

This will be the day when all of God's children will be able to sing with a new meaning: 'My country, 'tis of thee, sweet land of liberty, of thee I sing. Land where my fathers died, land of the pilgrim's pride, from every mountainside, let freedom ring.'

And if America is to be a great nation, this must become true. So let freedom ring from the prodigious hilltops of New Hampshire. Let freedom ring from the mighty mountains of New York. Let freedom ring from the heightening Alleghennies of Pennsylvania!

Let freedom ring from the snow-capped Rockies of Colorado!

Let freedom ring from the curvaceous peaks of California!

But not only that; let freedom ring from Stone Mountain of Georgia!

Let freedom ring from Lookout Mountain of Tennessee!

Let freedom ring from every hill and every molehill of Mississippi. From every mountainside, let freedom ring.

'Free at last! Free at last! Thank God Almighty we are free at last!'

When we let freedom ring, when we let it ring from every village and every hamlet, from every state and every city, we will be able to speed up that day when all of God's children, black men and white men, Jews and Gentiles, Protestants and Catholics, will be able to join hands and sing in the words of the old negro spiritual: 'Free at last! Free at last! Thank God Almighty, we are free at last!'

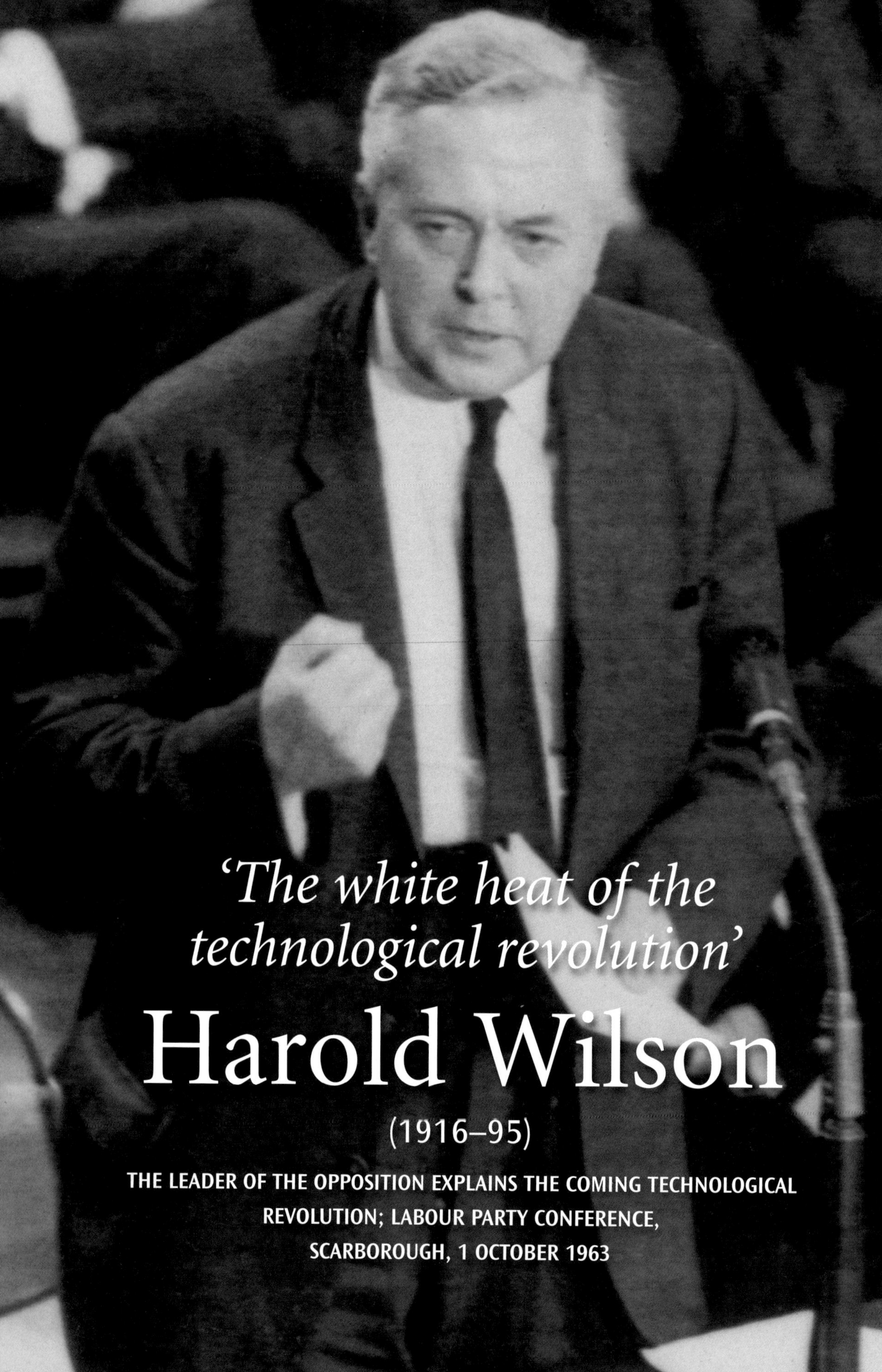

'The white heat of the technological revolution'

Harold Wilson

(1916–95)

THE LEADER OF THE OPPOSITION EXPLAINS THE COMING TECHNOLOGICAL REVOLUTION; LABOUR PARTY CONFERENCE, SCARBOROUGH, 1 OCTOBER 1963

In the year leading up to the general election of 1964 Harold Wilson delivered a series of speeches outlining a programme for government. Labour's recently elected leader needed to establish himself in the public mind and propose a compelling alternative to the Conservatives, who had been in power since 1951. Both aims were achieved to impressively brisk effect and Wilson's brief period as opposition leader forms one of his career high points.

The most celebrated of his 1963–4 speeches described the technological revolution's 'white heat' and portrayed the socio-economic changes which were required in order to extend the benefits of this modernizing process to the population at large. New national goals had to be identified, and these were to be planned and administered by experts who understood the contemporary challenge.

Wilson pilloried the Conservatives as reactionary incompetents indifferent to British needs and incapable of grasping the significance of 'science'. The fact that the 14th earl of Home emerged as Conservative leader in the month of this speech's delivery rather served his purpose. Wilson promised the self-conscious contrast: leadership by technocrats whose style and appeal were classless, and whose progress had been achieved through meritocratic effort rather than by exploiting 'aristocratic connections or the power of inherited wealth'.

Born in Yorkshire, the son of an industrial chemist, Wilson was raised a Congregationalist in the dissenting traditions of English religious non-conformity. Hard work and natural ability

HAROLD WILSON (1916–95)

1938–45 Fellow of University College, Oxford.

1943–4 Director of Statistics at Ministry of Fuel and Power.

1945 Elected MP (Labour) for Ormskirk in Labour's general-election victory.

1947 President of the Board of Trade.

1950 Elected MP (Labour) for Huyton, Merseyside.

1951–64 Labour in opposition.

Feb 1963 Elected Labour leader.

1964 Forms a government after Labour gains a majority of four in the general election.

1966 Labour gains majority of 96 in the general election.

1970 Loses general election to Conservatives.

1974 Forms minority administration after February general election; gains overall majority of three in subsequent October election.

1976 Resigns as prime minister.

1983 Created Baron Wilson of Rievaulx.

took him to Oxford, where he became a university teacher specializing in statistics. His political star shone early and he entered the Cabinet at the precocious age of 31. During Labour's years in opposition he associated initially with the party's left, before veering to the centre – and establishing a reputation as an adroit strategist whose tactics served both his party's cause and his own advancement.

Wilson was never particularly ideological, and although he accepted state nationalization of key industries as part of Labour's heritage, he did little to promote the policy. The extension of social opportunity, especially through education, was his natural territory and Wilson's premiership saw the establishment of the Open University (this speech's 'university of the air'). His advocacy of central planning to promote economic development was hardly a novelty in 1963 since interventionist policies had already enjoyed a vogue for almost two decades. But Wilson's dynamism and amiability had caught the public imagination and Labour's majority of four in 1964 was precursor to a landslide victory two years later.

High employment and general prosperity provided the background to Wilson's optimism about a regenerated Britain which also underwent rapid social change during his premiership: capital punishment was abolished, abortion laws were liberalized, homosexuality became decriminalized. Britain's prolonged economic crisis in the 1970s made for a darker picture. Industrial conflict's reality replaced this speech's anticipation of a benign leisure generated by scientific advance. Faith in 'democratic planning' and in government's capacity to create prosperity withered, and Wilson's skills were directed to the conciliation of factions within his party rather than to the goal of national revitalization.

‘One of the dangers of the old-boy network approach to life is the thought that it is international, that . . . we can always rely on a special relationship with someone or other to bail us out. From now on Britain will have just as much influence in the world as we can earn, as we can deserve. We have no accumulated reserves on which to live . . .

The period of 15 years from 1960 to the middle of the 1970s will embrace a period of technical change . . . greater than in the whole industrial revolution of the last 250 years . . .

If we try to abstract from the automative age, the only result will be that Britain will become a stagnant backwater, pitied and condemned by the rest of the world . . .

The danger, as things are, is that an unregulated private enterprise economy in this country will promote just enough automation to create serious unemployment but not enough to create a breakthrough in the production barrier . . .

Automation is not just one more process in the history of mechanization . . . The essence of modern automation is that it replaces the hitherto unique human functions of memory and of judgement. And now the computers have reached the point where they command facilities of memory and of judgement far beyond the capacity of any human being or group of human beings who have ever lived . . .

Since technological progress left to the mechanism of private industry and private property can lead only to high profits for a few, a high rate of employment for a few, and to mass redundancies for the many, if there had never been a case for socialism before, automation would have created it. Because only if technological progress becomes part of our national planning can that progress be directed to national ends.

'Britain will have just as much influence in the world as we can earn, as we can deserve'

So the choice is . . . between the blind imposition of technological advance . . . and the conscious planned purposive use of scientific progress to provide undreamed-of living standards and the possibility of leisure ultimately on an unbelievable scale . . .

We must organize British industry so that it applies the results of scientific research more purposively to our national production effort . . .

To train the scientists we are going to need will mean a revolution in our attitude to education . . . at every level . . .

Every one of us must accept a tremendous building programme of new universities, and . . . let us try and see that more of them are sited in industrial areas where they can . . . reflect the pulsating throb of local industry . . .

A university of the air . . . is a supplement to our plans. Nor . . . do we envisage this merely as a means of providing scientists and technologists . . . A properly planned university of the air could make an immense contribution to the cultural life of our country . . .

Scientific research in industry needs to be very purposively organized. That is . . . why we are going to establish a full Minister for Science . . .

Unless we can harness science to our economic planning, we are not going to get the expansion that we need . . . What is needed is structural changes in British industry . . . What we need is new industries and it will be the job of the next government to see that we get them. This means mobilizing scientific research in this country in producing a new technological breakthrough . . . We have spent thousands of millions . . . on misdirected research and development contracts in defence. If we were now to use the techniques of R and D contracts in civil industry, I believe we could . . . establish new industries which would make us once again one of the foremost industrial nations of the world . . .

We now need . . . to ensure that where new industries are established on the basis of state-sponsored research, the state will control the industries which result . . . We hold it as a basic principle that the profits which result from state-sponsored research should accrue in good measure to the community that created them.

These policies I think will provide the answer to the problem of Britain's declining industries and areas. Some of our declining industries will be revitalized, not on a basis . . . of uneconomic protection or subsidies, but revitalized by mobilizing these industries for new tasks . . .

'We are redefining and we are restating our socialism in terms of the scientific revolution'

The economic consequences of disarmament cannot be dealt with except on a basis of socialist planning. Advanced capitalist countries are maintaining full employment today only by virtue of vast arms orders and panic would be the order of the day in Wall Street and other stock markets, the day peace breaks out. We have announced that the Labour government will include a minister for disarmament, and among his duties will be to prepare for the economic problems that will follow hard on the heels of massive disarmament . . .

In all our plans for the future, we are redefining and we are restating our socialism in terms of the scientific revolution. But that revolution cannot become a reality unless we are prepared to make far-reaching changes in economic and social attitudes . . .

'The Britain that is going to be forged in the white heat of this revolution will be no place for restrictive practices'

The Britain that is going to be forged in the white heat of this revolution will be no place for restrictive practices or outdated methods on either side of industry . . . In the Cabinet room and the boardroom alike those charged with the control of our affairs must be ready to think and to speak in the language of our scientific age. For the controlling heights of British industry to be controlled today by men whose only claim is their aristocratic connections or the power of inherited wealth or speculative finance is as irrelevant to the 20th century as would be the continued purchase of commissions in the armed forces by lordly amateurs . . .

Our future lies not in military strength alone but in the efforts, the sacrifice, and above all the energies which a free people can mobilize for the future greatness of our country . . . Because we care deeply about the future of Britain, we must use all the resources of democratic planning, all the latent and underdeveloped energies and skills of our people, to ensure Britain's standing in the world.

’

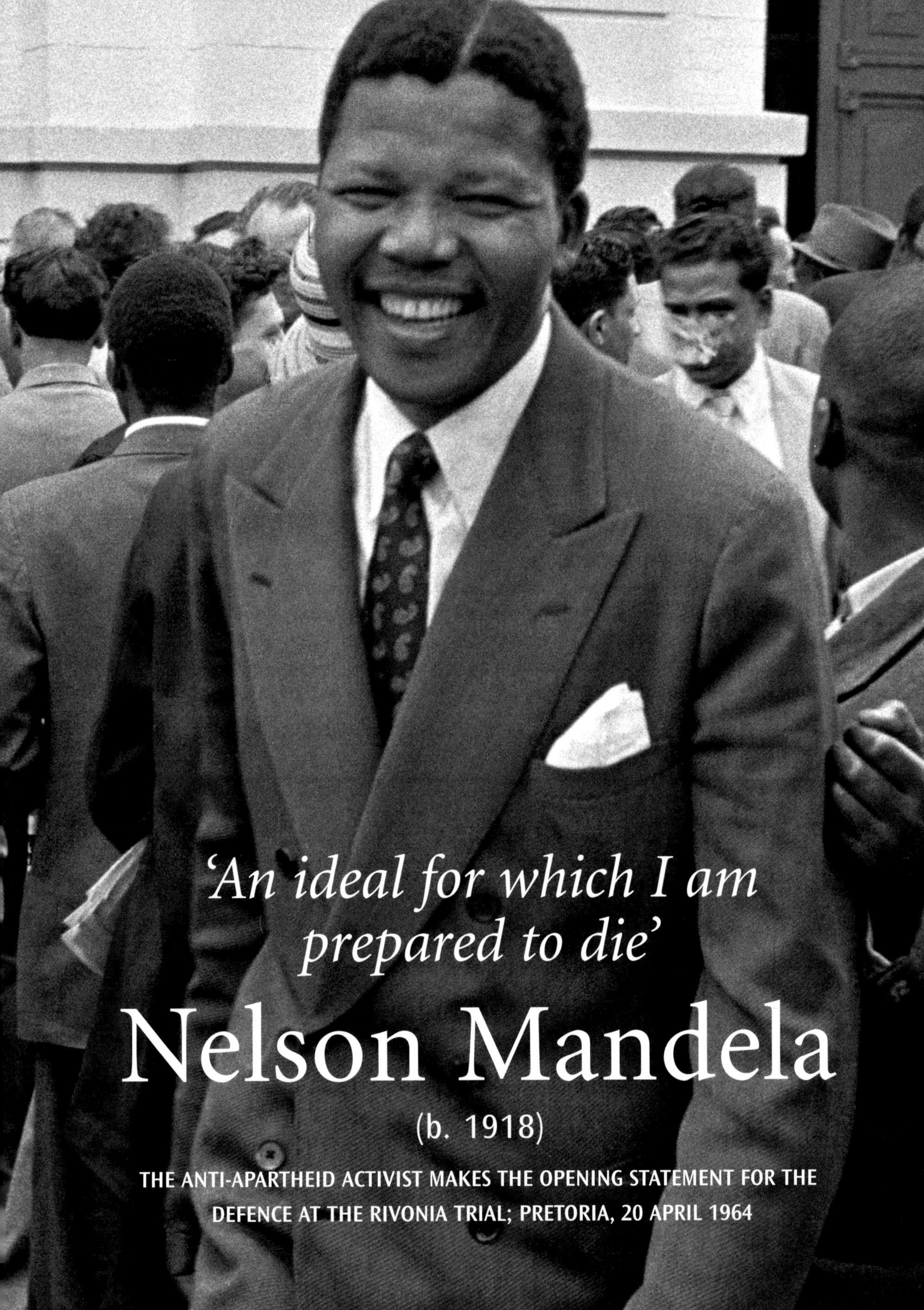

'An ideal for which I am prepared to die'

Nelson Mandela

(b. 1918)

THE ANTI-APARTHEID ACTIVIST MAKES THE OPENING STATEMENT FOR THE DEFENCE AT THE RIVONIA TRIAL; PRETORIA, 20 APRIL 1964

The formation of Umkhonto we Sizwe (Spear of the Nation), the armed wing of the previously non-violent African National Congress (ANC), marked a new and decisive stage in the history of South Africa's anti-apartheid movement. On 21 March 1960, 20,000 blacks had gathered outside the police station in the Johannesburg suburb of Sharpeville to protest against the pass laws which restricted their rights of movement within the country's overwhelmingly white urban areas. Police fired at the crowd, killing 69 protesters and wounding hundreds more, and the ensuing crisis created an acute problem of leadership for the ANC.

A new generation of black activists had emerged in the townships, those areas on the urban peripheries reserved for non-whites, and from the 1950s onwards they were urging a more vigorous assault on white supremacy. The ANC establishment, feeling threatened, had built alliances with other dissident groups, including communists, among South Africa's white, 'coloured' (racially mixed) and Indian communities. Having been banned after Sharpeville, the ANC then sought to reassert its authority in the eyes of black South Africans and to demonstrate its continued command of the strategic impetus. The establishment of an armed organization was part of this plan and the initial bombing campaign sought to sabotage South Africa's infrastructure and its military and industrial installations, rather than to take human life. Umkhonto would, however, adopt urban guerrilla warfare to bloody effect during the years of Nelson Mandela's imprisonment. In his earlier years Mandela had advocated Gandhi's methods of pacific protest, but as a co-founder and leader of Umkhonto he coordinated the sabotage programme and raised foreign funds for the campaign. He also organized paramilitary training in anticipation of the need for

NELSON ROLIHLAHLA MANDELA (b. 1918)

1912 South African Native National Congress is established (subsequently African National Congress, or ANC).

1937 Enrolls at Healdtown, a Wesleyan Methodist school in Eastern Cape province; subsequently follows the University of South Africa's correspondence courses and studies law at the University of Witwatersrand.

1943 Joins ANC.

1948 Afrikaaner-dominated National Party wins general election on a manifesto pledged to systematic apartheid.

1955 Congress of the People: a summit at which the ANC adopts chief elements of its anti-apartheid programme.

5 Dec 1956 Arrested with 155 others on a charge of treason; all are acquitted after a five-year trial.

1961 Co-founds Umkhonto we Sizwe.

7 Nov 1962 Sentenced to five years' imprisonment.

Oct 1963–June 1964 The Rivonia Trial.

Timeline continues on page 171

outright warfare, should the sabotage offensive fail to convert an intransigent government.

At the time of his trial Mandela was already serving a five-year prison sentence imposed in 1962 on charges of leading a strike and leaving the country without permission. While he was imprisoned, other ANC leaders were arrested at a farmhouse in Rivonia, a Johannesburg suburb. At the 'Rivonia Trial' charges of committing sabotage and planning acts of treason were brought against 11 activists in all, including defendants who had been arrested at the farmhouse. Mandela was indicted on the same counts and joined these defendants in the dock. Two of the accused managed to escape from prison while on remand. Mandela was among the eight sentenced to life imprisonment in 1964, and he was sent to Robben Island prison.

In presenting the case for his defence Mandela had the advantage of a legal mind trained in the presentation and assessment of evidence. Although facing a possible death sentence – which had been demanded by the prosecution – he presents a reasoned and dispassionate account of his motives and actions. Even when describing the oppression and poverty of South Africa's non-whites, it is the facts that matter to Mandela, and they were eloquent enough in themselves. That same quality of dispassion would enable him to rise above his immediate circumstances in the long years of captivity that lay ahead.

'I admit immediately that I was one of the persons who helped to form Umkhonto we Sizwe . . . All lawful modes of expressing opposition . . . had been closed by legislation, and we were placed in a position in which we had either to accept a permanent state of inferiority, or to defy the government . . .

In 1960 there was the shooting at Sharpeville, which resulted in the proclamation of a state of emergency and the declaration of the ANC as an unlawful organization. My colleagues and I, after careful consideration, decided that we would not obey this decree. The African people were not part of the government and did not make the laws by which they were governed . . . The ANC refused to dissolve, but instead went underground . . .

'The country was drifting towards a civil war in which blacks and whites would fight each other'

. . . it could not be denied that our policy to achieve a non-racial state by non-violence had achieved nothing, and that our followers were losing confidence in this policy and were developing disturbing ideas of terrorism . . . Already small groups had arisen in the urban areas and were spontaneously making plans for violent forms of political struggle. There now arose a danger that these groups would adopt terrorism against Africans, as well as whites, if not properly directed . . .

We felt that the country was drifting towards a civil war in which blacks and whites would fight each other . . . We did not want to be committed to civil war, but we wanted to be ready if it became inevitable . . . Sabotage did not involve loss of life, and it offered the best hope for future race relations . . . We believed that South Africa depended to a large extent on foreign capital and foreign trade. We felt that planned destruction of power plants, and interference with rail and telephone communications, would tend to scare away capital from the country . . . thus compelling the voters of the country to reconsider their position. Attacks on the economic life-lines of the country were to be linked with sabotage on government buildings and other symbols of apartheid. These attacks would serve as a source of inspiration to our people . . .

The Manifesto of Umkhonto was issued on the day that operations commenced . . . The whites failed to respond by suggesting change . . . In contrast, the response of the Africans was one of encouragement. Suddenly there was hope again . . . But we in Umkhonto weighed up the white response with anxiety. The lines were being drawn . . . We decided, therefore, in our preparations for the future, to make provision for the possibility of guerrilla warfare . . . I started to make a study of the art of war and revolution and, whilst abroad, underwent a course in military training . . .

Another of the allegations made by the state is that the aims and objects of the ANC and the Communist Party are the same . . . The ANC has never at any period of its history, advocated a revolutionary change in the economic structure of the country, nor has it, to the best of my recollection, ever condemned capitalist society . . . It is true that there has often been close cooperation between the ANC and the Communist Party. But cooperation is merely proof of a common goal – in this case the removal of white supremacy – and is not proof of a complete community of interests . . . Theoretical differences amongst those fighting against oppression is a luxury we cannot afford at this stage . . .

'We fight against two features which are the hallmark of African life in South Africa'

From my reading of Marxist literature . . . I have gained the impression that communists regard the parliamentary system of the West as undemocratic and reactionary. But . . . I have great respect for British political institutions and for the country's system of justice. I regard the British parliament as the most democratic institution in the world, and the independence and impartiality of its judiciary never fails to arouse my admiration. The American Congress, that country's doctrine of separation of powers, as well as the independence of its judiciary, arouses in me similar sentiments . . .

Basically we fight against two features which are the hallmarks of African life in South

Africa and which are entrenched by legislation . . . These features are poverty and lack of human dignity, and we do not need 'communists' or so-called 'agitators' to teach us about these things.

'White supremacy implies black inferiority'

South Africa is the richest country in Africa . . . But it is a land of extremes and remarkable contrasts. The whites enjoy what may well be the highest standard of living in the world, whilst Africans live in poverty and misery . . . The complaint of Africans, however, is not only that they are poor and the whites are rich, but that the laws which are made by the whites are designed to preserve this situation . . .

White supremacy implies black inferiority . . . whites tend to regard Africans as a separate breed. They do not look upon them as people with families of their own; they do not realize that they have emotions – that they fall in love like white people do . . . that they want to earn enough money to support their families properly . . .

Hundreds and thousands of Africans are thrown into jail each year under pass laws. Even worse than this is the fact that pass laws keep husband and wife apart and lead to the breakdown of family life . . . Children wander about the streets of the townships because they have no schools to go to . . . or no parents at home to see that they go to school, because both parents (if there be two) have to work to keep the family alive. This leads to a breakdown in moral standards, to an alarming rise in illegitimacy, and to growing violence . . .

'I have fought against white domination, and I have fought against black domination'

Africans . . . want equal political rights, because without them our disabilities will be permanent . . . It is not true that the enfranchisement of all will result in racial domination . . . The ANC has spent half a century fighting against racialism. When it triumphs, it will not change that policy . . .

I have fought against white domination, and I have fought against black domination. I have cherished the ideal of a democratic and free society in which all persons live together in harmony and with equal opportunities. It is an ideal which I hope to live for and to achieve. But if needs be, it is an ideal for which I am prepared to die. ’

'Extremism in the defence of liberty is no vice . . . moderation in the pursuit of justice is no virtue'

Barry Goldwater

(1909–98)

SPEECH ACCEPTING THE REPUBLICAN PARTY'S PRESIDENTIAL NOMINATION, DELIVERED AT THE REPUBLICAN NATIONAL CONVENTION, SAN FRANCISCO, 16 JULY 1964

'Extremism in the defence of liberty is no vice . . . moderation in the pursuit of justice is no virtue'

He rejoiced in the title of 'Mr Conservative' but this speech ended Barry Goldwater's hopes of being called 'Mr President'. This ringing flow of words is unique in America's political history, and the crisp delivery of its unambiguous message marked Goldwater out as a true original who rose above the platitudes of consensus politics. The object of his ire was twofold: the communist threat to both the US and democratic values worldwide; and the expansion of federal activity which, ever since F.D. Roosevelt's introduction of assorted 'New Deal' programmes, had transformed American lives and opinions. An inadequate response to the former, a supine acceptance of the latter: these had, in Goldwater's view, sapped the nation's moral fibre. This was not so much a politician as a prophet who, it seemed, had emerged out of Arizona's desert intent on rebuking an America which had fallen from its erstwhile state of grace. Goldwater's austerely bespectacled expression appeared to provide confirmation of a trigger-happy zealotry.

Prolonged acclamation followed the observation – lifted from Cicero and loosely rendered – to the effect that 'extremism in the defence of liberty is no vice'. But a politician's words to his disciples can turn into his opponents' useful weapons, and from now on Goldwater could be labelled a dangerous extremist who might start a nuclear war. 'In your heart you know he's right' ran the Republican campaign slogan – with the Democrats scripting the riposte: 'In your guts you know he's nuts.' His speech made Goldwater appear anarchic rather than just conservative, and Karl Heiss, the anti-state activist who scripted most of it, would later be charged with tax resistance by the Internal Revenue Service.

In that November's election Goldwater got only 38 per cent of the popular vote and carried, apart from Arizona, just five states. But Alabama, Georgia, Louisiana, Mississippi and South Carolina had all been Democrat previously, and his campaign marked the beginning of a profound political and ideological shift. The American South, previously

BARRY GOLDWATER (1909–98)

1930 Takes over running of family business, a department store in Phoenix, Arizona.

1942–5 Serves in US Air Force, attaining rank of major general.

1952 Wins US Senate seat for Arizona; re-elected in 1958.

1964 Becomes the Republican presidential candidate; loses November presidential election to Democratic incumbent Lyndon B. Johnson.

1968 Re-elected senator for Arizona, and again in 1974 and 1980.

Jan 1987 Retires from the US Senate, having served as chair of the Senate Intelligence and Armed Service Committee in his final term.

dominated by Democrats, would become the electoral base of a Republican Party enthused by many of Goldwater's stances. Republicans who adhered to the political centre, such as New York's governor Nelson Rockefeller, were sidelined and the party's representation in the northeast of the country withered away. In 1964 Republicans remained divided rather than converted en masse – hence Goldwater's reference to their discord – and Rockefeller came close to gaining the nomination. But the future belonged to Goldwater's heirs, and the presidencies of Ronald Reagan, George Bush and George W. Bush are inconceivable without his prior work as one of 'freedom's missionaries'.

He remained, though, intellectually independent, rather than a slave to party orthodoxy, and a libertarian defence of the individual conscience lent a grandly rugged unity to his career. Goldwater's radicalism flared up again late in life when he criticized the ban on gays serving in the military and voted in the Senate to uphold legalized abortion. Evangelical right-wing Christians were by then a forceful element within the electoral coalition which had swept his party to power, but the intolerance of those he labelled 'a bunch of kooks' appalled his nonconforming soul.

The Good Lord raised this mighty Republic to be a home for the brave and to flourish as the land of the free – not to stagnate in the swampland of collectivism, not to cringe before the bully of communism . . .

Our people have followed false prophets. We must, and we shall, return to proven ways – not because they are old, but because they are true. We must, and we shall, set the tide running again in the cause of freedom. And this party . . . has but a single resolve, and that is freedom – freedom made orderly for this nation by our constitutional government; freedom under a government limited by laws of nature and of nature's God; freedom – balanced so that liberty lacking order will not become the slavery of the prison cell; balanced so that liberty lacking order will not become the licence of the mob and of the jungle . . .

'Absolute power does corrupt, and those who seek it must be suspect and must be opposed'

We can be freedom's missionaries in a doubting world. But first we must renew freedom's mission in our own hearts . . .

We have lost the brisk pace of diversity and the genius of individual creativity. We are plodding at a pace set by centralized planning, red tape, rules without responsibility and regimentation without recourse . . .

Those who seek to live your lives for you, to take your liberties in return for relieving you of yours, those who elevate the state and downgrade the citizen must see ultimately a world in which earthly power can be substituted for divine will, and this nation was founded upon the rejection of that notion and upon the acceptance of God as the author of freedom.

Those who seek absolute power, even though they seek it to do what they regard as good, are simply demanding the right to enforce their own version of heaven on earth. And . . . they are the very ones who always create the most hellish tyrannies. Absolute power does corrupt, and those who seek it must be suspect and must be opposed. Their mistaken course stems from false notions of equality. Equality, rightly understood, . . . leads to liberty and to the emancipation of creative differences. Wrongly understood . . . it leads first to conformity and then to despotism . . .

It is the cause of Republicanism to resist concentrations of power, private or public, which enforce such conformity and inflict such despotism . . . It is our cause to dispel the foggy thinking which avoids hard decisions in the illusion that a world of conflict will somehow mysteriously resolve itself into a world of harmony . . .

'Only the strong can remain free . . . only the strong can keep the peace'

It is further the cause of Republicanism to remind ourselves, and the world, that only the strong can remain free, that only the strong can keep the peace . . .

The Republican cause demands that we brand communism . . . as the only significant disturber of the peace, and we must make clear that until its goals of conquest are absolutely renounced . . . communism and the governments it now controls are enemies of every man on earth who is or wants to be free . . .

I believe that we must look beyond the defence of freedom today to its extension tomorrow . . . I suggest that all thoughtful men must contemplate the flowering of an Atlantic civilization, the whole world of Europe unified and free, trading openly across its borders, communicating openly across the world . . .

I can see a day when all the Americas, North and South, will be linked . . . in a rising tide of prosperity and interdependence . . .

And I pledge that the America I envision in the years ahead will extend its hand in health, in teaching and in cultivation, so that all new nations . . . will not wander down the dark alleys of tyranny or to the dead-end streets of collectivism. We do no man a service by hiding freedom's light under a bushel of mistaken humility . . .

But our example to the world must, like charity, begin at home . . . We must assure a society here which, while never abandoning the needy or forsaking the helpless, nurtures incentives and opportunity for the creative and the productive . . .

This nation . . . should again thrive upon the greatness of all those things which we, as individual citizens, can and should do. During the Republican years, this again will be . . . a nation where all who can will be self-reliant . . .

We Republicans seek a government that attends to its inherent responsibilities of maintaining a stable monetary and fiscal climate, encouraging a free and competitive economy and enforcing law and order. Thus do we seek inventiveness, diversity and creativity within a stable order, for we Republicans define government's role where needed at many, many levels, preferably through the one closest to the people involved. Our towns and our cities, then our counties, then our states, then our regional contacts – and only then, the national government. That is the ladder of liberty, built by decentralized power . . .

Balance, diversity, creativity – these are the elements of Republican equation . . . This is a party . . . for free men, not for blind followers, and not for conformists.

Back in 1858 Abraham Lincoln said this of the Republican party – and I quote him, because he probably could have said it during the last week or so: 'It was composed of strained, discordant, and even hostile elements' in 1858. Yet all of these elements agreed on one paramount objective: to arrest the progress of slavery, and place it in the course of ultimate extinction.

'Balance, diversity, creativity – these are the elements of Republican equation'

Today, as then, but more urgently and more broadly than then, the task of preserving and enlarging freedom at home and safeguarding it from the forces of tyranny abroad is great enough to challenge all our resources and to require all our strength . . .

I would remind you that extremism in the defence of liberty is no vice. And let me remind you also that moderation in the pursuit of justice is no virtue . . .

Our Republican cause is not to level out the world or make its people conform in computer-regimented sameness. Our Republican cause is to free our people and light the way for liberty throughout the world . . .

I accept your nomination . . . and you and I are going to fight for the goodness of our land. ’

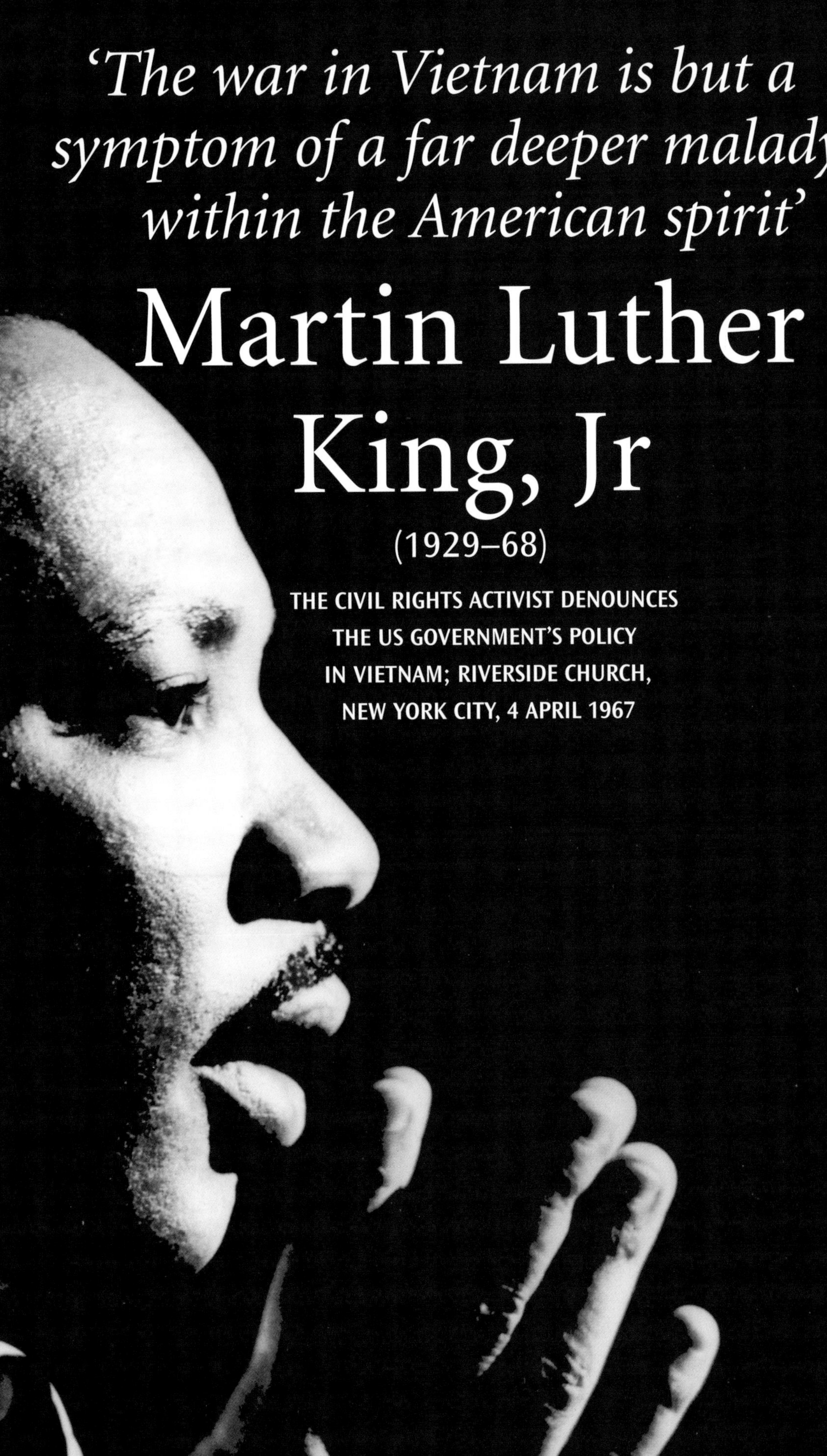

'The war in Vietnam is but a symptom of a far deeper malady within the American spirit'

Martin Luther King, Jr

(1929–68)

THE CIVIL RIGHTS ACTIVIST DENOUNCES THE US GOVERNMENT'S POLICY IN VIETNAM; RIVERSIDE CHURCH, NEW YORK CITY, 4 APRIL 1967

King's leadership of the civil rights movement was based on the principle of non-violence, and in 1964 he had been awarded the Nobel Peace Prize. His effectiveness as a campaigner resulted in a comprehensive civil rights bill which, on becoming law in July 1964, outlawed segregation in public places and forbad racial discrimination in any enterprise which used federal money. The Voting Rights Act of 1965 outlawed discriminatory procedures in voter registration and the American South started to adapt to the new agenda.

This speech, entitled 'Beyond Vietnam', was King's response to a new turbulence which threatened to undermine recent progress in securing civil rights. President Johnson was overseeing an immense expansion in federal activity, and the 'Great Society' programme of legislation aimed at promoting opportunity for the hitherto marginalized, whether they were black or white. But the administration was also responsible for a spiralling defence budget as a result of the US military intervention in Vietnam, where America was the ally of the independent South, run by President Diem's dictatorial regime, and opposed to the equally sovereign North, which proclaimed itself to be a communist state. King protested that money spent on the Vietnam War would be better spent on 'programmes of social uplift', but his fears were also aroused by what was now happening in the American inner cities, where waves of violence undermined his aspiration for a racially integrated US achieved by pacifist means. On 12 August 1965 the Watts area of Los Angeles, a ghetto of 80,000 blacks, erupted in six days of race riots, and the summer of 1966 saw similar violence in other northern urban centres. Poor housing, inadequate education and high unemployment had created a black proletariat which considered itself excluded from American society. The new kind of activism which emerged from this milieu of the wretched and forgotten preached anti-white 'black power', and its most prominent representative was Malcolm X (1925–65), who rejected racial integration and urged instead black self-dependence.

King's commitment to democracy was now matched by his equally engaged awareness of a globalized instability. The US, he thought, was quite simply ending up on the wrong, and tyrannical, side of the argument in too many places across the world. His hostility to the US government's support for Latin American dictatorships and their claim to protect 'social stability' prefigured two decades of similar protests by King's compatriots. Criticism of big business sounded a new note in his rhetoric, but King remained the committed preacher – a Christian clinician diagnosing that 'malady within the American spirit' of which the Vietnam War was but a symptom. In calling for a worldwide 'revolution of values' King spoke as both a Christian and an American. The gospel was universal since it transcended nationality and American democracy could, in its own way, also heal a broken world. Rooted in the principles of a democratic revolution, the US was uniquely qualified to proclaim those same values and apply them to contemporary effect in a global crusade against militarism, poverty and racism. Redeeming the world meant reclaiming America.

'The war in Vietnam is but a symptom of a far deeper malady within the American spirit'

I sometimes marvel at those who ask me why I am speaking against the war. Could it be that they do not know that the Good News was meant for all men . . . ? Have they forgotten that my ministry is in obedience to the one who loved His enemies so fully that he died for them? . . .

I must be true to my conviction that I share with all men the calling to be a son of the living God. Beyond the calling of race or nation or creed is this vocation of sonship and brotherhood . . . We are called to speak for the weak, for the voiceless, for the victims of our nation . . .

The Vietnamese people proclaimed their own independence in 1945 . . . Even though they quoted the American Declaration of Independence in their own document of freedom, we refused to recognize them. Instead, we decided to support France in its reconquest of her former colony . . .

'We are called to speak for the weak, for the voiceless, for the victims of our nation'

For nine years we vigorously supported the French in their abortive effort to recolonize Vietnam . . . We encouraged them with our huge financial and military supplies to continue the war even after they had lost the will. After the French were defeated, there came the United States . . . and the peasants watched as we supported one of the most vicious modern dictators, our chosen man, President Diem . . .

All the while the people read our leaflets and received the regular promises of peace and democracy and land reform. Now they languish under our bombs . . . They watch as we poison their water, as we kill a million acres of their crops . . . They wander into hospitals with at least 20 casualties from American firepower for one Vietcong-inflicted injury . . .

We have destroyed their two most cherished institutions: the family and the village . . . Now there is little left to build on, save bitterness . . .

I am as deeply concerned about our own troops there as anything else. For it occurs to me that what we are submitting them to in Vietnam is not simply the brutalizing process that goes on in any war where armies face each other and seek to destroy. We are adding cynicism to the process of death, for they must know after a short period that none of the things we claim to be fighting for are really involved. Before long they . . . surely realize that we are on the side of the wealthy, and the secure, while we create a hell for the poor.

Somehow this madness must cease. We must stop now. I speak as a child of God and brother to the suffering poor of Vietnam . . . I speak for the poor of America who are paying the double price of smashed hopes at home, and death and corruption in

Vietnam. I speak as a citizen of the world, for the world as it stands aghast at the path we have taken . . . In order to atone for our sins and errors in Vietnam, we should take the initiative in bringing a halt to this tragic war.

'I speak as a citizen of the world . . . as it stands aghast at the path we have taken'

The war in Vietnam is but a symptom of a far deeper malady within the American spirit . . . During the past ten years we have seen emerge a pattern of suppression which has now justified the presence of US military advisers in Venezuela. This need to maintain social stability for our investment accounts for the counter-revolutionary action of American forces in Guatemala. It tells why American helicopters are being used against guerrillas in Cambodia and why American napalm and Green Beret forces have already been active against rebels in Peru . . .

I am convinced that if we are to get on the right side of the world revolution, we as a nation must undergo a radical revolution of values . . . True compassion is more than flinging a coin to a beggar. It comes to see that an edifice which produces beggars needs restructuring.

'If we are to get on the right side of the world revolution, we as a nation must undergo a radical revolution of values'

A true revolution of values . . . will look across the seas and see individual capitalists of the West investing huge sums in Asia, Africa and South America, only to take the profits out with no concern for the social betterment of the countries . . .

A nation that continues year after year to spend more money on military defence than on programmes of social uplift is approaching spiritual death . . .

There is nothing except a tragic death wish to prevent us from reordering our priorities, so that the pursuit of peace will take precedence over the pursuit of war. There is nothing to keep us from moulding a recalcitrant status quo with bruised hands until we have fashioned it into a brotherhood . . .

We must not engage in a negative anti-communism, but rather in a positive thrust for democracy, realizing that our greatest defence against communism is to take offensive action in behalf of justice . . .

These are revolutionary times. All over the globe men are revolting against old systems of exploitation and oppression, and out of the wounds of a frail world new systems of justice and equality are being born. The shirtless and barefoot people of the land are rising up as never before. The people who sat in darkness have seen a great light . . .

The Western nations that initiated so much of the revolutionary spirit of the modern world have now become the arch anti-revolutionaries. This has driven many to feel that only Marxism has a revolutionary spirit . . . Our only hope today lies in our ability to recapture the revolutionary spirit and go out into a sometimes hostile world declaring eternal hostility to poverty, racism and militarism . . .

'Out of the wounds of a frail world new systems of justice and equality are being born'

A genuine revolution of values means in the final analysis that our loyalties must become ecumenical rather than sectional . . .

This call for a worldwide fellowship that lifts neighbourly concern beyond one's tribe, race, class and nation is in reality a call for an all-embracing and unconditional love for all mankind . . .

We can no longer afford to worship the god of hate or bow before the altar of retaliation . . .

We must find new ways to speak for peace in Vietnam and justice throughout the developing world, a world that borders on our doors. If we do not act, we shall surely be dragged down the long, dark and shameful corridors of time reserved for those who possess power without compassion, might without morality and strength without sight.'

'Socialism is an attitude of mind'

Julius Nyerere

(1922–99)

THE PRESIDENT OF TANZANIA DISCUSSES SOCIALISM ON BEING AWARDED AN HONORARY DEGREE BY THE UNIVERSITY OF CAIRO; EGYPT, 10 APRIL 1967

Throughout his period in office Julius Nyerere preached 'African socialism' – his idiosyncratic blend of rural values and left-wing intellectualism. He was known as *Mwalimu*, the Swahili for 'teacher', not just in his native Tanganyika but right across the African continent, and the didactic tone of this particular address typified Nyerere's speeches in general. The African countryside was, in his view, innately communal, since its characteristic social structure was supposed to be that of the *ujamaa*, or extended household. Tanganyika's rural population was therefore deemed to be naturally (albeit unselfconsciously) socialist – people who would adapt readily to their president's socio-economic experimentation.

In formulating his goals Nyerere was much influenced by British socialism's Fabian tradition – a school of thought with a high view of government and a progressivist zeal for organizing other people's lives. Nyerere's personal life was austere and his Catholic spirituality was reflected in his habit of regular fasting and daily attendance at mass. The sincerity of his political idealism and evident incorruptibility won him a vast and devoted personal following, and for many he was the face of Africa itself in its immediate postcolonial period. He won plaudits for his moderation when leading the movement for Tanganyika's self-determination, and an orderly transfer of power from the British colonial administration secured his installation as leader of a one-party state.

Nyerere's speech idealizes a traditional past when African workers owned their own tools or 'means of production' and travelled independently to markets where they could sell or

JULIUS NYERERE (1922–99)

1937 Enters Tabora Government School, and subsequently attends Makerere University, Uganda.

1949 Wins scholarship to Edinburgh University; graduates (1952) in economics and history, and teaches subsequently in Dar es Salaam.

1953 President of Tanganyika African Association, a group of public sector workers, which becomes in 1954 the Tanganyika African National Union, a body working for independence.

1958 Enters Colonial Legislative Council and elected (1960) chief minister.

1961 Tanganyika gains independence; becomes country's first prime minister.

1962 President of Tanganyika, which is now a republic.

1964 Zanzibar unites with Tanganyika to form Tanzania.

Feb 1967 Arusha Declaration.

1978 Declares war on Uganda, whose ruler Idi Amin is toppled in 1979.

1985 Resigns presidency amid economic chaos; successors adopt free-market policies.

1992 Tanzania becomes a multi-party democracy.

barter produce – their appropriate means of 'distribution and exchange'. Introduction of money had destroyed this primitive arcadia, and its particular economic structure could not be re-established. But communal ownership of the means of production, distribution and exchange would nonetheless recapture the cooperative values associated with this imagined past. Nyerere acknowledges that the effectiveness of such a system presupposes the existence of an incorruptible political and administrative elite, an insight which had not prevented him from issuing the Arusha Declaration and its embrace of an *ujamaa*-based socialism just months earlier. The document pledged his government to the 'villagization' of the rural economy: a previously scattered population farming small holdings would be congregated in village units designed to be large enough to provide communal services and increase production levels. Widespread resentment was aroused by this collectivization of farming when it was enforced in the mid-1970s and the programme was abandoned after a few years. The malign effects, however, were long-lived and the renamed Tanzania, having been a massive exporter of agricultural produce, became a net importer experiencing acute levels of poverty. Socialism in its *ujamaa* guise aimed to secure national self-sufficiency in all areas of the economy, and its application through the Basic Industrial Strategy led to the nationalization of banks and key industries. But there was little that was 'self-sufficient' about a country burdened by a massive national debt, plagued by balance of payments crises and dependent on International Monetary Fund loans. Nyerere's words had turned to dust.

Over time there have been many definitions of socialism . . . Unfortunately, however, there has grown up what I can only call a 'theology of socialism'. People argue – sometimes quite violently – about what is the true doctrine . . . I think that this idea that there is one 'pure socialism', for which the recipe is already known, is an insult to human intelligence. It seems to me that man has yet to solve the problem of living in society, and that each of us may have something to contribute to the problems it involves. We should recognize that there are books on socialism which can illuminate the problems, and books which chart a way forward from a particular point. But that is all . . .

'This idea that there is one "pure socialism", for which the recipe is already known, is an insult to human intelligence'

Yet I am not saying that socialism is a vague concept . . . For socialism the basic purpose is the well-being of the people and the basic assumption is an acceptance of human equality . . . The human equality before God which is the basis of all the great religions of the world is also the basis of the political philosophy of socialism. Yet socialism is not

Utopian . . . It is a recognition that some human beings are physically strong and others weak, that some are intellectually able whilst others are rather dull, that some are skilful in the use of their hands whilst others are clumsy. It involves, too, a recognition that every person has both a selfish and a social instinct, which are often in conflict. Socialist doctrine then demands the deliberate organization of society in such a manner that it is impossible – or at least very difficult – for individual desires to be pursued at the cost of other people . . .

'Socialism is not Utopian'

For a socialist state these requirements have both a negative and a positive aspect. Men must be prevented from exploiting each other. And at the same time institutions and organizations must be such that man's needs and progress can be cooperatively secured. There are two paths through which exploitation has been historically secured and which must therefore be blocked. The first was the use of naked force. Originally through physical strength, and then through a monopoly of weapons of force, men imposed their will upon others . . . The gradual growth of law, and the principle of equality before the law, ease the severity of oppression until the people are in a position to take control of their own destiny.

The second major means of exploitation has been through private property . . . The man whose means of living are controlled by another must serve the interests of this other regardless of his own desires or his own needs . . .

If a society is to be made up of equal citizens, then each man must control his own means of production. The farmer must own his own tools – his hoe or his plough. The carpenter must have his own saw and not be dependent upon the whims of another for its use. The tools of production must be under the control of the individual or group which depends upon them for life.

In African traditional life this was the normal routine . . . But there can be no going back to this system – which has now suffered considerably from the effects of a money economy . . .

'The farmer must own his own tools – his hoe or his plough'

In those areas of production where individual ownership of tools is impractical we are therefore forced to the conclusion that group ownership of the means of production is the only way in which the exploitation of man by man can be prevented. This communal ownership can be through the state, which represents every citizen, or through some other institution which is controlled by those involved – such as, for example, a cooperative or a local authority.

The same thing applies to the question of distribution and exchange. In small peasant societies it is possible for each grower or each producer to bring his goods to a central place and bargain . . . But the increasing specialization of production requires more sophisticated techniques. And once again, a private individual can get into a position where he controls the well-being of another. He can do this by his charges for transport, by his commission on sales, or by exploiting a monopoly position. Communal ownership of the means of distribution and communal enterprise in the act of bargaining can eliminate this kind of exploitation.

Yet although the facts of modern technology provide the final justification for the communal ownership of the means of production and exchange, it is not always and everywhere appropriate . . . It is possible, as we have found out in Tanzania, for farmers to be exploited even by their own cooperative and their own state if the machinery is not correct, or if the managers and workers are inefficient or dishonest . . .

For it is not good enough just to deprive people of the incentives of selfishness. Development requires that these should be replaced by effective social incentives . . . Public ownership may not necessarily and always be the correct answer for socialists at a particular time . . . A decision should depend on the circumstances and the prevailing attitudes – that is, on the success of socialist political education . . .

'It is not good enough just to deprive people of the incentives of selfishness'

In 1962 I said that socialism is an attitude of mind. I still believe this to be true . . . Without the correct attitudes, institutions can be subverted from their true purpose . . . There must be, among the leadership, a desire and determination to serve alongside of, and in complete identification with, the masses.

If the people are not honestly served by those to whom they have entrusted responsibility, then corruption can negate all their efforts and make them abandon their socialist ideas . . .

This is a technological age, and many decisions cannot be taken directly by the masses. Tremendous responsibilities therefore rest upon those of us who have had the privilege of higher education . . . Our function is to serve, to guide the masses through the complexities of modern technology – to propose, to explain and to persuade . . . And unless we who have the power – whether it be political or technical – remain at one with the masses, then we cannot serve them. ’

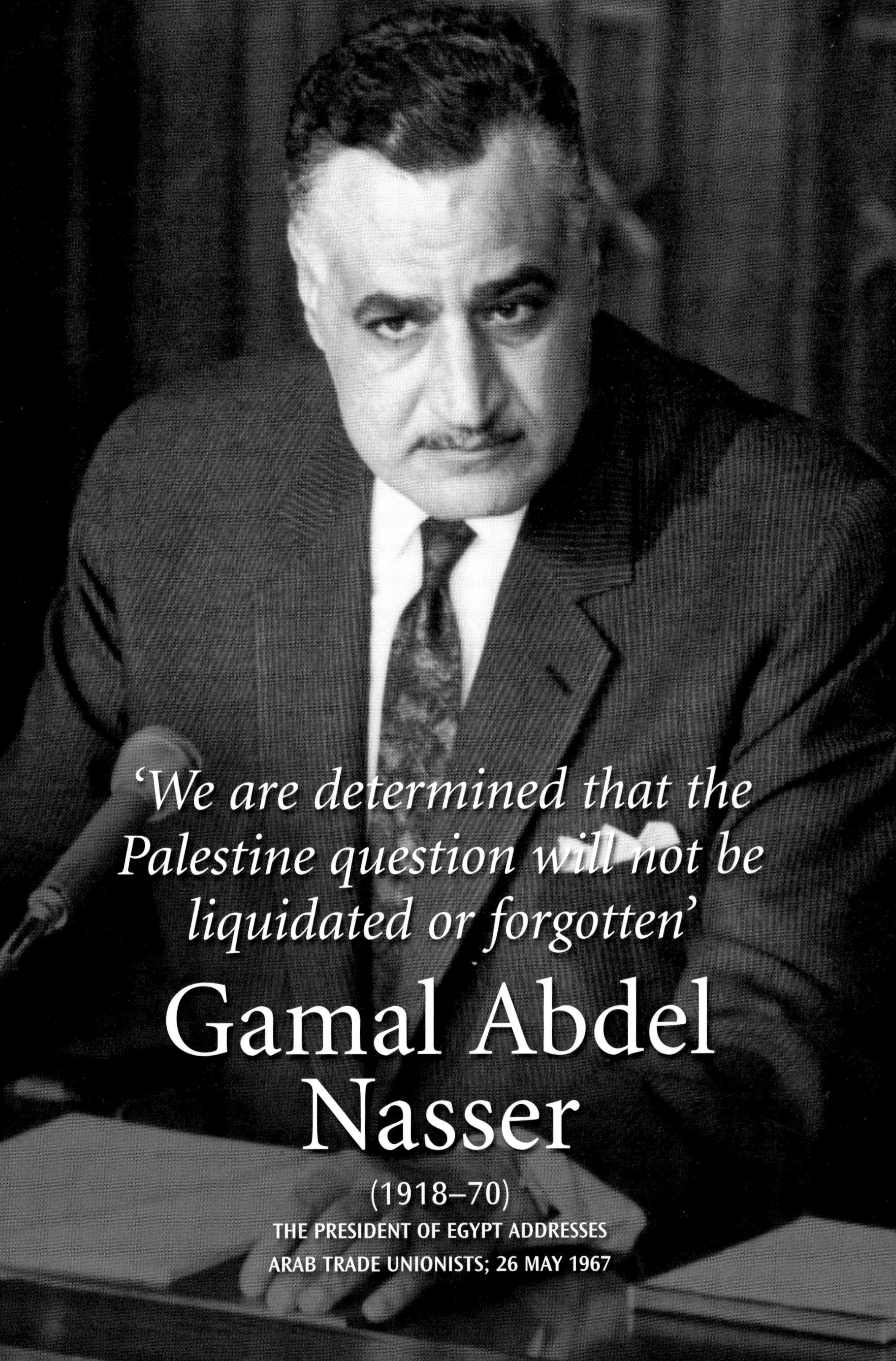
'We are determined that the
Palestine question will not be
liquidated or forgotten'
Gamal Abdel
Nasser
(1918–70)
THE PRESIDENT OF EGYPT ADDRESSES
ARAB TRADE UNIONISTS; 26 MAY 1967

These speeches are among Nasser's many declamations while preparing for war in the spring of 1967. He was speaking not just as Egypt's president but also as the advocate of pan-Arabism – the belief that the Middle East's Arab states should strive for unity.

'The 1961 secession' refers to Syria's decision to withdraw from the United Arab Republic, an unsatisfactory three-year experiment conjoining Egypt with Syria and scant proof of a 'union . . . achieved'. Over a decade had passed since the Suez episode enhanced Nasser's prestige and he was now under pressure to take military action to redress Palestinian grievances. The UN Emergency Force's presence in the Sinai during that period had stopped any remilitarization of the peninsula by either Israel or Egypt. On 16 May 1967 Nasser ordered UNEF's immediate withdrawal and Egyptian forces moved across the Sinai to take up positions on Israel's border. On 23 May he closed the Straits of Tiran to Israeli shipping, thereby blocking Israel's southern port of Eilat and the country's access to the Indian Ocean.

Nasser speaks here at the height of his influence. Muammar al-Gaddafi of Libya and Ahmed Ben Bella of Algeria were among the Arab leaders who emulated him. He ran Egypt through an efficient police and security apparatus, and in the early 1960s he nationalized most of the country's industrial, commercial and financial sectors. Though he disliked communism, he liked Soviet aid, and the USSR helped pay for the Aswan High Dam which boosted Egypt's electricity supplies. In these speeches he stirs pan-Arab sentiment to

GAMAL ABDEL NASSER (1918–70)

1939 Graduates from Egyptian Military Academy, Cairo.

1948–9 Serves in the Arab–Israeli War, and subsequently becomes an instructor at Cairo's Military Academy.

1949 Forms coordinating committee of the Free Officers Movement (FOM) and in 1950 becomes its head.

23 July 1952 The FOM seizes control of the Egyptian government, subsequently forming the Egyptian Revolutionary Command Council.

1954 Becomes president of Egypt.

1956–7 The Suez Crisis raises his authority.

1962 Promotes the Arab nationalist coup d'état establishing the Yemen Arab Republic.

1967 Egypt loses the Sinai as a result of the Six Day War (5–10 June).

1969 Dismisses more than one hundred judges.

1970 An estimated five million mourners attend his funeral in Cairo.

characteristic effect with his portrayal of an Arab civilization whose historic glories have been revived magnificently. Medieval crusaders are compared to modern Westerners contemptuous of Arab dignity. Injustice is about to be punished.

Jordan and Syria would wage war as Egypt's allies. Iraq, Saudi Arabia, Sudan, Tunisia, Morocco and Algeria committed troops and equipment. This was as pan-Arab as it could get. Israel responded to the threat pre-emptively and in the Six Day War (5–10 June 1967) smashed its enemies' offensive capacity in an awesome display of strategic power. The first wave of strikes on Egypt's airfields destroyed some 300 of her 450 combat aircraft, all Soviet-built and up to date. Within two days total losses of enemy aircraft amounted to 416, and the air forces of Jordan, Syria and Iraq played no further role in hostilities. Israel gained the River Jordan's West Bank – including East Jerusalem – the Golan Heights, the Gaza Strip and the entire Sinai Peninsula. Over half a million West Bank Palestinians now lived on Israeli land, and another 300,000 of them had fled to Jordan. Jordan and Egypt would eventually withdraw their claim to, respectively, the West Bank and Gaza. The Sinai was returned to Egypt in 1978 and Israel withdrew from Gaza in 2005.

The war shattered pan-Arabism and its largely secularist impulses would be replaced by those of Islamist fundamentalism. On 9 June 1967 Nasser tried to resign. Popular street protests persuaded him to stay but he never regained the self-confidence expressed in these grandiloquent phrases.

'

You, the Arab workers' federation, represent the biggest force in the Arab world. We can achieve much by Arab action, which is a main part of our battle. Despair has never found its way into Arab hearts and never will. What we see today in the masses of the Arab peoples everywhere is their desire to fight. The Arab people want to regain the rights of the people of Palestine.

We sustained heavy losses in 1956. Later, union was achieved. The 1961 secession occurred when we had barely begun to stand firmly on our feet. We were waiting for the day when we would be confident of being able to adopt strong measures if we were to enter the battle with Israel. Recently we felt that we could triumph. On this basis, we decided to take steps.

'The Arab people want to regain the rights of the people of Palestine'

Many people blamed us for the presence of the UN Emergency Force. Should we have listened to them, or rather built and trained our army while UNEF still existed? Once we were fully prepared, we could ask UNEF to leave. And this is what actually happened.

With regard to military plans, there is complete coordination of military action between us and Syria. We will operate as one army fighting a single battle for the sake of a common objective – the objective of the Arab nation.

'The problem today is not just Israel, but also those behind it'

The problem today is not just Israel, but also those behind it. If Israel embarks on an aggression against Syria and Egypt, the battle against Israel will be a general one and not confined to one spot on the Syrian or Egyptian borders. Our basic objective will be to destroy Israel. I probably could not have said such things five or even three years ago. Today I say such things because I am confident. I know what we have here in Egypt and what Syria has. I also know that Iraq has sent its troops to Syria; Algeria will send troops; Kuwait also will send troops. This is Arab power. This is the true resurrection of the Arab nation.

We are not states without status. Our states have thousands of years of civilization behind them – 7000 years of civilization. We shall not relinquish our rights. We want the front to become one united front around Israel. We will not relinquish the rights of the people of Palestine.

'This is the true resurrection of the Arab nation'

During the crusaders' occupation, the Arabs waited 70 years before a suitable opportunity arose and they drove away the crusaders. Some people commented that Abdel Nasser said we should shelve the Palestinian question for 70 years, but I say that as a people with an ancient civilization, as an Arab people, we are determined that the Palestine question will not be liquidated or forgotten. The whole question is the proper time to achieve our aims. We are preparing ourselves constantly. You are the hope of the Arab nation and its vanguard. As workers, you are actually building the Arab nation. The quicker we build, the quicker we will be able to achieve our aim. ’

'We are now ready to deal with the entire Palestine question'

THE EGYPTIAN PRESIDENT ADDRESSES MEMBERS OF THE EGYPTIAN NATIONAL ASSEMBLY; 29 MAY 1967

The circumstances through which we are now passing are difficult because we are not only confronting Israel but also the West, which created Israel and despised us Arabs and which ignored us before and since 1948. They had no regard whatsoever for our feelings, our hopes in life, our rights. The Arab nation was unable to check the West's course.

Then came the events of 1956 – the Suez battle. When we rose to demand our rights, Britain, France and Israel opposed us. We resisted, however, and proclaimed that we would fight to the last drop of our blood. God gave us success and God's victory was great.

'We would fight to the last drop of our blood'

Subsequently we were able to rise and build. Now, 11 years after 1956, we are restoring things to what they were in 1956. This is from the material aspect. In my opinion this material aspect is only a small part, whereas the spiritual aspect is the great side of the issue. The spiritual aspect involves the renaissance of the Arab nation, the revival of the Palestine question, and the restoration of confidence to every Arab and to every Palestinian. God will surely help us and urge us to restore the situation to what it was in 1948.

'The spiritual aspect involves the renaissance of the Arab nation'

Israel used to boast a great deal, and the Western powers, headed by the United States and Britain, used to consider us of no value. But now that the time has come, we must be ready for triumph and not for a recurrence of the 1948 comedies. Preparations have already been made. Now we are ready for the confrontation. We are now ready to deal with the entire Palestine question. We demand the full rights of the Palestinian people. Arabs throughout the Arab world are demanding these rights.

'The time has come, we must be ready for triumph'

The United States and Britain give no consideration to the entire Arab nation. Why? Because we have made them believe that we cannot distinguish between friend and foe. We must make them know that we know who our foes are and who our friends are and treat them accordingly. I wish to tell you today that the Soviet Union is a friendly power and stands by us as a friend. In all our dealings with the Soviet Union – and I have been dealing with the USSR since 1955 – it has not made a single request of us. The USSR has never interfered with our policy or internal affairs. This is the USSR as we have always known it. Last year we asked for wheat and they sent it to us. When I asked for all kinds of arms, they gave them to us. The war minister yesterday handed me a message from the Soviet premier Kosygin saying that the USSR supported us in this battle and would not allow any power to intervene until matters were restored to what they were in 1956.

Brothers, we will work for world peace with all the power at our disposal, but we will also hold tenaciously to our rights with all the power at our disposal. ’

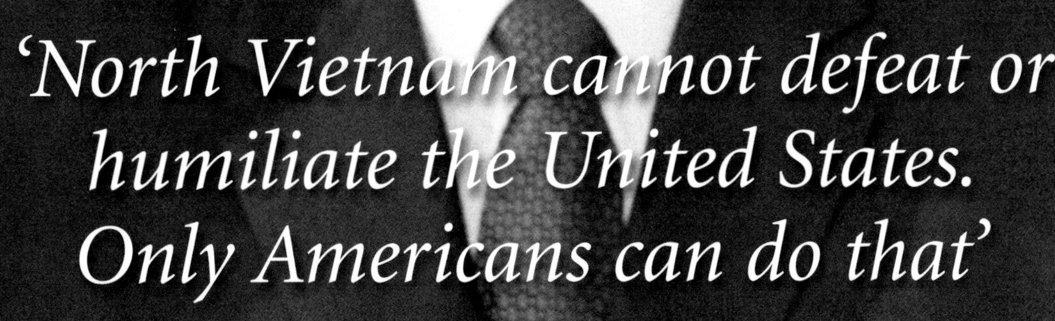

'North Vietnam cannot defeat or humiliate the United States. Only Americans can do that'

Richard Nixon

(1913–94)

THE US PRESIDENT SIGNALS A CHANGE OF COURSE IN VIETNAM; TELEVISED ADDRESS TO THE AMERICAN PEOPLE, 3 NOVEMBER 1969

During his presidential campaign Richard Nixon pledged that he would, if elected, end the Vietnam War, and the first reductions in US troop levels in South Vietnam were announced in June 1969. US foreign policy under Nixon abandoned the 'domino theory' which maintained that a North Vietnamese victory would inevitably lead to communist governments throughout southeast Asia. But he had also promised 'peace with honour', by which he meant the maintenance of US credibility as a superpower. This typically skilful address therefore deploys some of the vigorous anti-communist rhetoric which had marked Nixon's earlier career. Menacing states devoted to 'world conquest' would seek to profit from the US's humiliation were it to be defeated in South Vietnam, and America's 'national destiny' involved 'free-world leadership'.

The appeal to the 'silent majority' marked the latest evolution of a continuous Nixon theme: the contrast between a noisy 'liberal elite' and those hard-working, undemonstrative Americans who supplied the nation with its enduring identity. Nonetheless, few American citizens were taken in by the policy of Vietnamization and its application of the 'Nixon Doctrine'. Their country was retreating and the South Vietnamese army, however well trained by the departing ally and despite its liberal endowment with US military hardware, was obviously incapable of withstanding an all-out assault by the combined forces of the People's Army of Vietnam (PAVN) and the National Front for the Liberation of South Vietnam (the Vietcong guerrillas).

Two-thirds of the original US combat force of just over half a million had left South Vietnam by the end of 1971. But the need to maintain both the US's military authority and its diplomatic credibility meant that the administration had to mask the truth that

RICHARD NIXON (1913-94)

1937 Admitted to the US bar and practises law in California.

1946 Elected to US House of Representatives.

1948 As member of the House Un-American Activities Committee, exposes Alger Hiss, a State Department official, as a Soviet spy.

1950 Elected to US Senate.

1952 Elected vice president of the US.

1960 Becomes the Republican Party's nominee for the presidency; narrowly defeated by the Democratic candidate John F. Kennedy.

1962 Fails to be elected governor of California, informs journalists: 'You won't have Nixon to kick around anymore.'

1968 Elected president of the US.

9 August 1974 Resigns presidency.

Vietnamization really meant withdrawal. Nixon therefore seized the opportunity to extend the war to neighbouring Cambodia, which had been protected previously by its neutrality. By 1969 Prince Norodom Sihanouk, the country's ruler, was declaring that he wanted closer US relations, and General Lon Nol, who deposed him in March 1970, was pro-American. US and South Vietnamese forces were therefore able to attack PAVN and Vietcong troops encamped on Cambodia's eastern border with Vietnam. Operation Menu was conducted over 14 months during 1969–70, but few Americans listening to Nixon's address would have known of this massive bombing campaign. The president had ignored the need for Congressional approval and the operation's covert nature made it the first of his subversions of the US constitution.

Cambodia's bombing nonetheless did the trick for Nixon since it amounted to a shield behind which Vietnamization could proceed. Yet for the president that disengagement was but one element in a wider picture: the pursuit of détente, or the easing of tension, with the USSR and China. The Cambodian bombing was intended to show these communist states that America would be negotiating with them from a position of continued strength. Words, though, as well as deeds, still mattered in the conduct of such diplomacy and this speech's projection of US power was intended to be heard in Moscow and Beijing as well as in America.

'

Fifteen years ago North Vietnam, with the logistical support of communist China and the Soviet Union, launched a campaign to impose a communist government on South Vietnam by instigating and supporting a revolution.

In response to the request of the government of South Vietnam, President Eisenhower sent economic aid and military equipment . . . Seven years ago, President Kennedy sent 16,000 military personnel to Vietnam as combat advisers. Four years ago President Johnson sent American combat forces to South Vietnam.

Now, many believe that President Johnson's decision was wrong. And many others – I among them – have been strongly critical of the way the war has been conducted.

But the question facing us today is: Now that we are in the war, what is the best way to end it? . . .

For the South Vietnamese, our precipitate withdrawal would inevitably allow the communists to repeat the massacres which followed their takeover in the North 15 years before . . .

'Now that we are in the war, what is the best way to end it?'

For the United States, this first defeat in our nation's history would result in a collapse of confidence in American leadership, not only in Asia but throughout the world . . .

Our defeat and humiliation in South Vietnam without question would promote recklessness in the councils of those great powers who have not yet abandoned their goals of world conquest. This would spark violence wherever our commitments help maintain the peace – in the Middle East, in Berlin, eventually even in the western hemisphere . . .

'This first defeat in our nation's history would result in a collapse of confidence in American leadership'

For these reasons, I rejected the recommendation that I should end the war by immediately withdrawing all our forces. I chose instead to change American policy on both the negotiating front and battlefront . . .

– We have offered the complete withdrawal of all outside forces within one year.

– We have proposed a ceasefire under international supervision.

– We have offered free elections under international supervision with the communists participating in the organization and conduct of the elections . . .

Hanoi has refused even to discuss our proposals. They demand . . . that we withdraw all American forces immediately and unconditionally and that we overthrow the government of South Vietnam as we leave . . .

It has become clear that the obstacle in negotiating an end to the war . . . is the other side's absolute refusal to show the least willingness to join us in seeking a just peace . . .

At the time we launched our search for peace I recognized we might not succeed in bringing an end to the war through negotiation. I therefore put into effect another plan which will bring the war to an end regardless of what happens on the negotiating front.

It is in line with a major shift in US foreign policy which . . . has been described as the Nixon Doctrine . . .

'We Americans are a do-it-yourself people. We are an impatient people'

'North Vietnam cannot defeat or humiliate the United States. Only Americans can do that'

We Americans are a do-it-yourself people. We are an impatient people. Instead of teaching someone else to do a job, we like to do it ourselves. And this trait has been carried over into our foreign policy.

In Korea and again in Vietnam, the United States furnished most of the money, most of the arms and most of the men to help the people of those countries defend their freedom against communist aggression . . .

'In this administration we are Vietnamizing the search for peace'

I laid down three principles as guidelines for future American policy towards Asia:

– First, the United States will keep all of its treaty commitments.

– Second, we shall provide a shield if a nuclear power threatens the freedom of a nation allied with us or of a nation whose survival we consider vital to our security.

– Third, in cases involving other types of aggression, we shall furnish military and economic assistance when requested in accordance with our treaty commitments. But we shall look to the nation directly threatened to assume the primary responsibility of providing the manpower for its defence . . .

In the previous administration, we Americanized the war in Vietnam. In this administration we are Vietnamizing the search for peace . . . Under the new orders, the primary mission of our troops is to enable the South Vietnamese forces to assume the full responsibility for the security of South Vietnam . . .

We have adopted a plan . . . for the complete withdrawal of all US combat ground forces, and their replacement by South Vietnamese forces . . . As South Vietnamese forces become stronger, the rate of American withdrawal can become greater . . .

In speaking of the consequences of a precipitate withdrawal, I mentioned that our allies would lose confidence in America.

Far more dangerous, we would lose confidence in ourselves. Oh, the immediate reaction would be a sense of relief that our men were coming home. But as we saw the consequences of what we had done, inevitable remorse and divisive recrimination would scar our spirit as a people . . .

I know it may not be fashionable to speak of patriotism or national destiny these days. But I feel it is appropriate to do so on this occasion.

Two hundred years ago this nation was weak and poor . . . Today we have become the strongest and richest nation in the world . . . Any hope the world has for the survival of peace and freedom will be determined by whether the American people have the courage to meet the challenge of free-world leadership . . .

And so tonight – to you, the great silent majority of my fellow Americans – I ask for your support . . .

'To you, the great silent majority of my fellow Americans – I ask for your support'

Let us be united for peace. Let us also be united against defeat. Because let us understand: North Vietnam cannot defeat or humiliate the United States. Only Americans can do that.

Fifty years ago, in this room and at this very desk, President Woodrow Wilson . . . said: 'This is the war to end war.' His dream for peace after World War I was shattered on the hard realities of great power politics and Woodrow Wilson died a broken man.

Tonight I do not tell you that the war in Vietnam is the war to end wars. But I do say this: I have initiated a plan which will end this war in a way that will bring us closer to that great goal to which Woodrow Wilson and every American president in our history has been dedicated – the goal of a just and lasting peace. ’

'Mistakes, yes. But for personal gain, never'

Richard Nixon

(1913–94)

THE DISGRACED PRESIDENT MAKES HIS FAREWELL SPEECH TO WHITE HOUSE STAFF; WASHINGTON, 9 AUGUST 1974

In November 1972 Richard Nixon was re-elected president in a landslide which saw him carry 49 of the Union's 50 states and gain over 60 per cent of the popular vote. His record as one of the great reforming presidents in domestic and foreign affairs helps explain that victory. Nixon ended the Vietnam War, and his policies, based on realism rather than ideology, led to the establishment of US diplomatic relations with China. The treaty agreed between the US and the USSR in May 1972 on the limitation of anti-ballistic missile systems was a milestone in the history of détente. Many federal agencies, such as those regulating environmental protection and enforcing anti-drugs legislation, were established during the Nixon presidency, a period which marks a high point in the history of US governmental activism. Desegregation in the public schools of the American South became rapid and irreversible, and in February 1974 Nixon introduced a measure which would have forced employers to buy health insurance for their employees. But the Nixon White House also became synonymous with a paranoid style of government whose suspicions, resentments and illegalities were directly attributable to the president's own personality and fears.

At 11.35 a.m. on the day he delivered this speech Nixon formally resigned the presidency by signing a letter addressed to Secretary of State Henry Kissinger. Facing impeachment by the House of Representatives and almost certain conviction by the Senate, he had been forced out of office by the evidence of his complicity in the attempt to conceal his officials' involvement in the Watergate scandal. On 17 June 1972 five burglars were arrested after breaking into the headquarters of the Democratic Party's National Committee at the Watergate Hotel in Washington DC. Their links with the Committee to Re-elect the President (CREEP), a White House funding organization, led to Nixon being named an 'unindicted co-conspirator' by the grand jury investigating the affair. Watergate, however, meant more than just a single, bungled burglary since its investigation revealed an even wider pattern of 'dirty tricks', many of which related to Nixon's dislike of the media. Concerned about the leaking of governmental information to the press, from 1969 onwards he had been authorizing the illegal tapping of the phones of journalists and of administration officials. Nixon's legacy included a widespread loss of belief among Americans in the probity of US government but, following his successor's grant of an official pardon, criminal charges could not be brought against him.

This speech shows many of Nixon's finer qualities: personal resilience, an easy command of his audience and the unaffected eloquence of a born orator. The affecting description of his childhood and of his parents' struggles in life reveal the depths to his character – as well as explaining in part the edge to his personality. Formed by early adversity, Nixon always regarded himself as a loner, and even as president he had behaved like an outsider whose aims had to be achieved by stealth. That combative style had been both the making and the unmaking of the most complex president in American history.

'

You are here to say goodbye to us, and we don't have a good word for it in English. The best is *au revoir*. We will see you again . . . I ask all of you . . . to serve our next president as you have served me and previous presidents – because many of you have been here for many years – with devotion and dedication, because this office, great as it is, can only be as great as the men and women who work for and with the president.

This house, for example, I was thinking of it as we walked down this hall, and I was comparing it to some of the great houses of the world that I have been in. This isn't the biggest house . . . This isn't the finest house. Many in Europe, particularly, and in China, Asia, have paintings of great value, things that we just don't have here, and probably will never have until we are 1000 years old or older.

'This office, great as it is, can only be as great as the men and women who work for and with the president'

But this is the best house. It is the best house because it has something far more important than numbers of people who serve, far more important than numbers of rooms or how big it is, far more important than numbers of magnificent pieces of art. This house has a great heart, and that heart comes from those who serve . . .

Sure we have done some things wrong in this administration, and the top man always takes the responsibility, and I have never ducked it. But I want to say one thing: we can be proud of it – five and a half years. No man or woman came into this administration and left it with more of this world's goods than when he came in . . . Mistakes, yes. But for personal gain, never . . .

You are getting something . . . in government service that is far more important than money. It is a cause bigger than yourself. It is the cause of making this the greatest nation in the world, the leader of the world, because without our leadership the world will know nothing but war, possible starvation, or worse, in the years ahead. With our leadership it will know peace, it will know plenty . . .

You know, people often come in and say, ' What will I tell my kids?' They look at government and say it is sort of a rugged life, and they see the mistakes that are made. They get the impression that everybody is here for the purpose of feathering his nest. That is why I made this earlier point – not in this administration, not one single man or woman.

I remembered my old man. I think that they would have called him sort of a little man, common man. He didn't consider himself that way. You know what he was? He was a streetcar motorman first, and then he was a farmer, and then he had a lemon ranch. It was the poorest lemon ranch in California, I can assure you. He sold it before they found oil on it. And then he was a grocer. But he was a great man because he did his job, and every job counts up to the hilt, regardless of what happens.

Nobody will ever write a book, probably, about my mother. Well, I guess all of you would say this about your mother – my mother was a saint. And I think of her, two boys dying to tuberculosis, nursing four others in order that she could take care of my older brother for three years in Arizona, and seeing each of them die, and when they died, it was like one of her own. Yes, she will have no books written about her. But she was a saint.

Now, however, we look to the future. I had a little quote in the speech last night from T.R. [Theodore Roosevelt]. As you know, I kind of like to read books. I am not educated, but I do read books [laughter] and the T.R. quote was a pretty good one. Here is another one I found as I was reading, my last night in the White House . . . He was a young lawyer in New York. He had married a beautiful girl . . . and then suddenly she died, and this is what he wrote. This was in his diary:

> She was beautiful in face and lovelier still in spirit . . . When she had just become a mother, when her life seemed to be just begun and when the years seemed so bright before her, then by a strange and terrible fate death came to her. And when my heart's dearest died, the light went from my life forever.

That was T.R. in his twenties. He thought the light had gone from his life forever – but he went on. And he not only became president but, as an ex-president, he served his country always in the arena, tempestuous, strong, sometimes wrong, sometimes right, but he was a man.

And as I leave, let me say, that is an example all of us should remember. We think sometimes when things happen that don't go the right way; we think that when you don't pass the bar exam the first time – I happened to, but I was just lucky; I mean my writing was so poor that the bar examiner said, 'We have just got to let the guy through.' [Laughter] We think that when someone dear to us dies, we think that when we lose an election, we think that when we suffer defeat, that all is ended. We think, as T.R. said, that the light had left his life forever.

Not true. It is only a beginning always. The young must know it; the old must know it. It must always sustain us because the greatness comes . . . when you take some knocks, some disappointments, when sadness comes, because only if you have been in the deepest valley can you ever know how magnificent it is to be at the highest mountain.

And so, we leave with high hopes, in good spirits and with deep humility, and with very much gratefulness in our hearts. I can only say to each and every one of you, we come from many faiths, we pray perhaps to different gods, but really the same God in a sense . . . I want to say . . . always you will be in our hearts and you will be in our prayers. ’

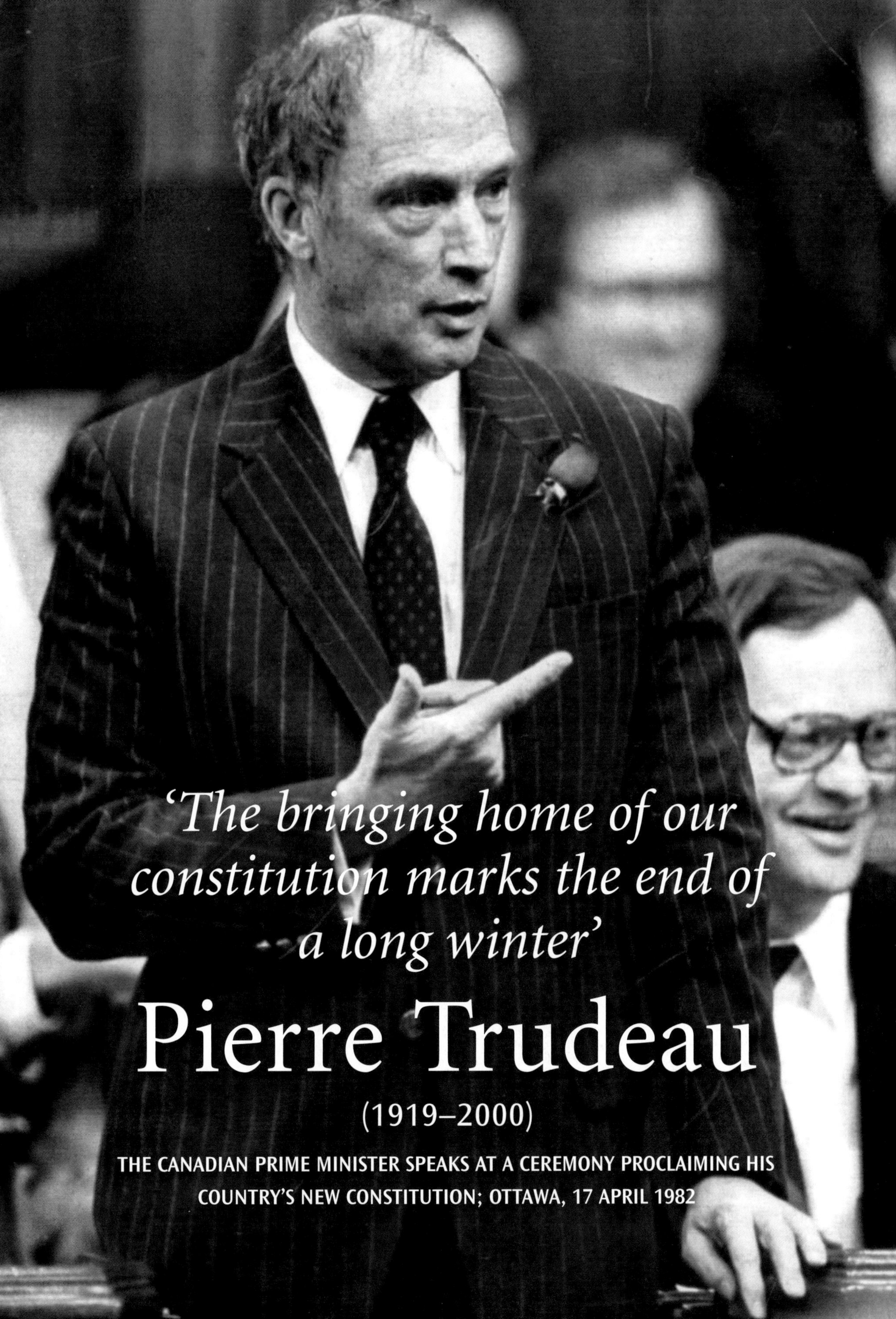
'The bringing home of our constitution marks the end of a long winter'
Pierre Trudeau
(1919–2000)
THE CANADIAN PRIME MINISTER SPEAKS AT A CEREMONY PROCLAIMING HIS COUNTRY'S NEW CONSTITUTION; OTTAWA, 17 APRIL 1982

Pierre Trudeau's intellectual agility and personal flair dominated late 20th-century Canadian history and helped to ensure the country's survival as a federal state. The 1982 Constitution Act is his most significant achievement, and the speech Trudeau delivered at its formal proclamation illustrates the clarity of his legal thought and an equally characteristic progressivism. Although Canada already had a bill of rights (1960), the incorporation of a 'Charter of Rights and Freedoms' in the new measure provided a more precise definition of individual freedoms and strengthened the judges' role in the interpretation and enforcement of its provisions. Taken as a whole, Trudeau's legislative package aimed at the entrenchment of a collective Canadian identity, and he eventually persuaded nine out of the ten provincial premiers to support the Canada Act, though their formal consent was not necessary. The government of Quebec never formally approved the measure.

Trudeau was a Quebecer formed by the province's francophone traditions at a time when the predominant milieu was one of conservative-minded clericalism. A Jesuit education at Montreal's Collège Jean-de-Brébeuf trained him in dialectical sharpness and encouraged his early leanings towards Quebec nationalism. He took a detached view of the Second World War in the course of which he was a reluctant conscript and never served overseas. During the postwar period, however, he became increasingly committed to the cause of individual rights and formed the view that their protection and advancement within Canada required the survival and strengthening of the country's federal government. Trudeau's early years as premier saw the passage of measures decriminalizing homosexuality, legalizing abortion and controlling gun ownership. The country became officially bilingual and the provision

PIERRE TRUDEAU (1919–2000)

1943 Graduates from Montreal University.

1946–7 Studies at École des Sciences Politiques, Paris.

1961–5 Associate Professor of Law, Montreal University.

1965 Joins Liberal Party; elected to the Canadian parliament.

1967 Appointed minister of justice.

1968 Becomes prime minister, having been elected Liberal Party leader, and wins subsequent (25 June) general election.

1972 Forms a minority government supported by the left-wing New Democratic Party.

1974 Re-elected prime minister; forms majority government.

1979 Liberal government defeated by Progressive Conservatives, whose government loses (Dec) a parliamentary motion of no confidence.

Feb 1980 Wins general election.

June 1984 Resigns premiership.

of federal services in both French and English sought to secure the two communities' rapprochement. The 'October Crisis' of 1970 tested Trudeau's leadership when the *Front de libération du Québec* embarked on a terrorist campaign, and his application of the War Measures Act – including arrest and detention without trial – confirmed his stature as a resolute leader. Quebec nationalism lost its extremist tinge but nonetheless retained its political edge.

Economic crisis in the 1970s threatened Trudeau's balancing act as he tried to reconcile the country's provinces to each other and to win support for the expansion of the federal government's welfare programmes. He introduced wage and price controls in 1975, and the National Energy Programme (1980) attempted to reduce spiralling rates of inflation and of interest by using Petro-Canada, a publicly owned company, to regulate the country's oil industry. The programme's promotion of lower prices was unpopular in oil-producing western Canada and, shorn of its commodity profits, the region developed its own separatist ambitions. Trudeau's personal and political unpopularity meant that not a single Liberal candidate was elected west of Manitoba in the 1980 election, though in Quebec a referendum of that year saw 60 per cent of those voting reject independence for the province. Québécois hostility to the Canada Act kept the sovereignty issue alive, however, and in the 1995 referendum 49.4 per cent voted for independence as opposed to 50.6 per cent who opted for the status quo. Protected in their rights by the Canada Act, Quebec's aboriginal peoples had voted overwhelmingly to endorse the union which had become their Canadian home.

Today, at long last, Canada is acquiring full and complete national sovereignty. The constitution of Canada has come home. The most fundamental law of the land will now be capable of being amended in Canada, without any further recourse to the parliament of the United Kingdom . . .

For more than half a century, Canadians have resembled young adults who leave home to build a life of their own, but are not quite confident enough to take along all their belongings. We became an independent country for all practical purposes in 1931, with the passage of the Statute of Westminster. But by our own choice, because of our inability to agree upon an amending formula at that time, we told the British parliament that we were not ready to break this last colonial link.

'The constitution of Canada has come home'

After 50 years of discussion we have finally decided to retrieve what is properly ours . . . It is my deepest hope that Canada will match its own legal maturity with that degree of political maturity which will allow us all to make a total commitment to the Canadian ideal.

I speak of a Canada where men and women of aboriginal ancestry, of French and British heritage, of the diverse cultures of the world, demonstrate the will to share this land in peace, in justice and with mutual respect. I speak of a Canada which is proud of and strengthened by its essential bilingual destiny, a Canada whose people believe in sharing and in mutual support, and not in building regional barriers. I speak of a country where every person is free to fulfil himself or herself to the utmost, unhindered by the arbitrary actions of governments.

The Canadian ideal which we have tried to live, with varying degrees of success and failure for a hundred years, is really an act of defiance against the history of mankind. Had this country been founded upon a less noble vision, or had our forefathers surrendered to the difficulties of building this nation, Canada would have been torn apart long ago. It should not surprise us, therefore, that even now we sometimes feel the pull of those old reflexes of mutual fear and distrust: fear of becoming vulnerable by opening one's arms to other Canadians who speak a different language or live in a different culture; fear of becoming poorer by agreeing to share one's resources and wealth with fellow citizens living in a region less favoured by nature.

'Had our forefathers surrendered to the difficulties of building this nation, Canada would have been torn apart long ago'

The Canada we are building lies beyond the horizon of such fears. Yet it is not, for all that, an unreal country, forgetful of the hearts of men and women. We know that justice and generosity can flourish only in an atmosphere of trust.

For if individuals and minorities do not feel protected against the possibility of the tyranny of the majority, if French-speaking Canadians or Native peoples or new Canadians do not feel they will be treated with justice, it is useless to ask them to open their hearts and minds to their fellow Canadians. Similarly, if provinces feel that their sovereign rights are not secure in those fields in which they have full constitutional jurisdiction, it is useless to preach to them about cooperation and sharing.

The constitution which is being proclaimed today goes a long way toward removing the reasons for the fears of which I have spoken. We now have a charter which . . . guarantees the basic rights and freedoms which each of us shall enjoy as a citizen of Canada.

It reinforces the protection offered to French-speaking Canadians outside Quebec, and to English-speaking Canadians in Quebec. It recognizes our multicultural character. It upholds the equality of women, and the rights of disabled persons.

The constitution confirms the long-standing division of powers among governments in Canada, and even strengthens provincial jurisdiction over natural resources and property rights. It entrenches the principle of equalization, thus helping less wealthy provinces to discharge their obligations without excessive taxation. It offers a way to meet the legitimate demands of our Native peoples. And, of course, by its amending formula, it now permits us to complete the task of constitutional renewal in Canada.

The government of Quebec decided that it wasn't enough. It decided not to participate in this ceremony, celebrating Canada's full independence. I know that many Quebecers feel themselves pulled in two directions by that decision. But one need look only at the results of the referendum in May 1980 to realize how strong is the attachment to Canada among the people of Quebec. By definition, the silent majority does not make a lot of noise; it is content to make history.

History will show, however, that in the guarantees written into the Charter of Rights and Freedoms, and in the amending formula, which allows Quebec to opt out of any constitutional arrangement which touches upon language and culture, with full financial compensation, nothing essential to the originality of Quebec has been sacrificed . . .

'We now have a charter which . . . guarantees the basic rights and freedoms which each of us shall enjoy as a citizen of Canada'

It must, however, be recognized that no constitution, no charter of rights and freedoms, no sharing of powers can be a substitute for the willingness to share the risks and grandeur of the Canadian adventure. Without that collective act of the will, our constitution would be a dead letter, and our country would wither away.

It is true that our will to live together has sometimes appeared to be in deep hibernation; but it is there nevertheless, alive and tenacious, in the hearts of Canadians of every province and territory. I wish simply that the bringing home of our constitution marks the end of a long winter, the breaking-up of the ice jams and the beginning of a new spring.

For what we are celebrating today is not so much the completion of our task, but the renewal of our hope; not so much an ending, but a fresh beginning. Let us celebrate the renewal and repatriation of our constitution; but let us put our faith, first and foremost, in the people of Canada, who will breathe life into it. ,

'I warn you that you will have pain'

Neil Kinnock

(b. 1942)

THE RISING STAR OF THE LABOUR PARTY SPEAKS ON THE EVE OF THE 1983 GENERAL ELECTION; BRIDGEND, SOUTH WALES, 7 JUNE 1983

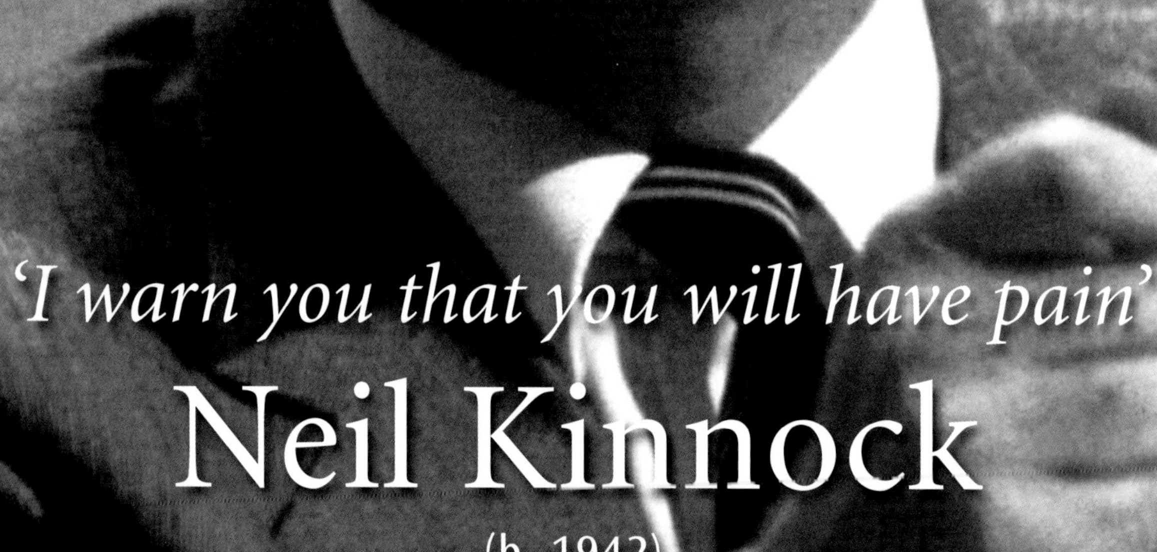

Social conflict, ideological economics and strident rhetoric marked the end of Britain's postwar consensus during Margaret Thatcher's premiership and belied the country's reputation for moderation, centrism and civility. The Conservative government elected in 1979 inherited an economy weakened by persistent strikes and plagued by high levels of unemployment and inflation, and it had sought to cure these ailments by pursuing 'free-market' policies. Neil Kinnock's warning, delivered during the 1983 general election, was based on the ensuing aggravation of social misery, especially in those areas of Britain, such as his own southeast Wales, where heavy industry had already been in steady decline for over two decades. An application of 'monetarism' – the belief that the money supply was inflation's sole determinant – had proved especially witless and reflected the prime minister's susceptibility to dogma. Monetarist counsel indicated that high interest rates would moderate a growth in the money supply and so reduce inflation. Experience contradicted theory and inflation continued to rise until the Thatcher U-turn of late 1981, when monetarism was abandoned and interest rates were reduced. Inflation began to fall, but by then an immense cost had been inflicted.

Labour's legacy of a million unemployed first of all doubled in the early 1980s and would then peak at 3.6 million. By 1983 manufacturing output had suffered a massive 30 per cent reduction compared to its level of five years earlier. Britain's underlying problem of an uncompetitive economy had resisted politicians' aspiring solutions since at least 1945. Kinnock spoke for the many who considered the Tory cure to be worse than the original

NEIL KINNOCK (b. 1942)

1965 Graduates from University of Wales, Cardiff

1966–70 Tutor at Workers' Educational Association.

1970 Elected MP (Labour) for Bedwellty (subsequently Islwyn), South Wales.

1979 Leads successful campaign against Labour government's proposals for Welsh devolution.

May 1979 Labour government defeated; subsequently joins Shadow Cabinet as Education spokesman.

Oct 1983 Elected Labour leader following party's general election defeat.

1987 Conservative government elected with majority of 101.

July 1992 Resigns as Labour leader following Conservative election victory with majority of 21.

1995–2004 Member of European Union Commission despite hostility to European integration in the 1970s.

1999–2004 Vice president of EU Commission.

2004 Appointed Chairman of the British Council.

2005 Becomes Baron Kinnock of Bedwellty, despite hostility to existence of House of Lords in the 1970s.

disease but whose numbers failed to prevent the government's re-election in 1983 with a 144 majority – though only 42.4 per cent actually voted Conservative.

The Labour Party which subsequently elected Kinnock to lead it was at a spectacularly low ebb. Those in work were benefiting from the return of economic growth, and the Thatcher cult of leadership had been emboldened by her zest during the Falklands War of 1982, when British forces retook the South Atlantic islands following an Argentinian invasion. Members of the far-left Militant Tendency had infiltrated Labour ranks and associated the party with extremism, while the formation of the Social Democratic Party had divided the British centre-left vote and thereby boosted the Tory majority. The personal edge to political debate was aggravated by pro-Thatcher newspaper editors who encouraged attacks on Kinnock's animated personality and verbose tendencies. Throughout these travails he remained resilient and often witty, and despite his left-wing origins Kinnock understood how and why his party had to change. Addressing the Labour conference in 1985, he attacked the local authority in Liverpool where Militant's influence had resulted in 'the grotesque chaos of a Labour council . . . hiring taxis to scuttle round a city handing out redundancy notices to its own workers'. By the 1987 election Labour had purged itself of such extremism and attained some aplomb in its communication and self-presentation, though its defeat of that year, like that of 1992, showed that preaching the need for 'the collective effort of the whole community' was a hard task in a post-socialist age.

If Margaret Thatcher is re-elected as prime minister, I warn you

I warn you that you will have pain –

When healing and relief depend upon payment.

I warn you that you will have ignorance –

When talents are untended and wits are wasted, when learning is a privilege and not a right.

I warn you that you will have poverty –

When pensions slip and benefits are whittled away by a government that won't pay in an economy that can't pay.

I warn you that you will be cold –

When fuel charges are used as a tax system that the rich don't notice and the poor can't afford.

I warn you that you must not expect work –

When many cannot spend, more will not be able to earn. When they don't earn, they don't spend. When they don't spend, work dies.

I warn you not to go into the streets alone after dark or into the streets in large crowds of protest in the light.

'I warn you not to go into the streets alone after dark or into the streets in large crowds of protest in the light'

I warn you that you will be quiet –

When the curfew of fear and the gibbet of unemployment make you obedient.

I warn you that you will have defence of a sort –

With a risk and at a price that passes all understanding.

I warn you that you will be home-bound –

When fares and transport bills kill leisure and lock you up.

I warn you that you will borrow less –

When credit, loans, mortgages and easy payments are refused to people on your melting income.

'If Margaret Thatcher wins I warn you not to be ordinary'

If Margaret Thatcher wins, she will be more a leader than a prime minister. That power produces arrogance, and when it is toughened by Tebbitry and flattered and fawned upon by spineless sycophants, the boot-licking tabloid Knights of Fleet Street and placemen . . . the arrogance corrupts absolutely.

If Margaret Thatcher wins –

I warn you not to be ordinary.

I warn you not to be young.

I warn you not to fall ill.

I warn you not to get old. ’

'We are democratic socialists. We care all the time'

THE LABOUR LEADER ADDRESSES THE PARTY FAITHFUL IN THE RUN-UP TO THE 1987 GENERAL ELECTION; LLANDUDNO, NORTH WALES, 15 MAY 1987

We are democratic socialists. We care all the time. We don't think it's a soft sentiment, we don't think it's 'wet'.

We think that care is the essence of strength.

And we believe that because we know that strength without care is savage and brutal and selfish.

Strength with care is compassion – the practical action that is needed to help people lift themselves to their full stature . . .

But where do we get that strength to provide that care?

Do we wait for some stroke of good fortune, some benign giant, some socially conscious Samson to come along and pick up the wretched of the earth?

Of course we don't.

We cooperate, we collect together, we coordinate so that everyone can contribute and everyone can benefit, everyone has responsibilities, everyone has rights . . . That is how we make the weak strong, that is how we lift the needy, that is how we make the sick whole, that is how we give talent the chance to flourish, that is how we turn the unemployed claimant into the working contributor . . .

When we speak of collective strength and collective freedom, collectively achieved, we are not fulfilling that nightmare that Mrs Thatcher tries to paint . . .

We're not talking about uniformity; we're not talking about regimentation; we're not talking about conformity – that's their creed. The uniformity of the dole queue; the regimentation of the unemployed young and their compulsory work schemes. The conformity of people who will work in conditions, and take orders, and accept pay because of mass unemployment that they would laugh at in a free society with full employment.

That kind of freedom for the individual . . . can't be secured by most of the people for most of the time if they're just left to themselves, isolated, stranded, with their whole life chances dependent upon luck! . . .

And now, Mrs Thatcher, by dint of privatization, and means test, and deprivation, and division, wants to nudge us back into the situation where everybody can either stand on their own feet, or live on their knees.

That's what this election is about as she parades her visions and values, and we choose to contest them as people with roots in this country, with a future only in this country, with pride in this country. People who know that if we are to have and sustain real individual liberty in this country, it requires the collective effort of the whole community.

Of course you hear the Tories talking about freedom. We'll be hearing a great deal of that over the next month from the same people who have spent the last eight years crushing individual freedoms under the weight of unemployment and poverty, squeezing individual rights with cuts and means tests and charges.

'They live in a free country, but they do not feel free'

I think of the youngsters I meet. Three, four, five years out of school. Never had a job. And they say to me, 'Do you think we'll ever work?'

They live in a free country, but they do not feel free.

I think of the 55-year-old woman I meet who is waiting to go into hospital, her whole existence clouded by pain . . .

And I think of the old couple who spend months of the winter afraid to turn up the heating, who stay at home because they are afraid to go out after dark, whose lives are turned into a crisis by the need to buy a new pair of shoes.

They live in a free country . . . but they do not feel free.

How can they – and millions like them – have their individual freedom if there is no collective provision?

How can they have strength if they do not have care?

Now they cannot have either because they are locked out of being able to discharge responsibilities just as surely as they are locked out of being able to exercise rights.

They want to be able to use both.

They do not want feather-bedding, they want a foothold.

They do not want cotton-woolling, they want a chance to contribute.

That is the freedom they want.

That is the freedom we want them to have. ’

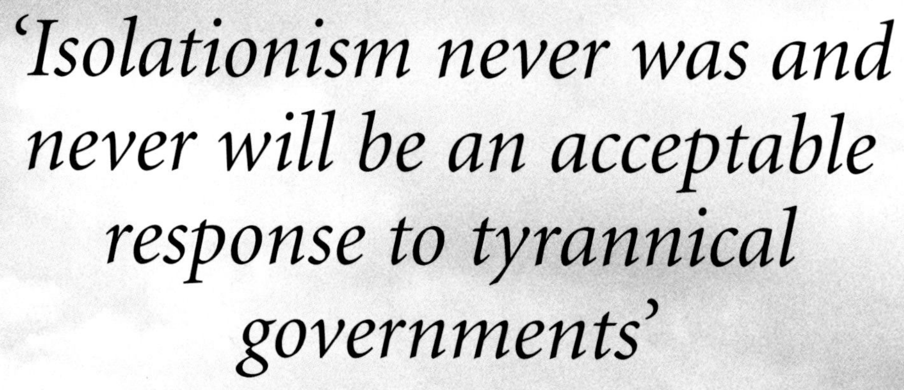

'Isolationism never was and never will be an acceptable response to tyrannical governments'

Ronald Reagan

(1911–2004)

THE AMERICAN PRESIDENT MARKS THE 40TH ANNIVERSARY OF THE D-DAY LANDINGS; US RANGER MONUMENT, POINTE DU HOC, FRANCE, 6 JUNE 1984

'Isolationism never was and never will be an acceptable response to tyrannical governments'

In the summer of 1984 Ronald Reagan was running for re-election, and this superbly crafted speech, written by the president's special assistant Peggy Noonan, encapsulated his administration's consistent foreign-policy goals. The commemoration of the D-Day landings required a particular tone of moral gravity blending sorrow with pride, remembrance of lives lost in battle as well as confidence in the justice of the Allied cause. Noonan's words and Reagan's faultless delivery avoided mere triumphalism and made a necessary connection: totalitarianism's fascist form had been defeated in 1944–5 but its communist expression continued to divide Europe. Freedom's business remained unfinished.

Reagan's own military service was of a specialized kind. In 1937, the year he signed a seven-year contract with Warner Brothers, Reagan enlisted in the US Army Reserve and was commissioned as a second lieutenant. Near-sightedness disqualified him from overseas service, and in 1942 he was assigned to the public relations division of the Army Air Force, working subsequently for the California-based First Motion Picture Unit. Reagan's critics mocked him as a mere B-movie actor whose second profession of politics provided him with an alternative theatre for the delivery of other people's words. This missed the point. Reagan's belief that communism was unnatural as well as wicked was genuine and not contrived, and his words were taken seriously because he clearly believed in them and acted accordingly. The USSR was an 'evil empire' (June 1982) tottering towards extinction and communism in general was 'another sad, bizarre chapter in human history whose last pages even now are being written' (March 1983). The sunny and optimistic temperament of this natural Californian helped him gain support for these militant assertions, and mockery as well as excoriation were well within his dramatic range.

RONALD REAGAN (1911–2004)

1947–52, 1959 President of the Screen Actors Guild.

1962 Switches allegiance from the Democratic Party to the Republicans.

1966 Elected governor of California and serves in office, 1967–75.

1976 Campaigns for the Republican presidential nomination but is defeated by the incumbent Gerald Ford.

1980 Gains Republican nomination and is elected US president.

1984 Re-elected president.

1986 Details emerge of covert arms sales to Iran to fund anti-communist Contra insurgents in Nicaragua, a policy specifically outlawed by Congress; 14 of his staff are subsequently indicted and 11 convicted.

Jan 1989 Leaves office.

1993 Awarded Presidential Medal of Freedom.

Nov 1994 Makes public that he is suffering from Alzheimer's disease.

Past, present and future are intercut to dramatic, even filmic, effect as the speech proceeds from its evocation of the beachhead scene of 40 years ago to the concluding peroration linking historic sacrifice with contemporary struggle and battles yet to be won. There is poetry, too, when the scene shifts across the Atlantic to the pen portrait of a prayerful hush as news of the invasion spreads through an expectant America. The speech is grounded in recollected emotion and renewed gratitude for valour displayed in a noble cause, and the connection made with its immediate audience of veterans is both poignant and dignified.

Soviet communism's collapse showed that America's hostile words worked – but money also talked. Reagan's first term saw a 40 per cent real-terms increase in the defence budget, and in 1983 he unveiled the Strategic Defence Initiative (SDI), a ground- and space-based system intended to provide the US with a defence shield against nuclear ballistic missiles. Though never fully developed, SDI's prevision of a US rendered invulnerable to nuclear attack alarmed the USSR, since it abolished any notion of an equivalence of offensive capacity. The fall of the Berlin Wall in 1989 signified the collapse of Soviet communism and of its satellite governments in Central and Eastern Europe. Regan's prediction had come true, and the US was the only superpower left.

We're here to mark that day in history when the Allied armies joined in battle to reclaim this continent for liberty . . . Here the Allies stood and fought against tyranny in a giant undertaking unparalleled in human history.

We stand on a lonely, windswept point on the northern shore of France. The air is soft, but 40 years ago at this moment, the air was dense with smoke and the cries of men, and the air was filled with the crack of rifle fire and the roar of cannon. At dawn, on the morning of 6 June 1944, 225 Rangers jumped off the British landing craft and ran to the bottom of these cliffs. Their mission was one of the most difficult and daring of the invasion: to climb these sheer and desolate cliffs and take out the enemy guns.

The Rangers looked up and saw the enemy soldiers shooting down at them with machine guns and throwing grenades. And the American Rangers began to climb . . . Soon, one by one, the Rangers pulled themselves over the top, and in seizing the firm land at the top of these cliffs, they began to seize back the continent of Europe. Two hundred and twenty-five came here. After two days of fighting, only 90 could still bear arms.

Behind me is a memorial that symbolizes the Ranger daggers that were thrust into the top of these cliffs. And before me are the men who put them there . . .

'What inspired all the men of the armies that met here?'

Forty summers have passed since the battle that you fought here. You were young the day you took these cliffs; some of you were hardly more than boys, with the deepest joys of life before you. Yet, you risked everything here . . . What inspired all the men of the armies that met here? We look at you, and somehow we know the answer. It was faith and belief; it was loyalty and love.

'There is a profound, moral difference between the use of force for liberation and the use of force for conquest'

The men of Normandy had faith that what they were doing was right, faith that they fought for all humanity, faith that a just God would grant them mercy on this beachhead or on the next. It was the deep knowledge – and pray God we have not lost it – that there is a profound, moral difference between the use of force for liberation and the use of force for conquest. You were here to liberate, not to conquer, and so you and those others did not doubt your cause. And you were right not to doubt.

You all knew that some things are worth dying for. One's country is worth dying for, and democracy is worth dying for, because it's the most deeply honourable form of government ever devised by man. All of you loved liberty. All of you were willing to fight tyranny, and you knew the people of your countries were behind you.

The Americans who fought here that morning knew word of the invasion was spreading through the darkness back home. They felt in their hearts . . . that in Georgia they were filling the churches at 4 a.m., in Kansas they were kneeling on their porches and praying, and in Philadelphia they were ringing the Liberty Bell . . .

'The Allies summoned strength from the faith, belief, loyalty and love of those who fell here'

When the war was over, there were lives to be rebuilt and governments to be returned to the people. There were nations to be reborn. Above all, there was a new peace to be assured. These were huge and daunting tasks. But the Allies summoned strength from the faith, belief, loyalty and love of those who fell here. They rebuilt a new Europe together . . .

In spite of our great efforts and successes, not all that followed the end of the war was happy or planned. Some liberated countries were lost. The great sadness of this loss echoes down to our own time in the streets of Warsaw, Prague and East Berlin. Soviet troops that came to the centre of this continent did not leave when peace came. They're still there, uninvited, unwanted, unyielding, almost 40 years after the war. Because of this, Allied forces still stand on this continent. Today, as 40 years ago, our armies are here for only one purpose – to protect and defend democracy . . .

We in America have learned bitter lessons from two world wars: it is better to be here ready to protect the peace than to take blind shelter across the sea, rushing to respond only after freedom is lost. We've learned that isolationism never was and never will be an acceptable response to tyrannical governments with an expansionist intent.

But we try always to be prepared for peace; prepared to deter aggression; prepared to negotiate the reduction of arms; and, yes, prepared to reach out again in the spirit of reconciliation . . .

It's fitting to remember here the great losses also suffered by the Russian people during World War II: 20 million perished, a terrible price . . . I tell you from my heart that we in the United States do not want war. We want to wipe from the face of the earth the terrible weapons that man now has in his hands. And I tell you, we are ready to seize that beachhead. We look for some sign from the Soviet Union that they are willing to move forward, that they share our desire and love for peace, and that they will give up the ways of conquest . . .

We will pray forever that some day that changing will come. But for now, particularly today, it is good and fitting to renew our commitment to each other, to our freedom, and to the alliance that protects it.

'We want to wipe from the face of the earth the terrible weapons that man now has in his hands'

We are bound today by what bound us 40 years ago, the same loyalties, traditions and beliefs. We're bound by reality. The strength of America's allies is vital to the United States, and the American security guarantee is essential to the continued freedom of Europe's democracies.

Here, in this place where the West held together, let us make a vow to our dead. Let us show them by our actions that we understand what they died for . . .

Strengthened by their courage . . . let us continue to stand for the ideals for which they lived and died. ’

'For the love of God: Please, make this nation remember how futures are built'

Mario Cuomo

(b. 1932)

THE GOVERNOR OF NEW YORK CALLS THE DEMOCRATS BACK TO THEIR CORE VALUES; DEMOCRATIC PARTY NATIONAL CONVENTION, SAN FRANCISCO, 16 JULY 1984

The 1980s were not the Democrats' decade. Jimmy Carter's evident decency and earnestness helped them regain the presidency in 1976, but the latter part of his period in office was overshadowed by the Iran hostage crisis. Islamic fundamentalists had stormed the US embassy in Tehran, where for 444 days they detained 52 American diplomats and were initially impervious to negotiation. Carter's inability to secure their release seemed to denote a more general loss of US authority in world affairs and the Democrats paid an electoral price. Hostility to federal expenditure, lower taxation and an aggressively anti-communist foreign policy: these were the keynotes of 1980s politics as provided by a resurgent Republican Party. The fact that the Iranians delayed the hostages' release until the first day of the Reagan presidency compounded the Democratic humiliation.

Democrats needed, therefore, some additional inspiration at their 1984 convention, and it was Mario Cuomo's address that provided them with a cogent reminder of their core values. He was already a popular figure with those liberal Democrats who admired his blend of compassion and efficiency. He consistently delivered a balanced budget during his 12 years as New York's governor and there were even occasional tax cuts. Public-sector investment spurred the private sector's economic development and job creation. Cuomo's gubernatorial budget expanded housing programmes for the homeless, funded treatment centres for drug addicts, and was notably pioneering in its provision for those suffering from AIDS and mental illness. This made his state into a surviving beacon of liberal values in an American political landscape being reshaped by a vigorous Republicanism. It was John Winthrop, the governor of the Massachusetts Bay Company, who coined the phrase 'city upon a hill' in a sermon of 1630, and Reagan's version of the phrase expressed a similar sense of America's exemplary destiny. Cuomo's extension of the metaphor portrayed the divisive consequences of 'Reaganomics' to graphic effect and led many to hope that he would run for the presidency.

MARIO CUOMO (b. 1932)

1953 Graduates from St John's University, New York City, a Catholic university from which he also graduates (1956) in law.

1956 Called to the New York bar.

1958 Enters legal practice.

1975 Appointed New York's Secretary of State by Governor Hugh Carey.

1978 Elected lieutenant governor of New York.

1982 Elected governor of New York, and serves three consecutive terms after being re-elected in 1986 and 1990.

1987 Announces that he will not contest the Democratic Party's nomination for the US presidency.

1994 Stands for re-election as governor defeated by Republican George Pataki.

When Carter left office, inflation was running at almost 12 per cent and unemployment stood at 7.5 per cent. The Republican corrective included large tax cuts which stimulated economic growth but limited government revenue. By 1984 Reagan was running an annual federal budget deficit of 200 billion dollars, and his eventual legacy included a national debt which increased from 700 billion to 3 trillion dollars. The background to Cuomo's speech, therefore, was the major recession of 1982 in the course of which American unemployment peaked at 10.8 per cent, although two years later it was evident that the economy was once again expanding. A total of 16 million new jobs were created during Reagan's presidency and US GDP grew at an annual rate of just over 3 per cent. But the recession had had an especially grievous impact on the urban poor, who found an eloquent advocate and defender in New York's governor. Cuomo's parents were Italian immigrants and his father had worked as a cleaner of sewers while saving enough money to open a grocery store in the New York borough of Queens. These struggles, and his family's Catholicism, made a profound impression on this unusually introspective politician, whose call to conscience expresses his intense conviction that 'the family of America' is built on inclusion and endeavour.

Ten days ago, President Reagan admitted that although some people in this country seemed to be doing well nowadays, others were unhappy, even worried . . . The president said that he didn't understand that fear. He said: 'Why, this country is a shining city on a hill.' And the president is right. In many ways we are a shining city on a hill.

But . . . there's another part to the shining city; the part where people can't pay their mortgages . . . ; where students can't afford the education they need and middle-class parents watch the dreams they hold for their children evaporate.

In this part of the city there are more poor than ever . . . And there are people who sleep in the city streets, in the gutter, where the glitter doesn't show . . . There is despair, Mr President, in the faces that you don't see, in the places that you don't visit . . .

'There are people who sleep in the city streets, in the gutter, where the glitter doesn't show'

The truth is that this is how we were warned it would be . . . 'Government can't do everything,' we were told, so it should settle for taking care of the strong and hope that economic ambition and charity will do the rest . . .

The difference between Democrats and Republicans has always been measured in courage and confidence. The Republicans believe that the wagon train will not make it to the frontier unless some of the old, some of the young, some of the weak are left behind by the side of the trail . . . We Democrats believe that we can make it all the way with the whole family intact . . .

Today our great Democratic Party, which has saved the nation from depression, from fascism, from racism, from corruption, is called upon to do it again – this time to save the nation from confusion and division, from the threat of eventual fiscal disaster, and most of all from the fear of a nuclear holocaust . . .

What chance would the Republican candidate have had in 1980 if he had told the American people that he intended to pay for his so-called economic recovery with bankruptcies, unemployment, more homeless, more hungry, and the largest government debt known to humankind? . . .

They said that they would make us and the whole world safer. They say they have: by creating the largest defence budget in history; by escalating to a frenzy the nuclear arms race; by incendiary rhetoric; by refusing to discuss peace with our enemies . . .

'We give money to Latin American governments that murder nuns, and then we lie about it'

We give money to Latin American governments that murder nuns, and then we lie about it . . . Our foreign policy drifts with no real direction, other than an hysterical commitment to an arms race that leads nowhere – if we're lucky. And if we're not, it could lead us into bankruptcy or war . . .

Where would another four years take us? . . .

We must ask ourselves what kind of country will be fashioned by the man who believes . . . that the laws against discrimination against people go too far; a man who threatens Social Security and Medicaid and help for the disabled. How high will we pile the missiles? . . .

We Democrats believe in a government strong enough to use words like 'love' and 'compassion' and smart enough to convert our noblest aspirations into practical realities . . .

We believe that while survival of the fittest may be a good working description of the process of evolution, a government of humans should elevate itself to a higher order.

'We Democrats believe in a government strong enough to use words like "love" and "compassion"'

Our government should be able to rise to the level where it can fill the gaps that are left by chance or by a wisdom we don't fully understand. We would rather have laws written by the patron of this great city, St Francis of Assisi, than laws written by Darwin . . .

We believe in a single fundamental idea that describes . . . what a proper government should be: the idea of family, mutuality, the sharing of benefits and burdens for the good of all . . . without respect to race, or sex, or geography, or political affiliation.

We believe that we must be the family of America, recognizing that at the heart of the matter we are bound one to another . . .

We Democrats created a better future for our children, using traditional Democratic principles as a fixed beacon, giving us direction and purpose, but constantly innovating, adapting to new realities . . .

We can do it again, if we do not forget that this entire nation has profited by these progressive principles; that they helped lift up generations to the middle class and higher; that they gave us a chance to work, to go to college, to raise a family, to own a house, to be secure in our old age . . .

'We Democrats created a better future for our children, using traditional Democratic principles as a fixed beacon'

The struggle to live with dignity is the real story of the shining city. And it's a story that I didn't read in a book, or learn in a classroom. I saw it and lived it, like many of you. I watched a small man with thick calluses on both his hands work 15 and 16 hours a day. I saw him once literally bleed from the bottoms of his feet, a man who came here uneducated, alone, unable to speak the language, who taught me all I needed to know about faith and hard work by the simple eloquence of his example. I learned about our kind of democracy from my father. And I learned about our obligation to each other from him and from my mother. They asked for a chance to work and to make the world better for their children, and they asked to be protected in those moments when they would not be able to protect themselves. This nation and this nation's government did that for them.

And that they were able to build a family and live in dignity and see one of their children . . . occupy the highest seat, in the greatest state, in the greatest nation, in the only world we would know, is an ineffably beautiful tribute to the democratic process.

And on 20 January 1985 it will happen again – only on a much, much grander scale. We will have a new president of the United States, a Democrat . . .

It will happen if we make it happen; if you and I make it happen. And I ask you now, for the good of all of us, for the love of this great nation, for the family of America, for the love of God: Please, make this nation remember how futures are built.

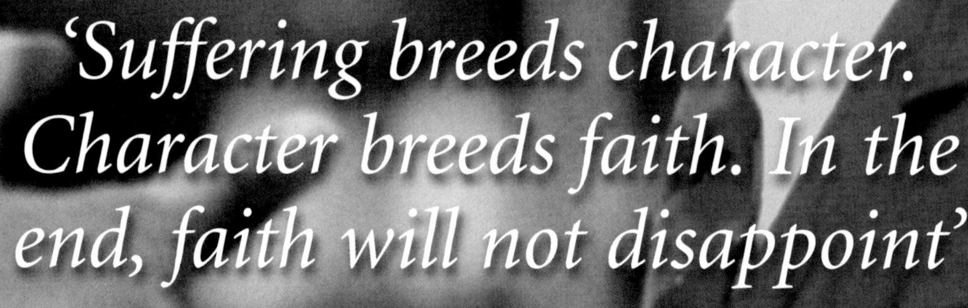

'Suffering breeds character. Character breeds faith. In the end, faith will not disappoint'

Jesse Jackson

(b. 1941)

THE DEFEATED CANDIDATE FOR THE DEMOCRATIC NOMINATION FOR THE US PRESIDENCY ADDRESSES HIS PARTY'S NATIONAL CONVENTION; SAN FRANCISCO, 18 JULY 1984

'Suffering breeds character. Character breeds faith. In the end, faith will not disappoint'

Jesse Jackson emerged as the civil rights movement's most significant leader during the years following the assassination of his mentor Martin Luther King, Jr. He too had been ordained into the Baptist ministry, and although his lush oratory lacked King's intellectual focus, Jackson communicated a direct passion which made a powerful impact on the Democratic Party. He was not the first African-American to contest the presidency, but Congresswoman Shirley Chisholm's 1972 campaign for the Democratic nomination had been largely symbolic. Jackson had no experience at this stage of elective public office and most observers thought initially that his presidential ambitions lacked a serious intent. Moreover, his aim of reversing tax cuts, reducing defence expenditure and expanding welfare went against the emergent political consensus. But a campaign conducted with typical verve gained Jackson 18.2 per cent of the total votes cast during the Democratic primaries, and the result ensured his subsequent status as a major force within his party. His feel for the Democrats' recent history undoubtedly helped him in this regard and is illustrated by this speech's reference to Hubert Humphrey. The former vice president (1965–9), defeated by Richard Nixon in the presidential election of 1968, was admired for his progressivism and fortitude, and the widespread feeling that Humphrey was the Democrats' great lost leader had survived his support for the war in Vietnam.

The need for black Americans to work together as part of a wider coalition was a major aspect of the King legacy. This included the furthering of North–South solidarity among civil rights activists, and in 1966 King asked Jackson to assume responsibility for the expansion into Chicago of the protests organized by the Southern Christian Leadership Conference (SCLC). Ralph Abernathy, who became head of the SCLC after King's assassination, clashed repeatedly with Jackson, who therefore decided to resign from the organization in December 1971 and to form his own movement. The result was Operation PUSH (People United to Save Humanity), a Chicago-based body which concentrated on

JESSE JACKSON (b. 1941)

1966 Leaves Chicago Theological Seminary to become a full-time civil rights activist.

1968 Ordained a Baptist minister.

Nov 1983 Announces candidacy for Democratic presidential nomination.

1984 Walter Mondale, Democratic presidential nominee, is defeated and President Reagan re-elected.

1988 Gains 6.9 million votes in the Democratic primaries as candidate for the presidential nomination; Vice President George Bush, the Republican candidate, defeats the Democrats' nominee Michael Dukakis.

1991–7 Shadow senator for the District of Columbia, an elective office whose holder lobbies for the District's admission as a Union state.

2000 Awarded Medal of Freedom by President Clinton.

promoting African-Americans' business opportunities and employment rights. In 1984 Jackson founded another movement, the Rainbow Coalition, which represented a very wide spectrum of interest groups. His description in this speech of an American quilt formed out of diversity but united by a common thread indicates the range of the Coalition, and in 1996, under his continued leadership, Jackson's two organizations merged.

Occasional diplomatic forays confirmed Jackson's patriotism. In 1983 he secured the release of an American pilot captured by the Syrians, and in the month before this speech's delivery he had negotiated the release of 22 US citizens being detained in Cuba. The acclaim that greeted his 1984 address and Jackson's subsequent energy in renewing, regrouping and moving on provided him with a springboard for another attempt at gaining the Democratic presidential nomination in 1988, when he gained 21 per cent of the vote in the party's primaries. But the emergence of Michael Dukakis, governor of Massachusetts, as the lacklustre party nominee showed the limits to the powers of persuasion that could be exerted even by Jackson's dazzling verbal pyrotechnics.

'

This is not a perfect party. We are not a perfect people. Yet, we are called to a perfect mission. Our mission: to feed the hungry; to clothe the naked; to house the homeless; to teach the illiterate; to provide jobs for the jobless; and to choose the human race over the nuclear race.

We are gathered here this week to nominate a candidate and adopt a platform which will expand, unify, direct and inspire our party and the nation to fulfil this mission. My constituency is the desperate, the damned, the disinherited, the disrespected and the despised. They are restless and seek relief . . .

Leadership must heed the call of conscience, redemption, expansion, healing and unity . . . Throughout this campaign, I've tried to offer leadership to the Democratic Party and the nation. If, in my high moments, I have done some good, offered some service, shed some light, healed some wounds, rekindled some hope, or stirred someone from apathy and indifference . . . then this campaign has not been in vain.

If, in my low moments, . . . I have caused anyone discomfort, created pain or revived someone's fears, that was not my truest self . . . Please forgive me. I am not a perfect servant. I am a public servant doing my best against the odds. As I develop and serve, be patient: God is not finished with me yet . . .

I went to see Hubert Humphrey three days before he died. He had just called Richard Nixon from his dying bed, and many people wondered why. And I asked him. He said: 'Jesse, from this vantage point, the sun is setting in my life, all of the speeches, the political conventions, the crowds and the great fights are behind me now. At a time like this you are forced to deal with your irreducible essence, forced to grapple with that which is really important to you. And what I've concluded about life,' Hubert Humphrey said, 'When all is said and done, we must forgive each other, and redeem each other, and move on.'

Our party is emerging from one of its most hard-fought battles for the Democratic Party's presidential nomination in our history. But our healthy competition should make us better, not bitter. We must use the insight, wisdom and experience of the late Hubert Humphrey as a balm for the wounds in our party, this nation and the world. We must forgive each other, redeem each other, regroup and move on.

'We must forgive each other, redeem each other, regroup and move on'

America is not like a blanket – one piece of unbroken cloth, the same colour, the same texture, the same size. America is more like a quilt: many patches, many pieces, many colours, many sizes, all woven and held together by a common thread. The white, the Hispanic, the black, the Arab, the Jew, the woman, the native American, the small farmer, the businessperson, the environmentalist, the peace activist, the young, the old, the lesbian, the gay and the disabled make up the American quilt.

Even in our fractured state, all of us count and fit somewhere. We have proven that we can survive without each other. But we have not proven that we can win and make progress without each other. We must come together . . .

The requirement for rebuilding America is justice. The linchpin of progressive politics in our nation will not come from the North; they, in fact, will come from the South . . .

If blacks vote in great numbers, progressive whites win. It's the only way progressive whites win. If blacks vote in great numbers, Hispanics win. When blacks, Hispanics and progressive whites vote, women win. When women win, children win. When women and children win, workers win. We must all come up together . . .

'There is a way out – jobs. Put America back to work'

There is a way out – jobs. Put America back to work. When I was a child growing up in Greenville, South Carolina, the Reverend Sample used to preach every so often a sermon relating to Jesus. And he said: 'If I be lifted up, I'll draw all men unto me.' I didn't quite understand what he meant as a child growing up, but I understand a little better now. If you raise up truth, it's magnetic. It has a way of drawing people . . .

If we lift up a programme to feed the hungry, they'll come running; if we lift up a programme to study war no more, our youth will come running; if we lift up a programme to put America back to work, and an alternative to welfare and despair, they will come running . . .

*'You must face reality – that which is.
But then dream of a reality that
ought to be – that must be'*

In this campaign, I've tried to be faithful to my promise. I lived in old barrios, ghettos, and reservations and housing projects. I have a message for our youth. I challenge them to put hope in their brains and not dope in their veins . . . Just because you're born in the slum does not mean the slum is born in you, and you can rise above it if your mind is made up . . .

I'm more convinced than ever that we can win. We will vault up the rough side of the mountain. We can win. I just want young America to do me one favour, just one favour. Exercise the right to dream. You must face reality – that which is. But then dream of a reality that ought to be – that must be . . . Use hope and imagination as weapons of survival and progress. Use love to motivate you and obligate you to serve the human family.

*'We must leave racial battle ground and
come to economic common ground
and moral higher ground'*

Our time has come. Our time has come. Suffering breeds character. Character breeds faith. In the end, faith will not disappoint. Our time has come. Our faith, hope and dreams will prevail. Our time has come. Weeping has endured for nights, but now joy cometh in the morning. Our time has come. No grave can hold our body down. Our time has come. No lie can live forever. Our time has come. We must leave racial battle ground and come to economic common ground and moral higher ground. America, our time has come. We come from disgrace to amazing grace. Our time has come. Give me your tired, give me your poor, your huddled masses who yearn to breathe free and come November, there will be change because our time has come. ’

'Anyone who closes his eyes to the past is blind to the present'

Richard von Weizsäcker

(b. 1920)

THE PRESIDENT OF WEST GERMANY ADDRESSES THE BUNDESTAG ON THE 40TH ANNIVERSARY OF THE END OF WAR IN EUROPE; BONN, 8 MAY 1985

This profound and measured account of guilt, innocence and suffering stands in the highest traditions of German, and European, statesmanship. President Richard von Weizsäcker was at this time West Germany's head of state, and that non-partisan role qualified him to speak on behalf of his compatriots. Personal experience lent an added significance to these words of a representative German.

The von Weizsäckers had given distinguished service to the Second Reich created in 1871, and the president's grandfather, state premier of Württemberg, was raised to the hereditary nobility in 1916. His father Ernst joined the German foreign office in 1920 and was ambassador to the Holy See from 1943 to 1945. In 1947 Ernst von Weizsäcker was arrested, charged with war crimes and, controversially, sentenced to a seven-year term of imprisonment by the US military tribunal held in Nuremberg. Richard von Weizsäcker, then a law student at Göttingen, acted as assistant defence counsel on behalf of his father, who was released as part of a general amnesty in 1950 but died the following year.

West Germany's rapid postwar development as a prosperous and stable democracy necessarily meant turning its back on the past. The 40th anniversary of the Third Reich's collapse was a public opportunity to start asking the question why Germany, at both an elite and a popular level, embraced totalitarianism in the interwar years. Some considered this process to be overdue, and student radicals in the 1960s had protested at the German establishment's indifference to the issues raised by the recent past. Von Weizsäcker's speech marked the start of a national self-examination which has continued ever since.

For the first time a senior German public figure stated explicitly that 8 May 1945 had been a 'day of liberation' for his compatriots. Given the scale of the national catastrophe, its anniversary could not be a day of celebration but it could be commemorated as 'the end of

RICHARD VON WEIZSÄCKER (b. 1920)

1939–45 Serves in the German army, and is wounded (1945) whilst campaigning in East Prussia.

1955 Gains his Juris Doctor, a professional doctorate in law, from University of Göttingen.

1967–84 Member of the Synod and Council of the German Evangelical (Lutheran) Church.

1954 Joins the Christian Democratic Union, a centre-right political party.

1969–81 Member of the Bundestag and (1979–81) its vice president.

1981–4 Governing mayor of West Berlin.

1984 Elected president of West Germany by the country's Federal Convention.

1989–94 Serves second term as president; presides over reunification of Germany and collapse of communist East Germany.

an aberration'. Germany's responsibility for starting the war is accepted, but the account of how the nation became the last victim of Nazism is both scrupulous and just: 'we became the victims of our own war.'

The personally cultivated and intellectually serious tone of this speech demonstrated qualities which had typified German society before Nazism and which re-emerged as distinguishing characteristics after 1945. Its religious emphasis is derived from von Weizsäcker's Protestant and Christian faith, an emphasis which explains why he thinks that 'Guilt is, like innocence, not collective, but personal.'

Western European moves towards a single currency and integrated political structures were gathering pace in the mid-1980s. Hence von Weizsäcker's subtle formulation: 'The new beginning . . . has brought both victory and defeat for the notion of freedom and self-determination.' The war was won by states who were defending their national independence. But avoiding its recurrence had involved a pooling of sovereignty. One reconciliation, however, that between East and West Germany, was yet to be achieved in 1985. Germany's return as 'one people and one nation', here prophesied, would become fact in just four years' time.

'Many nations are today commemorating the date on which World War II ended in Europe. Be it victory or defeat, liberation from injustice and alien rule, or transition to new dependence, division, new alliances, vast shifts of power – 8 May 1945 is a date of decisive importance for Europe.

We Germans are commemorating that date among ourselves, as is indeed necessary. We must find our own standards. We are not assisted in this task if we or others spare our feelings.

For us Germans, 8 May is not a day of celebration. Those who actually witnessed that day in 1945 think back on highly personal and hence highly different experiences. Some returned home, others lost their homes. Some were liberated, while for others it was the start of captivity. Many were simply grateful that the bombing at night and fear had passed and that they had survived. Others felt first and foremost grief at the complete defeat suffered by their country. Some Germans felt bitterness about their shattered illusions, while others were grateful for the gift of a new start.

Most Germans had believed that they were fighting and suffering for the good of their country. And now it turned out that their efforts were not only in vain and futile, but had served the inhuman goals of a criminal regime.

'There is every reason for us to perceive 8 May 1945 as the end of an aberration in German history'

Yet with every day something became clearer, and this must be stated on behalf of all of us today. The eighth of May was a day of liberation. It liberated all of us from the inhumanity and tyranny of the National Socialist regime.

There is truly no reason for us today to participate in victory celebrations. But there is every reason for us to perceive 8 May 1945 as the end of an aberration in German history, an end bearing seeds of hope for a better future.

'There is no such thing as the guilt or innocence of an entire nation'

At the root of the tyranny was Hitler's immeasurable hatred against our Jewish compatriots. Hitler had never concealed this hatred from the public, but made the entire nation a tool of it . . . The genocide of the Jews is unparalleled in history. The nature and scope of the destruction may have exceeded human imagination, but in reality there was, apart from the crime itself, the attempt by too many people . . . not to take note of what was happening. There were too many ways of not burdening one's conscience, of shunning responsibility, looking away, keeping mum.

There is no such thing as the guilt or innocence of an entire nation. Guilt is, like innocence, not collective, but personal. Everyone who directly experienced that era should today quietly ask himself about his involvement then.

The vast majority of today's population were either children then or had not been born. No discerning person can expect them to wear a penitential robe simply because they are Germans. But their forefathers have left them a grave legacy.

'Remembrance is experience of the work of God in history'

It is not a case of coming to terms with the past. That is not possible. It cannot be subsequently modified or made not to have happened. However, anyone who closes his eyes to the past is blind to the present. Whoever refuses to remember the inhumanity is prone to new risks of infection.

'Seeking to forget makes exile all the longer. The secret of redemption lies in remembrance.' This Jewish adage surely expresses the idea that faith in God is faith in the work of God in history. Remembrance is experience of the work of God in history. It is the source of faith in redemption. This experience creates hope, creates faith in redemption, in reunification of the divided, in reconciliation.

Hitler wanted to dominate Europe and to do so through war. The Soviet Union was prepared for other nations to fight one another so that it could have a share of the spoils. The initiative for the war, however, came from Germany.

In the course of that war the Nazi regime tormented and defiled many nations. At the end of it all, only one nation remained to be tormented, enslaved and defiled: the German nation. Time and again Hitler had declared that if the German nation was not capable of winning the war, it should be left to perish. The other nations first became victims of a war started by Germany before we became the victims of our own war.

The new beginning in Europe after 1945 has brought both victory and defeat for the notion of freedom and self-determination. Our aim is to seize the opportunity to draw a line under a long period of European history in which to every country peace seemed conceivable and safe only as a result of its own supremacy, and in which peace meant a period of preparation for the next war.

'Other nations first became victims of a war started by Germany before we became the victims of our own war'

Whereas at the end of the war many Germans tried to hide their passports or to exchange them for another one, German nationality today is highly valued. We may look back with gratitude on our development over these 40 years, if we use the memory of our own history as a guideline for our future behaviour.

– If we remember that mentally disturbed persons were put to death in the Third Reich, we will see care of people with psychiatric disorders as our own responsibility.

– If we remember how people persecuted on grounds of race, religion and politics and threatened with certain death often stood before the closed borders with other countries, we shall not close the door today on those who are genuinely persecuted and seek protection with us.

– If we reflect on the penalties for free thinking under the dictatorship, we will protect the freedom of every idea and every criticism, however much it may be directed against ourselves.

We Germans are one people and one nation. We feel that we belong together because we have lived through the same past. Reconciliation that transcends boundaries cannot be provided by a walled Europe but only by a continent that removes the divisive elements from its borders. We are confident that 8 May is not the last date in the common history of all Germans. ’

'Let Europe be a family of nations . . . relishing our national identity no less than our common European endeavour'

Margaret Thatcher

(b. 1925)

THE BRITISH PRIME MINISTER SETS FORTH HER VISION OF EUROPE; BRUGES, 20 SEPTEMBER 1988

'Let Europe be a family of nations . . . relishing our national identity no less than our common European endeavour'

European integration accelerated during the 1980s and the goal of 'an ever closer union' enshrined in the Treaties of Rome acquired closer definition. Six countries had joined the European Economic Community, established under the original 1957 treaties. By 1988, 12 member states belonged to an organization which had dropped the word 'economic' from its title and was evolving towards the European Union. The aspiration to remove national barriers to trade under the Single European Act (1986) met with approval in Britain, whose population habitually referred to the Community as the 'Common Market'. European Economic and Monetary Union (EMU), however, was a very different matter.

In the summer of 1988 a committee chaired by Jacques Delors, president of the European Commission, was working on plans to introduce a single currency and establish a central bank. Many British Conservatives, taking their cue from the premier's attitudes, protested that the sovereignty of the Westminster parliament, and thereby the country's independence, would be diminished were these innovations to apply to Britain. 'Thatcherism' maintained that the accretion of power by European institutions was a relentless and one-way process, and that its unacknowledged aim was the creation of a federal super-state. The speech led to 'Euro-scepticism' becoming respectable in Britain rather than merely dissident, and hostility to 'European federalism' shaped the consequent public debate.

Thatcher's broad brush portrayed a European 'political class' which was sceptical of capitalism and credulous about government compared to a British political tradition whose devotion to individual freedom and enterprise was more resilient. These convictions reflected her enthusiasm for entrepreneurial values, and Thatcher's flagship policy of privatizing

MARGARET THATCHER (b. 1925)

1946 Graduates in Natural Sciences from University of Oxford.

1953 Called to the Bar of England and Wales.

1959 Elected MP (Conservative) for Finchley.

1970–4 Education Secretary.

1972 Britain's Conservative government signs the Treaty of Accession to the European Economic Community.

Feb 1974 Conservatives lose the general election and are also defeated in the subsequent (Oct) election.

1975 Elected Conservative Party leader.

1979 Forms a government following general-election victory; re-elected in 1983 and 1987.

Nov 1990 Resigns the premiership, unwillingly, and becomes increasingly critical of her successor, John Major.

1990 Awarded Order of Merit.

1992 Resigns as MP, becomes Baroness Thatcher of Kesteven.

1995 Installed as Lady of the Garter, Britain's most ancient chivalric order.

nationalized industries impelled the British economy towards deregulation, greater competition and convergence with American business practice. The speech urges European governments to pay more towards NATO defence costs, as the US had been urging, and the claim that North America is also 'Europe', because of some migrants' origins, is enjoyably mischievous.

This undiplomatic offensive is suffused with Thatcher's suspicion of consensus – in this case that of a European leadership typified as arid, parochial and backward-looking – and the Community is summoned to wider horizons. That international perspective, however, is dominated by the Atlanticist attitudes of Britain and the US, countries which are presented as exemplary in their political wisdom and economic virtue.

Britain's opt-out clauses agreed under the Maastricht Treaty (1992) preserved the pound sterling and the Bank of England, but by then Thatcher had been rejected by a Conservative Party which feared her 'divisiveness'. Europe was central to that drama. In the summer of 1989 Nigel Lawson, as chancellor, and Geoffrey Howe, then foreign secretary, forced an isolated Thatcher to agree in principle to Britain joining the Exchange Rate Mechanism, the Single Currency's designed precursor. Howe resigned from the government in November 1990 and attacked her European convictions as one aspect of a persistent failure to consult her colleagues. Later that month the Cabinet forced her resignation. The strenuous individualism which is lauded in this speech and which marked its delivery had both made, and unmade, Margaret Thatcher's career.

Europe is not the creation of the Treaty of Rome. Nor is the European idea the property of any group or institution. We British are as much heirs to the legacy of European culture as any other nation . . . We in Britain are rightly proud of the way in which, since Magna Carta in the year 1215, we have pioneered and developed representative institutions to stand as bastions of freedom . . . But we know that without the European legacy of political ideas we could not have achieved as much as we did. From classical and medieval thought we have borrowed that concept of the rule of law which marks out a civilized society from barbarism.

'Europe is not the creation of the Treaty of Rome'

But we British have in a very special way contributed to Europe. Over the centuries we have fought to prevent Europe from falling under the dominance of a single power . . . Had it not been for that willingness to fight and to die, Europe would have been united long before now – but not in liberty, not in justice . . .

The European Community is one manifestation of European identity, but it is not the only one. We must never forget that east of the Iron Curtain, people who once enjoyed a full share of European culture, freedom and identity have been cut off from their roots . . .

Nor should we forget that European values have helped to make the United States of America into the valiant defender of freedom which she has become . . .

British involvement in Europe . . . is as valid and strong as ever. Yes, we have looked to wider horizons – as have others – and thank goodness for that because Europe never would have prospered and never will prosper as a narrow-minded, inward-looking club.

The European Community belongs to all its members. It must reflect the traditions and aspirations of all its members. Britain does not dream of some cosy, isolated existence on the fringes . . . Our destiny is in Europe, as part of the Community. This is not to say that our future lies only in Europe, but nor does that of France or Spain or, indeed, of any other member.

'Europe . . . never will prosper as a narrow-minded, inward-looking club'

The Community is not an end in itself. Nor is it an institutional device to be constantly modified according to the dictates of some abstract intellectual concept. Nor must it be ossified by endless regulation. The European Community is a practical means by which Europe can ensure the future prosperity and security of its people in a world in which there are many other powerful nations and groups of nations . . .

Willing and active cooperation between independent sovereign states is the best way to build a successful European Community. To try to suppress nationhood and concentrate power at the centre of a European conglomerate would be highly damaging . . . Europe will be stronger precisely because it has France as France, Spain as Spain, Britain as Britain, each with its own customs, traditions and identity. It would be folly to try to fit them into some sort of identikit European personality . . .

Working together more closely does not require power to be centralized in Brussels or decisions to be taken by an appointed bureaucracy. We have not successfully rolled back the frontiers of the state in Britain, only to see them re-imposed at a European level with a European super-state exercising a new dominance from Brussels . . . The Treaty of Rome itself was intended as a Charter for Economic Liberty. But that is not how it has always been read, still less applied. The lesson of the economic history of Europe in the 70s and 80s is that central planning and detailed control do not work and that personal endeavour and initiative do.

By getting rid of barriers, by making it possible for companies to operate on a European scale, we can best compete with the United States, Japan and other new economic powers emerging in Asia and elsewhere. And that means action to free markets, action to widen choice, action to reduce government intervention . . .

The key issue is not whether there should be a European Central Bank. The immediate and practical requirements are:

– to implement the Community's commitment to free movement of capital – in Britain, we have it;

– the abolition through the Community of exchange controls – in Britain, we abolished them in 1979;

– to establish a genuinely free market in financial services in banking, insurance, investment . . .

'Willing and active cooperation between independent sovereign states is the best way to build a successful European Community'

It would be a betrayal if, while breaking down constraints on trade within Europe, the Community were to erect greater external protection . . .

We have a responsibility . . . towards the less developed countries. They need not only aid; more than anything, they need improved trading opportunities if they are to gain the dignity of growing economic strength and independence . . .

The fact is things are going our way: the democratic model of a free-enterprise society has proved itself superior; freedom is on the offensive, a peaceful offensive the world over, for the first time in my lifetime.

We must strive to maintain the United States' commitment to Europe's defence. And that means recognizing the burden on their resources of the world role they undertake and their point that their allies should bear the full part of the defence of freedom, particularly as Europe grows wealthier . . . It is not an institutional problem. It is not a problem of drafting. It is something at once simpler and more profound: it is a question of political will and political courage, of convincing people in all our countries that we cannot rely for ever on others for our defence . . .

Let Europe be a family of nations, understanding each other better, appreciating each other more, doing more together but relishing our national identity no less than our common European endeavour. Let us have a Europe which plays its full part in the wider world, which looks outward not inward, and which preserves that Atlantic community – that Europe on both sides of the Atlantic – which is our noblest inheritance and our greatest strength. ’

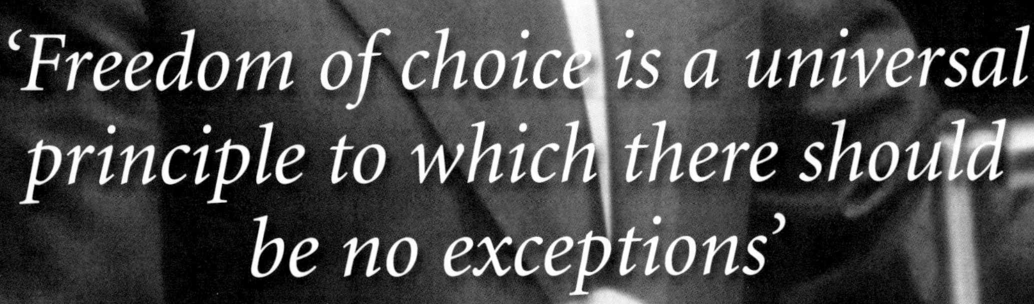

'Freedom of choice is a universal principle to which there should be no exceptions'

Mikhail Gorbachev

(b. 1925)

THE SOVIET LEADER ADDRESSES THE GENERAL ASSEMBLY OF THE UNITED NATIONS; NEW YORK, 7 DECEMBER 1988

Traces of Marxist-Leninist vocabulary could still be heard when Mikhail Gorbachev spoke in public. His rise through the Soviet Communist hierarchy had after all obliged him to espouse an official state doctrine which maintained that individuals' beliefs reflected their socio-economic 'interests', and that the consequent 'contradictions' were therefore 'objectively conditioned'. But these old categories of thought were now submerged within a wider programme of *glasnost* (openness) and *perestroika* (restructuring), which subverted practically everything the USSR had stood for ever since its establishment in 1922.

Gorbachev's conversion to democratization and free-market reforms meant that he was a new version of 'Soviet Man'. By the end of 1988 new laws allowed private ownership of businesses, and preparations were being made for the following year's multi-party elections. Foreign-policy changes reflected the USSR's inability to match US levels of defence spending, and Gorbachev hoped that a reduction in the arms budget would relieve the pressures on the Soviet economy. In December 1987 he therefore signed the Intermediate-Range Nuclear Forces Treaty (INF) with the US, which would eliminate the two countries' ground-launched ballistic and cruise missiles, both nuclear and conventional. This left the US and NATO with a strategic superiority over the USSR in respect of other nuclear weaponry. But the USSR's advantage in conventional weapons remained immense, and Gorbachev's announcement at the UN of a reduction in their numbers, along with a withdrawal of some forces from Eastern Europe and a deep cut in the number of Soviet soldiers, constituted an immense concession. The year 1988 also saw the start of the Soviet withdrawal from Afghanistan, where, following a 1979 invasion and subsequent occupation

MIKHAIL GORBACHEV (b. 1931)

1950–3 Studies at Moscow University.

1953 Joins Communist Party of the Soviet Union (CPSU).

1970 Appointed first secretary for the Stavropol region, northern Caucasus.

1971 Joins CPSU Central Committee.

1978 Appointed secretary of agriculture in Central Committee.

1980–91 Member of the Politburo.

1985–91 General secretary of CPSU.

April 1986 Chernobyl nuclear reactor explosion shows Soviet technological obsolescence.

March–April 1989 Democratic elections held for the Congress of People's Deputies.

1990–1 President of the Soviet Union.

1990 Awarded Nobel Peace Prize.

Aug 1991 Abortive coup attempts to stop USSR's dissolution.

25 Dec 1991 Resigns presidency.

in support of a Marxist regime, the USSR had become mired in a war waged by *mujahidin* 'freedom fighters'.

By refusing to lend Soviet support to the beleaguered government of the GDR (East Germany) Gorbachev ensured its swift collapse in November 1989, and the ensuing year of democratic revolutions witnessed the overthrow of communist regimes right across Central and Eastern Europe. The fast pace of change exhilarated Gorbachev's admirers, but in the short term his reforms aggravated the Soviet economic crisis rather than solving it. His speech notes resistance in 'certain influential circles', and these included internal critics who thought the reforms had diminished Soviet prestige and would lead to the USSR's dissolution. Gorbachev's ambition was for a new federal structure which would contain Russia and the other nationalities within a continuing union, and he was notably resistant to the independence of the Baltic states of Estonia, Latvia and Lithuania. But by 1991 he had been overtaken by events. Soviet reactionaries, hoping to preserve the old-style USSR, launched a putsch in August and detained the president at his dacha. The coup failed but Gorbachev's authority was diminished. By the time of his December resignation the ex-USSR had become the Commonwealth of Independent States, with the Russian Federation as just one among eleven autonomous countries. Gorbachev's UN address convinced the world community that a new era had started in the history of international relations, but by 2008 his earlier optimism had faded: 'We had ten years after the Cold War to build a new world order, and yet we squandered them.'

Two great revolutions, the French Revolution of 1789 and the Russian Revolution of 1917, have exerted a powerful influence on the actual nature of the historical process . . . That is a very great spiritual wealth, but . . . it is necessary to seek different roads towards the future . . . Today we have entered an era when progress will be based on the interests of all mankind . . .

The history of the past centuries and millennia has been a history of almost ubiquitous wars . . . They occurred in the clash of social and political interests and national hostility, be it from ideological or religious incompatibility . . . However, parallel with the process of wars . . . another process, just as objectively conditioned, was in motion and gaining force: the process of the emergence of a mutually connected and integral world.

'Force and the threat of force can no longer be, and should not be, instruments of foreign policy'

Further world progress is now possible only through the search for a consensus of all mankind, in movement towards a new world order . . . The formula of development 'at another's expense' is becoming outdated. In light of present realities, genuine progress by infringing upon the rights and liberties of man and peoples, or at the expense of nature, is impossible . . . Behind differences in social structure, in way of life, and in the preference for certain values, stand interests. There is no getting away from that, but neither is there any getting away from the need to find a balance of interests within an international framework . . . It is evident that force and the threat of force can no longer be, and should not be, instruments of foreign policy . . .

Freedom of choice is a universal principle to which there should be no exceptions . . . The variety of socio-political structures which has grown over the last decades . . . presupposes respect for other people's views, tolerance, a preparedness to see phenomena that are different as not necessarily bad or hostile . . .

The de-ideologization of interstate relations has become a demand of the new stage. We are not giving up our convictions, philosophy or traditions . . . Yet we are not going to shut ourselves up within the range of our values . . . Each should prove the advantages of his own system, his own way of life and values, but not through words or propaganda alone, but through real deeds as well. That is, indeed, an honest struggle of ideology, but it must not be carried over into mutual relations between states. Otherwise we simply will not be able to solve a single world problem; arrange broad, mutually advantageous and equitable cooperation between peoples; manage rationally the achievements of the scientific and technical revolution; transform world economic relations; protect the environment; overcome underdevelopment; or put an end to hunger, disease, illiteracy and other mass ills. Finally, in that case, we will not manage to eliminate the nuclear threat and militarism . . .

We must search jointly for a way to achieve the supremacy of the common human idea over the countless multiplicity of centrifugal forces, to preserve the vitality of civilization . . .

Our country is undergoing a truly revolutionary upsurge . . . In order to involve society in implementing the plans for restructuring, it had to be made more truly democratic. Under the badge of democratization, restructuring has now encompassed politics, the economy, spiritual life and ideology . . . We completed the first stage of the process of political reform with the recent decisions by the USSR Supreme Soviet on amendments to the Constitution and the adoption of the Law on Elections. Without stopping, we embarked upon the second stage of this, at which the most important task will be working on the interaction between the central government and the republics . . . and reorganizing the power of the Soviets locally . . .

Soviet democracy is to acquire a firm, normative base. This means such acts as the Law on Freedom of Conscience, on *glasnost*, on public associations and organizations, and on much else. There are now no people in places of imprisonment in the country who have been sentenced for their political or religious convictions . . .

Today I can inform you of the following: the Soviet Union has made a decision on reducing its armed forces. In the next two years, their numerical strength will be reduced by 500,000 persons, and the volume of conventional arms will also be cut considerably. These reductions will be made on a unilateral basis . . . By agreement with our allies in the Warsaw Pact, we have made the decision to withdraw six tank divisions from the GDR, Czechoslovakia and Hungary, and to disband them by 1991 . . . The Soviet forces situated in those countries will be cut by 50,000 persons, and their arms by 5000 tanks. All remaining Soviet divisions on the territory of our allies will be reorganized. They will be given a different structure from today's which will become unambiguously defensive . . .

Relations between the Soviet Union and the United States span 5½ decades . . . For too long they were built under the banner of confrontation . . . The USSR and the United States created the biggest nuclear missile arsenals, but after objectively recognizing their responsibility, they were able to be the first to conclude an agreement on the reduction and physical destruction of a proportion of these weapons, which threatened both themselves and everyone else. Both sides possess the biggest and the most refined military secrets. But it is they who have laid the basis for, and are developing a system of, mutual verification with regard to both the destruction and the limiting and banning of armaments production . . . We are talking first and foremost about consistent progress towards concluding a treaty on a 50 per cent reduction in strategic offensive weapons . . . ; about elaborating a convention on the elimination of chemical weapons . . . ; and about talks on reducing conventional weapons and armed forces in Europe . . .

'The Soviet Union has made a decision on reducing its armed forces'

The movement towards a nuclear-free and non-violent world is capable of fundamentally transforming the political and spiritual face of the planet, but only the very first steps have been taken. Moreover, in certain influential circles, they have been greeted with mistrust and are meeting resistance . . . Profound contradictions and the roots of many conflicts have not disappeared. The fact remains that the formation of the peaceful period will take place in conditions of the existence and rivalry of various socio-economic and political systems. However, the meaning of our international efforts, and one of the key tenets of the new thinking, is precisely to impart to this rivalry the quality of sensible competition in conditions of respect for freedom of choice and a balance of interests. '

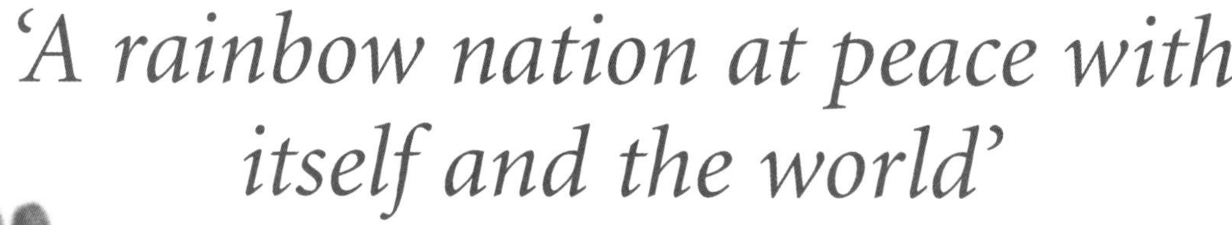

'A rainbow nation at peace with itself and the world'

Nelson Mandela

(b. 1918)

THE PRESIDENT OF SOUTH AFRICA PRAISES FREEDOM, PEACE AND RECONCILIATION IN HIS INAUGURAL SPEECH; PRETORIA, 10 MAY 1994

International opinion and economic forces had combined to undermine the 'pernicious ideology' described in Nelson Mandela's inaugural address as president, despite the apartheid regime's long-term commitment to the suppression of internal dissent. Over a thousand were injured and 176 killed in the township of Soweto in June 1976 during mass protests against the compulsory teaching of Afrikaans, and in September 1977 Steve Biko, a prominent activist, was killed while in police custody. South Africa's white leaders seemed indifferent to moral condemnation and diplomatic protests, but the facts of economic life were moving against them to decisive effect.

It was becoming clear to the state that apartheid was becoming increasingly unenforceable. This, however, did not stop it embarking on South Africa's most repressive period yet, from 1984 to 1989. South Africa's attempt to defeat the rebellion in its colony of Namibia, where an independence movement was being supported by Cuban troops and by neighbouring Angola, proved to be financially disastrous for the National Party's government. The withdrawal of South African forces from Namibia in 1988 prefigured the government's ultimate abandonment of authority, with the economy also suffering from the cumulative effect of UN sanctions and the disengagement of much international capital.

Mandela's inaugural address showed the grace and humanity which had by now made him one of the world's most universally admired individuals. His moral stature was emblematic of a more widespread climate of multiracial tolerance in many parts of the developed world during the late 20th century, and the terms of his speech, with its commitment to the extirpation of all forms of prejudice, make it a significantly humanist document. After his release from prison Mandela had committed himself, and the ANC, to the cause of reconciliation, and the organization's armed struggle was suspended. The multi-party

NELSON ROLIHLAHLA MANDELA (b. 1918)

Timeline continued from page 94

1982 Transferred from Robben Island to Pollsmoor prison.

2 Feb 1990 President F.W. de Klerk lifts the ban on the ANC and other anti-apartheid organizations.

11 Feb 1990 Released from Victor Verster prison, where he had been detained during the last 14 months of his captivity.

1991 Elected president of the ANC at its National Conference.

1992 A whites-only referendum approves the National Party continuing negotiations with the ANC.

June 1992 Boipatong massacre.

10 April 1993 Assassination of Chris Hani.

1993 Awarded Nobel Peace Prize, along with F.W. de Klerk.

27 April 1994 In South Africa's first one person, one vote general election the ANC gains 62.65 per cent of the vote.

1994–9 President of South Africa.

negotiations which followed from 1990 to 1994 were nonetheless often fraught. Following the massacre in the Boipatong township in June 1992, when the residents of a local hostel killed over 40 people, Mandela suspended negotiations with the government and blamed it for being implicated in the slaughter. The revelation of a far-right plot to derail South Africa's transition to a multi-party democracy – a conspiracy which claimed the life of the ANC's Chris Hani – concentrated minds and the parties resumed their talks on the way ahead. Following the general election of 1994 Mandela formed a 'government of national unity', which included representatives of all ethnic groups and in which F.W. de Klerk, formerly the state president, served as a vice president.

The ANC was now a party of government and had abandoned its earlier commitment to socialism, but labour disputes and high levels of violence still kept foreign investors away. South Africa remained a country scarred by the isolation and divisiveness which had been apartheid's explicit aim, but the compelling personality of its president showed how bitterness could be healed through forgiveness and by the provision of common purpose. As president, Mandela established the Truth and Reconciliation Commission in order to investigate human rights abuses in as non-partisan a way as possible. He also understood how important symbolic actions could be in the business of building a nation, and when South Africa hosted the Rugby World Cup in 1995, he encouraged the whole country to support the Springboks – the national side whose mostly white faces had once made them an intrinsic part of the old supremacy's sporting establishment. The Springboks won the tournament and the widespread local enthusiasm for the victory showed that a South African multiracial renaissance was a genuine possibility. Mandela's grace could also take a highly personal form. Dr Percy Yutar, the state prosecutor in the trial which had condemned him to life imprisonment in 1964, was invited by Mandela to lunch in the presidential palace and told that he had only been doing his job. It was a characteristic touch.

Today, all of us do, by our presence here, and by our celebrations in other parts of our country and the world, confer glory and hope to newborn liberty.

Out of the experience of an extraordinary human disaster that lasted too long, must be born a society of which all humanity will be proud.

Our daily deeds as ordinary South Africans must produce an actual South African reality that will reinforce humanity's belief in justice, strengthen its confidence in the nobility of the human soul and sustain all our hopes for a glorious life for all.

'Out of the experience of an extraordinary human disaster that lasted too long must be born a society of which all humanity will be proud'

All this we owe both to ourselves and to the peoples of the world who are so well represented here today.

To my compatriots, I have no hesitation in saying that each one of us is as intimately attached to the soil of this beautiful country as are the famous jacaranda trees of Pretoria and the mimosa trees of the bushveld.

Each time one of us touches the soil of this land, we feel a sense of personal renewal. The national mood changes as the seasons change.

We are moved by a sense of joy and exhilaration when the grass turns green and the flowers bloom.

That spiritual and physical oneness we all share with this common homeland explains the depth of the pain we all carried in our hearts as we saw our country tear itself apart in a terrible conflict, and as we saw it spurned, outlawed and isolated by the peoples of the world, precisely because it has become the universal base of the pernicious ideology and practice of racism and racial oppression.

We, the people of South Africa, feel fulfilled that humanity has taken us back into its bosom, that we, who were outlaws not so long ago, have today been given the rare privilege to be host to the nations of the world on our own soil.

'Each time one of us touches the soil of this land, we feel a sense of personal renewal'

We thank all our distinguished international guests for having come to take possession with the people of our country of what is, after all, a common victory for justice, for peace, for human dignity.

We trust that you will continue to stand by us as we tackle the challenges of building peace, prosperity, non-sexism, non-racialism and democracy.

We deeply appreciate the role that the masses of our people and their political mass democratic, religious, women, youth, business, traditional and other leaders have played to bring about this conclusion. Not least among them is my Second Deputy President, the Honourable F.W. de Klerk.

We would also like to pay tribute to our security forces, in all their ranks, for the distinguished role they have played in securing our first democratic elections and the transition to democracy, from bloodthirsty forces which still refuse to see the light.

The time for the healing of the wounds has come.

The moment to bridge the chasms that divide us has come. The time to build is upon us.

We have, at last, achieved our political emancipation. We pledge ourselves to liberate all our people from the continuing bondage of poverty, deprivation, suffering, gender and other discrimination.

We succeeded to take our last steps to freedom in conditions of relative peace. We commit ourselves to the construction of a complete, just and lasting peace.

We have triumphed in the effort to implant hope in the breasts of the millions of our people. We enter into a covenant that we shall build the society in which all South Africans, both black and white, will be able to walk tall, without any fear in their hearts, assured of their inalienable right to human dignity – a rainbow nation at peace with itself and the world.

As a token of its commitment to the renewal of our country, the new Interim Government of National Unity will, as a matter of urgency, address the issue of amnesty for various categories of our people who are currently serving terms of imprisonment.

We dedicate this day to all the heroes and heroines in this country and the rest of the world who sacrificed in many ways and surrendered their lives so that we could be free.

Their dreams have become reality. Freedom is their reward.

We are both humbled and elevated by the honour and privilege that you, the people of South Africa, have bestowed on us, as the first president of a united, democratic, non-racial and non-sexist South Africa, to lead our country out of the valley of darkness.

We understand it still that there is no easy road to freedom.

We know it well that none of us acting alone can achieve success.

We must therefore act together as a united people, for national reconciliation, for nation building, for the birth of a new world.

Let there be justice for all.

Let there be peace for all.

Let there be work, bread, water and salt for all.

Let each know that for each the body, the mind and the soul have been freed to fulfil themselves.

Never, never and never again shall it be that this beautiful land will again experience the oppression of one by another and suffer the indignity of being the skunk of the world.

Let freedom reign.

The sun shall never set on so glorious a human achievement.

God bless Africa!

'The Ireland I now inhabit is one that these Irish contemporaries have helped to imagine'

Seamus Heaney

(b. 1939)

THE IRISH POET'S ACCEPTANCE SPEECH ON RECEIVING THE NOBEL PRIZE FOR LITERATURE; STOCKHOLM, 7 DECEMBER 1995

On 31 August 1994 the Irish Republican Army (IRA) announced a cessation of its military operations with effect from midnight. One phase of the 'peace process' had ended and another had begun.

The Sunningdale Agreement of 1973, referred to here by Seamus Heaney, was a British government attempt at solving Northern Ireland's crisis: the local Stormont Assembly, suspended since 1972, was to be revived; the province's executive would be a devolved administration with the Unionist majority agreeing to share power with its local political opponents; Irish government ministers and Dáil representatives would sit alongside members of the Northern Ireland Executive and Assembly in a Council of Ireland. The Unionist leadership initially endorsed the agreement but the Protestant workforce rejected it. A general strike by the Ulster Workers' Council ensured the agreement's demise, and the province collapsed into the cycle of retaliatory Protestant–Catholic violence which had consumed the six counties ever since the onset of the 'Troubles' in 1968. The Downing Street Declaration of 15 December 1993 broke the impasse: the British government stated that it had 'no selfish strategic or economic interest in Northern Ireland' and the government of Éire formally agreed that a united Ireland required the consent of a majority of the Northern Irish electorate.

SEAMUS HEANEY (b. 1939)

1961 Graduates from Queen's University, Belfast.

1965 Publishes his first collection of verse, *Eleven Poems.*

1966–72 Lecturer in English literature, Queen's University, Belfast.

1970–1 Visiting lecturer, University of California, Berkeley.

1975 Publishes *North.*

1980 *Selected Poems 1965–1975.*

1982 Appointed part-time lecturer, Harvard University.

1984 Elected to the Boylston Chair of Rhetoric and Oratory, Harvard University.

1984 *Station Island; Sweeney Astray*, a translation from Middle Irish.

1988 *The Government of the Tongue* (collected essays).

1989–94 Professor of Poetry, University of Oxford.

1990 *New Selected Poems 1966–1987.*

1991 Publishes *The Cure at Troy*: a version of Sophocles' *Philoctetes*, and his verse collection *Seeing Things.*

1995 *The Redress of Poetry* (collected essays).

1995 Awarded Nobel Prize for Literature.

1998 *Opened Ground: Poems, 1966–1996.*

1999 *Beowulf: A New Translation.*

Heaney was right in thinking that a quarter century of 'hardening attitudes' was ending, but further progress remained tortuous. The Good Friday Agreement (10 April 1998) set the terms for a devolved and inclusive government, along with troop reductions and civil rights for the province's Catholic population. An elected Northern Ireland Assembly and a power-sharing executive came into being, with Unionists agreeing to work with the Irish republican Sinn Féin – a party with close IRA links. Continuing Unionist suspicions focused on the IRA's retention of weaponry, and the devolved arrangements were suspended between 2002 and 2007. In 2005 the IRA embarked on a complete decommissioning of its arsenal – a process overseen by an international commission. The reconciled leadership of Sinn Féin and of the Democratic Unionist Party formed a joint administration in 2007 and, following that year's elections, the Assembly reconvened. 'Operation Banner', the British army's operation in Northern Ireland, came to an end and the province was at peace.

In this speech Heaney traces the connection between his own imaginative evolution and the often tragic dimension to Ireland's politics. The heavily stressed lines of his verse in *North* communicate the tension of 1970s Ireland, and poetry's linguistic ability to heal constriction and transcend division has been a constant Heaney preoccupation. Born to a Catholic family in the rural North, he has found themes of epic significance in the region's landscape and its people's endurance, while the influence of both Anglo-Saxon and Irish-language literature on his poetry accounts for its distinctively 'northern' idiom. The straightening up that he described in Stockholm includes a poetic shift towards the spacious and lyrical, with *Station Island* showing Dante's influence and *Seeing Things* absorbing echoes of Virgil. His journey into 'the wideness of language' continues to transformative effect.

'

In the 1940s, when I was the eldest child of an ever-growing family in rural Co. Derry, we crowded together in the three rooms of a traditional thatched farmstead and lived a kind of den-life which was more or less emotionally and intellectually proofed against the outside world . . . When a wind stirred in the beeches, it also stirred an aerial wire attached to the topmost branch of the chestnut tree. Down it swept . . . right on into the innards of our wireless set where a little pandemonium of burbles and squeaks would suddenly give way to the voice of a BBC newsreader . . . We could pick up . . . the names of bombers and of cities bombed, of war fronts and army divisions . . . of casualties suffered and advances made. But even so, none of the news of these world-spasms entered me as terror . . . The wartime, in other words, was pre-reflective time for me . . .

Then as the years went on and my listening became more deliberate, I would climb up on an arm of our big sofa to get my ear closer to the wireless speaker . . . and in that intent proximity to the dial I grew familiar with the names of foreign stations . . . I had already begun a journey into the wideness of the world beyond. This in turn became a journey into the wideness of language . . . I credit poetry for making this space-walk possible. I credit poetry . . . for making possible a fluid and restorative relationship between the mind's centre and its circumference, between the child gazing at the word 'Stockholm' on the face of the radio dial and the man facing the faces that he meets in Stockholm at this most privileged moment . . .

I found myself in the mid-1970s in another small house. This time in Co. Wicklow south of Dublin, with a young family of my own and a slightly less imposing radio set, listening to the rain in the trees and to the news of bombings closer to home – not only those by the Provisional IRA in Belfast but equally atrocious assaults in Dublin by loyalist paramilitaries . . .

There are times . . . when we want the poem to be not only pleasurably right but also compellingly wise, not only a surprising variation played upon the world, but a retuning of the world itself . . . This is the want I was experiencing . . . in Co. Wicklow . . .

'There are times . . . when we want the poem to be not only pleasurably right but also compellingly wise'

Until the British government caved in to the strong-arm tactics of the Ulster loyalist workers after the Sunningdale Conference in 1974, a well-disposed mind could still hope to make sense of the circumstances, to balance what was promising with what was destructive . . . For the 20 long years between then and the ceasefires of August 1994, such a hope proved impossible. The violence from below was productive of nothing but a retaliatory violence from above . . . and people settled in to a quarter century of . . . hardening attitudes and narrowing possibilities that were the natural result of political solidarity, traumatic suffering and sheer emotional self-protectiveness . . .

'People settled in to a quarter century of . . . hardening attitudes and narrowing possibilities'

It is difficult at times to repress the thought that history is about as instructive as an abbatoir . . . Which is why for years I was bowed to the desk like some monk bowed over his prie-dieu, some dutiful contemplative . . . constrained by his obedience to his rule to repeat the effort and the posture. Blowing up sparks for meagre heat. Forgetting faith, straining towards good works . . .

Then finally and happily . . . I straightened up. I began a few years ago to try to make space in my reckoning and imagining for the marvellous as well as for the murderous . . .

The century has witnessed the defeat of Nazism by force of arms; but the erosion of the Soviet regimes was caused, among other things, by the sheer persistence, beneath the imposed ideological conformity, of cultural values . . . The way in which walls have come down in Europe . . . inspires a hope that new possibility can still open up in Ireland as well . . .

When the poet W.B. Yeats stood on this platform more than 70 years ago, Ireland was emerging from the throes of a traumatic civil war . . . Yeats barely alluded to the civil war in his Nobel speech . . . He came to Sweden to tell the world that the local works of poets and dramatists had been as important to the transformation of his native place and times as the ambushes of guerrilla armies; and his boast in that elevated prose was essentially the same as the one he would make . . . in his poem 'The Municipal Gallery Revisited'. There Yeats presents himself among the portraits and heroic narrative paintings which celebrate the events and personalities of recent history and all of a sudden realizes that something truly epoch-making has occurred:

> "This is not," I say,
> "The dead Ireland of my youth, but an Ireland
> The poets have imagined, terrible and gay."

And the poem concludes . . . :

> Think where man's glory most begins and ends,
> And say my glory was I had such friends.

. . . I ask you to do what Yeats asked his audience to do and think of the achievement of Irish poets and dramatists and novelists over the past 40 years, among whom I am proud to count great friends . . . The Ireland I now inhabit is one that these Irish contemporaries have helped to imagine . . .

When the bard Demodocus sings of the fall of Troy and of the slaughter that accompanied it, Odysseus weeps and Homer says that his tears were like the tears of a wife on a battlefield weeping for the death of a fallen husband:

> At the sight of the man panting and dying there,
> she slips down to enfold him, crying out;
> then feels the spears, prodding her back and shoulders,
> and goes bound into slavery and grief.
> Piteous weeping wears away her cheeks:
> but no more piteous than Odysseus' tears,
> cloaked as they were, now, from the company.

. . . The callousness of those spear shafts on the woman's back and shoulders survives time and translation . . . But there is another kind of adequacy which is specific to lyric poetry . . . It has to do . . . with the buoyancy generated by cadence and tone and rhyme and stanza . . . It is this which keeps the poet's ear straining to hear the totally persuasive voice behind all the other informing voices. Which is a way of saying that I have never quite climbed down from the arm of that sofa. ’

'Socialism or death!'

Fidel Castro

(b. 1926)

CUBA'S LEADER SPEAKS ON THE OCCASION OF THE 40TH ANNIVERSARY OF HIS COUNTRY'S SOCIALIST REVOLUTION; SANTIAGO DE CUBA, 1 JANUARY 1999

'Socialism or death!'

The regular delivery of speeches lasting several hours was one of the methods used by Fidel Castro in order to maintain high levels of revolutionary consciousness among Cuba's population and thereby to keep his grip on power. A Castro oration was never an event for the faint-hearted, and his audiences needed to be possessed of physical stamina as well as ideological rectitude.

His commemoration of the Cuban revolution's 40th anniversary showed that Castro, then in his 73rd year, could still combine Marxist doctrine with nationalist sentiment to potent effect, and the speech exemplifies some of his most characteristic certitudes. Cuba's revolutionary narrative merges with world historical trends, and Castro's urgent delineation of that process involves his listeners in a continuing struggle – one whose global victory is assured but whose successful resolution nonetheless requires their lasting commitment. Castro is speaking in the city where he first proclaimed victory for the revolution, and there is a theatrical quality to his re-creation of past emotions. He evokes the revolutionaries' nostalgia for the intensity of guerrilla solidarity, and their success is attributed to the force of ideas as well as cleverness in strategy. The revolution, in Castro's dramatic rendition, acquires its own secular liturgy: the sacrifices of the dead are remembered with gratitude and thanks are given for past victories. Financial markets' instability anticipates capitalism's collapse – and the world's subsequent salvation through socialism.

Castro's conviction of his own destiny was obvious right from the start of Cuba's revolution. At his trial in 1953, following the failure of an attack on the Moncada Barracks in Santiago de Cuba, he told the court: 'I warn you. I am just beginning . . . Condemn me. It does not matter. History will absolve me.' Once freed from prison, Castro formed the 26th of July Movement which, named after the day of that attack, organized the military struggle to overthrow President Fulgencia Batista, whose pro-American regime was closely associated with the Cuban elite's business interests.

FIDEL CASTRO (b. 1926)

1953 Sentenced to 15 years' imprisonment for participation in an attack (26 July) on Moncada Barracks, Santiago de Cuba; released under a general amnesty in 1955.

Dec 1956 Returns from Mexico to lead guerrilla warfare against the Cuban army.

1 Jan 1959 Proclaims victory of the Cuban revolution from a balcony on Santiago de Cuba's city hall; sworn in as premier (16 Feb).

1965 First secretary, Communist Party of Cuba.

1976 Becomes president of the Council of State (president of Cuba), and president of the Council of Ministers, following abolition of the office of premier.

Feb 2008 Resigns presidential offices and title of 'commander-in-chief' of Cuban armed forces.

The guerrilla army that Castro led to victory barely numbered 300 partisans, and his emphasis on the 'enormous difference in equipment and strength between the enemy and us' was no idle boast. He gained power as a nationalist resentful of US influence on Cuba, and the asceticism of Castro's revolutionary style was in conscious contrast to the lush decadence of Batista's corrupt government. Large-scale expropriation of Cuban property owned by US corporations, as well as agrarian reforms limiting individual land-ownership, placed the new Cuban regime on the extreme left, and the adoption of state socialism resulted in the emigration to the US of some one million Cubans whose many pressure groups became the fulcrum of the anti-Castro opposition. In December 1961 Castro officially declared himself to be a Marxist–Leninist and announced that Cuba would be ruled as a communist state. Two months later the US announced the imposition of a financial and commercial embargo on Cuba, a state which was now firmly allied with the USSR politically, economically and militarily. The 'special period', as Castro liked to call it, had started.

I am trying to recall that night of 1 January 1959; I am reliving and perceiving impressions and details as if everything were occurring at this very moment . . .

Our fleeting sadness at the moment of victory was nostalgia for the experiences we had lived through . . . We had to abandon our mountains, our rural life, our habits of absolute and obligatory austerity, our tense life of constant vigilance in the face of an enemy that could appear by land or air at any moment: a healthy, hard, pure life and one of great sacrifices and shared dangers, in which men become brothers and their best virtues flourish . . .

The enormous difference in equipment and strength between the enemy and us forced us to do the impossible . . . The infallible tactic of attacking the enemy when it was on the move was a key factor. The art of provoking those forces into moving out of their well-fortified and generally invulnerable positions became one of our commands' greatest skills . . . What we learned in the mountains and dense forest areas was applied in the lowland areas . . . The same method wound up being applied within the cities . . . That was how the plan was conceived to attack and take control of the garrison in the Santiago de Cuba plaza . . .

'Honour and eternal glory, infinite respect and affection to those that died to make possible the country's definitive independence'

Honour and eternal glory, infinite respect and affection to those that died to make possible the country's definitive independence: for all those who wrote that epic in the mountains, the plains and cities; to the underground guerrillas and fighters; to those who, after the triumph, died in other glorious missions or loyally gave up their youth and energies to the cause of justice, sovereignty and the redemption of their people . . .

The people of yesterday, illiterate and semi-literate, and with only a minimal political awareness, were capable of making the revolution, of defending the nation, of subsequently achieving an exceptional political consciousness and initiating a revolutionary process that is unparalleled in this hemisphere and in the world . . .

'Our eternal people have resisted 40 years of aggression, blockade, and economic, political and ideological warfare'

With the participation of three generations, our heroic people of yesterday and today, our eternal people have resisted 40 years of aggression, blockade, and economic, political and ideological warfare waged by the strongest and richest imperial power that has ever existed in the history of the world. The most extraordinary page of glory . . . has been written during these years of the special period, when we were left absolutely alone . . . 90 miles from the United States, and we decided to carry on.

Our people aren't any better than other peoples. Their historic greatness is derived from the singular fact of having been put to the test and having been able to withstand it. It's not a great people in and of itself; but rather a people which has made itself great, and its capacity to do so is born out of the greatness of the ideas and the righteousness of the causes it defends. There are no other causes like these, and there never have been . . .

The struggle begun on 1 January 1959 has inexorably turned into a struggle . . . for the interests of all humanity . . . But the solutions for humanity will not come from the good will of those who rule and exploit the world . . . The current system is unsustainable because it is based on blind and chaotic laws which are ruinous and destructive to society and nature . . . The most fanatical defenders of and believers in the market have converted it into a new religion. This is how the theology of the market emerged . . . Out of respect for the genuine religions practised honestly by billions of people throughout the world and out of respect for the genuine theologians, we could simply add that the theology of the market is sectarian, fundamentalist and not ecumenical . . .

'The most fanatical defenders of and believers in the market have converted it into a new religion'

New and unsuspected phenomena are emerging, ones which escape the control of governments and international financial institutions . . . The slightest carelessness can lead speculators to attack, devaluing the currency and liquidating hard currency reserves, built up over decades, in a matter of days . . . Absolutely no one is or can be safe. The wolves, grouped in packs and aided by computer programs, know where to attack, when to attack and why to attack . . .

The prevailing order flip-flops between inflation, recession, deflation, potential overproduction crises, and sustained slumps of basic products . . .

Economic crises and the absence of solutions within the established international economic system will destabilize many governments. We are living through a stage in which events move more quickly than consciousness of the realities under which we suffer. We must sow ideas and unmask deceit, sophism and hypocrisy, using methods and means which counteract the disinformation and institutionalized lies . . .

'May there be an end to the tyranny of an order that imposes blind, anarchic and chaotic principles'

May there be an end to the tyranny of an order that imposes blind, anarchic and chaotic principles, that is leading the human species towards the abyss . . .

The unfathomable differences between rich and poor within each country and between countries cannot continue growing. They must progressively diminish until they disappear. May merit, capacity, creative spirit, and what each individual actually contributes to the welfare of humanity, as opposed to theft, speculation and the exploitation of the weakest, determine differences. May humanism be genuinely practised, with concrete actions and not hypocritical slogans . . .

To all of our compatriots, and especially the young, I assure you that the next 40 years will be decisive for the world. Before you there are tasks that are incomparably more complex and difficult. New glorious goals await you; the honour of being Cuban revolutionaries demands it . . . In the ideological war, as in armed battles, there are casualties . . . I was recalling today that in the midst of the war . . . of all the young volunteers . . . one in ten was able to withstand it, but that one was worth ten, a hundred, a thousand. By strengthening awareness, forming character, educating the young in the difficult school of life in our era, sowing solid ideas, using arguments that are irrefutable, preaching through example and trusting in the honour of mankind, we can ensure that for every ten, nine remain in their battle posts alongside the flag, the revolution and the homeland. Socialism or death!

'By putting our money where our heart is . . . we will mould the world into a kinder, more loving shape'

Anita Roddick

(1942–2007)

THE FOUNDER OF THE BODY SHOP ADDRESSES THE INTERNATIONAL FORUM ON GLOBALIZATION; SEATTLE, 27 NOVEMBER 1999

During the late 20th century socialism was on the retreat both in the West and in large areas of the developing world. During this new phase in the evolution of market capitalism, global trading patterns became increasingly interlinked, and advances in information technology meant that deregulated financial markets could shift massive flows of capital across national boundaries within seconds. 'Globalization' boosted trade, encouraged productivity gains and lowered prices, but critics alleged that it exploited the low-paid, was indifferent to environmental concerns and subjected the Third World to a monopolistic form of capitalism. Many radicals within Western societies who wished to protest against this process joined voluntary bodies, charities and other non-governmental organizations, rather than the marginalized political parties of the left. The environmental movement itself grew out of the recognition that the world was interconnected, and an angry, if diffuse, international coalition of interests emerged. Anita Roddick was its impassioned advocate.

Roddick was an entrepreneur of genius who had pioneered 'ethical consumerism' through the Body Shop, the cosmetics company she had founded and which prohibited the use of animal-tested ingredients in the manufacture of its products. Feminist principle would lead her to castigate the traditional cosmetics industry as 'a monster selling unattainable dreams, one that lies, cheats and exploits women'. Having started as one shop in Brighton, the company became a multinational with some 2000 branches, but despite the dizzying scale of this expansion, Roddick stuck to 'fair trade' principles when dealing with her suppliers in evolving markets. The 'Queen of Green' campaigned against sweat shops and for workers' rights, and the Body Shop's use of locally sourced organic products aimed to support the economic base and cultural diversity of traditional societies. Roddick was a prominent supporter of debt relief for governments struggling to meet the conditions attached to International Monetary Fund and World Bank loans. She had a ready audience among the protesters who in November 1999 gathered in Seattle, where the ministerial

ANITA RODDICK (1942–2007)

1976 Founds Body Shop.

1990 Establishes Children on the Edge, a charity for the disadvantaged in Asia and Eastern Europe; co-founds *The Big Issue*, a magazine sold by the homeless and published on their behalf.

1984 Body Shop becomes a public company.

1990 Establishes Body Shop Foundation, a major donor to charities.

2003 Becomes Dame of the British Empire.

2006 Body Shop bought by L'Oréal, a company involved in animal testing and whose part-owner Nestlé has been criticized for its treatment of Third World producers; Roddick claims that the Body Shop will bring change within L'Oréal.

2007 Makes public that she has been diagnosed as having contracted hepatitis C following a 1971 blood transfusion.

conference of the World Trade Organization (WTO) was about to embark on a new round of international trade negotiations.

WTO officials pointed out that labour conditions and green issues were beyond their remit and that their sole aim was to discourage 'protectionism'. Government subsidies to endangered sectors and tariffs on competing imports were futile and reactionary measures. Economic development would eventually lead to higher-paid work, but in the meantime the only alternative to low-paid jobs in many areas of the Third World was no jobs at all. Roddick was vulnerable to these criticisms, but she was no mere 'New Age' theorist and had shown how business could provide moral leadership while also delivering a profit. Nuances of argument were lost, however, when over 40,000 protesters took to the Seattle streets on 30 November 1999 in a massive and pre-planned programme of civil disturbance which initially overwhelmed the local police and included acts of vandalism by anarchist groups. Order was restored later that day and the conference was able to convene. Negotiations, however, soon collapsed, with emerging economies rivalling older ones in their attachment to protectionist barriers.

We are in Seattle arguing for a world trade system that puts basic human rights and the environment at its core. We have the most powerful corporations of the world ranged against us. They own the media that informs us – or fails to inform us. And they probably own the politicians too. It's enough to make anybody feel a little edgy.

So here's a question for the world trade negotiators. Who is the system you are lavishing so much attention on supposed to serve? We can ask the same question of the gleaming towers of Wall Street or the City of London – and the powerful men and women who tinker with the money system which drives world trade. Who is this system for?

'The great global myth being that the current world trade system is for anything but money'

Let's look more closely. Every day the gleaming towers of high finance oversee a global flow of two trillion dollars . . . And the terrifying thing is that only three per cent of that has anything to do with trade at all. Let alone free trade between equal communities.

It has everything to do with money. The great global myth being that the current world trade system is for anything but money.

The other 97 per cent of the two trillion is speculation. It is froth – but froth with terrifying power over people's lives . . . We all of us, rich and poor, have to live with the insecurity caused by an out-of-control global casino with a built-in bias towards instability. Because it is instability that makes money for the money-traders . . .

I spend much of every year travelling around the world, talking to people in the front line of globalization: women, community farmers, children. I know how unrealistic these myths are. Not just in developing countries but right under our noses.

Like the small farmers of the USA . . . Globalization means that the subsidies go to the big farms, while the small family farms – the heart of so many American communities – go to the wall . . .

We have a world trading system that is blind to this kind of injustice. And as the powers of governments shrink, this system is, in effect, our new unelected, uncontrollable world government. One that outlaws our attempts to make things better . . .

The truth is that the WTO, and the group of unelected trade officials who run it, are now the world's highest court, with the right to overturn local laws and safety regulations wherever they say it 'interferes with trade'.

This is world government by default, but it is a blind government. It looks at the measurements of money, but it can't see anything else. It can recognize profits and losses, but it deliberately turns its face away from human rights, child labour or keeping the environment viable for future generations.

It is government without heart, and without heart you find the creativity of the human spirit starts to dwindle too . . .

The truth is that 'free trade' was originally about the freedom of communities to trade equally with each other. It was never intended to be what it is today. A licence for the big, the powerful and the rich to ride roughshod over the small, the weak and the poor . . .

'It is government without heart, and without heart you find the creativity of the human spirit starts to dwindle too'

Nobody could be more in favour of a global outlook than I am. Internationalism means that we can see into the dark corners of the world, and hold those companies to account when they are devastating forests or employing children as bonded labour. Globalization is the complete opposite, its rules pit country against country and workers against workers in the blinkered pursuit of international competitiveness.

Internationalism means we can link together at local level across the world, and use our power as consumers. Working together, across all sectors, we can turn businesses from private greed to public good. It means, even more important, that we can start understanding each other in a way that no generation has managed before.

Let's be clear about this. It's not trade we're against. It's exploitation and unchecked power . . . Businesses which forego profits to build communities, or keep production local rather than employing semi-slaves in distant sweatshops, risk losing business to cheaper competitors without such commitments, and being targeted for take-over by the slash-and-burn corporate raiders. Reinforced by the weight of the WTO . . .

Business has to be a force for social change. It is not enough to avoid hideous evil – it must, we must, actively do good . . . The rules have got to change. We need a radical alternative that puts people before profit . . . We must start measuring our success differently.

'Let's measure the success of places and corporations against how much they enhance human well-being'

If politicians, businesses and analysts only measure the bottom line – the growth in money – then it's not surprising the world is skewed. It's not surprising that the WTO is half-blind, recognizing slash-and-burn corporations but not the people they destroy. It's not surprising that it values flipping hamburgers . . . as a valuable activity, but takes no account of those other jobs – the caring, educating and loving work that we all know needs doing . . . Let's measure the success of places and corporations against how much they enhance human well-being . . . Measuring what really matters can give us the revolution in kindness we so desperately need. That's the real bottom line.

And finally, we must remember we already have power as consumers and as organizations forming strategic and increasingly influential alliances for change . . . If consumers won't buy, nothing on earth can make them. Just look at how European consumers have forced the biotech industry's back up against the wall.

We have to be political consumers, vigilante consumers. With the barrage of propaganda served up to us every day, we have to be. We must be wise enough so that – whatever they decide at the trade talks – we know where to put our energy and our money. No matter what we're told or cajoled to do, we must work together to get the truth out in cooperation for the best, not competition for the cheapest.

By putting our money where our heart is, refusing to buy the products which exploit, by forming powerful strategic alliances, we will mould the world into a kinder, more loving shape. ’

'Our policies only succeed when the realism is as clear as the idealism'

Tony Blair

(b. 1953)

THE BRITISH PRIME MINISTER ADDRESSES THE LABOUR PARTY IN THE WAKE OF 9/11; BRIGHTON, 2 OCTOBER 2001

'Our policies only succeed when the realism is as clear as the idealism'

This is the speech that propelled Tony Blair onto the world stage following his earlier successes in domestic politics. Labour had been recast in his own image as the face of competent and youthful modernity, and during those earlier years Blair was often criticized for being obsessed with presentation at the expense of policy. The rhythms of his speeches were staccato. Sentences were short. And often verbless. New Labour's series of sound bites were designed to capture media attention. And they did. Labour had long since been derided by the British press, but Blair's courtship of media proprietors and journalists transformed the way in which his party was portrayed. None of this would have happened, however, unless Labour's substance had changed. Clause IV of the party's constitution committed it to the classically socialist 'common ownership of the means of production and exchange'. Blair persuaded party members that this endorsement of state nationalization was irrelevant to Britain's economic needs and damaging to Labour's electoral prospects. The jettisoning of the clause in 1995 was a powerfully symbolic moment which prepared the way for a 'New Labour' converted to a free-enterprise economy. As premier, Blair encouraged the introduction of market-led solutions designed to promote individual choice and greater efficiency in public services. Personal rates of taxation remained low – by European standards – during his time in office, and a buoyant economy meant that his government presided over a massive increase in the health and education budgets. Personal ambition and wealth creation, rather than socialist ideology, became the Labour way of extending opportunity to 'the many, not the few'.

Blair's grasp of the significance of 9/11 was immediate, intuitive and intense. The terrorist attack on New York's Twin Towers would transform international relations and it was

TONY BLAIR (b. 1953)

1975 Graduates from University of Oxford; joins Labour Party shortly afterwards.

1976 Called to the Bar of England and Wales.

1983 Elected MP (Labour) for Sedgefield in Durham.

1988 Joins Labour Shadow Cabinet.

1992 Elected to Labour Party's National Executive Committee.

1992 Becomes shadow home secretary following Labour's defeat in the general election.

1994 Elected leader of the Labour Party.

1997 Becomes prime minister after Labour wins a landslide victory in the general election.

2001 Labour re-elected in general election.

2003 Awarded Congressional Gold Medal.

2005 Labour re-elected in general election.

Sept 2006 Forced to announce that he will resign within the next 12 months.

27 June 2007 Resigns premiership.

Britain's duty to support the US politically and militarily. US intelligence had concluded that the al-Qaeda network, led by Osama bin Laden, was responsible for the atrocity and that the attack had been planned from the organization's bases in Afghanistan, where it was being protected by a government run by the Taliban, an Islamist group. British naval forces were deployed in support of US air strikes launched against the bases five days after this speech's delivery. The Taliban government collapsed during the ensuing land war, in which British troops served alongside the US army, but despite the installation of a democratically elected government in 2004, the military coalition became involved in a prolonged war waged by Taliban guerrilla forces.

Blair's commitment to a morally directed foreign and military policy faced its most extreme test during the war in Iraq from 2003 onwards. President George W. Bush and his advisers had decided that the struggle against terrorism required the removal from power of Saddam Hussein, who, though a brutal president of Iraq and a threat to his neighbours, was not linked to the 9/11 attacks. Britain's military involvement in the campaign divided not just the Labour Party but the entire country. When Blair left office, the kaleidoscope he had described six years earlier remained shaken and the world had resisted his reordering.

In retrospect, the Millennium marked only a moment in time. It was the events of September 11 that marked a turning point in history, where we confront the dangers of the future and assess the choices facing humankind. It was a tragedy. An act of evil. From this nation goes our deepest sympathy and prayers for the victims and our profound solidarity with the American people. We were with you at the first. We will stay with you to the last . . .

'It was the events of September 11 that marked a turning point in history'

Our way of life is a great deal stronger and will last a great deal longer than the actions of fanatics . . . This is a battle with only one outcome: our victory not theirs . . . Be in no doubt: Bin Laden and his people organized this atrocity. The Taliban aid and abet him. He will not desist from further acts of terror. They will not stop helping him . . .

The action we take will be proportionate; targeted; we will do all we humanly can to avoid civilian casualties. But understand what we are dealing with . . . There is no compromise possible with such people, no meeting of minds, no point of understanding with such terror. Just a choice: defeat it or be defeated by it. And defeat it we must.

Today conflicts rarely stay within national boundaries. Today a tremor in one financial market is repeated in the markets of the world. Today confidence is global; either its presence or its absence . . . I have long believed this interdependence defines the new world we live in. People say: we are only acting because it's the USA that was attacked. Double standards, they say. But when Milosevic embarked on the ethnic cleansing of Muslims in Kosovo, we acted . . . and look what happened, we won, the refugees went home, the policies of ethnic cleansing were reversed . . .

And I tell you if Rwanda happened again as it did in 1993, when a million people were slaughtered in cold blood, we would have a moral duty to act there also . . . The power of the international community could, with our help, sort out the blight that is the continuing conflict in the Democratic Republic of the Congo, where three million people have died through war or famine in the last decade.

'The world community must show as much its capacity for compassion as for force'

A Partnership for Africa, between the developed and developing world, is there to be done if we find the will . . . We could defeat climate change if we chose to . . . With imagination, we could use or find the technologies that create energy without destroying our planet . . . And if we wanted to, we could breathe new life into the Middle East Peace Process and we must . . .

The world community must show as much its capacity for compassion as for force. The critics will say: but how can the world be a community? Nations act in their own self-interest. Of course they do. But what is the lesson of financial markets, climate change, international terrorism, nuclear proliferation or world trade? It is that our self-interest and our mutual interest are today inextricably woven together . . .

The issue is not how to stop globalization. The issue is how we use the power of community to combine it with justice . . . If we follow the principles that have served us so well at home – that power, wealth and opportunity must be in the hands of the many, not the few – if we make that our guiding light for the global economy, then it will be a force for good . . .

'Our self-interest and our mutual interest are today inextricably woven together'

The governing idea of modern social democracy is community. Founded on the principles of social justice. That people should rise according to merit not birth; that the test of any decent society is . . . the commitment to the poor and weak.

But values aren't enough . . . Our policies only succeed when the realism is as clear as the idealism. This party's strength today comes from the journey of change and learning we have made . . . We learnt that equality is about equal worth, not equal outcomes . . . On this journey, the values have never changed . . . But the means do change. The journey hasn't ended. It never ends . . .

When we act to bring to account those that committed the atrocity of September 11, we do so not out of bloodlust. We do so because it is just. We do not act against Islam. The true followers of Islam are our brothers and sisters in this struggle. Bin Laden is no more obedient to the proper teachings of the Koran than those crusaders of the 12th century, who pillaged and murdered, represented the teaching of the Gospel.

'The governing idea of modern social democracy is community'

It is time the West confronted its ignorance of Islam. Jews, Muslims and Christians are all children of Abraham. This is the moment to bring the faiths closer in understanding of our common values and heritage, a source of unity and strength.

It is time also for parts of Islam to confront prejudice against America, and not only Islam but parts of Western societies too. America has its faults as a society, as we have ours . . . But it is a free country, a democracy, it is our ally and some of the reaction to September 11 betrays a hatred of America that shames those that feel it.

So I believe this is a fight for freedom. And I want to make it a fight for justice too. Justice not only to punish the guilty. But justice to bring those same values of democracy and freedom to people round the world. And I mean: freedom, not only in the narrow sense of personal liberty but in the broader sense of each individual having the economic and social freedom to develop their potential to the full. That is what community means, founded on the equal worth of all.

The starving, the wretched, the dispossessed, the ignorant, those living in want and squalor from the deserts of northern Africa to the slums of Gaza, to the mountain ranges of Afghanistan: they too are our cause. This is a moment to seize. The kaleidoscope has been shaken. The pieces are in flux. Soon they will settle again. Before they do, let us reorder this world around us. ’

'Whatever the country, freedom of thought and expression are universal human rights'

Orhan Pamuk

(b.1952)

THE TURKISH NOVELIST DELIVERS THE INAUGURAL PEN ARTHUR MILLER FREEDOM TO WRITE MEMORIAL LECTURE AT THE WORLD VOICES FESTIVAL; NEW YORK CITY, 25 APRIL 2006

In an interview with the Swiss publication *Das Magazin*, published in February 2005, Orhan Pamuk was reported as saying of his native Turkey: 'Thirty thousand Kurds and a million Armenians were killed here. Hardly anyone dares to mention it. And so I do.' These words were used as evidence against him during the cause célèbre which forms the immediate background to this address.

Turkey's new penal code became effective in June 2005 and ultra-nationalist lawyers filed charges against Pamuk citing that legislation's Article 301, whose original wording made it a crime for the country's citizens to 'denigrate Turkishness'. Pamuk's trial started in December 2005, but the charges against him, which carried a penalty of between six months and three years' imprisonment, were dropped. The case involved a retrospective application of the penal code's provisions and, as a result, the Ministry of Justice's approval was required before prosecution could proceed. Mindful of its international reputation, and especially concerned about the progress of its application to join the European Union, the Turkish government refused to allow the case's prosecution.

Pamuk's fiction deals with East–West cultural cross-currents and draws much of its strength from a close observation of Istanbul, a city which straddles the European–Asian boundary. He describes modernity's unsettling impact on an ancient culture and is sensitive to the way in which traditionalist, non-Western societies fear their humiliation by a progressive, self-satisfied West. Public commitment did not come easily to Pamuk, a scrupulous stylist who values his art's detachment and whose pen resists activism's ready-made slogans.

This lecture describes the intellectual tensions of a natural aesthete impelled towards the recognition of difficult truths: writers cannot escape their context, and protest in the face

ORHAN PAMUK (b. 1952)

1976 Graduates from Istanbul University, following an earlier period studying architecture at Istanbul Technical University.

1982 Publishes first novel, *Cevdet Bey ve O ullari* (Cevdet Bey and Sons).

1985–8 Visiting Scholar at Columbia University, New York City.

1985 *Beyaz Kale* (trans. *The White Castle*, 1991) enjoys international success.

1990 *Kara Kitap* (trans. *The Black Book, 1995*).

1998 *Benim Adim Kirmizi* (trans. *My Name is Red,* 2001).

1998 Refuses Turkish government recognition as 'state artist'.

2002 *Kar* (trans. *Snow*, 2005).

2003 *Istanbul: Hatiralar ve Sehir* (trans. *Istanbul: Memories of a City*, 2006).

2006 Appointed Visiting Professor at Columbia University.

2006 Awarded Nobel Prize for Literature.

of repression is a moral necessity. Pamuk's remarks about the Kurds and Armenians were calculated to arouse a febrile national consciousness, but he spoke as a Turk convinced that his people had to confront certain facts, both historic and contemporary.

The Kurds were among the many nationalities seeking independence from the Ottoman Turkish empire, but their aspirations to independent statehood were frustrated. The empire's dissolution at the end of the First World War left the Kurds scattered across the contiguous boundaries of Iran, Iraq, Syria and the newly formed republic of Turkey. Conflict between the Turkish military and Kurdish secessionists has been intense in recent years, and use of the Kurdish language, legally prohibited by Turkey until 1991, remains subject to official restrictions. The First World War is also the background to the 'Armenian genocide': Ottoman Turkey, an Islamic culture, was at war with Russia, then still a Christian Orthodox civilization, and the Ottoman government suspected that the Christianity of its Armenian subjects inclined them to pro-Russian, and therefore treasonous, acts and sentiments. Neutral observers accept that between 1 and 1.5 million Armenians were killed between 1915 and 1917 as a result of an ethnic extermination authorized by the Ottoman imperial government. Pamuk was dealing with a 'forbidden topic', since the Turkish republic, as successor state to the Ottoman power, denied any such genocide. His concluding remarks may serve as a reminder why no one likes a missionary when he's armed.

'

In March 1985 Arthur Miller and Harold Pinter made a trip together to Istanbul. At the time, they were perhaps the two most important names in world theatre, but unfortunately it was not a play or literary event that brought them to Istanbul, but the limits being set on freedom of expression in Turkey . . . Whenever I've looked through the newspaper archives and the almanacs of that time . . . I soon come across the image that defines that era for most of us: men sitting in a courtroom, flanked by gendarmes, their heads shaven, frowning as their case proceeds. There were many writers among them, and Miller and Pinter had come to Istanbul to meet with them and their families, to offer them assistance, and to bring their plight to the attention of the world . . . A friend of mine and I were to be their guides . . .

Until then I had stood on the margins of the political world . . . but now, as I listened to suffocating tales of repression, cruelty and outright evil, I felt drawn to this world through guilt – drawn to it, too, by feelings of solidarity, but at the same time I felt an equal and opposite desire to protect myself from all this, and to do nothing in life but write beautiful novels . . .

I clearly remember one image: at one end of a very long corridor in the Istanbul Hilton, my friend and I are whispering to each other with some agitation, while at the other end, Miller and Pinter are whispering in the shadows with the same dark intensity. This image remained engraved in my troubled mind, I think, because it illustrated the great distance between our complicated histories and theirs, while suggesting at the same time that a consoling solidarity among writers was possible.

I felt the same sense of mutual pride and shared shame in every other meeting we attended . . . The writers, thinkers and journalists with whom we were meeting mostly defined themselves as leftists in those days . . . Twenty years on, when I see that half of these people – or thereabouts, I don't have the precise numbers – now align themselves with a nationalism that is at odds with Westernization and democracy, I of course feel sad . . .

Whatever the country, freedom of thought and expression are universal human rights. These freedoms, which modern people long for as much as bread and water, should never be limited by using nationalist sentiment, moral sensitivities or – worst of all – business or military interests . . . We must be alert to those who denigrate immigrants and minorities for their religion, their ethnic roots or the oppression that the governments of the countries they've left behind have visited on their own people.

'Our desire to understand those unlike us should never stand in the way of our respect for human rights'

But to respect the humanity and religious beliefs of minorities is not to suggest that we should limit freedom of thought . . . Our desire to understand those unlike us should never stand in the way of our respect for human rights.

I always have difficulty expressing my political judgements in a clear, emphatic and strong way – I feel pretentious, as if I'm saying things that are not quite true. This is because I know I cannot reduce my thoughts about life to the music of a single voice and a single point of view – I am, after all, a novelist, the kind of novelist who makes it his business to identify with all his characters, especially the bad ones. Living as I do in a world where, in a very short time, someone who has been a victim of tyranny and oppression can suddenly become one of the oppressors, I know also that holding strong beliefs about things and people is itself a difficult enterprise.

I do also believe that most of us entertain these contradictory thoughts simultaneously, in a spirit of good will and with the best of intentions. The pleasure of writing novels comes from exploring this peculiarly modern condition . . . we need to understand ourselves, our shady, contradictory, inner thoughts, and the pride and shame I mentioned earlier.

So let me tell another story that might cast some light on the shame and pride I felt 20 years ago while I was taking Miller and Pinter around Istanbul. In the ten years following their visit, a series of coincidences . . . led to my making a series of public statements on freedom of expression that bore no relation to my novels, and before long I had taken on a political persona far more powerful than I had ever intended. It was at about this time that the Indian author of a United Nations report on freedom of expression . . . came to Istanbul and looked me up . . . He asked me a question that still echoes strangely in my mind: 'Mr Pamuk, what is there going on in your country that you would like to explore in your novels but shy away from, due to legal prohibitions?' . . .

'When another writer in another house is not free, no writer is free.'

In the Turkey of ten years ago, there were many more subjects kept closed by laws and oppressive state policies than there are today, but as I went through them one by one, I could find none that I wished to explore 'in my novels'. But I knew, nonetheless, that if I said 'there is nothing I wish to write in my novels that I am not able to discuss', I'd be giving the wrong impression. For I'd already begun to speak often and openly about all these dangerous subjects . . . As I thought all this through, I was at once ashamed of my silence, and reconfirmed in my belief that freedom of expression has its roots in pride, and is, in essence, an expression of human dignity. I have personally known writers who have chosen to raise forbidden topics purely because they were forbidden. I think I am no different. Because when another writer in another house is not free, no writer is free . . .

Sometimes my friends rightly tell me or someone else, 'You shouldn't have put it quite like that; if only you had worded it like this, in a way that no one would find offensive, you wouldn't be in so much trouble now.' But to change one's words and package them in a way that will be acceptable to everyone in a repressed culture . . . is shaming and degrading.

The theme of this year's PEN festival is reason and belief . . . So let us now ask ourselves how 'reasonable' it is to denigrate cultures and religions, or, more to the point, to mercilessly bomb countries, in the name of democracy and freedom of thought . . . In the war against Iraq, the tyrannization and heartless murder of almost 100,000 people has brought neither peace nor democracy. To the contrary, it has served to ignite nationalist, anti-Western anger. Things have become a great deal more difficult for the small minority who are struggling for democracy and secularism in the Middle East. This savage, cruel war is the shame of America and the West. Organizations like PEN and writers like Harold Pinter and Arthur Miller are its pride. ’

'As of today, the time for denial, the time for delay, has at last come to an end'

Kevin Rudd

(b. 1957)

THE AUSTRALIAN PRIME MINISTER APOLOGIZES TO HIS COUNTRY'S INDIGENOUS PEOPLES FOR PAST WRONGS; CANBERRA, 13 FEBRUARY 2008

'As of today, the time for denial, the time for delay, has at last come to an end'

By tabling a parliamentary motion expressing contrition for the ill-treatment of Australia's indigenous peoples, Kevin Rudd was fulfilling a campaign promise. Labour's recent election win on a 5.4 per cent swing was substantial, and that decisive shift towards the centre-left made him prime minister. Rudd promised 'a new style of leadership' and a reserved manner distinguished him from the Australian political tradition's frequent exuberance. His fluency in Mandarin and diplomatic expertise qualified Rudd to speak authoritatively on Australia's strategic relationship with China and southeast Asia, and in running for office he had stressed his practical experience as both bureaucrat and businessman. When he spoke of the 'stolen generations' to the House of Representatives, the premier's seriousness of purpose did justice to the issues raised by 'one of the darkest chapters in Australia's history'. But his speech also displayed an imaginative grasp of their significance for Australia's future as well as her past. 'This unfinished business' was a question of natural justice, and the apology was presented as the final stage in Australia's dismantling of colonial attitudes. The era which had started with the white man's arrival had finished, and Rudd was ushering in a more inclusive epoch.

The indigenous population of Australia is descended from migrants who arrived from Asia at least 50,000 years ago. The 'Dreaming', or 'Dreamtime', referred to by Rudd describes the sacred period which, according to these peoples' traditional lore, preceded the earth's creation and whose mythic values subsist in the symbols and beliefs of the present. Enforced separation of indigenous children from their parents was first adopted as a policy in Australia under the provisions adopted by the colony of Victoria under its Aboriginal Protection Act (1869). Other Australian states would adopt the same means to ensure a common goal: the eventual 'breeding out' of the original population to ensure its eventual genetic, and cultural, assimilation to the white majority. Rudd's apology was extended to

KEVIN RUDD (b. 1952)

1981 Graduates in Asian Studies from Australian National University, Canberra.

1981–8 Career diplomat, Department of Foreign Affairs.

1989–92 Chief of staff to the premier of Queensland, Wayne Goss (Labour).

1992–5 Director general of the Cabinet Office, government of Queensland.

1996–8 Senior China consultant to the accountancy firm KPMG Australia.

1998 Elected member of the House of Representatives, Parliament of Australia.

2001–5 Shadow minister for foreign affairs.

2006 Elected leader of the Australian Labour Party.

2007 Labour wins the federal election (24 Nov), defeating the incumbent Liberal–National Party coalition government; sworn in as prime minister (3 Dec).

include the indigenous population of the Torres Strait Islands, which lie between the northern Australian coast and New Guinea, and who were subjected to the same measures.

Late 20th-century statistics for illiteracy, ill health and unemployment among the indigenous population offered a tragic commentary on an original policy goal of social 'improvement'. The report of the national inquiry into the 'stolen generations', published in 1997 as 'Bringing Them Home', concluded that Australian legislatures should express an official apology for the forcible removals. The state parliaments of Victoria, South Australia and New South Wales, and the parliament of the Northern Territory, proceeded to do so. But the then prime minister John Howard rejected the idea of a federal government apology.

Howard's opposition was motivated partly by a career-long rejection of multiculturalism but also by a concern that the Australian government would face claims for financial compensation if it apologized. Speaking shortly before the 2007 election, he nonetheless recognized that 'the crisis of indigenous cultural and social disintegration requires a stronger affirmation of indigenous identity and culture'. Howard had sensed the public mood, but it was Rudd who represented the new empathy. The motion, supported by the Liberal official opposition, was adopted unanimously by both the House and the Senate.

I move: That today we honour the indigenous peoples of this land, the oldest continuing cultures in human history. We reflect on their past mistreatment. We reflect in particular on the mistreatment of those who were stolen generations – this blemished chapter in our nation's history . . .

We apologize for the laws and policies of successive parliaments and governments that have inflicted profound grief, suffering and loss on these our fellow Australians. We apologize especially for the removal of Aboriginal and Torres Strait Islander children from their families, their communities and their country.

For the pain, suffering and hurt of these stolen generations, their descendants and for their families left behind, we say sorry.

To the mothers and the fathers, the brothers and sisters, for the breaking-up of families and communities, we say sorry.

And for the indignity and degradation thus inflicted on a proud people and a proud culture, we say sorry.

We the parliament of Australia respectfully request that this apology be received in the spirit in which it is offered as part of the healing of the nation.

For the future we take heart; resolving that this new page in the history of our great continent can now be written . . .

'For the pain, suffering and hurt of these stolen generations, their descendants and for their families left behind, we say sorry'

There comes a time in the history of nations when their peoples must become fully reconciled to their past if they are to go forward with confidence to embrace their future.

Our nation, Australia, has reached such a time.

That is why this parliament is today here assembled: to deal with this unfinished business of the nation, to remove a great stain from the nation's soul and, in a true spirit of reconciliation, to open a new chapter in the history of this great land, Australia . . .

There has been a stony, stubborn and deafening silence for more than a decade; a view that somehow we, the parliament, should suspend our most basic instincts of what is right and what is wrong; a view that, instead, we should look for any pretext to push this great wrong to one side, to leave it languishing with the historians, the academics and the cultural warriors, as if the stolen generations are little more than an interesting sociological phenomenon.

'There comes a time in the history of nations when their peoples must become fully reconciled to their past'

But the stolen generations are not intellectual curiosities. They are human beings, human beings who have been damaged deeply by the decisions of parliaments and governments. But, as of today, the time for denial, the time for delay, has at last come to an end . . .

Should there still be doubts as to why we must now act, let the parliament reflect for a moment on the following facts: that, between 1910 and 1970, between 10 and 30 per cent of indigenous children were forcibly taken from their mothers and fathers; that, as a result, up to 50,000 children were forcibly taken from their families; that this was the product of the deliberate, calculated policies of the state as reflected in the explicit powers given to them under statute . . .

We must acknowledge these facts if we are to deal once and for all with the argument that the policy of a generic forced separation was somehow well motivated, justified by its historical context . . . Let us remember the fact that the forced removal of Aboriginal children was happening as late as the early 1970s . . . It is well within the adult memory span of many of us . . .

It is for these reasons . . . that the governments and parliaments of this nation must make this apology – because, put simply, the laws that our parliaments enacted made the stolen generations possible. We, the parliaments of this nation, are ultimately responsible, not those who gave effect to our laws. And the problem lay with the laws themselves.

As has been said of settler societies elsewhere, we are the bearers of many blessings from our ancestors; therefore we must also be the bearer of their burdens as well. Therefore, for our nation, the course of action is clear: that is, to deal now with what has become one of the darkest chapters in Australia's history.

In doing so . . . we are also wrestling with our own soul . . . Until we fully confront that truth, there will always be a shadow hanging over us and our future as a fully united and fully reconciled people . . .

To the stolen generations, I say the following: as prime minister of Australia, I am sorry. On behalf of the government of Australia, I am sorry . . . We apologize for the hurt, the pain and suffering that we, the parliament, have caused you by the laws that previous parliaments have enacted. We apologize for the indignity, the degradation and the humiliation these laws embodied. We offer this apology to the mothers, the fathers, the brothers, the sisters, the families and the communities whose lives were ripped apart by the actions of successive governments under successive parliaments . . .

Our challenge for the future is . . . to embrace a new partnership between indigenous and non-indigenous Australians . . . The core of this partnership for the future is to close the gap between indigenous and non-indigenous Australians on life expectancy, educational achievement and employment opportunities . . .

Let us . . . allow this day, this day of national reconciliation, to become one of those rare moments in which we might just be able to transform the way in which the nation thinks about itself, whereby the injustice administered to the stolen generations in the name of these, our parliaments, causes all of us to reappraise, at the deepest level of our beliefs, the real possibility of reconciliation writ large: reconciliation across all indigenous Australia; reconciliation across the entire history of the often bloody encounter between those who emerged from the Dreamtime a thousand generations ago and those who, like me, came across the seas only yesterday . . .

It is for the nation to bring the first two centuries of our settled history to a close, as we begin a new chapter. We embrace with pride, admiration and awe these great and ancient cultures we are truly blessed to have among us, cultures that provide a unique, uninterrupted human thread linking our Australian continent to the most ancient prehistory of our planet . . .

Let us . . . write this new chapter in our nation's story together. ’

'This is your victory'

Barack Obama

(b. 1961)

SPEECH DELIVERED BY THE PRESIDENT-ELECT OF THE UNITED STATES AT A VICTORY RALLY IN GRANT PARK, CHICAGO, ILLINOIS, ON THE EVENING OF ELECTION DAY, 4 NOVEMBER 2008

The American news networks waited until the close of polling in California at 23.00 hrs (Eastern Time) before declaring the junior senator from Illinois to be the president-elect. But his victory was already evident as the results came in from Ohio and Iowa, Florida and Virginia, Pennsylvania and New Hampshire, key states which could now be shaded in blue, the Democrats' defining colour, rather than the red of the Republicans. John McCain, a once independent-minded Arizona senator and the Republicans' presidential candidate, had phoned to offer his congratulations. So had George W. Bush, a president struggling with the Wall Street banking crisis and a worsening economic recession. It was just after 23.00 when Barack Obama appeared to speak before a crowd of well over 125,000. His had been a candidacy blessed by good fortune as well as one guided by careful judgement. He had consistently opposed the US's unpopular involvement in the Iraq war and Obama's chief Democratic rival for the presidential nomination, Senator Hillary Clinton, had voted for the policy. She was adroit in the ways of the Democratic political machine but in 2008 the grinding gears of both major parties were being blamed for America's malaise. Obama was in his first term as a US senator, a fact which preserved the freshness of his appeal, and the record sums of money he raised for his campaign through the internet showed how modern technology could be used to rejuvenate political idealism.

Born in Honolulu to a Kenyan father and an American mother, Obama conformed to few political stereotypes. He was raised partly in Jakarta, following his parents' divorce and his

BARACK OBAMA (b. 1961)

1983 Graduates from Columbia University, New York City.

1985–8 Director of Developing Communities Project, Chicago.

1988–91 Harvard Law School; edits (1990) *Harvard Law Review.*

1992–2004 Lecturer at University of Chicago Law School.

1993 Joins the law firm Davis, Miner, Barnhill and Galland, and becomes a counsel (1996–2004).

1995 Publishes *Dreams from My Father: A Story of Race and Inheritance.*

1996 Elected to the Illinois Senate; subsequently re-elected (1998, 2002); resigns seat in Nov 2004.

July 2004 Delivers keynote address to the Democratic Party national convention; elected (Nov) to US Senate.

2006 *The Audacity of Hope: Thoughts on Reclaiming the American Dream.*

Feb 2007 Announces candidacy to become the Democratic nominee in the 2008 presidential election.

3 June 2008 Becomes the Democratic presumptive nominee.

4 Nov 2008 In the presidential election Barack Obama gains 53 per cent of the popular vote to John McCain's 46 per cent, and becomes president-elect of the US.

mother's marriage to an Indonesian national, and then by his grandparents in Honolulu. This international background was supplemented by an Ivy League education and his temperament was instinctively graceful, sure-footed and thoughtful. His own character exemplified the change that Obama promised his country as it turned its back on sectarian attitudes, and the elegant equipoise of his sentences urged America towards a deepening of the union between her states and among her peoples.

Obama's speech avoids triumphalism and reaffirms his central message: America's optimism will see her through and his cause of democratic change embodies the convictions of the many. It is therefore a mass movement which has won the victory and Obama's words are a celebration of that solidarity. There are, typically, subtle evocations of the lineage whose heir he had now become. Abraham Lincoln, 'a man from this state', is memorialized as the architect of a national unity which needs reassertion. John F. Kennedy's New Frontier lives on in the summons to 'a new spirit of patriotism' and the words of Martin Luther King supply a resonant internal echo. King had once told his audience that 'I want you to know, tonight, that we, as a people, will get to the promised land.' Thirty years later Obama told all Americans that though the road ahead was long, and the climb steep, he was confident of their eventual success. The 44th president had aligned himself with a noble pattern of thought and endeavour, a tradition which was now renewed by his own winged words and guided towards the cause of an American renaissance.

'If there is anyone out there who still doubts that America is a place where all things are possible, who still wonders if the dream of our founders is alive in our time, who still questions the power of our democracy, tonight is your answer.

It's the answer told by lines that stretched around schools and churches in numbers this nation has never seen . . . because they believed that this time must be different, that their voices could be that difference.

It's the answer spoken by young and old, rich and poor, Democrat and Republican, black, white, Hispanic, Asian, Native American, gay, straight, disabled and not disabled. Americans who sent a message to the world that we have never been just a collection of individuals or a collection of red states and blue states.

We are, and always will be, the United States of America.

It's the answer that led those who've been told for so long by so many to be cynical and fearful and doubtful about what we can achieve to put their hands on the arc of history and bend it once more toward the hope of a better day.

'Change has come to America'

It's been a long time coming, but tonight, because of what we did on this day in this election at this defining moment change has come to America . . .

I was never the likeliest candidate to this office. We didn't start with much money or many endorsements. Our campaign was not hatched in the halls of Washington. It began in the backyards of Des Moines and the living rooms of Concord and the front porticos of Charleston. It was built by working men and women who dug into what little savings they had to give $5 and $10 and $20 to the cause.

It drew strength from the young people who rejected the myth of their generation's apathy . . .

It drew strength . . . from the millions of Americans who volunteered and organized and proved that more than two centuries later a government of the people, by the people, and for the people has not perished from the earth.

This is your victory.

And I know you didn't do this just to win an election. And I know you didn't do it for me.

You did it because you understand the enormity of the task that lies ahead. For even as we celebrate tonight, we know the challenges that tomorrow will bring are the greatest of our lifetime – two wars, a planet in peril, the worst financial crisis in a century.

Even as we stand here tonight, we know there are brave Americans waking up in the deserts of Iraq and the mountains of Afghanistan to risk their lives for us.

There are mothers and fathers who will lie awake after the children fall asleep and wonder how they'll make the mortgage or pay their doctor's bills or save enough for their child's college education.

There's new energy to harness, new jobs to be created, new schools to build, and threats to meet, alliances to repair.

'This is your victory.'

The road ahead will be long. Our climb will be steep. We may not get there in one year or even in one term. But, America, I have never been more hopeful than I am tonight that we will get there . . .

What began 21 months ago in the depths of winter cannot end on this autumn night.

This victory alone is not the change we seek. It is only the chance for us to make that change . . .

It can't happen without you, without a new spirit of service, a new spirit of sacrifice.

So let us summon a new spirit of patriotism, of responsibility, where each of us resolves to pitch in and work harder and look after not only ourselves but each other.

Let us remember that, if this financial crisis taught us anything, it's that we cannot have a thriving Wall Street while Main Street suffers.

In this country, we rise or fall as one nation, as one people. Let's resist the temptation to fall back on the same partisanship and pettiness and immaturity that has poisoned our politics for so long.

Let's remember that it was a man from this state who first carried the banner of the Republican party to the White House, a party founded on the values of self-reliance and individual liberty and national unity.

Those are values that we all share. And while the Democratic Party has won a great victory tonight, we do so with a measure of humility and determination to heal the divides that have held back our progress.

As Lincoln said to a nation far more divided than ours, we are not enemies but friends. Though passion may have strained, it must not break our bonds of affection.

And to those Americans whose support I have yet to earn, I may not have won your vote tonight, but I hear your voices. I need your help. And I will be your president, too.

'Our stories are singular, but our destiny is shared'

And to all those watching tonight from beyond our shores, from parliaments and palaces, to those who are huddled round radios in the forgotten corners of the world, our stories are singular, but our destiny is shared, and a new dawn of American leadership is at hand.

To those who would tear the world down. We will defeat you. To those who seek peace and security. We support you. And to all those who have wondered if America's beacon still burns bright: tonight we proved once more that the true strength of our nation comes not from the might of our arms or the scale of our wealth, but from the enduring power of our ideals: democracy, liberty, opportunity and unyielding hope.

That's the true genius of America: that America can change. Our nation can be perfected. What we've already achieved gives us hope for what we can and must achieve tomorrow . . .

'Yes, we can.'

This is our time, to put our people back to work and open doors of opportunity for our kids, to restore prosperity and promote the cause of peace, to reclaim the American dream and reaffirm that fundamental truth, that, out of many, we are one; that while we breathe, we hope. And where we are met with cynicism and doubts and those who tell us that we can't, we will respond with that timeless creed that sums up the spirit of a people: Yes, we can.'

'

Index

Acknowledgements/credits

The author would like to thank Richard Milbank, the book's commissioning editor, and Ben Dupré, its copyeditor.

The publishers would like to thank the following for source material and permission to reproduce copyright material:

For speeches: p30 David Ben-Gurion, 'This is our native land; it is not as birds of passage that we return to it', 2 October 1947; p85 Martin Luther King, 'I have a dream', 28 August 1963, © 1963 Dr. Martin Luther King Jr; © renewed 1991 Coretta Scott King, reprinted by arrangement with The Heirs to the Estate of Martin Luther King Jr., c/o Writers House as agent for the proprietor New York, NY; p90 Harold Wilson, 'The white heat of the technological revolution', 1 October 1963; p95 Nelson Mandela, 'An ideal for which I am prepared to die', 20 April 1964; p100 Barry Goldwater, 'Extremism in the defence of liberty is no vice . . . moderation in the pursuit of justice is no virtue', 16 July 1964; p105 Martin Luther King, 'The war in Vietnam is but a symptom of a far deeper malady within the American spirit', 4 April 1967, ©1967 Dr Martin Luther King Jr, reprinted by arrangement with The Heirs of Martin Luther King Jr., c/o Writers House as agent for the proprietor New York, NY; p110 Julius Nyerere, 'Socialism is an attitude of mind', 10 April 1967; p136 Neil Kinnock, 'I warn you that you will have pain', 7 June 1983, and 'We are democratic socialists. We care all the time', 15 May 1987, reprinted by permission of the author; p147 Mario Cuomo, 'For the love of God: Please, make this nation remember how futures are built', 16 July 1984, reprinted by permission of the author; p152 Jesse Jackson, 'Suffering breeds character. Character breeds faith. In the end, faith will not disappoint', 18 July 1984; p177 Seamus Heaney, 'The Ireland I now inhabit is one that these Irish contemporaries have helped to imagine', 7 December 1995, © The Nobel Foundation 1995; p187 Anita Roddick, 'By putting our money where our heart is . . . we will mould the world into a kinder, more loving shape', 27 November 1999; p197 Orhan Pamuk, 'Whatever the country, freedom of thought and expression are universal human rights', 25 April 2006, reprinted by permission of The Wylie Agency (UK) on behalf of the author, translation © Maureen Freely; p207 Barack Obama, 'This is your victory', 4 November 2008.

Every effort has been made to trace and contact copyright holders. However, the publishers will be glad to rectify in future editions any inadvertent omissions brought to their attention.

For pictures: p. 8 Time & Life Pictures/Getty Images; p. 13 Keystone Archives/HIP/TopFoto; pp. 18, 23 Bettmann/Corbis; p. 28 Time & Life Pictures/Getty Images; p. 33 Bettmann/Corbis; p. 38 Time & Life Pictures/Getty Images; p. 43 Bettmann/Corbis; pp. 48, 53, 58 Getty Images; pp. 63, 68, 73 Bettmann/Corbis; p. 78 Topham Picturepoint; p. 83 Flip Schulke/Corbis; pp. 88, 93 Getty Images; p. 98 Ted Streshinsky/Corbis; p. 103 akg-images; p. 108 Topham Picturepoint; p. 113 Getty Images; pp. 119, 125 Bettmann/Corbis; p. 129 T Star/Keystone USA/Rex Features; p. 134 Topham Picturepoint; p. 140 Getty Images; p. 145 Wally McNamee/Corbis; p. 150 Bettmann/Corbis; p. 155 akg-images; p. 160 The Independent/Rex Features; pp. 165, 170 Getty Images; p. 175 Scanpix/PA Photos; p. 180 AFP/Getty Images; p. 185 Alisdair Macdonald/Rex Features; p. 190 Nils Jorgensen/Rex Features; p. 195 Ullstein Bild/TopFoto; p. 200 Alan Porritt/epa/Corbis; p. 205 AFP/Getty Images.

Quercus Publishing Plc
21 Bloomsbury Square
London
WC1A 2NS

First published in 2009

A catalogue record of this book is available from the British Library

Cloth case edition
ISBN 978 1 84724 836 7

Printed case edition
ISBN 978 1 84866 014 4

Paperback with flaps
ISBN 978 184724 919 7

Editor: Ben Dupré
Designer: Patrick Nugent
Picture researcher: Claudia Tate

Printed in UK

10 9 8 7 6 5 4 3 2 1